FIFTH EDITION

The Litigation Paralegal

A Systems Approach

WEST LEGAL STUDIES

 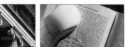

Options

Over 300 products in every area of the law: textbooks, CD-ROMs, reference books, test banks, online companions, and more—helping you succeed in the classroom and on the job.

Support

We offer unparalleled, practical support: robust instructor and student supplements to ensure the best learning experience, custom publishing to meet your unique needs, and other benefits such as West's Student Achievement Award. And our sales representatives are always ready to provide you with dependable service.

Feedback

As always, we want to hear from you! Your feedback is our best resource for improving the quality of our products. Contact your sales representative or write us at the address below if you have any comments about our materials or if you have a product proposal.

Accounting and Financials for the Law Office • Administrative Law • Alternative Dispute Resolution • Bankruptcy • Business Organizations/Corporations • Careers and Employment • Civil Litigation and Procedure • CLA Exam Preparation • Computer Applications in the Law Office • Contract Law • Court Reporting • Criminal Law and Procedure • Document Preparation • Elder Law • Employment Law • Environmental Law • Ethics • Evidence Law • Family Law • Intellectual Property • Interviewing and Investigation • Introduction to Law • Introduction to Paralegalism • Law Office Management • Law Office Procedures • Legal Nurse Consulting • Legal Research, Writing, and Analysis • Legal Terminology • Paralegal Internship • Product Liability • Real Estate Law • Reference Materials • Social Security • Sports Law • Torts and Personal Injury Law • Wills, Trusts, and Estate Administration

---

West Legal Studies
5 Maxwell Drive
Clifton Park, New York 12065-2919

For additional information, find us online at:
www.westlegalstudies.com

THOMSON
DELMAR LEARNING

FIFTH EDITION

The Litigation Paralegal

A Systems Approach

James W.H. McCord, J.D.
Professor Emeritus
Eastern Kentucky University

THOMSON
DELMAR LEARNING

Australia Canada Mexico Singapore Spain United Kingdom United States

WEST LEGAL STUDIES

The Litigation Paralegal: A Systems Approach, **Fifth Edition**
James W.H. McCord

Career Education Strategic Business Unit:
Vice President:
Dawn Gerrain

Director of Learning Solutions:
John Fedor

Managing Editor:
Robert L. Serenka, Jr.

Acquisitions Editor:
Shelley Esposito

Senior Product Manager:
Melissa Riveglia

Editorial Assistant:
Melissa Zaza

Director of Content & Media Production:
Wendy A. Troeger

Senior Content Project Manager:
Betty L. Dickson

Art Director:
Joy Kocsis

Director of Marketing:
Wendy Mapstone

Marketing Manager:
Gerard McAvey

Marketing Coordinator:
Jonathan Sheehan

Cover Design:
Joseph Villanova

Library of Congress Cataloging-in-Publication Data

McCord, James W.H.
   The litigation paralegal: a systems approach/ James W.H. McCord.—5th ed.
      p. cm.—(West legal studies)
   Includes index.
   ISBN 1-4180-1604-7
      1. Civil procedure—United States. 2. Legal assistants—United States—Handbooks, manuals, etc. I. Title.

KF8841.M39 2008
347.73'5—dc22

2006101408

NOTICE TO THE READER

To Sandy,

the love of my life,

and

in loving memory of my parents

Marks W. and Hazel C. McCord

CONTENTS

CHAPTER 4

Drafting the Complaint   139

CHAPTER 5

Filing the Lawsuit, Service of Process, and Obtaining a Default Judgment   178

PREFACE

Litigation is a vital and often dramatic component of our system of dispute resolution. *The Litigation Paralegal: A Systems Approach* and the closely integrated *Student Workbook* provide students and faculty with learning resources written specifically for them—resources combining the theories and principles of law with practical paralegal skills, paralegal ethics, and a sensitivity toward the goals and needs of the paralegal profession, all in the context of the law office.

This *Fifth Edition* is a painstakingly comprehensive revision impacting every chapter. The suggestions provided by reviewers, paralegals, colleagues, students, and attorneys have been carefully considered. Although the changes are numerous, the most significant address *electronic discovery and filing* and the associated ethical and practical responsibilities of the lawyer and the paralegal. New *revisions to the Federal Rules of Evidence and Civil and Appellate Procedure* are examined, as are the practice requirements of the *Health Insurance Portability and Accountability Act.* Relevant *new forms* have been added or substituted and others revised to reflect current practice. Web sites, assignments, key terms, and study questions have been updated as well. The attention to the application of state rules and practice is continued.

The text and workbook are further complemented by an expanded *Online Companion* and a revised instructor's manual.

This text is suited to several types of litigation students: the traditional college classroom student, the student in an online course, and the paralegal being trained in the law office as a litigation paralegal

ORGANIZATION OF TEXT

The Litigation Paralegal: A Systems Approach introduces students to the law office and takes them chronologically through the steps and tasks involved in litigation, from the facts of the cases they will be working on to judgment enforcement and appeal. Chapter by chapter they build proficiency in the specific tasks or competencies that are required of them as paralegals. The text places the student in a law office setting where the instructor assumes the role of the paralegal's supervising attorney. This office training procedure uses a systems approach in which the student develops a litigation system folder complete with forms, documents, checklists, rules, relevant Web sites, and practice tips. The system, completed by the end of the course, provides the student with a valuable resource.

Use of the system enhances the process of both teaching and learning litigation paralegal skills. Because a good system folder helps the student on the job and maybe even in securing a job, the system folder provides an extra incentive to do the Workbook Assignments thoroughly and accurately. It teaches the benefits of being organized and develops the confidence to create a system in any area of law. Utilization of the systems approach also reinforces the skills presented in the text. The text, workbook, and instructor's manual, however, are flexible and designed to accommodate approaches other than a systems approach.

FEATURES OF THE TEXT AND INTEGRATED WORKBOOK

In each chapter the student is given the following:

1. One or more specific litigation tasks
2. Substantive and procedural background on the task.

3. Guidelines and directions on how to perform the task
4. Examples from a sample case on how to perform the task
5. Helpful Web sites
6. Study questions to review and reinforce learning
7. Key terms for vocabulary building

The Workbook adds the following items from which to chose and customize an integrated course plan:

8. Chapter objective
9. Chapter outline
10. List of key terms to define
11. System folder assignments
12. Application assignments
13. Internet exercises
14. Additional learning exercises and discussion points
15. Chapter review test with answers

Application of Knowledge

Each chapter, according to its focus, contains a varying balance of exercises for in-class or out-of-class assignments and discussions.

System Folder Assignments structure the building of an impressive practice system of topically arranged forms, legal principles, rules, checklists, and other material. An outline of the system folder contents is in Appendix A.

Application Assignments require the application of legal principles to new fact situations or to practice skills.

Internet Exercises encourage familiarity with electronic research on relevant Web sites.

Chapter Review Tests can be used by instructors as a pre- or post-test, and students can use them to assess their progress and study for exams.

Other features of the text include:

- **Professional Associations and Resources**
  References to numerous relevant professional organizations, associations, and related Web sites, publications, standards, and other resources are provided.

- **Case Law and Other Authority**
  Citations refer to pertinent case law, statutes, rules, and American Bar Association standards.

- **Sample Practice Forms**
  Many practice forms, pleadings, motions, and other documents are included to provide familiarity with forms and to give a basis from which to work with state forms or to draft forms.

- **Checklists**
  Checklists give step-by-step guidance in specific practice situations and provide examples for developing additional checklists as needed.

- **Diagrams, Tables, and Charts**
  Visual aids facilitate learning, stimulate interest, and summarize and organize important information. Space is provided in exhibits for the addition of state-specific information.

- *Legal Terminology*
  Key legal terms are highlighted in bold and defined in the text as well as in the margins for quick access. They are also listed at the end of each chapter and in the Glossary at the end of the text.

- *Notable Quotations*
  Quotations related to law appear in the margins to emphasize ideas and provoke thought and discussion (and maybe a smile) about the subject matter.

NEW FEATURES AND CHANGES TO THE FIFTH EDITION

- *Most Significant Additions*
  The most significant additions include the integrated workbook bundled with the text, e-filing and service, e-discovery (including the duty to protect and preserve evidence) and related forms, HIPAA practice and forms, the Servicemembers Civil Relief Act, revised subpoena practice, courtroom decorum for paralegals, and the latest in courtroom presentation technology and practice.

- *Updated Helpful Web Sites*

- *General Resource Guide for Investigation on the Web*
  Chapter 3 contains an updated guide to law-related and other resources on the Web. Used as is or as a resource to be periodically updated in the law office, the guide is a valuable, categorized resource.

- *Updated Internet Exercises*

- *Case Examples*
  Recent case examples, including Supreme Court cases, are included throughout the text.

- *Updated Pleadings, Motions, and Time Limits Chart*
  This chart, located at the end of Chapter 6, has been expanded and updated to reflect recent changes in the federal rules of civil and appellate procedure.

- *Changes to the Federal Rules*
  The text identifies and explains important changes in the federal rules on civil procedure, evidence, and appeal. Those impacting on e-service and filing, e-discovery, attorney client privilege and trial preparation materials (work product), subpoenas, and citation of unpublished court opinions are most important.

- *American Bar Association Standards*
  Expanded discussions of ABA standards on e-discovery, Ethics 2000, and ABA Principles for Juries and Jury Trials (2005) are presented.

- *Other Changes*
  Other changes have been made in every chapter of the book to see that forms and checklists are current and that text and concepts are both current and clear. Additions include jurisdiction, class actions, federal tort claims practice, meta-data, high-low agreements, offer of judgment, types of verdict, practice tips, and other topics and procedures.

ANCILLARY MATERIALS

- The extensive **Instructor's Manual** is available both in print and on-line at **www.westlegalstudies.com** in the Instructor's Lounge under Resources. Written by the author of the text, the *Instructor's Manual* contains chapter objectives, instructional supplements, suggested class activities, an outline, a key term list, system folder assignments and answers, application assignments and answers, a test bank, and Power Point masters.
- **Student Workbook**—a new student workbook, bundled with the text, contains all assignments along with other features.
- **Online Companion**—a Web-based site for students enrolled in classes using this text is available, offering resources including links to useful Web sites, cases, and other materials.
- **Computerized Test Bank**—The Test Bank found in the *Instructor's Manual* is also available in a computerized format on CD-ROM. The platforms supported include Windows®—Windows 98, ME, 2000, XP or more recent version; Macintosh®—OS 8.6, OS 9.2 or OS X (10.2 or higher). Features include the following:
  - Multiple methods of question selection
  - Multiple outputs—that is, print, ASCII, and RTF
  - Graphic support (black and white)
  - Random questioning output
  - Special character support
- **Web page**—Come visit our Web site at **www.westlegalstudies.com**, where you will find valuable information specific to this book such as hot links and sample materials to download, as well as other West Legal Studies products.
- **Westlaw®**—West's on-line computerized legal research system offers students hands-on experience with a system commonly used in law offices. Qualified adopters can receive ten free hours of Westlaw®, which can be accessed with Macintosh and IBM PC and compatibles. A modem is required.

> Please note the Internet resources are of a time-sensitive nature and URL addresses may often change or be deleted.
>
> *Contact us at westlegalstudies@delmar.com*

ABOUT THE AUTHOR

James W. H. McCord earned his law degree at the University of Wisconsin-Madison and practiced civil and criminal law before becoming the first director of the Paralegal Program at Eastern Kentucky University. He has served as president of the American Association for Paralegal Education and as a member of the American Bar Association Commission on Approval of Legal Assistant Programs. He has published articles and other books on paralegals and paralegal education, including the coauthored *Criminal Law and Procedure for the Paralegal: A Systems Approach.*

ACKNOWLEDGMENTS

As is true with previous editions of this text, this fifth edition would not have been possible without the invaluable contributions of my wife and colleague Sandra McCord. She is an exceptionally capable manuscript editor, advisor, researcher, organizer, computer person, and so much more essential to the making of a quality text. I am grateful to many colleagues, paralegals, students in Dr. Elaine Tackett's litigation course, and others who have provided valuable comments and suggestions for improving the book.

My thanks go to Eastern Kentucky University for use of its impressive undergraduate law library and other resources and to the Department of Government and the Paralegal Program.

I am also grateful for the valuable contributions of the West Legal Studies team for this fifth edition: Shelly Esposito, Acquisitions Editor; Melissa Riveglia, Senior Product Manager; Lyss Zaza, Editorial Assistant; and Betty Dickson, Senior Content Project Manager.

Finally, I am indebted for the many hours spent by my busy colleagues for reviewing the previous editions and giving me valuable encouragement and suggestions:

Michele Bradford
Gadsden State Community College
Gadsden, AL

Elizabeth Mann
Greenville Technical College
Greenville, SC

Brian McCully
Fresno City College
Fresno, CA

Jill Bush Raines
Oklahoma University College of Law
Norman, OK

Sheryne Richardson
Clayton State College University
Morrow, GA

Kimberly Starks
Mississippi Gulf Coast Community College
Gulfport, MS

James W. H. McCord, J.D.
Professor Emeritus
Eastern Kentucky University

Welcome to the Law Office: Foundations for Litigation

INTRODUCTION

civil litigation
The process whereby one person sues another person in a court of law to enforce a right or to seek a remedy such as financial compensation.

Civil litigation is the process whereby one person sues another person in a court of law to enforce a right or to seek a remedy such as financial compensation. Established procedures facilitate the fair resolution of conflicts that might not otherwise be peacefully resolved. Our focus is civil litigation, suits between private citizens for wrongs such as the carelessness leading to an auto accident or the failure to follow the terms of a contract. We will not address criminal litigation, which is the government suing a person for specific violation of the criminal code such as murder and robbery.

The following cases are typical of the kinds of circumstances that spawn litigation. They are real in the sense that there are hundreds of cases just like these, involving human pain and deeply felt emotions.

In the chapters to come, paralegal tasks will be presented in the context of one or more of these cases. Case I, the *Forrester* case, will be the text's main reference. Some of the other cases will be used for task assignments. The remaining cases illustrate other kinds of litigation. The cases will also be used to place you in as realistic a law office setting as a textbook can create.

> "No two cases are exactly alike. A young attorney found two opinions in the New York Reports where the facts seemed identical although the law was in conflict, but an older and more experienced attorney pointed out to him that the names of the parties were different."
>
> —CUTHBERT W. POUND, AMERICAN JURIST, "AMERICAN LAW INSTITUTE SPEECH OF JUDGE POUND," 5 N.Y.

◙ **CASE I**

Forrester v. Hart and Mercury Parcel Service, Inc.

On her way to work Tuesday, February 26, Ann Forrester ducked her head against the cold wind and stepped gingerly across the ice patches on Highway 328 to put a letter in the mailbox. Her husband, William Forrester, and children, Sara, age four, and Michael, age eight, waited in the car in the Forrester driveway, ready to be dropped off at work, day care, and school.

Michael yawned and drew pictures on the frosty car window with his fingernail. Sara banged her new pink snowboots against the seat. "Cut that out, Sara!" William warned, then opened the car door to yell, "Hurry up, Ann, or we'll be late!" She didn't seem to hear.

Richard Hart, married and father of three teenage children, sang along with the radio as he drove his Mercury Parcel Service van the morning of February 26. After delivering this express package, he would take a breakfast break. It hadn't been fun driving in the wind and patchy ice from Ohio into the state of Columbia.

As the van topped a sharp crest in the road, Mr. Hart saw a woman on the right side of the road stepping out onto the highway. He pressed down on the brake pedal, but the van didn't stop.

The woman, Ann Forrester, looked up at the approaching van. Richard Hart hit the brake hard. The van skidded. Ann Forrester scrambled frantically, in vain. Mr. Hart could not bring the vehicle under control, and it struck Ms. Forrester, then smashed into a tree. ∎

◙ **CASE II**

Ameche v. Congden

Margie and Leroy Congden, owners of Maple Meadows Campground, were told that electrical outlets at some of the campsites weren't working. The Congdens groaned. It was the middle of the busiest season of the year.

Leroy confirmed that the problem included all sites from 30 to 39 and found that repair would necessitate digging a trench across the ten campsites to excavate the faulty wiring.

"We have to keep those sites available, at least until after Labor Day," Margie told Leroy. "There's no way we can notify all the people who have made reservations that we won't have a place for them, and there isn't another campground within one hundred miles."

Leroy made an appointment with an electrician to do the repairs after September 7, then ran a connecting line of extension cords from the outlet at site 40 to the affected sites. He was careful to string the cords along the gravel edge of the campsites away from traffic areas. The rubber casing on one of the cords was broken in several places, he noticed, but concluded it would not be a problem.

On the afternoon of August 21, Carl and Zoe Ameche set up their camper on site 36 of Maple Meadows Campground. Meanwhile, their six-year-old son, Zach, collected bugs and sticks and gathered gravel into piles.

When Carl finished with the camper, he noticed an extension cord connection lying on the ground near where his son was playing. He pulled the cord away from the campsite into a grassy area.

Mr. and Mrs. Ameche unpacked and relaxed in their camper, occasionally noticing a flickering of the camper light. Emerging later, they found the grassy area behind their campsite in flames. Carl found Zachary unharmed, trapped on the other side of the fire, and was able to carry him to safety, but received severe burns on his own arms and legs in the process. Since most campers had not yet checked in, there were no other injuries, but several campsites, some recreation facilities, and many of the venerable maple trees for which the camp was named, were destroyed. ■

▣ CASE III

Coleman v. Make Tracks, Inc.

Harold James, an executive at Make Tracks, Inc., propped his feet on his desk and looked out over the skyline of Legalville. He had finally brought his successful bicycle company into the motor age with the new three-wheeled all-terrain vehicle, Big Track, now being shipped to markets across the region.

James had pushed diversification to capture a more modern image for the company in a speed-conscious society. The positive reaction to television ads featuring the Big Track over bold computer graphics and rock music seemed to bear him out.

His friends had urged him to take the safer route, to stay with bicycles. After all, he had three kids to educate. He was glad he had not listened.

At the Coleman farm on Labor Day, September 4, laughter and wisecracks focused on Sean Coleman, the only child of Sam and Emma Coleman. His effervescent personality and athletic skills had made him a leader at Lafayette County High. His intelligence and academic record convinced adults in the community that he would go far. In two years he would be off to Columbia State University, where he planned to major in agriculture in preparation for managing the family farm.

Now Sean was celebrating with his friends—trading stories, eating hot dogs, and taking turns riding the new Big Track three-wheeled all-terrain vehicle that he had received for his recent sixteenth birthday.

"So, Hotshot," called Sean's best friend, Jason Hackett, "Let's see you ride that thing like they do on TV!"

Sean gave him a thumbs-up signal, and was off, riding up a nearby hill. Rapidly increasing speed, he hit full throttle at the steepest incline before the crest of the hill. The front wheel lifted off the ground, flipping the vehicle backward onto Sean. The county rescue squad rushed him to the hospital, unconscious. ■

▣ **CASE IV**

Briar Patch Dolls, Inc. v. Teeny Tiny Manufacturing Co.

Pandemonium broke out in the aisles of toy departments across the country. There were fewer than forty shopping days until Christmas, and the stock of popular Briar Patch Dolls was 30 to 60 percent short.

Briar Patch Dolls seemed to be an overnight craze, but it had taken Paul and Judy Heinz twelve years to build up from the cottage industry production of a few hand-sewn rag dolls for a local gift shop. The business had grown slowly and gradually until last year, when the Heinzes decided on a major expansion. They invested their last dollars in new equipment, employees, and a national advertising campaign that produced Christmas orders for 100,000 dolls—ten times last year's number. Production of the dolls proceeded on schedule.

Paul and Judy Heinz obtained clothing for the dolls from the Teeny Tiny Clothing Manufacturing Company, Inc., which made the trademark denim overalls worn by all Briar Patch Dolls. Three friends owned and operated Teeny Tiny Clothing and had expanded it to keep pace with Briar Patch. Although not all past contracts for the denim overalls had been filled on time, sales of the dolls had not been substantially hurt.

The general manager and primary force in the enterprise was Ethel Meyers, an energetic, creative woman. Her partners, Harriet Smith and Alice McGinnis, were mostly interested in supplementing their families' incomes while their children were in college.

In January of the prior year, a contract had been signed between Briar Patch Dolls and Teeny Tiny Manufacturing for 100,000 pairs of doll overalls, sewn to specification, to be delivered in increments of 25,000 on March 15, May 15, July 15, and September 15. Within thirty days of delivery, Briar Patch was to pay one dollar for each pair of overalls delivered in satisfactory condition.

On March 11, Ethel Meyers died. Teeny Tiny Manufacturing tried to meet the contract anyway. On March 15, 24,000 overalls were delivered, of which 5,000 were unsatisfactory. The other delivery dates were met as follows:

May 15:	15,000 pieces, 5,000 unsatisfactory
July 15:	10,000 pieces, 5,000 unsatisfactory
September 15:	7,000 pieces, 3,000 unsatisfactory
October 15:	3,000 pieces, 2,000 unsatisfactory

As a result of the delays, inadequate shipments, and defects, Briar Patch was able to fill only 40 percent of its orders. At a profit of ten dollars per doll, Briar Patch lost $600,000.

This year children's television programming is saturated with colorful ads for Jolly Lolly clown dolls, which have replaced Briar Patch Dolls as number one on children's Christmas lists.   ▪

▣ **CASE V**

Rakowski v. Montez Construction Co.

Darlene Rakowski was proud to be the first woman to be hired for a nonsecretarial position by Montez Construction Company. Adam Stroud, the foreman who hired her, said he really didn't think a woman was tough enough for the job, but she was determined to try.

As she arrived the first day, catcalls and whistles erupted from the crew. A couple of the men followed her, doing an exaggerated bump and grind. The sexual behavior ended after Ms. Rakowski complained to the foreman. Thereafter, however, Ms. Rakowski was assigned menial tasks, primarily fetch and carry orders on the ground. Rarely was she allowed to work with equipment on actual construction, although her vocational school training had prepared her to do so. Her usually competent work on these simple tasks elicited loud mocking from her co-workers and almost weekly profane outbursts from the foreman. His complaints never included instructions on how to do a better job, but rather references to Ms. Rakowski's stupidity and worthlessness, and were always made in front of other workers. When a male worker made mistakes, Mr. Stroud called him into his office for a quiet conference. Ms. Rakowski went to Mr. Stroud to complain about her treatment, and he responded that she was taking it too seriously.

As the incidents continued, Ms. Rakowski became more distraught, occasionally bursting into tears, which only intensified the mocking and jeering from her fellow workers. In desperation she went to Carlos Montez, owner of the company. He promised to look into the problem, and advised her to "loosen up."

Conditions did not change. Complaints about the quality of her work and her inability to lift certain items, follow directions, and operate tools safely were filed in her personnel record. She was not given the normal opportunity to rebut such charges. Very upset, Ms. Rakowski missed more and more work.

Having made her decision to look for another job, Ms. Rakowski travels from employment agency to employment agency with no success. She feels trapped, wondering, "What am I going to do?"   ■

OFFICE MANUAL

Successful litigation requires skill and efficiency. One tool for efficiency is the office manual or handbook. These books, in loose-leaf or electronic format, consist of information, policies, and procedures that help employees work more effectively from the first day forward. Paralegals may be assigned the task of writing an office manual.

The following section is an example of a manual designed to orient a new paralegal to the firm. This manual describes the structure and personnel of the law office and some of the essential procedures, such as timekeeping and billing, employed by most law firms. Thriving in a law office environment is crucial to your well-being and is addressed here as well. Learning processes employed in your training are introduced in the manual, as are the ethical and professional responsibilities that you must assume from the start. In short, the *Paralegal Handbook* addresses fundamentals essential to becoming an effective litigation paralegal. Following the handbook is a review of the U.S. court system and the somewhat complex issues of jurisdiction, venue, and related concepts.

THE PARALEGAL HANDBOOK

White, Wilson & McDuff

Attorneys at Law

Federal Plaza Building, Suite 700

Third and Market Streets

Legalville, Columbia 00000

(111) 555-0000

THE PARALEGAL HANDBOOK: OFFICE ORIENTATION AND ETHICS

STRUCTURE AND PERSONNEL

Titles/Diversity

This firm is structured like many other law firms in the United States. *Partners* are the attorney-owners of the law firm and share in its profits. *Senior partners* are the partners who have been with the firm the longest and often have the greatest ownership share. Attorneys who have not yet become partners and are salaried are *associates*. More experienced associates are sometimes given the title *senior associate*. *Staff attorneys* are hired for economic reasons and, unlike associates, have no expectation of becoming partners. *Temporary or contract attorneys* may be hired for a limited period of time to address a brief expansion of the firm's workload. Some attorneys may have the designation *of counsel*, which means they maintain an advisory capacity or refer clients to the law firm (or do both).

Personnel other than lawyers include paralegals, paralegal managers, law clerks, and legal secretaries. *Paralegals* (also called legal assistants) are educated in legal skills and provide legal services under the supervision of an attorney, or as otherwise permitted by law.[1] *Paralegal managers* (often experienced paralegals) administer paralegal hiring, training, and productivity. *Law clerks* work in the law office while completing their law degrees. Clerical and word processing services for the office are provided by *legal secretaries*. Small law offices may have fewer levels of employees, and large firms can have legal administrators, litigation managers, investigators, errand runners, and receptionists. A relatively new addition to some law firms is the *nonlawyer manager/executive*. Akin to corporate chief operating officers, these employees have executive authority for the firm's business policies and strategies.[2] Our office structure is typical of the small or medium-sized firm and is illustrated in the office organization chart in Exhibit 1:1.

Diversity in our office personnel at all levels enriches our work environment, improves communication with an increasingly diverse clientele, and is good for business. A rapidly growing list of businesses and major corporations is looking to hire law firms with diverse personnel, including women and minority partners. Congruently, we strive to develop corresponding policies and benefits, such as better access for the disabled plus child care, flex time, and family leave programs.[3]

The Changing Law Office

New technology and a global economy are offering both pressures and incentives for law offices to change their ways of doing business. Office executives face the challenge of keeping their firms competitive not only with firms across the courthouse square, but also with firms across the nation and world.

Seeking efficiency in both time and cost, increasingly sophisticated clients expect to access legal services through the Internet and even to bid on-line to set the cost of those services. **Multijurisdictional practices,** the provision of legal services in states other than the one for which the attorney is licensed, is fast becoming the norm [ABA Model Rules of Professional Conduct 5.5 and 8.5 (amended 2002)]. Predictors envision *multidisciplinary businesses* housing, for example, legal, accounting, real estate, engineering, or other departments in one firm. Although multidisciplinary practice is currently not permitted in most states, the realities of the e-world may force that change.[4] The e-world has also led to law firm use of Web pages and informative *blogs* (Web logs—topical chronological journals) to serve clients and market

multijurisdictional practice
The provision of legal services in states other than the one for which the attorney is licensed.

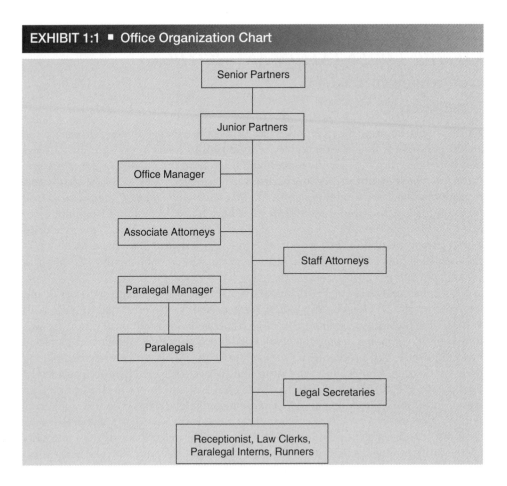

EXHIBIT 1:1 ■ Office Organization Chart

legal services. As a member of this office, you will become an important part of our efforts to compete on a new and broader scale.

The Work of the Firm

This firm is primarily engaged in civil litigation. Our cases include the following:

Personal injury cases arise when an individual has been physically injured from the negligence (carelessness) of another—for example, an automobile accident or a slip-and-fall case. This type of case accounts for most of the litigation work we do.

Malpractice cases involve alleged acts of negligence on the part of physicians, counselors, lawyers, or other professionals.

Product liability cases belong to a special type of personal injury case in which the individual has been physically injured by a defective product, such as an exploding beverage bottle, adulterated food, or unsafe machinery.

Contracts cases involve one party having suffered a loss from the failure of another party to meet the terms of an agreement between them. A typical contract case could involve the failure to complete construction of a house, or the failure to pay once construction is complete.

Corporation cases are brought by one corporation against another for such incidents as trademark violation or industrial espionage.

Antitrust cases deal with individuals, government, or a business suing another business for harmful trade practices, such as price discrimination, unfair competition, or monopolization of a market.

Securities cases arise from disputes regarding the ownership, value, or other issues regarding stocks, bonds, certificates, and other documentation of financial property.

Civil rights cases involve an individual or the government suing another party for violation of rights guaranteed by federal and state law. A typical civil rights litigation might involve race, sex, disability, or age discrimination.

Intellectual property cases primarily encompass disputes over patents, copyrights, and trademarks.

The percentage of federal civil cases resolved by trial dropped from 11 percent in 1962 to 1.8 percent in 2002. About 50 percent fewer state civil cases go to trial today than did in 1992. Also of note, persons suing in state civil cases won 55 percent of the time but only 27 percent of the time in medical malpractice cases.[5]

The Role of the Paralegal

The paralegal is an essential component in our delivery of legal services. You will spend the largest share of your time gathering and organizing factual information and drafting legal documents. You will also conduct legal research and investigation, assist at hearings and trials, oversee the timely scheduling and filing of matters, and help the office keep our clients informed as to the status of their cases. Unresponsiveness is among the most significant reasons a firm loses clients. Recently, our paralegals have begun to participate in case planning, client meetings, and firm marketing. Their familiarity with technology and the Internet makes them valuable to this firm's aggressive efforts to adapt to the e-world.

The firm bills clients directly for your services in the same manner we bill for the time of our attorneys. Court decisions, including the Supreme Court decision in *Missouri v. Jenkins,* 491 U.S. 274 (1989), confirm the legality and advantages of billing for paralegal time. A growing body of federal and state authority, plus Guideline 8 of the revised *ABA Model Guidelines for the Utilization of Paralegal Services (2004)* either sanction or strongly encourage such billing. A lower court's capping of paralegal fees at an amount lower than that paid attorneys in indigent cases was held by the Iowa Supreme Court to be an abuse of discretion [*Greatamerica Leasing Corp. v. Cool Comfort Air Conditioning and Refrigeration, Inc.,* 691 N.W.2d 730 (Iowa 2005)]. The basis, according to the court, should be what is reasonable in light of current market rates for paralegal fees and similar factors. Several federal and state statutes specifically authorize billing paralegal time.[6] We are not allowed to bill for the time of a legal secretary or clerk. The paralegal, therefore, is an important source of income and profit for the firm. Because you will be performing tasks formerly done by an attorney, but billed to the client at a lower rate, the client, too, will benefit from your work. *As long as you work efficiently, you will help this firm provide legal services to more people at a more reasonable cost. Therein lies the heart of the paralegal profession.*

The paralegal manager coordinates the paralegal staff and is the liaison between the partners and the paralegals. She allocates tasks to the paralegals. Should you have any questions or concerns about your position, please direct them to her. Any questions concerning a particular task should be directed to the attorney for whom the task is being completed. Assign typing to the designated person in the secretarial pool.

PARALEGAL HANDBOOK

"Ideas, ideals and great conceptions are vital to a system of justice, but it must have more than that—there must be delivery and execution. Concepts of justice must have hands and feet or they remain sterile abstractions. The hands and feet we need are efficient means and methods to carry out justice in every case in the shortest possible time and at the lowest possible cost."

—WARREN E. BURGER, ADDRESS, AMERICAN BAR ASSOCIATION, SAN FRANCISCO, VITAL SPEECHES, OCTOBER 1, 1972.

Paralegals at our firm are paid overtime, consistent with the Department of Labor's newly revised Fair Pay regulations of the Fair Labor Standards Act (effective August 2004). Overtime pay, though temporarily resolved by this act, remains an issue among paralegals. Some paralegals, because of their level of education and administrative responsibility, argue they are exempt from the overtime provisions; such exemption making them viewed more as professionals and eligible for flexible hours and pay bonuses. Other paralegals prefer set hours and argue that overtime pay protects them from not being compensated for after-hours work. Because the paralegal profession continues to evolve, requiring more specialized knowledge and higher levels of responsibility, the overtime issue will need to be revisited both for individual employees and for the profession as a whole.[7]

IMPORTANT LAW OFFICE PROCEDURES

Introduction

Every office has a variety of established procedures each new employee must learn. Procedures are necessary for the sake of efficiency, uniformity, and quality. Learning the required procedures will save you time and help you to survive and thrive in the law office. One of the first things you should do, therefore, is to locate and read the office procedures manual. It will provide information ranging from pay periods and sick leave to cash receipts and conference calls. Three procedures of particular importance are timekeeping, disbursement entry, and deadline control.

Timekeeping and Billing

billable hours
The time spent on a client's case that can be billed to the client.

Timekeeping is a procedure whereby attorneys and paralegals regularly record how much time they spend on a client's case or on other matters. A law firm is compensated for its work and analyzes its productivity (including that of each paralegal) on the basis of such records. The time spent on a client's case that can be billed to the client is called **billable hours.** The lawyer's fee, and hence the firm's income, is often based on billable hours. Some types of billing and fees are:

Hourly rate billing—a price based on the total number of hours worked at a specified per hour charge

Task-based billing—set prices for different types of tasks that may vary depending on the nature or difficulty of the task (phone call, travel, document drafting, etc.)

Flat fee billing—an overall, preset price to handle a matter from start to finish (frequently used for routine, high volume matters)

Contingency fee—an amount to be paid only if the client wins the case, usually a percentage of the money awarded to the client

Retainer fee—upfront payment to secure legal services and to cover anticipated costs and attorney fees

Value billing—a pricing method (increasingly demanded by many businesses and corporations) that requires the law firm to estimate what the legal representation will cost and what services, specifically, the client will pay for (used to bid for a prospective client's business and to help the client budget the cost of legal services).

Regardless of the type of billing, it is essential to keep accurate time and task records from the start. This process is computerized in most firms. A typical window is seen in Exhibit 1:2.

EXHIBIT 1:2 ■ Permanent Time Log

```
┌──────────────────────── Time/Bill ────────────────────────┐
│                                                             │
│  I.D. Code    [KS            ] [↓]      Related             │
│                                         Expense            │
│  Client       [Ann Forrester ] [ ]      Type    [        ] [↓] │
│                                                             │
│  File No.     [02-3010       ] [ ]      Amount  [        ]  │
│                                                             │
│  Date         [              ] [ ]                          │
│                                                             │
│  Service      [Phone Conference] [↓] [NC]                   │
│                                                             │
│  Start   [1255]    Total Time [.25]     Bill [$15.00]       │
│  Stop    [1310]    Rate/Hr    [60]                          │
│                    Flat Rate  [    ]                        │
│                                                             │
│  Description [Regarding her upcoming deposition: time, place, materials to │
│               review.                                     ] │
│                                                             │
└─────────────────────────────────────────────────────────────┘
```

Guidelines for Entering Your Time

1. Enter the client's name, the related file or account number, and the date of entry.
2. Enter your identification code.
3. Enter or click the type of service provided.
4. Click the NC box if time was spent on a nonbillable item such as a professional meeting or public service activity.
5. Enter the number of whole hours worked on the service plus any partial hours, usually in tenths of an hour (six minutes equals one tenth of an hour).
6. If the software permits, enter a description of the task that accurately conveys to the client the legitimacy of the work.
7. Enter information on any out-of-pocket expenses incurred that are to be reimbursed by the client, such as long-distance phone calls, mileage traveled, and on-line fees.

For efficiency in billing, we use the *American Bar Association Uniform Task-Based Management System* (UTBMS) [*http://www.abanet.org/litigation/utbms(1994)*], which includes standardized task (service) codes. This system is used by a number of law firms and requested by businesses and other clients.

Timekeeping software can generate a bill to the client, provide billing reports for each attorney and paralegal, and produce financial summaries for the firm as a whole. Some names in time and billing software are Timeslips™, Tabs 3™, Quick Books®, and PCLaw. Internet programs include Keystone Professional, DDI*Law®, Timesolv™, and Timesheet Professional®. Cutting-edge programs allow data entry by cellular phone and satellite, and let clients receive and review their bills online.

Electronic billing (e-billing) is the posting of billing information by the law office to a secure electronic host site for instant client access. Although attaching a bill to an e-mail is technically e-billing, the more important trend involves the use of vendor

"I dislike sending in professional charges to friendly people, but we have a saying here that offices like individuals have to live."

—REGINALD L. HINE, AMERICAN JURIST, CONFESSIONS OF AN UNCOMMON ATTORNEY, 1945.

electronic billing (e-billing)
The posting of billing information by the law office to a secure electronic host site for instant client access.

systems that permit the online sharing of billing information. Though e-billing's speed and flexibility in offering customized financial information to the client are advantages, they also increase costs.[8] E-billing often employs the ABA's UTBMS and the *Legal Electronic Data Exchange Standard* (LEDES) (*http://www.ledes.org.*), the standardized file format for the transfer of electronic information. Some vendors are Serengeti Tracker, TyMetrix, Data Cert, Inc., and IGD Systems.

Learning to produce accurate time and billing data is essential. Start by getting a few typical client bills and review them with an experienced paralegal or attorney. Consult, as well, on what is an appropriate balance of billable and nonbillable time.

Important ethical guidelines limit billing practices [ABA Comm. on Ethics and Professional Responsibility Formal Op. 379 (1993)]. The American Bar Association prohibits double billing. The opinion eliminates the practice of billing several clients the full amount for time spent on behalf of all the clients. For example, it is unethical to bill one client for three hours of flight time if two hours of that in-flight time is spent working on a brief for another client. Formerly, some law firms billed the first client for three hours at the full rate and the second client two hours at the full rate, creating unfair income for five hours of work instead of the real total time of three hours.

Other ethical concerns arise when a paralegal is encouraged to misrepresent clerical work (nonbillable) to a client as nonclerical and billable or some similar deception. Such practices are highly improper and can lead to serious consequences for both the attorney and the law office. Another current ethical issue is the unbundling of legal services. **Unbundling legal services** is the mutually agreed limitation of legal representation to one distinct step in a legal matter or process that may have numerous steps. For example, an attorney and a client may contract for the attorney to handle a trial but not the appeal, or draft a legal document but not file it or present it in court. Unbundling's rationale is to make legal services more affordable by allowing clients to do some things on their own or to contract for just what services they can afford. Because this flies in the face of traditional ethical standards that require lawyers to be responsible for the entire representation process, many states are revising their codes to permit reasonable, segmented representation.

Disbursement (Expense) Entry

Disbursements are expenses incurred on behalf of the client and can be directly attributed to that client's case. Disbursements include such things as phone calls, faxes, postage, photocopies, on-line research service, travel, filing fees, and others; record these expenditures on disbursement forms or computerized equivalents. Many time and billing software programs also have a disbursement feature. The ABA's Uniform Task-Based Management System provides standard disbursement (expense) codes. Exhibit 1:3 is an example of the format and data needed.

Guidelines for Recording Disbursements

1. Enter the client's name, file number, the date, and your initials or code.
2. Enter the expense type (photocopies, lodging, travel, etc.).
3. Enter the amount of the expense.
4. Enter comments to provide specific information.

The disbursement entries are collected manually or electronically for billing. This kind of recordkeeping leads to well-documented bills and reduces disputes over fees.

unbundling legal services
The mutually agreed limitation of legal representation to one distinct step in a legal matter or process that may have numerous steps.

EXHIBIT 1:3 ■ Permanent Disbursement Record

Expense	
I.D. Code	KS ↓
Client	Ann Forrester
File No.	02-3010
Date	
Type	photocopies ↓ NC
Price	**Quantity** **Total**
Description	Photocopies of deposition requested by client.

Deadline (Docket) Control

Hovering over every attorney and paralegal is the fear of making a mistake costing the client a significant sum of money or, even worse, the client's one lifetime opportunity to sue for just compensation or to challenge an unjust suit. Mistakes lead to malpractice (errors and omissions) claims that, if not settled, lead to costly malpractice lawsuits. Such claims raise the firm's insurance costs, damage reputations, and can result in disciplinary action by the state bar. One misconception, however, is that good attorneys and good paralegals do not make mistakes. The reality is that even the best make mistakes. Keep in mind, however, that a good paralegal knows that errors are likely and takes every precaution.

Studies tell us that some of the errors most often leading to malpractice claims include calendaring and deadline control errors, failure to know or properly apply the law, failure to do adequate research and investigation, faulty drafting of legal documents, failure to inform clients, incorrect or inadequate advice, conflicts of interest, and acts and omissions of associates and employees.[9] Personal injury practice (tort cases for plaintiffs) is the area of practice most subject to malpractice claims.[10]

Office procedures and systems, such as those for timekeeping and disbursements, reduce errors. One critical system is deadline control. Missed deadlines are the primary reason law offices are sued for professional malpractice. Every office must have a system ensuring that important deadlines are met. These systems, often called tickler systems, involve a regular calendaring (docketing) process. When the attorney or a paralegal in the office becomes aware of a deadline, it is entered onto a deadline control slip or computer equivalent. If every member of the legal team is responsible for recording or "noticing" a deadline, then the chance of an omission is greatly reduced. Electronic, rules-based calendaring products are gaining popularity. These products automatically calculate and calendar deadlines required by any relevant

---

EXHIBIT 1:4 ▪ Deadline Slip

```
┌─────────────────────────────── Docket Entry ───────────────────────────────┐
│                                                                             │
│   I.D. Code     [                 ] [ ]                                      │
│                                                                             │
│   Client        [                 ] [ ]      Time     [                 ]    │
│                                                                             │
│   File No.      [                 ] [ ]      Place    [                 ]    │
│                                                                             │
│   Date          [                 ] [ ]      Start    [                 ]    │
│   Entered                                                                   │
│                                                                             │
│   Deadline for  [                 ] [↓]      Due      [ 6/15/08        ]     │
│                                                                             │
│   Priority level [ 3 ]                       Reminder  1  [ 6/08/08 ]        │
│                                                                             │
│                                                         2  [ 6/13/08 ]       │
│   Remarks       [ First interview of Ann Forrester  ]                        │
│                 [                                   ]   3  [ 6/16/08 ]       │
│                 [                                   ]                         │
│                 [                                   ]                         │
│                                                                             │
└─────────────────────────────────────────────────────────────────────────────┘
```

state or federal rules of procedure, for example, when an important document must be filed in court within a specified number of days from a triggering event. If the trigger event changes, then the program can recalculate and reenter the needed dates. Exhibit 1:4 indicates what data is needed.

Guidelines for Entering Deadline Data

1. Enter the name of the client and the file number of the case to which the deadline applies.
2. Enter the task that must be completed. Some tasks require other related tasks to be done by other people in the firm, or software facilitates the assignment of deadlines to more than one employee. Enter this information.
3. Enter the deadline date and reminder dates for the particular task in the designated boxes.
4. Enter the start date (the day the task should be started) in the designated box.
5. Enter under "Remarks" any specific direction to assist in completing the task.
6. If done electronically, the data is automatically recorded in the firm's master calendar. If done manually, see that the required form is delivered to the person in charge of recording deadlines.

On each start date, the person responsible for the designated task will receive an electronic or other reminder and will receive increasingly urgent reminders until the task is done. The person charged with the task indicates its completion by initialing after "Done" on the form or as required by the deadline software. The deadline system should also include a post-deadline reminder that the target date was missed and some corrective action should be taken.

Notebook computers and handheld electronic devices facilitate the exchange of deadlines and other information to and from the office at other locations.

Technology Management

Our office increasingly expects our paralegals to function as technology managers. It is important for you not only to master technological procedures, but also to inform yourself of the latest software for carrying out procedures. Your knowledge of software, e-mail procedures and security, video conferencing, instant messaging, PIMs, and other means for us to communicate with each other and our clients make you a much more valuable employee.

E-Mail

Our office relies heavily on communication through our office computer network and the Internet. E-mail is a primary means of sending information, including many kinds of documents. Our office, like many others, requires its employees to sign an agreement with the following essentials:

1. We encourage the use of computers and electronic communication for the business of the firm.
2. Use e-mail for office business only and in an appropriate manner.
3. The firm reserves the right to monitor the use of e-mail by each employee.
4. Your e-mail passwords shall not be shared with any unauthorized person.
5. Inappropriate and offensive e-mail is prohibited.
6. Unauthorized use of e-mail and the Internet includes accessing or downloading pornography, hacking into computers, playing games, and compromising the security of the firm's confidential and other information.[11]

Technology Security

The security of our firm's records and our communication processes, including all electronic communication, is paramount. It is every employee's duty to protect client confidentiality, prevent identity theft, and ensure the integrity of our network and operating systems. Here are a few cautionary tips regarding security in general:

- When e-mailing confidential documents, use encryption or, at the very least, use the office's standard confidentiality disclaimer with intended recipient information and subject as the e-mail message and enclose the confidential document as an attachment only.
- Use a metadata removal program for documents being sent out of the office (metadata is invisible but retrievable electronic information about the preparation and history of a document that can be harmful in the hands of opponents or others).
- In addition to virus protection, use software that prevents others from invading your computer system with spyware, password crackers, network scanners, and the like.
- When out of the office, avoid the use of shared wireless or Internet café services except for routine, non-confidential communication.
- Confirm that your computer work is backed up regularly.
- If working at home on office business, be sure your home computer is also protected by a firewall and other needed security devices.
- Take great care to prevent the theft of portable electronic devices used for office business.[12]

Chapter 9 on document management contains an additional discussion of security.

TECHNIQUES FOR THRIVING IN THE LAW OFFICE

In addition to learning office procedures and following them closely, practicing the following techniques will help you thrive in the law office.

- Become acquainted with your fellow employees. Respect for others can foster better working relationships.
- Review your ethical responsibilities and those of the firm on a regular basis.
- Learn the chain of command in the office and the roles of your supervising attorney or paralegal manager, the secretaries and others to whom you will give assignments, and other members of the firm. Know where authority rests and who is responsible for what.
- Understand that you are a part of a team whose members are likely to have conflicting deadlines and schedules. The team's success requires appreciation for cooperation, mutual consultation, compromise, and the contributions of all its members.
- Know how to assign work. Decide to whom the work should be assigned and submitted, how much advance notice is normally required before the expected completion date, what procedure is appropriate in last-minute rushes, whether completion dates should be given, and whether special forms for delegating tasks are used. Compliance with these procedures will enhance your relationship with those to whom you assign work and will contribute to office efficiency.
- Submit work as error-free as possible. Take the time to check grammar, spelling, citations, form, brevity, accuracy, and clarity. When time permits, study the rules of good writing to improve your communications skills. Attention to detail is essential.
- Keep careful track of client files. Misplaced case files lead to frustration and can adversely affect our representation of a client. Follow strictly the office policy on checking out and returning files.
- When addressing clients, use Mr., Ms., Dr., or other appropriate titles. Avoid first names unless there is no doubt the situation makes it acceptable.
- Be sensible when using the telephone. How you conduct yourself when using the phone is a direct reflection on this firm. Exercise good common sense and be polite, businesslike, and brief. Ethically, it is important that everyone you speak with on the phone understand that you are not an attorney. Make this clear at the outset of the conversation whenever there might be any doubt. Plan ahead for phone calls; knowing what information you need helps keep conversations brief. Incomplete messages and misunderstandings on the phone can be a problem; it is a good idea to have people repeat addresses and phone numbers that you have given them and for you to repeat information that you receive.
- In addition, some phone conversations are important enough to confirm in writing the terms, dates, or arrangements discussed on the phone. If possible, do this immediately following the phone call. The letter serves as an important record of the conversation. In some instances, if a letter of confirmation seems inappropriate, a brief memo to the file may be useful.
- Learn to complete assignments efficiently. Each time you receive an assignment, be sure you thoroughly understand it and the time frame in which it must be completed. Obtain the facts underlying the task—know why you are doing the task. Ask questions to determine exactly what is required of you, especially if you have never done such an assignment before. Prioritize your

assignments according to deadline, how much time they will take, and other factors.

- ▪ Once you have the assignment in mind, decide the best way to complete the task. Use the guides and examples provided during your training. Ask the attorney for additional guidance. Do not try to reinvent the wheel on each assignment. If the information supplied to you is insufficient, seek examples in our legal form files, in the numerous form books, in the statutes, and in the state and federal rules. Ask the advice of others who have done similar work and would be glad to give you some suggestions. Keep a log of each of your assignments, indicating when the task was given and when it was completed. Such a log will help you build a system folder, described later in this handbook. It will also help you list specific skills on your resume should you decide to apply for an advanced position in this firm or elsewhere. It will be used in an annual evaluation of your work.

- ▪ Remember the importance of your work to our clients. On any job there will be times when you are tired or simply bored. These are times rife with the potential for error. Remind yourself that our clients rely heavily on us, and what we do has considerable impact on their lives and businesses.

- ▪ Reduce stress and its debilitating effects by learning not to take curtness and gruffness personally, understanding that this is a symptom of the pressure felt by others. Set your limits and stick to them. Use the firm's policies when necessary to defend yourself tactfully. Notify others well in advance of doctor's appointments and other personal business, then keep your personal appointments. Stay healthy by getting regular exercise, taking necessary breaks, anticipating crunch times and pacing yourself, getting adequate sleep, and avoiding those things that contribute to long-term debilitation such as abuse of alcohol and prescription and other drugs.[13]

- ▪ Dress professionally.

- ▪ Learn the criteria in your office for a job well done and those for advancement.

- ▪ Keep a sense of humor. While you need to regard your work seriously, it is equally important to be able to laugh, to see the humor in your own follies as well as in the situations in which you find yourself. Of all creatures, it is said, we alone have the gift for laughter; maybe that is why we have thrived.

THE TRAINING PROCEDURE

Procedure, Task Information, Assignments

You will begin your training with several cases currently being handled by this firm. You will work through the cases at a relatively slow pace, concentrating on the paralegal tasks one step at a time as they arise chronologically. For each assigned task, you will be given the following:

1. Information on the nature and purpose of the task to be performed
2. Directions or guidelines as to how to perform the task
3. Examples of the completed tasks
4. Opportunities to perform the task yourself
5. Evaluation of your work

During this training period, you will be performing the following duties:

1. Researching
2. Investigating

3. Interviewing
4. Organizing materials
5. Summarizing materials
6. Drafting documents, forms, and correspondence
7. Responding to questions on concepts, principles, and procedures

Developing a Litigation System

litigation system
A detailed procedure manual that is a chronological collection of the guidelines, forms, correspondence, checklists, procedures, and pertinent law for all steps in the litigation process.

A **litigation system** is a detailed procedure manual that is a chronological collection of the guidelines, forms, correspondence, checklists, procedures, and pertinent law for all steps in the litigation process. As a personal resource it provides advantages in efficiency, uniformity, accuracy, and quality. It will help you learn the benefits of being organized and can be easily updated. Because a good system folder will help you on the job, and perhaps in securing a job, the system folder should provide an extra incentive to do your assignments thoroughly and accurately. Regular use of the system approach will help reinforce the individual litigation skills presented in this text and will help develop confidence in your ability to create a system in any area of law.

Should your supervisor (instructor) choose to use the system development approach to your training, one of your continuous assignments will be to construct a paralegal's litigation system folder. A three-ring binder will serve as a convenient system folder. It should have enough tabbed dividers to accommodate the following divisions (also listed in the system folder contents in the appendix to this text). You may choose to computerize the system folder.

1. Quick reference information
   a. Pertinent office procedure
   b. General information (courts, names, addresses, deadlines, and so on)
2. Interview
3. Investigation
4. Pleadings and service of process
5. Discovery
6. Settlement
7. Pretrial
8. Trial
9. Post-trial
10. Appeal

As you are asked to do certain tasks, place the necessary information into the appropriate section of the system in chronological order. Your system will gradually take shape and should be complete by the conclusion of the training period.

In the upcoming weeks, you will be given numerous paralegal assignments. The workbook contains many such assignments from which your instructor or you may choose. They will help you apply and learn the material you have read. When doing the assignments, assume that you are in the state of Columbia, whose laws are the same as the laws of your state. Because most of your future work will be in *your state*, pay particular attention to the applications of this text and assignments to the practice of law in *your state*.

ETHICAL AND OTHER PROFESSIONAL RESPONSIBILITIES

Introduction

professional ethics
For attorneys, the rules of conduct that govern the practice of law.

Soon you will be working with cases and the people involved in those cases. In dealing with others, be ever mindful of the high standard of professional ethics to which your actions must conform. **Professional ethics,** as applied to attorneys, are the rules of conduct that govern the practice of law. Each person working for this firm is responsible for knowing what is expected and is to act accordingly. A breach of ethical standards will reflect badly upon this firm and may also lead to the disbarment of one or more of our attorneys. It may cost you your job and subject you to prosecution for the unauthorized practice of law.

Valuable resources relevant to your ethical responsibilities include your state's rules of professional conduct for lawyers, the *ABA's Model Rules of Professional Conduct* (1983), the *ABA's Model Guidelines for the Utilization of Paralegal Services* (2004), the *Code of Ethics and Professional Responsibility of the National Association of Legal Assistants, Inc.* (adopted 1975, revised 1979, 1988 and 1995), the National Federation of Paralegal Association's *Affirmation of Responsibility* (adopted 1977, revised 1981), and the ethics code of your state paralegal association. The guidance provided by these documents is quite consistent.

What a Paralegal May Not Do

Except as specifically permitted by law, paralegals *may not* perform any of the following functions:

1. Provide legal services directly to the public without the supervision of an attorney.
2. Give legal advice or counsel a client. **Legal advice** is independent professional judgment based on knowledge of the law and given for the benefit of a particular client.
3. Represent a client in court or other tribunal or otherwise act as an advocate for a client unless specifically permitted to do so by law or rule of court.
4. Accept or reject cases for the firm.
5. Set any fee for representation of a client.
6. Split legal fees with an attorney (bonuses and profit-sharing plans not tied to a specific case are permissible).
7. Be a partner with a lawyer if any of the activities of the partnership include the practice of law [exception: the District of Columbia ethics Rule 5.4(b)]. The American Bar Association rejected a proposal to relax the prohibition against fee sharing and multidisciplinary practice (July 2000).
8. Solicit cases for a lawyer.
9. Perform tasks that are the unauthorized practice of law as defined in the pertinent state. One state supreme court has stated that prior to any attempt on its part to better define and regulate the unauthorized practice of law, the state bar association must provide the court with demonstrable, quantifiable evidence of the extent of and harm caused by the unauthorized practice of law.[14] Note, as well, that the unauthorized practice of law is now a felony in Florida [Fla. Stat. § 454.23 (2004)], and other states are considering enacting such laws.

legal advice
Independent professional judgment based on knowledge of the law and given for the benefit of a particular client.

What a Paralegal May Do

Paralegals may perform a wide array of tasks and be confident their work will not create a breach of ethics if it meets certain criteria.

1. The task must be delegated by an attorney.
2. It must be performed under an attorney's supervision.
3. Paralegals must clearly designate their status as a paralegal.
4. The lawyer must retain a direct relationship with the client (the attorney must retain control over the relationship).
5. The task must involve information gathering or be ministerial and cannot involve the rendering of legal advice or judgment (unless the legal advice or judgment is provided by the paralegal directly to the attorney).

6. The work must be given final approval or be examined by the attorney.
7. The work must not have a separate identity but merge with the attorney's final work product.

In addition, the name of a paralegal may appear on a firm's business card and letterhead if the person is designated a paralegal.

Paralegals may represent clients at federal administrative hearings. This includes hearings of matters such as supplemental Social Security or black lung benefits. Some states have passed administrative procedure acts similar to that of the federal government permitting paralegal representation without attorney supervision.

American Bar Association studies have underscored the unmet legal needs of millions of U.S. citizens.[15] Expanding the range and responsibility of what paralegals are permitted to do under the supervision of an attorney could help meet these needs. A 1995 report from the American Bar Association Commission on Nonlawyer Practice specifically recommends this.[16] Meanwhile, various state legislatures or supreme courts continue to consider proposals to license or register paralegals. Whether paralegals should be licensed as a profession and be permitted to provide legal services beyond what they do now will continue to be hotly debated, especially in those states that reexamine the availability of legal services to their respective citizens.

California became the first state to enact legislation that not only defines a paralegal/legal assistant, but also requires a paralegal to have specific educational and experience qualifications, coupled with mandatory continuing legal education requirements [Cal. Bus. & Prof. Code § 6450–6456 (Deering 2001)]. No one other than a qualified paralegal may use the paralegal/legal assistant title. The legislation does not, however, expand what paralegals can legally do for clients.

Confidentiality, Honesty, Conflict of Interest, and Other Ethical Considerations

Paralegal ethical standards, for all practical purposes, are the same as those for attorneys. Attorneys, not paralegals, are disciplined by the bar for ethical breaches. Paralegals, however, are bound by the nature of their jobs to uphold each rule as if they were the attorneys.

Attorneys are bound by the ethical standards set by their state's highest court. Most states have adopted the American Bar Association's *Model Rules of Professional Conduct* (1983) with some local amendments. Studying the *Model Rules of Professional Conduct* provides a paralegal with an understanding of most of the ethical standards in effect in any particular state. Because some states have deleted or amended some of the ABA's rules, however, you should obtain a copy of your state's version of the ethical standards. These are available through state bar associations. Place these in the ethics section of your system folder. The following discussions highlight the portions of the *Model Rules* most important for you to learn at this point. Other sections of the rules will be presented as they arise in the context of a particular paralegal task. The following paragraphs incorporate changes to the Model Rules stemming from the report of the American Bar Association Commission on Evaluation of the Rules of Professional Conduct: Ethics 2000.

Confidentiality: A paralegal shall hold inviolate the confidences of a client. Nothing the client tells you or that you learn about the client may be revealed to anyone outside the office, not even to a spouse or parent. ABA Model Rule 1.6 states that a client's confidences shall not be revealed unless the client gives "informed consent" or the disclosure is "impliedly authorized to carry out the representation." An attorney *may* reveal confidential information to prevent "reasonably certain death or substantial bodily harm," to prevent a client's crime or fraud reasonably certain to cause substantial financial injury and furthered by the attorney's legitimate services (or to mitigate or rectify such injury), to get advice to assure ethical compliance, to defend an action or complaint against the attorney arising out of representation of the client, or to comply with "other law or court order."

Parallel state ethics rules regarding disclosure of confidential information may vary. Generally, to preserve confidentiality, a client's statement to you or other employees of the firm should not be made in the presence of outsiders. Exceptions to this rule of thumb will be discussed in Chapter 3 and subsequent discussions of attorney-client privilege. Further, the duty to protect confidentiality extends beyond the conclusion of the representation and even after the death of the client [Rule 1.9(c)(2)].

Today law office technology raises added concern about preserving confidential information. E-mail can be copied accidentally or forwarded to unintended recipients, so it must be used with great care. Nevertheless, the use of e-mail carries an expectation of privacy parallel to that of regular mail and standard phone-line conversations. Therefore, e-mail use does not violate Model Rule 1.6 [ABA Comm. on Ethics and Professional Responsibility, Formal Op. 413 (1999)]. Cellular phone transmissions are not as secure as e-mail, and their use for confidential conversations is risky. Although some protection against intentional interception and recording of wire, oral, and electronic communications is provided by the federal wiretap statute (18 U.S.C.A. 2510, *et seq.*), neither e-mail nor cellular phones or other wireless devices should be used for transmitting especially sensitive material. Giving third parties (often vendors) access to a law office's computers to remedy technology problems or to assist in electronic aspects of litigation requires great caution to protect client confidentiality.

The disposal of outdated hardware, often containing sensitive files, can lead to breaches of confidentiality. Offices should have procedures in place that truly erase or destroy residual computer files. Simply deleting files is not adequate.

Honesty: A paralegal must maintain the highest standards of professional integrity and avoid any dishonesty, fraud, deceit, or misrepresentation. This rule applies to all dealings with the client, judges, court employees, opposing attorneys, and the public. (See Rules 3.3, 3.4, 3.5, 3.6, 4.1, 4.3, 4.4, 8.1, 8.2, 8.3, and 8.4.)

Conflict of Interest: A paralegal should avoid and reveal any conflicts of interest. This requirement rests on the rationale that citizens must have faith in the legal system to seek the peaceful resolution of their disputes. Since conflicts of interest can dilute an attorney's allegiance to the client and damage independent professional judgment, they are barred by Model Rules 1.7–1.13. A paralegal must also be loyal to the client and avoid such conflicts [Rules 1.7 through 1.13, ABA Model Guideline 7 for the Utilization of Paralegal Services (2004), Comment to Guideline 1 (NALA Model Standards and Guidelines for Utilization of Legal Assistants), and EC-1.6(a)–(g) (NFPA Model Code of Ethics and Professional Responsibility and Guidelines for Enforcement)]. A conflict of interest would occur if this firm accepted a case to sue Mr. Hart, and then was hired by Mr. Hart to sue someone else. In this situation, confidential information learned from Mr. Hart in the second case could be used against him in the first case. In such circumstances, the second case should not be accepted.

In another example, if a client represented by the firm sued the O.K. Manufacturing Company, a conflict of interest would arise if the paralegal assigned to the case owned stock in the company. It is obvious that the paralegal may hesitate to do the best job possible when the outcome of the case could have an adverse effect on the paralegal's income. In such a situation, the paralegal should inform the supervising attorney of the conflict. A remedy for the conflict would be to take the paralegal off that case.

Law offices must be extremely sensitive to actual and potential conflicts of interest. Not only can violations lead to serious ethics sanctions, but also to costly and embarrassing disqualification from otherwise lucrative cases and the long-term representation of valued clients (Model Rule 1.10).

Hiring new personnel who have worked at another law firm is fraught with potential conflicts problems. For example, if a paralegal worked on behalf of Mr. Hart at the first firm, but now must handle cases against Mr. Hart at the second firm, a paralegal might be likely to use such confidential information gained from Mr. Hart while working for the first firm against him at the second firm. Remedies for this situation are to disqualify the law office because of the conflict or not to hire the transferring paralegal. These remedies are harsh and pose an unfair restraint on the freedom of employment. The preferred method to deal with such real or potential conflicts is to surround the new employee with an "ethical wall" that screens the employee from any contact with the case that causes the conflict. This approach is recommended by the ABA and has been adopted in most jurisdictions [Comment 4, Model Rule of Professional Conduct 1.10; ABA Committee on Ethics and Professional Responsibility, Informal Op. 1526 (1988); and ABA Model Guideline 7 for the Utilization of Paralegal Services (2004)]. In *Leibowitz v. the Eighth Judicial District Court of the State of Nevada*, 78 P. 3d 515 (Nev. 2003), the Nevada Supreme Court reversed a former decision that prohibited such screens for nonlawyer personnel, and reiterated the recommended criteria for a proper conflict of interest screen:

1. The new nonlawyer employee must be warned not to reveal any information relating to the representation of the former employer's client.
2. The employee must be told not to work on any matter the employee worked on for the former employer or on which the employee has information gained during the former employment.
3. The new firm should implement safeguards beyond the above warnings to see to it that the new employee does not work with matters worked on during the prior employment (such as notifying all office lawyers and paralegals that the relevant employee must not work on the specifically identified matter).
4. The new firm must inform the adverse party (or counsel) that their former employee has been hired and of the screening methods used.

The court in *Mulhern v. Calder,* 763 N.Y.S.2d 741 (Sup. Crt. 2003) reversed a lower court prohibition on nonlawyer screening because such screening was now permitted for lawyers. Also see *Schiessle v. Stephens,* 717 F.2d 417 (7th Cir. 1983) regarding ethical screens for lawyers.

Even in the few jurisdictions where screening is not yet permitted or in circumstances when screening is not likely to be effective (for example where the information has already been disclosed), disqualification of the law firm in the new case may still be avoided if the client from the new employee's previous office gives informed, written consent to the otherwise disqualified firm to go ahead with the representation despite the existing conflict (Model Rule 1.10 with reference back to Rule 1.7). A client can even waive future conflicts of interest if the proper procedures are followed [ABA Formal Opinion 436 (2005)].

If a paralegal, subsequent to working for one law firm, has been hired by another law firm, it is paramount for that paralegal not only to confirm the absence of conflicts in a new case with the current firm's clients and cases but also the absence of conflicts with any cases the paralegal worked on or clients worked for at the previous law firm. As discussed above, failure to make such checks or to report such information can have serious consequences. If a paralegal is given the responsibility to interview a prospective employee, any potential conflicts arising from the employment of the interviewee must be identified.

Malpractice: Lawyer malpractice cases involving significant amounts of money are on the rise.[17] Avoiding malpractice is a top priority that requires the attention of the entire law office staff. Carelessness by paralegals or others in the office can be expensive. In one case an important legal document was lost among other papers on a paralegal's desk, costing the paralegal's company over five hundred thousand dollars.[18] You can help prevent malpractice by paying close attention to details, double checking deadlines and other aspects of your work, employing standardized practice systems, adhering to ethical practices, avoiding the unauthorized practice of law, identifying troublesome cases and clients, keeping current on relevant changes in the law and procedure, asking questions, reporting concerns, and following other good employment practices.

Pro Bono Work: Firms appreciate assistance in efforts to provide free legal services to the poor, called **pro bono** work. The National Association of Legal Assistants, the National Federation of Paralegal Associations, and state and local paralegal associations encourage paralegals to participate in pro bono work. Doing probono work with the bar is beneficial to the law firm, the paralegal, and the person served.

pro bono
Free legal services provided to those unable to afford representation.

Other Professional Considerations

Some professional ethics are not found in the codes but are nevertheless quite important. In professional working relationships, mutual respect and loyalty between employer and employees is especially important. Publicly criticizing one's fellow workers or one's clients, who deserve the utmost courtesy, respect, and every effort on our part to preserve their dignity, is not consistent with professional loyalty. Relationships with clients must always be kept on a professional level. If a relationship becomes too personal, it threatens objectivity, confidentiality, and one's loyalty to the firm.

Professional loyalty to the firm extends to the practice of law, which supersedes loyalty to any specific individual. Attorneys are directed to call attention to the unethical practices of other attorneys [Model Rule 8.3 (where adopted)], or, in some instances of the illegal conduct of their own clients to avoid assisting in fraud or crime [Rule 4.1 (truthfulness in statements to others) subject to Rule 1.6 on revealing confidentiality] or perjury [Rule 3.3 (candor toward the tribunal)]. Similarly, a paralegal must be prepared to report unethical behavior to the appropriate person within the firm. In *Brown v. Hammond,* 810 F. Supp. 644 (E. D. Pa 1993), a paralegal who was fired for refusing to be involved in wrongful billing practices was allowed to sue for wrongful discharge.

Advertising of legal services in various forms raises ethical questions. For example, a law firm ad that featured a pit bulldog and displayed an 800-pit-bull phone number was sanctioned as unprofessional and unethical in *The Florida Bar v. Pape,* 918 So.2d 240 (Fla. 2005). Paralegals may be asked to draft proposals for firm advertisements or brochures. The various state bars have attempted to review such advertising with mixed success. The Supreme Court of the United States strengthened bar efforts to control advertising. In *Florida Bar v. Went For It, Inc.,* 115 S. Ct. 2371 (1995), the court upheld the constitutionality of a bar association rule prohibiting lawyers from sending direct-mail solicitation to victims or their families within thirty days of an accident. Some law firms are utilizing paralegals to place advertising on the Internet in the form of Web sites. It is best to check state bar ethics guidelines, including those on how to avoid creating inadvertent attorney/client relationships, prior to using the information highway for this purpose.

It is helpful for each of us to be mindful that our actions reflect upon this firm and the professions we each represent. We encourage you to go beyond this brief word of caution on ethics. Study ethics in more detail as you learn other litigation tasks. The more you know about the ethical responsibilities of the attorney and paralegal, the more likely you will be able to spot and avoid trouble. Additional ethical considerations will be highlighted as they arise in the chapters ahead.

YOUR PROFESSIONAL DEVELOPMENT

White, Wilson & McDuff has always encouraged its employees to improve themselves professionally. For that reason, our firm will support you in your efforts toward personal professional development. Keep informed of what is going on in your field; attend continuing education seminars; participate in paralegal associations; and subscribe to literature that will benefit your career. Here is a brief list of some organizations, their addresses, and pertinent literature. Seek information as well from the local affiliates of these national organizations and from your local and state associations.

- Your local paralegal association

- American Association for Paralegal Education

  19 Mantua Road
  Mt. Royal, NJ 08061
  (856) 423-2829
  Fax: (856) 423-3420
  E-mail: info@aafpe.org
  Web: http://www.aafpe.org
  Publications: *The Paralegal Educator; The Journal of Paralegal Education and Practice*

- American Bar Association

  321 North Clark Street
  Chicago, IL 60610
  (312) 988-5000
  E-mail: askaba@abanet.org
  Web: http://www.abanet.org

- ABA Standing Committee on Legal Assistants

  E-mail: legalassts@abanet.org
  Web: http://www.abanet.org/
      legalservices

- International Paralegal Management Association

  P.O. Box 659
  Avondale Estates, GA 30002-0659
  (404) 292-4762
  Fax: (404) 292-2931
  E-mail: info@paralegalmanagement.org
  Web:
  http://www.paralegalmanagement.org

- National Association of Legal Assistants

  1516 South Boston, #200
  Tulsa, OK 74119
  (918) 587-6828
  Fax: (918) 582-6772
  Web: http://www.nala.org
  Publication: *Facts and Findings*

- National Federation of Paralegal Associations

  2517 Eastlake Avenue East, Suite 200
  Seattle, WA 98102
  (206) 652-4120
  Fax: (206) 652-4122
  E-mail: info@paralegals.org
  Web: http://www.paralegals.org
  Publication: *National Paralegal Reporter*

- *Legal Assistant Today*

  James Publishing, Inc.
  3505 Cadillac Avenue, Suite H
  Costa Mesa, CA 92626
  (714) 755-5450
  (800) 440-4780
  Fax: (714) 751-2709
  Web: http://www.jamespublishing.com

COURTS AND JURISDICTION

INTRODUCTION

Moving beyond the foundations discussed in the office handbook, this section discusses the function, structure, and jurisdiction of both the federal and state court systems. Then it explains the relationship between jurisdiction and venue, and how these distinct concepts determine the choice of a proper court for a lawsuit.

BASIC COMPONENTS OF A COURT SYSTEM

The federal and state court systems have at least two types of courts in common: the trial court and the appellate court.

The Trial Court

The trial court is the real workhorse of the court system. This is where most lawsuits are filed. Trial courts decide questions of law and questions of fact. Questions of fact focus on what happened: How fast was Mr. Hart driving? Was the floor wet? Was the traffic light red? The jury, if there is one, or judge decides the questions of fact. Questions of law focus on the law or proper procedure to be applied to a particular case: Is the evidence admissible? Was the hearing conducted in a fair and impartial manner? Is the statute constitutional? Questions of law are always decided by the judge. Beyond deciding questions of law, the judge sees to it that the rules of evidence and procedure are applied fairly, that order and decorum are maintained, and that the trial progresses expeditiously. In addition to deciding questions of fact, juries or judges decide whether the party bringing the lawsuit has met its burden of proof. Following that decision, the judge enters a formal finding called a judgment.

Most cases are resolved in the trial court. Trial courts have a variety of names: county, district, superior, common pleas, traffic, circuit, city, justice of the peace, or even supreme court in New York state. The trial courts may also be divided into branches or specialized courts: criminal, juvenile, probate, or family court.

The Appellate Court

If a trial court judge commits an error, the losing party has the right to appeal the case to an appellate court. Grounds for appeal include incorrect application of the law, a verdict not supported by the weight of the evidence, and errors in procedural or other rulings. The appellate court considers questions of law only and does not retry the facts of the case. It decides cases by reading the legal arguments of the parties, listening to oral arguments, and reviewing the written transcript or video record of the trial.

The federal and state court systems each have a final court of appeal. This court is called the supreme court in most systems. Others call it the court of appeals, supreme judicial court, or supreme court of appeals. The published opinion of an appellate court becomes the rule of law (precedent) in the particular geographical jurisdiction of that court.

The Intermediate Appellate Court

Thirty-seven states and the federal system have an intermediate appellate court. Where it exists, this court stands between the trial court and the court of final review. Most appeals from the trial courts must go to the intermediate appellate court and

> "If respect for the courts and for their judicial process is gone or steadily weakened, no law can save us as a society. Lawyers, whatever their views on controversial decisions, must inspire respect for the judiciary."
>
> —WILLIAM T. GOSSETT, PRESIDENT, AMERICAN BAR ASSOCIATION; SPEECH, CANADIAN BAR ASSOCIATION, OTTAWA, SEPTEMBER 3, 1969.

are resolved there. Some cases, usually of considerable significance, are appealed from the intermediate appellate court and are accepted by the supreme court or court of final appeal for review.

JURISDICTION

Jurisdiction is the power or authority of a court to hear and decide the questions of law or fact (or both) presented by a lawsuit. Most courts have a *geographical jurisdiction*, meaning that they hear cases that arise within specific geographical boundaries. The boundaries may encompass the city limits for municipal courts or the entire nation for the U.S. Supreme Court. Court decisions become law only within the specific geographical boundaries in which the court has jurisdiction.

The court also has *personal (in personam) jurisdiction*. This means the court must have the power over the particular person named in the lawsuit to enter a judgment against that person. This is usually accomplished by serving a summons and a copy of the complaint on the person being sued (the defendant). Traditionally, state courts had personal jurisdiction only over defendants located in the state. Today more states are passing long-arm statutes that permit service in other states under prescribed circumstances. In federal courts, personal jurisdiction is gained by serving the necessary documents within the geographical district of the court. The Internet's worldwide reach has raised new questions regarding personal jurisdiction. Electronic contacts alone can be sufficient to establish personal jurisdiction. Personal jurisdiction and what types of minimum contacts are sufficient to establish it are discussed in more detail in Chapter 5.

In rem (property) jurisdiction is the authority of the court to attach (seize) property (real estate, jewelry, bank deposits, or other property) within its geographical jurisdiction to resolve claims to the property. *Quasi in rem jurisdiction* is the authority of a court to seize and use property (within its jurisdiction) of a defendant over whom it does not have personal jurisdiction to pay a judgment against the defendant entered in an action indirectly related or unrelated to the property. For example, a court may use a defendant's small piece of land located in state to satisfy a bank's judgment against the defendant who has moved out of state and who has failed to make car payments legally owed to the bank. Quasi in rem jurisdiction is normally used when a state does not have the needed long-arm statute to gain personal jurisdiction.

Relevant to personal jurisdiction is the concept of sovereign immunity. *Sovereign immunity* protects governments and people in government positions from being sued for conducting legitimate (even if injurious) government business. Although the federal and state governments have passed laws waiving this protection in some types of cases, the doctrine can deprive a court of the authority to adjudicate some matters.

Each court has some form of *subject matter jurisdiction*. This jurisdiction is defined by the nature or subject of the lawsuits handled by that court—for example, criminal, juvenile, civil, or appellate cases.

If a court has *general jurisdiction*, it can hear all types of cases. Most states have trial courts of general jurisdiction where subject matter jurisdiction is assumed unless one party can demonstrate that the court does not have the necessary subject matter jurisdiction.

Original jurisdiction indicates that cases first enter the system at this court level—they "originate" here. Therefore, a court having original jurisdiction over criminal cases is the first to hear and try criminal cases. Most trial courts are courts of original jurisdiction.

"To no one will we sell, to no one will we refuse or delay, right or justice."

—Magna Carta, 1215.

A court has *limited jurisdiction* if its authority to hear and decide cases is limited to specific types of cases. A court specifically labeled a traffic court can hear only traffic cases; criminal court, only criminal cases; and so forth. Limited jurisdiction becomes *exclusive jurisdiction* if a court is the only court permitted to handle a specific type of case.

Frequently the jurisdiction of a court is limited by the amount of money claimed in the lawsuit. For example, a state's lower court may have jurisdiction over all civil cases up to $5,000, with the higher trial court having jurisdiction over all civil cases involving more than that amount. Frequently this monetary value is referred to as the **jurisdictional amount** or amount in controversy.

Supplemental jurisdiction (28 U.S.C. § 1367) permits federal courts already having jurisdiction over a federal claim to hear a state claim if that claim is based on essentially the same facts as the federal claim. The federal court, under the same circumstances, may also add parties over which it would not otherwise have jurisdiction. Supplemental jurisdiction includes what has previously been called *pendent, pendent party*, and *ancillary jurisdiction*.

Another type of jurisdiction is *removal jurisdiction*. Most often this refers to the ability of federal district courts to remove cases from state courts to federal court if the federal court has jurisdiction to hear the case. Removal jurisdiction and procedure are discussed further in Chapter 6.

When two courts have jurisdiction on the same type of case, the courts are said to have *concurrent jurisdiction*.

The jurisdiction of each court is legally defined by the constitution and statutes of the governmental entity that creates the court. Other aspects of jurisdiction will be addressed later in this text.

FEDERAL COURTS AND THEIR JURISDICTION

Introduction

Article III of the Constitution establishes the main federal courts and their jurisdictions. These courts are called constitutional courts and their judges are tenured for life. The constitutional courts consist of the United States Supreme Court, the United States Court of Appeals, and the United States District Court.

Legislative courts are established by act of Congress under Article I of the Constitution. Their judges have set terms. These are the specialized courts such as the United States Claims Court and the United States Tax Court.

All federal courts have limited subject matter jurisdiction and can exercise their power only with specific authorization. This authorization requires a constitutional source (Article III or Article I) and an act of Congress (found as United States Code provisions).

United States District Court

The United States District Court is the trial court in the federal system. There are ninety-four district courts, with at least one in each state and territory. These courts have original jurisdiction in a number of areas, the two most important being federal question cases and diversity of citizenship cases. **Federal question** cases are "all civil actions arising under the Constitution, laws, or treaties of the United States" (28 U.S.C. § 1331). These cases require the determination of rights under federal law and interpretation of its provisions. For example, a statute that unduly restricts freedom of the press would raise a federal question under the First Amendment, or a person suing to challenge a denial to that person of certain Social Security

jurisdictional amount (amount in controversy)
Specific dollar amount that must be claimed in an action to meet jurisdictional minimum of a given court.

supplemental jurisdiction
The power of federal courts already having jurisdiction over a federal claim to hear a state claim and add parties if that claim is based on essentially the same facts as the federal claim.

federal questions
"[A]ll civil actions arising under the Constitution, laws, or treaties of the United States" (28 U.S.C. § 1331).

benefits would be raising a question about federal law (i.e., the Social Security regulations). The U.S. Supreme Court recently expanded the reach of federal question jurisdiction to even the most traditionally exclusive state law actions when, embedded in the state case, there is a substantial, disputed question of federal law [*Grable & Sons Metal Products Inc. v. Darue Engineering & Mfg.*, 125 S. Ct. 2363 (2005)].

diversity of citizenship
Jurisdictional requirement for U.S. District Court that parties of a lawsuit be citizens of different states.

The second most important area of original subject matter jurisdiction for the district court is **diversity of citizenship** cases. "The district courts shall have original jurisdiction of all civil actions where the matter in controversy exceeds the sum or value of $75,000, exclusive of interest and costs, and is between . . . citizens of different states" [28 U.S.C. § 1332(a)(2)]. The rationale for federal diversity jurisdiction is to provide a party in the case with access to a neutral federal court, rather than having to litigate in a state court that might be biased in favor of an opponent who is a resident of the state in which the state court is located.

Several issues arise under this provision. The district court does not have jurisdiction unless diversity is complete. Each defendant must be a citizen of a different state from each plaintiff.[19] For example, three plaintiffs, two from Kansas and one from Wisconsin, could sue four defendants, two from Missouri and two from Nebraska, assuming $75,000 in dispute; but the same plaintiffs could not sue in federal district court if just one defendant was from the same state as any of the plaintiffs. For the purpose of determining diversity jurisdiction, citizens of the District of Columbia are treated as if they were citizens of a state.[20]

domicile
A person's true, permanent home.

A citizen's state is defined as the state of domicile. The **domicile** is the true permanent home—the place to which one intends to return after being away—and is frequently determined by looking at a person's place of employment, site of voting or automobile registration, site of property, and the like.[21]

For purposes of diversity, a corporation is considered a citizen of both the state in which it is incorporated and the state where it has its principal place of business [28 U.S.C. § 1332(c)]. If a company is incorporated in several states, the modern view (though not accepted in all jurisdictions) is to treat it as a citizen of each of those states.[22] The "principal place of business" is the center of most of the corporation's activities, and if that isn't determinative, the site of the corporation's headquarters is.[23] A national bank is a citizen in the state "designated in its articles of association as its main office" [*Wachovia Bank, National Association v. Schmidt*, 126 S.Ct. 941 (2006)].

If a party is an insurance company, that company is a citizen not only of the state of incorporation and the state of its principal place of business, but also of the state of the insured [28 U.S.C. § 1332(c)]. The insured is the person protected under the policy.

Determining diversity in other situations can present other problems. If the organization is an unincorporated association, it is a citizen of each state where each of its members is domiciled. For partnerships, it is unclear whether limited partners are included in diversity questions. [*Carden v. Arkoma Associates*, 494 U.S. 185 (1990)]. Limited liability corporations (LLCs) are increasingly being treated as partnerships for diversity determinations [*Cosgrove v. Bartolotta*, 150 F.3d 729 (7th Cir. 1998)]. Where all of the parties in a business case are otherwise diverse, the fact that two of the opposing parties actually reside in the same foreign country is irrelevant to potential state court bias and, therefore, diversity is not defeated.[24] Class action (numerous individuals with a common legal interest, i.e., all users of a certain product) citizenship is generally in the state of the named representative.[25] Under the Class Action Fairness Act (CAFA) [Pub. L. No. 109–2, 119 Stat. 4 (2005)], however, federal diversity jurisdiction is satisfied in class action cases filed on or after February 18, 2005 if the case meets the special jurisdictional amount (see below) and at least one plaintiff is diverse from at least one defendant [28 U.S.C. § 1332 (d)(2), (6), (8)].

Here are other points on diversity jurisdiction. Diversity of citizenship must be alleged in the complaint (the document that states the claim) (28 U.S.C. § 1653). Once it is established, it cannot be altered by the parties' moving from state to state. It must exist, however, at the time a case is removed to federal court. Diversity jurisdiction is not defeated because the defendant claiming diversity fails to negate the existence of an unnamed potential defendant, who, if included, would defeat diversity jurisdiction [*Lincoln Property Co. v. Roche,* 126 S. Ct. 606 (2005)]. Diversity does not give federal district courts jurisdiction in domestic relations or probate matters.[26]

In addition to diversity being complete, the "amount in controversy" must meet the $75,000 requirement. Normally the district court will accept jurisdiction based on the allegation of amount in the complaint unless it is legally clear that the plaintiff cannot recover the required amount.[27] Federal jurisdiction is not lost if recovery is eventually less than the requirement, but costs may be assessed [28 U.S.C. § 1332(b)].

Here is how the "amount in controversy" is determined in several contexts:

1. If the suit is for a declaratory judgment or an injunction, it is most often the value or cost to the plaintiff if relief were denied.
2. In most actions, it is the amount of plaintiff's harm or the defendant's costs to comply.
3. If suing under a federal statute that permits recovery of attorney's fees, that amount can be added to make $75,000.
4. If the case is an installment contract case and it is the entire contract that is in dispute, it is the value of the entire contract; otherwise, it is just the amount that has accrued in the installments to date.
5. If the case involves one plaintiff against one defendant, it is the value of all claims against defendant (i.e., a combination of tort and contract claims).
6. If there are multiple plaintiffs, each plaintiff's claim must be $75,000 or more. The claims cannot be combined to make the amount. If one plaintiff meets the jurisdictional amount, however, other plaintiffs may be added whose claims are less than the requisite amount through the district court's application of supplemental jurisdiction [*Exxon Mobil Corp. v. Allapattah Servs.,* 125 S.Ct. 2611(2005)].
7. If multiple parties own property in common, it is the value of the property that is determinative (for three plaintiffs owning property in common, the value would not have to be $225,000).
8. In a class action, each person's claim must be in excess of the $75,000 amount. This requirement has been significantly modified in *Exxon Mobil v. Allapattah* and by CAFA. CAFA extends diversity jurisdiction in class actions where there is at least one plantiff and one defendant that are diverse *and* where the combined monetary claims of all plaintiffs exceed five million dollars [28 U.S.C. § 1332(d)(2), (6), (8)].
9. If there is a counterclaim, determination under current law is not clear.[28]

In addition to the federal question cases and diversity cases involving more than $75,000, federal district courts have original subject matter jurisdiction over the following:

1. Exclusive jurisdiction over all admiralty, maritime, and prize cases (28 U.S.C. § 1333).
2. All suits brought by the United States, its agencies, or officers (28 U.S.C. § 1345).

3. Suits against the United States or its officers (concurrent with U.S. Claims Court up to $10,000) (28 U.S.C. § 1346).
4. Suits to compel officers of United States to perform their duty (28 U.S.C. §1361).
5. Removal of suits against federal officers in state courts (28 U.S.C. § 1442).
6. Suits in Bankruptcy (28 U.S.C. § 1334).
7. Suits in patents, plant variety protection, copyrights, trademarks, and unfair competition (28 U.S.C. § 1338).
8. Suits involving Internal Revenue and customs duties (28 U.S.C. § 1340).
9. Suits in civil rights (28 U.S.C. § 1343).
10. Suits affecting ambassadors and other public ministers and consuls (28 U.S.C. § 1351).

State courts have concurrent jurisdiction with federal courts in all matters within federal jurisdiction, except if federal jurisdiction is exclusive, as in the case of copyright and patent law.

The district courts have subject matter, diversity jurisdiction over suits between citizens of a state and citizens or subjects of a foreign state [28 U.S.C. § 1332(a)(2)], where citizens or subjects of foreign states are "additional parties" on either side of the suit, and where a foreign state sues "citizens of a state or of different states" [28 U.S.C. § 1332(a)(3) and (4)]. This type of diversity jurisdiction involving foreign states and their citizens or subjects is called **alienage jurisdiction.**

alienage jurisdiction
A diversity jurisdiction involving foreign states and their citizens or subjects.

United States Court of Appeals

The United States Court of Appeals is the intermediate appellate court in the federal system. It is divided into thirteen courts consisting of eleven regional circuits, a Court of Appeals for the District of Columbia, and the U.S. Court of Appeals for the Federal Circuit. The courts of appeals have appellate jurisdiction over all appeals taken from final decisions of the United States District Court (28 U.S.C. § 1291). Each court of appeals hears appeals from the federal district courts in their respective circuits. The Court of Appeals for the Federal Circuit has exclusive subject matter jurisdiction over appeals in patent, trademark, and plant variety protection cases, plus appeals from the U.S. Claims Court and those involving government employment and international trade (28 U.S.C. § 1295). It reviews decisions of the U.S. Court of International Trade, the U.S. Claims Court, the U.S. Court of Veterans Appeals, and the decisions of the Board of Appeals or the Board of Patent Interferences of the Patent and Trademark Office, the Commission of Patents and Trademarks, and the Trademark Trial and Appeals Board.

The map in Exhibit 1:5 shows the geographical arrangement of the circuits for the U.S. Court of Appeals and their respective federal district courts. Determine from the map in Exhibit 1:5 the federal circuit and district courts that serve your state.

United States Supreme Court

The United States Supreme Court is the highest-level appellate court in the federal system. Its one chief justice and eight associate justices function as the authority on the Constitution and ensure the supremacy of federal law. Supreme Court jurisdiction is defined in Article III of the Constitution and cannot be increased or decreased by Congress. It has appellate jurisdiction over appeals from the United States Court of Appeals (28 U.S.C. § 1254) and from the highest-level appellate courts in each state if the appeal raises a question of federal law (28 U.S.C. § 1257). Since 1988,

EXHIBIT 1:5 ▪ U.S. Courts of Appeals and U.S. District Courts

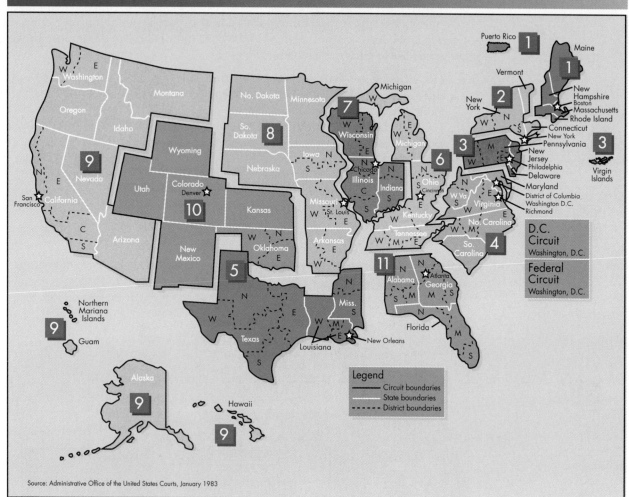

Source: Administrative Office of the United States Courts, January 1983

cases reach the Supreme Court almost exclusively by **writ of certiorari.**[29] This is a discretionary procedure that allows the Court to take only the cases that, in its opinion, have sufficient national significance to warrant its attention. The Court also uses the writ to resolve issues in which the courts of appeals are in serious conflict. Some constitutional matters come to the Court through a certification process distinct from the writ of certiorari.

The Supreme Court also has original jurisdiction in the following matters.

1. Controversies between two or more states (exclusive).
2. All actions or proceedings to which ambassadors, public ministers, and consuls of foreign states are a party.
3. All controversies between the United States and a state.
4. All actions or proceedings by a state against citizens of another state or against aliens.

Items 2–4 are subject matter jurisdictions held concurrently with lower federal courts.

writ of certiorari
A discretionary writ that allows the Supreme Court to take only cases that, in its opinion, have sufficient national significance to warrant its attention.

SPECIALIZED FEDERAL COURTS

Specialized federal courts are established as Article I legislative courts. Their judges have specified terms, usually fifteen years, and their salaries are not protected from congressional decreases as are those of the constitutional courts. The most important specialized courts are as follows:

1. The *United States Court of International Trade* decides disputes between citizens and the government on issues arising from import transactions (28 U.S.C. § 1581–85).
2. The *United States Court of Federal Claims* decides claims of U.S. citizens and foreign entities against the government based on federal law or contracts [28 U.S.C. § 1491(a)(1)] (some of this jurisdiction is concurrent with U.S. district courts, especially in Internal Revenue Service taxes improperly collected).
3. The *United States Tax Court* has original (trial) jurisdiction over taxpayer challenges to deficiency determinations of the Internal Revenue Service (26 U.S.C. § 6213).

EXHIBIT 1:6 ■ The Federal Court System

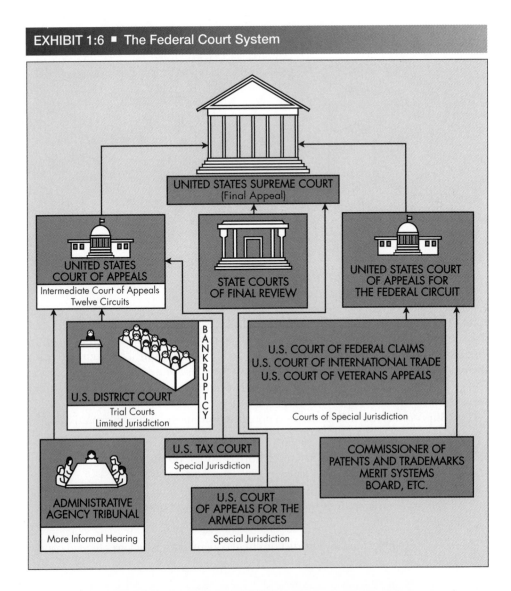

4. The courts and magistrate courts adjunct to the United States District Courts (28 U.S.C. §§ 7441–87) include the following:
   a. *federal magistrate courts* (whose judges are called magistrate judges)
   b. *bankruptcy courts*
   c. hearing of some private civil disputes and criminal matters
5. The *United States Court of Appeals for the Armed Forces* hears appeals from the Courts of Military Review (civil judges) (10 U.S.C. § 867).
6. The *United States Court of Veterans Appeals* reviews decisions of the Board of Veterans Appeals (38 U.S.C. § 4052).

See the diagram of the federal court system in Exhibit 1:6. Note the flow of appeals in the system.

STATE COURTS AND THEIR JURISDICTION

The diagram in Exhibit 1:7 illustrates of the structure of many state court systems. Note the flow of appeals in this diagram. Obtain or create a diagram of your state system, noting which courts function as trial courts (original jurisdiction) and as

EXHIBIT 1:7 ■ The State Court System

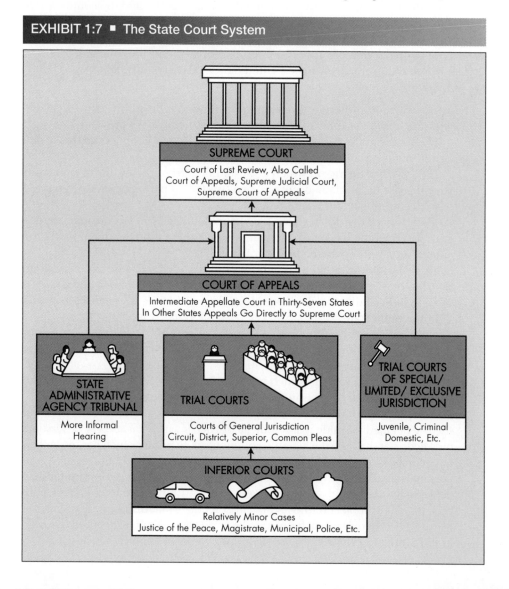

SUPREME COURT
Court of Last Review, Also Called Court of Appeals, Supreme Judicial Court, Supreme Court of Appeals

COURT OF APPEALS
Intermediate Appellate Court in Thirty-Seven States In Other States Appeals Go Directly to Supreme Court

STATE ADMINISTRATIVE AGENCY TRIBUNAL
More Informal Hearing

TRIAL COURTS
Courts of General Jurisdiction Circuit, District, Superior, Common Pleas

TRIAL COURTS OF SPECIAL/ LIMITED/ EXCLUSIVE JURISDICTION
Juvenile, Criminal Domestic, Etc.

INFERIOR COURTS
Relatively Minor Cases Justice of the Peace, Magistrate, Municipal, Police, Etc.

intermediate or final level courts of appeal (appellate jurisdiction). Be able to identify the subject matter jurisdiction of each of your state courts. This is important because most of your work will be done in state court.

State courts are considered courts of general jurisdiction. All legitimate claims, including most of those that can go into the federal courts, can be filed in the state courts of original jurisdiction. State court judges are elected, appointed, or some combination of the two. Note how your state's judges come to office and for what length of term.

An increasing number of state court systems have or are developing specialized courts such as family, drug, community crime, medical malpractice, and business/technology courts. These courts are designed to expedite specific types of cases and to develop judges with pertinent expertise.

VENUE

venue
"Neighborhood"; the geographical area in which a court with jurisdiction can hear a case; distinct from jurisdiction.

Venue, literally "neighborhood," is the concept that determines where a case should be heard. Generally it means the defendant's neighborhood and/or the neighborhood where the incident occurred giving rise to the legal claim in the lawsuit. In most states this means the county where the defendant resides and the county where the incident happened. Some states have passed statutes or rules of procedure that define what court has venue generally and in specific kinds of situations such as in probate or property matters. Learn the venue requirements for your state.

The venue requirements for the United States District Court, 28 U.S.C. § 1391, are as follows:

(a) A civil action wherein jurisdiction is founded only on diversity of citizenship may, except as otherwise provided by law, be brought only in

(1) a judicial district where any defendant resides, if all defendants reside in the same State

(2) a judicial district in which a substantial part of the events or omissions giving rise to the claim occurred, or a substantial part of property that is the subject of the action is situated, or

(3) a judicial district in which any defendant is subject to personal jurisdiction at the time the action is commenced, if there is no district in which the action may otherwise be brought.

(b) A civil action wherein jurisdiction is not founded solely on diversity of citizenship may, except as otherwise provided by law, be brought only in

(1) a judicial district where any defendant resides, if all defendants reside in the same State

(2) a judicial district in which a substantial part of the events or omissions giving rise to the claim occurred, or a substantial part of property that is the subject of the action is situated, or

(3) a judicial district in which any defendant may be found, if there is no district in which the action may otherwise be brought.

(c) For purposes of venue under this chapter, a defendant that is a corporation shall be deemed to reside in any judicial district in which it is subject to personal jurisdiction at the time the action is commenced. In a State which has more than one judicial district and in which a defendant that is a corporation is subject to personal jurisdiction at the time an action is commenced, such corporation shall be deemed to reside in any district in that state within which its contacts would be sufficient to subject it to personal jurisdiction if that district were a separate State, and, if there is no such district, the corporation shall be deemed to reside in the district within which it has the most significant contacts.

(d) An alien may be sued in any district.

(e) A civil action in which a defendant is an officer or employee of the United States or any agency thereof acting in his official capacity or under color of legal authority, or an agency of the United States, or the United States, may, except as otherwise provided by law, be brought in any judicial district in which

(1) a defendant in the action resides

(2) a substantial part of the events or omissions giving rise to the claim occurred, or a substantial part of property that is involved in the action is situated, or

(3) the plaintiff resides if no real property is involved in the action. Additional persons may be joined as parties to any such action in accordance with the Federal Rules of Civil Procedure and with such other venue requirements as would be applicable if the United States or one of its officers, employees, or agencies were not a party.

The summons and complaint in such an action shall be served as provided by the Federal Rules of Civil Procedure except that the delivery of the summons and complaint to the officer or agency as required by the rules may be made by certified mail beyond the territorial limits of the district in which the action is brought.

(f) A civil action against a foreign state as defined in section 1603(a) of this title may be brought

(1) in any judicial district in which a substantial part of the events or omissions giving rise to the claim occurred, or a substantial part of property that is the subject of the action is situated

(2) in any judicial district in which the vessel or cargo of a foreign state is situated, if the claim is asserted under section 1605(b) of this title

(3) in any judicial district in which the agency or instrumentality is licensed to do business or is doing business, if the action is brought against an agency or instrumentality of a foreign state as defined in section 1603(b) of this title, or

(4) in the United States District Court for the District of Columbia if the action is brought against a foreign state or political subdivision thereof.

Venue is distinct from jurisdiction. It does not address which court has personal or subject matter jurisdiction. Rather, it addresses a location that should be fair to the parties and is likely to be close to witnesses, evidence, or the property in question. It might help to think that subject matter jurisdiction presents the question of *which court* handles this kind of case. Personal jurisdiction asks against *whom* can this court enforce a judgment, and venue asks *where*, in relationship to the parties, the event, or the property, can this case be heard.

As in the case of jurisdictional requirements, the general venue requirements at both the state and federal levels are further defined by statutes specific to a particular type of case or circumstance. For example, 28 U.S.C. §§ 1394 and following address venue in bank, internal revenue, forfeitures, and other matters. Section 1392 states that venue in actions of a "local nature" (such as in *in rem* or trespass actions where the property is tied to a specific, as opposed to a "transitory" locale) where the property is located in different districts in the same state rests in any of those federal districts. Section 1391(g) controls venue in large multiparty (multijurisdictional) actions as defined in § 1396. In probate matters, state court venue is typically where the estate is located.

TRANSFER OF CASES, FORUM NON CONVENIENS

Under 28 U.S.C. § 1404 and similar state laws, courts have the discretion to transfer a case to a more convenient court if the current court is inconvenient, even though the plaintiff may have met all the jurisdiction and venue requirements. This is a legal concept known as *forum non conveniens*. If a defendant demonstrates that the current forum is truly inconvenient (unfair, too costly, too far from evidence, and so on) and that another court exists with all the requisite jurisdiction and venues, then the court may transfer the case to the better forum.

If venue is improper, the court can dismiss the case or transfer it to a court that has venue [28 U.S.C. § 1406(a)]. Objection to venue, if not made early in the suit, will be waived, unlike objections to subject matter or personal jurisdiction.

Accurate determinations of jurisdiction and venue can range from being quite simple to exceptionally complex. Thorough research relevant to the parties and facts of each particular case is critical. Because you may be asked to participate in that process, your understanding of these fundamentals is important knowledge for the rest of this course and, eventually, for the law office. The next section will help you derive a better understanding of the application of jurisdiction and venue to choosing an appropriate court.

CHOOSING A COURT: THE RELATIONSHIP BETWEEN JURISDICTION AND VENUE, AND OTHER CONSIDERATIONS

Here is a review of the factors that must be taken into consideration in deciding which court can hear a matter. First, the court must have subject matter jurisdiction. Most state courts, unless they are specialized courts, are courts of general jurisdiction and can hear most matters. The federal courts have limited jurisdiction and can hear only those matters defined by law for them to hear.

Once it is determined which courts have subject matter jurisdiction, it must be determined which courts have venue. Keep in mind that in most states, venue rests with the court in the county where the defendant resides and in the county where the incident occurred giving rise to the lawsuit. Some state statutes define the venue for specific matters. Federal venue is defined in 28 U.S.C. § 1391 and subsequent sections as delineated on pages 34–35 in the section on venue. Recall that for venue purposes, corporations, insurance companies, national banks, aliens, foreign states, and actions in which a defendant is the United States or one of its officials or agencies, are treated specially, and the specific statute should be consulted.

Of the courts that have both subject matter jurisdiction and venue, it must be determined which, if any, of these courts have personal jurisdiction (or in the case of property such as real estate, which has *in rem* jurisdiction over the property). To gain personal jurisdiction over the defendant, the defendant must be served with a summons and complaint. The summons is generally valid only in the geographical area over which the court has authority. Generally, therefore, federal district courts can serve a summons on persons only in the district in which the court sits. State courts can get personal jurisdiction only over persons within the boundaries of the state in which that court sits. State statutes called long-arm statutes can extend personal jurisdiction beyond a state's borders to persons living in other states if those persons have had or do have sufficient contact with the state seeking personal jurisdiction. For example, if Florida has passed a long-arm law to reach across state boundaries, a motorist from New York driving in Florida generally is deemed to be subject to the personal jurisdiction of the Florida courts for wrongful acts (negligence) while operating a motor vehicle in Florida. This is true even if the motorist has returned to New York. In diversity cases, the law of the state in which the federal court sits determines the reach of the federal court. In addition, specific federal statutes may give the federal district courts personal jurisdiction beyond each court's district boundaries. Long-arm statutes will be discussed further in Chapter 5.

Corporations are subject to personal jurisdiction in any state where the law invokes personal jurisdiction if the cause of action arises out of the corporation's "doing business," "transacting business," or registration to do business in that state. Usually, if a corporation regularly does business in a state, it is subject to personal jurisdiction in the state. If the corporation is subject to personal jurisdiction in a state, it is also deemed subject to personal jurisdiction of the U.S. district court in that state.

Now, how good are you at applying these general rules to determine in which courts an action can be filed? Assume that X, a California resident, wants to sue Y, a resident of western New York, for $80,000 in damages stemming from an automobile accident in northern California. Which courts have subject matter jurisdiction? At least the state trial courts of California and New York have the original and general jurisdiction to hear the case. The federal district courts in the Northern District of California and the Western District of New York have the needed limited subject matter jurisdictions, that is, diversity jurisdiction involving more than $75,000.

Which courts have venue? One California state trial court has venue—the trial court located in the county where the accident occurred. A New York trial court has venue in the county where Defendant Y resides. Federal venue rests in the Northern District of California because this is a diversity of citizenship case and in such cases venue is located where a substantial part of the events or omissions arose. Federal venue also rests in the Western District of New York because, in diversity cases, venue exists where any defendant resides when all defendants reside in the same state.

Assuming there is no long-arm statute, which courts can get personal jurisdiction? Courts normally can get personal jurisdiction only in the state or federal district in which they sit. Only the New York state trial court and the federal district court for the Western District of New York have the defendant residing in their geographical boundaries. Therefore, X must bring suit in either the New York state court or the federal court for the Western District of New York. A chart showing which courts can hear the case of *X v. Y* looks like this:

	Subject Matter Jurisdiction	Venue	Personal Jurisdiction
California State Court	Yes	Yes	No
California Federal Court	Yes (Diversity)	Yes	No
New York State Court	Yes	Yes	Yes
New York Federal Court	Yes	Yes	Yes

With this information, the attorney would have to consider the judges in each court, possible bias in state court, convenience to witnesses and evidence, and all other factors that would work either in X's favor or to X's disadvantage in deciding which of the two courts would be best.

If, in the prior action, Z is also a defendant and lives in Utah, where could X sue? Add the following to the previous breakdown:

	Subject Matter Jurisdiction	Venue	Personal Jurisdiction
Utah State Court	Yes	Yes (for Z only)	Yes (for Z only)
Utah Federal Court	Yes	Yes (for Z only)	Yes (for Z only)
N.Y. Federal Court	Yes	Yes (for Y only)	Yes (for Y only)

Utah cannot qualify for joint federal venue because not all of the defendants reside in Utah, no personal jurisdiction exists over all the defendants, and the substantial events or omissions did not occur there. This is also true for the federal court in New York. Therefore, no federal court will work for suing both defendants simultaneously or individually, so X must sue Y and Z separately in their respective state or federal courts. Note that in federal actions with one defendant, all the defendants reside in one state. Therefore, venue exists in the district of the defendant's residence.

X could sue Y and Z in California state or federal court only if California had a long-arm guest motorist statute giving California courts personal jurisdiction over out-of-state residents involved in automobile accidents in California.

If the original X and Y example involved a federal question, such as a violation of a constitutional right, the federal venues would be the same as in the preceding diversity example. State venue would exist in the county in which the action arose and where the defendant resides (the proper county in New York.) But again, without a long-arm statute, only the district court in New York and the state court in New York have personal jurisdiction.

This time, try to determine where A and B can sue under the following circumstances. A resides in Wyoming and B resides in Colorado. They wish to sue C, a corporation, for a contract violated in Colorado in the amount of $100,000. C is incorporated in Delaware and has its principal place of business in Colorado. Take a minute to work this out before reading on. Test your understanding.

If you sued in Delaware and Colorado state courts, you are correct. Here is why. Each state in question has subject matter jurisdiction. Diversity jurisdiction for a federal court action does not exist—diversity must be complete, and B is from Colorado and so is defendant C (principal place of business). Without diversity jurisdiction, the federal courts are out of the picture. Since state venue normally exists in the county of the defendant's residence as well as the county where the action arose, venue exists in Delaware and Colorado. The only state courts with personal jurisdiction are those where the defendant resides—in this case Delaware and Colorado, if Colorado state law holds that the principal place of business is sufficient for personal jurisdiction to exist. The action, therefore, can be heard in state courts in Colorado or Delaware.

But what if C's principal place of business is Chicago, Illinois, instead of Colorado? Then we have plaintiffs from Wyoming (A) and Colorado (B) and a defendant (C) from Delaware (state of corporation) and Illinois (principal place of business). Because of general jurisdiction, each of the named states has subject matter jurisdiction. Federal diversity jurisdiction exists in each of the district courts—the districts of Colorado, Wyoming, Northern Illinois, and Delaware. State venue exists in Delaware and Illinois (residence of defendant) and in Colorado (where case arose). Federal venue, under

28 U.S.C. § 1391(c), for a *defendant* corporation lies in any district in any state where under that state's law the corporation does enough business that the state has personal jurisdiction over the corporation. Personal jurisdiction can be obtained at least in Delaware and in Illinois and, if there is enough business, in Colorado and Wyoming. Federal venue, therefore, would exist in these states and double in Colorado because that is where the cause arose. A chart of the possibilities appears as follows:

	Subject Matter Jurisdiction	Venue	Personal Jurisdiction
Colorado State Court	Yes	Yes	? (depends on contacts)
Wyoming State Court	Yes	No	? (depends on contacts)
Delaware State Court	Yes	Yes	Yes
Illinois State Court	Yes	Yes	Yes
Colorado Federal Court	Yes	Yes	? (depends on contacts)
Wyoming Federal Court	Yes	?	? (depends on contacts)
Delaware Federal Court	Yes	Yes	Yes
Illinois Federal Court	Yes	Yes	Yes

Plaintiffs would definitely have four courts to choose from and possibly as many as eight because of the defendant corporation venue rule and the expanded personal jurisdiction through corporate contacts in the state.

Once jurisdiction and venue are determined, the final choice of which state or federal court to file the action in is based on several additional factors: which of the courts in question tend to award the highest or lowest monetary amounts, which courts move cases along the fastest or slowest, which court is closest to or has personal jurisdiction over key witnesses, how do the judges compare, will the law applied be different and, if so, which law will best benefit the client. Paralegals are occasionally asked to research such comparative factors.

A CASE ROADMAP

Exhibit 1:8 sets out the various steps in handling a case from start to finish. Although you will be learning the process in more detail later, this case roadmap will help you to know where you are headed when working on a case. You should photocopy this diagram and place it in your system folder.

SUMMARY

The *Paralegal Handbook* introduced you to the law firm, its structure, the kinds of cases it handles, the role of the paralegal, office procedures, ethical considerations, and the methods to be employed in your training. In addition, the handbook has emphasized techniques for thriving in the law office and your professional development. You have also reviewed courts, jurisdictions, and venue. These fundamentals are essential to a good beginning to your career.

Consider the story of a man who encountered three workers. Stepping up to the first worker, the man asked, "What are you doing?" The first worker replied, "Making

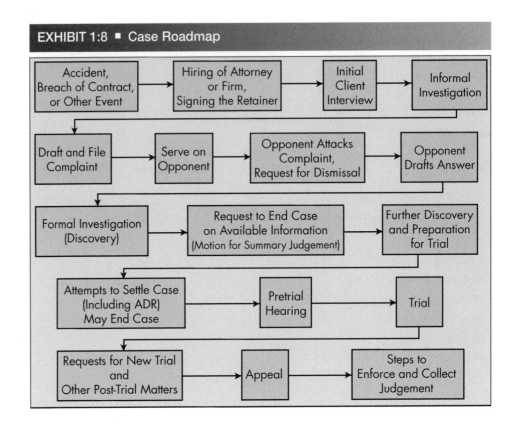

EXHIBIT 1:8 ■ Case Roadmap

a buck." Going on to the second worker, he repeated the question, "What are you doing?" The second worker said, "Laying bricks." Then the man approached the third worker and asked again, "What are you doing?" To this the third worker replied, "Building a cathedral."[30]

Although your work may range from the routine and mundane to the challenging and creative, be aware that, like the third worker, you are part of a larger scheme of things. Brick by brick, you are building cases that provide a service to your clients while enhancing your profession and the legal system in which you work.

▣ WORKBOOK

System Folder Assignments, other exercises, a chapter outline, a review test, and other study aids are located in the accompanying workbook.

▣ HELPFUL WEB SITES (some sites require fees)

http://www.uscourts.gov
  Administrative Office of the United States Courts

http://www.ncsconline.org
  National Center for State Courts

http://www.law.com
  Latest legal developments, updated daily; practice area sections

http://www.abanet.org
  American Bar Association, current information on areas of law practice

http://www.state.FL.us
  Substitute your state's abbreviation for "FL;" state government Web sites, state statutes and cases

http://www.legalethics.com
General ethics codes, state and professional codes, Internet ethics issues

http://www.lectlaw.com
Sections on paralegals, ethics, expert witnesses, and consultants; humor

http://www.lawjobs.com
Listings of employment opportunities in legal fields by state

http://www.martindale.com
http://www.lawyersforless.com
Examples of legal exchanges, Web-based sites to unite lawyers and prospective clients

(See the previous section in this chapter for the Web sites of the national associations related to the paralegal field.)

QUESTIONS FOR STUDY AND REVIEW

Use the following study questions as a summary of the terms, definitions, concepts, and procedures in this chapter, and to prepare for an exam on these materials.

1. What is a partner, an associate, and a staff attorney?
2. Define *paralegal*.
3. What is the "chain of command" at White, Wilson & McDuff?
4. State the benefits of having diverse personnel.
5. Define *civil litigation*.
6. What are some of the profound effects the Internet is having and will have on the practice of law?
7. What is the difference between a personal injury case based on negligence and a product liability case? An antitrust and a civil rights case?
8. Why is a paralegal valuable to a law firm? Identify significant legal authority on billing for paralegal time.
9. Define the various billing types and describe the steps in the timekeeping procedure. What is task-based billing?
10. Describe the steps in the deadline control procedure.
11. Why are timekeeping and deadline control important?
12. What are some ethical concerns regarding timekeeping and billing?
13. What is the significance of office electronic security? List related security tips.
14. What are the techniques for thriving in the law office?
15. What is a litigation system and why is it beneficial?
16. Define *professional ethics* in the context of the practice of law.
17. Why are professional ethics so important to a law firm?
18. What are the things a paralegal may not do?
19. What are the seven criteria that assure a paralegal's actions will not be or cause a breach of ethics?
20. State the ethical standard on preserving client confidentiality.
21. What is a conflict of interest and the rationale for the relevant ethical standards?
22. What are the criteria for a proper conflict of interest screen according to the *Leibowitz* case?
23. Why are professional integrity and honesty so important?
24. What is meant by the term *professional loyalty* as applied to your fellow workers? The client? The practice of law?
25. What is personal professional development? Why is it important?
26. What are the characteristics of the common components of court systems in the United States?
27. What is jurisdiction? Define the various kinds of jurisdiction: geographical, personal, general, and so on.
28. What are the names and jurisdictions of the various levels of courts in both the federal and your state system?
29. What federal circuit is your state in?
30. What three things must a court have in order to hear a case and bind a party to the court's decision? Be able to apply these concepts to determine what court or courts can hear a lawsuit depending on domiciles of the parties and other factors.
31. Be able to explain why and give examples of when a court might have personal jurisdiction but still not be able to hear a case.

KEY TERMS

alienage jurisdiction	electronic billing	legal advice	professional ethics
billable hours	(e-billing)	litigation system	unbundling legal services
civil litigation	federal questions	multijurisdictional	venue
diversity of citizenship	jurisdictional amount	practice	writ of certiorari
domicile	(amount in controversy)	pro bono	

◼ ENDNOTES

1. To see interesting differences in the definitions of para-legals and legal assistants, see the Web sites of the national associations listed in this chapter and consult your state's laws, cases, and court rules.

2. Ritchenya A. Shepherd, *Nonlawyers Running Firms*, Nat'l L.J., Sept. 18, 2000, A1.

3. *See* Roy S. Ginsberg, *Making the Business Case for Diversity*, Wis. Law., June, 2005, 20, and for a discussion on award-winning law firm personnel programs see Debra Levy Martinelli, *Best of Both Worlds*, Leg. Assist. Today, Mar./Apr. 2004, 48–51.

4. *See* Joseph L. Kashi, *Structuring and Managing a Virtual Law Firm*, Law Office Computing, Dec./Jan. 2001, 70; *Resolution in Response to the Seize the Future Conference*, Inside the Bar (State Bar of Wisconsin), Jan. 2001, 5; Dianne Molvig, *Bakke's Law of Change*, Wis. Law., July 2000, 4; and Mark Voorhees, *Step Right Up: Lawyers for Sale*, Nat'l L.J., May 13, 2000.

5. The federal statistics are reported in *The Vanishing Trial*, Nat'l L.J., Jan. 12, 2004, 6 (citing an ABA symposium); the state figures are from Leonard Post, *Report: Civil Trials Fall by Half*, Nat'l L.J., June 21, 2004, 4, citing the Bureau of Justice report, *Civil Trial Cases and Verdicts in Large Counties, 2001*.

6. For example, Bankruptcy, 11 U.S.C. § 330 (a)(1); Civil Rights, 42 U.S.C. § 1988; Sherman Anti-Trust 15 U.S.C. § 1 *et seq.;* Cal. Prob. Code § 10811(b), *et seq.;* and Ind. Code § 1-1-4-6.

7. Eighty percent of paralegals responding indicated an increase in their responsibilities in the 2004 National Utilization and Compensation Survey (NALA): Marge Dover, *Survey Says . . .*, Facts & Findings Career Chronicle, 2004, 36.

8. James Evangelista, Teresa Stange, and Kelley Johnston, *Electronic Billing Offers Advantages*, Nat'l. L.J., Sept. 26, 2005, S1, S6–S7; Terry Carter, *Thrifty Litigation*, A.B.A. J., Aug. 2005, 34–39.

9. *See* American Bar Association, Profile of Legal Malpractice Claims 2000–2003, 2005.

10. *Id.*

11. For a more thorough statement of these policies, see Mark Dichter and Michael S. Burkhardt, *Electronic Interaction in*

the Workplace: Monitoring, Retrieving, and Storing Employee Communications, http://morganlewis.com/art61499.htm.

12. Mark Bassingthwaighte, *Ten Technology Traps and How to Avoid Them*, The Risk Manager (Lawyers Mutual Insurance Co. of Kentucky), Sum. 2005, 1–4.

13. For a discussion of these and other tips see C. Houston Ebert, *Stress in the Legal Profession*, Bench and Bar, June, 2004, 29; Shari Caudron, *Understanding Law Firm Culture*, Legal Assistant Today, Jul/Aug. 1995, 52; Jennifer Moore, *Keeping Focused: Total Time Management*, Legal Assistant Today, Jul/Aug. 1995, 56, 59.

14. Memorandum from Wisconsin Supreme Court to Board of Governors of the State Bar of Wisconsin regarding Rules Petition 03–05.

15. *See* report of ABA Comm. on Nonlawyer Practice, Nonlawyer Activity in Law Related Situations: A Report with Recommendations (Aug. 1995).

16. *Id.*, 161.

17. Emma Schwartz, *Malpractice: Law Firms Hit with More Lawsuits*, Nat'l. L.J., May 16, 2005, 11.

18. Rebecca Thompson Nagel, *Paralegal's Messy Desk Costs Company Half Million Dollars*, Legal Assistant Today, Jan./Feb. 1999, 24.

19. *Owen Equipment & Erection Co. v. Kroger*, 437 U.S. 365, 373 (1978).

20. *National Mutual Insurance Co. v. Tidewater Transfer Co.*, 337 U.S. 583 (1949).

21. *See* Chemerinsky, Federal Jurisdiction 250 (1989) and Wright, Miller & Cooper, Federal Practice and Procedure § 13B, 530–33 (1984).

22. Chemerinsky, *supra* note 23, 250.

23. *Id.*

24. *Tango Music LLC v. DeadQuick Music Inc.*, 348 F.3d 244 (7th Cir. 2003).

25. *Id.*, 251.

26. *Id.*, 252–53.

27. *Saint Paul Mercury Indemnity Co. v. Red Cab Co.*, 303 U.S. 283, 288 (1983).

28. *Id.*, 256–58.

29. Pub. L. No. 100–352, 102 Stat. 662 (1988).

30. J. Jeans, Trial Advocacy 48 (1975).

 For additional resources, visit our Website at **http://www.westlegalstudies.com.**

The Initial Interview

Note: If you have not yet studied torts and contracts, an expanded discussion of torts and contracts and the pertinent principles of law is included in Appendices B and C.

INTRODUCTION

Today, you have the opportunity to begin working on a case. (Please reread Case I.) Mr. White has met with Ann Forrester, who will be coming to the office for her initial interview for a personal injury negligence case. It may not always fall to the paralegal to do the interview alone. Sometimes the paralegal assists the attorney, sometimes the attorney and paralegal interview jointly, and sometimes the attorney conducts the interview alone. Increasingly, however, offices place this responsibility on the paralegal. It is your job to prepare and conduct the interview with Ms. Forrester.

The client interview is a significant step. First, it sets the tone for the entire relationship between the prospective client and the law firm. The client should leave feeling comfortable with the relationship and confident that matters will be handled competently. Second, it sets the tone for the critical relationship between the client and the paralegal that may last months or even years. Third, it is the important beginning of investigation, a fact-gathering process requiring other interviews and techniques that will be discussed in the chapters to follow. The initial client interview and subsequent interviews determine the basis of the lawsuit (or its defense), the firm's acceptance of the case, and the fee.

THE INTERVIEW PLAN

You will need to set up an interview plan in order to derive maximum benefit from the time spent with the client. Use the following Interview Plan Checklist in developing your interview plan.

INTERVIEW PLAN CHECKLIST

Step 1 Review all available information on the case.

Step 2 Locate or develop an appropriate interview form.

Step 3 Select a location for the interview.

Step 4 Determine what information the client should bring.

Step 5 Schedule the interview (tentatively); check with attorney.

Step 6 Anticipate and arrange for any special needs.

Step 7 Review pertinent ethical and tactical considerations.

Step 8 Review recommended interview techniques.

Step 9 Prepare orientation and instruction materials for the client.

Step 10 Prepare any forms for the client's signature.

Step 11 Prepare the interview site.

THE INTERVIEW PLAN IN DETAIL

Step 1

Review all available information on the case. Check the file for news clippings, police reports, and any other readily available information. Any background you gain about the incident will direct you in researching additional information.

"The love of justice is simply, in the majority of men, the fear of suffering injustice."

—LA ROCHEFOUCAULD, *MAXIMES*, 1665.

Further, attorneys have learned to be cautious about what cases they accept and what clients they represent. The case's potential for a successful outcome, likely profitability, and compatibility with the attorney's expertise are all important considerations. Important, as well, are the potential client's character, honesty in business dealings, caliber as a witness, and ability to work easily and cooperatively with others. Information that you can gather that enables your attorney to screen out bad clients and cases can save a lot of expense, time, and headache down the line. Gathering information about persons and businesses is discussed in Chapter 3.

Step 2

Locate or develop an appropriate interview form. An interviewer needs to identify what information is needed from the client and what questions will best elicit that information. A form questionnaire can save preparation time and serve as a guide for the interviewer. Such forms can usually be found in the firm's form files, or in trial practice manuals readily available at the firm or local library. Our firm has an interview form for personal injury–automobile negligence cases. See Exhibit 2:1 and Exhibit 2:2.[1] Read the form carefully; it will raise your awareness of what needs to be covered in this type of case.

Exhibit 2:1 • Checklist Form: Client Background Information

Please type or print neatly. If more space is needed, please use back or extra sheets.

1. Why did you choose this office? _____

2. Have you hired any other attorney on this matter? _____

3. _____   **4.** _____
            Name   Soc. Sec. No. (last 4 digits)

5. _____
       Address, including county   Zip Code   Years at

List prior addresses and approximate dates on back

6. _____ **7.** _____ **8.** _____ **9.** _____ **10.** _____
   Home Phone   Work Phone   Date of Birth   Age   Sex

11. _____ **12.** _____ **13.** _____
    Maiden Name   Other Names Used   Nationality, Race, Religion

14. _____
        If minor, guardian's name and address

15. S __ M __ D __ W __ Other __   **16.** _____   **17.** _____
     Marital Status   Spouse's Name   Date of Birth

18. _____   **19.** _____   **20.** _____
    Address, if different from 3 above   Home Phone   Work Phone

21. _____   **22.** _____
    Spouse's Place of Employment   Spouse's Job Title

(continued)

Exhibit 2:1 • Checklist Form: Client Background Information (*continued*)

23. _____

_____

_____

      Children's Names   Ages   Addresses

24. _____ **25.** If other marriages, list date, spouse, and children on back.

    Date of Marriage/Divorce

26. _____

    If divorced, status of maintenance or child support

27. _____

      Other Close Relative   (Name, Address, Phone)

28. Current_____

_____

     Employer   Address   Job Title/Salary   Phone   Dates

    List others on back

29. _____

    If self-employed, nature of business, address, phone, partners, salary or approximate income

30. Education: highest grade or degree completed _____

_____

      School   Dates   Degree   Area of Study

31. Gross Income _____ **32.** Attach tax returns from the last three years.

33. Property: List all real estate owned/if held solely, jointly, etc./value, mortgage, etc.

_____

34. If requested, attach a list of personal property (bank accounts, stocks and bonds, autos, furniture, etc.).

35. If you have been involved in any prior litigation, please give details, type of action, plaintiff-defendant, attorney, court, year, result.

_____

_____

Source: Reprinted with permission. Courtesy of Agnes M. Elliott.

Use the interview form as an aid; *do not rely on it entirely*. Each case is unique, and you will need to add or delete questions as appropriate.

Some cases will require you or the attorney (or both of you) to develop a special interview form or set of questions to cover in the interview. Until you become more experienced, this should be done in close consultation with the attorney working on the case. In order to develop your own questionnaire, you will need to review the file to identify the cause of action. If necessary, ask the attorney to identify the cause of action: negligence, breach of contract, sexual harassment, or other.

Exhibit 2:2 ■ Checklist Form: Automobile Accident

PARTIES—GENERAL INFORMATION

( ) Plaintiff _____ Age _____ Sex _____ Phone _____

( ) Address _____ City _____ County _____ State _____ Zip _____

( ) Bus. Address _____ City _____ County _____ State _____ Phone _____

( ) Ins. Carrier _____ Address _____ Phone _____

　　Amt. Ins. Liab. _____ P.D. _____ Med. _____ Collision _____

　　Uninsured Motorist _____ Any Coverage Deductible? Which? _____

　　_____

( ) Defendant 1. _____ Age _____ Sex _____ Phone _____

( ) Address _____ City _____ County _____ State _____ Phone _____

( ) Bus. Address _____ City _____ County _____ State _____ Phone _____

( ) Ins. Carrier _____ Address _____ Phone _____

　　Amt. Ins. Liab. _____ P.D. _____ Med. _____ Collision _____

　　Uninsured Motorist _____ Any Coverage Deductible? Which? _____

　　_____

( ) Co-Defendants 2. _____ Age _____ Sex _____ Phone _____

　　　　　　　　　 3. _____ Age _____ Sex _____ Phone _____

( ) Address 2. _____ City _____ County _____ State _____ Phone _____

　　　　　　 3. _____ City _____ County _____ State _____ Phone _____

( ) Bus. Address 2. _____ City _____ County _____ State _____ Phone _____

　　　　　　　　 3. _____ City _____ County _____ State _____ Phone _____

( ) Ins. Carrier 2. _____ Address _____ Phone _____

　　　　　　　 3. _____ Address _____ Phone _____

　　Amt. Ins. Liab. 2. _____ P.D. _____ Med. _____ Collision _____

　　　　　　　　 3. _____ P.D. _____ Med. _____ Collision _____

　　Uninsured Motorist 2. _____ Any Coverage Deductible? Which? _____

　　　　　　　　　　 3. _____ Any Coverage Deductible? Which? _____

　　2. _____

　　3. _____

FACTS OF ACCIDENT

( ) Date of Accident _____ Time _____ Material Facts _____

　　_____

　　_____

　　_____

　　_____

(continued)

Exhibit 2:2 ■ Checklist Form: Automobile Accident (*continued*)

Res Gestae Statements _____
_____

( ) Type of Case (Check Applicable Subject Matter)
( ) Animals   ( ) Assault & Battery   ( ) Drainage & Pollution   ( ) Employer, Employee, & Independent Contractor   ( ) False Imprisonment   ( ) Fraud & Deceit   ( ) Invitees & Licensees   ( ) Malicious Arrest or Prosecution   ( ) Malpractice   ( ) Municipal   ( ) Product Liability   ( ) Real Estate   ( ) Slander or Libel   ( ) Transportation—Airplane, Automobile, or Train   ( ) Trespass   ( ) Wrongful Death   ( ) Workers' Compensation   ( ) Other _____

( ) Diagram accident scene if physical facts are important
_____
_____

( ) Indicate & note on diagram. Answer Yes or No where applicable.
( ) Width of streets or roads measured _____
( ) Number of lanes _____ Any peculiar curves or hills _____
( ) Yellow lines _____ Stop signs or traffic devices _____
( ) Skid marks _____ Position of vehicles after accident _____
( ) Type of road surface—asphalt or concrete _____
( ) Dry or wet _____ Weather—fog, rain, drizzle, sleet, or snow _____
_____
( ) Visibility—good or bad _____ Day, night, dusk, or dawn _____
_____
( ) Clear or cloudy _____ Other _____
( ) Ascertain if pictures were taken of accident scene _____
( ) When _____ By whom _____
( ) Address _____ Phone _____
( ) If not, take pictures of accident scene immediately
( ) Place pictures obtained or taken in evidence file
( ) Miscellaneous comments _____
_____

( ) Automobile information
( ) Plaintiff Vehicle
( ) Year _____ Make _____ Model _____ Color _____
( ) Cylinders _____ Horsepower _____ Weight _____ Manuf. I.D. _____
( ) Tag No. _____ Power or regular steering _____ Brakes _____
( ) Defects of vehicle—Brakes _____ Lights _____ Motor _____
Steering _____ Tires _____ Other _____
Comments as to condition _____

Exhibit 2:2 ■ Checklist Form: Automobile Accident (*continued*)

( ) Location of Vehicle—Garage _____
    Address _____ Phone _____
    Were Pictures Taken of Automobile _____
    When _____ By Whom _____
    Address _____ Phone _____
( ) If not, take pictures at garage & place in evidence file
    Taken by _____ When _____ Address _____
( ) Note alleged speed prior to collision
( ) Indicate impact points on vehicle diagram & note interior damage

Right Side
Length _____ ft.   Front Width _____ ft.   Rear   Left Side

( ) Owner of plaintiff vehicle _____ Age _____ Sex _____
( ) Address _____ City _____ State _____ Phone _____
( ) Business Address _____ City _____ State _____ Phone _____
( ) Ins. Carrier _____ Address _____ Phone _____
    Amt. Ins.—Liab. _____ P.D. _____
    Med. _____ Collision _____
    Uninsured Motorist _____ Any coverage deductible? Which? _____
    _____
( ) Driver plaintiff vehicle _____
( ) Relationship to owner _____
    Driving with permission _____
( ) Destination & purpose _____
( ) Impediments of driver—Intoxication _____ Glasses _____
    Hearing _____ Other physical defects _____
    Passengers—Seat location in vehicle
    _____
    _____
( ) Defendant Vehicle
    ( ) Year _____ Make _____ Model _____ Color _____
    ( ) Cylinders _____ Horsepower _____ Weight _____ Manuf. I.D. _____
    ( ) Tag No. _____ Power or regular steering _____ Brakes _____
    ( ) Defects of vehicle—Brakes _____ Lights _____ Motor _____
    Steering _____ Tires _____ Other _____

(*continued*)

Exhibit 2:2 ■ Checklist Form: Automobile Accident (*continued*)

Comments as to condition _____

( ) Location of vehicle—Garage _____

    Address _____ Phone _____

    Were pictures taken of automobile? _____

    When _____ By whom _____

    Address _____ Phone _____

( ) If not, take pictures at garage & place in evidence file

    Taken by _____ When _____ Address _____

( ) Note alleged speed prior to collision _____

( ) Indicate impact points on vehicle diagram & note interior damage _____

Right Side   **Front**   **Rear**   **Left Side**
Length _____ ft.   Width _____ ft.

( ) Owner of defendant vehicle _____ Age _____ Sex _____

( ) Address _____ City _____ State _____ Phone _____

( ) Business Address _____ City _____ State _____ Phone _____

( ) Ins. Carrier _____ Address _____ Phone _____

    Amt. Ins.—Liab. _____ P.D. _____

    Med. _____ Collision _____

    Uninsured Motorist _____ Any coverage deductible? Which? _____

    _____

( ) Driver defendant vehicle _____

( ) Relationship to owner _____

    Driving with permission _____

( ) Destination & purpose _____

( ) Impediments of driver—Intoxication _____ Glasses _____

    Hearing _____ Other physical defects _____

    Passengers—Seat location in vehicle

    _____

    _____

    _____

( ) Traffic violations by plaintiff & defendant

    Charges against   Court   Hearing date   Result

    _____

    _____

Exhibit 2:2 ■ Checklist Form: Automobile Accident *(continued)*

( ) Get copy of traffic court testimony if recorded & place in evidence file

( ) Witnesses to accident including parties

Witnesses	Address	County	State	Age	Phone

( ) Statement record—Use checklist in taking statements

Last Name Witness	Taken by Plaintiff	Given to Defendant	Written, Recorded, When? or Oral	Copy Retained
Plaintiff				
Defendant				

( ) Place all statements in evidence file

( ) Impeachment of parties & witnesses (note unfavorable military record)

Name	Crime Conviction	Date	Good or Bad Character

( ) Parties' prior accidents

Plaintiff _____

_____

Defendant _____

_____

MEDICAL

( ) Plaintiff—Summary of Injuries? (Indicate degree of disability—Restriction of activities in work, sports, etc.)

_____

_____

_____

(continued)

Exhibit 2:2 ■ Checklist Form: Automobile Accident (*continued*)

( ) <u>Note Injuries on Diagram</u>

Parietal
Temporal
Zygomatic
Occipital
Cervical vertebrae (7)
Lumbar vertebrae (5)
Ilium
Sacrum
Pubis
Ischium
Femur
Patella
Tibia
Fibula
Tarsals (7)
Metatarsals (5)
Phalanges (14)

Frontal
Maxilla
Mandible
Clavicle
Scapula
Sternum
Ribs
Thoracic vertebrae (12)
Humerus
Ulna
Radius
Carpals (8)
Metacarpals (5)
Phalanges (14)

( ) <u>Indicate Plaintiff's Area of Pain</u>

( ) Symptoms
  ( ) Headaches
  ( ) Dizziness
  ( ) Nausea
  ( ) Nervousness
  ( ) Insomnia
  ( ) Appetite
( ) Head
  ( ) Brain
  ( ) Forehead
  ( ) Ears
  ( ) Eyes
  ( ) Nose
  ( ) Mouth
  ( ) Teeth
( ) Neck
  ( ) Muscles
  ( ) Spine
  ( ) Throat
( ) Chest
  ( ) Heart
  ( ) Lungs
  ( ) Ribs
( ) Abdomen
( ) Internal Injuries
( ) _____
_____
( ) Arms (Rt. or Left)
  ( ) Upper
  ( ) Forearm
  ( ) Elbows
  ( ) Wrist
  ( ) Hands
  ( ) Fingers

( ) Trunk
  ( ) Shoulders
  ( ) Spine
  ( ) Thoracic
  ( ) Scapula
  ( ) Lumbar
  ( ) Sacrum
  ( ) Coccyx
  ( ) Pelvis
  ( ) Hips
( ) Legs (Rt. or Left)
  ( ) Thighs
  ( ) Upper
  ( ) Lower
  ( ) Knees
  ( ) Ankles
  ( ) Feet
  ( ) Toes
( ) Indicate Radiations of Pain
( ) Note Cuts, Bruises, Burns, Bumps, Sutures, Fractures, Missing Teeth, Swelling, Contusions, Points of Bleeding, Unconsciousness, etc.

PLAINTIFF MEDICAL & PAIN AREAS

( ) Same information for defendant's injuries (if any)

( ) Ambulance, hospital, & doctor service, findings & treatment

( ) Ambulance service—By whom? _____ Other _____

Any first aid administered? If so, what? _____

Note time ambulance arrived at accident scene _____

Exhibit 2:2 ■ Checklist Form: Automobile Accident (*continued*)

( ) Hospitals   Address   Phone   Period of treatment   Surgery

1. _____

Treatment_____

_____ X-Rays taken? When? _____

2. _____

Treatment_____

_____ X-Rays taken? When? _____

3. _____

Treatment_____

_____ X-Rays taken? When? _____

( ) Doctors   Address   Phone   Period of Treatment   Surgery

1. _____

Diagnosis, Treatment, & Prognosis _____

_____ X-Rays taken? When? _____

2. _____

Diagnosis, Treatment, & Prognosis _____

_____ X-Rays taken? When? _____

3. _____

Diagnosis, Treatment, & Prognosis _____

_____ X-Rays taken? When? _____

4. _____

Diagnosis, Treatment, & Prognosis _____

_____ X-Rays taken? When? _____

( ) Summary comments as to percentage of disability & patient prognosis

_____

_____

PRIOR MEDICAL TREATMENT—PLAINTIFF & DEFENDANT

( ) Plaintiff—Prior Medical Treatment

Doctors & Hospitals   Address   Phone   Period of Treatment

1. _____

2. _____

3. _____

Treatment _____

_____

( ) Note relationship of prior to present injuries _____

_____

_____

(*continued*)

Exhibit 2:2 ■ Checklist Form: Automobile Accident (*continued*)

( ) Prior claims of any nature? When? Where? _____
_____
_____

( ) Defendant—prior medical treatment

Doctors & Hospitals	Address	Phone	Period of Treatment

1. _____
2. _____
3. _____

Treatment _____
_____

( ) Note relationship of prior to present injuries _____
_____
_____

( ) Prior claims of any nature? When? Where? _____
_____
_____

( ) Summary degree of prior disability
  ( ) Plaintiff _____
  ( ) Defendant _____

DAMAGES—PLAINTIFF

( ) Plaintiff employment subsequent & prior to accident

Subsequent to	Dates	Position	Annual Earnings	Per Diem

Prior to (last 2 yrs.)	Dates	Position	Annual Earnings	Per Diem

( ) Education & Job Training—   ( ) Elementary   ( ) High School   ( ) College   ( ) Graduate
  ( ) Other _____
_____

( ) Family Situation

Spouse & Children	Relationship	Age

Exhibit 2:2 ■ Checklist Form: Automobile Accident (*continued*)

( ) Computation of General Damages—Note age of injured party _____

   ( ) Pain & suffering (past, present, & future) estimate of party—value assessed per day

   $ _____ × _____ Days = $ _____ × Life Expectancy _____ = $ _____

( ) Diminution capacity to labor as element of pain & suffering

   (past, present, & future) estimate of party-value assessed per day

   $ _____ × _____ Days = $ _____ × Life Expectancy _____ = $ _____

   ( ) Loss of consortium (estimate of party) value assessed per day

( ) Computation of special damages (Date accident _____)

   $ _____ × _____ Days = $ _____ × Life Expectancy _____ = $ _____

   ( ) Loss of Earnings

      ( ) Past & present to date of trial—days in hospital _____

      ( ) Past & present continued (At home _____ Returned to work—Date _____)

      ( ) Total Days _____ × Per Diem Wages $ _____ = $ _____

      ( ) Annual Average Earnings $ _____ Capacity Reduced _____%

         Disability $ _____ × _____ Use Annuity Table _____%

         Column to reduce to present cash value or × _____ Life Expectancy

         (for gross when reduction not required) $ _____

( ) Hospitals, Nurses, Doctors, Drugs (Supports & Braces), & Ambulance Expenses

Hospitals	Period	Amount	
_____		$ _____	
_____			
_____			
		$ _____	$ _____

Nurses	Period	Amount	
_____		$ _____	
_____			
		$ _____	$ _____

Doctors	Period	Amount	
_____		$ _____	
_____			
_____			
_____			
_____			
		$ _____	$ _____

Pharmacy	Period	Amount	
_____		$ _____	
_____			
		$ _____	$ _____

(*continued*)

Exhibit 2:2 ■ Checklist Form: Automobile Accident (*continued*)

Ambulance	Period	Amount	
_____	$ _____		
	$ _____	$ _____	
( ) Funeral Expenses—Mortician's Name & Address _____			
_____	$ _____		
( ) Property Damage			
( ) Automobile—fair market value before	$ _____	$ _____	
Less fair market value after accident	$ _____	$ _____	
Diminution in value	$ _____	$ _____	
( ) Reasonable Hire _____ Days × Rental Value	$ _____	$ _____	

Source: Reprinted with permission. Courtesy of Agnes M. Elliott.

Research the cause of action and identify the elements that need to be proven to establish a case or its defense. Jury instruction books and legal encyclopedias will provide a quick overview of the key elements for a particular cause of action and its defenses. In regard to the *Forrester* case (Case I), assume that your research has produced the following information:

A Brief Look at the Substantive Law of Negligence. Law is divided into two major areas: substantive law and procedural law. **Substantive law** defines the duties owed by one person to another. **Procedural law** defines the rules and steps that must be followed in a lawsuit. The substantive law of negligence states that all individuals have a duty to conduct themselves in their activities so as not to create an unreasonable risk of harm to others. The elements that must be proven to show that negligence exists include the following:

1. *Duty:* the existence of a **duty** of due care owed by one person to another. For example, in Case I, Mr. Hart had a duty to drive the van without creating an unreasonable risk of harm to any other drivers or pedestrians, such as Ms. Forrester.

2. *A breach of that duty:* failure to conform to the required standard of care. The required standard of care is that which is reasonable under the circumstances. What is reasonable is a matter of experience and common sense. For example, if Mr. Hart were speeding, especially on icy roads, and/or was not paying close attention to the road, his conduct would fall short of what is reasonable under the circumstances to protect others.

3. *The cause of the injury:* that the conduct in question was the natural and **proximate** (probable) **cause** of the resulting harm. Some states define it as a substantial cause of the injury. If Ms. Forrester could have crossed the road safely had it not been for Mr. Hart's excessive speed, then Mr. Hart's speed would be the natural and proximate cause of Ms. Forrester's injuries.

4. *Injury in fact:* an actual injury or loss must have resulted from the incident. If Ms. Forrester, for example, suffers a broken hip as a result of the negligent act, then that is sufficient to provide this fourth element of negligence. It is also important that the injury be a foreseeable consequence of the negligence and not some quirk.

substantive law
Law that defines the duties owed by one person to another.

procedural law
Law that defines the rules and steps that must be followed in a lawsuit.

duty
In tort law, due care owed by one person to another.

proximate cause
In tort law, the cause-and-effect relationship that must be established to prove that the conduct in question was the substantial cause of the injury in question.

The defenses to negligence include the following:

1. *Comparative negligence* is the law in the majority of states and in Columbia (unless your instructor indicates otherwise). The doctrine of comparative negligence permits a plaintiff who is contributorily negligent to recover, but the award is reduced proportionately by the percentage of the plaintiff's negligence. For example, if Ms. Forrester stepped onto the highway without looking, then slipped as she tried to retreat, a jury might find her 30 percent negligent. If Mr. Hart was driving too fast to stop, a jury might find him 70 percent negligent. If Ms. Forrester's damages came to $100,000, the award would be reduced by 30 percent to $70,000. In some states, Ms. Forrester would be barred from any recovery if her comparative negligence was found to exceed 50 percent. Some states still use the term *contributory negligence* for this doctrine, although it is a modified version of contributory negligence (see number 3).

2. *Assumption of risk* states that plaintiffs may not recover for damages if they knowingly place themselves in danger. For example, if Ms. Forrester had decided to stay in the middle of the road and thumb her nose at any oncoming vehicle, she would be assuming the risk of injury, and Mr. Hart would have a defense to Ms. Forrester's action for negligence.

3. *Contributory negligence* is an important concept even though most states have abolished it as a defense. If the action of the plaintiff, the person suing for injuries, was a contributing factor in the accident, the plaintiff cannot recover her losses from the defendant, the person being sued. For example, if a jury found that plaintiff Ms. Forrester had contributed to her own injuries by failing to look both ways before crossing the highway, she would be barred from any recovery, even if defendant Mr. Hart was found to be primarily responsible for the accident. The harshness of this rule explains why it has been abolished in many states. Assume that contributory negligence is not the law in Columbia unless your instructor indicates otherwise.

4. *Last clear chance* is a doctrine that permits parties to recover damages who normally could not because of their contributory negligence. In that sense, it is a defense to the defense of contributory negligence. It applies when the plaintiff, through her own negligence, is placed in the defendant's path so that the defendant has the last clear chance to avoid an accident. If the defendant does not react as a reasonable person should (and therefore is negligent), causing injury to the plaintiff, the plaintiff may recover regardless of her initial contributing negligence. For example, assume that Ms. Forrester carelessly ran across the ice on the road, slipped, and fell, leaving her directly in the path of Mr. Hart's van. Also assume that Mr. Hart had a last clear chance to avoid the accident. If he was inattentive and did not avoid the accident, Ms. Forrester could still recover damages in spite of her own negligence.

After identifying the elements of the action, draft questions that elicit information that will help prove or disprove the elements or defenses. Forming questions to elicit information is a matter of applying common sense to the elements that must be proved. For example, to determine whether the defendant has created an unreasonable risk of harm to the plaintiff under the circumstances, the interviewer would need to find out what the circumstances were. The question should be asked, "What are all the possible circumstances that might have a bearing on the accident?" Each factor that comes to mind should be listed.

Circumstances possibly affecting an accident include the following:

time (such as rush hour, dusk, night)
weather (such as cold, rainy, foggy)
lighting (such as bright, dim, dark)
road conditions (such as slippery, dry, oily, rough)
road structure (such as lanes, narrow shoulders, curve, straight, level)
location of parties (including specific measurements in feet, inches)
dress of parties (as pertinent to cause of accident)
condition of parties (such as intoxicated, drugged, tired)
disabilities of parties (such as poor eyesight, poor mobility, poor hearing)
obstructions (such as limitations on view of parties, bushes, trees, terrain, sun glare)
traffic (such as heavy, light)
caution signs (including all traffic signals, barricades, posted signs, etc.)
relevant ordinances (such as speed limit, school zone, crosswalk)
helplessness of parties (facts indicating parties' inability to avoid or extract themselves from the peril)

The next question is, "Is there any evidence that an unreasonable risk of harm was created [carelessness]?"

Evidence of creating an unreasonable risk of harm includes the following factors:

speed of vehicle(s)
    plaintiff's opinion
    underlying basis for opinion (observability)
    skid marks (length and location)
    time intervals and distances to estimate speed
    police report information
attentiveness of defendant
    plaintiff's view of defendant
    witness's view of defendant
    direction driver was looking
    distractions at point in road
    time interval between when driver should have observed plaintiff and first attempt to brake or take evasive action
    distance between point where driver should have first seen plaintiff and start of skid marks
    lack of skid marks
    sounding of horn
obstructions under the control of defendant
    broken windshield
    frost, condensation, ice on windshield
    stickers
    car ornaments
unsafe vehicle
    immediate loss of control (brakes, steering, bald tires)
    lack of skid marks (brakes)
    high engine roar (stuck accelerator)
    dipped down on one side (springs, shock absorbers, overload)

"It warms the very sickness in my heart, That I shall live and tell him to his teeth, 'Thus diddest thou.'"

—SHAKESPEARE, HAMLET, IV, 7, 1600–01.

Creating questions or areas for inquiry is a brainstorming process that raises a variety of possibilities. This process should be repeated for each of the elements as well as the defenses. Complete your interview form with the following information:

- Add the standard general information questions (name, address, phone) found on most interview forms to complete the new interview form.
- Have the attorney review the draft interview form and make suggestions for other questions.
- Amend the form where appropriate.

Once you understand this method of creating an interview form, you should be able to create a form or expand an existing one in any area of law.

Step 3

Select a location for the interview. Most interviews will take place in the convenience of the office. This gives the interviewer control over outside interruptions and assures privacy, which is a paramount consideration. A disabled, elderly, or ill client, however, may require a personal visit. Sometimes it is advantageous to conduct all or part of an interview at the scene of the accident or where a view of some evidence would be particularly helpful. Before conducting an outside interview, however, obtain approval from the supervising attorney. This is important not only for reasons of cost, but also because outside interviews, depending on the circumstances, heighten safety concerns and expose the interviewer to accusations of misconduct. When the client is contacted to schedule the appointment, determine whether the site you have chosen is convenient.

Step 4

Determine what information the client should bring. Before calling the client, review the interview form and make a list of those items the client should bring to the interview. Typically in a personal injury case the client should bring all medical bills and dates of treatment; accident reports; pertinent names, addresses, and phone numbers; a diagram of the accident; and any other relevant documents. Even if a client does not have access to some of these items, it is important to tell the client to obtain as much of the needed information as possible prior to the interview.

In contract cases, the client should bring key dates surrounding the contract; the time, place, and nature of negotiations preceding the contract; the names, addresses, and phone numbers of people present during the negotiation or during discussion if it was an oral contract (lawyers, all parties, accountants, and so on); points of disagreement and how they were resolved; all drafts of the contract and the contract as signed by the parties; all papers, correspondence, memoranda, and so on, relating to the contract; anything indicating an attempt to modify the contract; and any documentation relating to actual damages or attempts to minimize damages.

Step 5

Schedule the interview; provide for some flexibility in its length. This allows for a more relaxed atmosphere for the client, and provides the opportunity for the interviewer to take more time should circumstances warrant it.

When telephoning the client to set the time for the interview, schedule the appointment as soon as possible because of case filing deadlines, the need to establish an attorney-client relationship to the exclusion of other interested firms, and to provide an opportunity to demonstrate a sincere interest in the client and the case. Use the phone conversation to assess whether the client has any special disabilities or needs that could affect the interview and for which arrangements need to be made. Inform the client about the availability of interpreters and the state of handicapped accessibility to your office, including parking, ramps, doorways, office space, proximity of properly equipped restrooms, and other considerations. The time of the interview should be coordinated with the supervising attorney to allow the attorney to meet with the client prior to the interview. This meeting helps establish the attorney-client relationship and may be used to answer the client's questions about the firm's fees. Occasionally this meeting with the attorney is not possible and the paralegal is directed to proceed accordingly.

Following the phone conversation, fill out a deadline control slip noting any tasks, such as preparation of a letter confirming the appointment or preparation of any documents to be signed by the client at the interview. Note the date on your calendar as well as Mr. White's calendar, and that of the secretary or receptionist who will greet Ms. Forrester. Then draft or dictate a letter confirming the appointment. You may choose to draft your own letter or copy a similar letter from another file. Have your supervising attorney review the letter and send it. An example of such a letter is shown in Exhibit 2:3. This letter can be easily adapted for a contract dispute or other type of case.

Step 6

Anticipate and arrange for any special needs. These might include arranging for an interpreter, having a diagram board ready, preparing for unique ethnic or occupational jargon, or reviewing special medical terminology. If a child is to be interviewed, a few toys might be helpful. Some evidence suggests that young children talk more freely in a play setting and describe what happened to them more easily when using a doll or other props for demonstration purposes.

Step 7

Review pertinent ethical and tactical considerations. The paralegal handbook has already set out for you some of the significant ethical considerations you must keep in mind while interviewing any client. It might be useful to review those prior to each interview until you have such considerations firmly in mind.

The interview is a time when clients want to ask you questions: What does my case look like? Will I be liable? What is your fee? Don't you think I ought to sue? Anticipate such questions and prepare a response. Use the opportunity to make clear your status as a paralegal and your ethical limitations. Your response to the previous questions could be the following:

I am sorry, but I am not permitted to answer that question because it calls for legal advice. Paralegals are not permitted to give legal advice, but Mr. White will be glad to respond to that question. I will pass your questions on to him.

Avoid tape-recording or having the client sign a written statement, unless otherwise directed by your supervising attorney. The opponent may be able to acquire the client's recorded statement under some state rules of civil procedure and would try

Exhibit 2:3 ▪ Confirmation of Appointment Letter

WHITE, WILSON & McDUFF
ATTORNEYS AT LAW
FEDERAL PLAZA BUILDING, SUITE 700
THIRD AND MARKET STREETS
LEGALVILLE, COLUMBIA 00000
(111) 555 - 0000

June 24, ____

Ms. Ann Forrester
1533 Capitol Drive
Legalville, Columbia 00000

Your Case File No. PI 3750

This is to remind you of your appointment on Wednesday, June 29, at 2:30 p.m. at our office. The purpose of the appointment is to discuss in detail the accident you were involved in on February 26 of this year. The appointment is for an hour, or more if necessary.

Please bring the items checked in the following list, if they are available:

(X) Last four digits of social security number
(X) Insurance carrier, policy limits, address, and phone number
(X) Name(s) of the other party or parties and any information you have about them, including insurance carrier
(X) Photos of accident, injuries, or other damage
(X) Photos of accident scene
(X) Diagram of accident and location
(X) News clippings regarding accident
(X) Names, ages, birth dates of spouse and dependents
(X) Description of vehicle(s) in accident, license number, owner, damage
(X) Medical bills, attending physicians, medical insurance, medical history
(X) Occupation and salary information, time lost
(X) Accident or injuries subsequent to this incident
(X) Any correspondence regarding accident
(X) Names, addresss, and phone numbers of other witnesses
(X) Be prepared to describe accident
( ) Other _____

We appreciate your gathering as much of the information as you can. I look forward to meeting you. In the meantime, I can be reached at 555 - 0000.

Terry Salyer

Litigation Paralegal

to use that statement against the client. You may take notes of the interview and record your impressions of the facts and the client's demeanor and truthfulness. Such records are normally protected under the attorney-client privilege.

Ethical and practical considerations require that you run a conflict of interest check on the potential or recently accepted client or verify that one has been completed. Do not assume that a check has been done. Law offices maintain paper or electronic conflict check sheets that include, but are not limited to, the office's personnel and close relatives; current, potential, and former clients; the adversarial parties; the type of case; names and information relevant to any business transactions facilitated by the firm; and other relevant conflict information. To avoid disqualification of the entire firm or other problems as a result of information obtained during a consultation or an initial interview, the following practices may be helpful, *if approved in advance by your attorney*:

1. Make a pre-interview call to the prospective client to determine what the nature of the case is and the names of persons or entities involved, while also stressing to the person not to reveal any confidential information in the process.
2. Have the potential or new client sign a form consenting that no information disclosed during this preliminary stage will prevent the firm from representing a different client in the matter (ABA Model Rules of Prof'l Conduct R. 1.18, cmt. 5).

If a conflict is uncovered, report it immediately. Normally, the office will decline or withdraw from the representation.

Step 8

Review recommended interview techniques. The following techniques have proven useful:

1. Have the client meet with the attorney first, giving the attorney the opportunity to explain the role of the paralegal and what that means to the client in reduced cost. The attorney can then introduce the paralegal. This sequence should help develop client confidence in the firm's professionalism and in the paralegal.
2. Make the client comfortable. Offer refreshments and break the ice with light, pleasant conversation.
3. Be friendly and respectful. Address the client as Mr., Mrs., Ms., or Dr., as appropriate.
4. Create a private environment free of interruptions. Have your calls held. If necessary, place an Interview in Progress sign on the office door.[2]
5. Explain the purpose of the interview and let clients know you need their help.
6. Inform the client that you, the attorney, and any employees of the law office are required to protect the information provided by the client and that such information is held in the strictest confidence. Explain that honesty is essential and that it can be disastrous to hold back any information, no matter how personal or embarrassing it might be. On the other hand, explain that it is human to forget, and it is not unusual that something forgotten now can be recalled later. Discuss, also, that it is normal for people to want to fill in gaps in their memory; that they need to be careful about presenting information they do not remember clearly.
7. Express confidence about what you are doing. Thorough preparation and planning will help you be more confident. It is equally important to avoid

trying to impress the interviewee with all of your legal knowledge and vocabulary.

8. Avoid being condescending. Try to put yourself in the client's position and think how you would like to be addressed.

9. Take accurate, detailed, and legible notes.

10. Be a good listener. Silences during the interview process are inevitable and can be productive periods of thought and recall.[3] Avoid the temptation to end the silence quickly. Be patient, supportive, and accepting. Encourage the expression of feelings, and avoid making value judgments.[4]

11. Be mindful of the client's body language or idiosyncratic mannerisms and note them for the attorney. Body language is important because of the jury's potential reaction to it. Be cautious, however, in interpreting body language; such interpretation is not a precise science.

12. Let clients tell their stories. It is important to them. Come back later to pick up significant details.

13. Use open narrative questions such as "What happened? What happened next?" This allows clients to proceed at their own pace and encourages a freer flow of information, which is more conducive to fact gathering.

14. Avoid questions that suggest an answer. For example, "Ms. Forrester, you did look both ways before you stepped onto the highway, didn't you?" This is a **leading question** and encourages clients to respond as they perceive you want them to respond, and not necessarily with the truth. This type of question restricts the flow of information.

15. Avoid "why" questions, which are often viewed by the interviewee as a sign of disapproval.[5] A less confrontational approach might be "Try to help me understand this," or "Would you please elaborate on your reasons for doing that?"

16. Probe the accuracy of judgments regarding items such as speed, distance, color, time, or size. Determine, if possible, the basis of the judgment or test its accuracy through example or comparison to some similar item or distance.

17. Be mentally prepared to deal with sensitive or personal matters in a forthright yet empathetic manner. Avoid skirting the issue or using euphemisms. Such shyness or hesitancy on the part of the interviewer can encourage dishonesty.[6]

18. Deal tactfully but directly with suspected dishonesty. Do not be afraid to indicate that a response doesn't seem to stand up or to follow from the other evidence.

19. Restate the client's information when necessary to make sure you understand: "Now let me see if I have this right. You said you stepped out . . . ?"

20. Be thorough in asking about the accident or other alleged wrongs and any damages. Cover how the injury or loss affected the family's life or, in a business or contract case, how the action affected the business, its customers, and other factors.[7] The more details you can obtain, the better.

leading question
Question phrased in such a manner as to suggest the desired answer (e.g., "It was raining that night, wasn't it?").

An important interview of a young child or a mentally challenged person requires special techniques. Review pertinent resource material on how to proceed or use a specially trained interviewer.

Interviewing is an art that requires practice and experience. Techniques that work well for some people do not work well for others. Experiment and develop your own style.

Step 9

Prepare orientation and instruction materials for the client. Clients will normally have a variety of questions concerning the litigation process as well as what will be expected of them. Some firms have developed a videotape that the client views either before or after the initial interview to provide guidance and information to the client. If the client hires the firm, make sure the client leaves with information on the following matters.[8] It is best to have this information in a brochure previously approved by the attorney to avoid any questions about giving legal advice.

1. The attorney is your legal advocate whose function is to assume responsibility for your case and represent you to the best of the attorney's ability.
2. The paralegal assists your attorney in handling your case, providing you with a more thorough preparation at a lower cost.
3. You will need to provide your attorney with *all* the information you can gather and recall about the incident, your injuries and losses, and any statements you have made to others.
4. It may be necessary to provide your attorney with intimate personal information. Expect that the information you give will be held in the strictest of confidence consistent with the highest standards of professional loyalty.
5. Refrain from making any statements to others about the incident or about your injuries or losses. Such statements may be used against you in court and could weaken your case. Refer any inquiries or requests to your attorney.
6. Do not sign any documents releasing others from liability or accepting payments for injuries. Do not file an accident report without first checking with your attorney.
7. Begin a daily medical journal in which you will record the condition of your injuries and medical treatment. Daily references to pain, suffering, sleeplessness, limitations on normal activity, changes in condition, and trips to the hospital or physician should be noted. Keep a record of your expenses: mileage, prescriptions, drugs, crutches, wheelchair, private nurse, and so on.
8. Record all employment losses: days missed; lost pay and benefits; and missed raises, promotions, merit pay, and bonuses. Also note the date of your return to work and any subsequent effects your injuries have on your ability to do your job.
9. Make a record of all damages to property and estimates for repair. Do not discard, give away, or sell such property without consulting your attorney.
10. List your expenses in hiring others to perform domestic work and maintenance or child care needed as a result of your injuries.
11. Apprise your attorney or paralegal of your medical, property, and disability insurance coverage in order that steps may be taken to inform the companies of the incident and claims may be made. You do not want to waive your right to a claim; such claims may provide necessary cash for living expenses. Money paid by your insurance company will be reimbursed to the insurance company if it is awarded to you in the lawsuit for the same damages previously paid for by the insurance.
12. You should be aware that most cases are settled before trial; your case may be settled through negotiation prior to trial.
13. The filing of a case is important because it keeps the case moving, provides access to the opponent's information, and encourages a more timely resolution

of the matter. Once a case is filed, it may take from one year to several years before it comes to trial. No settlement will be agreed upon without your full knowledge and acceptance.

14. Keep the paralegal informed of any new information that arises or that you recall. Inform us of any change in address, extended vacation plans, and so on. Refrain from asking others questions about your case. This frequently leads to confusion and incorrect information. If you have questions about your case, please ask us. We will be glad to help.

15. Prior to trial you will be called to the office to review information and to prepare for trial. You may be asked to provide sworn testimony about the incident at a deposition. This is required by law. You will be given time to prepare for this deposition. You may also be asked to undergo an examination by a physician chosen by the opponent in order to verify your injuries. This is permitted by law.

16. Your case may not end following a decision by the court. Frequently appeals are filed before a case is final. This can take a long time.

Step 10

Prepare any forms for the client's signature. The interview is a good time to have the client sign several documents, including the fee arrangement, which the attorney and the client should have discussed. Remember, it is the unauthorized practice of law for a paralegal to negotiate or set legal fees. There are two typical fee agreements. The first is for representation based on an hourly rate. Prepare an explanation for the client concerning how the hourly rate will be broken down for billing purposes, such as by one-quarter, one-sixth, or one-tenth of an hour. The second is for representation based on a percentage of the award won by the plaintiff, allowing for no fee if the plaintiff does not win. This is called a **contingent fee.**

contingent fee
Legal fee for representation based on a percentage of the award won by the plaintiff and allowing for no fee if the plaintiff does not win.

Many client-attorney fee disputes arise because the nature of the fee was not made clear to the client from the beginning and because the fee arrangement was not put in writing. Be prepared to explain the fee contract and have the client sign the written fee agreement. In some firms only the attorney will take this responsibility, but even then the paralegal may be responsible for drafting the fee agreement (see Exhibit 2:4 and Exhibit 2:5).[9] Some flexibility in the fee agreement is preferable. For example, the following language was held appropriate:

> Your ultimate fee may vary depending on the time limitations imposed by you, the questions involved, the skill requisite to perform the legal service properly, or the amount involved and the results obtained [Silva v. Buckley, not reported in S.W.3d, WL 23099681 (Tenn.Ct.App. 2003)].

Court rules dictate the nature and limits of contingent fee agreements in some states.

While addressing fee agreements, a cautionary word regarding law office Web sites is in order. Because you may become responsible for the office's Web site, note that such sites can, intentionally or unintentionally, create an attorney/client relationship. If the firm's intent is not to create such a relationship via the Web site, the site should contain a clear statement that any initial information conveyed to the firm will not be treated as confidential. Conversely, if the intent is to facilitate the creation of an attorney/client relationship via this electronic format, it is best to set out a clear agreement that requires the prospective client to acknowledge having read and agreed to the language by clicking an acceptance button. The agreement should include language that protects the firm if there is a conflict of interest or other reasons for declining the representation.[10]

EXHIBIT 2:4 ■ Fee Agreement

LEGAL REPRESENTATION AGREEMENT

I hereby employ the firm of _____, with the understanding that attorney _____

will represent me and provide legal services for me in: _____

_____

_____

and I authorize the firm to commence an action in this matter as may be advisable in the judgment of the firm, subject to my approval. I also understand that the law firm may assign other or additional attorneys to represent me, with my approval, as may be required from time to time.

Attorney's fees and expenses

I agree that the following method is to be used for determining the proper amount of legal fees:

1. FEES:

The attorney's fees for services performed under this agreement shall be based upon a rate of $____ per hour. Hourly billing will be to the tenth (1/10th) of an hour. (If more than one attorney, or paralegal, at differing rates, then so specify.)[a]

2. RETAINER: (Choose one):

A. In order to secure the time and services of the attorney for this matter, I agree to make an initial, nonrefundable payment in the amount of $___ toward my attorney's fees and expenses. I understand this is the minimum fee I will be charged for services and expenses.

B. In order to secure the time and services of the attorney for this matter, I agree to make an initial payment in the amount of $___ toward my attorney's fees and expenses. This retainer fee shall be a credit against hourly attorney's fees and costs advancements. It will be refunded to the extent it has not been utilized for this purpose.

3. COSTS:

A. I authorize my attorney to retain any individual and entities to perform services necessary for investigation or completion of legal services. I agree to pay the fees or charges of every person or entity hired by the attorney to perform necessary services.

B. I acknowledge that my attorney may incur various expenses in providing services to me. I agree to reimburse the attorney for all out-of-pocket expenses paid. If I am billed directly for these expenses, I agree to make prompt direct payments to the originators of the bills. Such expenses may include, but are not limited to, service and filing fees, courier or messenger services, recording and certifying documents, depositions, transcripts, investigations, witnesses' fees, long-distance telephone calls, copying materials, overtime clerical assistance, travel expenses, postage, notarial attestations, and computer research.

Billing

I agree to the following schedule of billing:

1. Fees, charges, and expenses will be billed on at least a monthly basis as they accrue.

2. The retainer shall be paid in full upon the execution of this agreement. The retainer shall be a credit against monthly bills.[b]

3. I agree to make payments promptly. I understand that failure to make payments is sufficient reason for the attorney to withdraw from representing me in this matter, whether or not litigation has been commenced. I will be notified in writing prior to any withdrawal. I agree that a letter to my last known address is sufficient notice.

Consultations

I understand that personal and telephone consultations with my attorney shall be part of my representation and I will be billed by the attorney for the time spent on such consultation.

EXHIBIT 2:4 ▪ Fee Agreement (*continued*)

Discharge of attorney

I may, if unsatisfied with the services for any reason, discharge the attorney at any time; however, it is understood that the attorney will be paid or arrangements will be made for the payment of all fees and costs.

Representation

It is expressly agreed and understood by me that no promises, assurances, or guarantees as to the outcome of this matter have been made by the attorney. Payment is not contingent upon the outcome of this matter.

I have read this fee agreement, and have had opportunity to discuss it with my attorney or any other attorney. I understand, agree and accept all of the terms within this agreement.

Dated this _____ day of _____, _____

Attorney _____ Client _____

[a]Note that any additional reservation of right to increase the fee in the future for increased hourly rates must be specifically stated.
[b]Modify paragraph if retainer is nonrefundable. Any other agreement on applying or retaining the retainer should be specifically drafted.
Source: Reprinted with permission of the Wisconsin Bar Association.

EXHIBIT 2:5 ▪ Contingent Fee Agreement

1. I, _____, having been injured on _____, hereby agree to retain _____, of the law firm of _____ as my attorney to make claims or bring suit against anyone necessary.

2. My attorney is to receive ___% of the gross settlement or judgment for legal services. This percentage will increase to ___% of the gross settlement or judgment in the event of an appeal of the final judgment to the court of appeals or supreme court. My attorney is hereby given a continuing lien in my claim and the proceeds thereof for the amount of the contingent fee, pursuant to Wis. Stats. section 757.36.

3. I UNDERSTAND THAT I COULD RETAIN THE ATTORNEY TO REPRESENT ME IN THIS ACTION AND COMPENSATE HIM/HER ON AN HOURLY BASIS, BUT I EXPRESSLY DECLINE TO DO SO, SUBJECT TO PARA. 8.

4. I also have been informed that I am responsible to pay for costs and disbursements including, but not limited to:

_____
_____

My attorney may, but is not obligated to, advance these and other costs he or she believes are reasonable and necessary for preparing and presenting any claim. Any costs advanced by the attorney for which he or she was not reimbursed shall be paid to the attorney for costs within 30 days of receiving a written statement thereof.

5. I understand that if no recovery is obtained for me, no attorneys' fees shall be due; however, I will remain responsible for costs and disbursements. I also understand that settlement shall not be made without my approval or the approval of my guardian.

6. I understand that by signing this agreement, I am promising not to release the names of any experts and/or consultants hired in regard to my case. I further understand that the names of any experts and/or consultants hired in regard to my case are the property of the attorney and law firm and are not my property. I expressly agree that my attorney may promise experts/consultants that their names and/or reports will not be revealed to anyone, including me.

7. I understand that my attorneys may withdraw if they believe my case lacks merit or is not fiscally responsible to pursue.

(*continued*)

EXHIBIT 2:5 ■ Contingent Fee Agreement (*continued*)

8. I understand that in the event that, contrary to the advice of my attorneys, I instruct my attorneys to discontinue the matter, the matter shall be discontinued and I shall pay the law firm a reasonable hourly rate, plus expenses, for the time they have expended on my behalf.

9. I have read and my attorney has explained the above eight points of this agreement and I understand the same.

Dated: _____ Client _____

Witness: _____

(Law Firm) _____

Attorney _____

Source: Reprinted with permission of the Wisconsin Bar Association.

Signed documents are of considerable assistance to the paralegal in subsequent investigative work. Among these forms are authorizations signed by the client permitting those holding confidential information, such as doctors and employers, to release that information to the lawyer. Exhibit 2:6 is a standardized release form designed to cover a variety of needed information. It can be used when one is not yet sure of the entire range of items that will be needed.

Medical records and other highly private health care information are now protected under the Health Insurance Portability and Accountability Act (HIPAA), 45 CFR §§ 164.501, et. seq. Therefore, any authorization to release medical information that you might need your client to sign must comply with federal requirements and any provisions of parallel state law that are more protective than HIPAA. See Chapter 3 for an example of an authorization to disclose protected health care information form. Some health care providers insist that you use their release forms. If you deal regularly with certain providers, consider getting a supply of their forms (or preferably an electronic copy) to have readily available.

In the following chapters, other specialized authorization forms are presented and discussed. For a particular situation, these may be preferable to a form that attempts to meet all needs.

Step 11

Prepare the interview site. Use your office or a conference room, if preferable. You will need to make sure the site is neat and clear of all other files so confidentiality of other clients is preserved. A clean, neat area and desk suggest to clients that you have everything under control. In addition, the clients will realize that you have set aside this time especially for them. We all like to feel important, and clients are no exception. If your office and your manner convey to clients that they are important, your interview will be that much more productive.

Make sure the office is arranged in a way you feel will be most comfortable for the client (facing each other across a desk, side by side at a table, or seated in chairs set in a conversational arrangement) and is equipped with everything you and the client will need. You should have paper for taking notes and drawing diagrams, extra pens or sharpened pencils, tissues, and ice water, coffee, and tea. Increasingly, paralegals use portable electronic keypads with small display screens for note taking. Some software provides simultaneous audio recording while taking notes. Be sure to have your

EXHIBIT 2:6 ■ Standardized Release Form (not medical)

WHITE, WILSON & MCDUFF
ATTORNEYS AT LAW
FEDERAL PLAZA BUILDING, SUITE 700
THIRD AND MARKET STREETS
LEGALVILLE, COLUMBIA 00000
(111) 555 - 0000

Address

Date

RE: (Name of client, date of birth)

This form authorizes _____ to release to my attorney, White, Wilson & McDuff, or their designated representative, all of the following information about me as indicated (X), and to discuss it, send it, make it available for inspection, or photocopy it as they may request.

( ) Employment records: description of position, length of employment, pay, benefits, absences, performance, accumulated sick leave, etc.

( ) Academic and school records: attendance dates; evaluations; grade performance; psychological, aptitude, and achievement tests; class ranking; teachers, etc.

( ) Military records

( ) All state and federal tax returns for the years _____

( ) Other: _____

_____   _____
Client   Date

_____
Address

own diagram present if you intend to work from that, and any photographs or other items you will be using or referring to. All the forms you drafted should be at hand for the client's signature.

In addition, you will want to remind the secretary or receptionist to hold your calls and to help head off other interruptions.

As a part of your preparation, be sure you know the procedure to follow in the event of an emergency. It does happen, though rarely, that the interviewee will faint, have a heart attack or seizure, or otherwise experience a medical emergency. The office should have a regular procedure that you should know so that you can react quickly and confidently to such a situation.

You have now gone through a fairly thorough preparation process for the interview. The interview, whether it is your first or one hundred and first, will go more smoothly, and the client will have more confidence in you because of it. With this kind of preparation, little can go wrong.

THE INTERVIEW

You are now prepared to conduct the initial interview with Ms. Forrester. The following are some examples of how you might conduct the interview. Assume that Ms. Forrester has already met with Mr. White and that he brings the client to your office. (Ms. Forrester is in a wheelchair.)

THE INTRODUCTION

Mr. White:	Ms. Forrester, I would like you to meet Terry Salyer, the paralegal who will be assisting me with your case. Terry, this is Ms. Ann Forrester, who, as you know, suffered injuries in a car-pedestrian accident this past year and is seeking our firm's assistance.
Paralegal:	How do you do, Ms. Forrester? We have spoken on the phone, and I have looked forward to meeting you.
Mr. White:	I'll leave you with Terry, who will be asking you some important questions. We will meet again later. It was good to see you.

Another frequent scenario for an introduction occurs when the secretary or receptionist informs you that your appointment has arrived. Clear your desk and go out to meet the client, letting her know that you are eager to meet and work with her.

Paralegal:	Please come into my office. I would be happy to fix a cup of coffee or tea for you. We also have some soft drinks. Would you care for anything?
Ms. Forrester:	Not now, thank you, maybe later.

Close the office door, return to your chair, and speak briefly about the weather, ask about her family, or about how she is doing with the wheelchair. Explain your role as a paralegal and the purpose of the interview. Ask for the information that Ms. Forrester was requested to bring.

Paralegal:	Thank you for taking the time to gather this material. It will be very helpful. I have some questions I need to cover with you. You can start by telling me your full name.
Ms. Forrester:	Ann Brooke Forrester.
Paralegal:	Your home address is 1533 Capitol Drive, Legalville, Columbia, Zip 00000?
Ms. Forrester:	Yes.

You can now proceed to work through the questions on the form you have prepared, listening carefully, recording all pertinent information, and drawing from the information brought in by the client as needed.

Assume that Ms. Forrester goes on to describe the accident summarized as follows. It was a partly sunny, windy, cold morning. There was ice on the road in front of the Forrester house. Ms. Forrester crossed the highway to mail a letter. The point of crossing sits in a depression in the road with knolls rising to the east and west, obscuring some vision. A van came over the east knoll, slid and hit Ms. Forrester, who was seriously injured.

> "It is not uncommon for ignorant and corrupt men to falsely charge others with doing what they imagine that they themselves, in their narrow minds and experience, would have done under the circumstances."
>
> —JOHN H. CLARKE, *VALDEZ v. UNITED STATES*, 224 U.S. 432, 450 (1917).

QUESTIONS ON CIRCUMSTANCES OF THE ACCIDENT

Now you need to focus on specific details. The following questions demonstrate the level of detail necessary to see whether evidence establishes the required elements of proof of breach of duty. (*P* stands for paralegal and *F* stands for Ms. Forrester.)

P: Ms. Forrester, you mentioned in your description of the accident that the road was icy. I'd like to go back to that. Did you personally observe that the road was icy?

F: Yes, when I walked across the road.

P: Was it icy enough for you to alter your normal walk?

F: Yes, I kind of shuffled over the icy patches.

P: The ice did not cover the entire road?

F: That's right.

P: Was the ice thick?

F: No, just a thin layer, like heavy frost. Some had already begun to melt in the sun and other areas were completely dry.

P: Did you notice the condition of the road on the downslope from where the van approached?

F: Not really. It was in the early morning shadows, however, and what ice was there probably did not melt.

P: On what do you base that opinion?

F: Several days before the accident we had similar weather. That slope remained icier because of the shadows.

P: Is there anyone besides yourself and the defendant who might have observed the ice on the road?

F: Yes.

P: Their names and addresses, please.

The questioning must be detailed. Listen carefully and take advantage of the opportunity to get witnesses' names on this particular point. It is a good idea when receiving such names to use a local phone directory immediately to confirm the spelling of the names as well as addresses and phone numbers.

P: Ms. Forrester, I would like to go back to what you said about the van seeming to keep coming at you. Did the defendant see you first, or did you see the defendant first?

F: I am not sure; however, when I looked up, the van was already coming down the slope, so the defendant should have seen me first.

P: When you first saw the van, was there any indication that the driver was taking evasive action?

F: No, in fact, the van just kept coming for what must have been at least four seconds, it felt that long. Before it hit me I heard a skidding sound and the van began to fishtail.

P: Describe what you mean by "fishtail."

F: The rear of the van began to move sideways—back and forth.

It is important that you call attention to words that might not be clear (in this case, *fishtail*) and ask for further explanation. It is also a good idea to clarify the meaning of all words you do not understand or that may be misused by the client.

THE ISSUE OF COMPARATIVE OR CONTRIBUTORY NEGLIGENCE

P: Earlier, you mentioned wearing a warm winter coat with a high, furry collar. Was the collar high enough to go over your ears?

F: Yes, it was.

P: Do you always wear it that way?

F: No, but I did on this day. The wind was cold, and I pulled my collar up and tucked my head into it.

P: Did you tuck your head into it far enough that your vision was obscured?

F: It was not obscured looking forward, but, yes, it was, I guess, on the sides.

P: By "sides" do you mean your peripheral vision?

F: Yes.

P: Help me on this. You said "I guess," referring to the coat's obstruction of your vision. Was your side vision obscured?

F: Yes, it was.

P: Would you have seen the van sooner had you not pulled the coat up around your head?

F: I don't know. It's possible. I did look to the left and then the right before stepping onto the road.

P: What were you looking at once you stepped onto the road?

F: The road immediately in front of me. I did not want to slip on the ice.

Note several things. First, a high collar might be a hearing obstruction. Second, the client said she tucked her head into the collar, raising the possibility of a sight obstruction. And third, responses such as "I guess" are insufficient. Tactfully press the client for a more precise response.

THE EXTENT OF INJURY AND SENSITIVE INQUIRY

The following questions come after a fairly extensive description by the client of severe injuries to the left hip, pelvic region, lower back, and left leg. The client has stated that she is nearly paralyzed on her left side from the waist down. At this point in the interview, the client begins to weep. The paralegal gets up from behind the desk, comes over to the client, and offers tissues.

P: Ms. Forrester, I know these must be very difficult times for you. Let's take a short break. How about a glass of water or maybe some soda?

(Ms. Forrester nods. Leave the room to give the client a few moments of privacy and time to regain her composure. Bring her a glass of water.)

P: May I get you anything else?

F: No, but thank you. I feel better now.

P: I realize it must be difficult to talk about your injuries. The more you can help me with information, however, the better job we can do for you.

F: I understand. Let's go on.

P: Ms. Forrester, have you had any problems as a result of the injuries regarding normal bodily functions?

F: Yes, I have some difficulty controlling my bladder.

P: I need to make sure I understand this correctly. You urinate regardless of any effort to control the urination process on your part?

F: That is correct.

P: Now, it is important for me to determine how this inconvenience and anxiety affect you.

"[Law] is not a profession at all, but rather a business, service station, and repair shop."

—Adlai E. Stevenson, 1900–1965, quoted in Walter Johnson and Carol Evans, *The Papers of Adlai Stevenson*, 1972.

Go on to explore the details, including any sense of humiliation, frustration, or degradation. Do not let the sensitivity of the issue stop the detailed inquiry. In most cases, sensitive issues must be dealt with forthrightly, using straightforward vocabulary. Avoid euphemisms.

One thing to be observed in reading through these interview segments is the need to ad-lib questions. Such questions will follow naturally if you listen carefully and keep in mind the elements of the action as well as the defenses.

DEALING WITH DIFFICULT CLIENTS

Every law office has its difficult clients. Learning to deal with them is an important skill that allows you to remain in control. Psychologists recommend a method for defusing angry clients, called "pace and lead."[11] Instead of becoming defensive or telling a client to calm down, acknowledge a client's anger with words and body language (pacing). For example, a client stands up and angrily responds to the need to sign more documents. Using "pacing," the paralegal stands up and says in a similarly angry tone of voice something like, "Isn't it awful, form after form. You would think it could be simpler." Then the paralegal "leads" the client toward less anger and more productivity by saying in a less angry tone, "We eliminate forms whenever we can, but we must use these forms currently required by the court. We're working on simplifying this process." Then, pointing to the document, the paralegal says in a calm but sympathetic voice, "Please start reading here and sign down here." "Pace and lead" keeps you and the client on the same side.

Another type of angry client is the abusive one who rants, demeans, and gives orders. Allowing this person to vent may diminish the anger. Above all, stay calm and realize this is not personal. If the anger persists, a prearranged interruption such as a phone call from the secretary or a colleague who needs to see you immediately can provide a brief cooling down period. Irate telephone callers should be told to calm down or be disconnected.

Techniques for dealing with the compulsive drop-in or frequent telephone caller include keeping him or her focused on what, if anything, is new and pertinent information. Lengthy social chit-chat can be derailed by asking, "How can I help you?" It is perfectly proper to indicate that you have another matter that you must attend to or, if the client is in your office, combine that approach with getting up and ushering him or her to the door.

The "I-can't-be-bothered-executive" may require direct contact from your supervising attorney or the plying of a high ranking assistant to that executive.[12]

Some clients are seductively dependent and feed your ego, while others can be sexually aggressive. Resolute and objective professional conduct soon deflects these attentions. There are times, however, when even the most professional individual is vulnerable to such attention. Such times require awareness and disciplined professionalism. Seeking assistance from experienced colleagues can be helpful, as can some of the available resource books on working with difficult people and on violence in the workplace.

CONCLUDING THE INTERVIEW

In concluding the interview, give the client a list of all the information that remains for the client to gather. Also remind the client to notify you of any new information regarding the accident, witnesses, injuries, and so on. Provide the client with the client information brochure. It might be helpful to give the client her own file folder in which to keep records and documents over the course of the lawsuit. Attach your business card to the folder. Then explain the documents that need to be executed and have them signed. After one last reminder to the client not to make any statements about the case and not to discuss the case with others, the interview can be concluded. Some interviewers choose at this time to turn off the billing clock and visit informally with the client to show their interest in the client. This is an effective technique, especially if used sincerely. Tell clients that you will keep them informed periodically of the progress in their case.

CONFIRMING THE STATUTE OF LIMITATIONS

statute of limitations
Law stating the time limit in which an action must be filed. If the time limit is not met, the defendant has a defense to the action, and the case will be dismissed.

Once you have found out the date of the occurrence and the nature of the action, it is important to check the **statute of limitations.** This may have been done already, but if not, it should be done now. The statute of limitations is the date by which an action must be filed. If it is not filed by the required time, the defendant has a defense to the action, and the case will be dismissed. Rarely is there an excuse of sufficient degree for a judge to permit an action to be filed after the required date. Therefore, the paralegal must unfailingly check the statute of limitations for the particular type of action involved. The time periods vary depending on the type of action and the state. Usually someone in the office will have previously made a quick-reference list of the common time limits. If not, statute books will list the time limits under the topic Statute of Limitations or by the type of case: negligence, contract, product liability, and so on.

The time period involved in the statute of limitations is a specified time such as one year or two years. When claims are based on federal laws with unspecified statutes of limitations, federal courts must look to parallel limits in the law of the state in which they are located. Title 28 U.S.C. § 1658 sets a uniform four-year limit in all such actions based on federal laws enacted after December 30, 1990. Normally the statute of limitations starts with the date of the injury, accident, breach of contract, and so on. In such circumstances, the lawsuit must be filed before one year elapses if it is a one-year statute of limitations or before two years elapse if it is a two-year statute, and so forth. If the precise origin of the injury is not apparent or the symptoms of the injury are not likely to manifest themselves for some time after the event that caused them (for example, in black lung cases in coal mining or in cancer cases caused by exposure to toxic substances), then the statute begins to run at the time the symptoms were first noticeable or at a time a reasonable person should have noticed the symptoms or problem. This may not occur until many years later. Information that places a person on notice that a problem exists, however, cannot simply be ignored. For example, in *Winters v. Diamond Shamrock Chemical Co.*, 149 F.3d 387 (5th Cir. 1998), *cert. denied* 526 U.S. 1034 (1999), extensive media coverage caused the statutory time to run because it "notified" the plaintiff to the extent that she should have investigated any link between her cancer and exposure to Agent Orange. The action must be started before the statute runs; it does not have to be concluded in that time. The statute of limitations is so significant that it should be conspicuously noted on the front of the case file and placed in the deadline calendaring system.

If, after careful calculation, it appears the statute of limitations has run, notify your supervising attorney immediately. There may still be life in the lawsuit. For instance, the defendants' ten-day out-of-state vacation during the two-year statutory limit allowed the personal injury plaintiff to file a lawsuit two days late [*Johnson v. Rhodes*, 733 N.E.2d 1132 (Ohio 2000)]. A defendant's misleading and false statements, which were relied on by the plaintiffs and resulted in delay in the filing of the plaintiffs' suit, were sufficient to extend the time limit in *Wall v. Construction and General Laborers' Union Local 230*, 224 F.3d 168 (2d Cir. 2000). If a lawsuit is filed within the prescribed time limit but is dismissed, it is treated as if no action had been filed [*Elmore v. Henderson*, 227 F.3d 1009 (7th Cir. 2000)].

SUMMARIZING THE INTERVIEW

From the notes and the interview form, prepare a summary of the interview. A summary sheet appears in Exhibit 2:7; the completed version is in Exhibit 2:8. Enter one copy of the summary into the file and give another copy to the supervising attorney.

KEEPING THE CLIENT INFORMED

A significant improvement paralegals have brought to the law office is increased communication with clients. Lack of communication from the law office is a frequent complaint of clients. Therefore, with the attorney's approval, the paralegal should assume the primary responsibility of keeping the client well informed. Schedule a report letter to be sent to the client at least once a month. Try to respond to all the client's inquiries as soon as possible and acknowledge receipt of any information sent to you by the client. This personal attention assures clients that they are not merely a case file number.

In this regard, knowing how to design a letter with good news or bad news is important. Here are a few tips. Your letter should be brief, polite, and, above all, easily understood. Good news is best stated first with any necessary explanation to follow.[13]

EXHIBIT 2:7 ■ Summary Sheet: Initial Interview of Client

File no.:   Date opened: Interviewer:
Client: (M) Spouse: (C) Children, ages: (P)Phone:
Party opponent(s):
Date of incident:
Type of Action: Statute of limitations:
Summary of facts of action:
Noteworthy facts related to elements of action:
Noteworthy facts related to possible defenses:
Witnesses:
Summary of injury and treatment to date:
Total medical bills to date:
Summary of business or wage loss:
Total business or wage loss to date:
Evaluation of client as witness:
Other comments:
Things to do:

EXHIBIT 2:8 ■ Summary Sheet: Initial Interview of Client (completed)

File No.: PI 3750   **Date opened:** 6/23/__   **Interviewer:** T.S. 6/29/__
Client: (P) Ann Forrester   (M) William Forrester   (C) Michael, 8   (P) 555 - 1111
     Sara, 4

Party opponent(s): (D) Richard Hart (Ohio resident)
     Mercury Parcel Service (Ohio resident, Hart's employer)

Date of incident: 2/26/__
Type of action: P.I. negligence, auto-pedestrian
Statute of limitations: 2/26/__
Summary of facts of action:
     P walked across Highway 328 three miles west of Legalville, Columbia, to mail letter. Coming back, P was struck by van owned by Mercury Parcel Service. Crossing point was in depression in road obscuring long-range vision of both pedestrian and driver. Road had patchy ice. D was driving about 40 mph in 35-mph zone. P was struck on left side and thrown to side of road. Van went off and struck tree.
Noteworthy facts related to elements of action:
Breach of duty: P states D going too fast for icy conditions, slid on ice. Also P states D delayed evasive action and may have been inattentive. P says her husband felt D looked quite tired. According to P's husband, van windshield partially fogged over.
Noteworthy facts related to possible defenses:
Comparative negligence: P was in hurry to mail letter to leave for work, had head tucked into coat and vision to side obscured. Thinks she looked left, not sure; did look to right. Didn't see van until it was headed down slope toward her. Didn't hear van coming.
Witnesses:
     Ms. Freda Schnabel saw accident from crest of opposite hill while driving her car toward accident. Her address is 1625 Capitol Dr.
P's husband, William Forrester, also saw some of accident.
Officer Jeremy Burton was first police officer on scene.
Summary of injury and treatment to date:
     Several fractures to left hip, pelvis, and left leg. Partial paralysis on left side from waist down. Loss of bladder control. Considerable pain in injured area. Permanent disability likely, currently confined to wheelchair. Emergency treatment: 2/26/__ Good Samaritan Hospital, 4600 Church St., Legalville, Columbia.
Treating physician(s): Albert Meyer, M.D., orthopedic surgeon
     Medical Arts Building, 4650 Church St.
Consultant: Robert S. Ward, M.D., urology
Total medical bills to date: $40,000
Summary of business or wage loss:
     Full-time teacher, Legalville Board of Education, $34,000 annually.
     Unable to work since accident. Note: Wage loss could be substantial if injury permanent.
Total business or wage loss to date: $ 17,000
Evaluation of client as witness: Client is pleasant, intelligent, and should be good witness.
Other comments: Client wanted to know if she should file a lawsuit. I explained she needed to discuss this with Mr. White, who whould be meeting with her.
Things to do: Gather medical records, interview witnesses, locate van.

Dear Ms. Rakowski:

I am pleased to inform you that the Montez Construction Company has agreed to meet to discuss a settlement of your lawsuit.

To take the best advantage of this opportunity, Ms. Wilson needs you to be present . . . .

Bad news requires the greatest tact and, if possible, should be sandwiched between more positive language that conveys a positive attitude toward the client and the case.[14]

Dear Ms. Rakowski:

Ms. Wilson and I enjoyed our chance to meet with you last Friday in preparation for the settlement conference with the Montez Construction Company. Unfortunately, the company representatives have cancelled that meeting.

Although Ms. Wilson is tied up in a trial this week, she wants you to know she will continue to pursue the matter vigorously on your behalf and will call you to discuss the latest developments.

Communication is also critical at the start of the case to document and make it absolutely clear to a person seeking legal representation by the law office that either the firm is accepting or rejecting the case. Ethical, malpractice, and other concerns make this essential. Normally, the office has copies of such letters. You may be asked to draft a version of the letter. Wording for a disengagement (or nonengagement) letter might appear as follows.

Dear Mr. Beckley,

Thank you for coming to our law office on (specific date) and meeting with me to discuss your legal concern. We understand the importance of this matter to you. Upon further review, however, our office must decline representing you in the matter.

(Language can be added about having not formed a legal opinion in the matter and the importance to the person of seeking the advice of another attorney as soon as possible because of any applicable statute of limitations).

Again, this letter is to notify you that we will not represent you in this matter. Enclosed are the documents that you left with us.

SUMMARY

The initial interview forms the basis for the client/law firm relationship and provides information essential to determining a cause of action or defense. The importance of the interview and its interactive nature cause some paralegals to feel intimidated or uneasy about this process. Take comfort from knowing, however, that experience and thoughtful planning can ease your anxiety and greatly increase your effectiveness. A good interview plan checklist, well-designed and thorough interview forms, and knowledge of the applicable area of law facilitate a smooth interview.

Interpersonal skills such as a sensitivity to the needs of the client and being able to anticipate and deal with difficult personalities will bring a human quality to your work that will be appreciated by both clients and supervisors. If you add to this your understanding of the significance of client screening, conflict of interest checks, HIPAA compliant medical releases, the statute of limitations, and an ability to capture critical information in a concise summary, your service to the client and the law office at this stage will be truly professional.

◼ WORKBOOK

System Folder Assignments, other exercises, a chapter outline, a review test, and other study aids are located in the accompanying workbook.

◼ HELPFUL WEB SITES

http://www.atanet.org
  American Translators Association, lists of translator and interpreter services by language and area of expertise, e.g., legal specialties, medicine, science, engineering

http://www.google.com
  a good search engine
http://www.abanet.org/lpm/lpt/articles/mgt04054.html
  2005 article on difficult clients and other resources

◼ QUESTIONS FOR STUDY AND REVIEW

1. For what reasons is the initial interview with the client important? What should be considered when screening a potential client?
2. Why is planning an interview important?
3. What are the eleven steps in the interview plan? Explain how each step is accomplished.
4. Explain how to develop an interview form.
5. Identify and define the four legal elements that must be proved by the plaintiff in a negligence case.
6. What is the difference between contributory negligence and comparative negligence? Which of these two doctrines is the rule of law in your state?
7. What is the doctrine of last clear chance? What is the assumption of risk? Give examples of each.
8. How does one develop pertinent questions for an interview?
9. Create ten questions probing the existence and nature of injuries suffered in an occurrence.
10. What are some of the considerations in selecting a location for the interview?
11. Why is scheduling a flexible time for the interview important?
12. What types of things should the client bring to the interview?
13. What is the simple process for developing a form letter?

14. Identify the special needs one should anticipate in planning an interview.
15. What special ethical and tactical concerns must a paralegal be aware of when interviewing a client?
16. Restate as many of the interview techniques as you can.
17. In the "Information to be Given to the Client" checklist, which suggestions, if not followed, may adversely affect the client's case?
18. What is a fee agreement and why do so many client v. attorney fee disputes occur? What is good practice regarding law office Web sites and fee agreements?
19. What federal law governs a medical facility's release of a client's medical information to a paralegal?
20. List those things to be considered in preparing the interview site.
21. Review all the steps necessary to prepare for and conduct an entire interview.
22. What is a statute of limitations? When should it be checked? When does a statute of limitations begin tolling in various circumstances?
23. How do you use "pace and lead" and other techniques to deal with a difficult client?
24. How should you summarize or evaluate an interview?
25. How can the paralegal play a key role in keeping the client informed of the status of the client's case?
26. What is a disengagement letter and why is it important?

◼ KEY TERMS

contingent fee
duty
leading question

procedural law
proximate cause

statute of limitations
substantive law

▣ ENDNOTES

1. ELLIOTT & ELLIOTT, A TORT RESUME FOR USE IN PROSECUTION AND DEFENSE OF ALL DAMAGE CLAIMS 1ff.
2. THE NATIONAL ASSOCIATION OF LEGAL ASSISTANTS, NALA MANUAL FOR PARALEGALS AND LEGAL ASSISTANTS, 175 (4th ed. 2005).
3. SHAFFER, LEGAL INTERVIEWING AND COUNSELING 117 (1976) (quoting suggestions by Annette Gerret).
4. *Id.*, 117–18.
5. *Id.*, 80 (quoting Alfred C. Kinsey).
6. *Id.*, 124 (quoting Alfred Benjamin).
7. Kathleen M. Reade, *Conducting Effective Client Conferences,* LEGAL ASSISTANT TODAY, May/June 1994, 59–60.
8. Suggested in part by J. JEANS, TRIAL ADVOCACY 2nd ed., 156–166, (1993).
9. Katzman, *Using Written Fee Agreements,* WIS. LAW., Dec. 1990, 15, 16; reprinted with permission of the Wisconsin Bar Association.
10. David Hricik, *Ethics in the Digital Age: Conflict Can Lie Just Below the Surface of Online Communication,* L.OFF. COMPUT'G, Dec./Jan. 2005, 67.
11. Dr. Noelle Nelson, *Managing the Difficult Client,* FACTS & FINDINGS, Feb. 1994, at 20; reprinted from LEGAL MGMT., Sept./Oct. 1993.
12. Stacy Hunt, *Taming the Beast,* LEGAL ASSISTANT TODAY, Jul./Aug. 1999, 82.
13. Mary Barnard Ray, *Writing Good News and Bad News Letters,* WIS. LAW., Sept. 1997, 45.
14. *Id.*, 46.

For additional resources, visit our Website at **http://www.westlegalstudies.com.**

Evidence and Investigation

INTRODUCTION

For your next assignment, Mr. White wants you to do the investigation of the *Forrester* case and the *Ameche* case.

Investigation is the formal and informal process of gathering information to determine what the facts are in a case. Formal investigation involving exchanges of information between opposing attorneys as governed by court rules and sanctions is called *discovery*. This is the focus of Chapters 7 through 9. Chapter 3, however, focuses on informal investigation. Fact gathering in informal investigation is achieved by interviewing the client (Chapter 2), interviewing witnesses, and reviewing documents, records, physical evidence, and test results. The purposes of the investigation are numerous and include the following:

1. To identify and locate the factual evidence that may be used by both sides to support or defeat each element of a cause of action
2. To locate persons and property
3. To establish expert opinion evidence
4. To develop evidence to discredit (impeach) a witness or opponent
5. To determine if there is sufficient factual evidence to support or defend the cause of action at trial or to form the basis for a settlement
6. To find additional evidence if necessary
7. To preserve evidence for trial
8. To organize the evidence for trial

Investigation requires the search of all the evidence, pro and con, and is so important a process that cases are won or lost on the degree of diligence devoted to investigation.

THE RELATIONSHIP OF EVIDENCE LAW TO INVESTIGATION

INTRODUCTION

The primary purpose of investigation is to accumulate evidence for trial. That evidence must be evaluated to determine if it is admissible—whether it can be used in a court of law. Although investigative decisions should be made in close consultation with the supervising attorney, the more the paralegal knows about the rules of evidence, the more assistance the paralegal can provide. An efficient investigator uses a fundamental knowledge of the rules of evidence to evaluate the usefulness and admissibility of the evidence as it is gathered. Knowledge of the rules also guides the investigator to the most valuable evidence, thus saving time and money. Job satisfaction is enhanced if the paralegal understands the underlying reasons for investigative tasks.

EVIDENCE IN GENERAL

Evidence is a distinct body of law that defines and regulates what information may be presented at trial. It is the information that the trier (jury or judge) uses to decide whether the plaintiff has proved the case. The rules of evidence help to ensure the fairest possible trial through the efficient presentation of reliable and understandable evidence. Truth and justice are the rules' ultimate goals. The rules of evidence for the federal system are the Federal Rules of Evidence, cited as FED. R. EVID. Many state systems have adopted the Federal Rules of Evidence, and the rules of most

> "We should not investigate facts by the light of arguments, but arguments by the light of facts."
>
> —MYSON OF CHEN, ONE OF THE SEVEN SAGES, CA. 600 B.C., QUOTED IN BURTON STEVENSON, *HOME BOOK OF PROVERBS, MAXIMS AND FAMILIAR PHRASES*, 1948.

testimonial evidence
Spoken or signed, elicited from a witness.

documentary evidence
Paper evidence such as letters, contracts, or medical records.

real evidence
The thing itself, physically present as opposed to being described, such as a scar, implement, or live view of the accident scene.

demonstrative evidence
Depiction or representation of something such as a photo of a scar or a diagram of the accident scene.

direct evidence
Evidence that is directly observable and proves the truth asserted.

circumstantial evidence
Evidence that suggests the existence of some other occurrence or thing.

admissible evidence
Evidence that may be presented in court because it complies with the rules of evidence that it must be relevant.

relevant
Admissible in court, of consequence to the determination of the action, and tending to prove or refute a fact of consequence.

material
Of consequence to the determination of the action.

other states have much in common with the Federal Rules. This section focuses on the Federal Rules of Evidence. Compare it with your state rules of evidence.

Evidence is broadly classified into four types: Testimonial, documentary, real, and demonstrative. **Testimonial evidence** is spoken or signed, and has been elicited from a witness. **Documentary evidence** is paper evidence such as letters, contracts, and medical records. **Real evidence** is the thing itself, physically present as opposed to being described, such as a scar, weapon, or live view of the accident scene. **Demonstrative evidence** is a depiction or representation of something, such as a photo of a scar or a diagram of the accident scene.

Evidence within each of these categories is either direct or circumstantial. **Direct evidence** is directly observable and proves the truth asserted. In Case I, for example, if the neighbor saw the van hit Ms. Forrester, a statement to that effect in court by the neighbor would be direct evidence that the van did hit Ms. Forrester. On the other hand, if the neighbor saw a damaged van and Ms. Forrester lying near it, a statement to the effect by the neighbor would be circumstantial evidence that the van hit Ms. Forrester. **Circumstantial evidence** suggests the existence of some other occurrence or thing. Both types of evidence may be valuable to a case.

ADMISSIBLE EVIDENCE

Admissible evidence may be presented in court because it complies with the rules of evidence. To be admissible, evidence must be **relevant.** Relevance has two components: the evidence must be **material**—of consequence to the determination of the action— and it must tend to prove or refute a fact of consequence (FED. R. EVID. 401). Being of consequence to the determination of the action (materiality) means that it bears a meaningful relationship to the determination of the issues at hand. For example, if the issue is whether Mr. Hart was careless when operating his van, would the color of his hair be of consequence to the determination of the issue? No. Would Mr. Hart's testimony that he was driving at thirty miles per hour be of consequence to the action? Yes. Speed in conjunction with the circumstances can be an indication of carelessness or carefulness; therefore, the testimony is material.

To be relevant, however, evidence must also tend to prove or refute a fact of consequence. If the fact of consequence is that Mr. Hart was traveling at thirty miles per hour, would his testimony that he was driving about thirty miles per hour tend to prove or refute this fact? Yes, it helps prove he was going thirty miles per hour (a fact of consequence). Therefore, the testimony meets both tests and is relevant and generally admissible. Among the most frequently heard objections are those asserting that the evidence is immaterial or irrelevant.

INADMISSIBILITY OF SOME TYPES OF RELEVANT EVIDENCE
Evidence Based on Prejudice, Confusion, or Delay

probative value of evidence
The degree to which evidence tends to prove or actually proves something.

Even relevant evidence is not always admissible. The evidence is inadmissible if the **probative value of evidence**—its strength to prove what it purports to prove—is outweighed by other factors deemed harmful to the trial process. These factors are identified in Rule 403 of the Federal Rules of Evidence and similar provisions in state rules of evidence. The rule states:

> Although relevant, evidence may be excluded if its probative value is substantially outweighed by the danger of unfair prejudice, confusion of the issues, or misleading the jury, or by considerations of undue delay, waste of time, or needless presentation of cumulative evidence. (Fed. R. Evid. 403)

The danger of unfair prejudice means that relevant evidence can be excluded if it is likely to cause a jury to decide an issue because it evokes undue sympathy, contempt, horror, or strong emotion. If a judge, for example, believed that a photograph showing Ms. Forrester's little girl crying over her injured mother would so evoke the jurors' sympathy that it would distract them from the actual injury portrayed in the photograph, the judge could exclude the photograph despite its relevance. The key is whether the danger of unfair prejudice substantially outweighs the probative value of the evidence.

If the evidence is likely to create confusion—that is, create unnecessary side issues or simply be too complex for most jurors—it may be excluded under this rule. Or if the evidence is too misleading and likely to cause jurors to place more weight on the evidence than fairness dictates, it may be excluded. For example, a jury may put too much credence on the results of a lie detector test or an unscaled model of the scene of an accident.

The remaining concerns under Rule 403 are directed at saving time and money in the trial. Thus, if the probative value of evidence is substantially outweighed by its consumption of court time, it can be excluded. Similarly, if it wastes time or is merely a repetitious accumulation of evidence already adequately presented, the court may exclude it. Another consideration here is if repeated or extended presentations on a certain point would cause jurors to unduly emphasize its importance, such evidence may be limited or excluded if its probative value is substantially outweighed by its detrimental effect.

Character Evidence

Evidence of a person's character or a particular trait offered as proof that a person's conduct conformed to that trait on a particular occasion is inadmissible (FED. R. EVID. 404). One major exception to this rule occurs when character, or a trait of character, is an element of a claim. To illustrate, a defense to an action for making false and damaging statements about another would be to prove that the statements are true. Hence, evidence of truthfulness and specific instances of such conduct would be admissible [FED. R. EVID. 405(b)]. When evidence of character is admissible, a witness may testify to the reputation of the person or render an opinion on the person's character [FED. R. EVID. 405(a)]. In these situations, inquiry into specific instances of relevant conduct is permissible on cross-examination of the witness. Any permissible testimony on reputation or opinions on a person's character focuses on reputation in the subject's neighborhood (residence) or among associates.

Evidence of Habit or Routine Practice

Evidence of habit or routine to prove that conduct on a specific occasion conformed to the habit or routine is generally admissible (FED. R. EVID. 406). **Habit** is the semiautomatic, repeated response to a specific situation. Brushing one's teeth each morning or automatically fastening the seat belt every time one rides in a car are examples of habit. **Routine (custom)** is the equivalent of habit for organizations. Products may be routinely inspected for defects, accounts routinely inspected for improper expenditures, and prospective employee references routinely checked. It is the nearly invariable regularity of habit and routine that makes them valid as evidence. Acts similar to the act in question, however, are not generally admissible as evidence because they may be remote in time to the occurrence in question or may lack the reliability of the invariable frequency of actions characterized as habit or routine.

habit
The semiautomatic, repeated response to a specific situation.

routine (custom)
The equivalent of "habit" for organizations.

Evidence of Offers to Compromise, Insurance, and Remedial Measures

Evidence of offers to compromise or statements or conduct pursuant to compromise are inadmissible, as evidence of insurance coverage and subsequent repairs to correct a defect that caused damages(FED. R. EVID. 408).

Evidence of Past Sexual Conduct, Past Sexual Crimes

Generally, evidence of a victim's past sexual conduct is not admissible. Evidence of a defendant's past sexual crimes is admissible in a civil case alleging sexual assault or molestation. Because of the significant exceptions to these general rules, the specific rule must be consulted when working with such cases (FED. R. EVID. 412–415).

Illegally Obtained Evidence

Courts can exclude evidence in civil cases, as well as in criminal cases, if it was illegally obtained. For example, since Georgia prohibits unauthorized interception of cordless telephone conversations, evidence from such an interception by a neighbor could not be used by a husband against his wife. The evidence was ruled inadmissible in *Barlow v. Barlow*, 526 S.E.2d 857 (Ga. 2000).

PRIVILEGES

Privilege makes inadmissible certain communications of a confidential nature because of their social utility: attorney-client, priest-penitent, physician-patient, social worker-client, and husband-wife.

The attorney-client privilege protects confidential communication made by the client to the attorney in the course of legal representation. Its rationale lies within the very foundations of the legal system, that the peaceful prevention and resolution of disputes begins with individuals confidently and, necessarily, confidentially seeking professional legal advice. The privilege is the client's, but it may also be invoked by the attorney. The privilege can be waived either voluntarily by the client or by an accidental revelation of the communication caused by the attorney's or paralegal's carelessness. Such involuntary revelation by the law firm is a serious breach of confidentiality and may result in legal action against the firm, not to mention loss of the client's lawsuit. Because of the serious consequences of such carelessness, paralegals must guard against such slips as mixing protected information with other information sent to an opponent, discussing confidential information where third parties might overhear it, asking the client questions in the presence of a third party, and leaving files (both physical and electronic) in places accessible to third parties.

In *State v. Ingraham*, 966 P.2d 103 (Mont. 1998), the defendant was charged with several felony counts related to a traffic accident. After the accident, the defendant was driven home by his friend, a paralegal who worked as an independent contractor for the defendant's father, who was an attorney. The defendant told the paralegal that the accident was caused by his dogs' trying to jump into the driver's seat of his vehicle. The court ruled that the incriminating statement was not protected by the attorney-client privilege because such a relationship had not been established and the statement was made to a friend, not a person acting in a legal capacity, which was further proved by the fact that the paralegal was not paid for this time.

Third party consultants, such as accountants, language translators, scientists, and others hired to assist in furthering a client's legal matter are, as a general rule, encompassed by the privilege. When the purpose of the consultation is less clearly tied to acquiring knowledge needed for the planning and strategy of the litigation, however, the application of the privilege is less clear. Also in such circumstances when confidential information is mixed with other information, the purpose of the consultation may be unclear, and the attorney-client privilege deemed waived. For example, the use of a media or a public relations expert in a high profile case might create such a problem. Therefore, prior to participating in third party consultations, seek guidance from your supervising attorney on what, if any, confidential information can be shared.

The attorney-client privilege does not apply if the client sues the attorney and the attorney needs the privileged information to defend against the suit. Furthermore, most jurisdictions do not extend the privilege to cover a client's requests for information on how to commit a fraud or other crime.

Despite the fundamental value of the attorney-client privilege, it has come under significant erosive pressures. The perceived importance of successfully prosecuting large corporate fraud, controlling terrorism, and addressing other wrongdoing has, in the view of some, necessitated the subordination of the privilege. The obvious concern is whether such subordination will undermine client confidence and forthrightness when disclosing information to the client's attorney and paralegal. A discussion of the related concept of attorney work product, which has also come under such pressure, is discussed in the ethics section of this chapter.

The physician-patient privilege protects confidential information about a patient's medical condition and treatment. The information may not be revealed by the physician unless the privilege is waived by the patient or unless the patient puts his or her medical condition in issue, such as in a medical malpractice suit or a personal injury suit. Similar protections and exceptions apply to the priest-penitent relationship.

Husband-wife (spousal, marital) privilege protects communications between married persons. Where recognized, one spouse can invoke the privilege to prevent the other from revealing this information. A spouse may also refuse to testify against a spouse. There is a growing legal debate on whether this privilege should be expanded to partners in a long-term relationship.

A journalist-confidential source privilege exists in most states and Washington DC but not in the federal system.

All of these privileges can be invoked after termination of the relationship if the communication in question occurred during the existence of the privileged relationship.

Another privilege that can be invoked in civil litigation is the privilege against self-incrimination. The Fifth Amendment to the U.S. Constitution allows a person to refuse to reveal information or to testify when such information is evidence of a crime committed by the person or may lead to such evidence. The privilege does not apply if the person has been convicted of the crime or has been granted immunity from prosecution of the crime.

The law of the local jurisdiction must be consulted for unique rules on privileged communications.

EVIDENCE ADMISSIBLE FROM A PARTY

The relevant admission of an opposing party (party-opponent) is admissible. It may be oral, written, or nonverbal conduct. The admission is generally damaging to the party making the admission and suggests a belief or position inconsistent with the

> "Truth and false-
> hood, it has been
> well said, are not
> always opposed to
> each other like
> black and white,
> but oftentimes,
> and by design,
> are made to
> resemble each
> other so as to be
> hardly
> distinguishable;
> just as the coun-
> terfeit thing is
> counterfeit
> because it resem-
> bles the genuine
> thing."
>
> —SIR ANTHONY CLEASBY,
> ENGLISH JURIST, *JOHNSON V.*
> *EMERSON,* 6 L.R. EX. CA.
> 357 (1871).

one the admitting party is taking at trial. This damaging nature, however, is not a requirement for admission. Therefore, the often-used designation of "admission against interest" is a misnomer under the federal rule and similar state rules.[1] According to Federal Rule of Evidence 801(d), such an admission is admissible under the following rules:

1. If it is the party-opponent's own statement either in an individual or a representative capacity (if the latter, the statement must be relevant to the context of the representation; both types of admissions can include relevant pleas of guilty)
2. If the opponent has in words or conduct manifested an adoption or belief in the truth of the statement or manifested such belief by remaining silent when normally a denial would be expected
3. If the statement is by a person authorized by the party-opponent to make such a statement (a party's books and records may be entered under this rule)[2]
4. If the statement is made by a party-opponent's agent or servant concerning a matter in the scope of his or her agency or employment
5. If the statement is made by a co-conspirator in the course of the conspiracy

RULES REGARDING THE TESTIMONY OF A WITNESS

Requirement of Firsthand Knowledge

The testimony of witnesses must be based on firsthand knowledge. In other words, the witnesses must have seen, heard, smelled, touched, or otherwise directly observed the subject of their testimony (FED. R. EVID. 602).

Opinion

Federal courts (FED. R. EVID. 701) and those of many states allow laypersons to give opinions. One such type of opinion is based on perceived facts leading to opinions on speed, weight, height, distance, and so on. A second type of opinion is that of a skilled lay observer. This opinion is based on repeated observations permitting identification of a specific signature or voice, or an assessment of the sanity of a person the observer knows.

Language was added to Rule 701 to prevent experts in specialized or scientific fields (FED. R. EVID. 702) from giving expert opinion disguised as lay opinion.

Expert Opinion

Highly specialized experts are permitted to give their opinions on matters at issue that relate to their field (FED. R. EVID. 702). Doctors, for example, are permitted to give their opinion regarding an injury, the cause of an injury, and the prognosis (outlook). Typically, engineers and scientists are among those experts permitted to give opinions.

The court will permit expert opinion if the "scientific, technical, or other specialized knowledge will assist the trier of fact to understand the evidence or to determine a fact in issue" (relevance) and if the witness is "qualified as an expert by knowledge, skill, experience, training, or education" (reliability). This test was confirmed as the appropriate standard for expert opinion in *Daubert v. Merrell Dow Pharmaceuticals, Inc.,* 113 S. Ct. 2786 (1993). The Supreme Court said the expert's reasoning or methodology must be scientifically valid and able to be applied to the facts in issue. Factors such as the method's rate of error, whether the method lends itself to testing and peer review, and whether it has gained general acceptance in the scientific community should be considered.

In 1999 the Supreme Court ruled that these reliability tests are not limited to the testimony of scientific experts [*Kumho Tire Co. Inc. v. Carmichael,* 526 U.S. 137 (1999)]. Federal Rule of Evidence 702 was subsequently amended to require the same level of court examination for all types of expert testimony. The resulting standard for determining the admissibility of expert opinion evidence in the federal system and states with parallel provisions is that (1) the testimony must be relevant and helpful, (2) the expert must be specially qualified, (3) the methodology used by the expert must be reliable, and (4) the evidence must be capable of being applied and actually be applied reliably to the facts of the case. Once expert testimony is found admissible, the opponent can still cross-examine the witness to test the opinion. Despite *Daubert, Kumho,* and the subsequent revision of Rule 702, a significant minority of states still rely on an earlier standard of admissibility set out in *Frye v. U.S.,* 293 F. 1013 (D.C. Cir. 1923). The *Frye* (general acceptance test) permits admissibility if the scientific method used or principle relied on is generally accepted in the relevant field.

Should you be assigned a task that requires you to better understand the language of a rule of evidence, consult the advisory committee's notes, which explain each rule and any changes in the rule in more detail. For example, the advisory committee's notes for Rule 702 explain not only the rationale behind the rule, but also that an expert may not base an opinion on the principles of astrology, necromancy, or clinical ecology, because these "junk sciences" are unfounded.[3]

The importance of Rule 702 cannot be overstated, particularly for the plaintiff. If the plaintiff's expert's testimony is key to the case, but later on appeal is found to have been improperly admitted by the trial court, the appellate court can enter judgment for the defendant. The plaintiff loses, therefore, and there is no second chance [*Weisgram v. Marley Co.,* 120 S. Ct. 1011 (2000)]. One useful fee-based resource for finding court opinions and other information on admissibility of expert opinion is http://www.dauberttracker.com.

Evidence of Character and Conduct of a Witness

A paralegal needs to remember that the jury's perception of a witness's truthfulness (credibility) may make the difference between winning and losing a case. Therefore, any evidence that bears on the truthfulness of a witness should be noted.

Under the Federal Rules of Evidence, it is permissible for others to enter an opinion on a witness's truthfulness or reputation for truthfulness. Specific conduct that bears on a witness's truthfulness may be inquired into by the attorneys but cannot be proved by independent evidence. Criminal convictions less than ten years old are also significant if the possible punishment was for more than one year in prison or the crime reflected dishonesty or untruthfulness [FED. R. EVID. 609(a)]. Religious beliefs are not admissible to show credibility. Rules 607 and 610 of the Federal Rules of Evidence apply to evidence of a witness's character and conduct.

Prior Statements of a Witness

A paralegal should take note of any statements of a witness on matters likely to be important at trial that may be used to challenge or support a witness's truthfulness. For example, if a witness testifies that Mr. Hart's van was going forty-five miles per hour at the time of the accident, and the same witness told a police officer that the van was going about twenty-five miles per hour, the prior inconsistent statement could be damaging to the witness's credibility.

Capacity to Observe, Record, Recollect, or Narrate

Any witness may be examined for the ability to observe, record, recollect, or narrate in order to demonstrate any weaknesses. Extrinsic evidence—evidence other than the testimony of the witness in question—may be used to prove such weaknesses. Mental capacity, intelligence, distractions, distance from the event observed, lighting conditions, influence of drugs or alcohol, and a multitude of other matters that affect reliability may be inquired into or proved by other evidence. Children are permitted to testify if the judge is satisfied that the child has a basic understanding of the importance of telling the truth and is able to observe, recall, and convey information.

Hearsay and Exceptions

Hearsay is evidence that relies on the firsthand observation of another person rather than the person testifying. For example, Ms. Schnabel, the neighbor, might testify that Mr. Forrester told her that Mr. Hart's van was going forty-five miles per hour. Since that statement is based on Mr. Forrester's observation and not on the firsthand observation of Ms. Schnabel, it is hearsay as to the speed of the van. Hearsay is considered unreliable and is generally inadmissible. The paralegal, therefore, must not rely on hearsay but should seek out the original firsthand source for needed evidence.

There are, however, some important exceptions to the hearsay rule. These are found in the Federal Rules of Evidence, beginning with Rule 801(d), and in similar state rules.

Prior statement of a witness: A statement previously made by a witness is admissible at trial if the witness is subject to cross-examination and any of the following elements are present:
  1. The statement is inconsistent with the witness's trial testimony and given under oath.
  2. The prior statement is consistent with the witness's testimony and is offered to meet an attack on the declarant's honesty or motives.
  3. The statement was one identifying a person after seeing the person.

Admission by party opponent: A previous statement made by a party may be admitted against that person by the opponent. See the preceding section, "Evidence Admissible from a Party."

Present sense impression: A statement made during or immediately after an event is observed or a condition is described is admissible. (Example: Mr. Johnson said, "That car is going too fast to make that curve!")

Excited utterance: An excited utterance is admissible. (Example: "My husband said, 'Look out! That car is coming into our lane!'")

Then-existing mental, emotional, or physical conditions: This exception is designed to admit some evidence other than conduct to reveal a person's state of mind regarding intent, plan, motive, emotion, and pain. (Example: "Ms. Forrester said, 'My hip hurts so much I can barely stand it.'" Example: "Mr. Hart said, 'I'll get those brakes fixed next month.'") Statements that are present sense impressions, excited utterances, or about then-existing mental, emotional, or physical conditions are called **res gestae statements.**

res gestae statements
Statements that are present sense impressions, excited utterances, or about then-existing mental, emotional, or physical conditions.

Statement made to receive a medical diagnosis: (Example: "Ms. Forrester said to me [doctor], 'My left hip is very painful.'") Such a statement is admissible.

Recorded recollection: A statement recorded when a witness's memory was fresh is admissible when the witness cannot recall the contents of the statement.

Records: Records kept in the regular course of business, such as motel registration or time cards, are admissible.

Statement of reputation: If it concerns family history, boundaries, or a person's character, such a statement is admissible.

Court judgment: A conviction of fraud, for example, would be admissible if offered to prove any fact essential to the case.

Unavailability of witness: Some hearsay evidence is admissible only if the declarant is unavailable to testify (Fed. R. Evid. 804). Unavailability means the witness is dead, is unavailable through reasonable efforts, refuses to testify or is protected from testifying, or can't remember.

Former testimony: If a witness is unavailable at trial, the witness's former testimony is admissible as long as it was subject to cross-examination at the time by one having a similar interest to the opponent's.

Statements under belief of impending death (dying declarations):   A statement made by a person who believed his or her death was imminent is admissible when offered to show the person's belief regarding the cause or circumstances of death. Under common law, the person must have died; in the Federal Rules, the person must be unavailable.

Statements against interest: The law has assumed that a person would not make a statement against his or her financial, business, or legal interest unless it were true. Therefore, when a witness is unavailable, that witness's previous statement against his or her interest is admissible.

Computer data must be scrutinized to determine whether it is hearsay and whether it meets one of the hearsay exceptions. For example, if a person enters data such as accounting records, a graph, or summaries into a computer, this data is hearsay. The fact that a person enters into a computer checkbook that a bill was paid on a specified date does not prove it was paid on that date. But purely computer generated data, such as that generated by an automated phone number recording system, is not entered by a person, and therefore, is not hearsay. The latter is inherently more reliable than the former.

RULES REGARDING PHYSICAL EVIDENCE AND AUTHENTICATION

Physical evidence is evidence that one can see, hear, touch, or otherwise perceive firsthand: the scene of an accident, a contract or other written instrument, an x-ray, the viewed injuries or scars of the plaintiff, or a photograph. Because such evidence is perceived firsthand by the trier of fact and not through the description of a witness, it can be very persuasive. Physical evidence needs to be authenticated in order to be admissible. In other words, it must be shown to be what it purports to be. Therefore, the paralegal must also determine what is necessary to have that evidence authenticated. Rule 901(b) of the Federal Rules of Evidence suggests several ways that evidence can be authenticated:

1. Testimony of a witness who has knowledge that a matter is what it is claimed to be. (Example: "I made the entries in the log describing which deliveries Mr. Hart was to make the day of the accident, and that is the log.")

2. Testimony of a nonexpert on someone's handwriting. (Example: "I have seen Mr. Hart's signature many times, and that is his signature.") This method can apply to voice identification as well.
3. Testimony of an expert witness based on adequate comparison. (Example: "I have examined exhibit A and several samples of handwriting known to be Mr. Brown's; it is my opinion that exhibit A is Mr. Brown's handwriting.")
4. Testimony about distinctive characteristics. (Example: "My wife's coat was all handsewn, and the aunt who made it sewed her initials, B.J., into the lining. Yes, that is my wife's coat.")
5. Testimony about a telephone conversation determining whether the other person was the person in question. (Example: "I called Richard Hart at the extension number listed for him at the Mercury Parcel Service, and he answered and said, 'This is Richard Hart.'")

chain of custody
The chronological record tracing a piece of evidence to the event that has resulted in the action, proving that it is the item in question.

If an item of evidence is not unique, such as an automobile tire, it can be shown to be the tire in question by establishing a **chain of custody.** A chain of custody is a chronological history of the storage or use (or both) of an item since the event in question. Testimony demonstrating a complete chain should remove reasonable doubt as to the authenticity of the item.

Scientific evidence resulting from blood, breathalyzer, and other scientific analyses requires testimony that the theory underlying the test is valid and the equipment used is reliable.

Some evidence is self-authenticating, requiring only a government seal, official attestation, or the signature of an official in charge of such documents. Federal and state documents and public records come under this category. Official publications, such as books and pamphlets, are self-authenticating, as are newspapers and periodicals, trade inscriptions, notarized documents, commercial paper, or any other signature or document declared so by act of Congress.

best evidence rule
Rule that allows only the original document or item to be admitted (exceptions are allowed for practical reasons).

The content of writings, recordings (including mechanical recordings), and photographs (including x-rays, motion pictures, and videotapes) also require authentication. These things fall under the **best evidence rule** (FED. R. EVID. 1002). By this rule, only the original document or item is admissible. This is to prevent admission of altered or fraudulent copies. Therefore, an investigator must strive to secure the original item. In some circumstances, however, copies may be substituted. This is so when the authenticity of the original is not in question, when use of a duplicate will not be unfair to the other party, or when the original is lost or destroyed (unless in bad faith by the proponent). Writings, recordings, or photographs too voluminous for practical court use may be summarized.

In the past, business records were authenticated by a witness. Now United States and foreign business records can be authenticated in federal court by affidavit [FED. R. EVID. 902(11) and 902(12)] as long as the opponent is given proper notice [FED. R. EVID. 903(11)].

The age of digital technology has made once reliable documents, photographs, audiotapes and videotapes, and other evidence susceptible to undetectable alteration. Authentication of such evidence today may require proof of a chain of custody.

Courts are increasingly applying the authentication requirements of Rule 901 to computer evidence. This evidence could consist of a variety of business or other records, or models for recreating data or simulating an event. If the computerized evidence is (1) a complete record of data rather than an attempt to fill in gaps in the data, (2) is based on simple rather than complex manipulation of data, (3) is a routine process, and (4) is easily verifiable, that is, testable, then the computer evidence is likely to be admissible.[4] The more computer evidence departs from each of these four criteria, the more difficult authentication becomes. More detailed authentication requires an examination of the data input process, how the data is processed by the computer, and whether the output is what it is represented to be.[5]

Official government Web sites are self-authenticating. Occasionally, however, information on the site may be successfully challenged [*State v. Davis*, 10 P.3d 977 (Wash. 2000)]. In *Davis*, population statistics on the state's Web site were ruled to be hearsay.

OTHER EVIDENTIARY CONCEPTS

Judicial Notice

Judicial notice permits a judge to admit certain evidence without authentication. Such evidence can be judicially noticed if it is a fact not subject to reasonable dispute and meets one of two criteria: (1) the fact must be commonly known in the territorial jurisdiction of the court, or (2) the fact is readily verifiable through undisputed sources (FED. R. EVID. 201). By eliminating the need for authentication, judicial notice saves time and expense. A court might take judicial notice of acts and records of the court, geographic and historical facts, matters of public record, or the viability of the underlying basis for a scientific test, such as for the presence of alcohol in the blood.

judicial notice
Admission of evidence without authentication, either a fact commonly known in the territorial jurisdiction of the court or a fact readily verifiable through undisputed sources.

Stipulations

A **stipulation** is an agreement between the parties that permits evidence to be admitted as true without authentication. Stipulations are formally received by most courts because they save time and often reduce the need for witnesses. For example, in a contract dispute, the parties might stipulate that the signatures are authentic or that the contract is the original, eliminating the need of proof of these facts.

In other than an evidentiary context, a stipulation is a specific condition parties agree to in a contract or other legal document or in an agreement on procedural matters, such as where to depose (examine) a witness (FED. R. CIV. P. 29).

stipulation
Formal agreement between opposing parties to a lawsuit regarding matters pertinent to the lawsuit, such as to admit certain evidence without testimony.

Burden of Proof

Even in the earliest stages of investigation, understanding which party has the **burden of proof** and on which points will allow the paralegal to be of more assistance in ferreting out evidence useful to the client's case. Since the plaintiff is the accuser and the one seeking a remedy, the law places the burden on the plaintiff to plead and prove the allegations set out in the complaint. Only when the plaintiff has satisfied the minimum burden does it become necessary for the defendant to rebut the plaintiff's evidence with evidence of his or her own. The defendant, however, bears the burden of proving affirmative defenses. An **affirmative defense** shows that the defendant is not liable even if the plaintiff's claim is assumed to be true. Self-defense, payment of debt, and assumption of risk are examples of affirmative defenses. If a party is in a position to have the only knowledge of a fact, that party bears the burden on the fact.

In civil cases, the person who bears the burden of proof must meet that burden by a **preponderance of the evidence.** "Evidence preponderates when it is more convincing to the trier than the opposing evidence," and the burden is met by "proof which leads the jury to find that the existence of the contested fact is more probable than its nonexistence."[6]

burden of proof
The obligation to prove the allegations; usually falls to the accuser.

affirmative defense
Defense showing that the defendant is not liable even if the plaintiff's claim is assumed to be true and for which the defendant bears the burden of proof.

preponderance of the evidence
Evidence that is more convincing to the trier than the opposing evidence; meets the requirement for the burden of proof in civil cases.

clear and convincing evidence
A higher standard of proof than preponderance of the evidence; requires that the matter be shown to be highly probable.

proof beyond a reasonable doubt
Proof that is so strong it excludes any other reasonable hypothesis or explanation—almost a certainty.

presumption
A mechanism that allows a jury to presume a fact is true based on indirect evidence if it might be awkward or difficult to prove by direct evidence. For example, mailing a letter creates the presumption it was received. A presumption stands unless it is rebutted.

In some types of civil cases (citizenship, fraud, mutual mistake, and content of lost deeds), the standard is proof by clear and convincing evidence. **Clear and convincing evidence** is a higher standard of proof than "preponderance of evidence" and requires that the matter be shown to be highly probable.

Criminal cases require the highest burden of proof: proof beyond a reasonable doubt. **Proof beyond a reasonable doubt** is proof that is so strong it excludes any other reasonable hypothesis or explanation—almost a certainty.

Presumption

An evidentiary **presumption** is a mechanism created by rule of law that presumes a specific fact to be true when certain other preliminary evidence is established. Thus, if it is proved that Ann Forrester mailed a letter to Richard Hart, and the letter was never returned to Ann Forrester as unclaimed, it is presumed that Richard Hart received the letter. The presumption of an unestablished fact, that Hart received the letter, avoids difficult, time-consuming, or awkward proofs. Unless Hart comes forth with evidence to rebut the presumption, such as, "I never received the letter," the jury will be instructed that the delivery has been established.

SOURCES FOR RESEARCHING EVIDENCE LAW

Keep in mind that rules of evidence are more complex than can be covered here, and occasions arise in the law office when you will need more information on a particular rule of evidence. When you do, there are several sources to consider: *Wigmore on Evidence,* the hornbook *McCormick on Evidence,* and the legal encyclopedias. The Federal Rules of Evidence with Advisory Committee Notes and the evidentiary statutes and rules of each state should not be overlooked. Imwinkelried's book, *Evidentiary Foundations,* can be useful as a quick guide to what evidence is necessary to establish proper foundation. An evidentiary foundation is that testimony necessary to establish that a person was in a position to have observed or have knowledge of the facts to which he or she will be testifying. It establishes firsthand knowledge. Some of the sources mentioned above, including the Federal Rules of Evidence, can be found on Westlaw® or Lexis®. A Web site that provides links to the rules is http://www.uscourts.gov/rules/index.html. You can get to some state rules through www.state.[state abbreviation].us.

PLANNING THE INVESTIGATION

INTRODUCTION

With some of these evidentiary concepts and principles in mind, you can begin the investigation. The three stages in the investigation procedure include planning the investigation, gathering the evidence, and preserving the evidence.

Thorough planning is extremely important to a good and efficient investigation. Some cases can be characterized as bottomless pits that sap the energy and time of the paralegal and the financial resources of the client. Proper planning allows for a thorough yet sensible approach that works to the benefit of paralegal and client alike.

A sound approach to planning an investigation should include the following steps:

1. Review the file and other available information.
2. Identify the essential elements of proof as defined by the appropriate substantive law.

3. Identify what facts will be needed to prove each of these elements.
4. Determine what sources, including witnesses, may provide those facts.
5. Record the investigation plan.
6. Consult with the attorney in selecting the most appropriate sources and methods of investigation to be followed.

REVIEW THE FILE AND OTHER AVAILABLE INFORMATION

Review the file to familiarize yourself with the client, the facts, the cause of action, and the leads to evidence and witnesses. For now, review the factual descriptions of Case I and the summary of Ms. Forrester's interview.

IDENTIFY THE ESSENTIAL ELEMENTS OF PROOF

The realization that evidence is gathered to prove or disprove the specific elements of a cause of action permits the paralegal to immediately narrow and focus the investigation. Chapter 2 explained the process of identifying the key elements of a cause of action through research, particularly research in a good jury instruction book. To review, the elements that our client, Ms. Forrester, must prove are:

1. Duty of care (as dictated by conditions)
2. Breach of duty (carelessness)
3. Injury
4. Causal relationships between breach and injury
5. Damages

In addition, Ms. Forrester must disprove comparative negligence.

IDENTIFY WHAT FACTS WILL BE NEEDED

Drawing from practical experience and common sense, list facts that need to be gathered to prove the elements in the case. Typical facts for several key elements are listed in the following table:

Breach of Duty	Injuries	Comparative Negligence
Carelessness	Fractures	Attentiveness
Road conditions	Pain	Obstructions to sight and sound (coat)
Mechanical defects	Disabilities	Haste (carelessness)
Speed of van	Insomnia	
Driver's condition		

DETERMINE WHAT SOURCES, INCLUDING WITNESSES, MAY PROVIDE FACTS

Sources of Information and Evidence

Identifying possible sources for information and evidence is a process of applying the information already gathered in the file, as well as a knowledge of investigative sources of information and common sense. Some typical sources of information and evidence for a personal injury investigation are included in Exhibit 3:1.

> "Half an answer also tells you something."
>
> —JEWISH FOLK SAYING, QUOTED IN JOSEPH L. BARON, *A TREASURY OF JEWISH QUOTATIONS*, 1956.

EXHIBIT 3:1 ■ Checklist of Evidentiary Sources

For Negligence Cases

Source	Likely Information
Client	Occurrence, other witnesses, damages, etc.
Witnesses	Occurrence, other witnesses, injuries, etc.
Scene of accident	Obstructions, distances, special circumstances, surveillance tapes
Police reports	Details of accident, witnesses, officer at scene, photos, sobriety tests
Event data recorder ("black box", if available)	Digitally preserved information at time of accident on engine speed, braking, air bag deployment, malfunctions
Department of Motor Vehicles	Accident reports, driving records
News accounts (newspapers, microfilm, videotapes)	Details, witnesses, reporters
Reporters (notes)	Details, photos, witnesses
Emergency personnel (ambulance crew, paramedic, tow truck operator)	Details, injuries
Fire marshal (reports)	Causes of fire, witnesses
Transcripts of related trials or hearings (criminal, traffic)	Statements of witnesses and parties, admission
U.S. Weather Bureau	Official weather reports
Licensing and inspection authorities	Code and licensing violations
Police agencies (local police, FBI)	Criminal records for impeachment
Internet and public or university library	General reference information
	Directories for scholarly and professional associations
	Experts in pertinent field, consultants
	Business information
	Corporate information
	Federal and state agencies
	Census reports
Hospital	Names of nurses, doctors, technicians; x-rays, medications, related medical records, pain and suffering, bills
Physicians	Consulting physicians, treatment history, diagnosis, prognosis, disabilities, pain and suffering, bills
Physical therapists	Disabilities, necessary treatment, likelihood of success
Close relatives, friends, and neighbors	Effects of the injury, disabilities
Medical literature	Injuries, medication, side effects, prognosis

EXHIBIT 3:1 ■ Checklist of Evidentiary Sources (*continued*)

Department of Vocational Rehabilitation	Expert witnesses, statistics on job rehabilitation and earning potential
Injured party's employer	Performance records, wages, firings, promotion potential

Federal Agencies

Federal Aviation Administration (FAA), (202) 426-4000, www.faa.gov	Airline accidents, safety standards
Department of Transportation, (202) 426-4043, www.dot.gov	Vehicle and driver safety standards
National Highway Traffic Safety Administration, www.nhtsa.gov	Vehicle complaints, investigations, recalls
National Oceanic and Atmospheric Administration, (310) 655-4000, www.noaa.gov	Certified weather reports
National Climatic Data Center, Asheville, NC, www.ncdc.noaa.gov	Certified weather information by state
Department of Agriculture, (202) 655-4000, www.usda.gov	Aerial photos, plants, wildlife
Department of Interior (Geologic Survey), www.doi.gov	Maps
Internal Revenue Service, (202) 566-4021, www.irs.gov	Former tax rates and schedules
Census Bureau, (202) 372-2000, www.census.gov	Demographic statistics
Occupational Safety and Health Administration, (OSHA) (202) 523-8165, www.osha.gov	Job safety standards
Agency for Toxic Substances and Disease Registry, www.atsdr.cdc.gov (See also the medical and other sites listed in this exhibit.)	Toxicity, sites, advisories

State Agencies

www.state.[your state's two-letter abbreviation].us	
Department of Transportation	Traffic flow, highways, bridges, signals, signs
Department of Labor and Industry	Industrial safety rules and regulations, statistics
Department of Geology	Geological surveys
Office of Secretary of State (corporations)	Corporate addresses, officers
Department of Insurance	Auto liability coverage, insurance company requirements
Department of Business and Professions	Licensing requirements of trades and businesses
Bureau of Vital Statistics	Certified records of birth, death, divorce, etc.
Department of Revenue	Personal property licenses, taxes, ownership, transactions
Wright and Allen, *The National Directory of State Agencies,* Information Resource Press	Directory of state agencies

(*continued*)

EXHIBIT 3:1 ■ Checklist of Evidentiary Sources *(continued)*

County and Local Agencies

Check county (parish), city, or town Web sites for local agencies.

Courthouse (clerk's offices)	Lawsuits, criminal cases, property ownership, liens, UCC filings (also see Exhibit 3.2)
Tax Assessor's Office	Ownership, location, taxes, and assessed value of property
Voter Registration	Voter's address, age, sex, race, and voting precinct
District, County, or City Attorney's Office	Criminal records, location of person
Coroner's Office	Cause of death and related hearings, records
Chamber of Commerce	Local businesses, services, literature
Department of Public Works and Traffic	Street blueprints, timing of traffic lights, expert witnesses, statistics
Universities and colleges	Experts in a variety of fields

Electronic Investigation and the Internet: Law and General Topic Research

Obtaining the best information most efficiently lies at the heart of successful litigation. Researching information is easier and yet more complex today than ever before because of computer or electronic research. Inexperienced electronic researchers can waste expensive billable hours "surfing" the numerous electronic sources trying to find something helpful. Knowledgeable electronic researchers first locate the specific sources most pertinent to the investigation of their case through general guides to electronic research. Networking with colleagues in the office or through electronic bulletin boards (e-mail lists) may produce more specialized sources.

Exhibit 3:2 is a general resource guide for investigation on the Web to help you make more efficient use of the information highway. Update frequently.

EXHIBIT 3:2 ■ General Resource Guide for Investigation on the Web

(Consult also government, court, paralegal association, and ethics Web sites at the end of Chapter 1)

General Web Directories and Search Engines

For information not normally found by common search engines:

htpp://lii.org   http://aip.completeplanet.com
   Librarians Internet Index

Common search engines

---

www.yahoo.com	Blog directories:
www.google.com	www.blogsearchengine.com
www.altavista.com	www.bloglines.com
www.excite.com	www.technorati.com
www.hotbot.com	

EXHIBIT 3:2 ■ General Resource Guide for Investigation on the Web *(continued)*

Law Search Engines

www.findlaw.com
free service owned by Westlaw
www.lawresearch.com
www.lawreader.com
www.virtualchase.com
www.lawguru.com
www.ilrg.com
Internet Legal Resource Guide
www.internetlawyer.com
www.lawofficecomputing.com

www.law.cornell.edu
federal and state statutes, decisions, rules, etc.
www.westlaw.com
www.lexis.com
free service at www.lexisone.com
www.loislaw.com
(Legal dictionaries)
www.duhaime.org
www.lectlaw.com/d-a.htm
(Verdicts)
www.verdictsearch.com

Government Resources

www.uscourts.gov
www.firstgov.gov
official links to U.S. and some state sites
www.governmentguide.com
www.fedworld.gov
list of government resources
www.fedstats.gov
links to federal statistics
www.census.gov
Census Bureau
www.whitehouse.gov
www.house.gov
www.senate.gov
http://thomas.loc.gov
pending and passed legislative bills by topic or title
www.gpoaccess.gov

federal documents from the U.S. Government
Printing Office
www.nfoic.org
federal and state freedom of information requests
www.forms.gov
official U.S. forms
www.ntis.gov
National Technical Information Service
http://faxxon.cifnet.com/faxxon
links to Secretary of State homepages for all
50 states
www.loc.gov
Library of Congress

Investigative Resources

www.merlindata.com
index of investigative research sites

www.militarysearch.org
military status of any person

Consumer and Product Information

www.cpsc.gov
Consumer Product Safety Commission
www.pueblo.gsa.gov
Consumer Information Center
www.consumer.gov
U.S. Consumer Gateway (resources by subject)

www.nhtsa.gov
National Highway Traffic Safety Administration
(vehicle complaints, investigations, recalls)
www.ansi.org
American National Standards Institute
www.nacaa.net
National Association of Consumer Agency
Administrators

Environmental/Occupational Safety

www.epa.gov
Environmental Protection Agency
www.osha.gov
Occupational Safety and Health Administration

www.cdc.gov/niosh/about.html
National Institute for Occupational Safety and Health
www.atsdr.cdc.gov
Agency for Toxic Substances and Disease Registry

(continued)

EXHIBIT 3:2 ▪ General Resource Guide for Investigation on the Web (*continued*)

Business, Labor, and Employment

www.doc.gov
  U.S. Department of Commerce
www.dol.gov
  Department of Labor
www.sba.gov
  Department of Commerce, Small Business
  Administration
www.uspto.gov
  U.S. Patent and Trademark Office
www.bbb.org
  Better Business Bureau
www.ftc.gov
  Federal Trade Commission

www.hoovers.com
  Hoovers (information on public companies)
www.law.cornell.edu/uniform/vol7.html
  Uniform Securities Act
www.companylink.com
  data on companies
www.corporateinformation.com
www.incspot.com
  U.C.C./corporate filings
www.sec.gov
  U.S. Securities and Exchange Commission

People/Business Locators

www.anywho.com
www.accurint.com
  fee: extensive personal information
www.reversedirectory.langenber.com
www.knowx.com
www.databaseamerica.com
www.switchboard.com
http://people.yahoo.com
www.ancestry.com
  social security death index
www.bop.gov
  Bureau of Prisons, find prison inmates

(Assets)
www.searchsystems.net
  registered assets such as real estate, cars,
  boats, planes, etc.; also criminal records,
  bankruptcies, and liens
www.carfax.com
  a car's history

(Credit Reports)
Note: personal credit checks are illegal except those
authorized by Fair Credit Reporting Act

Climate Reports

www.noaa.gov
  National Oceanic and Atmospheric
  Administration

www.ncdc.noaa.gov
  National Climatic Data Center

Maps/Aerial Photos

www.usda.gov
  Department of Agriculture (also plants and
  wildlife)

www.doi.gov
  Department of the Interior (Coastal and Geologic
  Survey)

Experts/Prior Testimony

www.dauberttracker.com
  expert evidence cases
www.expertpages.com
  organized by topic and state
www.almexperts.com/expertwitness
www.hg.org
  legal directories

www.trialsdigest.com/research/dlinfo.shtml
  (fee service)
www.tasanet.com
  Technical Advisory Service for Attorneys
Vocational Experts:
www.abve.net
www.rehabpro.org

EXHIBIT 3:2 ■ General Resource Guide for Investigation on the Web *(continued)*

News and Media

www.factiva.com
  extensive news and business information
www.newspaperlinks.com
http://newslink.org/menu.html
www.arl.org/scomm/edir/archive.html
  Association of Research Libraries Directory of
  Electronic Publications

www.excite.com
  customized news clipping searches
http://go.com
www.dialogselect.com

(For a local newspaper, use a general search engine and type in the name of the newspaper to see if articles are on-line.)

Public Records (birth, death, marriage, etc.)

(See Investigative Resources, this exhibit)
www.knowx.com
  background public information about businesses,
  persons, assets

http://vitalrec.com/index.html
  birth, death, marriage, and divorce
  records

Medical/Pharmacy

www.cdc.gov
  U.S. Center for Disease Control
www.fda.gov
  U.S. Food and Drug Administration
www.ama-assn.org/laps/amahg.htm
  doctor finder

www.merck.com
  Merck Manual of Diagnosis and Therapies
www.nlm.nih.gov
  National Library of Medicine (access Medline
  free by choosing Pub Med)
www.jdmd.com
  medical abbreviations, medical and dental mal
  practice consultants, glossary

Statistical Resources

www.fedstats.gov
http://tracfed.syr.edu
www.nces.ed.gov
  National Center for Education Statistics
www.scoi.com
  anatomical/orthopedic information
www.kumc.edu
  University of Kansas medical information and links

www.rarediseases.org
www.tbi.org
  information on traumatic brain injury
www.healthtouch.com
  prescription drugs
www.rxlist.com
  prescription drugs

Vehicle Value

www.kbb.com

Writing and Fact Resources

www.stands4.com/opaui.asp
  guide to lists of acronyms, abbreviations, and
  initialisms
www.odci.gov/cia/publications/factbook
  world factbook
www.almanac.com
  Old Farmers Almanac
www.onelook.com
  multiple specialized dictionaries

http://convert.french-property.u.k./index.htm
  measurement units conversion tables
www.timezoneconverter.com
www.thesaurus.com
  Roget's Thesaurus
www.itools.com/research_it/research_it.html
  dictionary, rhymer, translator, area codes,
  currency converter, others

(continued)

EXHIBIT 3:2 ■ General Resource Guide for Investigation on the Web *(continued)*

Miscellaneous	

www.fedex.com/us/tracking
www.winzip.com
    software for compressing large files or folders
    to disk
	www.ebay.com
	searches can turn up illegally obtained or other
	useful physical evidence

> "The Good, the True and the Beautiful! Alas, the Good is so often untrue, the True so often unbeautiful, and Beautiful so often not Good."
>
> —Isaac Goldberg

METHODS FOR GATHERING INFORMATION OR EVIDENCE

Once the potential sources of information have been identified, choose the method most suitable to obtain that information. Consider efficiency as well as expense; spending a great amount of money and time may not be justified if the amount in controversy is small. Use the following resources:

- The scene of the incident. In many cases, not just personal injury cases, a specific location may offer significant evidence. A visit to the location (office, scene of accident, factory) is essential. Remember to check for business or traffic control surveillance tapes.
- The telephone. Pinpointing the best source of information, especially if it involves leaving the office, interviewing people, going through files, and so on, can be a costly and time-consuming process. A preliminary assessment of these sources by telephone can reduce the amount of time and money spent. For example, if several people witnessed a particular occurrence, it might be wise to call each of them for a preliminary interview to determine whether an in-person visit is warranted.
- Mailed requests. Some information is obtainable through a relatively inexpensive request by correspondence. Medical, school, employment, and agency records can frequently be obtained in this manner if the request includes the proper authorization to release the information. Examples of particular requests by correspondence will be covered later in this chapter.
- The Internet. An increasing amount of information is available on the Internet for free. Although some of the private databases charge monthly or usage fees, the cost can be relatively inexpensive compared with more cumbersome and traditional methods of gathering information. Any office having a personal computer, a modem, and the necessary software can access a database. Should you find yourself without access to the Internet, many public and university libraries provide such services to the public. The average search takes about ten to twenty minutes, and costs are reasonable.
- Personal interview. In most circumstances involving key witnesses, there is no substitute for a personal interview. Personal interviews take time, careful planning, and skill. Because of costs, it may not be feasible to interview less important witnesses in person. The phone can be a big help in this case. It is better, however, to err on the side of too much interviewing than on too little. Interviews produce good evidence as well as the opportunity to assess the ability of the witness to testify.
- Professional research and search services. At times, it pays to hire professional search services. These companies provide a highly experienced and well-trained staff who have access to information unavailable to you. Although these services are often expensive,

they should be employed when the information sought is critical or needs to be gathered quickly. A variety of professional search services are available: PARASEC (www.parasec.com, 800-533-7272) provides document retrieval from anywhere in the country, including county services. It will also conduct searches of records and statements filed with secretaries of state. Corporation Service Company (www.incspot.com, 800-872-4636) offers a wide array of corporate information search services.

- Private investigators. Some firms use private investigators to do their factual investigation. Others use investigators only in certain situations. Investigators are not overly expensive, and using one may make it unnecessary for the office's paralegal to testify about the evidence-gathering process. A list of 14,000 independent investigative agencies with ratings is available through Investigators Anywhere (www.investigatorsanywhere.com, 800-338-3463).

- Legal and topical research. An important part of any investigation involves going to the Internet, CD-ROM library, law library, or general library to locate pertinent statutes, rules, and regulations; news articles; scholarly articles on particular points of law, investigation, and use of evidence; medical information; commercial information; sources for expert witnesses; and other sources. A local library's copy of the city directory is useful for tracking individuals. An older directory may list a phone number that is now unlisted. Also note that Westlaw, Lexis, and other subscription legal research services now offer non-subscription, single search services for a reasonable flat fee.

- Photos and video. Photography and videotaping not only preserve evidence but may also be the only way to effectively gather and demonstrate evidence. A relatively inexpensive digital camcorder with basic editing capabilities can help you create a compelling settlement request. If the photo or video is critical for trial, a professional photographer may be employed.

- Scientific tests. Re-creations, chemical analysis, and other forms of testing may be the only way to support the theory of the plaintiff or defense. The employment of state and private laboratories is normally essential in such circumstances.

- Experts. Related to testing, the use of scientists, professors, engineers, mechanics, medical personnel, and other experts in the relevant field is increasingly essential to win cases. Sometimes victory hinges on which side has the best expert. Associations of experts such as TASA (Technical Advisory Service for Attorneys) offer American and foreign experts in thousands of fields, as well as in alternative methods of resolving disputes (www.tasanet.com, 800-523-2319).

- Freedom of Information Act requests. FOIA requests are inexpensive and can provide valuable information from federal and state agencies. It is best to consider such requests early in the litigation process. A more detailed discussion of FOIA requests is addressed in the context of discovery in Chapter 9.

RECORD THE INVESTIGATION PLAN

Keeping in mind evidentiary considerations, the elements of the cause of action or its defenses, the potential sources of information, and the methods and costs of gathering that evidence, write out the detailed investigation plan as demonstrated in Exhibit 3:3.

EXHIBIT 3:3 ■ Investigative Plan

Possible to Prove or Acquire	Possible Source of Information	Method	Cost
Defendant Mercury Express—financial status, service agent, home office, etc.	Dun's Market Identifiers Corporation Service Co.	Internet search Professional search service	
Breach of Duty			
Weather conditions	Certified copy of weather conditions from National Climatic Data Center	Mail/Internet	
Mechanical defect	Inspection of vehicle Police report Vehicle maintenance records Mechanic who services vehicle	Hire mechanic Mail Mail request Phone/interview (deposition)	
Condition of driver	Police report Police officer Copy of breathalyzer report Ms. Schnabel (witness)	Mail Phone/personal interview Mail Clerk of court file Personal interview	
Conditions at scene	Scene of accident	Visit scene (photograph)	
Plaintiff's injuries			
Immediate injuries, broken bones, etc.	Doctors' reports Emergency room records Hospital records X-rays Doctors' testimony	Mail Mail Mail Mail Interview, letter, reports evaluated	
Immediate and long-term disabilities	Doctors' reports (follow-up visits) Doctors' testimony Ms. Forrester Mr. Forrester Nurse Friends	Mail Interview (after reports evaluated) Initial interview Interview Phone (followed by interview) Phone (followed by interview)	
Pain	Ms. Forrester's testimony (pain log) Mr. Forrester Nurse Hospital and doctors' reports Doctors' testimony Ambulance assistants Ms. Schnabel (witness)	Initial and follow-up interviews Interview Phone (follow-up interview) Mail Interview Phone Interview	
Comparative Negligence			
Attentiveness of plaintiff (haste of plaintiff)	Police report Insurance and Mercury accident reports Ms. Forrester Mr. Forrester Ms. Schnabel Mr. Hart	Mail Mail (discovery) Interview Interview Interview Deposition	
Obstruction of sight and sound by coat worn by plaintiff	Coat itself Possible re-creation tests with coat at scene University consultant	Obtain from Ms. Forrester (Suggestions from supervising attorney) Phone	

Note: This table is for illustrative purposes. It is not complete as to possible facts to prove, sources, or methods.

CONSULT WITH THE SUPERVISING ATTORNEY

Take the completed investigation plan to the attorney. A brief discussion should be held to determine the most feasible approach regarding sources, methods, and available time and money. You will be better able to assist in making decisions about sources and methods as you gain experience. The investigation plan should be amended as indicated by the attorney. At this time it should be made clear who is responsible for carrying out each step of the investigation, especially if the attorney regularly assumes some of this responsibility or if the office employs investigators.

ETHICAL AND RELATED CONSIDERATIONS

ETHICS

Investigation brings the paralegal into more contact with the public than at any other stage of litigation. The manner in which the paralegal approaches and conducts these contacts will reflect upon the reputation of the client, the firm, the paralegal, and the paralegal profession. If the contacts are thoughtful and ethical, the process will benefit the firm and help establish a responsive network of individuals who will be willing to help in future cases. Conversely, if the contacts are tactless and unethical, the consequences will be uncooperative witnesses, unsatisfactory information, a loss of confidence in the paralegal and the firm, and possible disciplinary action. Therefore, when investigating a case, keep in mind the following ethical considerations.

Be thorough in preparing and investigating a case, an important aspect of "competency" required in Rule 1.1 of the Model Rules of Professional Conduct. Similarly, be diligent and prompt to avoid the loss of important evidence (Rule 1.3). Exercise independent judgment so as not to become unduly influenced by the client or the client's directives to engage in unlawful or even unethical conduct. Know the limits to the scope of representation (Rule 1.2). Good investigation is essential for you to keep your client informed and able to make knowledgeable decisions (Rule 1.4). Seek all the evidence, both pro and con, and report your findings so the attorney can adequately advise the client—even if this includes information the client does not want to hear (Rule 2.1).

While investigating and researching, be aware of the attorney's as well as your own obligation to be candid with the court. Inform the attorney of any relevant evidence that is false or appears false; record all legal authority so the attorney can inform the court of clear opposing authority if the other side fails to present it; avoid inflating the importance of any evidence that might make the attorney appear to be presenting false statements to the court; correct false evidence presented to the court by informing the attorney; and in cases where there is only one side (ex parte), see to it that the attorney can present all material facts, both pro and con, to the court [Rules 3.3(a) and 3.3(d)].

Fairness to the opposition is also essential. Avoid any act that obstructs others' access to evidence or unlawfully alters, destroys, or conceals evidence [Rule 3.4(a)(b)]. It is also unethical to instruct a third person to refrain from speaking to or from giving information to the opposition unless the person is an employee or agent of the client [Rule 3.4(f)]. Paralegals can be involved in cases that attract public attention; in such circumstances and as a general rule, make no comments to the press. Attorneys may do so, but under strict guidelines (Rule 3.6). False statements to others on important facts are violations of the code [Rule 4.1(a)]. In some

"Prepare your
proof before you
argue."

—Jewish folk saying,
quoted in Joseph L.
Baron, *A Treasury of
Jewish Quotations*, 1956.

circumstances, there is a duty to speak up to prevent a client from committing fraud or a crime [Rule 4.4(b)]. If you are aware that your client is planning a fraudulent contract or agreement, the supervising attorney should be informed so remedial measures can be taken.

When speaking with others, always identify yourself as a paralegal from your firm or office so there can be no misunderstanding of your title or purpose. If the need arises to speak with a person who is represented by an attorney, speak with that person only with the permission of or through that person's attorney (Rule 4.2). If the person is not represented by an attorney, avoid implying your neutrality and correct any misunderstanding about whom you represent (Rule 4.3). Remember that you may not violate the rights of others (stealing a key document or harassing a potential witness, for example) or do anything for the purpose of embarrassment, delay, or to burden another (Rule 4.4). Keep in mind that to breach any of these ethical standards could subject your supervising attorney to disciplinary action, since the attorney is responsible for the ethical conformance of each employee (Rule 5.3).

Also, be aware of provisions of federal and state law that may come into play when conducting investigations. For example, the Fair Credit Reporting Act strictly governs and penalizes the request for and the unauthorized use of personal credit reports. Equally restrictive prohibitions are found in the Electronic Communications Privacy Act, the Health Insurance Portability and Accountability Act, and other federal and parallel state laws. Carefully reviewing the investigation plan with your attorney often flags such concerns.

ATTORNEY'S WORK PRODUCT (TRIAL PREPARATION MATERIALS)

Further, be aware of the law regarding an attorney's work product. Under Rule 26 of the Federal Rules of Civil Procedure and the rules of most states, a party may obtain from another party information that is relevant to the subject matter involved in the action. This information includes the existence, description, nature, custody, condition and location of any books, documents, or other tangible things, and the identity and whereabouts of persons having knowledge of disclosable matter. This exchange of information is called discovery.

Excepted from discovery under Rule 26(b)(3) are the mental impressions, conclusions, opinions, or legal theories of the attorney or the attorney's agent. Typically, this includes written or recorded notes, memoranda, interviews, and investigative and other reports. This exception is called the **attorney's work product** (**trial preparation materials**). As a tactical measure, each party will try to protect as much material as possible from discovery while trying to discover as much as they can from the opponent. The primary concern is to recognize that the work product exception exists to prevent divulging information that should not or need not be disclosed. Attorney work product is further discussed in the context of discovery in Chapter 7.

**attorney's work product
(trial preparation materials)**
The attorney's mental impressions, conclusions, opinions, or legal theories concerning a case; not discoverable.

REVEALING INFORMATION TO A WITNESS

It is possible for a witness or other source of information to turn the tables on the investigator by finding out more from the investigator than the investigator does from the source. Some investigators, especially novices, seem to feel that if they generously answer the questions of the other person, the other person will in turn generously answer their questions. This approach is unproductive and can lead to the revealing of confidential or undiscoverable information. Avoid this situation by stating that you are bound to preserve confidentiality and may not discuss what you know about the case. The majority of witnesses will accept this explanation with no effect on their willingness to participate.

GATHERING THE EVIDENCE

INTRODUCTION

When you have in mind an investigation plan as well as an awareness of ethical, evidentiary, and other considerations, it is time to actually gather the information. The three significant investigative procedures that will be emphasized in this section include gathering reports, records, and other documents; investigating the scene of the accident; and taking the statements of witnesses.

GATHERING REPORTS, RECORDS, AND OTHER DOCUMENTS

Medical Records

The investigation plan indicates that evidence needs to be gathered regarding the injuries of the plaintiff, including pain and suffering. A complete plan would also call for evidence of doctor and hospital bills. The task at hand is to gather that information. The most common method of verifying the plaintiff's injuries and bills is to request the medical records and doctors' reports describing the treatment rendered. Such records will not only help prove the plaintiff's case but also provide a well-documented record that will be useful in settling the case.

> "And I would sooner trust the smallest slip of paper for truth, than the strongest and most retentive memory, ever bestowed on mortal man."
>
> —JOSEPH HENRY LUMPKIN, *MILLER ET AL. V. COTTON ET AL.*, 5 GA. 341, 349 (1848).

Records regarding the treatment of the plaintiff in Case I, Ms. Forrester, can be obtained, typically, by writing the medical records librarian of the hospital, in this case the Good Samaritan Hospital in Legalville, Columbia. As long as such requests are accompanied by the HIPAA compliant authorization to release medical information executed by Ms. Forrester at the time of her initial interview, there should be no difficulty in obtaining the desired information. The medical authorization must be current. If the authorization is not current, it will have to be reexecuted. If the patient about whom information is requested is dead, a minor, or otherwise incapacitated, the authorization must be signed by the executor or administrator of the patient's estate, the child's parent or guardian, or the incapacitated person's guardian or other legal representative. The defendant's paralegal can get these records, pursuant to HIPAA, in four ways: by obtaining (1) the patient's signed authorization through the plaintiff's attorney, (2) a judicial or administrative order, (3) a subpoena signed by a judge, or (4) a subpoena or discovery request with (a) assurances of notice to the patient with time to object, or (b) assurances that reasonable efforts have been made to get a qualified protective order (an order indicating how the records, once disclosed, will be protected). The methods for defense to obtain medical records are discussed further in the context of discovery in Chapters 8 and 9. The state statutes on medical records should be consulted as well. HIPAA preempts relevant state law unless the state's provisions are more protective. Beyond the one set of records the patient is entitled to without cost, the hospital will charge a per-page fee for the reports. In many jurisdictions, the medical records librarian is not required to send the records unless the fee is paid in advance. Most record requests are phrased as "any and all records" pertaining to the treatment for an injury occurring on a specific date; but it is preferable to mention specifically emergency room reports, outpatient reports, and the face sheet of the patient's chart (which contains good background information plus a physician diagnosis in some cases), since these records will not necessarily be automatically included in the response. The available records include:

- Physician's discharge summary
- Emergency room and outpatient reports
- Patient's chart
- History and physical information
- Reports from operating room
- Pathology reports
- X-ray reports (summary plus film impression)
- Lab reports (summary)
- Progress notes by physician or interns
- Doctors' orders to nurses regarding medication and other care
- Consulting physicians' reports
- Nurses' notes

The following records are not usually requested; however, they can prove useful in specific situations or in malpractice cases. Because these records technically belong to the hospital, a subpoena may be needed to obtain them.

- Incident reports (if previous records reflect a fall or other accident)
- Statistical reports (by physician, disease, type of patient, etc.)
- Departmental records (radiology, physical therapy, etc.)
- Committee minutes and reports (problems and solutions)
- Peer review (licensing and accreditation reports)

Prior to making a request for records, contact the records librarian (or designated privacy officer) to find out the fee and any particular rules or procedures that should be followed. The institution may insist that you use its authorization form. Draft a letter to the medical records librarian of the hospital, giving the full name, address, and date of birth of the person whose records are requested. The use of full social security numbers is now widely discouraged. Enclose the authorization for release of protected health information (HIPAA). Special authorization forms for release of psychotherapy notes and records for treatment and diagnosis of HIV and chemical dependency may be required. An example of a form letter adapted to Ms. Forrester's case is included in Exhibit 3:4. An example of an Authorization to Release Protected Health Information form is shown in Exhibit 3:5.

Another source of valuable medical information is a narrative medical report prepared by the treating physician or physicians. A request for such a narrative is a simple matter, but not without pitfalls. Doctors may charge a substantial fee for such summaries, which frequently contain unneeded information. The better practice is to obtain the hospital records first, review them, and then request from the physician the specific information needed.[7] Since the paralegal and the firm are likely to be working periodically with the physician and nurse or assistant, it is a good idea to develop a pleasant relationship with them. Noting the name of the physician's nurse for your file, for example, will expedite future contacts. Such connections can be helpful when gathering information.

When requesting information from a doctor, many paralegals use a standardized letter. Unfortunately, such a letter is likely to lead to a rather general or incomplete response. A letter to the doctor needs to be as specific as possible and based on detailed information gathered from the medical records and the complaints identified by the client. It is a good idea to confirm with the client each matter complained of to the doctor so the report will be complete. An example of such a letter

EXHIBIT 3:4 ▪ Request for Medical Records (Cover Letter)

WHITE, WILSON & McDUFF
ATTORNEYS AT LAW
FEDERAL PLAZA BUILDING, SUITE 700
THIRD AND MARKET STREETS
LEGALVILLE, COLUMBIA 00000
(111) 555-0000

Ms. Betty Noble
Medical Records Librarian
Good Samaritan Hospital
4600 Church Street
Legalville, Columbia 00000

Re: Medical Records of Ms. Ann Forrester
                1533 Capitol Dr., Legalville, Columbia 00000
                Birth date: 4/25/__

Dear Ms. Noble:

The firm of White, Wilson, and McDuff has been retained to represent the above-named individual.

Enclosed is a current Authorization to Release Protected Health Information executed by our client. I request a copy of all of your medical records on Ms. Forrester. The enclosed authorization includes all Health Insurance Portability and Accountability Act requirements (45 CFR §164.508) as indicated below.

Core Elements:
(i) A specific and meaningful description of the information to be used or disclosed;
(ii) Your name (or facility's name) identifying you as the person(s), or class of persons, authorized to make the requested disclosure;
(iii) The name of the attorney and law office identifying us as the person(s), or class of persons, to whom the covered entity may make the disclosure;
(iv) A description of the purpose of the requested disclosure;
(v) An expiration date or event (with statement that neither has occurred); and
(vi) Signature of the patient and date (or signature of patient's personal representative and description of representative's authority to act for the individual).

Required Statements:
(i) The patient's right to revoke the authorization in writing plus any exceptions to the right to revoke and how to revoke the authorization;
(ii) The inability of you or your facility to condition treatment, payment, enrollment or eligibility for benefits on the signing of this authorization; and
(iii) The potential for information disclosed pursuant to the authorization to be subject to redisclosure by the recipient and no longer be protected by the privacy regulations.

Miscellaneous Elements:
(i) The authorization may not contain any material information that is false, and
(ii) An authorization for psychotherapy notes may not be combined with other types of authorization.

[Add any other state-specific requirements, e.g. some state statutes or regulations require medical records (or one complete copy) to be provided free.]

On receipt of the records, our firm will submit reasonable payment for any preparation fee.

Thank you for your assistance.

Sincerely,

Terry Salyer
Paralegal

Enclosure: Authorization to Release Protected Health Information

EXHIBIT 3:5 ■ Authorization to Disclose Protected Health Information: Plaintiff (HIPAA Compliant)

AUTHORIZATION TO DISCLOSE PROTECTED HEALTH INFORMATION

TO: (Health Care Provider/Address)
RE: (Client/DOB)

AUTHORIZED RECIPIENT: (Law Firm/Address) or its representatives.

RECORDS TO DISCLOSE [Pursuant to the Health Insurance Portability and Accountability Act, 45 CFR § 164.508 (and, where appropriate, cite any relevant state statute)]: ALL medical records including but not limited to: history, physical, dental, outpatient, inpatient, medication, laboratory, pathology, physical therapy and other rehabilitation, mental health, psychiatric (psychotherapy notes excepted), chemical dependency, HIV, billing, health insurance, Medicaid, and Medicare records; physician, nurse, progress, emergency and operating room orders, notes, and reports; discharge summary; and summary reports and films of X-rays, MRIs, and other scanning devices regarding my medical treatment rendered by you and all such information maintained in my medical file. [Although psychotherapy notes are not included in this request, please inform authorized recipient if such notes exist.]

PURPOSE: To authorize you to release all my medical information to my attorney for the purpose of civil litigation. You may rely on a photocopy of this authorization as if it were the original.

EXPIRATION: This authorization expires in [three years (or state date or event)] from the date of signature.

REVOCATION: I know I may revoke this authorization at any time by submitting a signed, written notice of revocation to the health care provider listed above and to my attorney.

REDISCLOSURE: I know the information disclosed pursuant to this authorization is subject to redisclosure by the authorized recipient and no longer protected under the Federal Privacy Rule.

FURTHER AUTHORIZATION: You are also authorized to speak confidentially with my law firm or any of its representatives and provide deposition and trial testimony.

CONDITIONS: I know treatment, payment, and enrollment or eligibility for benefits cannot be conditioned on whether I sign this authorization.

_____
[client signature]
[If personal representative,
sign and describe authority]

_____
[date]

appears in Exhibit 3:6. Occasionally a doctor needs a follow-up letter such as in Exhibit 3:7.

If the plaintiff has died, another report of value is the autopsy report, which represents the findings of the medical examiner or coroner on the cause of death and the medical evidence to support the conclusion. Such reports may be obtained through the office of the coroner or medical examiner. Funeral costs and related records should also be obtained.

EXHIBIT 3:6 ■ Request for Physician's Narrative Medical Summary

White, Wilson & McDuff
Attorneys at Law
Federal Plaza Building, Suite 700
Third and Market Streets
Legalville, Columbia 00000
(111) 555-0000

Albert Meyer, M.D.
Medical Arts Building
4650 Church St.
Legalville, Columbia 00000

Re: Ms. Ann Forrester, 1533 Capitol Drive, Legalville, Columbia 00000
Birthdate: 4/23/__

Dear Dr. Meyer:

Ms. Forrester has retained this office to represent her regarding injuries sustained from being struck by a van on February 26, ___. Ms. Forrester suffered multiple fractures of the pelvis and left leg, and also had spinal and internal injuries. As a result of these injuries, Ms. Forrester is currently bound to a wheelchair and may not be able to return to work for some time.

To assist Ms. Forrester, we would appreciate it if you would send us a report on the following:

1. Your diagnosis of Ms. Forrester's mental, emotional, and physical injuries
2. Your opinion as to the cause of Ms. Forrester's injuries
3. A description of the treatment given Ms. Forrester
4. Likely degree of pain and discomfort related to such injuries
5. Mental, physical, and emotional limitations as they relate to employment, recreational activities, and enjoyment of life
6. Future treatment needed
7. Prognosis
8. Likelihood of Ms. Forrester being able to return to work. If so, when?

In addition, please send an itemized bill for all your services related to these injuries.

The necessary authorization is enclosed. Upon receipt of your report, this office will promptly pay any preparation fee.

Please keep us informed regarding Ms. Forrester's future visits to your office and any change in condition or prognosis.

Thank you for your cooperation.

Terry Salyer
Paralegal

Enclosed: Authorization to Release Protected Health Information

cc: Ms. Ann Forrester

EXHIBIT 3:7 ■ Request for Medical Update

White, Wilson & McDuff
Attorneys at Law
Federal Plaza Building, Suite 700
Third and Market Streets
Legalville, Columbia 00000
(111) 555-0000

Albert Meyer, M.D.
Medical Arts Building
4650 Church St.
Legalville, Columbia 00000

Re: Ms. Ann Forrester, 1533 Capitol Drive, Legalville, Columbia 00000
Birthdate: 4/23/__

Dear Dr. Meyer:

Your report of September 9, ___ on Ms. Forrester was very helpful. Six months have passed since that report, and we need an update. Please provide us with detailed information on the following:

[List those points where specific elaboration is needed beyond the first request. Add a catchall question asking for information on any new or otherwise significant developments.]

Please include copies of itemized bills for your services to Ms. Forrester since September 9. A copy of the appropriate authorization should be in your files.

Thank you again for your assistance.

Terry Salyer
Paralegal

cc: Ms. Forrester

Employment Records

Another area of importance to Ms. Forrester's case is her loss in gross wages as a result of the accident. Such losses are recoverable and can make up an important part of a damage claim. That is why Ms. Forrester was asked to execute the authorization for release of employment information at the initial interview. Send a copy of the authorization along with a request letter to the personnel office where Ms. Forrester is employed. Remember that a person may have more than one employer or source of income. The letter should request a brief history of annual earnings, current salary or hourly wage, days of work missed since the accident, and overtime and bonuses missed. Request information on disability insurance to assist the client in meeting expenses.

If the client is self-employed, an average weekly gross income would have to be determined from the client's tax records or from the client's accountant. Keep in mind the following formula: average gross weekly income, less normal costs not incurred because of injury (such as the purchase or sale of goods, phone bills, and mileage), equals weekly amount claimed.[8]

In serious injuries, or in the case of death, loss of future earnings is also an important component of damages. Inquiry should be made about labor contracts that dictate pay into the next several years; possible loss or reduction in fringe benefits; any schedule of eligibility for promotion, bonuses, overtime, stock options, and profit sharing; and other special considerations. In addition, it is wise to seek the assistance of a qualified vocational expert or economist (or both) to form a sound claim for future loss of earnings or to challenge such a claim. One source of assistance is the American Board of Vocational Experts.

Other Records

Other records or documents may be obtained on behalf of the client as long as the proper authorizations have been signed. Information from the federal as well as some state governments may be obtained through forms and procedures described in the particular Freedom of Information Act.

Check Documents

Check documents immediately. Regardless of what information is requested, you will need to ensure that the information received is correct and clear. Requests for corrections or explanations should be made immediately where errors exist or information is unclear. It is also important to have a guide to reading medical records, a medical dictionary, or a guide to the vernacular of the particular subject area. Do not assume that these words are correctly used or that someone else in the office, particularly the attorney, will be able to decipher the language. See Chapter 9 and Appendix D on interpreting medical records and medical terminology.

INVESTIGATING THE SCENE OF THE ACCIDENT

Viewing the scene of the accident or source of the claim at the time of the injury (or as soon thereafter as possible) is essential to sound investigation. Secondhand reports and photos are certainly useful, but they do not substitute for a personal visit to the scene.

Advance planning helps you spend your time at the scene more efficiently. A quick review of the information in the file including the summary of the client's interview and the elements of proof critical to the case helps focus attention on the most important facts. It also helps to anticipate the need of any special investigative tools.

Some typical tools are necessary for investigating the scene. A quad-ruled tracing paper pad and clipboard are useful for diagramming the scene of the accident. (See Exhibits 3:11–3:13 for tips on diagramming an accident.) Tape measures of varying length and a walk-along, wheeled measuring device for longer distances are essential. A reliable 35mm camera with flash still provides the best quality photos. A digital camera, however, provides cheaper photos, instant photo review and retakes, and easy importability into documents such as a settlement proposal. A color video camera, if available, would certainly be helpful. Other useful tools that conjure up visions of Sherlock Holmes include a flashlight, magnifying glass, compass (to ensure accurate directions), tape recorder, stopwatch, protractor (for measuring angles), labeling tags, and various sizes of plastic bags (for storing evidence). Occasionally a specific type of case may require some other useful instruments.

A checklist form of things to note and record at the scene appears in Exhibit 3:8.

EXHIBIT 3:8 ▪ Accident Scene Checklist

1. Nature of area: urban, rural, intersection, highway, school zone, other _____
2. Weather (if at scene soon enough to observe) _____
3. Other conditions: visibility _____

   road surface _____

   lanes _____

   curves _____

   grade _____

   speed limit _____

   other _____

4. Witness   Position to view accident   View, obstructions

   _____   _____   _____

   _____   _____   _____

   _____   _____   _____

5. Possible distractions that might cause inattention _____
6. Measurements of critical distances[a]

   skid marks _____

   road width _____

   distance vehicle traveled after impact _____

   distance from witness position to scene _____

   other _____

7. Traffic control

   signs _____

   lane markings _____

   other _____

8. Sun or other lighting conditions at time of day accident occurred

   from plaintiff's position _____

   from defendant's position _____

   from witness's position _____

   other _____

9. Temporary conditions

   construction _____

   parked vehicles _____

   other _____

10. Flow of traffic, same time of day, same day of week _____

[a]A handy formula for converting speed to distance (and vice versa) is mph $\times$ 1.5 = ft. per sec.

EXHIBIT 3:8 ■ Accident Scene Checklist *(continued)*

11. All possible causes of accident _____
    _____

12. Evidence of damage
    vehicles _____
    signs _____
    trees _____
    buildings _____
    other _____

13. Photograph and videotape important items noted above from different angles to show relevant conditions or defects such as a pothole in the street, uneven sidewalk, slippery spots, etc.

14. Carefully note pertinent directions (N, NE, E, SE, S, SW, W, NW) _____

15. Locations of other possible witnesses regularly at the scene
    homes _____
    businesses _____
    joggers _____
    dog walkers _____
    farm workers _____
    maintenance or public works people _____
    other _____

16. Other physical evidence relevant to case _____

17. Special needs
    expert to view scene _____
    professional photographer to capture lighting, angles (good source: International Council of Evidence Photographers) _____
    _____
    _____
    aerial photograph _____
    other _____

18. Carefully preserve evidence.

ACQUIRING THE STATEMENTS OF WITNESSES

Locating the Witnesses

Locating witnesses as soon as possible is important to investigation. Memories fade quickly, making it difficult for witnesses to recall important details. Witnesses also tend to develop an attachment to the side that contacts them first, creating an impediment for the opposing investigator. Being first to the witness gives you an advantage. The following list contains ideas for locating witnesses:

- Ask the client, other known witnesses, the reporting police officer, emergency personnel, and so on.
- Review photographs for bystanders, license numbers, and other leads.
- Locate news reporters, camera operators, and free-lance photographers.
- Visit the scene at the same time of day and week to locate persons who might routinely frequent the area (joggers, walkers, delivery personnel, school crossing guards).
- Canvass the immediate area for local residents and businesses, or farm workers in rural areas.
- Place an ad in the local newspaper with a photo of the accident, asking witnesses or people with information to call.

If only a photo of the person is available,

- Canvass the area asking people who are likely to know many people, such as local politicians and officials, police, bankers, or school officials.
- Place an ad with the photo requesting information.

If only a name is available,[9]

- Use the telephone book, voter registration lists, or the city directory.
- Consult postal officials (you may need to use post office Freedom of Information form 1478 for forwarding address).
- Call contacts at utility companies and public service offices.
- Check with local credit bureaus (you may find restrictions or conditions).
- Check with the motor vehicle and licensing bureau.

If only the name and occupation are available,[10]

- Contact the personnel office of a likely employer (possible restrictions).
- Speak with co-workers.
- Seek information from the licensing agency if it is a regulated profession.
- Contact unions or trade associations.

If only the avocation or school is known,

- Contact sports leagues or hobby societies.
- Consult alumni groups.

See Exhibit 3:2 for good person and business locator Web sites.

If a witness is particularly critical and hard to locate, the office may have no choice but to hire a private investigation firm to locate the person.

Locating Expert Witnesses

Sometimes a case may involve the highly complex and technical principles of medicine, mechanics, engineering, electronics, or other fields. In such cases it may be necessary to locate an expert witness, not only to interpret information but also to translate it to a jury and to give an opinion relevant to the issues. The supervising attorney or the senior member of the firm will make the decision to hire an expert. The decision is an important one because hiring an expert can be expensive.

Nevertheless, it may fall to the paralegal to locate an expert. Some ways to locate an expert are as follows:

- Check with colleagues about experts used in previous cases and the office's list of experts.
- Ask the client about experts in the client's field, if relevant.
- Locate pertinent articles in professional journals or books on the topic and contact the authors (frequently considered experts in the field).

- Ask other firms who have had similar cases to recommend an expert they have used.
- Contact professional societies.
- Contact the applicable department or research facility at a college or university.
- Contact pertinent government agencies (local, state, and national) that often employ experts in a particular field.
- Check national legal newspapers, bar association, and paralegal publications for advertisements by experts. Request references and names of former clients.
- Check the expert Web sites in Exhibit 3:2.

Planning the Interview

Once the potential witness is located, it may be best to call the witness to see what information can be obtained. This step should be bypassed if the witness is evasive or seems likely to be so. If a personal visit is necessary to have the witness sign a written statement, the interview should be planned. The planning process and techniques are essentially the same as those for planning and conducting an interview with the client (see Chapter 2).

Determining the purpose of the interview is absolutely necessary. Some witnesses are interviewed to provide a broad look at events—the witness to the accident, for example. Other witnesses, such as the mechanic who checked the brakes on Mr. Hart's truck, will be interviewed to explore entirely different information, possibly with a narrow focus. Each witness is therefore sought out for a purpose, and that purpose should clearly dictate the extent and nature of preparation.

As an initial step in planning the interview, locate or develop any helpful forms and checklists. The law firm often has copies of such forms. These forms are designed to make sure the interviewer covers the essentials. Exhibit 3:9 is the Witness Information Cover Sheet to be filled out at the interview and used later for quick reference.

Exhibit 3:10, Checklist for Witness Interview, is easily adaptable to any personal injury case. It can be used as a guide during questioning and as a check to see that

---

EXHIBIT 3:9 ■ Witness Information Cover Sheet

1. _____ 2. _____ 3. _____
    Date   Interviewer   Place

4. _____ 5. _____ 6. _____
    Client   File No.   Type of Case

7. _____ 8. For Def. _____ Pltf. _____
    Full Name of Witness

photo

9. Summary of Statement _____

_____

_____

10. Availability _____

BACKGROUND

11. _____ (_____) 12. _____
    Address, City, County, State, Zip Code   Years at   Alias/Maiden Name

(continued)

EXHIBIT 3:9 ▪ **Witness Information Cover Sheet** (*continued*)

13. _____ _____ 14. Citizen (_____) (_____) 15. _____
    Home Phone   Work Phone   Yes   No   Nationality/Race

16. _____ 17. _____ 18. _____ 19. _____
    Date of Birth   Age   Sex   If Minor, Guardian's Name

20. _____ 21. _____
    Close Relative or Friend (Not Immediate Family)   Address/Phone

22. S___ M ___ D ___ W ___ Other ___ 23. _____
                                           Spouse's Full Name

24. _____ 25. _____ 26. _____
    Spouse's Address If Other Than 11.   Spouse's Place of Employment   Phone

27. _____ 28. Children's Names, Ages, Addresses (other than 11)
    Spouse's Job Title

    a. _____ ( ) _____
    b. _____ ( ) _____
    c. _____ ( ) _____

29. List other marriages on back.

EMPLOYMENT

30. _____
    Witness's Employer   Address   Job Title

31. _____ 32. _____ 33. _____
    Supervisor   Phone   Date Started Employment

34. Other Jobs: Employer/Address/Phone/Supervisor/Dates/Job Title
    a. _____
    b. _____
    c. _____

35. Education: School/Address/Degree or Diploma/Date
    a. H.S _____
    b. Voc. _____
    c. Coll. _____
    d. Grad. _____
    e. Other _____

36. Experience as Witness (___) (___) _____ _____ _____
                             Yes   No   Date   Location   Type of Case

37. Ever been convicted of fraud, theft, or other dishonesty? Give details.

_____

_____

EXHIBIT 3:10 ▪ Checklist for Witness Interview

☐ 1. Complete Witness Information Cover Sheet.

☐ 2. Identify taker of statement, time, date, place.

☐ 3. Witness's activity just prior to accident: ☐ location ☐ time ☐ date
☐ witness's activity ☐ view of scene ☐ distance from scene
☐ obstruction ☐ location of plaintiff and defendant
☐ activity of plaintiff ☐ activity of defendant ☐ others present
☐ names ☐ their location ☐ activities
☐ other possible witnesses ☐ others in vehicle
☐ key issue questions

☐ 4. Setting at time of accident:
☐ time ☐ weather ☐ lighting conditions ☐ road conditions
☐ wind ☐ unforeseen obstructions (repair work, children, animals, fallen trees or rocks, etc.)
☐ dangerous conditions
☐ traffic flow ☐ speed limits ☐ traffic signs
☐ school zone ☐ intersection ☐ type of road ☐ hills
☐ curves ☐ shoulders ☐ any unusual or particularly notable activity of parties or others (recklessness, inattentiveness, evidence of influence of alcohol or drugs, etc.)
☐ speed of vehicles ☐ distance between plaintiff and defendant
☐ vehicle window obstructions ☐ other conditions of importance
☐ when witness's attention first drawn to plaintiff and defendant
☐ other key issue questions

☐ 5. The accident:
☐ time ☐ general description of sequence
☐ attempt to evade (sound horn, brake, head for shoulder, etc.)
☐ skidding ☐ sounds of contact
☐ detailed description of what happened to plaintiff and defendant (thrown from car, hit windshield, fell, etc.)
☐ detailed description of what happened to vehicles
☐ exact point of contact ☐ exact position of parties at time of contact ☐ position of other people ☐ opinion as to cause of accident
☐ diagram ☐ other key issue questions

☐ 6. Setting after accident:
☐ witness's description of scene (diagram)
☐ position of plaintiff and defendant ☐ position of vehicles
☐ injuries and damage (persons and property)
☐ description of sequence of events after accident
☐ time of arrival and activity of all emergency personnel
☐ care rendered at scene to injured ☐ other persons and witnesses present after accident, including reporters, photographers, investigators ☐ cleanup activities (name of tow truck)
☐ who, if anyone, made or recorded statements ☐ conversations overheard (parties, witnesses, emergency personnel, etc.)
☐ opinion as to truthfulness and character of parties and witnesses
☐ witness's record of character and honesty ☐ any conversation with any of the parties since accident about accident or injuries
☐ other key issue questions

☐ 7. Record statement and have witness read, sign, and date it.

☐ 8. Check to see if witness made statements about the accident to anyone else. If so, to whom and what kind (oral, written, recorded)?

☐ 9. Assess witness's abilities
☐ voice ☐ sincerity ☐ power of observation ☐ confidence
☐ appearance ☐ appreciation of importance of truthfulness
☐ recognition of evidence, persons, photos, etc. ☐ objectivity
☐ truthfulness ☐ vulnerability to impeachment
☐ willingness to testify ☐ availability for trial

all significant items have been covered in the interview prior to drafting the written statement.

In addition to using this general questionnaire, the paralegal needs to take the planning stage further by developing questions that focus on the key issues of the case as they relate to elements and defenses in the case. For example, in Ms. Forrester's case, some initial questions must be probed in detail with one key witness, Ms. Schnabel. Some of these questions for each of the key elements in negligence are as follows:

Element. *Duty (defined by conditions at the time).*

Issue. *Was ice a factor in determining degree of caution required?*

Questions. *Was ice on the road the morning of the accident? How much of the road near the scene and at the scene of the accident was covered by ice? Where was the ice? Had you experienced any difficulty on the ice yourself? Did your tires slip? Did you have control problems?*

Element. *Breach of duty.*

Issue. *Was Mr. Hart driving too fast under the icy conditions?*

Questions. *How fast were you driving? How fast do you normally drive at that point? How fast was Mr. Hart driving? From your observations, how did the ice affect or enter into the accident? In your opinion, was Mr. Hart driving too fast for the icy conditions? Explain the basis for your answer.*

Element. *Breach was proximate cause of injury.*

Issue. *Was Mr. Hart's speed under the icy conditions the cause of Ms. Forrester's injuries?*

Questions. *In your opinion, what was the primary cause of the accident? Explain. Do you feel there were any other contributing causes? If so, what were they? Explain. Which cause was most significant? Explain.*

This question-planning process should be followed for any issues that might prove pivotal in the success of the case. Other key factors in the *Forrester* case include speed related to obstructions caused by the hills, inattentiveness of pedestrians, position of pedestrians, reaction times of the drivers, evidence of mechanical defects, and so on. Questions need to be planned to gather information on the key points of contention for each of the elements. This requires thorough preparation. Such preparation will help clarify the objectives of the particular interview and will make the interview much more valuable to the outcome of the case.

Another part of the planning process is deciding where the interview should take place. Occasionally a witness will agree to come to your office, but more than likely the interview will take place in the home, at the witness's place of employment, in a restaurant, in a car, or at the scene of the accident. Whenever possible the location should offer as much freedom from outside interruption and influence as possible. Witnesses should not be interviewed together, because one witness can influence or taint the statements of the other.

As in the initial interview, special problems or needs should be anticipated. Will you need a translator? Will you need a special setting for an interview with a child? Should you arrange for someone else to be present if the witness is likely to be hostile or accuse you of unethical behavior? Will the witness expect to be paid? (Expert witnesses expect to be paid.) Check the office for the local practice and appropriate fee. Be sure that the fee is approved before incurring the expense.

Conducting the Witness Interview

Because the personality and attitude of each witness can be quite different, there is probably no standard method of approaching a particular witness. You will have to draw upon experience, intuition, and common sense as the situation dictates. Some pointers are worth remembering, however. Courtesy should be of the first order. Calling ahead to arrange the interview is an important consideration. In circumstances such as in the case of a hostile witness when it may be better not to call, you should choose a time likely to be convenient to the witness. Make it clear to the witness who you are, your status, which party you represent, and your purpose. If the witness is a friend of your client, or simply neutral, introducing some information about your client that will evoke sympathy may encourage the witness to help you. Keep in mind, however, the ethical responsibility not to be misleading or deliberately dishonest and to preserve client confidentiality.

If witnesses are unwilling or hesitant to grant the interview, emphasize that you need their help and that it could be instrumental in bringing this matter to a quick, just, and less costly resolution. Cooperation now might reduce the time they would have to spend in the future. Also, delaying the interview may cause memory to fade, and valuable evidence will be lost. If this doesn't work, tell the witness that your firm can subpoena them to testify under oath, and it would be easier and more convenient to go ahead now than to do so under the subpoena. If this strategy fails, there is probably little choice but to withdraw and consider having them formally deposed, as discussed in Chapter 8.

The Witness Information Cover Sheet (see Exhibit 3:9) should be completed at the outset and clipped to the witness's statement. When organizing items for settlement or trial, you may refer to the cover sheet for a quick review of the witness and what he or she had to say.

The investigator's approach to the interview will depend on the witness. Some will want to tell you the entire story, while others will need regular questioning to focus their thoughts and to keep them on relevant information. Take notes, but listen carefully; do not be so concerned about your next question that you do not listen carefully to the answer to your last one. When you are not clear on a point, restate what the witness has said and ask if you have understood correctly. Be ready to employ the variety of interview techniques designed for the initial interview in Chapter 2. Do not try to compose a statement for the witness until you are sure that you know the information well.

The following are sections of an interview with Ms. Forrester's neighbor, Ms. Schnabel. The purpose of this example is to illustrate an approach to setting up an interview, a sequence to follow, a way to elicit detailed facts instead of beliefs, and a method to implement aspects of the interview plan (most particularly the key issue questions).

Illustrative Interview: Case 1

Setting Up the Interview

Setting: The doorstep of the witness's home (*I* stands for interviewer; *W* stands for witness).

 I: Good afternoon, Ms. Schnabel. I'm Terry Salyer, a paralegal with the law firm of White, Wilson and McDuff. I'm the one who spoke with you on the phone earlier this week. I appreciate your willingness to talk with us. As you know, we are trying to help Ms. Forrester recover compensation for the terrible injuries inflicted on her in an accident last February.

W: Well, I have been thinking about this, and my husband feels that I should-
     n't get involved. We are terribly busy and I just don't have the time to be
     going to court. I'm really not sure how helpful I can be anyway. I'd like to
     help Ms. Forrester, but I think I'd better stay out of it.

I: I can understand your concern, Ms. Schnabel, but one of the things we hope
     to accomplish in interviewing you is to get a better picture of what hap-
     pened. It is likely that what you tell me could actually shorten this case, pos-
     sibly make your testimony at a trial unnecessary, and allow for an early and
     just settlement of this matter. Frankly, it may be better for everyone involved
     in this incident, especially Ann Forrester, for you to tell us what you observed
     now, than to wait until months down the road when you might have to tes-
     tify in court and you have forgotten much of what happened. I ask you to
     put yourself in Ms. Forrester's place—if you were she, not only would you
     want the help, but you would need it. I'll make every effort to be as brief
     as my job will permit. May I come in?

W: Well, I guess so. My husband won't like it, but I'll do what I can.

I: Thank you. You have a lovely home.

W: Thank you. Please sit down.

I: I'll be asking you several questions about what you observed at the accident
     and then ask you to reconfirm what you said in a written statement. I have
     several background questions to ask you. [Follow the Checklist for Witness
     Interview, or use the checklist to make sure you have covered everything
     at the conclusion of the interview.]

Questions Regarding Witness's Activity Prior to Accident

I: Ms. Schnabel, do you remember the date on which the accident involving
     Ms. Forrester occurred?

W: Yes, it was February 26, the day after my husband's birthday.

I: What were you doing that morning immediately prior to the accident?

W: I was driving my grandchildren to school.

I: What way did you go that morning?

W: I turned onto Highway 328 and headed toward town.

I: What direction would that be?

W: East.

I: What was the weather like that morning?

W: It was a cold, windy morning. I recall that the road was slippery. [It might
     be best to finish questions about the weather, and then go on to questions
     about it being slippery.]

Questions Regarding the Conditions at the Time of the Accident

I: Could you describe in more detail what you mean by "slippery"?

W: Yes, there were patches of ice on the road. I remember that my wheels spun
     when I turned onto the highway. I noticed several more slippery spots, so
     I drove quite slowly.

I: How far did you drive before you came to where you observed the accident?

W: Oh, about a quarter of a mile.

I: Were there other slippery spots on that quarter mile of road?

W: Yes, there were several.

I: What percentage of the road was slippery?

W: Oh, I'd say about 20 percent.

I: Was there ice on both sides of the road?

W: Yes.

Questions Regarding the Accident

I: Ms. Schnabel, would you please draw me a diagram of the accident location?

W: Yes.

I: Using the diagram, describe the sequence of events of the accident itself.

W: Ann Forrester was walking on the road toward her house. The van was coming down the hill in her direction. Suddenly, the back of the van began to swerve from side to side. Ms. Forrester tried to get out of the way, but the van kept sliding into the middle of the road and hit her. Ms. Forrester was thrown to the side of the road.

Using Follow-up Questions to Gain Greater Factual Detail

I: How close was the van to Ms. Forrester when it started to skid and turn?

W: Pretty close.

I: Please state the distance in feet.

W: About thirty-five to forty feet.

I: What would you estimate to be the distance between your front window and your mailbox? [This gives an indication of the witness's judgment of distance. The actual distance can be measured later.]

W: Around sixty to seventy feet.

I: Was there any observable attempt by the driver of the van to warn Ms. Forrester or to avoid the accident?

W: Not that I recall.

I: Not even a sounding of the horn?

W: No.

I: Not any braking?

W: Well, yes. It sounded like the wheels locked on the van. There was some sliding and some skidding.

I: Describe those sounds, please.

Probing Further for Details

I: Could you see the driver of the van just before the accident?

W: Not really.

I: Were the windows of the van fogged over?

W: I really didn't notice.

I: How fast was the van going when you first saw it?

W: He seemed to be going pretty fast.

I: How fast was that?

W: Oh, I'd say about forty to forty-five miles per hour.

I: Help me understand how you arrived at that estimate.

W: Well, thirty years of driving for one thing, but also because the van came over the hill so quickly and seemed to cover the ground between it and Ann so fast, even after the driver tried to brake the van.

I: What was the distance between the van when you first saw it crest the hill and Ms. Forrester?

W: I'd say about one hundred feet—maybe a little more.

I: Did you see if Ms. Forrester looked before she stepped onto the road?

W: No, she was already on the road when I came over the hill.

I: Where was Ms. Forrester's attention directed when you first saw her?

W: I can't be certain, but she seemed to be looking at the road.

I: Please describe that in more detail.

W: She was looking down and straight ahead.

I: Was her head tucked into her coat collar?

W: I kind of recall her collar being up around her neck and ears—but I'm really not sure.

(Note the absence of expressions such as "poor Ms. Forrester" or "poor Ann," which might suggest a strong bias held by Ms. Schnabel, thus weakening the possible effectiveness of her testimony at trial.)

The remaining part of the interview concerns the witness's impression of the situation immediately after the accident. Here, a good investigator would concentrate on the witness's observation of injuries to either party, especially on any overt indications of pain and suffering endured by Ms. Forrester. Prior to writing the statement, review the checklist to make sure all areas of the planned inquiry have been covered.

I: Ms. Schnabel, is there anything else you would like to add? [This avoids accusations of restricting what the witness was allowed to say.]

W: Not that I can think of.

I: Ms. Schnabel, I will take what you have told me and draft a written statement for you to review and sign. This will take me a few minutes, so if you have something to do in the meantime, please go ahead and I will let you know when we are ready to resume.

Drafting the Statement

The statement of a witness is taken for several reasons, as we have seen in other contexts. It tells the attorney what facts can be corroborated or refuted, which determines what the issues in the case will be and how good the evidence will be on those issues. More directly, the statement serves as a record of the witness's recollection of the facts, which can be used months and even years later to refresh the memory of the witness. It commits the witness to his or her story. It can also be used in cross-examination to impeach the testimony of a witness who later contradicts the earlier statement. Statements of opposing parties can also serve as admissions that can be used against them in court. In addition, if a statement is sufficiently convincing and corroborates key facts, it may help bring about an early settlement of the case.

There are several different ways to record a statement. One method is to have witnesses write their own statements and sign them. This process is inexpensive, but few witnesses are willing to do this, and if they are, the information often lacks factual detail. Another method is to have a court reporter (stenographer) accompany the paralegal and record the statement. This approach may be particularly helpful when interviewing an adverse party or witnesses partial to the opposition. It is not, however, recommended for witnesses favorable or partial to the client because any initial inaccuracies or misjudgments of the witness will be recorded prior to any corrections, making the witness appear uncertain.[11] This method is also more expensive. Another method is to bring a neutral third party to hear the interview and sign the statement as a verification witness, or to record in a memorandum what the witness said, especially if the witness refuses to sign a statement. The advantage to these last two methods is that they provide a neutral third party to refute any statements by the witnesses that they did not read the statements, that the words in the statements are not their words, or that improprieties occurred. Without the neutral third party, the paralegal might have to testify to refute such an allegation. Unfortunately, the paralegal has a specific interest in the case and would probably not be viewed by the jury as a neutral witness. Sometimes it is best to have a reluctant or adverse witness sign a statement in the form of a sworn affidavit. These are harder to refute later.

The most common method involves interviewing the witness and drafting a statement for the witness to read and sign. In addition to these methods, statements may be taken by audio or video recorder or recorded over the telephone. Tape recordings or phone recordings should be conducted only with the full knowledge and permission of the witness and should be done so as to guarantee that the recordings are not subsequently tampered with or altered.

Tips for Taking and Drafting an Effective Statement

1. Visit the scene of the accident first to gain insights that will aid in taking a statement.
2. Note facts as opposed to beliefs ("twenty feet" as opposed to "too close").
3. Avoid references to automobile insurance; they can make the statement inadmissible.[12]
4. Take statements from likely witnesses who say they didn't see anything; a change in their stories will subject them to impeachment.
5. Note, but do not include in the statement, the names of other witnesses. (The jury may wonder why some of these people are not called later at trial.)[13]
6. Do not pay a witness for a statement without the attorney's approval. Fees for a statement are viewed skeptically by jurors, but reimbursement for expenses actually incurred by a witness, such as travel or missed work, is typical.[14]
7. Do not probe further when you receive a favorable answer to a question, especially if the interview is witnessed by a court reporter or other third party. Further inquiry often reveals weaknesses or qualifications, which may impede a favorable settlement. (There are two schools of thought here. One says if you get what you need for settlement, stop. If you need more information later for trial, go back. The other school says get all the information you can at this point—even if it hurts. Ask your supervising attorney for guidance on this one.)
8. Do not give the witness a copy of the statement unless told to do so by the attorney. (It could fall into the opponent's hands.)[15]
9. Use diagrams to aid the witness's explanations.
10. Avoid a witness's tendency to use qualifiers such as "I think," "maybe," and "could have," which weaken a favorable statement.[16]
11. Draft the statement in the best light for the client without being misleading or inaccurate, or substituting the interviewer's vocabulary and grammar for that of the witness.

The statement should be drafted in the following sequence:[17]

1. Begin with a background paragraph to identify the witness, address, date, time, marital status, occupation, and so on. If you use a form such as the Witness Information Cover Sheet, more detailed background is not necessary in the statement.
2. A second section should state the date of the accident, the setting prior to the accident, the witness's purpose in being there, and so on.

3. A third section should describe the sequence of events as observed by the witness (the accident or other occurrence).
4. A fourth section describes what happened following the accident.
5. Conclude with a brief statement to be signed: "I, _____, have read the above statement comprising _____ pages, and it is true to the best of my knowledge. I have initialed each page and sign this in the presence of _____ this _____ day of _____, _____."

If the witness is partial to the client and really wants to help, the statement could be drafted at the office and returned for signature at some later time. Otherwise, it is best to complete the process at the interview.

ILLUSTRATIVE STATEMENT

I am Freda C. Schnabel and I reside at Box 20, Route 328, Legalville, Columbia. I was born on May 16, ____, and am fifty-eight years of age. I am married, have three grown children, and am a housewife. I worked as a department store clerk for eight years.

On February 26, ____, about 7:35 a.m., I was driving my grandchildren to school. We went east on Highway 328. It was a cold, windy day and there were patches of ice along the road. About 20 percent of the highway was covered with ice. Because of the ice, I was driving twenty-five to thirty miles per hour. As we got to Forrester's house, I saw Ms. Forrester crossing the road at a low spot in the highway. We were at a rise in the highway about 250 feet west of the spot where Ms. Forrester was crossing. There is another rise in the highway a little more than 100 feet east from the same low spot. Until the car reaches the top of either rise, the driver cannot see the bottom of the low spot. There are other hills and low spots and some tricky curves on Highway 328 east of the point where the accident took place.

I started to slow down for Ms. Forrester. A white van on the downslope east of Ms. Forrester came on down the hill a ways. I'd estimate its speed to be about forty to forty-five miles per hour. It started to swerve from side to side. Ms. Forrester hesitated, not knowing which way to go. She then headed for my lane, which was the south side of the road. I heard a few squeals of tires as the van veered toward the middle of the road. I heard a thud and saw Ms. Forrester thrown to the side of the road where she landed like a sack of potatoes—very still and limp. The van kept veering left, crossed over my lane and hit a tree.

I pulled my car over to the side of the road near the van. The driver got out of the van. He was limping and had a cut on his forehead. Ms. Forrester was lying face up. She kept screaming, "God help me, it hurts, oh, God, I'm dying, please help me." I told Mr. Forrester to call an ambulance and that I'd stay with his wife. Soon my grandchildren got some blankets to cover Ms. Forrester. She was bleeding at her left side and leg. I remember her left foot pointing inward at an odd angle. The ambulance eventually arrived and took Ms. Forrester and her husband. I offered to stay with the children.

I did get a chance to see the driver of the van a little later at the scene. He appeared tired—his face was pale; he had a five o'clock shadow; his voice was hoarse; and I noticed his clothes were wrinkled.

I, ____, have read the above statement comprising ____pages and it is true to the best of my knowledge. I have initialed each page and sign this in the presence of Terry Salyer, this 3d of September, ____.

The witness should then read the statement. Corrections should be made where needed, and the witness should indicate approval of the correction by initialing the correction. If a major change is required, or one that suggests uncertainty where you do not want uncertainty, the statement may need to be redrafted. This is where a laptop computer and printer could be useful. The witness should initial each page to verify that he or she has read each page, and then sign at the end of the statement. A third party might also sign to indicate that this is the witness's statement and was read and signed in the third party's presence.

Concluding the Interview

You might ask to take a photograph of the witness, which can be helpful in assessing the witness's impact on the jury and in recognizing the witness at a later time. Get a second phone number in case the witness moves or changes jobs. Thank the witness for the assistance and leave a business card. Remind the witness to call you if he or she will be moving or will be gone for any extended period of time, or if additional information is recalled.

After the interview, review your interview notes and check the witness's statement for inaccuracies, typos, and leads that should be followed immediately. Make note of the leads and enter them on your deadline calendar. Unpursued leads can be damaging to the case and embarrassing to the paralegal and the firm, especially if a settlement negotiation or trial is imminent and you realize that the lead should have been followed up months ago.

After reviewing your notes and the witness's statement, summarize the essence of the witness's statement in the appropriate place on the Witness Information Cover Sheet. Place the completed sheet and statement in the client's folder.

PRESERVING EVIDENCE

Learning to preserve evidence is essential for a good paralegal. Techniques for preserving evidence are examined in the following material:

PRESERVING ELECTRONIC EVIDENCE

Electronically stored evidence and, thus, its preservation are extremely important in many types of litigation. The unique nature of such evidence, including the ease with which it is generated, altered, erased, or otherwise corrupted, has created problems for the courts in determining what is good evidence and what should be done to sanction litigants who fail to preserve or, worse, deliberately destroy such evidence. Although the preservation of electronic evidence will be addressed further in discovery, a few words about it here are in order. Even at the initial investigative stage, the paralegal should know that a growing body of case law indicates:

- the duty to preserve electronic evidence commences when
  a. dictated by a specific statute, e.g. Internal Revenue Service and Occupational Safety and Health Administration requirements; or
  b. the party first knew or should have known that the evidence is potentially relevant to pending or future litigation; and
- once commenced, the duty requires a party to prevent the destruction or corruption of that evidence, e.g. implementing strict e-mail policies, suspending routine e-document destruction or alteration procedures, notifying all relevant employees of such a "freeze", and designating a party's employee to coordinate preservation procedures with counsel.[18]

Further, be mindful that simply booting up and accessing data can alter electronic evidence. Therefore, an electronic data preservation (e-discovery) expert may need to be hired. Such a person can make uncorrupted copies of e-mails or other relevant evidence. Once the relevant data is copied, the computers can be put back into daily use. Subsequent to retrieval, the key to preserving the copied evidence is having a chain of custody of the evidence to assure a court and a jury that it is authentic and free from intentional or unintentional tampering. E-discovery experts often offer such chain of custody preservation services.[19] Emerging federal and state rules of civil procedure increasingly govern the preservation of electronic information, particularly in regard to discovery.

The following sections are excerpted from the NALA *Manual for Legal Assistants.*[20]

IDENTIFICATION

Identifying potential evidence is perhaps the most difficult duty of the investigator. An investigator at an accident scene works under certain time constraints before the cleanup activity begins, and there is always a substantial amount of confusion regarding the circumstances of the event as well as the number and variety of people interested in the matter. Police, fire department, and public safety personnel all have responsibilities in any accident involving major property damage or injury to life.

The first step most investigators follow at an accident scene is to preserve that scene as best they can through immediate photography and/or sketches. This frequently requires a quick orientation sketch on which a diagram of the camera angles and distances is plotted. [See Exhibit 3:11.] One technique for creating good proportionate sketches is to carry a quad-ruled tracing paper pad. After a basic sketch with the major geographic features (whether of an intersection or a room) is made, it is torn off the pad and slipped beneath the next sheet. Retrace the major features and add the specific data desired for that sketch. One sketch may be the photo reference sketch; another might be the positions of the vehicles (if it is a traffic collision); and a third may be a clear basic sketch with the data supplied by each percipient witness. That data might include the location of the witness, the first point at which the witness saw each vehicle, and the locations of other vehicles or witnesses. These witness sketches can be amplified by adding trees, shrubs, buildings, parked vehicles and supplemented by the investigator standing where the witness was to determine whether the story of the witness is physically possible. A composite sketch can be used to locate each witness graphically. [See Exhibit 3:12.]

The diagram may be used to record such things as skid marks, significant buildings, vegetation, safety control devices, and the relationships of the objects involved in the incident. At an explosion scene, for instance, where a gas heater is considered to be the origin of the explosion, a photograph including both the thermostat and heater in one picture is desirable, if possible. If not, a sketch must be used to carefully reconstruct that relationship, keying the multiple photographs together with the sketch.

At accident scenes involving automobiles, the locations of the roadways, traffic control devices, visual obstructions (trees, fences, bridges, parked cars), skid marks, point of impact, and positions at rest of the involved vehicles are essential. While photographs can do this to a certain extent, detailed sketches are also necessary. [See Exhibit 3:13.] In extremely important cases, these details should be surveyed by a qualified surveyor to ensure the accuracy and later admissability of the sketch at trial.

Unfortunately, the investigator is rarely able to get to the accident scene before the vehicles are removed. The investigating police department usually makes a diagram of the accident scene, which is attached to the police accident report. Such a report and diagram can be obtained from the police department and will assist the investigator in creating additional sketches. Police departments also sometimes prepare accident reconstruction reports and diagrams that can be excellent resources for scale drawings.

PHYSICAL EVIDENCE

Every time an object is identified as potential evidence, the investigator faces the problems of how to acquire, preserve, and identify it for future reference and retrieval for introduction at trial, and create the foundation for its admissibility. In many cases, the investigator does not have legal title to the evidence he or she wishes to take into custody. Frequently, the ownership of the item is in question, and the propriety of taking custody calls the investigator's judgment to the test. In most cases of doubt, take custody of the documents, objects, or things and leave a receipt indicating the investigator's name and identity and the means by which people can contact the investigator if they wish to exert their ownership rights in the matter. Often police, fire, or safety investigators will be on the scene, and notification can be left with them if they allow the investigator to take possession of the item.

CONTROL AND RETRIEVAL

Possession of the item of evidence carries the responsibility of control and assuring the future identification of the object as being *that very item*. The investigator imposes upon the object some minor but unique marking to allow absolute and unequivocal identification of that particular object as being the one taken into custody on the date and at the time involved. The investigator thus must create a document that details the manner of taking custody and of marking this item for future reference as well as establishing the first step in the chain of evidence, which will terminate with the introduction of the item at trial. Many investigators carry copper wire and lead seals with a sealing tool. The wire is passed around the object, then through the seal. The sealing tool squeezes the seal tightly around the wire and can impress designs, a logo, or numbers on the soft lead. For larger objects, nylon cable-ties can be obtained in a range of sizes. Some objects are too large or unsuitable for such seals, and a unique marking can be engraved on the object; initials and the date are best. Small objects can be placed inside plastic bags or envelopes and sealed with tape on which the date and initials can be written. Any system may be used, so long as it provides a means of distinguishing that one object from all others similar to it and a credible basis for testifying that the object is the one collected as evidence on a given date.

From the time that object is identified as potential evidence, its custody must be substantiated by a document trail showing every transfer of custody from the point of the incident or event to the trial. That chain is based on the investigator or legal assistant creating that first step in proper, ethical, and careful manner and recording each subsequent transfer in detail.

Caveat: Documents pose a special identification and storage problem for the investigator. They are most valuable to the attorney in their unaltered state. . . .

EXHIBIT 3:11 ■ Photograph Index Sketch

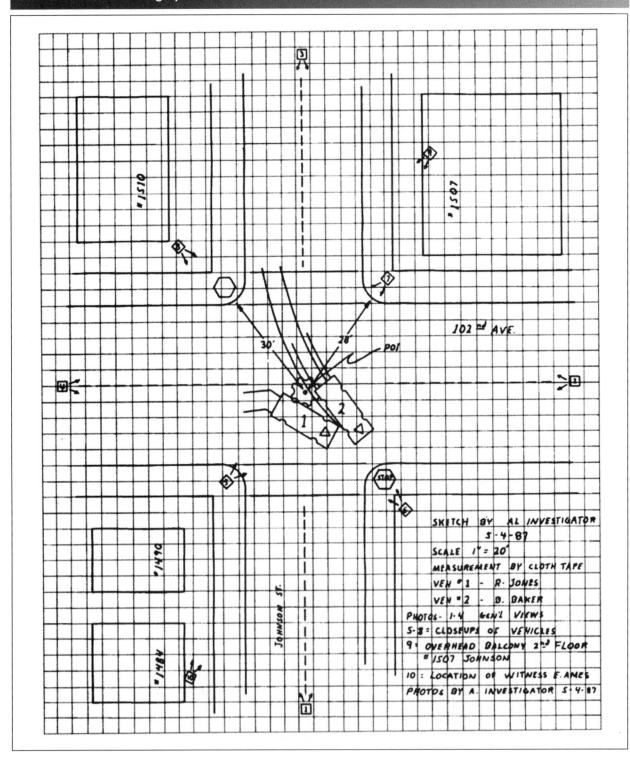

EXHIBIT 3:12 ■ Witness Location Sketch

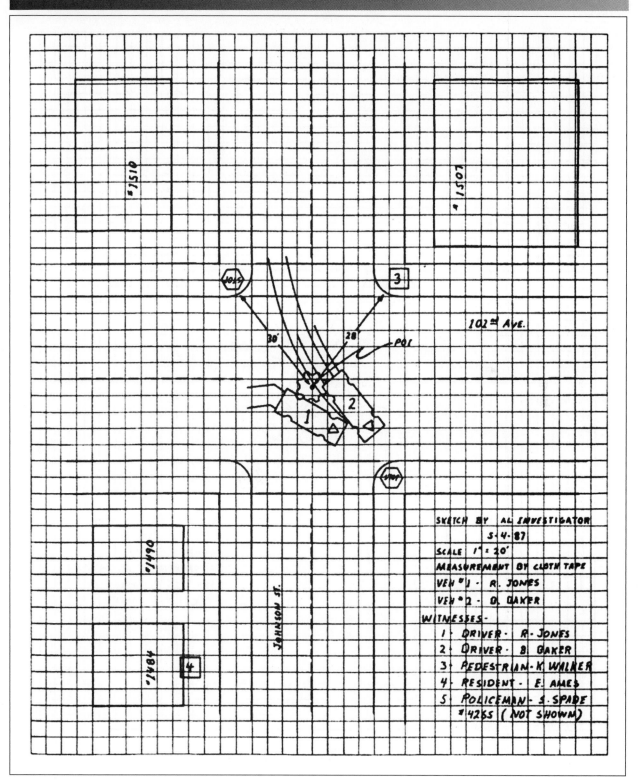

EXHIBIT 3:13 ■ Basic Scene Sketch

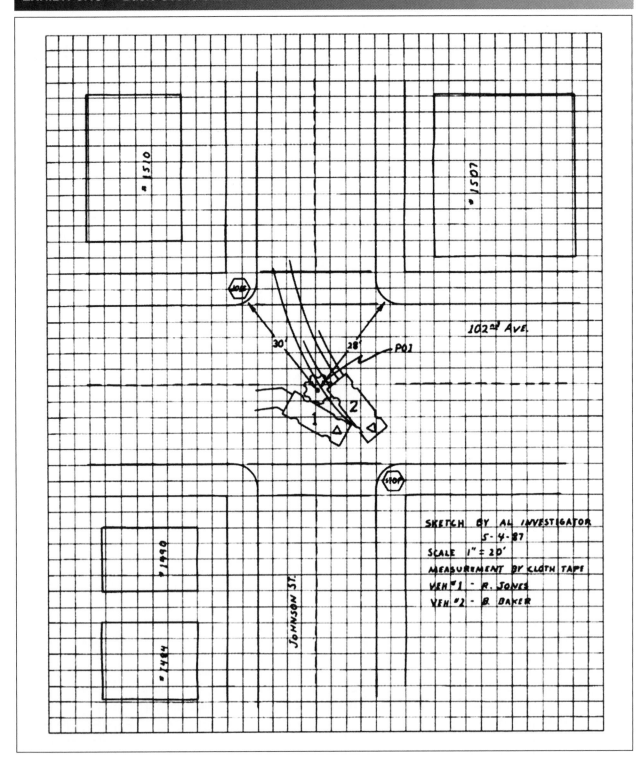

A [good] technique is to place the document in a transparent envelope (or even an opaque paper one) and apply the "EXHIBIT _____" or "ATTACHMENT _____" label to the envelope together with a thorough description of the document (date, document type, author, addressee, topic or title, number of pages, and any attachments), as well as a short statement of the source of the document, the custodian, and the relevance of the document to the case. Alternatively, a "face sheet" can carry this information. A photocopy of the document can be used as a "work copy" during preparation of the case.

Underlining, marginal annotation, or writing on the document cannot be allowed to happen to the *original* document (whether the true original, a duplicate true copy, or a photocopy). *Evidence* must be preserved in the *discovered state*. If a copy is made, it *must be marked as a copy,* preferably with a marginal label "Copy of a document in the file _____vs. _____." This avoids the problem of creating yet another piece of *evidence* that could confuse the future admissability of the original document at the trial. . . .

STORAGE

Once the document or object is in custody, . . . the investigator or the attorney must provide a safe and controlled environment within which the object is stored. Each event between the time of taking custody and its introduction to trial where people wish to examine the object should be recorded in detail to include the date and time, the person authorizing the particular examination or movement, the person benefiting from such activity or movement, the duration, and the return of the object to the place of storage. Anyone taking possession of the object must sign for it with a statement that it will be safeguarded and returned or preserved in the exact same condition. Polaroid photos may be appropriate for memorializing the transfer. A suitable form for controlling evidence is shown in Exhibit 3:14.

TESTING AND EXAMINATION

Often evidence . . . must be tested, examined, or disassembled to validate it as evidence. Sometimes the examination, disassembly, or test will damage or destroy the object. If this situation arises, the attorney will ensure that the adversary and all other parties to the action have an opportunity to have representatives present. The investigator generally is charged with taking custody of the item, removing it to the place of examination, and documenting the steps of the examination. . . . The whole process may be recorded through the use of still photographs, movies, or videotape. The investigator records the presence of all witnesses, including their full identification and their association with their respective parties in the matter. All experts should be fully identified as to name, address, specialty, and employer. Remember, any examination, testing, or disassembly of the item that destroys or changes the physical characteristics of the item and is not accomplished with the knowledge, consent, and participation of all of the parties may prevent the use of any developed information at trial.

SURVEILLANCE AND ACTIVITY CHECKS

Occasionally, there will be a need to verify the activities of certain parties to a lawsuit. This type of investigation is usually done when plaintiffs or claimants

EXHIBIT 3.14 ■ Evidence Log

Evidence Log		
Case:	Event:	
Evidence:		
How Acquired:	Date:	
	By:	
Identifying Marks: By:_____ Date: _____		
Storage Location:		

Custodian	Date	Released To	Date/Purpose

are alleging disabilities that either preclude them from certain activities or limit abilities to perform particular tasks.

Surveillance should be conducted by trained investigators who have the experience and equipment to properly perform this type of investigation.

Sometimes the alleged disabled party can be caught working around the yard or involved in sporting activities with little or no sign of physical limitations. A serious limp that was quite obvious in the doctor's office sometimes can miraculously disappear outside. Videotaped proof of these activities can be later used in the courtroom to raise questions of truthfulness in regard to the alleged disabilities. However, this kind of investigation may be expensive and may yield no useful information.

Divorce and child custody disputes may require "domestic" surveillance. In states where grounds for divorce are required, surveillance may be used to establish the needed evidence to determine certain grounds, such as adultery. Surveillance in child custody cases may yield helpful evidence regarding the fitness of the adverse parent.

Activity checks are usually conducted by talking with neighbors or other persons who make frequent observations of the plaintiff or claimant. Though these checks may provide helpful information, they will often alert the plaintiff or claimant that an investigation is being conducted. For this reason, activity checks should be done as the last or later part of the investigation.

DEMONSTRATIVE EVIDENCE

Demonstrative evidence in the form of sketches, drawings, or surveys created as a means of preserving transitory physical evidence in retrievable form will require a certain amount of documentation for use at future times. The presence of a scale and the date and the name of the person who rendered the drawing is essential. The means and method of making the measurement represented in the drawing will be subject to question and must be supported by the proper foundation. The date of the examination and measurements is essential, particularly if it is different from the date of the event in question. It is helpful to support these drawings with photographs of the same area.

Demonstrative evidence that is a model, a replica, a reconstruction, or an exact duplicate of the object involved in the case requires the same recording of the dates, times, scale, methods of calculation, sizes, and measurements. The accuracy of the representation probably still will be subject to questioning. . . .

Sketches and Drawings

Certain injury litigation cases and regulatory agency actions can benefit from the use of renderings by artists. Medical illustrators are talented at clarifying what otherwise might be very difficult explanations of X rays (even if produced as positives) by converting them into easily understood colored drawings at relatively little cost. Illustrators can show a proposed development or project in simplified (even idealized) form to assist the presentation for permits, zoning actions, and so forth. Models and illustrations are increasingly computer generated.

Photography

Photography is both a blessing and a curse in litigation. It is a truism that almost any photograph related to an event is potentially admissable at trial. The opposite side of the coin is that almost any photograph may be subject to argument over its admissability. The judgment of the person taking the photograph and his or her expertise are always subject to question. The average investigator or legal assistant who chooses to take his or her own photographs rather than to employ professional photographers must be prepared to defend the representations in the photographs. For this reason, many investigators have resorted to snapshots taken with simple, nonadjustable or instant cameras. If the investigator is an expert, he or she understands that the use of an adjustable lens camera that allows shooting wide-angle, normal-angle, and telephoto views of the same scene alters perspective as focal length changes. In order to ensure that the investigator defend the photographic representation, he or she should employ some form of photo log.

For every photograph taken, the focal length, f-stop, film speed, film type, filters, and whether or not artificial lighting equipment was used should be recorded. If possible, each photograph should be related to a sketch indicating the location of the camera and the direction it was pointed to get the view in the photograph. [See Exhibit 3:11.]

The use of filters is arguable at best and difficult to explain to a jury. At worst, the photograph will be excluded. If filters are used, an unfiltered shot of the same view should be made. A great deal of judgment must be exercised by the investigator or legal assistant in deciding whether or not to shoot photographs.

Obviously, if the client is a plaintiff and the accident investigation involves an automobile collision with injury, photographs of the amount of blood spilled in the vehicles may be desirable. If the client is a defendant, gory photographs can be no help at all. It is not enough to take them and destroy them because then the photographs and the destruction must be explained. The skilled legal assistant considers the evidentiary value of each photograph he or she intends to take—both its benefits and its detriments—and then decides whether the benefits outweigh the detriments.

Counsel for plaintiffs often find photographs of bodily injuries very early in the incident are shockingly persuasive to the jury to demonstrate the obvious pain and suffering caused by the injury. It is important to consider the type of camera and film used in making these photographs. For instance, a black-and-white photograph of a person showing massive bruises of an extremely dark nature may be the result of the use of film specially sensitive to the color red and generating a higher contrast than otherwise may be present. Similarly, color photographic film can show red, blue, or green very strongly, depending on the representation desired by the person taking the photograph.

The use of lighting will often have an effect on the photograph. Daylight provides one form of reflected light accepted, while incandescent light tends to throw a warmer red-toned color on the same object. Fluorescent light tends to provide more yellow-green, and flash bulbs, depending on their size and nature, affect the color quality of the image produced. Infrared film can be highly informational in cases involving vegetation growth, decline, and death or in heat gain and loss disputes.

When the investigation begins some time after the incident, a wide variety of sources of photographs should be explored. The police often take photographs, as do fire departments, coroner's officers, and newspapers, wire services, and freelance photographers. The more important, dramatic, and longterm incident produces a veritable flood of photographs to which the legal assistant can gain access. Occasionally, a neighborhood canvass can locate snapshots of the immediate area.

It is always possible, and often desirable, to employ a professional photographer to take selected photographs for specific purposes. They are relatively expensive, but professionals can usually qualify their photos for introduction as evidence. Be specific in the request for the number, sizes, type of film, and views desired. Every photograph should benefit the case or the understanding of the jury.

Do not ignore the possibilities of overhead views obtained through aerial photos from a wide variety of sources. The U.S. Coast and Geologic Survey has a tremendous collection of recent and historical aerial photos in different scales. The U.S. Department of Agriculture, too, uses aerials in its studies. Forestry departments, state and federal highway projects or departments, and city and county public works and planning departments turn more and more to aerial photographs for planning, zoning, and traffic study work. Many have aerial photographs of diverse locations. Any area subject to land management or reclamation probably has been photo-mapped by the U.S. Department of the Interior. These governmental sources generally provide fine, full-frame prints at nominal cost but with a bureaucratic time delay problem. Using private aerial photograph sources often permits enlargements of all of a negative or only a portion, at the lawyer's election. The cost is a little greater for the custom work but is well worth it.

Individually, photographs from an upper-story window or rooftop can be helpful. A photograph from a chartered airplane may be desirable. It is difficult for these photographs to be used to scale, however, and that is one of the major benefits of professional aerial photographs—the exact determination of scale.

PRESERVING RECORDED STATEMENTS

Earlier in this chapter, the use of recording equipment for statement taking was discussed, together with its benefits and hazards. The preservation of the recorded statement is a special problem since it is a form of evidence. A special storage facility for such recordings should be maintained, together with a numbering system, a log, a cross-reference to the case file, and a suspense device to dispose of the recording following resolution of the case. An easy system combines the last two digits of the year, the initials of the investigator, and the number of the tape (an increasing sequential series) to be affixed to the tape.

REVIEWING THE INFORMAL INVESTIGATION

Investigation may continue in its various stages, including continuing to follow leads and gathering documents, right up until trial. After this initial stage of informal investigation, however, the attorney will want a report on how you have progressed. Providing a simple summary of what you have found on each of the elements will accomplish this task. Often the attorney will simply review the file containing the client interview, medical and other records, a description and diagrams of the scene, photos, statements of the witnesses, and any other gathered information. From the review of this information, the attorney can determine whether initial steps toward settlement should be taken and whether a complaint should be filed to start the action. A discussion of settlement practice is reserved for Chapter 10.

SUMMARY

Because a lot of material is covered in this chapter, note the material that is clearly reference material so you can find it in the future as needed. Focus on those concepts and terms that are significant and will be helpful when you are not next to your office computer nor in a law library—when you are talking with a client or out in the field gathering evidence, for example. The study questions at the end of this chapter will help identify most, but not all, of this material.

The purposes of investigation can be summed up as the need to provide your client with the knowledge to make informed decisions and to provide your attorney with the best available evidence to assess and hopefully win the case. Investigation of any type is not likely to be effective, however, without a good grasp of the rules of evidence, what is admissible and what is not, as set out in both the state and federal rules. Generally, evidence must be relevant, which means it must be material and tend to provide or refute a fact of consequence. But even relevant evidence may not be admissible because of its prejudicial or detrimental nature. Unreliable evidence such as hearsay is excluded except when its source or nature suggests reliability.

Understanding the rules of evidence helps you develop a plan for investigation, from understanding the elements of the law that must be proved or refuted to developing a list of likely sources for obtaining information. Learning your ethical responsibilities is extremely important in giving you a mooring in safe harbor at troubling moments. In investigation, a paralegal needs to be thorough, prompt, objective, and honest; must avoid falsehoods, misrepresentations, and the revealing of attorney-client privileged information; and must remain independent in professional responsibility. To do otherwise can jeopardize the case and the attorney's and paralegal's reputations. Consult your supervising attorney before conducting any investigation.

Gathering the evidence requires a knowledge of where to look, the most efficient methods and technologies, and the relationship between the economics of the case and the cost of the investigation. Interviewing witnesses is a critical part of this process and requires diligence, planning, and tact. Drafting a good statement that is an accurate reflection of the witness's point of view is an art that improves with practice.

Finding all the evidence in the world is of little value if you do not know how to preserve it. This can be done by diagramming, photographing, storing, testing, and properly inventorying all evidence. Evaluate the evidence and report to the attorney on what has been gathered so decisions about filing or defending a lawsuit can be made.

▣ WORKBOOK

System Folder Assignments, other exercises, a chapter outline, a review test, and other study aids are located in the accompanying workbook.

▣ HELPFUL WEB SITES

For this chapter, see Exhibit 3:1 and Exhibit 3:2.

▣ QUESTIONS FOR STUDY AND REVIEW

1. What are the purposes of investigation?
2. Why does an investigator need to understand the relationship between investigation and evidence law?
3. Define *evidence law.*
4. Give examples of testimonial, documentary, real, and demonstrative evidence.
5. What is the difference between direct and circumstantial evidence?
6. What requirements must be met for evidence to be admissible?
7. What is relevant evidence?
8. When will relevant evidence not be admissible?

9. What are the rules of evidence (for federal and for your state) governing the following areas?

Character	Hearsay
Habit or routine	Physical evidence
Privilege	Authentications
Requirement of witness to testify	Best evidence
	Judicial notice
Admission of party opponent	Reputation for truthfulness
	Past sexual conduct and past sexual crimes
Lay opinions	
Expert opinion	

10. What indicators suggest computer generated evidence will be relatively easy to authenticate? More difficult to authenticate?
11. Define *preponderance of evidence* and *clear and convincing evidence.*
12. Define *presumption of evidence.*
13. What are some typical sources for the rules of evidence?
14. Why is it necessary to plan an investigation thoroughly?
15. What are the six stages in planning an investigation?
16. What is the purpose of the information in Exhibit 3:1? How do you identify potential sources of information and evidence in a particular case? Review the categories of Web sites in Exhibit 3:2.
17. What are the major methods of investigation, and what should be considered in selecting a particular method?
18. What information should go into a written investigation plan?
19. Discuss the major ethical and related concerns (including attorney's work product) that are particularly applicable to investigation.
20. How should a paralegal gather medical and employment information about the client? What recommendations should be followed?
21. Why is it essential to immediately check documents that have been returned pursuant to the paralegal's request?
22. What procedures should be followed in investigating the scene of an accident?
23. List some good techniques for finding a witness and for finding an expert witness.
24. Why is it important to interview a witness as soon as possible after the accident?
25. What needs to be done to plan a witness interview?
26. Why are the elements of a cause of action important to planning an interview?
27. How does an interviewer gain the cooperation of a witness?
28. Describe useful techniques in interviewing a witness. (Review the appropriate section of Chapter 2.)
29. What are the purposes of taking a statement?
30. How does a paralegal draft a good statement?
31. Why should a paralegal review a statement immediately after it has been taken?
32. Describe the purpose for preserving evidence and some good techniques for preserving evidence.

◉ KEY TERMS

admissible evidence	circumstantial evidence	material	relevant
affirmative defense	clear and convincing evidence	preponderance of the evidence	res gestae statement
attorney's work product (trial preparation materials)	demonstrative evidence	presumption	routine
	direct evidence	probative value of evidence	stipulation
best evidence rule	documentary evidence	proof beyond reasonable doubt	testimonial evidence
burden of proof	habit	real evidence	
chain of custody	judicial notice		

◉ ENDNOTES

1. GRAHAM, FEDERAL RULES OF EVIDENCE IN A NUTSHELL 318 (4th ed. 1996).
2. *Id.*, 320.
3. Edward J. Imwinkelried, *Expert Witness: Rule 702's Reach,* NAT'L L.J., Nov. 20, 2000, A18; FED. R. EVID. 702 advisory committee's note.
4. Gregory P. Joseph, *Federal Practice: Computer Evidence II,* NAT'L L.J., April 5, 1999, B14.
5. *Id.*
6. MCCORMICK, MCCORMICK ON EVIDENCE (5th ed. 1999).
7. Memo from C. Wilson to J. McCord (March 23, 1986).
8. WEINSTEIN, INTRODUCTION TO CIVIL LITIGATION 59 (2d ed. 1986).
9. NATIONAL ASSOCIATION OF LEGAL ASSISTANTS, NALA MANUAL FOR PARALEGALS AND LEGAL ASSISTANTS, 193–195 (4th ed. 2005).
10. *Id.*
11. ALAN E. MORRILL, TRIAL DIPLOMACY 175 (2d ed. 1972).
12. Lay, *A Trial Lawyer Speaks to the Investigator,* 2 PRACTICAL LAWYER 68–81 (1956) (quoted in STATSKY, TORTS: PERSONAL INJURY LITIGATION 151 [1982]).

13. CAROLE A. BRUNO, PARALEGAL'S LITIGATION HANDBOOK 122 (1980).

14. MORRILL, *supra* note 11, 172.

15. BRUNO, *supra* note 13, 123.

16. MORRILL, *supra* note 11, 174.

17. *Id.*

18. Stephen D. Whetstone and Kara A. Millonzi, *Latest 'Zubulake' Ruling Imposes Harsh Sanctions*, NAT'L L. J., Sept. 13, 2004, S3.

19. Sharon D. Nelson and John W. Simek, *Don't Let Electronic Evidence Bury Your Firm*, LEGAL ASSISTANT TODAY, May/June 2004, 62, 66.

20. NATIONAL ASSOCIATION OF LEGAL ASSISTANTS, MANUAL FOR LEGAL ASSISTANTS, 174–183 (2d ed. 1992), reprinted with permission of Delmar Learning, a division of Thomson Learning: http://www.thomsonrights.com.

 For additional resources, visit our Web Site at **http://www.westlegalstudies.com.**

CHAPTER

4

Drafting the Complaint

INTRODUCTION

THE TASK: DRAFT A COMPLAINT

Now that you have gathered some significant evidence through informal investigation, your next task assignment from Mr. White is to draft complaints for the *Forrester* and *Ameche* cases. Mr. White will review and sign the complaints.

Before you draft the complaints for these cases, you will learn the purposes for the complaints, the structure and components of both state and federal complaints of various kinds, how to ensure each complaint states a cause of action, and how to properly include exhibits and appendices. Further, you will practice drafting complaints according to a checklist, learn about pleading for an injunction (another form of action), and continue to expand your litigation system.

Learning to draft effective complaints and similar pleadings is an art; like other arts it takes time and, above all, practice. This art is an important one. If done well, the complaint is succinct, adequate, and permits the action to proceed. If done poorly, the complaint will lead to costly delay, negative impressions of the advocate's ability, and worst of all, dismissal and possible loss of the client's cause of action. Like other skills addressed in this text, learn this one well and your value to the firm and the client increases significantly.

DEFINITION AND PURPOSE

due process of law
Fair, prescribed judicial proceedings that must be followed before a person may be deprived of life, liberty, or property; guaranteed by the Constitution.

The Fifth Amendment and the Fourteenth Amendment to the Constitution of the United States guarantee that a person shall not be deprived of "life, liberty, or property, without **due process of law**." Most civil lawsuits attempt to deprive the defendant of money or other property. Therefore, the procedure used in deciding whether that person will be deprived of that property must meet the requirement of due process. In other words, the procedure must be fair. One way to ensure fairness is to require that all parties be informed of the basis of the lawsuit, initially accomplished through formal documents called pleadings that must be filed in court.

pleadings
Formal documents filed in a lawsuit that inform all parties of the basis for and defenses to the lawsuit; normally include the complaint, answer, counterclaim and reply, answer to cross-claim, and third-party complaint and answer.

Pleadings are formal documents that state and clarify the issues in a case by setting out the claims and defenses of the parties. A variety of state and federal pleadings are allowed by the respective rules of each jurisdiction. Some pleadings are claim pleadings; they state a claim against the other party. These pleadings include the complaint, counterclaim, cross-claim, and third-party complaint. Other pleadings are defense pleadings that respond to the claim and may state defenses. They include the answer, reply to counterclaim, answer to cross-claim, and a third-party answer. Most of these pleadings are discussed in subsequent chapters.

complaint
The formal document used to commence a lawsuit; tolls the statute of limitations, identifies parties, and states the cause of action the plaintiff alleges against the defendant.

The first of the pleadings, and the focus of this chapter, is the **complaint**. The purpose of the complaint is to (1) commence the lawsuit and toll the statute of limitations, (2) introduce the cause of action, (3) invoke the court's jurisdiction, and (4) present the facts, thus (5) informing the defendant about who is suing him or her, for what reason, and for how much money or other award. This gives the defendant "notice" and the opportunity to respond to the allegations and to prepare adequately for trial. Thus, the complaint helps ensure fairness and compliance with procedural due process.

AN EXAMPLE

In preparing to draft a complaint, it is useful to obtain a copy of a previously filed complaint. One can be obtained from another case file, the firm's form file, a previously compiled system folder, or from form books in the law library. Most state rules of civil procedure and the Federal Rules of Civil Procedure provide examples of complaints. Some states and local courts require the use of a specific complaint form.

A sample complaint, with sections labeled for illustrative purposes only, appears in Exhibit 4:1.

EXHIBIT 4:1 ■ Sample Complaint (State)

	STATE OF COLUMBIA CAPITOL COUNTY CIRCUIT COURT
(caption)	MARY E. JOHNSON, Plaintiff v. Civil Action, File No. 00000 ARTHUR HENDRICKS, Defendant JURY TRIAL DEMANDED
	COMPLAINT FOR NEGLIGENCE
	The Plaintiff states that:

(body)	1. The court has jurisdiction in this matter under Section 403A, Title 23 of the Columbia Revised Statutes.
	2. Plaintiff is a paralegal and resides at 43 South Senate Avenue, Legalville, in Capitol County, Columbia.
	3. Defendant is a baker and lives at 500 Maple Street, Legalville, in Capitol County, Columbia.
	4. Defendant owns and operates the Deli Bakery at 508 Maple Street, Legalville, in Capitol County, Columbia.
	5. On August 23, ____, at said bakery, Defendant sold Plaintiff a chocolate eclair, which was negligently prepared containing pieces of glass.
	6. Plaintiff ate said pastry, receiving the following damage:
	   a. Great pain and suffering
	   b. Internal injuries
	   c. Medical and hospital bills
	   d. Loss of income

(prayer for relief)	WHEREFORE, Plaintiff demands judgment in the amount of ten thousand dollars ($10,000), together with the costs and disbursements of this action.
	
	Plaintiff demands trial by jury.
	
	                        _____
	                        Plaintiff's Attorney
	                        407 E. Second Avenue
	                        Legalville, Columbia

(verification)	State of Columbia
	County of Capitol
	Mary Johnson, on oath, deposes and states that she has read the foregoing complaint and that the matters stated therein are true to the best of her knowledge, information, and belief.
	
	                        _____
	                        Mary Johnson
	                        Subscribed and sworn to before me
	                        this 12th day of October, ____
	
	                        _____
	                        Notary Public
	                        My commmission expires: _____

THE COMPLAINT IN DETAIL

CAPTION

The caption of the complaint is the heading that identifies the location of the action, the court, the docket or file number, and the title of the action. The title includes the parties and sometimes the nature of the action (e.g., complaint for negligence). Although the paralegal may be of considerable assistance in determining the court, the parties, and other specifics for the caption, the attorney must make the final decision on such matters.

Rule 10 of the Federal Rules of Civil Procedure designates what must be included in a pleading filed in federal court. Form 1 and subsequent forms in the Federal Rules appendix of forms give recommended examples. Likewise, parallel state and local practice rules and forms should be consulted. If the complaint is to be filed electronically (discussed in Chapter 5), the caption should state "Electronically Filed."

Parties

plaintiff
The party bringing the lawsuit.

defendant
The party being sued for an alleged wrong.

The caption of the complaint must designate the parties to the lawsuit. The parties include the **plaintiff**, the party bringing the lawsuit (suing the other party), and the **defendant**, the party being sued for an alleged wrong. Parties can include individuals, corporations, unincorporated associations, partnerships, government entities, representatives of a person or an estate, and others. A potential defendant whose identity will be learned later in an action can be identified as "John or Jane Doe." Some potential parties may be immune from suit because of sovereign immunity; others might be reachable only through a required administrative procedure, such as in workers' compensation claims; and still others, particularly government agencies, may require notification of a claim or intent to sue before an action can be brought. Strategy issues regarding jurisdiction, venue, who can afford to pay damages, and other matters make the choice of defendant important and occasionally complex.

Real Party in Interest

real party in interest
The one who has the right to sue by law—for example, the injured party or legal representative of that party.

The plaintiff must be a real party in interest [Rule 17(a)]. A **real party in interest** is the one who has the right to sue by law. For example, Columbia state negligence law gives those injured in negligence cases the right to sue to be compensated for their injuries. Therefore, Ms. Forrester is a real party in interest and has the right to sue. In some circumstances the injured party may be unable to sue—for example, a child, or a deceased person. When this situation occurs, the law allows a parent of the child or administrator for the deceased to be the plaintiff. Since these legal representatives have the right to sue by law, they are the real party in interest and can sue in their own names [Rule 17(a)]. The real party in interest requirement simply determines who is the right person or persons to bring a particular lawsuit.

Standing to Sue

standing to sue
Requirement that only plaintiffs who suffer or will suffer real or direct injury may sue.

Standing to sue is a legal concept that allows a plaintiff to pursue a lawsuit only if that plaintiff has suffered or will suffer a direct or actual injury. Our adversarial system of justice requires a party to have such a significant interest in the case that the party will pursue the interest aggressively. This requirement meets the constitutional demand of Article III, Section 2 that courts decide real controversies, not hypothetical ones. For example, Ms. Forrester's sister may suffer anxiety over her sister's injury, but her concern will not normally reach the degree needed to have standing to sue either for her sister's injuries or her own anxiety over the injuries.

Capacity to Sue or Be Sued

A party must have the **capacity** to sue or be sued [Rule 17(b)]. Persons have such capacity unless they are under the age of majority (eighteen in most states), are incompetent, insane, or dead. Although minors and incompetent persons may lack capacity to sue, they can be named as defendants. The law of each state determines whether a person has the capacity to sue. Capacity in the federal courts is determined by the law of the state in which the person resides (domicile). In those cases in which persons do not have legal capacity, they may sue or be sued through a legal representative such as a parent for a minor or a spouse as the representative for the estate of the deceased. If the person does not have a legal representative or needs an independent representative just for the action such as in a child custody case, then a **guardian ad litem** (or "next friend") is appointed by the court [Rule 17(c)]. When a party dies or becomes incompetent during a lawsuit, another party may be substituted as long as it is done within ninety days of notice of the death to the court (Rule 25).

Corporations are considered "persons" under the law, and therefore have the capacity to sue and be sued. Consequently, because Mercury Parcel Service corporately owns the van that caused Ann Forrester's injuries and is also the employer of Richard Hart, it can be sued as a codefendant.

Joinder of Parties

In setting up a complaint, be aware of who should and can be added as parties to a lawsuit, which is governed by federal and state rules. You should consult both while studying this section. The federal rules on **joinder of parties** aim to reduce litigation and protect people's legal rights by including all the parties in one lawsuit who have a legal interest arising out of the same event. If a matter is going to be resolved, it should be resolved in a manner that is just for all concerned; no party of significance should be left out.

Federal Rule of Civil Procedure 19(a) requires joinder when a person is subject to service of process (discussed in Chapter 5) and whose joinder will not deprive the court of jurisdiction, such as where the new party will defeat diversity jurisdiction. Further, joinder is required when it is necessary to grant complete relief to the existing parties, or the party to be joined claims an interest in the action that, if left unaddressed, will leave the interest completely or partially unprotected or is likely to cause any existing party to bear unjust multiple or inconsistent obligations.

If a required party cannot be joined, such as when the party cannot be served or when joinder would defeat diversity jurisdiction, the court must consider whether to dismiss the suit and how dismissal will impact all of the interested parties. For example, failure to dismiss the action may subject the defendant to multiple lawsuits from different plaintiffs in different jurisdictions.

Federal and state rules also allow the joinder of multiple plaintiffs and defendants on a permissive (voluntary) basis. Federal Rule of Civil Procedure 20(a) permits the joinder of any plaintiffs and any defendants when claims for or against the potential parties arise out of the same occurrence and stem from any common questions of law or fact. This rule does not require those joined to have the exact same interest in the lawsuit. For example, Mr. Forrester may join Ms. Forrester's lawsuit, not because he suffered the injuries to his wife, but because he was deprived of his wife's affection and service.

capacity
Requirements of age, competency, and so on, for a party to be allowed to sue or be sued.

guardian ad litem
Representative for a party who lacks the legal capacity to sue or be sued; serves for the duration of the action.

joinder of parties
The uniting of parties making claims or defending against an action as co-plaintiffs or co-defendants.

Joinder is encouraged, and the rules are broadly interpreted to permit it. When joining parties, however, you must consider how adding the new party will impact on jurisdictional matters. When joinder is voluntary, the action will not be dismissed if a party elects not to join a potential party (Rule 21).

As a practical matter, plaintiffs will join defendants to increase the chances of gaining more compensation. Ms. Forrester is much more likely to gain a large sum of compensation from Mercury Parcel, Mr. Hart's employer, than from Mr. Hart himself. The defendant best able to pay damages is frequently called the "deep pocket." Some states, such as Wisconsin, have enacted laws that limit the liability of "deep pockets" according to a threshold percentage of liability or their degree of fault. The U.S. Congress has looked hard at this issue as well. Therefore, check your state and federal law regarding joint and several liability to determine if any limits have been imposed.

Defendants can join other parties as well. This issue is discussed in Chapter 6, which deals with defending a lawsuit.

A 1990 law, 28 U.S.C. §1367, reinforces the authority of federal courts to join cases or parties that have no federal jurisdiction independent of the original federal case. When considering adding such claims or parties, consult this statute and the pertinent Federal Rules of Civil Procedure.

Interpleader

interpleader
The joining of those parties that have the same claim against a third party; done to limit the liability of the third party.

Rule 22, the **interpleader** rule, permits a plaintiff to join as defendants those parties who have claims against the plaintiff when the plaintiff is exposed to multiple liability. For example, if defendant A has a claim to the plaintiff's property as does B, the plaintiff may interplead B as a defendant and let the court decide who gets the property. If done in separate suits, the plaintiff could be found liable to both parties.

In addition to Rule 22, a similar interpleader mechanism is available under 28 U.S.C.A. §1335 (statutory interpleader). If interpleader is being considered, consult this statute for its more liberal diversity amount ($500 instead of $75,000), different venue requirements, and other differences.

Class Actions

class action
A suit by or against an entire class—whose members are too numerous for a joinder—represented by one or a few individuals.

Class actions are permitted under Rule 23. For such actions, one or more members of a class may sue or be sued as representative of the entire class, rather than joinder of all members of the class, if the following elements are present:

- The members of the class are too numerous for joinder.
- There are common questions of law and fact.
- The claims of the representative are typical of those of the class.
- The representative will protect the interests of the class.
- Separate actions would be likely to bring inconsistent results.
- Separate actions might hinder or preclude the action of the other members of the class.
- The adverse party has acted or failed to act in a manner applicable to the entire class.
- A class action is the superior action under the circumstances.

If the elements are met, the court will certify the class and order that the action proceed as a class action. Class actions provide a unique legal mechanism whereby a citizen's relatively small and financially impractical claim can be combined with the claims of similarly wronged parties to make the lawsuit not only practical but also potent. This type of lawsuit has been particularly useful in cases involving securities fraud, antitrust, product liability, and deceptive marketing practices. Class actions have also been used to design workable settlements for large companies facing potentially countless individual lawsuits, particularly in mass product liability cases of national scope. A district court's order granting or denying class action certification can be appealed immediately (interlocutory appeal) rather than having to wait until the trial is concluded [FED. R. CIV. P. 23(f)]. Conflicting court approaches to class action cases and congressional perceptions of abuse led to revisions of Rule 23 (2003) and the passage of the Class Action Fairness Act, which expanded federal jurisdiction (see Chapter 1). See the forms of various types of complaints at the end of this chapter for an example of a complaint for a class action suit.

Intervention

Rule 24 permits a party to intervene in an action either as a plaintiff or as a defendant when specifically permitted by U.S. law; when the action may impede or impair the intervenor's interest, which is otherwise unrepresented by the existing parties; or when the applicant's claim or defense raises the same question of law or fact as the existing claim. Intervention is accomplished by a *motion to intervene* [Rule 24(c)]. If an intervenor can show the requisite interest in the litigation [Rule 24(a)(2)], there is no separate need for the intervenor to establish standing [*San Juan County, Utah v. U.S.*, 420 F.3d 1197 (10th Cir. 2005)].

"Et al."

"Et al." is an abbreviation for the Latin *et alii*, meaning "and others." Rule 10(a) of the Federal Rules of Civil Procedure and parallel state rules require that all parties to an action be listed in the caption. Pleadings that come after the complaint, however, may state the name of the first party on each side followed by the *et al.* abbreviation. This can save paper and time in actions involving numerous parties.

Sample Captions

Here are examples of caption formats for a variety of circumstances and parties. Note that some states require the caption of the complaint to include the addresses of the parties. Consult current local practice, because privacy concerns may limit addresses to city, county, and state only. Add these examples of captions to your system folder.

Example of Caption: State Court

STATE OF COLUMBIA   CAPITOL COUNTY   CIRCUIT COURT

ANN FORRESTER, Plaintiff
      v.   Civil Action, File No. <u>1000</u>
RICHARD HART and
MERCURY PARCEL SERVICE, INC., Defendants

COMPLAINT FOR NEGLIGENCE

(continued)

"The Legislature has the power to decide what the policy of the law shall be, and if it has intimated its will, however indirectly, that will should be recognized and obeyed. The major premise of the conclusion expressed in a statute, the change of policy that induces the enactment, may not be set out in terms, but it is not an adequate discharge of duty for courts to say: We see what you are driving at, but you have not said it, and therefore we shall go on as before."

—OLIVER WENDELL HOLMES, *JOHNSON V. UNITED STATES*, 163 F. 30 (1ST CIR. 1908).

Example of Caption: Federal Court

UNITED STATES DISTRICT COURT FOR THE EASTERN DISTRICT
OF COLUMBIA Civil Action, File Number <u>1001</u>

ANN FORRESTER,

                                 Plaintiff

     v.

RICHARD HART and
MERCURY PARCEL SERVICE, INC.,

                                 Defendants

COMPLAINT

Party Caption for Suit by Minor or Person Under Disability

BARRY SMITH,
a minor by his parents and guardians,
SAMUEL and EDNA SMITH,

                                 Plaintiff

     v.

JOHNSON MOTORS, INC.,

                                 Defendant

Party Caption for Suit by Deceased Person

HAROLD WEBER
Executor of the estate of
[(or) Personal Representative for the Estate of]
MARY WEBER,

                                 Plaintiff

     v.

FRANCIS LONG,

                                 Defendant

Party Caption for Suit by Multiple Parties

SAMUEL HARRIS
       and
IRENE BOND,

                                 Plaintiff

     v.

EDWARD SUMMER,
SPIKES, INC.,
       and
JOHNSON MANUFACTURING COMPANY, INC.,

                                 Defendant

Party Caption for Subsequent Pleading in Preceding Case

SAMUEL HARRIS, et al.,

                                 Plaintiff

     v.

EDWARD SUMMER, et al.,

                                 Defendant

THE BODY OF THE COMPLAINT

Jurisdictional Allegations

As discussed in Chapter 1, jurisdiction is the authority of a court to decide a case and enforce its decisions. Subject matter jurisdiction is the court's authority to hear certain types (subjects) of cases. An allegation of jurisdiction must be included in complaints filed in federal courts, because those are courts of limited subject matter jurisdiction. A plaintiff must demonstrate to a federal court through the jurisdictional allegation that the court has the subject matter jurisdiction to hear the case.

Although the trial courts of most states are courts of general jurisdiction, it is best to allege jurisdiction unless you are absolutely positive that your state rules do not require such an allegation. More than likely, you will need the names and domiciles of the parties, the cause of action and its location, a reference to any controlling jurisdictional state statute, and any jurisdictional amount. This information is stated in the first paragraphs of the complaint.

Since paralegals are often responsible for drafting complaints, they must know the jurisdictional requirements for the pertinent court and take care that the amount or other jurisdictional requirements are properly alleged. The final determination of whether the client's case meets the jurisdictional requirement, and what court the case should be filed in, will be left to the attorney. Nevertheless, it is important to know the jurisdictional fundamentals needed for drafting jurisdictional allegations and for understanding the attorney's choices. A review of these fundamentals as discussed in Chapter 1 may be useful at this time.

Typical formats for allegations of subject matter jurisdiction for a complaint to be filed in federal district court follow:

Jurisdictional Allegation of Diversity

Sample 1

1. Jurisdiction of this court is based on diversity of citizenship and the amount in controversy exceeds the sum of $75,000, exclusive of interest and costs.

Sample 2

1. Plaintiff is a [citizen of the State of Columbia] [corporation incorporated under the laws of the State of Columbia having its principal place of business in the state of Columbia] and defendant is a corporation incorporated under the laws of the State of [Ohio] having its principal place of business in [Ohio] [a state other than the State of Columbia]. The matter in controversy exceeds, exclusive of interest and costs, the sum of $75,000.
Sample 2 is based on Form 2(a) in the appendix of forms of the Federal Rules of Civil Procedure.

Note that diversity for a corporation is based on two locations: the state of incorporation and the state where the corporation has its principal place of business. If either of those locations is the same as that of the opposing party, diversity does not exist.

Jurisdictional Allegation for Federal Question Cases

1. The action arises under [the Constitution of the United States, Article _____, Section _____]; [the _____ Amendment to the Constitution of the United States, Section _____], [the Act of _____, _____ Stat. _____; U.S.C., Title _____ § _____]; [the Treaty of the United States (here describe the treaty)].

The preceding example is based on Form 2(b) in the appendix of forms of the Federal Rules of Civil Procedure. Jurisdictional amount is no longer alleged in federal question cases.

Jurisdictional Allegation for Cases Arising Under Federal Statute

Sample 1

1. The action arises under the Act of ___, Stat. ___, U.S.C., Title ___, § ___.

Sample 2

1. The action arises under the National Environmental Policy Act of 1969, § 102; ___ Stat. 852; 42 U.S.C. § 4332 (1970).

Samples 1 and 2 are based on Form 2(c) in the appendix of forms.

In those states where jurisdictional allegations are required, the following format may be appropriate:

Jurisdictional Allegation for Cases Arising Under State Statute Where Jurisdictional Amount Is Necessary

1. The jurisdiction of this court arises under Section 335, Title 17, of the State Code of Columbia. The amount in controversy exceeds $2,500, exclusive of interest and costs.

Note: In the prior example, it was necessary to allege the $2,500 in order to get into the state circuit court, in this case the highest-level trial court in the state. The sample complaint at the beginning of this chapter contains an example of a jurisdictional allegation for cases arising under state statutes not requiring a jurisdictional amount.

Identification of the Parties

The complaint should state the domicile of the plaintiff and the defendant. Jurisdictions and form books vary on whether "domicile" requires you to include the complete address of the parties or simply the city, county, and state. The following examples include addresses:

---

2. Plaintiff resides at 301 South Short Street, in the City of Legalville in the County of Capitol in the State of Columbia.

3. Defendant resides at 5130 West North Avenue, in the City of Lancaster in the County of Capitol in the State of Columbia.

In some jurisdictions it is necessary to state the names and addresses of the parties in the complaint to demonstrate that the court has proper venue. This is true if venue is to be based on the convenience of the parties. If venue is to be based on the location of the incident precipitating the lawsuit, then that location (state, city, and county) must be made clear in the body of the complaint. In the federal system, proper venue does not have to be alleged in the complaint; it is considered a matter for the defendant to raise.[1] Venue may be waived by the defendant; jurisdiction may not be.

Allegations (Cause of Action)

Introduction

The allegation section is the heart of the complaint. It states the *claim upon which relief may be granted*, often called the **cause of action**. The writing of this section of the complaint is critical to the initial success of the plaintiff's lawsuit, for if it is not done correctly, either the action will be dismissed or the complaint will have to be amended.

cause of action
Statement of the claim upon which relief may be granted in an action.

What Must Be Alleged

The specific answer to what must be alleged lies in the law of each jurisdiction. It would be comforting to all of us if drafting an adequate body of a complaint were an exact science. Unfortunately, an adequate complaint often depends on the history of pleadings in a particular jurisdiction, that is, the case law on adequate pleading and the rules of civil procedure for the pertinent court. Therefore, regardless of the specific points to be covered here, it is absolutely essential that you become familiar with what is acceptable in the court in which the action will be filed. Reviewing copies of successful pleadings previously filed in that court can be helpful, but researching the rules of procedure and the case law applicable to that particular court is preferable. Regardless of the differences among jurisdictions, some factors are applicable to most complaints.

Think of the claim as a syllogism.[2] A syllogism is a logical formula for an argument based on three parts: a major premise, a minor premise, and a conclusion. The major premise is the rule of law. It is stated like this: if A, B, and C exist, then the plaintiff is entitled to relief X. The minor premise consists of the facts to support the rule of law: that A, B, and C exist. Then the conclusion is: since A, B, and C exist, the plaintiff is entitled to X. Let us look at this from the perspective of a negligence case.

The rule of law or major premise in a negligence case would develop this way: if (A) there is a duty to the plaintiff, (B) a breach of that duty occurred, (C) injury or damage to the plaintiff resulted, and (D) the breach of duty was the substantial cause of injury, the plaintiff is entitled to compensation for the resulting damages.

In order to have in mind the major premise underlying a successful complaint, *you must know the applicable rule of law for the claim and each element of that rule of law* (duty, breach, injury, etc.). Chapter 2 discussed how you can research the elements of the rule of law in jury instruction books, legal encyclopedias, and the particular statute involved.

The minor premise in the syllogism is that A, B, and C exist. In terms of a negligence action, it is stated as follows: (A) the defendant was operating a motor vehicle on the highway and had a duty to drive safely; (B) the defendant drove negligently by speeding, failing to keep proper lookout, and failing to keep his vehicle under control; (C) the plaintiff suffered several broken bones, internal injuries, and considerable pain; and (D) the plaintiff's injuries were substantially caused by the defendant's breach of duty (allowing his vehicle to strike her). In brief, these facts support the allegation that A, B, C, and D exist. In other words, *you must state facts to satisfy each element of the rule of law*. These facts must be alleged in the body of the complaint, for if the alleged facts can be proven to exist through evidence presented by the plaintiff at trial, then the minor premise is established, bringing the syllogism to its conclusion (the designated relief to the plaintiff). Should the drafter carelessly omit facts needed to support one of the required elements of the rule of law, the syllogism is incomplete, and the complaint is defective and subject to dismissal.

Keep in mind that the major premise—the rule of law and each of its elements—is not stated in the body of the complaint. Its function is to determine what facts must be alleged in the complaint and what remedy is available. The complaint drafted with an understanding of these logical and necessary relationships will be a superior complaint.

Guidelines and Techniques for Drafting the Body of the Complaint

In addition to thinking through the legal syllogism, there are several other guidelines and techniques that you should have in mind before drafting the body of the complaint.

- Be aware of any applicable court rules that because of privacy concerns restrict the personal identification information that can be stated in a complaint, pleading, or other court document. Federal and parallel state and local practice impose the use of only the last four digits of a social security number; the initials of minors; the year of birth (no specific date); and city, county, and state of the home address. Federal court policy on privacy is at http://www.privacy.uscourts.gov. Proposed Federal Rule of Civil Procedure 5.2 incorporates the policy on privacy (Dec. 2007).

- Be clear and concise. Get to the point quickly, state it simply, and eliminate all unnecessary words and phrases. Avoid archaic, redundant, and obscure legalese. Do not get caught in the trap of perpetuating the obscure language found on many legal forms and documents. Judges, juries, and others will read the complaint or hear it being read. If it is unnecessarily wordy or obscure, it will waste time and be a source of irritation for those people you want on your client's side.

- Which of the following would you rather read?

Complaint Example 1
Comes now the above named plaintiff, by his attorney, Albert Grey, for his complaint, respectfully shows to the court and alleges as follows: At all times hereinafter mentioned, Plaintiff was and still is a resident of Legalville, Columbia, residing at 201 Short Street.

Complaint Example 2
Plaintiff resides and has resided in the City of Legalville in the County of Capitol in the State of Columbia.

Several good books on plain English and effective legal writing are: Wydick's *Plain English for Lawyers*, Good's *Mightier Than the Sword*, Goldfarb and Raymond's *Clear Understandings*, Stark's *Writing to Win: The Legal Writer*, and Garner's *Elements of Legal Style*.

- Use brief, numbered paragraphs. Short paragraphs are best for the sake of clarity, and the numbers provide easy reference. Avoid complex, run-on paragraphs by limiting each paragraph to a single idea.
- Be an advocate when drafting. Strive for language that is assertive, persuasive, evokes sympathy for the client, and conveys a confident attitude toward the claim. "The Plaintiff was hit by the van" is colorless and evokes little emotion. "The van struck the Plaintiff, throwing her to the side of the road" would be a more assertive statement. On the other hand, do not overdo it. You do not want to sound phony or theatrical.
- Avoid impertinent, scandalous, or immaterial language. A complaint is not to be used for harassment or any other improper purpose (Rule 11). If language is improper, it subjects the complaint to attack and the inappropriate language will be stricken [Rule 12(f)]. Furthermore, the use of such language makes suspect the motive of the plaintiff and the judgment of the law firm.
- Organize the paragraphs of the complaint so that they flow logically. A complaint should tell an interesting, chronological story. One paragraph should lead into the next. This order not only makes the complaint read more smoothly, but also enhances clarity and effectiveness.
- Reveal no more of the facts than necessary. Your client gains no advantage by having the complaint reveal too much. To do so may simply show weaknesses or contradictions in the case, or even suggest defenses to the opposition.
- Do not state evidence or conclusions. It is not the purpose of the complaint to prove the case. Allegations such as "The Defendant had 300 feet in which to avoid the accident, according to skid marks, but did not apply his brake until only 100 feet were left" do not belong. A conclusion such as "Defendant breached his duty of care" is excluded because it serves no useful function other than possibly to prejudice a jury. Some conclusions such as "Defendant negligently operated the vehicle" have been accepted as useful to a general understanding of the specific cause of action. Regardless, including evidence or conclusions will make the body of the complaint intolerably long-winded as well as subject to attack. Stick to alleging the facts.
- Be truthful. Keep in mind at all times when drafting pleadings that the supervising lawyer is under a serious ethical responsibility of truthfulness and can be severely disciplined for pleadings that reflect a disregard for the truth. Model Rule 3.3(a)(1) of the American Bar Association's Model Rules of Professional Conduct, which has been adopted by most states, requires truthfulness in pleadings.
- When the truth of the matter is uncertain but there is some basis for a statement, make the statement on the basis of information and belief. For example: "On information and belief, Defendant Hart was an employee of the Mercury Parcel Service at the time of the accident."
- Do not anticipate defenses. When the facts of a case may raise defensive issues, such as contributory negligence, payment of the debt, or self-defense, the complaint should not include any direct attempt to address those concerns. An allegation that "Plaintiff did not fail to keep a lookout prior to crossing the street" or "Plaintiff was exercising due care for her safety at all times prior to the accident" are subjects to be raised by the defendant and not the plaintiff.

- When there is uncertainty or alternative parties or causes, that uncertainty is permissible in the complaint. Suppose a piece of rodent was found in some corn served to a customer at a restaurant. The culprit could be the packager of the corn or the server of the corn. An acceptable allegation in the complaint would be: "Defendant City Cafe or Defendant Green Grower Canning Company negligently or willfully allowed animal remains to be mixed with corn served to the Plaintiff at said cafe, causing Plaintiff to become violently ill."
- Do not state the law. It is not the function of the complaint to serve as a vehicle to argue the law or to cite cases in support of the client's case. The law, however, should appear in the complaint in the following instances: if the action is brought pursuant to the specific provisions of a particular statute, administrative rule, or ordinance; and if the action is brought in one state and the plaintiff is relying on the law of another state.
- It is better to state the various types of damages incurred by the plaintiff in one concise paragraph as opposed to several wordy paragraphs when permitted by the rules of the particular jurisdiction.

> As a consequence of Defendant's negligence and the aforesaid resulting injuries, the Plaintiff has incurred, and will incur, substantial monetary losses for hospital and medical care, loss of income and benefits, and property damage.

The law in some jurisdictions, however, requires that each type of damage be stated separately and in detail, including the specific part of the body that was injured. The rules on damages do differ and need to be consulted. One must be careful as well to allege damages in an amount sufficient to meet any jurisdictional amount.

- State separate claims or theories for claims in separate counts: Count One for negligence, Count Two for breach of warranty, and Count Three for battery. Each count will have its own separate body of allegations, damages, and demand for judgment. Information alleged in the introductory paragraphs or that would be repeated from Count One, may be incorporated in the other counts. For example:

COUNT THREE

Plaintiff hereby incorporates by reference the allegations contained in paragraphs 1 through 7 of Count One.

Fact (Code) Pleading

fact pleading
The requirement that the body of a pleading state in detail the facts in support of each element of the rule of law or claim.

Columbia, as is true of a number of other states, requires **fact pleading.** The body of the complaint must state the ultimate facts (the minor premise) in support of each element of the rule of law or claim (the major premise). In other words, sufficient detail must be alleged to tell the defendant the basis of the complaint. The difficulty in this type of complaint is knowing what is enough without unnecessarily revealing too much. The answer to this dilemma lies in the experience, rules, cases, and statutes of the particular jurisdiction in which the claim will be filed. An example of an adequately alleged claim for Columbia follows. The labels on the left side of the page are for your guidance and are not part of the complaint. **Note:** Some jurisdictions use Roman numerals to number the paragraphs in the complaint.

Sample Allegation Section of a Negligence Complaint for a Fact Pleading State

date/time duty/conditions venue connection to other defendants	**4.** On February 26, _____, at approximately 7:30 A.M., Defendant Hart was operating a motor vehicle on a hilly and partially icy section of Highway 328 about three miles west of the City of Legalville, County of Capitol, in the State of Columbia. Defendant Hart was driving a vehicle owned by Defendant Mercury Parcel Service for whom Hart is an employee and for whom he was working at all times in the course and scope of his employment.
breach of duty alternative theories	**5.** Defendant Hart operated his vehicle in a negligent manner and without regard for Plaintiff by: (a) operating the vehicle at an excessive rate of speed under the circumstances; (b) failing to exercise a proper lookout and attentiveness; (c) failing to exercise adequate control of said vehicle; and (d) otherwise failing to exercise due and adequate care under the circumstances.
substantial cause of injury	**6.** As a direct consequence of Defendants' negligence, Plaintiff was struck down and seriously injured by Defendants' vehicle as she was walking south across Highway 328.
injuries	**7.** As a result of said negligence, Plaintiff suffered fractures of the left leg and hip; damage to the lower spine; torn muscles, tendons, tissue, and nerves; insomnia; inability to walk; confinement to a wheelchair; intense depression; and other maladies; all of which, now and in the future, will cause her intense pain, great suffering, and considerable inconvenience.
damages	**8.** As a consequence of Defendants' negligence and the aforesaid injuries, the Plaintiff has incurred and will incur the loss of considerable sums of money for hospital and medical care, loss of income and benefits, property damage, and domestic expenses.

[Compare to the traditional allegation of damages in paragraphs 8–10]

Alternative

medical expenses (damages)	**8.** As a further consequence of the injuries, Plaintiff has been and will continue to be obligated to pay large sums of money for medical and hospital bills.
other damages	**9.** As a result of these injuries, Plaintiff has and will continue to be unable to fulfill her daily duties and will be unable to do so for an indefinite time, to her loss.
other damages— loss of income	**10.** As a further consequence of Defendants' negligence, Plaintiff has been unable to pursue her regular or any other employment and will be unable to do so for an indefinite period of time causing her considerable loss of income and benefits. The allegations above are for illustrative purposes only and do not exhaust other possible causes of action against the defendants.

Notice Pleading

The Federal Rules of Civil Procedure, which have been adopted by many state jurisdictions, require a briefer form of pleading called **notice pleading.** One purpose of notice pleading is to eliminate some of the uncertainty and resulting litigation concerning what factual allegations are sufficient. Notice pleading simply informs the defendant of the claim and the general basis for the claim (notice). Rule 8(a) of the Federal Rules of Civil Procedure states that the body of the complaint must contain "a short and plain statement of the claim showing that the pleader is entitled to relief."

notice pleading
Abbreviated form of pleading authorized by the Federal Rules of Civil Procedure and parallel state rules.

Rule 8(c)(1) states: "Each averment of a pleading shall be simple, concise, and direct. No technical forms of pleadings or motions are required." Form 9 in the Federal Rules sets out the necessary allegations. The following is based on Form 9:

Sample Allegation Section of Negligence Complaint for Federal or Other Notice Pleading Jurisdiction

2. On February 26, _____, on Highway 328 in Capitol County, Columbia, Defendant negligently drove a motor vehicle striking down Plaintiff who was then crossing Highway 328.
3. As a result, Plaintiff fractured her left leg and hip bones and was otherwise seriously injured. She has been prevented from transacting her business, and has suffered and will continue to suffer great physical and emotional pain. In addition, she has incurred and will continue to incur expenses for medical attention and hospitalization in the sum of $750,000.

Note: Despite the brevity of the body of the complaint, there are effective allegations on each essential element of the syllogism.

Some specialized rules on pleading are found in parts of Rules 8, 9, and 10. Most notably, Rule 9 on "pleading special matters" requires the equivalent of fact pleading (pleading specifically and with particularity) in cases of fraud or mistake. Failure to do so may result in the opponent asking the court to dismiss the case.

REMEDIES AND THE PRAYER FOR RELIEF (DEMAND FOR JUDGMENT)

Following the allegation section, the complaint should contain a prayer for relief (demand for judgment), which is commonly referred to as the "wherefore" clause. This clause demands that judgment be entered for the plaintiff and that relief be granted accordingly.

Some of the typical remedies that the plaintiff may demand are damages, recovery of property, injunctions, and specific performance.

general damages
Damages that are a natural and direct result of the defendant's wrong, such as pain and suffering, humiliation, and loss of enjoyment of life.

1. Damages are sums of money awarded to compensate the plaintiff for a variety of injuries and losses. **General damages** are those damages that are a natural and direct result of the defendant's wrong and the resulting injury—for example, pain and suffering or emotional trauma. General damages do not have to be pleaded in the complaint in order to prove them at trial. Pain and suffering, emotional distress, and loss of consortium are frequently grouped under the term noneconomic damages. About half of the states now have caps (upward limits) on the monetary amount that can be awarded a plaintiff. A few state high courts have declared such caps unconstitutional.

special damages
Damages that are incurred because of the defendant's wrong and the actual result of the injury, but not the necessary result, such as medical bills, lost wages, or property loss.

Special damages are damages that are incurred but do not necessarily follow from the defendant's wrong. For example, pain is the natural and direct consequence of being struck (general damage), but one does not necessarily incur hospital bills for being struck, so the hospital bill would be a special damage. It is the result of the injury but not necessarily the natural result. Other special damages could be doctors' fees, loss of income, loss of profits in a contract situation, and property damage. Special damages must be specifically alleged in most jurisdictions, including the federal courts.

Exemplary (punitive) damages are damages awarded to the plaintiff when the defendant's conduct is particularly aggravated, malicious, or reckless. Such damages are designed to punish the wrongdoer and to deter similar conduct. For example, if a manufacturer sold a product which it knew could cause serious injury because of a defect, an injured party could receive exemplary damages. The award is in addition to all other damages. Some states have enacted laws placing caps on punitive damages, as well as noneconomic damages.

Because some punitive damage awards have been excessive, questions regarding the fundamental fairness of punitive damages have attracted considerable legislative and judicial attention. In *State Farm Mutual Auto Ins. Co. v. Campbell*, 123 S.Ct. 1513 (2003) the Court reiterated that, as a matter of due process, punitive damages are constitutional if they are reasonable. The key factors include the degree of reprehensibility of the relevant conduct, the ratio of punitive to compensatory damages (usually should be a single digit ratio), and sanctions (such as criminal penalties) for comparable misconduct. Watch for the U.S. Supreme Court decision due in *Phillip Morris v. Williams* (No. 05-1256). This decision will further test the criteria for punitive damage stated in *State Farm* and may include a decision on whether a court can impose large punitive awards for reprehensible conduct that impacts on persons other than the defendant.

2. Recovery of property is a remedy available to a plaintiff when property has been wrongfully taken, transferred, sold, or otherwise kept from its rightful owner. In such cases, the property may be seized (attached) by the court and returned to the rightful owner. The eviction of a tenant is an example of a recovery of property remedy.

3. Injunctions are remedies designed to prevent future harm and, in some cases, correct past harm. **Prohibitory injunctions** order the defendant to refrain from a specific course of conduct, and **mandatory injunctions** require the defendant to continue or take some course of conduct. For example, an ornate fence divides the property of two new residents of a subdivision. Neighbor A wants the fence torn down, claiming it to be his fence. Neighbor B loves the fence and wants it to remain. Owner B can get an injunction against A ordering A not to tear the fence down until it can be determined who owns it. Injunctions are discussed in more detail at the end of this chapter.

4. **Specific performance** is a remedy unique to contract law. Instead of granting damages when a breach of contract occurs, the court can require the offending party to live up to the specific terms of the contract regarding a unique piece of property. If one party agrees to sell an original painting and then reneges, damages are of little value to the party who wanted the painting. In this case, the court may require the seller to surrender the painting called for by the contract.

Rule 8(a) of the Federal Rules of Civil Procedure requires a demand (wherefore) clause. Should a complaint contain more than one claim or count, each count needs to have a separate "wherefore" clause. The plaintiff is not bound by the relief requested if it is inappropriate or inaccurate as revealed later in trial. The court, however, may not grant the plaintiff more than that requested in the complaint if the defendant defaults (fails to oppose the action) according to Rule 54(c). It is good practice to add a catchall phrase such as the one at the end of the following sample prayer for relief.

exemplary (punitive) damages
Damages awarded to a plaintiff beyond actual loss as punishment for conduct of the defendant that is particularly aggravated; also called punitive damages.

prohibitory injunction
Order that informs a defendant to refrain from a specific course of conduct.

mandatory injunction
Requirement that the defendant perform conduct specified by the court.

specific performance
In breach of contract cases, the requirement of the offending party to fulfill specific terms of the contract regarding a unique piece of property.

> ### Sample Prayer for Relief (Demand)
>
> WHEREFORE plaintiff demands judgment against defendant in the sum of seven hundred and fifty thousand dollars ($750,000), together with the costs and disbursements of this action and for such other relief as the court deems just and equitable.

A BRIEF GUIDE TO CAUSES OF ACTION AND REMEDIES

Knowing what elements to allege and what remedies to claim is essential to drafting complaints. Exhibit 4:2 contains a brief guide to the common causes of action and their respective remedies.

EXHIBIT 4:2 ■ Causes of Action and Remedies[3]

Breach of Contract

In any type of contract action, the existence of the contract and the type of contract must be proven. The law recognizes three types of contracts.

1. Oral contracts

In the complaint, the plaintiff must allege the terms of the contract including the consideration for the contract.

2. Written contracts

The plaintiff must allege the terms of the contract or attach a copy of the contract to the complaint as an exhibit.

3. Implied contracts

An implied contract may exist when, despite no formal agreement, the actions of the parties cause the court to find that a contract exists. For example, a person operating a restaurant may be found by the court to have an implied contract to provide the public with healthy, wholesome food. If the patrons in the establishment are suddenly struck with hepatitis, a suit for breach of this implied contract may result.

In a suit of breach of implied contract, the following facts must be alleged in the complaint:

— The performance by the plaintiff of the contract terms or the excuse for his [or her] nonperformance;
— The facts which caused the defendant to fail to fulfill his [or her] part of the contract; and
— The damages suffered by the plaintiff as the result of the defendant's nonperformance.

Remedies available

- *General damages:* Compensation for the injuries suffered by the plaintiff directly stemming from the defendant's breach.
- *Special damages:* Compensation for the "out-of-pocket" expenses suffered by the plaintiff due to the breach, such as loss of earnings, medical expenses, and injury to property.
- *Attorney's fees:* Attorney's fees are available in any contractual action if called for under the terms of the contract.
- *Costs of suit:* Costs of suit are available in any action at the discretion of the court.
- *Liquidated damages:* Some contracts include in their terms a "liquidated damages" provision, spelling out specific sums payable by a party upon breach of the contract. These provisions may have an effect on the damages awarded to the plaintiff.

EXHIBIT 4:2 ■ Causes of Action and Remedies[3] (*continued*)

- *Exemplary damages:*   Recently, some state courts have recognized and approved the award of exemplary or punitive damages in a breach of contract case, if the breach is found by the court to have been "willful or malicious." Exemplary damages are awarded by the court to punish the defendant because of the particularly reprehensible nature of his actions.
- *Prejudgment interest:*   Some contracts have provisions for the payment of interest by the defendant on any sums which are to be found due and owing to the plaintiff.

Anticipatory Breach of Contract

If one party to a contract unilaterally repudiates the contract before the time of performance, the injured party may either:

- Wait until the time for performance of the contract, and bring suit for breach of contract; or
- Bring immediate suit for anticipatory breach of contract.

The defendant's repudiation of the contract may take one of two forms: (1) Expressed, when defendant's repudiation is clear, positive, and unequivocal; or (2) Implied, when the actions of the defendant make performance of the contract impossible.

An example of this cause of action would be a farmer who contracts with a laborer to plow [a] field on a given date. Prior to the date of the plowing, the laborer communicates to the farmer [a refusal to] plow the field (expressed anticipatory breach), or the farmer learns that the laborer will be out-of-town on the date set for the plowing (implied anticipatory breach). In either of the [these] instances, the farmer will have a cause of action for anticipatory breach of contract. In bringing suit for anticipatory breach of contract, all the following elements must be pled:

- Existence of a contract;
- The actions of the defendants which caused the anticipatory breach;
- That these actions happened before the time of performance of the contract;
- That the plaintiff has performed his duties under the contract; and
- That plaintiff has been injured by the actions of the defendant.

Remedies available

The following remedies are available in an action for anticipatory breach of contract:

- *Compensatory damages:*   The measure of the compensatory damages is the amount that will fully compensate the plaintiff for the damages caused by the breach, or that will result from the breach in the ordinary course of events.
- *Future damages:*   The plaintiff is entitled to any damages that he may foresee as the result of the breach, but only at their present value.
- *Limitation on damages:*   The damages awarded for anticipatory relief are limited to "reasonable damages." No punitive or exemplary damages may be awarded, nor can the plaintiff receive a greater amount than he [or she] would if the contract had been performed.

Specific Performance

The remedy for a cause of action for specific performance is a court order that the contract in question be performed exactly as it was written and negotiated. This remedy is not available for the following types of contracts:

- Personal service contracts;
- Contracts to employ another;
- Contracts for acts which the party charged with performing the act has no legal power to do at the time of the contract. An example of this bar would be a contract to sell a piece of property before the selling party had in fact purchased it; and
- Agreements to obtain the consent of a third party.

(continued)

EXHIBIT 4:2 ▪ Causes of Action and Remedies[3] (*continued*)

The elements making up the specific performance cause of action are:

- Existence of the contract;

As well as containing the elements listed in [Breach of Contract], the complaint must also state that performance of the contract was possible for both parties.

- That the plaintiff has performed his [or her] duties under the contract;
- That the defendant has failed to perform his [or her] duties under the contract; and
- That the plaintiff has an inadequate remedy at law. This means that an award of money will not compensate the plaintiff for the damages suffered. It is this element that separates a cause of action for specific performance from a cause of action for breach of contract.

Remedies available

The following remedies are available in an action for specific performance:

- In general:
— An order for performance of the contract; and
— An adjustment for the losses suffered by the parties because of the delay in performance.

- In actions involving real property:
— Rents and profits which would have accrued to the plaintiff had he obtained the property under the contract;
— The buyer of real property may be awarded interest on any money deposited in escrow;
— The seller of real property may be awarded interest on any money he would have received had the property been bought; and
— The seller may recover the upkeep expenses of the property, such as taxes and insurance costs.

- Injunctive relief.

Injunctive relief is an order by the court that an action be done or to prevent someone from performing a specified action.

Contractual Reformation

Contractual reformation is a request to the court to change the terms of a contract because of an error made by the parties. The elements to prove this cause of action are:

- Existence of the contract;
- The mistake which arose between the parties; and
- The grounds for the reformation which include:

— Mutual mistake of fact; or
— Fraud, which occurs when one party falsely represents that modifications will be made to the written agreement conforming with the original agreement between the parties.

Remedies available

The sole remedy for a cause of action for contractual reformation is correction of the error made in the contract.

Rescission

This action calls upon the court to cancel a contract on any of the following grounds:

- The agreement was made under a mistake of fact or law;
- That the party requesting the rescission was mentally incompetent;

EXHIBIT 4:2 ■ Causes of Action and Remedies[3] (continued)

- That there was a material breach of the contract;
- That all parties to the contract agreed to the rescission;
- That the agreement was induced by fraud, duress, menace, or undue influence; or
- That the contract was unlawful or against the public interest.

The elements which must be pled in the complaint are:

- Existence of a contract;
- The grounds for the rescission as listed; and
- That the plaintiff suffered a material injury.

Remedies available

The following remedies are available in an action for rescission:

- *Implied damages:*   This remedy includes the repayment of any contractual consideration provided by the plaintiff and all incidental damages that may have been suffered as the result of the contract.
- *Attorney's fees:*   In a rescission action, the court may award attorney's fees, even if not called for in the contract.
- *Exemplary damages:*   These may be awarded if it is found that the defendant fraudulently induced plaintiff to enter into the contract.

Quantum Meruit (Unjust Enrichment)

This cause of action arises when the defendant fails to pay for goods or services supplied by the plaintiff at the request of the defendant. The elements necessary to plead this cause of action are:

- The defendant requested plaintiff's performance;
- The plaintiff performed the services requested:
- The services rendered by the plaintiff had a fair and reasonable value; and
- The defendant(s) failed to pay for the goods or services rendered.

Remedies available

The following remedies are available in an action for quantum meruit:

- Damages equal to the value of the goods and services rendered;
- Special damages, which include the costs incurred by plaintiff in attempting to enforce the contract;
- Attorney's fees;
- Costs of suit; and
- Liquidated damages, if called for in the contract.

Negligent Torts Causes of Action

The types of torts in this classification include the following:

- Personal injury
- Wrongful death
- Attorney malpractice
- Medical malpractice
- Infliction of emotional trauma
- Wrongful termination

In any negligent tort, the following elements must be pled:

- The existence of a duty owed by the defendant to the plaintiff

There is no hard and fast rule for determining the existence of a duty. The general rule is the question: how would a "reasonable" person have acted in the role of the defendant? If this reasonable person would have

(continued)

EXHIBIT 4:2 ■ Causes of Action and Remedies[3] (*continued*)

performed differently than the defendant and would have taken steps to prevent or lessen the injury suffered by the plaintiff, then a duty exists for the defendant to act in the same manner.

- Breach of the duty
- Plaintiff suffered an injury caused by defendant's breach of duty

Remedies Available in a Negligent Tort Action

In any negligent tort action, the plaintiff may recover the following:

- *Compensatory damages:* The plaintiff may recover damages for the detriment suffered as a result of the defendant's negligent conduct.
- *Lost earnings:* Plaintiff may recover any wages lost because of the defendant's negligent conduct. The amount of lost earnings to be awarded to the plaintiff is based upon the plaintiff's possible future earnings, not past income.
- *Lost profits:* This remedy is available when it can be proven that the plaintiff had a reasonable expectation of earning profits based upon prior earnings.
- *Injury to personal property:* The plaintiff can be awarded damages based upon the damage and the loss of use of personal property.
- *Personal injuries:* The plaintiff can recover damages to compensate for the injuries incurred because of defendant's negligent actions and any injuries the plaintiff can reasonably expect to incur in the future.
- *Pain and suffering:* Plaintiff can recover for past pain and suffering, and if [the] injury is permanent, for the pain and suffering expected to occur in the future.
- *Emotional distress:* Recoverable by the plaintiff in most states only if he [or she] has suffered a physical injury.
- *Loss of consortium:* Recoverable by spouse of the plaintiff for loss of the love and affection of a spouse.
- *Exemplary damages:* Exemplary or punitive damages are available where it can be shown that the defendant acted with malice or criminal indifference.

Relief Available in a Wrongful Death Action

The damages available in wrongful death actions differ from those available in other negligent torts as follows:

- *General damages:* In most states, the monetary damages awarded in a wrongful death action are based upon a formula which takes into account the future monetary contributions and the value of any personal service, training, or advice that may have been given by the decedent to heirs.
- *Spousal damages:* A surviving spouse may recover for the loss of the defendant's love and affection and the value of future earnings.
- *Parental damages:* The parents of a deceased child may recover for loss of the child's comfort and society. The parent's future costs for the child's support and education may be discounted in the award.
- *Emotional and mental distress:* Damages for these factors are available when death is not instantaneous.
- *Exemplary damages:* The laws of most states disallow the awarding of exemplary damages in a wrongful death action.
- *Funeral expenses:* The decedent's survivors are entitled to the reasonable cost of all funeral expenses.
- *Damages otherwise available to the decedent:* The administrator of the decedent's estate is permitted to maintain any action on behalf of the decedent that would have accrued had the decedent survived, such as an action for damage to personal property. Such actions are usually joined in the wrongful death complaint.

EXHIBIT 4:2 ■ Causes of Action and Remedies[3] (continued)

Other Torts

Aside from the negligence torts, a class of tort relates to the conduct of business and business relationships.

Unfair Competition

To bring an action for unfair competition, the following facts must be pled in the complaint:

- The plaintiff must be engaged in a business affected by the interference of the defendant;
- The defendant must have engaged in improper conduct, an unlawful, unfair, or fraudulent business practice or have been engaged in unfair, untrue, or misleading advertising; and
- Defendant's conduct must have resulted in injury to the plaintiff.

Remedies available

The following remedies are available in unfair competition actions:

- *Injunctive relief:* Injunctive relief is available to the plaintiff where the court finds that general damages will not fully compensate the plaintiff.
- *Restoration of property:* The court may order the defendant to provide an accounting of the monies or property earned by the defendant from the unfair competition and that any such monies be paid to the plaintiff.
- *Exemplary damages:* These damages are awarded if the court finds the defendant's actions to have been malicious.

Inducing Breach of Contract

To bring an action for inducing breach of contract, the following conditions must be pled:

- The existence of valid contract between the plaintiff and a third party;
- Knowledge of the existence of the third party contract by defendant;
- Defendant's intention to cause the breach of the third-party contract;
- Breach of the contract by the third party;
- That the defendant was the cause of the breach of contract; and
- Injury to the plaintiff resulted.

Remedies available

The following remedies are available in an action for inducement of breach of contract:

- Injunctive relief;
- General damages;
- Special damages, including any damage to plaintiff's good will; and
- Exemplary damages on the showing of maliciousness by the defendant.

Tortious Interference with Prospective Economic Advantage

To bring an action for tortious interference with prospective economic advantage, the following facts must be pled in the complaint:

- *Existence of relationship between the plaintiff and a third party:* This relationship must contain the possibility of an economic or monetary benefit accruing to the plaintiff.
- *Knowledge of this relationship by the defendant:* This includes relationships of which the defendant has direct knowledge and those that the defendant *should have reasonably known to have existed.* For example, if there are only two manufacturers of a certain type of widget, the defendant can reasonably be expected to know that any third party using these widgets obtained them from one of the two sources.

(continued)

EXHIBIT 4:2 ■ Causes of Action and Remedies[3] (continued)

- The defendant's intent to interfere with the economic relationship;
- Disruption of the relationship; and
- Injury to the plaintiff caused by the disruption.

Remedies available

The following remedies are available in an action for tortious interference with prospective economic advantage:

- Injunctive relief;
- General damages;
- Special damages, including any damage to plaintiff's goodwill (goodwill is defined as the manner in which a business is perceived by the public); and
- Exemplary damages on the showing of maliciousness by the defendant.

Misappropriation of Trade Secrets

To bring an action for misappropriation of trade secrets, the following facts must be pled in the complaint:

- Existence of a trade secret: An exact definition of a trade secret is not possible. However, it must be a scientific or technical process which gives the possessor a unique advantage over a competitor. It has also been held that certain elements of the retail trade, such as customer lists, constitute trade secrets.
- Defendant must owe a duty not to disclose the information;
- Disclosure of the secret by the defendant; and
- Damage suffered by the plaintiff by the disclosure.

Remedies available

- Injunctive relief;
- Compensatory damages including the loss of value to plaintiff's business suffered because of defendant's disclosure; and
- An accounting of all profits earned by the defendants because of the misappropriation.

Source: Copyright James Publishing, Inc. Reprinted with permission of the publisher.

SEPARATE COUNTS

Rule 18 of the Federal Rules of Civil Procedure states that a "party asserting a claim to relief . . . may join . . . as many claims . . . as he has against an opposing party." Rule 8(e)(2) also permits claims to be set out in separate statements or counts.

A single occurrence may result in several claims for relief. In the rodent-in-the-corn example mentioned earlier, the victim had at least two claims against each of the defendants. One claim was for willful or negligent conduct stated in the alternative. The other was for a breach of warranty that the food was edible and safe. The negligence claim could be alleged as Count One and the breach of warranty claim as Count Two. It is also possible, as in our contract case (Case IV, in which the doll clothing company was unable to fulfill its obligation to the dollmaker), that instead of one contract, there could be several contracts, each with a specific delivery date: May 15, July 15, September 15, and October 15. Each of these contracts could be joined in one complaint and alleged in four individual counts. Another possibility exists in the *Forrester* case. If Ann's husband had been joined as one of the parties, the complaint could also allege that William Forrester has suffered and will continue to suffer the loss of consortium (marital affection) of his wife due to the negligence of the defendant. The form of the second count is demonstrated next. **Note:** The phrase "incorporate by reference" is item one of the sample separate count. This phrase is a drafting mechanism that saves time and space by integrating previous material as if it were restated in its entirety but without having to restate it.

Note: Each separate count should have a separate "wherefore" clause.

Sample Separate Count

Count Two

1. Plaintiffs hereby incorporate by reference paragraphs 1 through 6 of Count One.
2. Because of Defendants' negligence, Plaintiff William Forrester has suffered loss of the consortium of his wife, Ann Forrester, in the amount of twenty thousand dollars ($20,000).

WHEREFORE, Plaintiff William Forrester demands judgment against Defendant in the sum of twenty thousand dollars ($20,000) and costs and for such other relief as this court may deem just and proper.

DEMAND FOR JURY TRIAL

Rule 38(b) of the Federal Rules indicates that a demand for a jury may be placed in the complaint. This demand is advisable in both federal and state courts. Verify with the attorney the desirability of making a demand for a jury trial before including it in the complaint. The demand can be made later (ten days after service of the last pleading), but by putting the demand in the complaint, a strategic and embarrassing oversight can be avoided. The demand should be in a conspicuous place, such as in the lower right corner of the caption or at the end of the "wherefore" clause above the attorney's signature, as shown in the next sample. State rules and local practice may vary.

Sample Subscription and Demand for Jury Trial

Plaintiff demands trial by jury.
October,

_____

Arthur White
White, Wilson & McDuff
Attorneys at Law
Federal Plaza Building
Suite 700
Third and Market Streets
Legalville, Columbia 00000
(111) 555-0000

SUBSCRIPTION (RULE 11)

Federal Rule of Civil Procedure 11(a) and parallel state rules require that the complaint (and other pleadings and motions) be signed by the attorney or, if the party is not represented by an attorney, by the party. The address and phone number must be included. Unsigned papers are subject to being stricken if the defect is not corrected immediately after notice of the problem [Rule 11(a)]. As electronic filing of case documents increases (see Chapter 5), electronic signatures are increasingly considered valid. The attorney's assigned electronic identification name and password are sufficient in some courts. Confirm local practice.

The signing of the complaint or other pleading has serious implications. The paralegal should not present the document to the attorney for signature unless it is the product of thoughtful deliberation and investigation. Although it is the attorney who signs the document, the paralegal is often relied on to make some initial judgment as to whether the pleading meets the rules. If it does not, and the attorney signs it, the attorney and the law firm are subject to serious sanctions for ethical violations, in addition to penalties. Rule 3.1 of the Model Rules of Professional Conduct prohibits frivolous pleadings and motions, and Rule 4.4 forbids conduct with no substantial purpose other than to embarrass, delay, or burden another. Be acutely aware of the following Federal Rule 11(b) provisions:

> (b) Representations to Court. By presenting to the court (whether by signing, filing, submitting, or later advocating) a pleading, written motion, or other paper, an attorney or unrepresented party is certifying that to the best of the person's knowledge, information, and belief, formed after an inquiry reasonable under the circumstances,—
>
> (1) it is not being presented for any improper purpose, such as to harass or to cause unnecessary delay or needless increase in the cost of litigation;
>
> (2) the claims, defenses, and other legal contentions therein are warranted by existing law or by a nonfrivolous argument for the extension, modification, or reversal of existing law or the establishment of new law;
>
> (3) the allegations and other factual contentions have evidentiary support or, if specifically so identified, are likely to have evidentiary support after a reasonable opportunity for further investigation or discovery; and
>
> (4) the denials of factual contentions are warranted on the evidence or, if specifically so identified, are reasonably based on a lack of information or belief.

VERIFICATION

The certification method used in the federal system and many states makes verification unnecessary in those jurisdictions. Where verification is required, it consists of a brief affidavit sworn to by the party stating that the party has read the pleading, and it is true except for statements made on information and belief. The purpose of the verification is to deter the filing of false claims by imposing the threat of criminal prosecution for false swearing. Check your state practice on whether notarization is required for the verification.

As already mentioned, the filing of a pleading, especially a complaint, is a serious matter that can have a serious impact on the lives of others. When the pleading is sworn to and signed by the client, special care should be given to see that the client reads it carefully; is given the opportunity to ask questions; is asked to raise the right hand and repeat the oath; and is asked to sign the pleading. Above all, if you act as notary, you must witness the client's signature to affirm that the oath was sworn and signed in your presence.

"A doctrine capable of being stated only in obscure and involved terms is open to reasonable suspicion of being either crude or erroneous."

—Sir Frederick Pollock, 1845–1937, quoted in Mark De Wolfe Howe, *Holmes-Pollock Letters*, 1946. St. B. Ass'n Bull. 265, 267 (1933).

Sample Pleading Verification

State of Columbia
County of Capitol
    Ann Forrester, being first duly sworn on oath according to law, deposes and says that she has read the foregoing complaint and that the matters stated therein are true to the best of her knowledge, information, and belief.

_____
Ann Forrester

Subscribed and sworn to before me this 1st day of October, _____

_____
Notary Public

My commission expires January 1, _____.

EXHIBITS AND APPENDICES

At times, exhibits or an appendix attached to the complaint can be helpful. It is required in some jurisdictions, most commonly in contract cases where the contract or a copy of the contract is included. Exhibits normally include contracts, promissory notes, bills of lading, correspondence, and other documents at issue. An appendix often is used to further explain technical language used in the documents. Exhibits and appendices can be helpful to the parties, but especially to the judge and jury.

Exhibits or appendices are attached following the verification or certification, and essentially become a part of the complaint. The drafter includes references to the attachments in the body of the complaint, as shown in the following example.

6. That the Defendant prepared a contract that was entered into with the Plaintiff on June 15, _____, a copy of which is attached and marked "Exhibit A," and incorporated into this complaint.

The exhibits and appendix could appear as follows (first page after verification or certification):

Agreement between Plaintiff and Defendant.

EXHIBIT A

[here insert language of contract]

APPENDIX A

[here insert explanatory note or term defined]

"Extraordinary Whole Life 13" refers to a special insurance policy that . . . "

A cost bond must be included with civil complaints in some states. This assures the court that the plaintiff is able to pay court costs if awarded to the other side.

When all aspects of the complaint are ready, they should be placed in their proper order. The paralegal sees to it that the necessary copies are prepared by the legal secretary or copy clerk, including one for the file, one for each defendant, and the original for the court.

SYSTEM CHECKLIST FOR DRAFTING A COMPLAINT

PREPARATION

- [ ] If the complaint is to be filed in state court, consult state rules for differences from the federal rules. Remember that each court may also have its local rules.
- [ ] Review the file for the names and addresses of the parties, the type of claim, and so on.
- [ ] Confirm in what court the action should be filed.
- [ ] Confirm the existence of venue, subject matter jurisdiction, and personal jurisdiction.
- [ ] Research the necessary elements for each cause of action to be alleged.
- [ ] Formulate those elements into a legal syllogism to form the body of each count of the complaint. (If A, B, and C exist, then plaintiff is entitled to X.)
- [ ] Identify the facts needed to support each element of the syllogism.
- [ ] Identify the appropriate remedies.
- [ ] Consult with the supervising attorney to confirm all of the preceding points.
- [ ] Make corrections as the attorney indicates, and do further research or investigation as needed.
- [ ] Check your system folder for appropriate samples of both federal and state complaints or sections thereof.
- [ ] Obtain one good copy of a recent complaint for the type of claim or claims to be alleged and for the specific court in which the action is to be filed.
- [ ] Check local court rules for size of paper, backing sheets, color, and any other requirements.

> "Fools and stub-born men make wealthy lawyers."
>
> —SPANISH PROVERB, H. L. MENCKEN, *A NEW DICTIONARY OF QUOTATIONS*, 1946. ST. B. ASS'N BULL. 265, 267 (1933).

DRAFTING

- [ ] Draft the caption.
  - [ ] Indicate the court (branch, if several branches) and its location.
  - [ ] Indicate the parties, the joinder thereof; check spelling and the addresses if included; capacity, real party in interest, and so on. Federal Rule 17(a)(b)(c), 19(1), 20(1); State rule ___; system folder page ___.
  - [ ] Apply pertinent rules on redaction (editing) to protect personal identity information.
  - [ ] Indicate the docket or court file number of the action if available, or leave an appropriate space.
  - [ ] Indicate the type of complaint (negligence, breach of contract, etc.).
  - [ ] Include the references to federal and state rules and forms on drafting. Federal Rule 10(a), Form 1; State Rule ___, Form ___; system folder page ___.
  - [ ] Include a demand for jury trial if so instructed.
- [ ] Draft simple, concise, and direct statements. Avoid repetition and legalese.
- [ ] Use double spacing; quoted matter should be single spaced.
- [ ] Draft the jurisdictional allegation, if required, including any monetary amount. Federal Rule 8(a)(1), Form 2; State Rule ___; system folder page ___.
- [ ] Make sure all allegations regarding venue, if required, are included (not necessary in the federal system): location of incident and addresses of parties. State Rule ___; system folder page ___.

- ☐ Draft the body of the complaint.
  - ☐ Include facts to support each element of the claim.
  - ☐ Use brief, numbered paragraphs limited to one idea. Federal Rule 10(b); State Rule ___; system folder page ___.
  - ☐ Add just enough detail to meet the minimum requirement for fact pleading or for notice pleading, depending on applicable rules. Federal Rule 8(a)(2), 8(e)(1), Forms 3-17; State Rule ___; system folder page ___.
  - ☐ Do not state evidence or conclusions.
  - ☐ Avoid impertinent, scandalous, or immaterial language. Federal Rule 11, 12(f); State Rule ___.
  - ☐ Be truthful; make sure there are provable facts to support a good-faith allegation. Model Rule 3.3(a)(1).
  - ☐ State those allegations that are uncertain but have some basis on information and belief.
  - ☐ Do not anticipate defenses.
  - ☐ Plead hypothetically, in the alternative, and state uncertainty when necessary. Federal Rule 8(e)(2); State Rule ___; system folder page ___.
  - ☐ Do not plead the law, except (1) when the action is under a specific statute or administrative rule, or (2) when the action is in one state but relies on the law of another state.
  - ☐ List various damages in one paragraph, unless local rules or practice dictates otherwise.
  - ☐ Check to see that all separate claims are alleged and all separate counts included. Federal Rule 8(e)(2), 18; State Rule ___; system folder page ___.
  - ☐ Check to see that paragraphs flow logically and tell an interesting and easy-to-read story.
  - ☐ Choose assertive, persuasive words to evoke sympathy and convey confidence.
  - ☐ Check that all incorporations by reference (including exhibits and appendixes) have been accurately stated where needed.
- ☐ Draft special matters as they arise.
  - ☐ Aver the capacity of the parties unless not required by local rules. It is not required in the federal system [Rule 9(a)].
  - ☐ Aver the circumstances supporting the allegation of fraud or mistake with particularity [Rule 9(b)].
  - ☐ Aver malice, intent, knowledge, or other condition of the mind generally [Rule 9(b)].
  - ☐ Aver the performance of all conditions precedent generally [Rule 9(c)]; aver the denial of performance with particularity.
  - ☐ Aver that an official document was issued or act done in compliance with the law [Rule 9(d)].
  - ☐ Aver a judgment or decision of domestic or foreign court, administrative tribunal, or of a board of officers without alleging facts showing jurisdiction to render it.
  - ☐ Aver time and place [Rule 9(f)].
  - ☐ Aver specifically any special damages [Rule 9(g)].
- ☐ Draft the prayer for relief (demand for judgment).

> "The court should be a place where anybody can come—whatever they have in their pocket—and be able to file a complaint in simple fashion and at least have somebody give consideration to it and give them an opportunity to be heard."
>
> —THOMAS T. CURTIN, JUDGE, U.S. DISTRICT COURT, *NEW YORK TIMES*, OCTOBER 7, 1971.

- [ ] State relief in the alternative when necessary. Federal Rule 8(a)(3); State Rule ___; system folder page ___.
  - [ ] damages   [ ] recovery of property
  - [ ] injuries   [ ] specific performance   [ ] other
- [ ] Draft the subscription and see to it that the attorney's address and phone number are included. Federal Rule 11(b); State Rule ___; system folder page ___.
- [ ] Draft verification if required (not required in federal pleadings). Federal Rule 11(b); State Rule ___; system folder page ___.
- [ ] Have the client swear to the truthfulness of the complaint and sign it in your presence if you are a notary.
- [ ] Attach exhibits and appendices.
- [ ] See that the complaint is typed with sufficient copies.

SAMPLE COMPLAINTS

Drawing from the checklist and information in the chapter, a fact-pleading complaint in the *Forrester* case appears as follows:

Complaint for Ann Forrester Case

STATE OF COLUMBIA   CAPITOL COUNTY   CIRCUIT COURT

ANN FORRESTER and
WILLIAM FORRESTER,
    Plaintiffs

                                      Civil Action, File No. <u>1000</u>

    v.

RICHARD HART and
MERCURY PARCEL SERVICE, INC.,
    Defendants   Plaintiff Demands Trial by Jury.

COMPLAINT FOR NEGLIGENCE

The Plaintiffs make the following allegations:

1. The jurisdiction of this court is based on the amount in controversy in this action which is more than $2,500.
2. Plaintiff Ann Forrester is a teacher and homemaker and resides at 1533 Capitol Drive, Legalville, in Capitol County, Columbia.
3. Plaintiff William Forrester is the husband of Ann Forrester and resides with her.
4. Defendant Richard Hart is a driver employed by Defendant Mercury Parcel Service, Inc., and resides at 1223 Penny Lane, Cincinnati, Ohio.
5. Defendant Mercury Parcel Service, Inc., is incorporated in the state of Delaware with its principal place of business located at 603 Stoker St., Cincinnati, Ohio.
6. On February 26, _____, at approximately 7:30 A.M., Plaintiff Ann Forrester was walking across a hilly and partially icy section of Highway 328 in the City of Legalville, County of Capitol, in the State of Columbia.

(continued)

7. At that time, Defendant Hart was driving a van on behalf of his employer and the owner of the van, Defendant Mercury Parcel Service, Inc.

8. Defendant Hart operated the van negligently by:

(a) driving the vehicle at an excessive rate of speed under the circumstances;

(b) failing to exercise a proper lookout;

(c) failing to exercise adequate control of said vehicle; and

(d) otherwise failing to exercise due and adequate care under the circumstances.

9. As a direct consequence of the Defendants' negligence, the Plaintiff was struck down by the Defendants' van and seriously injured.

10. Because of said negligence, the Plaintiff suffered fractures of the left leg and hip; damage to the lower spine; torn muscles, tendons, tissue, and nerves; insomnia; paralysis that confines her to a wheelchair; depression; and other maladies, causing her intense pain and great suffering and considerable inconvenience which will continue in the future.

11. As a consequence of the Defendants' negligence and the aforesaid injuries, the Plaintiff has incurred and will incur substantial monetary losses for hospital and medical care, loss of income and benefits, domestic services, and property damages to her coat and clothing.

WHEREFORE the Plaintiff demands judgment in the amount of seven hundred and fifty thousand dollars ($750,000), together with the costs and disbursements of this action and for such other relief as this court may deem just and proper.

COUNT TWO

12. The Plaintiffs hereby allege and incorporate by reference paragraphs 1 through 9 of Count One.

13. Because of the Defendants' negligence, Plaintiff William Forrester has suffered the loss of consortium with his wife, Ann Forrester, in the amount of twenty thousand dollars ($20,000).

WHEREFORE, Plaintiff William Forrester demands judgment against the Defendants in the sum of twenty thousand dollars ($20,000) and costs and for such other relief as this court may deem just and proper.

_____

Arthur White

White, Wilson & McDuff

Attorneys at Law

Federal Plaza Building

Suite 700

Third and Market Streets

Legalville, Columbia 00000

(111) 555-0000

STATE OF COLUMBIA
⎫
⎬ SS.
⎭
County of Capitol

Ann Forrester and William Forrester, being duly sworn on oath according to law, depose and state that they have read the foregoing complaint and that

(continued)

the matters stated therein are true to the best of their knowledge, information, and belief.

_____
Ann Forrester

_____
William Forrester

Subscribed and sworn to before me this 1st day of October, _____.

_____
Notary Public

My commission expires January 1, _____

[attach exhibits if any]

This complaint is for illustrative purposes and does not exhaust all possible causes of action against the defendants.

Examples of complaint forms for other types of actions follow. Keep in mind that these forms are for your guidance and that any particular case may require important amendments.

Contract

Elements of a claim for breach of contract include the following:

A. A promise by Defendant, e.g., to pay money or do something by a certain date
B. Consideration for promise, e.g., $25,000
C. Performance of condition by Plaintiff, e.g., payment of $25,000
D. Defendant's breach, i.e., failure to perform promise by a certain date
E. Plaintiff injury, e.g., loss of $25,000 plus additional cost to enforce performance of promise

The syllogism would be: If A, B, C, D, and E exist, then the plaintiff is entitled to damages. Facts should be alleged in the body of the complaint to show A through E exist.

Form: Complaint for Breach of Contract

[include caption] Jury Trial Is Demanded
The Plaintiff makes the following allegations:

1. That the court has jurisdiction over this matter because the Plaintiff is a resident of the State of Columbia, and the Defendant is a resident of the State of Ohio, and the amount in controversy exceeds seventy-five thousand dollars ($75,000), exclusive of interest and costs.

(continued)

2. That on [date], a written contract was entered into by the Plaintiff and the Defendant in which the Defendant agreed to ___ [state promise].
3. That the agreed upon consideration for said promise was payment to the Defendant of ___.
4. That a copy of said contract is attached to this complaint as "Exhibit A" and incorporated herein by reference.
5. That the Plaintiff ___ [state the Plaintiff's performance of condition, e.g., rendered payment] and all other conditions precedent have occurred or have been performed by the Plaintiff.
6. That the Defendant failed to ___ [restate promise] even though the Plaintiff made a demand on the Defendant to do so.
7. That as a consequence of the Defendant's breach of contract, the Plaintiff has ___ [state the injury or injuries, e.g., purchased at a higher price, lost profit, interest, lost other contracts].

WHEREFORE, the Plaintiff demands judgment against the Defendant for the sum of ___ dollars with interest at the rate of ___ per annum from the date of the Defendant's breach, together with the Plaintiff's costs and disbursements.

_____
Attorney for Plaintiff
[Address]
[Phone]

Form: Complaint on a Promissory Note

1. Allegation of jurisdiction
2. The Defendant, on or about June 1, 1935, executed and delivered to the Plaintiff a promissory note [in the following words and figure: (*here set out the note verbatim*)]; [a copy of which is hereto annexed as Exhibit A]; [whereby the Defendant promised to pay the Plaintiff on order on June 1, 1936, the sum of ___ dollars with interest thereon at the rate of six percent per annum].
3. Defendant owes the Plaintiff the amount of said note and interest.

WHEREFORE, the Plaintiff demands judgment against the Defendant for the sum of ___ dollars, interest, and costs.

Signed:_____
Attorney for Plaintiff

Address: _____
[Phone]

Source: Fed. R. Civ. P. Form 3

Form: Complaint for Antitrust Action[4]

[Title of Court and Cause]

The plaintiff, ___, a corporation, (hereinafter referred to as "B___"), by ___ & ___, its attorneys, complains of the defendant, ___, a corporation (hereinafter referred to as "G___") as follows:

1. *[Allegations of jurisdiction based on federal statute and diversity of citizenship.]*

2. Defendant G___, a ___ corporation, has its principal place of business at ___, and is a manufacturer and seller of watch bands and other merchandise to the wholesale jewelry trade in the State of ___ and in various other states in the United States of America, and is and has been at all times referred to herein engaged in interstate commerce between various states and including such commerce between States of ___ and ___. By reason thereof, the defendant G___ is subject to and bound by the provisions of the Sherman Antitrust Act, being Sections 1 through 33, inclusive, Title 15, United States Code Annotated.

3. The plaintiff, B___, a ___ corporation, has its principal place of business in ___, and is engaged in the wholesale jewelry trade in the State of ___ and in various other States of the United States of America.

4. Prior to ___, ___, the plaintiff B___ had been appointed and had acted as a wholesale distributor of G___'s products to the retail jewelry trade in the State of ___ and in various other States of the United States of America.

5. At all times while plaintiff had been so appointed and engaged as a wholesale distributor for defendant G___, plaintiff followed and adhered to G___'s announced policy of selling G___ products to retailers at G___'s factory suggested list prices.

6. On ___, ___, G___, through its Vice President in Charge of Marketing and its Chicago representative, advised plaintiff B___ that the philosophy of G___ is that all watch bands sold by a G___ distributor, whether manufactured by G___ or by its competitors, must be sold by the G___ distributor at the factory suggested selling prices, and that to continue to be a G___ distributor, B___ would have to price other factory lines, that is, watch bands manufactured by G___'s competitors and sold by B___, at factory suggested selling prices, and not at prices otherwise determined by B___.

7. B___ refused so to do, and G___'s Vice President in Charge of Marketing thereupon, then and there, and on the same day, and at the same conference, on, to-wit, ___, ___, summarily advised B___ that B___'s distributorship of G___'s products was terminated and G___ would no longer sell B___ any G___ merchandise because of B___'s refusal to comply with G___'s policy regarding the price at which B___ sold watch bands manufactured and sold by G___'s competitors.

8. That the defendant, G___ thereby attempted to engage in a wrongful and unlawful combination and conspiracy,

   a. To prevent and restrict the sale and distribution of G___'s products, by reason of its refusal, for the unlawful reason stated by G___ as aforesaid, to sell its products to B___;

   b. To prevent and restrict the sale and distribution of products manufactured and sold by G___'s competitors;

(continued)

   c. To, and did, discriminate against a wholesale distributor, to-wit, B___, who would not combine and conspire with G___ to price competitors' lines as directed and dictated by G___;

   d. To force and compel B___ to enter into a contract or agreement providing for the establishment and maintenance between wholesalers of minimum resale prices on products competitive to the G___ line; and

   e. To force and compel B___ to enter into a contract or agreement providing for the establishment and maintenance of minimum resale prices between persons, firms, or corporations in competition with each other; and that such acts have unreasonably restrained, do unreasonably restrain, and will continue unreasonably to restrain trade and commerce in violation of the anti-trust laws of the Untied States of America above cited.

9. That by reason of G___'s wrongful and unlawful termination of B___'s distributorship of G___ products and its refusal to thereafter sell such products to B___ for the reason forbidden by the antitrust laws, as aforesaid, and in restraint of trade and commerce, as aforesaid, the plaintiff, B___, has been injured in its business and property to an amount in excess of ___ (___), and hereby demands of the defendant G___ threefold the damages by it sustained, and the costs of this action, including a reasonable attorney's fee to be fixed and determined by this Court.

> _____
> Plaintiff
> By _____
> President

Form: Complaint for Class Action[5]

Class Action Allegations—Action for Damages
[Fed. R. Civ. P. 23(a), (b)]

2. Plaintiffs bring this action on behalf of themselves and, under Federal Civil Procedure Rule 23(a) and (b)(3), on behalf of all other Lake ___ lakeshore landowners and lakeshore lessees similarly situated and located in the Towns of ___ and ___, County of ___, State of ___; the said lakeshore landowners and lakeshore lessees in the Towns of ___ and ___ number approximately two hundred (200), and it is therefore impracticable to bring them all before Court.

3. There are questions of law and fact common to the entire class of lakeshore landowners and lakeshore lessees similarly situated and located in the Towns of ___ and ___; the claims of the Plaintiffs herein are typical of the claims of the said class; and the Plaintiffs will fairly and adequately protect the interest of and represent said class; the common questions of law and fact predominate over any questions affecting only individual members, and a class action is superior to other available methods for the fair and efficient adjudication of this controversy.

(continued)

4. The Plaintiffs, ___ and ___, are the owners of certain lands and premises having lake frontage on the easterly edge of Lake ___ in the Town of ___, ___, namely, all the same lands and premises conveyed to the Plaintiffs ___ by Warranty Deed of ___, dated ___, ___, and recorded in ___, said lands including over ___ feet of lakeshore frontage.

5. The Plaintiffs, ___ and ___, are the owners of certain lands and premises having lake frontage on the easterly edge of Lake in the Town of ___, ___, being all and the same lands and premises conveyed to the Plaintiffs ___ by Deed of ___, dated ___, ___, and recorded in ___, said lands and premises including over ___ feet of lakeshore frontage.

Source: Reprinted with permission of West Group.

INJUNCTIONS

At times the attorney will instruct the paralegal to draft a request for an injunction or temporary restraining order to accompany the complaint. This is necessary in some circumstances to prevent further deterioration in the subject of the lawsuit, or some other violation of a party's rights. For example, if a defendant is sued over

---

EXHIBIT 4:3 ■ Motion for Preliminary Injunction—General Form

[Fed R. Civ. P. 65(a)]

[*Title of Court and Cause*]

Plaintiffs, _____and _____, move the Court for a preliminary injunction in the above entitled cause enjoining the defendants, and _____and _____, their agents, servants, employees, and attorneys, [and those persons in active concert or participation with them] from _____

_____

The grounds in support of this motion are as follows:

1. _____
2. _____

Unless restrained _____and _____will immediately [*state action defendants will take unless restrained*].

Immediate and irreparable injury, loss, and damage will result to the plaintiffs by reason of the threatened action of the defendants, as more particularly appears in the verified complaint filed herein and the attached affidavit of _____. The plaintiffs have no adequate remedy at law.

If this preliminary injunction be granted, the injury, if any, to defendants herein, if final judgment be in their favor, will be inconsiderable and will be adequately indemnified by bond.

[Add if appropriate: Plaintiffs further move the Court that the trial of this action on the merits be advanced and consolidated with the hearing of this motion for preliminary injunction. The grounds in support of consolidation are as follows: *Add matter similar to matter in second paragraph of form in § 5272*].

_____
Attorneys for Plaintiffs
Address: _____

Source: Reprinted with permission of West Group.

EXHIBIT 4:4 ■ Motion for Temporary Restraining Order

[Fed. R. Civ. P. 65(b)]

[Title of Court and Cause]

Plaintiff moves this court to grant [(1) forthwith and without notice to defendant or his attorney] a temporary restraining order restraining and enjoining the defendant [his agents, servants, employees, and attorneys, and those persons in active concert and participation with him] from [*describe actions sought to be enjoined by motion*] pending a hearing and disposition of plaintiff's motion for a preliminary injunction filed herein on ___, ___, [and scheduled by the court for a hearing on defendant or his attorney on ___, ___] on the ground that immediate and irreparable loss, damage, and injury will result to plaintiff [(2) before defendant or his attorney can be heard in opposition] and before [notice can be served and] a hearing can be had on plaintiff's motion for a preliminary injunction, if defendants are permitted to [*describe actions sought to be enjoined*], as more fully appears from plaintiff's verified complaint herein and the attached affidavits of ___ [(3) and the attached certificate of applicant's attorney certifying the efforts which have been made to give defendant notice, and the reasons notice of this motion should not be required].
[Date]

_____
Attorneys for Plaintiffs
Address: _____

Source: Reprinted with permission of West Group.

---

a boundary dispute, a preliminary injunction may be in order to prevent the defendant from cutting down trees on the disputed property until the suit is resolved.

Rule 65 sets out the difference between a preliminary injunction and a temporary restraining order. The important thing to remember, however, is that these documents are filed to require the other party either to do or refrain from doing some act. Without such action, the plaintiff could possibly suffer irreparable harm.

The injunction or temporary restraining order should be filed with the complaint along with a proposed order prohibiting or demanding the action in question. The request is often supported by a memorandum of law. A surety bond must also be filed with the court.

Exhibit 4:3[6] and Exhibit 4:4[7] are examples of forms for injunction and the temporary restraining orders.

SUMMARY

Drafting good pleadings is an important art that increases your value to the law firm. The first pleading to be drafted in litigation is the complaint. It introduces the cause of action, invokes the court's jurisdiction, presents the facts of the case, and provides due process notice to the defendant. A complaint consists of three main parts: the caption, the body, and the prayer for relief. What must be stated in these sections is established by court rules, the nature of the action, remedies available, and techniques of drafting. Sample forms and a checklist for drafting complaints are provided in the chapter as guides to be adapted for state or federal court. The assignments for the chapter emphasize your need to practice applying the techniques and procedures outlined in the chapter.

In addition, you have learned about the pleadings needed to file for an injunction. An injunction may be sought as a lone action or as a remedy in conjunction with another action. Its purpose is to request a court to prohibit the action of another or to command that the other party take some action. Injunctions are an important tool in our legal system to prevent damage before it occurs. Sample motions for an injunction have been provided for your use. Familiarity with and practice at each of the tasks presented in this chapter will increase your ability and confidence as a paralegal.

▣ WORKBOOK

System Folder Assignments, other exercises, a chapter outline, a review test, and other study aids are located in the accompanying workbook.

▣ HELPFUL WEB SITES

http://www.westlaw.com; www.lexis-nexis.com; and http://www.uscourts.gov
  federal and state rules of civil procedure

http://www.ojp.usdoj.gov/bjs/civil.htm
  Bureau of Justice Statistics, civil litigation

http://www.hotdocs.com
  a fee-based electronic aid for drafting a variety of documents (a number of forms available free with a free registration)

http://www.llrx.com/courtrules
  law and technology resources, links to federal and state court rules, forms, and dockets

▣ QUESTIONS FOR STUDY AND REVIEW

1. What is procedural due process of law?
2. What is the relationship between due process and a complaint?
3. Describe the various sections of a complaint, their contents, and the functions of each section.
4. What are the minimum requirements in order for a person to be eligible to sue or be sued? What happens when a person has grounds for a lawsuit but does not have the legal capacity to sue?
5. What is the federal and your state rule on joinder of parties in a lawsuit?
6. Why is jurisdiction important to the drafter of a complaint?
7. What are class actions and in what ways can they be beneficial?
8. What caption information might be restricted to protect the privacy of the parties?
9. What role do jurisdictional amounts play in both federal and state courts?
10. What are the necessary components of an adequate jurisdictional allegation?
11. Why is venue important to the drafter of a complaint? When venue must be alleged, what specifically needs to be included?
12. What should a paralegal do to be sure that a claim is properly alleged in a particular jurisdiction?
13. What is a syllogism? A major and minor premise? How can it be useful to the drafter of a complaint?
14. For an adequate allegation of a claim, what must a paralegal know about the legal basis of such a claim?
15. Review the guidelines and techniques for drafting the body of the complaint.
16. What ethical consideration must a paralegal keep in mind when drafting a complaint? Cite the disciplinary rule.
17. What is the difference between fact pleading and notice pleading?
18. What federal rules set out guidelines for pleading?
19. How can a paralegal determine the extent of facts to allege in a fact-pleading jurisdiction?
20. What is the difference, if any, between a prayer for relief, a demand for judgment, and the "wherefore" clause?
21. What are damages?
22. What is the difference between general and special damages? Which must be alleged with particularity (applicable rule)?
23. What are noneconomic damages?
24. Describe and define the other common forms of relief: recovery of property, injunction, and specific performance.

25. What factors are used to determine whether punitive damages are reasonable?
26. What does it mean to have multiple counts in a complaint? Should there be a "wherefore" clause in each count?
27. What is the proper method of incorporating paragraphs of one count into another?
28. What must a paralegal keep in mind regarding a demand for a jury trial? What federal rule applies?
29. What does an attorney certify in signing a complaint where verification is not required?
30. What is the proper procedure for notarizing a verification?
31. What is the purpose of an appendix to a complaint? What is the proper way to reference either an exhibit or an appendix?
32. Review the system checklist for drafting a complaint.
33. Be prepared to draft both a fact and a notice complaint.

▣ KEY TERMS

capacity
cause of action
class action
complaint
defendant
due process of law

exemplary (punitive) damages
fact pleading
general damages
guardian ad litem
interpleader

joinder of parties
mandatory injunction
notice pleading
plaintiff
pleadings
prohibitory injunction

real party in interest
special damages
specific performance
standing to sue

▣ ENDNOTES

1. MOORE, TAGGART & WICKER, MOORE'S FEDERAL PRACTICE § 0.140, 1–4 (2d ed. 1959).
2. The following discussion on the syllogism is drawn in part from KARLEN, PROCEDURE BEFORE TRIAL IN A NUTSHELL 45–48 (1972).
3. PHILLIP J. SIGNEY, LITIGATION PARALEGAL (1991).
4. WEST'S FEDERAL FORMS § 1585, v. 2A, with permission of West Group.
5. *Id.*, § 3065, v. 3.
6. *Id.*, § 5271, v. 4.
7. *Id.*, § 5297, v. 4.

For additional resources, visit our Web site at **http://www.westlegalstudies.com.**

Filing the Lawsuit, Service of Process, and Obtaining a Default Judgment

INTRODUCTION

THE TASKS: FILING THE LAWSUIT, SERVING THE SUMMONS, OBTAINING A DEFAULT JUDGMENT

Mr. White has met with Ms. Forrester and reviewed her case. She has decided to go forward with her lawsuit. You have been assigned the following tasks:

1. Prepare the necessary documents to file the action.
2. File the documents with the court clerk.
3. Serve each defendant with the summons and complaint.
4. If the defendant does not respond, prepare the necessary documents to obtain a default judgment.

PURPOSE OF THE TASKS

Filing the lawsuit is the first formal step in the litigation process. It establishes the date when the case officially begins, and all deadlines in the case ultimately stem from that date. If the claim has not been filed prior to the running of the statute of limitations, the opposition has a defense to the action and the case will be dismissed. The filing of the action informs the court of the suit and makes the claim a matter of public record.

Service of process (delivery of a copy of the summons and complaint) officially notifies the defendant of the lawsuit and the defendant's need to respond (answer). Service also gives the court personal jurisdiction over the defendant, which is necessary for the court to impose a binding judgment on the defendant. Discussion of the default judgment is reserved for later in this chapter.

service of process
Delivery to the defendant of official notification of the lawsuit and of his or her need to respond; delivery of a copy of the summons, complaint, writs, and other documents to another party.

PREPARING DOCUMENTS FOR FILING AN ACTION AND FOR SERVICE OF PROCESS

DETERMINE WHAT DOCUMENTS ARE NEEDED

There are several ways to determine what is needed to file an action. One method is to ask an experienced paralegal or attorney in your law firm. Another method, until you are familiar with the requirements, is to visit the clerk of the court in which the action will be filed. The clerk will explain to you what is needed and will probably give you copies of some of the forms you will need. Do not be afraid of appearing uninformed. The clerks are there to help you and want you to have a good start.

This visit will acquaint you with the clerk's personnel, who will be of considerable help to you in the years to come. If you treat these individuals with courtesy and respect, remembering that they are also under pressure and time constraints, your relationship with the clerk's office should develop on a pleasant and productive basis.

Consult the court filing and service requirements in the Federal Rules of Civil Procedure (FED. R. CIV. P.) and parallel state rules. An excellent Web site for the rules, their latest and proposed revisions, and committee commentary is http://www. uscourts.gov. State rules may be available through the Web sites of your state courts, a state law library, a state law school library, or a commercial site such as Westlaw or Lexis. Frequently, courts have their own local rules in addition to the standard rules that dictate what documents must be prepared and filed. Confirm with the attorney the method of service of process to be used.

GATHER AND PREPARE THE DOCUMENTS NECESSARY FOR FILING AND SERVICE

Introduction

Once the required documents are identified, draft the necessary information into the forms, or, in some cases, draft the entire document. Note that the latest edition of federal court forms can be found at the uscourts Web site. Your state court site may have forms as well. Gather or prepare the following forms:

Complaint

The complaint has been prepared, but this is a good time to check its accuracy and to see that it has been signed by the attorney or verified by the client as required by the jurisdiction and that the necessary copies have been prepared. Blue backings may be required by the state; they are not required in federal court, and are impractical if the document will be delivered electronically.

Summons

summons
A document issued by the court that informs the defendant of the action and requires the defendant to respond or appear by or at a designated time; when served, gives the court personal jurisdiction over the defendant.

A **summons** is a document issued by the court that informs the defendant of the action and requires the defendant to respond or appear by or at a designated time. When served on the defendant, it gives the court personal jurisdiction over the defendant. Federal Rule of Civil Procedure 4(a) provides the requirements for a valid summons in federal court. All states have similar requirements. The summons is signed by the clerk of court, bears the seal of the court, identifies the court and the parties, is directed to the defendant, states the name and address of the plaintiff's attorney, states the time within which the defendant must appear and defend, and provides notice that failure to respond will result in a default judgment being entered for the plaintiff in the amount demanded.

Most clerks have preprinted copies of the summons. Obtain a copy of the summons, and see that it is properly and accurately filled out. Exhibit 5:1 is a federal summons completed for the Ann Forrester case. Note any differences in your state summons. Rule 4(b) permits the listing of multiple defendants on the summons. Copies must be prepared for each defendant.

Civil Cover Sheet

A Civil Cover Sheet should be prepared for each civil case filed in federal district court. Some states require the completion of a similar form. Exhibit 5:2 is a completed version of the federal Civil Cover Sheet. Always make sure that this cover sheet is signed by the attorney.

Notice of Lawsuit and Request for Waiver of Service of Summons; Waiver of Service of Summons

Rule 4(d) allows plaintiffs in actions filed in federal court to reduce the cost and time involved in serving the summons by placing a duty on the defendant to waive service of the summons. This process requires two documents to be provided and prepared by the plaintiff. The first is the Notice of Lawsuit and Request for Waiver of Service of Summons. It is addressed directly to the defendant, if an individual, or else to an officer or agent authorized to receive service. It identifies the court in which the action has been filed and the docket number, informs the defendant of the consequences of compliance and failure to comply with the request, sets forth the date the request is sent, and states that

EXHIBIT 5:1 ■ Summons in a Civil Action

AO 440 (Rev. 8/01) Summons in a Civil Action

United States District Court

————————————— DISTRICT OF —————————————

ANN FORRESTER and
WILLIAM FORRESTER, Plaintiffs

V.

RICHARD HART and
MERCURY PARCEL, INC., Defendants

SUMMONS IN A CIVIL ACTION

CASE NUMBER:

TO: (Name and Address of Defendant)

Richard Hart
1223 Penny Lane
Cincinnati, OH

YOU ARE HEREBY SUMMONED and required to serve upon

PLAINTIFF'S ATTORNEY (name and address)
Arthur White
White, Wilson & McDuff
Attorneys at Law
Federal Plaza Building, Suite 700
Third and Market Streets
Legalville, Columbia 00000

an answer to the complaint which is herewith served upon you, within _____20_____ days after service of this summons upon you, exclusive of the day of service. If you fail to do so, judgment by default will be taken against you for the relief demanded in the complaint. Any answer that you serve on the parties to this action must be filed with the Clerk of this Court within a reasonable period of time after service.

J. D. Walterson	10/2/--
CLERK	DATE

BY DEPUTY CLERK

(continued)

EXHIBIT 5:1 ■ Summons in a Civil Action *(continued)*

AO 440 (Rev. 8/01)   Summons in a Civil Action

RETURN OF SERVICE

	DATE
Service of the Summons and Complaint was made by me[1]	
NAME OF SERVER	TITLE

Check one box below to indicate appropriate method of service

☐ Served personally upon the defendant. Place where served: _____

_____

☐ Left copies thereof at the defendant's dwelling house or usual place of abode with a person of suitable age and
discretion then residing therein.
Name of person with whom the summons and complaint were left: _____

☐ Returned unexecuted: _____

_____

_____

☐ Other (specify): _____

_____

_____

STATEMENT OF SERVICE FEES

TRAVEL	SERVICES	TOTAL

DECLARATION OF SERVER

I declare under penalty of perjury under the laws of the United States of America that the foregoing information
contained in the Return of Service and Statement of Service Fees is true and correct.

Executed on _____   _____
                   Date   *Signature of Server*

                                        _____
                                                  Address of Server

1) As to who may serve a summons see Rule 4 of the Federal Rules of Civil Procedure.

EXHIBIT 5:2 ▪ Civil Cover Sheet (Completed Form)

JS 44 (Rev. 11/04)

CIVIL COVER SHEET

The JS 44 civil cover sheet and the information contained herein neither replace nor supplement the filing and service of pleadings or other papers as required by law, except as provided by local rules of court. This form, approved by the Judicial Conference of the United States in September 1974, is required for the use of the Clerk of Court for the purpose of initiating the civil docket sheet. (SEE INSTRUCTIONS ON THE REVERSE OF THE FORM.)

I. (a) PLAINTIFFS

Ann Forrester and
William Forrester

DEFENDANTS

Richard Hart and
Mercury Parcel Service, Inc.

(b) County of Residence of First Listed Plaintiff ___Capitol___
(EXCEPT IN U.S. PLAINTIFF CASES)

County of Residence of First Listed Defendant ___Hamilton___
(IN U.S. PLAINTIFF CASES ONLY)
NOTE: INLAND CONDEMNATION CASES, USE THE LOCATION OF THE LAND INVOLVED.

(c) Attorney's (Firm Name, Address, and Telephone Number)
Arthur White
White, Wilson & McDuff
Federal Plaza Building, Suite 700
Third and Market Streets
Legalville, Columbia 00000

Attorneys (If known)
Harold Ott
Ott, Ott, and Knudsen
444 Front Street
Cincinnati, OH

II. BASIS OF JURISDICTION (Place an "X" in One Box Only)

☐ 1 U.S. Government Plaintiff
☐ 2 U.S. Government Defendant
☐ 3 Federal Question (U.S. Government Not a Party)
☒ 4 Diversity (indicate Citizenship of Parties in Item III)

III. CITIZENSHIP OF PRINCIPAL PARTIES (Place an "X" in One Box for Plaintiff and One Box for Defendant)
(For Diversity Cases Only)

	PTF	DEF		PTF	DEF
Citizen of This State	☒ 1	☐ 1	Incorporated or Principal Place of Business In This State	☐ 4	☐ 4
Citizen of Another State	☐ 2	☒ 2	Incorporate and Principal Place of Business In Another State	☐ 5	☐ 5
Citizen of Subject or a Foreign Country	☐ 3	☐ 3	Foreign Nation	☐ 6	☐ 6

IV. NATURE OF SUIT (Place an "X" in One Box Only)

CONTRACT	TORTS		FORFEITURE/PENALTY	BANKRUPTCY	OTHER STATUTES
☐ 110 Insurance	**PERSONAL INJURY**	**PERSONAL INJURY**	☐ 610 Agriculture	☐ 422 Appeal 28 USC 158	☐ 400 State Reapportionment
☐ 120 Marine	☐ 310 Airplane	☐ 362 Personal Injury –	☐ 620 Other Food & Drug	☐ 423 Withdrawal	☐ 410 Antitrust
☐ 130 Miller Act	☐ 315 Airplane Product	Med. Malpractice	☐ 625 Drug Related Seizure	28 USC 157	☐ 430 Banks and Banking
☐ 140 Negotiable Instrument	Liability	☐ 365 Personal Injury –	of Property 21 USC 881		☐ 450 Commerce
☐ 150 Recovery of Overpayment	☐ 320 Assault, Libel &	Product Liability	☐ 630 Liquor Laws	**PROPERTY RIGHTS**	☐ 460 Deportation
& Enforcement of Judgment	Slander	☐ 368 Asbestos Personal	☐ 640 R.R. & Truck	☐ 820 Copyrights	☐ 470 Racketeer Influenced
☐ 151 Medicare Act	☐ 330 Federal Employers'	Injury Product Liability	☐ 650 Airline Regs.	☐ 830 Patent	and Corrupt Organizations
☐ 152 Recovery of Defaulted	Liability	**PERSONAL PROPERTY**	☐ 660 Occupational	☐ 840 Trademark	☐ 480 Consumer Credit
Student Loans	☐ 340 Marine	☐ 370 Other Fraud	Safety/Health		☐ 490 Cable/Sat TV
(Excl. Veterans)	☐ 345 Marine Product	☐ 371 Truth in Lending	☐ 690 Other	**SOCIAL SECURITY**	☐ 810 Selective Service
☐ 153 Recovery of Overpayment	Liability	☐ 380 Other Personal	**LABOR**	☐ 861 HIA (1395ff)	☐ 850 Securities/Commodities/
of Veteran's Benefits	☒ 350 Motor Vehicle	Property Damage	☐ 710 Fair Labor Standards	☐ 862 Black Lung (923)	Exchange
☐ 160 Stockholders' Suits	☐ 355 Motor Vehicle	☐ 385 Property Damage	Act	☐ 863 DIWC/DIWW (405(g))	☐ 875 Customer Challenge
☐ 190 Other Contract	Product Liability	Product Liability	☐ 720 Labor/Mgmt. Relations	☐ 864 SSID Title XVI	12 USC 3410
☐ 195 Contract Product Liability	☐ 360 Other Personal		☐ 730 Labor/Mgmt. Reporting	☐ 865 RSI (405(g))	☐ 890 Other Statutory Actions
☐ 196 Franchise	Injury		& Disclosure Act		☐ 891 Agricultural Acts
REAL PROPERTY	**CIVIL RIGHTS**	**PRISONER PETITIONS**	☐ 740 Railway Labor Act	**FEDERAL TAX SUITS**	☐ 892 Economic Stabilization Act
☐ 210 Land Condemnation	☐ 441 Voting	☐ 510 Motions to Vacate	☐ 790 Other Labor Litigation	☐ 870 Taxes (U.S. Plaintiff	☐ 893 Environmental Matters
☐ 220 Foreclosure	☐ 442 Employment	Sentence	☐ 791 Empl. Ret. Inc.	or Defendant)	☐ 894 Energy Allocation Act
☐ 230 Rent Lease & Ejectment	☐ 443 Housing/	**Habeas Corpus:**	Security Act	☐ 871 IRS—Third Party	☐ 895 Freedom of information Act
☐ 240 Torts to Land	Accommodations	☐ 530 General		26 USC 7609	☐ 900 Appeal of Fee Determination
☐ 245 Tort Product Liability	☐ 444 Welfare	☐ 535 Death Penalty			Under Equal Access to Justice
☐ 290 All Other Real Property	☐ 445 Amer. w/Disabilities –	☐ 540 Mandamus & Other			☐ 950 Constitutionality of State
	Employment	☐ 550 Civil Rights			Statutes
	446 Amer. w/Disabilities –	☐ 555 Prison Condition			
	Other				
	☐ 440 Other Civil Rights				

V. ORIGIN (Place an "X" in One Box Only)

☒ 1 Original Proceeding
☐ 2 Removed from State Court
☐ 3 Remanded from Appellate Court
☐ 4 Reinstated or Reopened
☐ 5 Transferred from another district (specify)
☐ 6 Multidistrict Litigation
☐ 7 Appeal to District Judge from Magistrate Judgment

VI. CAUSE OF ACTION

Cite the U.S. Civil Statute under which you are filing (Do not cite jurisdictional statutes unless diversity):

Brief description of cause: 28 USC 1332, 1441 Action for damage to pedestrian due to negligent operation of motor vehicle.

VII. REQUESTED IN COMPLAINT:

☐ CHECK IF THIS IS A CLASS ACTION UNDER F.R.C.P. 23

DEMAND $ 750,000

CHECK YES only if demanded in complaint:
JURY DEMAND: ☒ Yes ☐ No

VIII. RELATED CASE(S) IF ANY

(See instructions):
JUDGE _____
DOCKET NUMBER _____

DATE
10/21/--

SIGNATURE OF ATTORNEY OF RECORD
Arthur White

FOR OFFICE USE ONLY

RECEIPT# _____ AMOUNT _____ APPLYING IFP _____ JUDGE _____ MAG.JUDGE _____ the defendant has thirty days (sixty if located in a foreign country) in which to return the waiver. The notice and request must be sent to each defendant. Exhibit 5:3 is Federal Form 1A, Notice of Lawsuit and Request for Waiver of Service of Summons.

The second document is the Waiver of Service of the Summons. It includes the case caption, docket number, court, and date the request was sent. The plaintiff sends to the defendant two copies of this waiver to be signed, along with means of return (self-addressed, stamped envelope). If the defendant returns the signed waiver, the period in which to answer the complaint is extended from the usual twenty days to sixty days (ninety, if out of the country). Exhibit 5:4 is Federal Form 1B,

---

EXHIBIT 5:3 ■ Notice of Lawsuit and Request for Waiver of Service of Summons

AO 398 (12/93)

NOTICE OF LAWSUIT AND REQUEST FOR
WAIVER OF SERVICE OF SUMMONS

TO: (A)_____
as   (B)_____ of (C) _____

A lawsuit has been commenced against you (or the entity on whose behalf you are addressed.) A copy of the complaint is attached to this notice. It has been filed in the United States District Court for the (D) _____ District of _____ and has been assigned docket number (E) _____.

This is not a formal summons or notification from the court, but rather my request that you sign and return the enclosed waiver of service in order to save the cost of serving you with a judicial summons and an additional copy of the complaint. The cost of service will be avoided if I receive a signed copy of the waiver within (F) _____ days after the date designated below as the date on which this Notice and Request is sent. I enclose a stamped and addressed envelope (or other means of cost-free return) for your use. An extra copy of the waiver is also attached for your records.

If you comply with this request and return the signed waiver, it will be filed with the court and no summons will be served on you. The action will then proceed as if you had been served on the date the waiver is filed, except that you will not be obligated to answer the complaint before 60 days from the date designated below as the date on which this notice is sent (or before 90 days from that date if your address is not in any judicial district of the United States).

If you do not return the signed waiver within the time indicated, I will take appropriate steps to effect formal service in a manner authorized by the Federal Rules of Civil Procedure and will then, to the extent authorized by those Rules, ask the court to require you (or the party on whose behalf you are addressed) to pay the full costs of such service. In that connection, please read the statement concerning the duty of parties to waive the service of the summons, which is set forth at the foot of the waiver form.

I affirm that this request is being sent to you on behalf of the plaintiff, this _____ day of _____, _____.

_____
Signature of Plaintiff's Attorney
or Unrepresented Plaintiff

A — Name of individual defendant (or name of officer or agent of corporate defendant)
B — Title, or other relationship of individual to corporate defendant
C — Name of corporate defendant, if any
D — District
E — Docket number of action
F — Addressee must be given at least 30 days (60 days if located in foreign country) in which to return waiver

EXHIBIT 5:4 ▪ Waiver of Service of Summons

AO 399 (Rev. 10/95)

WAIVER OF SERVICE OF SUMMONS

TO: _____

(NAME OF PLAINTIFF'S ATTORNEY OR UNREPRESENTED PLAINTIFF)

I, _____, acknowledge receipt of your request

(DEFENDANT NAME)

that I waive service of summons in the action of _____,

(CAPTION OF ACTION)

which is case number _____ in the United States District Court for

(DOCKET NUMBER)

the _____ District of _____.

I have also received a copy of the complaint in the action, two copies of this instrument, and a means by which I can return the signed waiver to you without cost to me.

I agree to save the cost of service of a summons and an additional copy of the complaint in this lawsuit by not requiring that I (or the entity on whose behalf I am acting) be served with judicial process in the manner provided by Rule 4.

I (or the entity on whose behalf I am acting) will retain all defenses or objections to the lawsuit or to the jurisdiction or venue of the court except for objections based on a defect in the summons or in the service of the summons.

I understand that a judgment may be entered against me (or the party on whose behalf I am acting) if an answer or motion Under Rule 12 is not served upon you within 60 days after _____. or within

(DATE REQUEST WAS SENT)

90 days after that date if the request was sent outside the United States.

_____   _____

(DATE)   (SIGNATURE)

Printed/Typed Name: _____

As _____ of _____

(TITLE)   (CORPORATE DEFENDANT)

Duty to Avoid Unnecessary Costs of Service of Summons

Rule 4 of the Federal Rules of Civil Procedure requires certain parties to cooperate in saving unnecessary costs of service of the summons and complaint. A defendant located in the United States who, after being notified of an action and asked by a plaintiff located in the United States to waive service of summons, fails to do so will be required to bear the cost of such service unless good cause be shown for its failure to sign and return the waiver.

It is not good cause for a failure to waive service that a party believes that the complaint is unfounded, or that the action has been brought in an improper place or in a court that lacks jurisdiction over the subject matter of the action or over its person or property. A party who waives service of the summons retains all defenses and objections (except any relating to the summons or to the service of the summons), and may later object to the jurisdiction of the court or to the place where the action has been brought.

A defendant who waives service must within the time specified on the waiver form serve on the plaintiff's attorney (or unrepresented plaintiff) a response to the complaint and must also file a signed copy of the response with the court. If the answer or motion is not served within this time, a default judgment may be taken against that defendant. By waiving service, a defendant is allowed more time to answer than if the summons had been actually served when the request for waiver of service was received.

Waiver of Service of Summons. Check your state and local rules to see if a parallel waiver of service of summons has been adopted. Also, confirm whether the Notice of Lawsuit and Request for Waiver of Service of Summons and the Waiver of Service of Summons can be delivered and executed electronically.

A defendant who fails to waive service of the summons must bear the cost of service, including the plaintiff's related attorney fees, unless good cause is shown. Good cause does not include a belief that the complaint is unfounded. A defendant who returns the waiver retains all defenses and objections to the complaint, including those regarding jurisdiction and venue.

The plaintiff's attorney may elect not to use the notice and waiver process, especially if the statute of limitations is about to expire, and no time remains to send and receive a waiver.

Request for Service of Process

Although most federal service is by waiver or effected by any person over 18 not a party, the U.S. marshal located in each federal district may be requested through the court to make service. The marshal must serve process when the plaintiff is indigent (**in forma pauperis**) or a seaman [Rule 4(c)(2)]. The U.S. government is no longer required to use the marshal or appointed server.

in forma pauperis
"In the manner of a pauper"; permission given to a poor person to sue without liability for costs.

When the marshal does serve process, Form USM-285, Process Receipt and Return, must be completed by the law firm and filed with the action. An example of this form is shown in Exhibit 5:5. This form is available through the marshal's office or at http://www.usmarshals.gov. The fee for the marshal's service is minimal, but must be included when filing the Process Receipt and Return.

Many state courts also require the filing of a request for service of process. Filed with the clerk of the state court, this request is then given to the local sheriff or constable with the summons and complaint. Determine whether a request for service is required in your state and place a copy of the request form in your system folder.

Motion for Special Appointment to Serve Process

In some circumstances your attorney may decide that service should be made by a process server specially appointed by the court [Rule 4(c)(2)]. If so, prepare the motion. Exhibit 5:6 is an example of the motion.[1]

Affidavit of Service of Summons and Complaint

When service is performed by a specially appointed process server, an affidavit of service must be completed pursuant to Rule 4(l). There are times when your state court may also require such an affidavit. An affidavit appropriate for federal court is shown in Exhibit 5:7.

Consent to Exercise of Jurisdiction by Magistrate Judge

This document is drafted only on the specific direction of the attorney. Its purpose is to inform the court that the parties agree to have the matter tried by a federal magistrate judge rather than the district court judge. If so directed, this document should be prepared and presented to the clerk at the same time the complaint is filed as dictated by local federal practice. It will then have to be signed by the defendant and returned to the clerk of court. Exhibit 5:8 is the form for consent to exercise of jurisdiction by a United States magistrate judge.

EXHIBIT 5:5 ■ Process Receipt and Return

U.S. Department of Justice
United States Marshals Service

PROCESS RECEIPT AND RETURN
*See Instructions for "Service Process by the U.S. Marshal"
on the reverse of this form*

PLAINTIFF	COURT CASE NUMBER
DEFENDANT	TYPE OF PROCESS

SERVE AT
{ NAME OF INDIVIDUAL, COMPANY, CORPORATION, ETC., TO SERVE OR DESCRIPTION OF PROPERTY TO SEIZE OR CONDEMN

ADDRESS *(Street or RFD, Apartment No., City, State and Zip Code)*

SEND NOTICE OF SERVICE COPY TO REQUESTER AT NAME AND ADDRESS BELOW:	Number of process to be served with this Form - 285	
	Number of parties to be served in this case	
	Check for service on U.S.A.	

SPECIAL INSTRUCTIONS OR OTHER INFORMATION THAT WILL ASSIST IN EXPEDITING SERVICE *(Include Business and Alternate Addresses. All Telephone Numbers, and Estimated Times Available for services):*
Fold   Fold

Signature of Attorney or other Originator requesting service on behalf of:	☐ PLAINTIFF ☐ DEFENDANT	TELEPHONE NUMBER	DATE

SPACE BELOW FOR USE OF U.S. MARSHAL ONLY – DO NOT WRITE BELOW THIS LINE

I acknowledge receipt for the total number of process indicated. *(Sign only first USM 285 if more than one USM 285 is submitted)*	Total Process	District or Origin No.	District to Serve No.	Signature of Authorized USMS Deputy or Clerk	Date

I hereby certify and return that I ☐ have personally served, ☐ have legal evidence of service, ☐ have executed as shown in "Remarks", the process described on the individual, company, corporation, etc., at the address shown above or on the individual, company, corporation, etc., shown at the address inserted below.

☐ I hereby certify and return that I am unable to locate the individual company, corporation, etc.. named above *(See remarks below)*

Name and title of individual served *(if not shown above)*	☐ A person of suitable age and discretion then residing in the defendant's usual place of abode.	
Address *(complete only if different than shown above)*	Date of Service	Time am / pm
	Signature of U.S. Marshal or Deputy	

Service Fee	Total Mileage Charges *(including endeavors)*	Forwarding Fee	Total Charges	Advance Deposits	Amount owed to U.S. Marshal or	Amount of Refund

REMARKS:

PRIOR EDITIONS MAY BE USED   **1. CLERK OF THE COURT**   **FORM USM-285 (Rev. 12/15/80)**

EXHIBIT 5:6 ▪ Motion for Special Appointment to Serve Process

THE UNITED STATES DISTRICT COURT FOR THE CENTRAL DISTRICT OF COLUMBIA

Civil Action, File No. _____,

_____,
Plaintiff

v.

_____,
Defendant

Motion for Special Appointment to Serve Process

Pursuant to Rule 4(c)(2), Federal Rules of Civil Procedure, _____ moves this Court to specifically appoint _____ to serve the _____ on _____ in this action. Said person to be appointed is not less than eighteen years of age and is not a party to this action. Said appointment will bring a savings in costs to the United States Marshal.

_____
Attorney

Order

IT IS ORDERED this ____ day of ____, ____, that ____ be appointed to serve the ____ on ____ in this action. Proof of such service shall be made by affidavit in accordance with Rule 4(l), Federal Rules of Civil Procedure.

By the Court

_____
United States District Court Judge

Nongovernmental Corporation Disclosure Statement

If your client is a nongovernmental corporation, Rule 7.1 now requires a disclosure statement to be filed with the court. Two copies must be filed on the party's first appearance or action in the case. The statement must disclose any parent corporation and any publicly held corporation owning 10 percent or more of the party's stock or state that there is no such corporation.

OBTAIN THE CHECK FOR THE FILING FEES

After the documents are prepared and checked for accuracy and necessary signatures, a check for the filing fee should be obtained. Each firm will have its own procedure in this regard. If the procedure is not in the office procedures manual, ask an experienced secretary or the office manager. If the action is to be filed in state court, include any necessary service of process fee, which is paid to the clerk in some states and directly to the sheriff or process server in others. If the summons is to be served in a foreign jurisdiction, the fee is generally paid directly and in advance for serving the documents. The U.S. district court filing fee for a civil action is $250.

EXHIBIT 5:7 ▪ Affidavit of Service of Summons and Complaint

UNITED STATES DISTRICT COURT FOR
THE CENTRAL DISTRICT OF COLUMBIA CIVIL ACTION

File No. _____

_____
Plaintiff

v.   Affidavit of Service of Summons and Complaint

_____
Defendant

I served a copy of the summons and complaint in the above matter by __[type of service]__ at   [time] on the ___ day of _____, _____, on

Name _____

Address where served _____

_[signature of process server]_____
Name
Signed and sworn to before me on:

_____

_____

Notary Public
My commission expires on _____

EXHIBIT 5:8 ▪ Consent to Exercise of Jurisdiction by a United States Magistrate Judge, Election of Appeal to District Judge

UNITED STATES DISTRICT COURT
_____District of_____

Plaintiff
v.

Defendant

NOTICE, CONSENT, AND ORDER OF REFERENCE—
EXERCISE OF JURISDICTION BY A UNITED STATES
MAGISTRATE JUDGE

Case Number:

NOTICE OF AVAILABILITY OF A UNITED STATES MAGISTRATE JUDGE
TO EXERCISE JURISDICTION

In accordance with the provisions of 28 U.S.C. §636(c), and Fed.R.Civ.P. 73, you are notified that a United States magistrate judge of this district court is available to conduct any or all proceddings in this case including a jury or nonjury trial, and to order the entry of a final judgment. Exercise of this jurisdiction by a magistrate judge is, however, permitted only if all parties voluntarily consent.

(continued)

EXHIBIT 5:8 ■ Consent to Exercise of Jurisdiction by a United States Magistrate Judge, Election of Appeal to District Judge *(continued)*

You may, without adverse substantive consequences, withhold your consent, but this will prevent the court's jurisdiction from being exercised by a magistrate judge. If any party withholds consent, the identity of the parties consenting or withholding consent will not be communicated to any magistrate judge or to the district judge to whom the case has been assigned.

An appeal from a judgment entered by a magistrate judge shall be taken directly to the United States court of appeals for this judicial circuit in the same manner as an appeal from any other judgment of this district court.

CONSENT TO THE EXERCISE OF JURISDICTION BY A UNITED STATES MAGISTRATE JUDGE

In accordance with provisions of 28 U.S.C. §636(c) and Fed.R.Civ.P. 73, the parties in this case consent to have a United States magistrate judge conduct any and all proceedings in this case, including the trial, order the entry of a final judgment, and conduct all post-judgment proceedings.

Party Represented	Signature	Date
_____	_____	_____
_____	_____	_____
_____	_____	_____
_____	_____	_____

ORDER OF REFERENCE

IT IS ORDERED that this case be referred to _____
United States Magistrate Judge, to conduct all proceedings and order the entry of judgment in accordance with 28 U.S.C. §636(c) and Fed.R.Civ.P. 73.

_____   _____
         Date   United States District Judge

NOTE: RETURN THIS FORM TO THE CLERK OF THE COURT <u>ONLY IF</u> ALL PARTIES HAVE CONSENTED <u>ON THIS FORM</u> TO THE EXERCISE OF JURISDICTION BY A UNITED STATES MAGISTRATE JUDGE.

FILING THE LAWSUIT

TRADITIONAL METHODS OF FILING

When all the required documents have been prepared, checked for accuracy, and signed, it is time to file the action. Although filing the summons, complaint, and subsequent papers is occasionally done in a rush, it is a simple procedure. The prepared documents are taken to the clerk of the court in which the action is to be filed. Personal delivery of the papers to the clerk is the most common method of filing, but using certified mail to send the summons, complaint, and other necessary documents to the clerk is permitted.

The clerk stamps the date on the original complaint and, in the federal system, immediately assigns the action a civil case number and possibly a judge. The action commences in federal court upon the delivery of the complaint to the clerk (Rule 3). In some state courts, the action does not commence until a summons and a copy of the complaint are served upon the defendant.

The court clerk then issues a summons with the court seal and the clerk's signature. The clerk in federal court then asks what method of service will be used. This is done to see that all needed documents are presented. A summons for each defendant is then either returned to be served on the defendant (federal court) or delivered to the sheriff or process server for service (state court).

For all practical purposes, the procedure is the same in all federal district courts. State court procedures vary, but are similar.

E-FILING

Electronic filing or **e-filing** is a court-approved, Internet-based system for filing, serving, and accessing legal documents. It eliminates trips from the law office to the court house, reduces paper and photocopying costs, provides 24-hour access for attorneys and clients, and facilitates filing documents and viewing case files from locations other than the law office. Ideally, the e-filing system immediately confirms the filing of a document and its service on the opponent, and it calculates the required court fees and electronically transfers the funds. Savings to clients may be as much as seventy-five percent of traditional filing costs. Savings in reduced clerk of court time and document storage may be even greater for taxpayers.[2] Federal Rule of Civil Procedure 5(e) and parallel state rules authorize the filing of documents by electronic means. Rule 77(d) authorizes the court to use electronic means to notify parties of the entry of a court order or judgment.

E-filing systems normally have a closely associated system that provides both the public and attorneys with access to electronic court documents. A number of states have e-filing and public access systems. The e-filing system for U.S. district courts, bankruptcy courts, the courts of appeals, the Court of International Trade, and the Court of Federal Claims is the Case Management/Electronic Case Filing system (CM/ECF). It provides electronic docket management with Internet filing of most case documents. In addition to 24-hour access, its benefits include instant creation of docket entries, notification of any new entry to the parties in the case with hyperlinks to the new document and the pertinent case, and an instant filing confirmation receipt for the attorney's file. The automatic notification of the new entry is called Notice of Electronic Filing (NEF). It constitutes service of the document.

The federal court public access component is Public Access to Court Electronic Records (PACER). Anyone, including attorneys and their clients, with a PACER account and password can access PACER to locate and view federal court documents in specific cases. Only court-registered attorneys with a PACER account and a separate required login protocol and a password can access CM/ECF to file and view case documents. A PACER account is free, and parties receive one free, downloadable copy of a filed document with nominal fees for other documents. The court can order that some documents be sealed, which requires the documents to be filed in hard copy only and then sealed by the court. Sealed documents are unavailable through the e-system. The electronic docket will reflect that the sealed document has been filed.

Technical components needed to use the federal system include a recent computer operating system, a relatively fast Internet connection, a recent version of Netscape or Internet Explorer, word processing software, a personal e-mail account, and both Adobe Acrobat Reader and Acrobat Writer (or similar software) to view and create documents in portable document format (PDF). A scanner is needed to image any documents not in electronic form so they can be converted to PDF for filing.

Many federal courts (and your state courts may) now require cases to be filed electronically. Paralegals are likely to do the filing. Seek what training is available from your state or federal district court. A tutorial in e-filing is offered on the Web site of most federal district courts. The Web sites also offer the latest version of the CM/ECF User's Manual. Further, attorneys are permitted to bring paralegals to the hands-on

e-filing
A court-approved, Internet-based system for filing, serving, and accessing legal documents.

training sessions offered by the federal district courts. Regardless of whether you are filing documents in a state or federal e-filing system, the process is reasonably uniform. See Exhibit 5:9 for a Checklist for E-Filing.[3]

Although pleadings, motions, and other court documents can be filed electronically in the federal system, check your local system for what documents can be e-filed. Some federal district courts do not initiate cases electronically until the complaint is filed in the traditional manner. Many of these courts are not yet equipped to accept credit card payment of the filing fee, so check with the respective court clerk to be sure that e-filing of the complaint is acceptable and, if so, what payment procedure is required. Once a case is filed, the parties are designated, and the case is assigned a number, subsequent documents can be filed electronically.

Note this important rule about serving e-filed documents. The initial summons, which notifies the defendant that a lawsuit has been filed, must be served according

---

EXHIBIT 5:9 ▪ Checklist for E-Filings

WORD DOCUMENT

1) "Electronically Filed" is stated in the caption of the pleading.
2) There is a completed certificate of service. (signature (s/John Doe), dated etc.)
3) There is an "s/(attorney's typed name)" with the attorney's name typed on the signature line.

PDF DOCUMENTS

1) If the main document is created with a word application, it must be **converted** to PDF format instead of printed and scanned to create the PDF.
2) The main pleading is a **separate** PDF document from any attachments, and each exhibit is a separate PDF document.
3) There are no missing pages. All pages are in order and right side up.
4) Every page is legible. (The main document and all attachments)

ELECTRONICALLY FILING THE PLEADING

1) The attorney's name on the signature line must match the name of attorney logged into ECF.
2) Choose the correct case.
3) Check the case number and caption of the case on top of each screen.
4) Choose the most accurate/appropriate event.
5) If this is a multi-part **motion,** multiple reliefs should be chosen.
6) All attachments must be filled inidvidually and separately from one another, and named appropriately.
7) For each document filed or electronically attached, verify that you are filing the correct document by opening the PDF document at the "Browse" screen with Acrobat Reader before the document is uploaded into ECF.
8) A proposed order must be a separate document and accompany the motion as an electronic attachment, not as a separate entry.
9) When filing a "Motion for leave to file a document," the subject document is to be filed as an electronic attachment to the Motion, NOT as a separate entry.
10) Describe all attachments completely and concisely.
11) If given the opportunity to create a link to an existing event, do so when appropriate.
12) Use the optional text box, when given the opportunity, to further describe your pleading. Rule of thumb: the docket text should accurately reflect the title of the pleading being filed.
13) If you use the optional text box, make certain that information added should not be a separate entry.

to the traditional procedures outlined in Rule 4 (see next section). Under Rule 5(b)(2)(D), all other documents designated by the rules to be served on the parties may be served by electronic means, *if* the person served has given written consent [5(b)(2)(D)]. The pertinent note of the Committee on Rules of Practice and Procedure states that the consent may be electronic, it cannot be implied, and it should specify its scope and duration. E-service is complete on transmission, unless the party making service learns that the service failed [5 (b)(3)].

SERVICE OF PROCESS

Once the action is filed, it is essential to serve the summons and a copy of the complaint on the defendant in order for the court to gain personal jurisdiction over the defendant. In state court this is usually necessary to begin the action. The court's judgment is not binding against the defendant unless personal jurisdiction has been obtained by service of process. Consequently, it is an extremely important step.

Under Rule 4(c) the plaintiff must serve the summons and a copy of the complaint on each defendant within 120 days [Rule 4(m)] of filing the complaint. Failure to do so shall result in dismissal of the action unless good cause for failure to comply can be shown to the court. In some states, the responsibility for service of the summons rests with the clerk of court. If service is the clerk's responsibility, it is best to provide information on the best place(s) and time to find the defendant.

The methods of service vary depending on the court (state or federal), the type of defendant, and the location of the defendant (in state, out of state, or in another country).

REFERENCE GUIDE AND CHECKLIST FOR METHODS OF SERVICE

SERVICE ON INDIVIDUALS IN A STATE OR IN A JUDICIAL DISTRICT OF THE UNITED STATES

1. *Mail (state):*   Service on individuals by mail is permitted in a number of states. Check state practice carefully.
   a. Place a copy of the summons and complaint in an envelope addressed to the defendant or, if previously agreed to, to the defendant's attorney.
   b. Include a return-addressed envelope and two copies of an acknowledgment of service form, if your state requires it.
   c. Use first-class mail if an acknowledgment of service is used.
   d. When no acknowledgment is used, mail the documents to the defendant by registered or certified mail, return receipt requested. Mark the green certified mail card "Restricted Delivery Only" if you want only the named person to receive the envelope.
   e. The date the acknowledgment is signed is the date of service. If certified mail is used, the date of delivery marked on the return receipt is the date of service.
   f. Fill out the Return of Service on the original summons and file it (plus any signed acknowledgment) with the clerk.
2. *Waiver of Service of Summons, Federal Rule 4(d)*
   a. Dispatch by first class mail or other reliable means a Notice of Lawsuit and Request for Waiver of Service of Summons, two copies of the Waiver of Service

> "I'm sick and tired of hearing about the number of cases disposed of when we discuss the judicial system. The chief justice should know that the job of the courts is not to dispose of cases but to decide them justly. Doesn't he know that the business of courts is justice?"
>
> —JIM R. CARRIGAN, JUSTICE, SUPREME COURT OF COLORADO, *LOS ANGELES HERALD-EXAMINER,* AUGUST 3, 1977.

of Summons, a copy of the complaint with the date of filing stamped on it, and a return-addressed, stamped envelope to each defendant.
   b. The defendant has thirty days from the date the request is sent (sixty days if the defendant is outside any judicial district of the United States) to return the waiver.
   c. On receipt of the signed waiver, place it in your case file. No return of service is filed.
3. *Other Federal Service:* Rule 4(e) states that, unless otherwise provided by federal law, service on an individual (other than an infant or an incompetent person) may be made by the following means:
   a. Through the method of service used in the state within which the federal district court is located or that used in the state where service is made ("effected"); or
   b. Personal service
4. *Personal Service/Federal Rule 4(e)(2) and State:* The rules governing personal service are similar among jurisdictions, but the pertinent rules should be checked for any unique features. Personal service is achieved in the following manner:
   a. Locate the defendant and personally hand a copy of the summons and complaint to the defendant or an agent authorized by appointment or law to receive service of process.
   b. If the defendant is not available, leave a copy of the summons and complaint at the individual's residence with a person of suitable *age* (fourteen in many jurisdictions) and *discretion* residing there. Leaving the complaint with another person is not permitted in some states.
   c. Serve the documents during reasonable hours, including Sundays and holidays, or during the night shift if that is when the defendant works.
   d. Fill out the return of service on the original summons, make a copy for your records, and file the summons with the clerk.
5. *Service on Infants or Incompetent Persons*
   a. Serve according to the state law where service is to be attempted [Rule 4(g)].
   b. If in a foreign country, follow the steps for service of individuals in a foreign country [Rule 4(f)].
   c. Normally, serve the legal guardian or appointed representative.

SERVICE ON INDIVIDUALS IN A FOREIGN COUNTRY [RULE 4(F)]

Unless a waiver of service of summons has been obtained, service on an individual in a foreign country should be effected in the following manner:

1. Determine whether the pertinent foreign country is a party to any international agreement or treaty governing service of process, such as the Hague Convention on the Service Abroad of Judicial and Extrajudicial Documents. For the terms and parties, see the last volume of *The Martindale Hubbell Law Directory* or other international sources.
2. Follow the procedures outlined in the agreement [Rule 4(f)(1)].

If there is no applicable agreement, then follow Rule 4(f)(2).

1. Provided that service is "reasonably calculated to give notice," make service in the manner prescribed by the law of the foreign country; or
2. As directed by the foreign authority in response to a letter of request or a letter rogatory. A letter rogatory is a request from a court in one country to a court in another asking the foreign court to examine a witness according to that court's own rules (see FED. R. CIV. P. 28); or

3. Unless prohibited by the law of the foreign country,
    a. by actual delivery of a copy of the summons and complaint; or
    b. by signed receipt mail dispatched by the clerk of court; or
4. By other means directed by the court

SERVICE ON CORPORATIONS AND ASSOCIATIONS [RULE 4(H)]

1. If waiver of service has not been obtained, serve according to the law of the state in which the United States district court is located; or
2. Serve a copy of the summons and complaint to an officer, a managing or general agent, or to any other agent authorized by appointment or by law to receive service [Rule 4(h)]. If the law authorizing the agent to receive service requires it, mail a copy of the summons and complaint to the defendant. In many states, the secretary of state is the statutorily designated official. Most secretary of state offices keep a current list of business officers or agents designated to receive service. This information can also be obtained through Westlaw and Lexis databanks.

SERVICE ON THE UNITED STATES [RULE 4(I)]

1. Serve the U.S. attorney for the district in which the action is brought, or an assistant U.S. attorney or clerical employee designated by the U.S. attorney in writing filed with the clerk of the court [Rule 4(i)], or
2. Send a copy of the summons and complaint by registered or certified mail to the civil process clerk at the office of the U.S. attorney and send a copy of the summons and complaint by registered or certified mail to the attorney general of the United States in Washington, D.C.; *and*
3. In any action attacking the validity of an order of an officer or agency of the United States not made a party, also send copies by registered or certified mail to the officer or agency.
4. Serve any U.S. officer, agency, or corporation in the manner previously described [Rule 4(i)(1)] and by also sending a copy of the summons and complaint by registered or certified mail to the officer, agency, or corporation.

Note that there are special practice considerations related to commencing an action for damages against the United States under the Federal Tort Claims Act (28 USC §§ 2671–80). The act's procedure can save time and litigation costs. The act has a *two year* statute of limitation. Prior to filing a court action, the injured party must file an administrative claim with the relevant agency using form SF-95, including the evidentiary documents to support the claim. Once the administrative claim is filed, there is a six-month waiting period before an action can be filed in federal court. If the administrative claim is denied, the plaintiff has six-months from the date of notice of denial to file an action in U.S. district court.

SERVICE ON A FOREIGN, STATE, OR LOCAL GOVERNMENT

1. Serve a foreign government or entity pursuant to 28 U.S.C. § 1608.
2. Serve a state, municipal, or other government agency by effecting delivery on its chief executive officer or as prescribed by state law.
3. Note that some government entities require a person contemplating an action to file a demand by claim or other form with the entity before filing a lawsuit. This procedure can be found in the applicable laws.

SERVICE OUTSIDE THE GEOGRAPHICAL BOUNDARIES OF THE STATE OR FEDERAL DISTRICT COURT/LONG-ARM STATUTES

long-arm statutes
Laws giving a court personal jurisdiction over nonresident persons or corporations in specified circumstances.

At one time it was difficult, if not impossible, to serve defendants who resided beyond the borders of a particular state or who had passed briefly through the state and had caused injury. This injustice has been corrected in most states with the passage of **long-arm statutes.** These laws give a court personal jurisdiction over nonresident persons or corporations in specified circumstances. The key to these statutes is whether the defendant has sufficient minimum contacts with the state to justify personal jurisdiction and whether the statute provides constitutionally based "fair play," which includes such due process concepts as adequate notice of the action and a fair opportunity for the defendant to be heard [*International Shoe Co.* v. *Washington,* 326 U.S. 310 (1945)]. Under such statutes, courts have been able to gain jurisdiction over nonresident motorists and operators of planes and vessels, persons who commit torts in the state, property owners, foreign corporations and manufacturers, and persons who contract to sell goods or services in the state. The principles applied by courts in such circumstances have now been extended to gain jurisdiction over a party's Internet contact with a state [*Zippo Manufacturing Co. v. Zippo Dot Com. Inc.,* 952 F. Supp. 1119 (W.D. Pa. 1997)]. The more the nonresident has used the Internet to gain access (particularly commercial access) to the state's markets, the more likely the court will find the needed minimum contacts resulting in personal jurisdiction. Where the defendant had a Web site on which state residents could order products but had not, the contacts were insufficient to support personal jurisdiction [*Quality Improvement Consultants Inc. v. Williams,* F. Supp.2d not reported, WL543393 (D. Minn. 2003)]. Where a defendant's Web site and state commercial contacts were individually inadequate for personal jurisdiction, combining the two can be adequate [*Toys "R" Us Inc. v. Step Two S.A.,* 318 F.3d 446 (3d Cir. 2003)]. Similar principles are being used for jusrisdiction in international Internet lawsuits. Also, when a foreign defendant's contacts with a particular state are insufficient for personal jurisdiction, such jurisdiction may be gained by looking at its contacts with the United States [FED. R. CIV. P. 4(k)(2)]. Courts have upheld the validity of long-arm statutes on the logic that the cause of action should be remedied where the harm occurred as long as the minimum contacts are present and the nonresident is treated fairly (given due process).

The long-arm statute identifies which public official in the state must be served. For example, out-of-state corporations doing business in the state are typically served through the state's secretary of state, insurance companies through the commissioners of insurance, and out-of-state motorists through the commissioner of highways. Prior to filing an action using the long-arm statute, read the state's long-arm statute to determine which official should be served and with what documents.

The federal courts follow the long-arm procedure of the state in which the federal district court is located [Rule 4(k)(1)(A)]. A few federal long-arm provisions provide for nationwide personal jurisdiction in cases involving antitrust and securities laws as well as interpleader actions, which resolve a special type of property dispute. It pays to consult the specific statute under which a federal claim is brought to see if such extended jurisdiction exists. In addition, Rule 4(k)(1)(B) gives a federal district court jurisdiction over parties later added to an action (Rules 14 and 19) who reside within 100 miles of the district court in which the action was filed regardless of state boundaries. Even absent state court jurisdiction, in respect to claims arising under federal law, personal jurisdiction can be achieved by actual service of the summons or waiver if it is consistent with the Constitution and federal laws.

Here is a typical procedure for gaining service of process under a long-arm statute:

1. The original and two copies of the complaint are filed with the clerk of court.
2. The clerk issues the summons and mails two copies of the summons and complaint by certified mail to the secretary of state or other designated officer.
3. The secretary of state's office sends a copy of the summons and complaint to the nonresident defendant by certified mail, return receipt requested.
4. On return of the receipt, the secretary of state's office certifies to the clerk of court that service has been made.
5. If the secretary of state's office cannot gain service, the state statute normally sets out alternatives for service.

Some secretary of state Web sites now provide computerized tracking of summonses served through that office.

SERVICE IN IN REM AND QUASI IN REM CASES

An **in rem action** is an action involving the attachment of property to resolve claims to the property, and is based in the state's sovereign authority over property within its borders. The property can include real estate; tangibles such as automobiles, jewelry, or art; and intangibles such as bank deposits, stocks, and promissory notes. If, for example, a man dies having a will that leaves his property to his wife but also leaves substantial evidence of his intent to leave a secret condominium to his mistress of many years, who should own the condominium? The mistress might sue in the court in the jurisdiction where the condominium is located, using an in rem action to determine who owns the property. The action is against the property and service is gained by the method outlined in the governing state or federal statute or by delivery of the summons and complaint to the person holding the property [Rule 4(n)(1)].

A **quasi in rem action** is one in which the court uses the property of a defendant over whom it does not have personal jurisdiction to pay a judgment against the defendant entered in an action indirectly related or unrelated to the property. For example, assume A has a court judgment against B for B's failure to pay A for an automobile A sold to B. B now lives out of state and the court cannot gain personal jurisdiction over B. B, however, owns a small piece of land in-state. A can sue B in a quasi in rem process to have the state court seize B's property and sell it to pay on the debt for the automobile. If A's action is successful but the land is worth less than the car debt, A can recover only the value of the land, because the court does not have personal jurisdiction over B or any of his other assets. An *in rem* action is against the property, a *quasi in rem* action is brought against the owner of the property. One might characterize *quasi in rem* statutes as "short-arm" statutes. *In rem* and *quasi in rem* jurisdiction can no longer be based simply on the state's traditional authority over the property within its borders. The constitutional prerequisites of jurisdiction set out in *International Shoe* must also be applied in nonresident *in rem* and *quasi in rem* cases [*Shaffer v. Heitner*, 433 U.S. 186 (1977)]. On a showing that service cannot be made on a defendant by any method outlined in the rules, the court may seize the property according to the law of the state in which the district court is located [Rule 4(n)(2)].

In such cases, many jurisdictions authorize **constructive service,** which involves publication of the summons in a newspaper of general circulation in the area where the property is located. The newspaper will generally provide an affidavit of publication and the attorney will file an affidavit of compliance plus copies of the publication. Some publication statutes deem personal service of the defendant in another state to be adequate publication.

in rem action
An action involving the attachment of property to resolve claims to the property.

quasi in rem action
An action in which the court uses the property of a defendant over whom it does not have personal jurisdiction to pay a judgment against the defendant entered in an action unrelated to the property.

constructive service
Service of process other than direct service, such as through a newspaper of general circulation.

substituted service
Any type of service of process other than actual, personal service, such as through mail, waiver, publication, or legal representative.

Substituted service is any type of service other than actual, personal service. Service by mail, waiver, publication, or through an attorney or other legal representative are all means of substituted service.

Setting up a quick-reference guide or checklist for the methods of service for your state may be helpful. Particularly note that the time allowed after filing the complaint within which to serve the summons may vary from the federal 120-day limit. Also, the sheriff may or may not be the person who effects personal service.

IMMUNITY FROM SERVICE OF PROCESS

In some instances, a person may not be legally served with a summons and complaint because of immunity from service of process. Commonly, defendants and witnesses attending a trial, or traveling to or from the trial, are immune from service. So too are defendants brought into a state by force or served in some fraudulent manner.

LOCATING "INVISIBLE" DEFENDANTS

In most instances, you will be asked to locate the defendant as early in the case as possible to determine how and where service can be made. Even a sheriff or process server will need directions. Therefore, it is helpful to know ways to locate people who are difficult to find. Chapter 3 sets out several methods, including Internet resources, to locate hard-to-find witnesses; many of those methods are applicable to locating hard-to-find defendants. Here are some of the better techniques for locating the "invisible" defendant:

Checklist for Locating Defendants

1. If you are trying to ascertain the registered agent for service of process on a corporation, call the secretary of state's corporate division for your state and the state in which the corporation is likely to be incorporated or have its principal place of business. Many of the techniques used to locate individuals are applicable to corporations and other business organizations.
2. Check telephone and city or county directories. Use Internet directories such as www.switchboard.com, www.whowhere.lycos.com, and locator services through Westlaw and Lexis, or try a fee service such as www.ussearch.com or www.gisusdata.com. The fees are reasonable, and some services do not charge if the search is unsuccessful.
3. Send an envelope addressed to the last known address of the defendant with the words "Forwarding Address Requested" written in the lower left-hand corner of the envelope. The envelope should have the firm's return address on it and the necessary return postage enclosed.[4] The post office may require the submission of Form 1478 for a forwarding address under the Freedom of Information Act.
4. Send a plain envelope addressed to the defendant by registered mail marked "Return Receipt Requested" and check the box on the green card entitled "Show to whom, date, and address of delivery." The mail carrier will request the defendant to sign the card.
5. Contact the defendant's former landlord or neighbors to obtain a new address, the name of the moving company, or the names of relatives or friends who might know the new address or provide additional information. Sources providing such information include churches, schools, or colleges attended;

former employers, present employer, co-workers; professional or trade associations; health insurance carriers; sports clubs, civic clubs, country clubs, and veterans' organizations; and banking institutions.

6. Check voter registration lists, tax rolls, land transfer records (for names of persons involved in recent property transfers who might know the defendant's whereabouts, such as a buyer, a real estate agent, or a bank employee), civil and criminal court records, and vital statistics records.

7. Check with utility, telephone, cable television, newspaper, and other community-based companies for the address.

8. Check with credit and banking institutions. One way to locate the institutions used by the defendant is to ask a former employer to review old paychecks for the name of the bank where the checks were cashed. Review the bank's checking account records for businesses, services, and organizations paid by the defendant.[5]

9. Contact the pertinent state's auto registration and driver's licensing division.

10. Check with local tax accounting firms.

11. Place an ad in the newspaper with a reward for information that leads to the location of the defendant.

12. Hire a private investigator. Consider having the investigator appointed to serve process under relevant state or federal [4(c)(2)] rules, especially where the sheriff or marshal cannot locate the defendant.

A word of caution is in order here. Prior to contacting employers, neighbors, relatives, and so on, review the consumer protection and collection laws for your jurisdiction, including the Fair Debt Collections Practices Act (15 U.S.C. § 1692). Note especially the section on what constitutes harassment or otherwise illegal collection practices. If you do not, you may find yourself in violation of the law and subject to serious penalty.

Should your office use professional process servers, it helps to have access to a pertinent directory. One such directory is Deponet, an international directory of quality-assured court reporting firms and process servers (1-800-337-6638), www. deponet.com/about_us.html.

OTHER SERVICE OF PROCESS

Rule 4.1 covers methods for service of process other than a summons or a subpoena (Rule 45). Service shall be by U.S. marshal, deputy marshal, or by an appointed person. Orders of contempt of a federal decree or injunction can be served nationwide, and other orders of civil contempt can be served in the state in which the district court is located or within 100 miles of that court. Check the appropriate rules for your state practice.

FILING AND SERVICE OF PLEADINGS AND PAPERS SUBSEQUENT TO THE COMPLAINT

Once the lawsuit is started, pleadings, motions, notices, orders, and other documents must be served on the adverse party. Rule 5 of the Federal Rules of Civil Procedure sets out the procedure to follow for serving documents subsequent to the complaint. The original and supporting documents together with a certificate of service are filed with the clerk of court "within a reasonable time after service" [Rule 5(d)]. Some courts permit the filing of documents by fax or other electronic means [Rule 5(e)]. Rule 5(b) has been amended to permit service by electronic or

default judgment
Judgment rendered against the defendant for the damages specified in the claim without the case going to trial, based on the defendant's failure to respond to the complaint within the time limit.

other specified means with the consent of the person being served. One copy of the documents should be served on each of the parties.

When it becomes clear that a party is represented by an attorney, service shall be on the attorney [Rule 5(b)]. Service is achieved by mailing a copy of the document to the attorney's last known address; if no address is available, then by delivering it to the clerk of court. Service is also achieved by handing it to the attorney, leaving it at the attorney's office with a clerk or other person in charge, leaving it in a conspicuous place, or leaving it at the attorney's usual place of abode with a person of suitable age and discretion. Further, service by fax is now common. The court, on its own motion, may alter some requirements of service if there are an unusually large number of defendants [Rule 5(c)].

KEEP GOOD RECORDS OF SERVICE

Keep good records of the filing, service, and receipt of service of all the outgoing and incoming pleadings, notices, subpoenas, and motions in the entire case. Certified mail, Return Receipt Requested provides green receipts for the necessary documentation. If an item is delivered by hand, a receipt that lists the delivered item, the date it was delivered, and the signature of the person acknowledging receipt should be used. These receipts should be attached to a file copy of the pertinent document. If you are acknowledging service on behalf of your firm (check to see when, if ever, your attorney wants you to do this), keep one copy of the acknowledgment or signed receipt in the client's file with the pertinent document.

OBTAINING A DEFAULT JUDGMENT

INTRODUCTION

If the defendant does not file an answer to the complaint or a motion attacking the complaint or otherwise respond in the prescribed time period, the defendant is in default and a **default judgment** may be entered against the defendant without a trial. In other words, the plaintiff wins the action and is awarded the requested relief. Your task is to draft the required documents and obtain the default judgment.

THE PROCEDURE AND NECESSARY FORMS

Default judgments help clear the court docket of cases that would otherwise languish for lack of a desire to defend or for some other reason. Their purpose is not to give the plaintiff an advantage, and for that reason they incorporate some due process safeguards for the defendant. These safeguards include satisfactory proof of service of the summons and complaint and the opportunity to have the default set aside if there is adequate justification.

Most states and the federal courts require a two-step process. The first step is the filing of a request to the clerk of court for entry of default [Rule 55(a)]. The request for entry of default normally requires an affidavit stating that the defendant has failed to respond to the summons or otherwise has failed to appear in the action within the required time period. This step is significant because the entry of default generally prevents the defendant from doing anything further to contest his or her liability. Therefore, it is advantageous to prepare the necessary request so it can be filed as soon as the twenty days or other applicable time period has elapsed or when directed to do so by your supervising attorney. See Exhibit 5:10 for examples of these forms.[6]

EXHIBIT 5:10 ■ Request for Entry of Default

REQUEST TO CLERK FOR ENTRY OF DEFAULT

The plaintiff requests the clerk for the _____ *[name of court]*_____ to enter the Defendant's default in the above entitled action. The Defendant has failed to appear or otherwise answer the complaint, and is therefore in default as set out in the accompanying affidavit.

_____

Attorney for Plaintiff
(Address)
(Phone number)

AFFIDAVIT OF DEFAULT IN SUPPORT OF REQUEST FOR ENTRY OF DEFAULT

State of _____ ⎫
                      ⎬ ss.
County of _____ ⎭

_____, being duly sworn, deposes and says;

1. That s/he is Plaintiff's attorney and has personal knowledge of the facts set forth in this affidavit.

2. That the Plaintiff, on the _____ day of _____, _____, filed his complaint against the Defendants.

3. That the Defendants were served with a copy of the summons and the Plaintiff's complaint, on the _____ day of _____, _____.

4. That more than 20 days have elapsed since the Defendants were served with the summons and the complaint.

5. That the Defendants have failed to answer or otherwise defend as to the Plaintiff's complaint, or serve a copy of any answer or other defense which it might have had, upon _____ and _____, attorneys of record for the said Plaintiff.

6. That this affidavit is executed in accordance with Rule No. 55(a) of the Federal Rules of Civil Procedure, for the purpose of enabling the Plaintiff to obtain an entry of default against the Defendants.

[Jurat]

_____

Attorney for Plaintiff

Source: Reprinted with permission of West Group.

Step two requires the filing of a request for entry of a default judgment. Note the distinct difference between the entry of default, which simply establishes the point in time of the default, and the judgment, which is a determination that the plaintiff has won the action and is entitled to a specific amount of money or other remedy. Step two is the request for this judgment.

In some jurisdictions both the request for entry and request for default judgment are done simultaneously with the filing of the request for entry of default. In other jurisdictions the filing of the request for entry of default has been eliminated. Some jurisdictions have a statutory waiting period before the judgment can be requested, and in others a default judgment may be lost if it is not pursued within a statutory period of time. Consult the specific rules of the court in which you have filed the action to determine the exact procedure and time limits. It is best to file for the judgment at the first possible opportunity.

Once the default is entered, the federal rules provide for two approaches to obtain the default judgment. If the suit is for a sum certain, meaning not readily challengeable nor subject to reasonable dispute, the request for judgment is submitted to the clerk with an accompanying affidavit attesting to the amount. Judgment is then entered by the clerk. Exhibit 5:11 is an example of a request for default judgment by the clerk with an accompanying affidavit.

Federal law and some states require submission of an affidavit of nonmilitary service, as shown in Exhibit 5:12.[7] The Servicemembers Civil Relief Act (50 U.S.C. App. §§ 501–596) prohibits the entry of a default judgment against military personnel on active duty. Also draft a judgment for signature unless told not to do so. See an example in Exhibit 5:13.

EXHIBIT 5:11 ■ Request for Entry of Default Judgment by Clerk

REQUEST FOR ENTRY OF DEFAULT JUDGMENT BY CLERK WITH SUPPORTING AFFIDAVIT

The Plaintiff in the above entitled action requests the clerk of *[name of court]* to enter judgment by default against the Defendant *[name of defendant]* in the amount of [*state sum*], plus interest at the rate of [*state rate*], and costs.

_____
Attorney for Plaintiff
(Address)
(Phone number)

AFFIDAVIT

State of _____ }
                           } ss.
County of _____   }

[name of attorney], being duly sworn, deposes and states:
1. That s/he is the attorney for Plaintiff in the above entitled action.
2. That Defendant's default in this action was entered on *[date default entered]*.
3. That the amount due Plaintiff from Defendant is a sum certain in the amount of [*state amount*].
4. That the Defendant is not an infant, incompetant person, or in military service.
5. That the amount indicated is justly owed Plaintiff no part of which has been paid.

_____
Attorney for Plaintiff

[Jurat]
(A brief statement of amount due may be included.)

EXHIBIT 5:12 ■ Affidavit of Nonmilitary Service of Defendant

[Fed. R. Civ. P. Rule 55(b)]
[*Title of Court and Cause*]

State of _____

County of _____
    I, _____ being first duly sworn, on oath state:
    1. My age is [*legal age*] years.
    2. I reside at No. ____, _____ Street in the City of_____, State of _____.
    3. My occupation is attorney at law.
    4. I am the duly authorized agent for the plaintiff in the above entitled and numbered cause and as such have full knowledge of the facts relating thereto.
    5. With reference to the matter in issue in the above cause, I have conversed with the defendant _____ over the telephone; that at the said time said defendant _____ was at his place of business in the City of _____, and I have had representatives of this office call on him for the purpose of inducing him to comply with the demand set forth in the complaint filed herein; that from all of said facts, this affiant says that the said defendant _____ is engaged in the business of _____ in the City of _____, and is not in the military service of the United States.

                                                   _____

    Subscribed and sworn to before me this _____ day of _____, _____.
    Notary Public
    _____

Source: Reprinted with permission of West Group.

EXHIBIT 5:13 ■ Judgment of Default

[*Title of Court and Cause*]

JUDGMENT

    Defendant _____ having failed to answer plaintiff's complaint or otherwise appear in this action and having his/her default entered, and on plaintiff's application and affidavit that defendant owes plaintiff the sum of _____ ($_____),
    It is ORDERED and ADJUDGED
    that plaintiff _____ recover from defendant _____ the sum of _____ ($_____), with _____ percent interest from (date) _____ and costs of the action.

                                                    _____
                                                  Clerk of Court
                                                   Dated _____

EXHIBIT 5:14 ■ Notice of Motion for Default Judgment by Court to Defendant Who Has Appeared in Action

[Fed. R. Civ. P. Rule 55(b)]
[*Title of Court and Cause*]

Take notice, that the plaintiff will move this court, at _____ Building in the city of _____, on the _____ day of _____, ____, at _____ o'clock in the _____ noon, or as soon thereafter as counsel may be heard, for a default judgment for the relief demanded in the complaint.
   [*Date*]

                                                _____,
                                                Plaintiff's Attorney
                                                Address:_____

[*Address to defendant's attorney.*]

Source: Reprinted with permission of West Group.

If the claim is not for a sum certain, the request for default judgment is submitted to the court for determination [Rule 55(b)(2)]. Similar documents are required. The court may require a hearing in which evidence is required to prove the amount of the damages. If the defendant has appeared in the action or enters a special appearance to be heard on the damage issue, or when the defendant is a minor or incompetent, notice of the application for judgment must be served on the defendant at least three days prior to the hearing on the application. The form appears in Exhibit 5:14.[8]

When the documents are completed, signed, and notarized, they should be filed with the clerk of court, and any required notice served on the defendant. If the court holds a hearing on the application, additional preparation on behalf of the attorney may be required.

Once the default judgment is entered, enforcement of the judgment is obtained in the same manner as for any other judgment (see Chapter 12). The plaintiff is limited to the amount of damages requested in the complaint and may not increase the amount.

DEFAULT AND MULTIPLE DEFENDANTS

Exercise special caution when seeking a default judgment when only one defendant is in default. Some jurisdictions permit only one judgment in an action, which might preclude proceeding against the other defendants. This situation is avoided in some jurisdictions by placing language in the judgment that states this judgment will be "joint and several" with any judgments granted against the remaining defendants. Seek the advice of your supervising attorney after checking the pertinent rules and cases.

CHECKLIST FOR DEFAULT JUDGMENT

Stage One

- Check calendar (deadline control system) for upcoming expiration of deadline to answer or otherwise defend case.
- Review case file and date and proof of service.
- If defendant defaults, take action to file request and affidavit with clerk as soon after default (twenty-first day in most jurisdictions) as possible or when directed to do so by your attorney.

- Draft entry of default and affidavit.
- Attach copies of proof of service of summons and complaint.
- Have the documents signed and notarized.
- File with clerk and obtain clerk's entry of default.

Stage Two

- As soon after entry of default as local rules and statutes permit or when directed to do so by your attorney, take action to request judgment of default. (Note: If there are multiple defendants and not all are in default, consult with attorney.)
- If the award is for a sum certain, draft a request for entry of default judgment by the clerk [Rule 55(b)(1) and your state rule].
- If the award requested is not for a sum certain, draft a request for entry of default judgment by the court [Rule 55(b)(2) and your state rule].
- Include the attorney's affidavit, the affidavit regarding military service, breakdown of debt, affidavit of costs, proof of service if required, and the judgment.
- Have appropriate documents signed and notarized.
- Deliver to clerk of court.
- Obtain date for hearing if needed.
- If hearing is required, draft notice of hearing on application and have it signed and served on defendant at least three days prior to hearing [Rule 55(b)(2)].
- Notify all nondefaulting defendants of application for judgment or as directed by attorney.

> "A piece of paper blown by the wind into a law-court may in the end only be drawn out again by two oxen."
>
> —CHINESE PROVERB, S. G. CHAMPION, *RACIAL PROVERBS*, 1938.

SETTING ASIDE A DEFAULT JUDGMENT

Despite any excellent forms you may have drafted to obtain a default judgment, the defendant may be able to have a default judgment set aside [Rule 55(c)]. If so, the defendant can attack the complaint or file an answer as if the twenty-day period had not expired. The court will set aside the default judgment for *good cause*. Those things constituting good cause are enumerated in Rule 60(b):

(1) mistake, inadvertence, surprise or excusable neglect; (2) newly discovered evidence which by due diligence could not have been discovered in time to move for a new trial under Rule 59(b); (3) fraud . . . , misrepresentation, or other misconduct of adverse party; (4) the judgment is void; (5) the judgment has been satisfied, released, or discharged or a prior judgment upon which it is based has been reversed or otherwise vacated, or it is no longer equitable that the judgment should have prospective application; or (6) any other reason justifying relief from the operation of the judgment.

In more concrete terms, good cause might exist if a person has been incapacitated due to illness or injury, and is unable to attend to business; or if the attorney is ill or unavailable.

The motion must be made in reasonable time (up to one year from the date of judgment) for items 60(b)(1), (2), and (3). The form for a motion to set aside a default judgment appears in Exhibit 5:15. We will discuss motion practice in more detail in the next chapter.

Military personnel covered under the Servicemembers Relief Act have up to 90 days after release from active duty to reopen any default judgment entered against them while they were deployed.

EXHIBIT 5:15 ■ Motion to Set Aside Default Judgment

THE UNITED STATES DISTRICT COURT FOR THE _____ DISTRICT OF _____

Civil Action, File No. _____

_____,
                          Plaintiff

          v.   MOTION TO SET ASIDE DEFAULT
                                                       JUDGMENT (NOTICE OF MOTION)
_____,
                          Defendant

The Defendant moves the Court for an order to set aside the default judgment entered in the above action
on _____, ____, on the grounds that _____
      [date]
_____
_____

                                                          _____
                                                          Attorney for Defendant
                                                          (Address)

SUMMARY

Chapter 5 focuses on the specific tasks you must perform to commence a lawsuit officially, serve the opponent properly, and get a judgment should the defendant default. The purpose of filing the lawsuit is to notify the court and the defendant of the action and to establish its official beginning date.

You determine what documents are needed to file the action and see that they are prepared, signed, and copied. A complaint is always needed, as is a summons unless the federal waiver of service of summons is used. The original documents are then filed with the clerk of the appropriate court, who stamps or otherwise verifies the filing of the complaint and assigns it a case number. A summons is issued for each defendant.

Subsequently, the plaintiff acquires personal jurisdiction over each defendant through service of a copy of the complaint and a summons or waiver. This can be accomplished by closely following the state or federal rules; the exact process is determined by whether the defendant is a person, a corporation, an out-of-state citizen, or a foreign citizen. Citizens and corporations of other states may be served under an applicable long-arm statute if adequate minimal contacts make the application of the statute constitutional. Constructive service requiring publication may be available to the plaintiff, especially in *in rem* actions.

If the defendant is properly served and fails to answer the complaint or otherwise defend the action, the plaintiff may seek a default judgment. Such a judgment ends the case and awards the plaintiff the sum or damages sought plus costs. No trial is held. Consult local rules of court and local form books to determine default procedure. Request the entry of default and judgment as soon as the law permits or as directed by your supervising attorney. If there is good cause for the defendant's default, the judgment may be set aside.

▣ WORKBOOK

System Folder Assignments, other exercises, a chapter outline, a review test, and other study aids are located in the accompanying workbook.

▣ HELPFUL WEB SITES

http://www.Deponet.com/about_us.htm/
international directory of process server firms, also lists court reporters

http://www.uscourts.gov/cmecf/cmecf.html
court links to CM/ECF information and tutorials

http://www.privacy.uscourts.gov
http://www.ussearch.com
http://www.gisusdata.com
people locating companies (fee)

▣ QUESTIONS FOR STUDY AND REVIEW

1. Name the government Web site where federal court rules and forms can easily be found.
2. What purposes are achieved by filing the action and service of process?
3. What event marks the commencement of a lawsuit in the federal court system? What usually commences the action in most state systems?
4. What is the best method of determining which documents and how many are needed to properly file a civil lawsuit?
5. Although the complaint has been drafted, what should be checked on the complaint before filing?
6. What is the purpose of the waiver of service of summons? What documents are needed for it? What documents are needed for service of process in your state?
7. Be able to prepare each of the documents needed for filing an action and for service of process in both the federal and state court systems.
8. Who should sign the Civil Cover Sheet?
9. What forms are needed to secure service by the U.S. marshall or by a process server specially appointed by the court?
10. What is the filing fee to file a civil action in federal court? In your state court?
11. What does it mean for the clerk of court to issue a summons?
12. What is the clerk of federal court likely to ask the paralegal at the time of filing?
13. The court cannot gain personal jurisdiction over the defendant until what happens?
14. What are the advantages of e-filing over traditional methods of filing?
15. Define CM/ECF and PACER; describe the benefits and procedures for both the e-filing and e-access processes.
16. What are the federal rules and restrictions on electronic services of process?
17. What is the practical goal of service of process? What are the federal and your state time limits for service?
18. What are the required procedures to achieve service of process in each of the situations outlined in the Reference Guide and Checklist for Methods of Service?
19. What are long-arm statutes? What injustice do they attempt to remedy? What is meant by "minimum contacts" and constitutional "fair play"?
20. What classes of persons and businesses will the long-arm statute reach in your state?
21. What is (are) the method(s) of service required to comply with the long-arm statutes in your state?
22. Do federal statutes permit nationwide service of process?
23. Define *in rem* and *quasi in rem* jurisdiction. Why isn't the state's sovereign control over property enough to exercise either type of jurisdiction? Who is served process in an *in rem* action?
24. How is service of process generally achieved in your state court system? What items are needed?
25. Define substituted and constructive service of process.
26. Who is immune from service of process and when?
27. What are ten techniques or sources for locating hard-to-find defendants?
28. How does a paralegal keep good records of service?
29. What is a default judgment?
30. What is the benefit to the plaintiff of a default judgment?
31. What are the applicable rules and procedures for obtaining a default judgment?
32. Be able to draft the necessary forms to obtain a default judgment for both state and federal court.
33. How and why may a default judgment be set aside?

▣ KEY TERMS

constructive service	in forma pauperis	quasi in rem action	substituted service
default judgment	in rem action	service of process	summons
e-filing	long-arm statute		

▣ ENDNOTES

1. Adapted from Exhibit 4:18, M. WEINSTEIN, INTRODUCTION TO CIVIL LITIGATION 94 (2d ed. 1986).
2. West Group, *E-Filing Research*, 2 (2000), at www.westfile.com/library/divint.htm.
3. UNITED STATES DISTRICT COURT, EASTERN DISTRICT OF KENTUCKY, ATTORNEY'S CHECKLIST FOR E-FILING (2006), http://www.kyed.uscourts.gov.
4. Memo from J. Burton to J. McCord (March 27, 1986).
5. CAROLE A. BRUNO, PARALEGAL'S LITIGATION HANDBOOK 39 (2d ed. 1993).
6. Affidavit adapted from WEST'S FEDERAL FORMS, § 4663, v. 4 (1992), with permission of West Group.
7. *Id.*, § 4672.
8. *Id.*, § 4670.

 For additional resources, visit our Website at **http://www.westlegalstudies.com.**

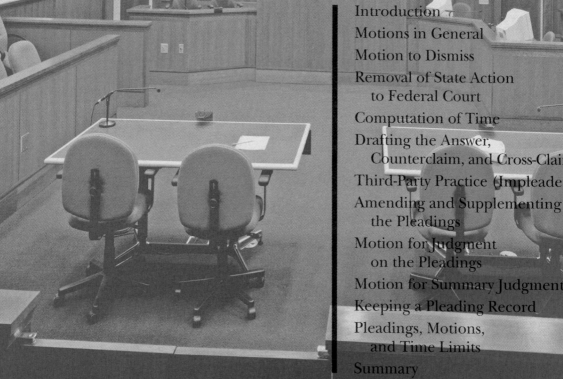

Defending and Testing the Lawsuit: Motions, Answers, and Other Responsive Pleadings

INTRODUCTION

When the complaint is received, the defendant may do one or more of the following: do nothing and default, attack the complaint through appropriate motions, file a notice of removal to have the case removed from state court to federal court, or file an answer. The opponent may respond, amend, oppose, or reply as necessary.

Beyond this stage of the pleadings, both sides may test the lawsuit with the hope of ending it through a motion for judgment on the pleadings and a motion for summary judgment. We will look at motion practice through the chronology of tasks in the typical lawsuit, first through the defendant's motion to dismiss and other motions attacking the complaint.

MOTIONS IN GENERAL

INTRODUCTION

motion
A request for a court order granting relief to the moving party.

order
A directive from a judge requiring some act or restraint from some act in a lawsuit.

A **motion** is a request to the court for an order granting relief favorable to the moving party. An **order** is a directive from a judge requiring some act or restraint from some act in a lawsuit—for example, an order to dismiss the case. Motions may be made before, during, and after trial. It is frequently the task of the paralegal to draft motions and supporting documents and to research the law in support of the motion.

PURPOSE

Motions have many purposes; for example, to obtain judicial relief such as dismissal of the action, exclusion of evidence, new trial, and so on; to narrow the issues for trial; and to establish a record for appeal. The first of these purposes needs no explanation. The second, to narrow the issues for trial, reflects that motions are used for a variety of matters, some central to the cause of action that may eliminate the lawsuit altogether, and some of lesser impact to clarify and refine the lawsuit. The third purpose, to establish a record for appeal, indicates that motions raise questions of law that affect the outcome of the case and must be decided by the judge. The judge's decision on these questions is often appealed. The motion establishes that an issue was raised in a proper and timely manner, preserving the right to have the issue heard on appeal.

REQUIREMENTS AND COMPONENTS OF THE MOTION

The requirements and components of a motion set out in this section are common to many courts. Local practice may vary, however, so carefully check local rules and practice.

Federal Rule 7(b) and parallel state rules set out the basic requirements for a motion: It must be made in writing, unless it is made at trial or hearing; its grounds must be stated with particularity, setting forth the order sought; it should have the same caption as the complaint with the exception that *et al.* (meaning "and others") may be used after the name of the first plaintiff or defendant rather than a list of all the other parties; and addresses are not necessary. Rules 7(b)(3) and 11 require that all motions be certified by the attorney's signature and include the attorney's address. It is good practice to include the attorney's phone number as well.

"In case of defence 'tis best to weigh The enemy more mighty than he seems."

—SHAKESPEARE, *HENRY V*, II, 4, 1598–99

In addition to the motion, a notice of motion must be prepared. The purpose of the notice is to inform the opponent that a motion has been filed and will be heard by the court at a specified time and place. Due process requires that the adverse party be given notice and, therefore, a fair chance to prepare for the hearing and to refute the motion. The Federal Rules permit the motion and notice to be combined in one document called the notice of hearing on the motion [Rule 7(b)].

The motion is usually a single document that concisely states the nature of the request. A separate document, called a **memorandum of law (memorandum of points and authorities)** or a **brief,** is attached to the motion. This accompanying document is a statement of the relevant legal authority (such as statutes, rules, and case decisions) and how it should be applied to the issues and facts in the case. Generally, a brief is more formal and more complex than a memorandum of law, but some jurisdictions use the terms interchangeably in motion practice. Affidavits setting forth additional facts not in the complaint may also be appended to the motion or brief as exhibits. An **affidavit** is a written statement sworn to by the signer. The signer is called the **affiant.**

PROCEDURE: FILING, SERVICE, AND TIME LIMITS

When the documents are prepared and signed, the motion must be filed and served on the opponent's attorney consistent with the procedure set out in Rule 5 (including e-filing) and as discussed in "Filing and Service of Pleadings and Papers Subsequent to the Complaint" in Chapter 5.

A motion must be served not less than five days before the scheduled hearing on the motion [Rule 6(d)]. Three days must be added to the time limit if service is by mail or electronic means [Rule 6(e)]. State requirements may vary. Affidavits may be served no later than one day before a hearing on the motion [Rule 6(d)]. The adverse party may file a responsive affidavit or memorandum. Check local rules for the specific time limits.

MOTION TO DISMISS

TASK

Mr. McDuff has just received the complaint in a case similar to Ms. Forrester's. In the new case, however, our firm represents the defendant, Allen Howard. Mr. McDuff would like you to look over the complaint to see if it can be attacked. After your review, Mr. McDuff will go over the complaint. If there are weaknesses in the complaint, your task will be to draft a motion to dismiss the opponent's complaint.

PURPOSE

The purpose of a motion to dismiss is to have the court dismiss the complaint and, thus, the lawsuit. Grounds for this motion include failure to state a claim for which relief can be granted, lack of jurisdiction, improper venue, defective service, and so on, to be discussed later. Filing the motion to dismiss or related objections to the complaint is also a common tactic to gain time to prepare the required answer to the complaint, because the time limit to answer is suspended until the motion is decided. This tactic is not ethically defensible when the basis for the motion is without substance (frivolous) and is submitted solely for delay.

memorandum of law (memorandum of points and authorities)
A document, normally shorter and less formal than a brief, stating the relevant legal authority and how it should be applied to the issues and facts of a case.

brief
A document stating the relevant legal authority and how it should be applied to the issues and facts of a case.

affidavit
A written, sworn statement.

affiant
The person who signs an affidavit.

If the complaint is dismissed, the plaintiff will probably respond by amending the complaint. Occasionally, however, the plaintiff is unable to correct the defect, and the case ends, much to the delight of the defendant. The savings in cost, time, and anxiety can be substantial. In other words, if the opponent can be kept out of court, our client cannot lose the lawsuit.

It is always best to check with your supervising attorney before drafting a motion to dismiss the complaint. Tactical reasons may exist for not filing the motion, especially if a defect can be easily corrected. The motion may alert the plaintiff to a weakness in the case that can be exploited to better advantage at a later stage in the case. A **demurrer** is the document used in some states to dispute the sufficiency of the complaint or other pleading. Its purpose is essentially the same as a motion to dismiss the complaint.

demurrer
A document used in some states to dispute the sufficiency of the complaint or other pleading.

DETERMINING WHAT TO ATTACK

If the motion to dismiss is for failure to state a claim, what weaknesses should you look for? If you will recall our discussion on drafting complaints (Chapter 4), the key to a successful complaint is a logical syllogism based on a rule of law, such as, if A, B, and C exist, then the plaintiff is entitled to remedy X. This rule is the major premise. The minor premise is stated in the complaint: A + B + C do in fact exist, therefore the plaintiff should receive remedy X. A syllogism opens two avenues for attack. The first is to determine whether a required element of the minor premise is missing in the complaint, that is, whether a required element—A, B, or C—in the rule of law has not been supported by alleged facts. If so, the minor premise is incomplete and the complaint fails to state a claim. The second avenue of attack is to look beyond the complaint to the major premise. The complaint may be based on an inaccurate or misconceived reading of the law. If so, there can be no claim. The court occasionally does, however, decide to accept a new rule of law.

Let us look at the body of the negligence complaint filed against Mr. Howard.

4. On September 2, _____, Defendant was operating a motor vehicle on South Maple Drive.
5. Defendant operated said vehicle in a negligent manner by failing to maintain a lookout and by failing to keep his automobile under control.
6. Plaintiff suffered great pain, broken ribs, and head injuries.
7. As a result of said injuries, plaintiff has incurred and will continue to incur doctor and hospital bills and loss of income and benefits.

Assume that you have researched the rule of law for a cause of action for negligence and find it to be: if A (duty) + B (breach) + C (injury) + D (breach is substantial cause of injury) exist, plaintiff is entitled to damages. Now apply the law to the complaint at hand to see if facts have been alleged to support each of the required elements of negligence. Paragraph four indicates that the defendant was operating a motor vehicle, which requires a duty of care toward others; therefore, a proper allegation of duty is present. Paragraph five alleges facts to show a breach of that duty. Paragraphs six and seven state facts in support of an injury to the plaintiff. So far, so good. But what is missing? The plaintiff has failed to allege facts to demonstrate D, that the defendant's breach of duty was a substantial cause of the plaintiff's injury. Because an entire element of the law is unalleged and unsupported, the complaint does not state a claim and is subject to a motion to dismiss. It is true that the omission may be easily corrected. On the other hand, there may not be a substantial connection between the defendant's negligence and the plaintiff's injuries, or the plaintiff may not have sufficient facts to demonstrate the connection. If the latter is true, the motion to dismiss will end the case against your client.

The body of the negligence complaint against Mr. Howard might read:

4. On September 2, _____, Defendant was operating a motor vehicle on South Maple Drive.
5. Defendant operated said vehicle in a negligent manner by failing to maintain a lookout and by failing to keep his automobile under control.
6. Plaintiff no longer feels safe operating a vehicle on South Maple Drive.

Here the complaint alleges that A + B + E (plaintiff's fear) exist, therefore the plaintiff is entitled to X damages. Research shows the underlying rule of law to be that A + B + $C + D$, not E, invoke the right to a remedy. The complaint does not match the law. Because it is based on an erroneous reading of the law, the major premise implied in the complaint does not hold up, and no cause of action is stated.

In the previous examples, the complaint is missing the proper allegations to state a claim on which relief can be granted. A third avenue of attack arises when the complaint alleges too much, revealing a defense to the action. Consider this premise: if A + B exist, and if W does not exist, then the plaintiff is entitled to relief. The existence of an element W, such as self-defense, would be a defense to the action. If in the factual allegation of the complaint, the plaintiff states that he was struck while lunging at the defendant, it might be sufficiently clear that W (self-defense) does exist. The motion to dismiss for failure to state a claim would be granted. Although oversimplified for purposes of illustration, these examples can be useful as a basic pattern in applying a syllogism to attack a complaint.

Prior to drafting the motion to dismiss the complaint, inform the supervising attorney of any apparent weaknesses in the opponent's complaint. This gives the attorney a chance to review the complaint, identify other weaknesses that need to be pursued, and assign any legal research needed to develop a basis for the motion founded in legal authority.

DRAFTING THE DOCUMENTS

Mr. McDuff agrees that the opponent's complaint is inadequate and assigns you the tasks of researching the legal basis for the motion to dismiss, writing a rough draft memorandum in support of the motion to dismiss, and drafting the motion to dismiss the complaint. You are also aware that the motion must be filed and served within the time permitted by the rules.

When any needed research is complete, draft the motion to dismiss the complaint. Exhibit 6:1 is an example of such a motion. Draft the notice of motion using the format demonstrated in Exhibit 5:14 and Exhibit 6:22. In case a state uses the demurrer, it appears in Exhibit 6:2. In some states a demurrer must contain the supporting authority for the demurrer, often eliminating the need for a memorandum of law.

The remaining task is the writing of the rough draft memorandum of law in support of the motion. Although the memorandum should be drafted with the highest standards, it is useful to consider it a rough draft to emphasize to both yourself and the attorney that the memorandum needs to be reviewed and probably revised by the attorney before filing at the courthouse. Keep in mind that Rule 32.1 of the Federal Rules

"I long have said there is no such thing as a hard case. I am frightened weekly but always when you walk up to the lion and lay hold the hide comes off and the same old donkey of a question of law is underneath."

—Oliver Wendell Holmes (1841–1935) quoted in Mark De Wolfe Howe, *Holmes-Pollock Letters*, 1946.

EXHIBIT 6:1 ▪ Motion to Dismiss Complaint

STATE OF COLUMBIA   CIRCUIT COURT   CAPITOL COUNTY

MARY ANN JAMES,
                        Plaintiff
                  v.   Civil Action, File No. <u>22222</u>
ALLEN HOWARD,
                        Defendant

MOTION TO DISMISS COMPLAINT

Defendant moves the court pursuant to Rule 12 (b)(6) of the Columbia Rules of Civil Procedure to dismiss the action because the complaint fails to state a claim against the Defendant upon which relief can be granted.

_____
James McDuff
Attorney for Defendant
(Address)

EXHIBIT 6:2 ▪ General Demurrer

STATE OF COLUMBIA   CIRCUIT COURT   CAPITOL COUNTY

MARY ANN JAMES,
                        Plaintiff
                  v.   Civil Action, File No. <u>22222</u>
ALLEN HOWARD,
                        Defendant

DEMURRER

Defendant demurs to Plaintiff's complaint, specifying:

That said complaint does not state facts sufficient to constitute a cause of action against Defendant.
    WHEREFORE, Defendant prays that Plaintiff be awarded nothing by reason of his complaint and that he be dismissed with his costs of suit paid by Plaintiff.

_____
James McDuff
Attorney for Defendant
(Address)

---

of Appellate Procedure now permits the citing in federal court of unpublished opinions issued after January 1, 2007. Exhibit 6:3 is a brief example of how a rough draft memorandum of law might look in Mr. Howard's case. Examples of the format for affidavits are found in Exhibit 5:12 and Exhibit 6:23.

In some jurisdictions the court requires that the motion be accompanied by a draft of the order for the judge to sign. Including this draft is a good idea even if it is not required. Exhibit 6:4 is an example of such an order. If your client is a nongovernmental corporate party, two copies of the parent and publicly held corporation

EXHIBIT 6:3 ■ Memorandum of Law in Support of Defendant's Motion to Dismiss Complaint

STATE OF COLUMBIA	CIRCUIT COURT	CAPITOL COUNTY

MARY ANN JAMES,

               Plaintiff

          v.   } Civil Action, File No. <u>22222</u>

ALLEN HOWARD,

               Defendant

MEMORANDUM OF LAW
IN SUPPORT OF DEFENDANT'S MOTION TO DISMISS COMPLAINT

Defendant argues to the court that the Plaintiff's complaint should be dismissed on the grounds that it does not state a claim against the Defendant on which relief can be granted. In support of said motion, Defendant states the following:

That Plaintiff's complaint does not allege facts in support of a critical element of a claim for negligence. A long-standing precedent in the state of Columbia is the case of *Winthrop v. Walters*, 200 Col. 392, 105 W.W. 63 (1934).* That case established the rule of law that a civil complaint must allege and state facts in support of each element of the cause of action, and that failure to do so made the complaint defective and upheld the lower court's dismissal of the complaint for its failure to state a cause of action.

In the recent case of *Arnold v. Taggie*, 592 Col. 365, 354 S.W.2d 615 (1992)* where the plaintiff failed to allege that the defendant's negligent operation of a van was the cause of plaintiff's injuries, the court held the dismissal of the complaint for failure to state a cause of action was proper.

Plaintiff's complaint in this action does not allege that the Defendant's conduct caused her injuries, nor does it allege any facts to support such a conclusion.

Therefore, Plaintiff's complaint is defective and should be dismissed.

Date _____

                                             _____

                                             James McDuff
                                           Attorney for Defendant
                                           (Address)
                                           (Phone number)

* Citations in this memorandum are fictitious.

disclosure statement must be prepared to accompany the defendant's first appearance in the case before the district court (Rule 7.1).

Each of these documents should be proofed for accuracy, reviewed by the attorney, revised as needed, and then signed by the attorney. Obtain a hearing date from the clerk and, when possible, confirm the date with the plaintiff's attorney. Place the date on the notice of motion and serve one copy of it, the motion, and any accompanying documents, such as a memorandum of law and affidavits, on the plaintiff's attorney as previously indicated. Check local practice for any variations in procedure. Immediately after service on the other party, file the original documents and a certificate of service with the clerk. Have one set of the documents stamped by the clerk with the filing date for your firm's file. If e-filing, follow the procedures of the relevant court or jurisdiction.

Remember that in the Federal Rules and those of most states, the defendant must respond within twenty days of receipt of the complaint. This time limit may be extended

EXHIBIT 6:4 ■ Order Granting Motion to Dismiss Complaint

STATE OF COLUMBIA   CIRCUIT COURT   CAPITOL COUNTY

MARY ANN JAMES,
                          Plaintiff
                  v.   } Civil Action, File No. 22222
ALLEN HOWARD,
                          Defendant

ORDER

On ____[date]____ Defendant motioned this Court for an order dismissing Plaintiff's complaint for failure to state a cause of action. The Court considered the motion, memoranda of law, and oral arguments heard by this Court on ____[date]____.

For GOOD CAUSE SHOWN, this Court finds that facts in support of several elements of the cause of action are insufficiently alleged failing to state a cause of action and that Defendant's motion to dismiss should be granted. SO ORDERED.

Date _____

                                                    _____
                                                              Signature of Judge

to 60 or 90 days if the federal waiver process is used [Rule 12(a)(1)(A) and (B)]. Any motion must be served not later than five days before the time specified for the hearing on the motion, unless the rules or order of the court indicate otherwise [Rule 6(d)]. Local rules should always be checked. The opposing party may file a responsive memorandum of law to which the original moving party may reply.

Occasionally, one side or the other in a lawsuit may need an extension of time for some good reason. The paralegal may have the responsibility of drafting the necessary documents. Consult local practice for the proper procedure and forms. Many jurisdictions require a request to extend time to be made by motion. This motion is necessary if the other party will not agree to an extension. If the parties agree to the extension, one option is a joint application for an order extending the time. A joint application leads to a court order that eliminates any potential disputes regarding whether a request for extension was granted. Include an order extending the time for the court to sign. Exhibit 6:5 is an example of a joint application for an order extending the time.

OTHER MOTIONS TO DISMISS

The most common motions to dismiss are contained in Rule 12(b) of the Federal Rules of Civil Procedure:

1. Lack of jurisdiction over the subject matter
2. Lack of jurisdiction over the person
3. Improper venue
4. Insufficiency of process
5. Insufficiency of service of process
6. Failure to state a claim upon which relief can be granted (previously discussed in this chapter)

EXHIBIT 6:5 ■ Joint Application for Extension of Time

STATE OF COLUMBIA   CIRCUIT COURT   CAPITOL COUNTY

MARY ANN JAMES,

                    Plaintiff

          v.   Civil Action, File No. 22222

ALLEN HOWARD,

                    Defendant

JOINT APPLICATION FOR EXTENSION OF TIME

Counsel for Plaintiff and Defendant in the above action jointly request the Court to issue an order granting Plaintiff an extension of time to October 1, _____, to respond to Defendant's memorandum of law in support of the motion to dismiss the complaint in this action.

Date _____

                                        _____
                                        Attorney for Plaintiff
                                        (Address)
                                        (Phone number)

                                        _____
                                        James McDuff
                                        Attorney for Defendant
                                        (Address)
                                        (Phone number)

Note that Rule 12(b) and parallel state rules indicate that if a motion to dismiss for failure to state a claim is accompanied by affidavits or other supporting documents, the court shall treat the motion as a motion for summary judgment. A motion for summary judgment is, essentially, a request to decide the case on the basis of the documents without going to trial. In such circumstances, the plaintiff needs to respond with counter affidavits or other documents.

Although it is beyond the scope of this book to discuss separate examples of each of the 12(b) motions, the motion procedure previously discussed in this chapter applies to these motions as well as other motions presented in this text. Referral to a form manual, such as West Group's *Federal Legal Forms* or *American Jurisprudence Pleadings and Practice Forms* (rev. ed.), should provide you with any examples of the forms that you might need. Numerous forms, including some state-specific forms, are available on Westlaw and Lexis. Federal or state digests should provide leads to the case precedents needed to draft a memorandum in support of any of these 12(b) motions. High-powered commercial services such as Westlaw.Litigator provide law offices with quick, electronic access to sample pleadings, motions and other forms, supporting briefs, and other litigation resources.

Form 19 of the Federal Rules gives an example of a motion to dismiss for failure to state a claim, for lack of service of process, for improper venue, and for lack of jurisdiction under Rule 12(b). Form 19 is duplicated in Exhibit 6:6.

The Federal Rules and the rules of those states adopting the Federal Rules permit Rule 12(b) motions to be filed as part of the answer or other appropriate pleadings, or they may be filed separately as illustrated in this chapter.

> **EXHIBIT 6:6 ▪ Federal Rules of Civil Procedure Form 19: Motion to Dismiss, Presenting Defenses of Failure to State a Claim, Lack of Service of Process, Improper Venue, and Lack of Jurisdiction Under Rule 12(b)**

The defendant moves the court as follows:

1. To dismiss the action becuse the complaint fails to state a claim against defendant upon which relief can be granted.

2. To dismiss the action or in lieu thereof to quash the return of service of summons on the grounds (a) that the defendant is a corporation organized under the laws of Delaware and was not and is not subject to service of process within the Southern District of New York, and (b) that the defendant has not been properly served with process in this action, all of which more clearly appears in the affidavits of M.N. and X.Y. hereto annexed as Exhibit A and Exhibit B respectively.

3. To dismiss the action on the ground that it is in the wrong district because (a) the jurisdiction of this court is invoked solely on the ground that the action arises under the Constitution and laws of the United States and (b) the defendant is a corporation incorporated under the laws of the State of Delaware and is not licensed to do or doing business in the Southern District of New York, all of which more clearly appears in the affidavits of K.L. and V.W. hereto annexed as Exhibit C and D respectively.

4. To dismiss the action on the ground that the court lacks jurisdiction because the amount actually in controversy is less than seventy-five thousand dollars exclusive of interest and costs.

Signed: _____
Attorney for Defendant

Address: _____

Notice of Motion

To: _____
Attorney for Plaintiff

_____

Please take notice that the undersigned will bring the above motion on for hearing before this Court at Room _____, United States Court House, Foley Square, City of New York, on the _____ day of _____, _____, at 10 o'clock in the forenoon of that day or as soon thereafter as counsel can be heard.

Signed: _____
Attorney for Defendant

Address: _____

OTHER MOTIONS ATTACKING THE COMPLAINT

The Motion to Strike

Two other motions are commonly used to attack the complaint: a motion to strike and a motion to make more definite and certain. Rule 12(f) states, "Upon motion . . . the court may order stricken from any pleading any insufficient defense or any redundant, immaterial, impertinent, or scandalous matter." Hence, the purpose of the motion to strike is to keep pleadings lean, to the point, and free of spurious and prejudicial language. The motion to strike can be an effective mechanism to keep pleadings sensible and fair.

The Motion to Make More Definite and Certain

Rule 12(e) of the Federal Rules authorizes a motion when the complaint or other pleading is so vague or so devoid of facts that it is difficult to determine if a claim for relief or a defense to a claim has been stated. This motion is similar in function to a *special demurrer,* which is still used in some states to attack the complaint for insufficiency of facts. A request for a **bill of particulars,** which asks the opponent for more details, is used in some states. The purpose of the motion to make more definite and certain, the special demurrer, and the bill of particulars, however, is essentially the same: to provide the opponent with sufficient facts to determine the claim or defense and the opportunity to respond.

bill of particulars
A request for the opponent to make an ambiguous pleading more definite and certain.

You can assist the supervising attorney by reviewing outgoing or incoming pleadings for such defects, calling them to the attention of the attorney, and drafting the necessary motions and supporting documents. Rule 12(e) requires that the motion to make more definite and certain specify the defects complained of and the details desired.

Review the following excerpts from a complaint filed in federal district court. Do grounds exist for either a motion to strike or a motion to make more definite and certain?

Count One

1. . . .
2. Defendant negligently drove a vehicle against Plaintiff who was crossing the highway.
3. As a result, Plaintiff was injured to the sum of twenty thousand dollars.
   WHEREFORE . . .

Count Two

4. . . .
5. Defendant negligently caused injury to Plaintiff.
6. As a result, Plaintiff has suffered serious emotional trauma to the sum of thirty thousand dollars.
   WHEREFORE . . .

This example demonstrates how problems may arise when a complaint is poorly drafted or without substance. Counts I and II of this complaint could be subject to a motion to make more definite and certain for several reasons: There is no date specified in the complaint, no location is given, and no facts are presented to support the claim that the defendant was driving negligently. The defendant can only guess at the accusation. Without more detail, it may be impossible to determine if there is a defense. For example, the defendant may have been in South America at the time of the alleged accident. The motion to make more definite and certain eliminates guesswork for the defendant regarding the basis for the claim. It is not to be used to provide details to the defendant such as weather conditions, names of witnesses, and other facts that can be found out in discovery. The motion to make more definite and certain appears in Exhibit 6:7.

A motion to strike will not be allowed unless there is a clear reason to do so. In the preceding example it appears as if Count Two may be a restatement of Count

EXHIBIT 6:7 ▪ Motion to Make More Definite and Certain

[*Caption omitted*]

MOTION TO MAKE MORE DEFINITE AND CERTAIN

Defendant, pursuant to Rule 12(e) of the Federal Rules of Civil Procedure, moves this court for an order requiring Plaintiff to provide a more definite statement of the claim against the Defendant.

As grounds, Defendant states the Plaintiff's complaint is so vague and ambiguous that Defendant cannot reasonably frame a response thereto.

The complaint is defective for the reasons stated below:

1. In both Counts One and Two Plaintiff does not state on what date the alleged incident occurred.
2. Nor does Plaintiff indicate the location of said occurrence, and
3. Insufficient facts are alleged in support of the claim of negligence or any other cause of action.

Defendant requests Plaintiff provide the following:

1. The date of the alleged incident.
2. The specific location of the incident, and
3. Facts describing how the Defendant was negligent.

(Attorney's signature, address, and telephone number)
(Notice of motion omitted)

I, but alleging a different injury, emotional trauma. The statement of two counts could make the jury think the defendant had committed two wrongs instead of one. Assuming that the motion to make more definite and certain revealed that Count II simply repeated Count I, a motion to strike under Rule 12(f) for redundant material is in order. Emotional trauma would then be included in the damages clause to Count I. Exhibit 6:8 is such a motion.

Apply what you learn in reviewing pleadings for weaknesses to improve the drafting of your own complaints and other pleadings.

ETHICS REMINDER

Remember that the attorney's signature on a pleading, including a motion, certifies that the attorney has read the document, that it is well grounded in fact, that it

EXHIBIT 6:8 ▪ Motion to Strike Redundant, Immaterial, Impertinent, or Scandalous Matter from Pleading

(*Caption omitted*)

MOTION TO STRIKE

Defendant, pursuant to Rule 12(f) of the Federal Rules of Civil Procedure moves the court for an order striking Count Two of the Plaintiff's complaint on the grounds that it is redundant, repeating the same cause of action as Count One, causing confusion and prejudicing Defendant at trial.

(Attorney's signature, address, and telephone number)
(Notice of motion omitted)

is warranted by law or a good-faith argument to alter the law, and that it is not offered for any improper purpose (Rule 11). Keep this in mind while drafting and reviewing pleadings.

RESPONSE TO MOTIONS

When the plaintiff receives the defendant's motion, check to see if it was filed within the time limit provided by the applicable state or federal rule; that it contains the requisite information (in writing), particular grounds, relief sought, and any necessary affidavit [Rule 7(b)]; and that it contains the necessary signatures under Rule 11 or similar state rule.

To respond, you may need to research the matter (and brief it if the court has required it) and draft any opposing affidavit. After consulting with the attorney and obtaining needed signatures, serve the response to the motion before the hearing on the motion and according to the time limits set in local practice rules of the pertinent court. Any legal authority or supporting evidence that you have gathered becomes the basis for a possible oral argument before the judge. Some matters raised by motion are sufficiently routine that opposition and response are not necessary, or they may be resolved without a hearing, using a consent or agreed order signed by all parties. Check with your supervising attorney. If the motion to dismiss is denied, the defendant must proceed to file an answer; if successful, either the case will be dismissed with the possibility of a new start if the defect can be corrected, or the court may permit the plaintiff an opportunity to amend the complaint without dismissal.

REMOVAL OF STATE ACTION TO FEDERAL COURT

TASK

Mr. McDuff wants you to draft the necessary documents and follow the necessary procedure to have Alan Howard's case removed from the state court to the federal district court. This task can be important to the defendant's case, but the task itself is relatively simple.

PURPOSE

The objective of removal is to have the case transferred from state court to federal court jurisdiction. The defendant is given this privilege under 28 U.S.C. § 1441 *et seq.* It affords the defendant the same opportunity that the plaintiff has to choose either the state or federal court when their respective jurisdictions are concurrent. A case may not be removed unless the federal district court has original jurisdiction over the subject matter of the lawsuit. An attorney may choose federal court for a variety of strategic reasons:

1. A different judge, considering that federal judges have more control over the case and may comment on the evidence
2. A more competent jury (it is generally harder to get excused from federal jury duty) from a wider geographical area than a county or parish
3. A chance to have the case removed to an even more convenient federal court through the liberal transfer and venue rules within the federal system
4. A more liberal set of discovery, evidence, and pleading rules in federal court than in some state courts
5. A docket that may be less crowded in federal district court than in state court

> "Of every hundred cases, ninety win themselves, three are won by advocacy, and seven are lost by advocacy."
> —A FOUNTAIN, *WIT OF WIG*, 1980.

Although some of these considerations can be quite complex, the end result can be an increased likelihood of winning the case.

CASES THAT MAY BE REMOVED

The United States Code Title 28 § 1441(a) states that

> any civil action brought in a state court of which the district courts of the United States have original jurisdiction, may be removed by the defendant or the defendants, to the district court of the United States for the district and division embracing the place where such action is pending.

Therefore, if federal original subject matter jurisdiction exists, as it does in diversity of citizenship and federal question cases, then the case may be removed. Note, however, that if a defendant is a citizen of the state where the action is brought, the purpose for diversity jurisdiction (avoiding bias against a nonresident) does not exist; therefore, removal is not permitted [1441 U.S.C. § 1441(b)]. Only defendants have the right of removal, and all defendants must agree to the removal. Removal is a statutory and not a constitutional right, so any close questions about the appropriateness of removal are to be decided against removal. The United States and its agencies and officers may remove an action to federal court [28 U.S.C. § 1442(a)]. Civil rights cases in which a person is denied the opportunity to have a federal right honored because of some unique aspects of state law can be removed to federal court (28 U.S.C. § 1443). Cases that may not be removed include workers' compensation cases, specified actions against railroads, some actions against interstate (common) carriers, and civil actions based on § 40302 of the Violence Against Women Act of 1994 [28 U.S.C. §1445(a–d)].

The right to remove a case must exist when the action is commenced and at the time of the notice of removal. Cases subject solely to state jurisdiction may be joined with a separate and independent federal question (not a diversity) case for removal [28 U.S.C. § 1441(c)]. Without this right, the defendant might be forced to stay in state court to avoid the extra cost of litigating related matters in both state and federal court. Finally, as mentioned in Chapter 1, the Class Action Fairness Act makes it easier to remove class action cases from state courts.

PROCEDURE

The procedure for removing a case to federal court is governed by 28 U.S.C. § 1446. This statute requires the following procedure:

1. File a "notice of removal" in the federal district court encompassing the area where the state action is pending. The notice must be signed in compliance with Rule 11 of the Federal Rules of Civil Procedure, and a copy of all "process, pleadings, and orders served on . . . defendants" must be attached to the notice [28 U.S.C. § 1446(a)].
2. The notice is a "short plain statement of the grounds for removal" [§ 1446(a)]. It should state:
   a. The statute conferring federal jurisdiction
   b. Facts in support of federal jurisdiction
   c. The date of receipt of the initial pleadings in the state action
   d. The applicable removal statute [28 U.S.C. § 1446(b)]
   e. That all defendants have joined in the removal action

"An incompetent attorney can delay a trial for years or months. A competent attorney can delay one even longer."

—EVELL J. YOUNGER, ATTORNEY GENERAL, CALIFORNIA, *LOS ANGELES TIMES*, MARCH 3, 1971.

3. The notice of removal must be served on all parties and filed within thirty days after commencement of the state action or, if the original action is not removable but becomes removable, thirty days after amendment or service of papers from which it can be determined that the action has become removable.

4. A copy of the notice must be "promptly" filed with the state court; the state court must proceed no further.

5. If the time limit for responding to the initial pleading has expired, the defendant has five days from the date the notice is filed to file any motion, objection, or answer to the plaintiff's complaint [Rule 81(c)].

The plaintiff can challenge the removal through a motion to remand (send) the case back to the state court because of defects in the removal process. This motion must be filed within thirty days after the filing of the notice of removal [28 U.S.C. § 1447(c)]. With some exceptions, a U.S. district court's order to remand a case to state court is not appealable [28 U.S.C. § 1447(d)]. The district court's subject matter jurisdiction can be challenged any time up to the entry of judgment. If after removal the plaintiff joins additional defendants whose joinder defeats subject matter jurisdiction, the district court may deny joinder, or it may permit joinder and remand the case to state court [28 U.S.C. § 1447(e)]. Although attorney fees and costs incurred on removal may be awarded to the plaintiff if the case is subsequently remanded, the U.S. Supreme Court has ruled that such awards are not automatic, especially if there was an objectively reasonable basis for the removal [*Martin v. Franklin Capital Corp.*, 126 S.Ct. 704 (2005)]. Exhibit 6:9[1] is a suggested format for the notice of removal.

EXHIBIT 6:9 ■ Notice of Removal

[28 U.S.C.A.§§] 1441, 1446]

[Title of Federal Court and Cause as in State Court]

To: The United States District Court for the _____ District of _____, _____ Division; and to: _____ Counsel for Plaintiff(s) from: _____, Counsel for Defendants.

1. Pursuant to 28 U.S.C. §§ 1441 and 1446(b) take notice that the above entitled action is removed to the above mentioned United States District Court.

2. The above entitled action was commenced in the _____ Court of _____ county, State of _____ and is now pending in that court. Process was served on the petitioner on the _____ day of _____, _____. A copy of the plaintiff's _____ (complaint, declaration or other initial pleading) setting forth the claim for relief upon which the action is based was first received by the petitioner on the _____ day of _____, _____.

3. The action is a civil action for _____ [*state briefly nature of case*] and the United States District Court for the District of _____ has jurisdiction by reason of the diversity of citizenship of the parties.

4. Plaintiff is a citizen of the State of _____ and defendant is a citizen of the State of _____. The matter in controversy exceeds, exclusive of costs and disbursements, the sum [*or value*] of $75,000. No change of citizenship of parties has occurred since the commencement of the action.

5. All defendants have joined in this removal action (if applicable).

6. Copies of all process, pleadings and orders served upon petitioners are filed herewith.

Dated _____, _____

_____
Attorney for Petitioner

Address:_____

Source: Reprinted with permission of West Group.

Computation of Time

In this chapter we have discussed a variety of procedures and responses that require one side or the other in the lawsuit to meet a deadline imposed by the rules: "within twenty days," "not less than five days before the hearing," or some other limit. You must be able to compute these time periods accurately, either to comply with the deadlines or to know when the adverse party is not in compliance. Federal Rule 6(a) states what days should be included or excluded in calculating the time period. The day the pleading is served or mailed, and the day the hearing is held, for example, are not counted. The last day of any time period may not fall on a Saturday, Sunday, or a legal holiday. When it does, the next regular business day is considered the final day of the period. When the period of time is *less than eleven days*, Saturdays, Sundays, and legal holidays shall not be counted. The legal holidays include New Year's Day, Martin Luther King, Jr.'s Birthday, Presidents' Day, Memorial Day, Independence Day, Labor Day, Columbus Day, Veterans' Day, Thanksgiving Day, Christmas Day, and any other days so designated by the president or Congress, or by the state in which the district court is held. When working in state court, the state's rule on time should be consulted.

Confusion arises if the rule or order states the time as "two months" rather than "sixty days" or "to" July 1 rather than "until" July 1. In these instances it is best to consult local rules. If they are unclear, consult the judge or a knowledgeable clerk. Generally speaking, however, "two months" means the specific number of calendar days in each of the next two months (twenty-eight, thirty, or thirty-one days). Two months from a specific date is that same numerical date—say the fourth—two months later (two months from June 4 = August 4). Sixty days is simply sixty calendar days starting with the first day after service or other required act. "To" a certain day usually means "up to" and does not include the designated day. "Until" normally means until the close of business on the specified day. An enlargement of time that has been granted by the court begins at the time the original time limit expires (i.e., if the answer was originally due on October 1, a thirty-day extension would run through October 31). It bears no relationship to the date on which the court grants the motion to extend the time.

Here is a formula for computing the due date: date of service + the number of days in the prescribed time period – the number of days in the month if the days in the time limit exceed the number of days left in the month = due date. To calculate the due date for an answer to a complaint served on September 20, the formula would work as follows:[2]

Date of Service: September	20
Plus prescribed time limit	20
Total	40
Minus days in September	30
Due Date	10th of October (unless Saturday, Sunday or holiday, then add days to next business day)

Remember that when service is by mail, electronic, or other means set out in Rule 5(b)(2)(B), (C), or (D), three days are added after the prescribed period would otherwise expire under subdivision (a) [Rule 6(e) as revised]. Saturdays, Sundays, and legal holidays are included in counting the three days. The new language that refers to when the prescribed period would otherwise expire is significant. For example, if the initial time limit is 20 days and ends on a Saturday, Rule 6(a) requires service on the next day that is not a Saturday, Sunday, or legal holiday. If the Monday is a legal holiday, then the "prescribed period" ends on Tuesday. The three-day mail extension after the prescribed period adds Wednesday, Thursday, and Friday. Friday is the final day to complete service of the document or other requirement. Failure to calculate time accurately can result in some serious consequences including default, loss of a claim or defense, payment of penalties or costs, and possible malpractice claims against the law firm. Always check local rules for any unique requirements.

DRAFTING THE ANSWER, COUNTERCLAIM, AND CROSS-CLAIM

TASK

For the purposes of this section, assume that you are a paralegal in the firm of Ott, Ott, and Knudsen, which is representing Mercury Parcel Service. You receive the following interoffice memo:

Memo to: Chris Sorenson

From: Lynn Ott
Subject: Forrester v. Hart and Mercury Parcel
Date: October 1, _____

We have twenty days to file an answer to the complaint against our client, Mercury Parcel. Please draft the answer including a counterclaim against Ms. Forrester for her negligence that resulted in injury to Mr. Hart, our need to replace him temporarily, and damage to our van. Please ask me if you need any assistance.

The **answer** is a formal pleading filed in response to the complaint. It identifies the issues to be contested and contains a statement of what the defendant admits and denies and what defenses to the claim, if any, will be presented.

GENERAL REQUIREMENTS

Time

Prior to drafting the answer, the paralegal must note the deadline for filing the answer or a motion attacking the complaint. Federal Rule 12(a) requires a defendant to serve an answer or a motion attacking the complaint

- within twenty days after being served with the summons and complaint, or
- if service of process has been properly waived [Rule 4(d)], within 60 days after the date when the request for waiver was sent (90 days if the defendant was served beyond the jurisdiction of any federal district court), or
- within 60 days of service on the U.S. attorney if the defendant is the United States or an officer or agency of the United States.

If a motion attacking the complaint was filed by the defendant, then an answer must be served on the plaintiff within ten days of notice of the court's decision on the motion [Rule 12(a)(4)(A)] or, if the court grants a motion for a more definite statement, within ten days after service of the revised complaint. Consult your state rules for different requirements.

Style and Content of the Answer

The answer should be drafted similarly to the complaint:

- Be clear and concise [Rules 8(b) and (e)(1)].
- Use numbered paragraphs addressing, point by point, the elements of the complaint, each paragraph being a statement of a single set of facts [Rule 10(b)].

answer

A formal pleading filed in response to the complaint; identifies the issues to be contested and contains a statement of what the defendant admits and denies and what defenses to the claim, if any, will be presented.

- Avoid impertinent, scandalous, or immaterial language [Rule 12(f)].
- Follow the complaint logically.
- Reveal no more facts than necessary.
- Avoid evidence and conclusions.
- Be truthful [Rule 11 and Disciplinary Rule 7–10(a)].
- State that the defendant lacks knowledge or information sufficient to form a belief as to the truth of the matter alleged, if that is the case [Rule 8(b)]. The court treats this as a denial.
- State separate defenses in separate paragraphs.

The difference between notice pleading and fact (code) pleading applies to answers as it does to complaints. An answer drafted for a code pleading jurisdiction requires more detail than an answer for a notice pleading jurisdiction. Check local procedure and forms for guidance.

STRUCTURE OF THE ANSWER

Introduction

The answer may have several components: legal defenses, admissions, denials, affirmative defenses, counterclaims, and cross-claims. After reviewing the complaint, the defendant's attorney indicates to the paralegal what needs to be done. This may be done electronically, or the attorney may scribble directions on a copy of the complaint. For complex complaints, use a color-coded system, for example: yellow highlight for facts admitted; blue for facts denied; and pink for allegations lacking knowledge to form a belief. The paralegal for the plaintiff would also find this method useful for keeping track of what has been admitted or denied by the defendant.[3]

Defenses

Defenses using the Rule 12(b) motion to dismiss for failure to state a claim, for lack of jurisdiction, for insufficient process, and others are commonly filed as separate motions. They may also be a part of the answer [Rule 12(b)(1) and (2)], where they are set out following the caption. If these defenses have not been filed separately, the attorney should be consulted to see if they are to be added to the answer. This practice is important because a defense of lack of personal jurisdiction, improper venue, insufficiency of process, or insufficiency of service of process is waived unless raised in the first responsive pleading [Rule 12(h)(1)] or unless the court permits an amendment under Rule 15(a).

Denials

Rule 8(d) requires a party in a responsive pleading to deny the allegations of the other party or they will be deemed admitted. The answer, therefore, should contain a section where the opponent's allegations are denied, if the facts justify the denial. General denials, however, are discouraged by the rules of most jurisdictions. A general denial is a brief statement that denies all allegations and claims of the plaintiff. Because it fails to narrow the contested issues and encourages a sweeping, thoughtless response, it is not favored by the courts. Instead, Rule 8(b) requires the denials to be written in short, plain terms with a separate admission or denial for each of the plaintiff's allegations. The denial should make clear what language in what paragraph of the complaint is being denied.

Plaintiff's allegation:

4. Defendant's vehicle was traveling in excess of the speed limit at the time of the accident.

Defendant's corresponding answer would use the same paragraph number as the complaint and state a short, plain denial:

4. Defendant denies allegation of paragraph 4 of the complaint.

Or if the defendant agreed with the allegation, the response would be:

4. Defendant admits the allegation of paragraph 4 of the complaint.

It may be necessary to split a response and admit some and deny some of the allegation [Rule 8(b)].

Plaintiff's allegation:

5. Defendant is the owner of said van which struck Plaintiff.

Defendant's response:

5. Admitted in part and denied in part. It is admitted that Defendant owns said van. It is denied that said van struck the Plaintiff.

If the defendant has insufficient knowledge or information to form a belief as to the truth of the matter, then the response should so state [Rule 8(b)]. However, this type of denial should be made in good faith and not simply to avoid an admission, reveal a denial, or cover up an unwillingness to investigate the fact. The penalty assessed in such circumstances is a finding that the allegation is admitted [*Nieman v. Long*, 31 F. Supp. 30 (E.D. Pa. 1934)]. A response based on lack of knowledge follows.

Plaintiff's allegation:

6. As a result of Defendant's negligence plaintiff has suffered loss of employment.

Defendant's response:

6. Defendant lacks knowledge sufficient to form a belief as to the truth of the allegation in paragraph 6 of Plaintiff's complaint, and therefore denies same.

Denials should not be ambiguous. For example, if the plaintiff alleges that the defendant is the owner of the car that struck the plaintiff at the corner of Jefferson and Wells streets, and the defendant simply states "denied," it is impossible to know what is being denied—ownership of the car, location of the accident, or the fact that the car struck the plaintiff. The denial should be more specific. Denials that state facts suggesting a defense, but in fact are not really defenses, are called **argumentative denials.** For example, if the plaintiff alleges an accident occurred in Gary, Indiana, on the evening of March third and the defendant replies, "Defendant was in Chicago on March 3," there is an implication that the defendant was elsewhere. However, that is not necessarily the case, since the person could travel to both places on the same day. This type of answer is only confusing and should be avoided.

argumentative denials
Denials that state facts suggesting a defense, but in fact are not really defenses.

Here are some other suggestions for drafting successful denials.[4] If the defendant faces making a multitude of denials covering words as well as phrases, it might be easier to state the defendant's own version of the facts, using the following format:

As to paragraph _____ of the complaint, [Defendant] alleges that [own version of facts].
Except as so alleged, Defendant denies the remaining allegations of paragraph _____.

When the term of a contract or other document is characterized in the pleading, it is best to deny the opponent's characterization and state that the documents speak for themselves.

When a co-defendant faces allegations or counts addressed to the other defendant, the language of Rule 8(b) does not excuse the defendant from denying claims asserted against a co-defendant. The following response is suggested:

As to paragraph _____of the complaint, [Defendant] denies having sufficient knowledge to form a belief.

Paragraphs _____ to _____ [of Plaintiff's complaint] do not apply to this Defendant, but insofar as they do refer to, may refer to, or may apply to this Defendant, each allegation is denied.

If lack of capacity is alleged or performance of a condition precedent is denied, such must be done specifically and with particularity as required by Rule 9 on pleading special matters.

Exhibit 6:10 summarizes the denials available and their purposes.

Affirmative Defenses

An affirmative defense says, "There are facts present which defeat the plaintiff's claim." These facts are not denials; they are "new matters" and say, "Even if all of the plaintiff's allegations are true, the defendant has a defense to the claim and should prevail." Affirmative defenses are waived in federal court if not asserted in the answer.

Affirmative defenses are defined by substantive law. Each action or claim established by substantive law has one or more defenses that will defeat the claim. A civil action for battery can be defeated by proving self-defense; slander by proving the statement is true; negligence by proving contributory negligence (where it still exists as a defense) or assumption of risk; and so on.

It is the responsibility of the defendant's attorney to determine whether the substantive law provides a defense to the claim, and whether sufficient facts support a good allegation of that defense. Just as each element of a claim must be supported by facts in the complaint, so too, must each element of an affirmative defense be supported by facts in the answer.

The attorney may tell you what defenses, if any, are to be drafted into the answer. Nevertheless, you need to know how to determine what defenses are available to the claim and what facts must be alleged to support the elements of the defense. The procedure for locating defenses is similar to the procedure for locating the elements of a claim as described in Chapter 4.

- Identify the descriptive word for the claim (negligence, contract, antitrust, etc.).
- In the index to the appropriate jury instruction book, look up the descriptive word for the claim and search for the subcategory on defenses or a separate section in the index on affirmative defenses. Turn to the designated instruction, which should define the affirmative defense and set out the elements that must be proven. *Am Jur Proof of Facts* is also a good source for this information.
- Go to a legal encyclopedia and look up the descriptive word for the claim and the subcategory under that topic on defenses. Here the defenses are defined and the elements set out.
- If the claim is defined by statute, consult the index of the annotated statutes to find the pertinent statute and defenses.

EXHIBIT 6:10 ▪ Forms of Denial in Pleadings

TYPE	FORM [each answer after "reasonable inquiry" must be accurate and submitted in good faith (Rule 11)]	EFFECT
Deny	Defendant denies the allegations of paragraph _____ of the complaint, or Denied (depending on jurisdiction).	Denies each allegation of that paragraph; any allegation not denied is admitted [Rule 8(d)].
Without knowledge	Defendant is without knowledge or information sufficient to form a belief as to the allegation that (state specific allegation) of paragraph _____ of the complaint.	Works as denial but provides flexibility as more information comes to light. Defendant has burden to make "reasonable inquiry."
Admit in part	As to paragraph _____, defendant admits to operating the van on (date) but denies the balance of the allegations in the paragraph.	Makes the admission specific, but denial of remainder of paragraph avoids having to list and possibly omitting a response to some of the items.
Leave to proof	As to paragraph _____, defendant neither admits or denies but leaves plaintiff to his/her proof.	Works as denial by requiring plaintiff to prove facts at trial.
Own allegation	Defendant denies the allegation in paragraph _____ and alleges (own version of facts).	Gives defendant the opportunity to be free from certain implications of plaintiff's langauge and to state more accurately what happened.
No answer/ conclusion of law	The allegation in paragraph _____ of the complaint improperly states a conclusion of law.	Protects defendant but points out that pleadings are not to allege conclusions of law, just facts in support of the conclusions.
Denial on information and belief	Defendant, on information and belief, denies the allegation in paragraph _____ of the complaint.	Generally used by corporations to deny based on the best information they have at the time from their employees. Permits change if necessary.
Not applicable to defendant	Paragraphs _____ to _____ of the complaint do not apply to this defendant, but insofar as they do refer to, may refer to, or may apply to this defendant, each allegation is denied.	Provides notice that defendant feels the allegation does not apply to this defendant but protects defendant in case it is intended to apply.

- Review the applicable digest of cases under the topic of the affirmative defense. These cases may shed light on what elements must be alleged and typical fact situations that invoke the defense.

Compare this information with the facts known about the case at hand, determining what defenses are applicable and what facts, if any, support an allegation of the defense.

Federal Rule 8(c) sets out the defenses that must be alleged affirmatively:

accord and satisfaction	contributory negligence
arbitration and award	discharge in bankruptcy
assumption of risk	duress
estoppel	payment
failure of consideration	release
fraud	res judicata
illegality	statute of frauds
injury by fellow servant	statute of limitations
laches	waiver
license	any other avoidance or affirmative defense

For the definitions of these terms, see Appendices B and C on torts and contracts and a legal dictionary. Note that a proposed amendment to Rule 8(c) removes discharge in bankruptcy as an affirmative defense (Dec. 2007).

Federal Rule 8(e)(2) indicates that affirmative defenses may be pleaded in the alternative, hypothetically, and even inconsistently. Therefore, in a negligence case a defendant might admit to the negligence but allege the running of the statute of limitations, or might allege that the plaintiff is comparatively negligent as well as having assumed the risk.

Affirmative defenses are placed immediately after the denials in the answer and appear as follows.

FIRST AFFIRMATIVE DEFENSE
Plaintiff did not file this action before the one-year statute of limitations elapsed.

SECOND AFFIRMATIVE DEFENSE
Plaintiff signed a release on November 8, ____, relieving Defendant of all liability in this matter.

In some states the affirmative defenses fall in a section on the answer titled "New Matter." The length and detail of the affirmative defense depend on the practice in a particular jurisdiction. In a notice pleading jurisdiction, the defenses may be stated quite briefly. In a code or "fact" pleading state, more detail may be required.

Under modern rules of pleading, the plaintiff is not required to plead responsively to the defenses. They are assumed to be controverted. The plaintiff, however, may choose to attack the defenses in the same manner as the defendant attacks the complaint: through a motion to strike or to dismiss, or through a demurrer in some jurisdictions.

Wherefore Clause

The answer includes a "wherefore" clause:

> WHEREFORE, Defendant demands a jury trial, requests that Plaintiff's complaint be dismissed, and that judgment be entered for the Defendant for his/her costs and disbursements.

A single "wherefore" clause is all that is necessary in most jurisdictions regardless of the inclusion of affirmative defenses or the number of affirmative defenses. Some attorneys prefer and some local practices require one "wherefore" clause after the denials and another after the affirmative defenses. Verify the local practice. The demand for a jury trial should be included in the answer; some drafters prefer to place it in the caption, while others place it in the "wherefore" clause. In some states a demand for a jury trial must be made in a separate document called a *notice of issue*.

Counterclaims

The **counterclaim** is a claim asserted by the defendant against the plaintiff, which is often included in or with the answer. It may arise out of the same circumstances as the plaintiff's claim or from unrelated circumstances. It is a suit within a suit. For example, a bishop used tennis courts at the United States Naval Academy on a regular basis for a number of years. He was never charged for his use of the courts. When the bishop injured his leg playing tennis, he sued the Naval Academy for negligence. The Naval Academy in turn counterclaimed against the bishop for all the accumulated fees owed the academy for use of the court.[5]

counterclaim
A claim asserted by the defendant against the plaintiff, often included in or with the answer.

Rule 13 of the Federal Rules of Civil Procedure permits two basic types of counterclaims: compulsory and permissive.

Compulsory counterclaims arise out of the original circumstances leading to the plaintiff's action against the defendant. For example, if Mercury Parcel thought Ann Forrester was responsible for the auto-pedestrian accident, it could counterclaim against Ms. Forrester for the loss of business and damage to their van. Since this claim arose out of the same transaction as Ms. Forrester's claim, Federal Rule 13(a) requires it to be brought in the answer. If not asserted, the claim could not be raised against the plaintiff in a separate lawsuit. The purpose of this rule is to have all claims related to a single occurrence resolved at one time. In some states where the Federal Rules have not been adopted, there are no compulsory counterclaims.

Counterclaims may also be brought against the plaintiff for claims unrelated to the original action [Rule 13(b)]. Assume that Ann Forrester had owed money for services provided to her by Mercury Parcel. Mercury Parcel could assert a *permissive counterclaim* against Ms. Forrester for the debt. The purpose of this rule is to use the one suit to resolve all outstanding matters between the parties rather than doing so through separate lawsuits. The defendant, however, may choose to assert the claim in a separate lawsuit and is not barred from doing so. If the claim is asserted in the answer, the traditional rule has been that an independent source of jurisdiction for the unrelated action must be asserted. Increasingly, however, federal courts hold that under 28 U.S.C. § 1367 (supplementary jurisdiction) an independent jurisdictional basis for a permissive counter claim is not required [*Jones v. Ford Motor Credit Co.*, 358 F.3d 2005 (2nd Cir. 2004) and *Channell v. Citicorp National Services Inc.*, 89 F.3d 379 (7th Cir. 1996)]. In *Channell*, a "loose factual connection" to the original claim was constitutionally sufficient. A court will not permit the original action to be left in limbo for failure of the court to get jurisdiction over the counterclaim.

Counterclaims are added to the answer following the "wherefore" clause after the affirmative defenses. Appropriate portions of the complaint may be incorporated by reference. The claim must be drafted according to the same rules as the body of the complaint and assert facts necessary to support the elements of the claim.

The defendant may add other parties besides the plaintiff [Rule 13(h)], and the amount of the claim may exceed that of the original action [Rule 13(c)]. Should a counterclaim against the plaintiff arise after the answer has been filed, or if the defendant realizes that a counterclaim has been inadvertently missed, Rules 13(e) and (f), respectively, permit the subsequent filing of those claims by leave of the court. There is a filing fee for the counterclaim.

The counterclaim is subject to the same attack and motions as the complaint, and the plaintiff is required to reply to the counterclaim with denials and defenses in the same fashion that the defendant answers the complaint. The plaintiff's response to the counterclaim is called a reply and must be served on the defendant within twenty days after service of the answer and counterclaim [Rule 12(a)]. A counterclaim against the plaintiff does not give the plaintiff the right to remove a state action to a federal court [*Shamrock Oil & Gas Corp. v. Sheets*, 313 U.S. 100 (1941).

Cross-Claims

When two or more persons are sued in an action, it is not unusual for one party to believe a co-party should bear the liability. For example, if a builder of an office building is sued over defects in the building, the builder may believe that any damages owed the plaintiff were caused by and should be the responsibility of his co-defendant, the architect who designed the building. In such circumstances, the builder may file a cross-claim against the architect. Rule 13(g) permits a **cross-claim** to be filed against a co-party only if the cross-claim arises out of the original action or a counterclaim or relates to any property that is the subject matter of the original action. Cross-claims, therefore, do not require an independent source of jurisdiction. A party may choose to cross-claim or sue independently.

cross-claim
A claim by one party against a co-party in the same action.

A cross-claim must meet all the pleading requirements of any other claim. It is placed in the answer after the counterclaim or may be placed in a separate document. A cross-claim does not require a summons for service.

Should the original action be dismissed or otherwise disposed of, the court will still try a remaining cross-claim or counterclaim. If a cross-claim or counterclaim is made a part of the answer, the title of the document should be changed from "Answer" to "Answer, Counterclaim, and Cross-Claim."

If either a counterclaim or cross-claim or both are drafted into the answer, an additional "wherefore" clause is required in the answer, demanding judgment to be entered for the person bringing the claims for the sum requested, plus costs and interest. Generally, a party receiving a cross-claim has twenty days to answer.

Certification and Verification

All that is required to certify the answer under the federal rules of pleading is the signature, address, and telephone number of the defendant's attorney [Rule 11(a)]. An electronic signature is valid for filing by electronic means. If the state rules require verification, the defendant must read the pleading, sign it, and have it notarized. As you may recall, a verification is the defendant's sworn statement that the defendant has read the pleading and that all the facts alleged are true or otherwise stated on information and belief. For this reason, it may be best not to plead inconsistent facts where verification is required.[6] Local practice should be determined.

SAMPLE ANSWER, COUNTERCLAIM, AND CROSS-CLAIM

The general requirements and components of an answer have been reviewed. The task assigned is to draft an answer for Mr. Hart to the complaint filed against him by Ms. Forrester and her husband. The Forresters' complaints (both notice and code-pleading examples) appear in Exhibit 6:11 and Exhibit 6:13. Following each complaint is the corresponding answer (see Exhibit 6:12 and Exhibit 6:14). Note the difference between the two answers in the factual detail required. Exhibit 6:15 is another example of a fact complaint.

EXHIBIT 6:11 ■ Forrester Complaint: Notice Pleading

UNITED STATES DISTRICT COURT FOR THE EASTERN DISTRICT OF COLUMBIA
Civil Action, File No. _____

ANN FORRESTER
  and
WILLIAM FORRESTER,

             Plaintiffs

     v.

RICHARD HART
  and
MERCURY PARCEL SERVICE, INC.,

             Defendants

COMPLAINT FOR NEGLIGENCE
Jury Trial Demanded

COUNT I

1. Plaintiffs are citizens of the State of Columbia and Defendant Hart is a citizen of the State of Ohio; Defendant Mercury Parcel Service, Inc., is a corporation incorporated under the laws of the State of Delaware, having its principal place of business in the State of Ohio. The matter in controversy exceeds, exclusive of interest and costs, the sum of $75,000.
2. On February 26, ____, on Highway 328 in Capitol County, Columbia, Defendant Hart, an employee of Defendant Mercury Parcel, Inc., negligently drove a motor vehicle striking down Plaintiff who was crossing said highway.
3. As a result, Plaintiff fractured her left leg and hip bones and was otherwise seriously injured; has been prevented from transacting her business; has suffered, and continues to suffer, great pain of body and mind; has incurred, and will continue to incur, expenses for medical attention and hospitalization, all to the sum of $750,000.

WHEREFORE Plaintiff demands judgment against Defendant in the sum of $750,000.

COUNT II

4. Plaintiff William Forrester hereby alleges and incorporates by reference paragraphs 1 through 3 of Count One.
5. Because of Defendant's negligence, Plaintiff has suffered loss of the consortium of his wife, Ann Forrester, in the amount of $20,000.

WHEREFORE, Plaintiff demands judgment against the Defendant in the sum of $20,000.

_____
Arthur White
Attorney for Plaintiffs
(Address)
(Phone number)
_____

EXHIBIT 6:12 ▪ Answer and Counterclaim to Forrester Complaint: Notice Pleading

UNITED STATES DISTRICT COURT FOR THE EASTERN DISTRICT OF COLUMBIA
Civil Action, File No. ____

ANN FORRESTER
  and
WILLIAM FORRESTER,

              Plaintiffs

     v.

RICHARD HART
  and
MERCURY PARCEL SERVICE, INC.,

             Defendants

DEFENDANTS' ANSWER
AND COUNTERCLAIM

COUNT I

1. Admitted.
2. Denied that Defendant drove vehicle negligently.
3. Defendant lacks knowledge sufficient to form a belief regarding the truth of the allegation in paragraph 3 of Plaintiff's complaint, and therefore denies same.

FIRST AFFIRMATIVE DEFENSE

Plaintiff was more than 50 percent negligent in causing the accident, and is therefore barred from recovery.

COUNT II

4. No answer required.
5. Denied.

COUNTERCLAIM

On February 26, ____, on Highway 328 in Capitol County, Columbia, Plaintiff Ann Forrester negligently tried to cross the road in front of Defendant's vehicle, causing injury to Defendant Hart.

As a result of plaintiff's negligence, Defendant Hart suffered lacerations and contusions and lost days of work all to the sum of $2,200.

SECOND COUNTERCLAIM

Defendant Mercury Parcel incorporates by reference the facts as alleged in the first counterclaim and alleges the Plaintiff's negligence caused damage to the defendant's vehicle and required the hiring of an extra employee for one week all to the sum of $4,250.

WHEREFORE, Defendants request that Plaintiffs' action be dismissed and demand judgment against the Plaintiffs for $2,200 for Defendant Hart and $4,250 for Defendant Mercury Parcel Service, Inc., plus interest and costs.

_____
Attorney for Defendants
(Address)
(Phone number)

EXHIBIT 6:13 ■ Fact Complaint for Forrester Case

STATE OF COLUMBIA   CAPITOL COUNTY   CIRCUIT COURT

ANN FORRESTER
  and
WILLIAM FORRESTER,
                    Plaintiffs

          v.   Civil Action, File No. _____

RICHARD HART
  and
MERCURY PARCEL SERVICE, INC.,
                    Defendants   Plaintiff Demands Trial by Jury

COMPLAINT FOR NEGLIGENCE

Plaintiffs allege the following facts:

1. The jurisdiction of this court is based on the amount in controversy in this action which is more than $2,500.
2. Plaintiff Ann Forrester is a teacher and homemaker and resides at 1533 Capitol Drive, Legalville, in Capitol County, Columbia.
3. Plaintiff William Forrester is the husband of Ann Forrester and resides with her.
4. Defendant Richard Hart is a driver employed by Defendant Mercury Parcel Service, Inc., and resides at 1223 Penny Lane, Cincinnati, Ohio.
5. Defendant Mercury Parcel Service, Inc., is incorporated in the State of Delaware with its principal place of business located at 603 Stoker St., Cincinnati, Ohio.
6. On February 26, ____, at approximately 7:30 A.M., Plaintiff Ann Forrester was walking across a hilly and partially icy section of Highway 328 in the City of Legalville, County of Capitol, in the State of Columbia.
7. At that time, Defendant Hart was driving a van on behalf of his employer and the owner of the van, Defendant Mercury Parcel Service, Inc.
8. Defendant Hart operated the van negligently by:
   a. driving the vehicle at an excessive rate of speed under the circumstances;
   b. failing to exercise a proper lookout;
   c. failing to exercise adequate control of said vehicle; and
   d. otherwise failing to exercise due and adequate care under the circumstances.
9. As a direct consequence of Defendant's negligence, Plaintiff was struck down by Defendant's van and seriously injured.
10. Because of said negligence, Plaintiff suffered fractures of the left leg and hip; damage to the lower spine; torn muscles, tendons, tissue and nerves; insomnia; paralysis that confines her to a wheelchair; depression; and other maladies, all of which cause her intense pain, great suffering, and considerable inconvenience, and will continue to do so in the future.
11. As a consequence of defendant's negligence and the aforesaid injuries, the Plaintiff has incurred, and will incur, considerable expense for hospital and medical care, loss of income and benefits, domestic services, and property damage to her coat and clothes.

WHEREFORE, Plaintiff demands judgment in the amount of seven hundred and fifty thousand dollars ($750,000), together with the costs and disbursements of this action and for such other relief as this court may deem just and proper.

(continued)

EXHIBIT 6:13 ▪ Fact Complaint for Forrester Case *(continued)*

COUNT II

12. Plaintiffs hereby allege and incorporate by reference paragraphs 1 through 9 of Count I.
13. Because of Defendant's negligence, Plaintiff William Forrester has suffered loss of the consortium of his wife, Ann Forrester, in the amount of twenty thousand dollars ($20,000).

WHEREFORE, Plaintiff William Forrester demands judgment against Defendants in the sum of twenty thousand dollars ($20,000) and costs and for such other relief as this court may deem just and proper. (verification)

_____

Arthur White
White, Wilson, and McDuff
Attorneys at Law
Federal Plaza Building
Suite 700
Third and Market Streets
Legalville, Columbia 00000
(111) 555-0000

EXHIBIT 6:14 ▪ Answer and Counterclaim to Forrester Complaint: Code (Fact) Pleading

STATE OF COLUMBIA   CAPITOL COUNTY   CIRCUIT COURT

ANN FORRESTER
  and
WILLIAM FORRESTER,
                    Plaintiffs

     v.   Civil Action, File No. _____
RICHARD HART
  and
MERCURY PARCEL SERVICE, INC.,
                Defendants   Jury Trial Demanded

DEFENDANTS' ANSWER, NEW MATTER, AND COUNTERCLAIM

1. Admitted.
2. Admitted.
3. Admitted.
4. Admitted.
5. Admitted.
6. Admitted.
7. Admitted.
8. Denied. Defendant specifically denies negligence in the following areas:
   a. Driving the vehicle at an excessive rate of speed under the circumstances.
   b. Failure to exercise a proper lookout.
   c. Failure to exercise adequate control of vehicle.
   d. Failure to exercise due and adequate care under the circumstances.
9. Admitted in part, denied in part. Defendant admits the Plaintiff was struck by Defendant's van and denies the balance of the allegations in the paragraph.
10. Denied. Defendant, after reasonable investigation, lacks sufficient knowledge to form a belief regarding the truth of Plaintiff's allegation of injuries, and therefore denies same.

EXHIBIT 6:14 ■ Answer and Counterclaim to Forrester Complaint: Code (Fact) Pleading *(continued)*

11. Denied. Defendant, after reasonable investigation, lacks sufficient knowledge to form a belief as to the truth of Plaintiff's allegation of loss of money, and therefore denies same.

WHEREFORE, Defendants request the Plaintiffs' complaint be dismissed and that judgment be entered for Defendants for their costs and disbursements.

NEW MATTER

12. Defendants incorporate by reference paragraphs 1 through 11 of their answer.
13. Defendant alleges that Plaintiff is more than 50 percent responsible for the accident and resulting injuries and therefore barred from recovery due to the following:
    a. Failing to stop, look, and listen for oncoming traffic prior to stepping onto the highway.
    b. Failing to maintain a lookout for oncoming vehicles while crossing said highway.
    c. Not taking care for her safety and the safety of others in light of the ice on the highway.

WHEREFORE, Defendants request that Plaintiff's complaint be dismissed and that judgment be entered for Defendants for their costs and disbursements.

ANSWER TO COUNT II

14. No response to Plaintiff's paragraph 12 is required.
15. Denied. Defendants specifically deny being negligent or responsible for Plaintiff's alleged injuries. Defendant, after reasonable investigation, lacks suficient knowledge to form a belief regarding the truth of Plaintiff's allegation of loss of consortium of his wife and the amount of the loss.

WEREFORE, Defendants request that Plaintiffs' complaint be dismissed and that judgment be entered for Defendants for their costs and disbursements.

NEW MATTER COUNT II

16. Defendants incorporate by reference paragraphs 12 and 13 of their answer alleging the Plaintiff is more than 50 percent responsible for the accident and is barred from recovery.

WHEREFORE, Defendants request that Plaintiffs' complaint be dismissed and that judgment be entered for Defendants for their costs and disbursements.

DEFENDANTS' COUNTERCLAIM

17. Defendants incorporate by reference paragraphs 1 through 16 of their answer.
18. On February 26, ____, Plaintiff Ann Forrester negligently walked onto Highway 328 in Capitol County, Columbia by failing to take the following precautions:
    a. Stop, listen, and look for oncoming traffic
    b. Maintain a lookout while crossing said highway.
    c. Exercise due care for her own safety and that of others in light of the ice on the highway.
19. As a result of Plaintiff's negligence, Defendant Hart had to take emergency evasive action, unsuccessfully avoiding Plaintiff, and causing his vehicle to leave the road and strike a tree.
20. Because of Plaintiff's negligence, Defendant Hart suffered lacerations to his head and legs, bruises to various parts of his body and head, intense emotional anxiety, insomnia, and substantial pain and suffering.
21. As a further consequence of Plaintiff's negligence and the aforesaid injuries, Defendant Hart has incurred the expense of hospital and medical care, and a loss of income totaling two thousand two hundred dollars ($2,200).

COUNT II

22. Defendants incorporate by reference paragraphs 1 through 21 of their answer.

(continued)

EXHIBIT 6:14 ■ Answer and Counterclaim to Forrester Complaint: Code (Fact) Pleading *(continued)*

23. Becaue of Plaintiff Ann Forrester's negligence, Defendant Mercury Parcel Service suffered damage to their delivery van and expenses necessitated by a replacement employee for Mr. Hart for one week, totaling four thousand two hundred and fifty dollars ($4,250).

   WHEREFORE, Defendants demand judgment against Plaintiff Ann Forrester for Defendant Hart in the amount of $2,200, and for Defendant Mercury Parcel Service in the amount of $4,250, plus their costs and disbursements.

_____
Attorney for Defendants
(Address)
(Phone number)

State of Columbia   ⎫
                     ⎬ ss.
Capitol _____   ⎭

   Richard Hart, being duly sworn on oath according to law, deposes and states that he has read the foregoing Answer and Counterclaim, and that the matters stated therein are true to the best of his knowledge, information, and belief.

_____
Richard Hart

Subscribed and sworn to before me this _____ day of _____, ____.

_____
Notary Public

My commission expires January 1, ____.

State of Columbia   ⎫
                         ⎬ ss.
County of Capitol _____ ⎭

   Sandra Franz, being duly sworn on oath according to law deposes and states that she is the president and duly authorized representative of Mercury Parcel Service, Inc., and has read the foregoing Answer and Counterclaim, and that the matters stated therein are true to the best of her knowledge, information, and belief.

_____
Sandra Franz

Subscribed and sworn to before me this _____ day of _____, ____.

My commission expires January 1, ____.

_____
Notary Public

EXHIBIT 6:15 ■ Fact Complaint Case II

STATE OF COLUMBIA   CAPITOL COUNTY   CIRCUIT COURT

CARL AMECHE
   and
ZOE AMECHE,

             Plaintiffs

     v.   Civil Action, File No. _____

MARGIE CONGDEN
   and
LEROY CONGDEN,

           Defendants   Plaintiffs Demand Trial by Jury

COMPLAINT FOR NEGLIGENCE

Plaintiffs allege that:

1. The jurisdiction of this court is based on the amount in controversy in this action which is more than $2,500.
2. Plaintiff Carl Ameche is an accountant and resides at 222 2nd Street, Thorp, Ohio.
3. Plaintiff Zoe Ameche is the wife of Carl Ameche and resides with him.
4. Defendants Margie and Leroy Congden are the owners of the Maple Meadows Campground and reside at the campground which is located at Star Route 2, Highway 66, in the city limits of Legalville, Capitol County, Columbia.
5. On August 21, ____, Plaintiffs rented campsite 36 in the Maple Meadows Campground.
6. Defendants had negligently placed a worn extension cord running to campsite 36.
7. As a direct consequence of the Defendants' negligence, a fire was started that encircled the Plaintiffs' son, Zachary, requiring Carl Ameche to place himself in peril in order to rescue his son.
8. Because of said negligence, Carl Ameche suffered severe burns to his face, hands, and legs that have caused him intense pain, suffering, physical disability, considerable inconvenience, and permanent scarring.
9. As a consequence of the Defendants' negligence and the aforesaid injuries, Carl Ameche has incurred and will incur considerable expense for hospital and medical care, loss of income and benefits, and property damage to his clothing and camper.

WHEREFORE, Plaintiff demands judgment in the amount of three hundred and fifty thousand dollars ($350,000), together with the costs and disbursements of this action, and for such relief as this court may deem just and proper.

COUNT II

10. Plaintiffs hereby allege and incorporate by reference paragraphs 1 through 8 of Count I.
11. Because of the Defendants' negligence, Plaintiff Zoe Ameche has suffered loss of consortium of her husband, Carl Ameche, in the amount of fifteen thousand dollars ($15,000).

WHEREFORE, Plaintiff Zoe Ameche demands judgment against Defendants in the sum of fifteen thousand dollars ($15,000), together with costs, and for such relief as this court may deem just and proper.

                            _____
                            Arthur White
                            White, Wilson, & McDuff
                            Attorneys at Law
                            Federal Plaza Building
                            Suite 700
                            Third and Market Streets
                            Legalville, Columbia 00000

(verification)

Assume for illustrative purposes that Richard Hart and Mercury Parcel Service are each represented by different attorneys and that Richard Hart has decided to cross-claim against Mercury Parcel. The cross-claim is placed in Hart's answer after the counterclaims, and the drafted language appears as follows:

CROSS-CLAIM

22. Defendant incorporates by reference paragraphs 1–21 of his answer.

23. Sometime during the week of February 20, Defendant Mercury Parcel Service negligently failed to check and maintain the van driven by Defendant Hart on February 26 as required by (state any applicable statutes or regulations).

24. Because of Defendant Mercury Parcel's negligence, the brakes on said vehicle were not functional, causing the wheels to lock and the vehicle to go out of control. The malfunctioning caused said vehicle to strike Plaintiff Ann Forrester, go off the highway, and strike a tree.

25. As a consequence of Defendant Mercury Parcel's negligence, Plaintiff and Defendant have both suffered the injuries and loss of income set out in the complaint and answer.

WHEREFORE, Defendant Hart demands judgment be entered against Defendant Mercury Parcel for him for $2,200 and for any liability Defendant Hart is required to pay Plaintiffs as a consequence of this lawsuit.

THIRD-PARTY PRACTICE (IMPLEADER)

INTRODUCTION

third-party practice (impleader)
The filing of a third-party complaint by the original defendant against a person not yet named a party to the lawsuit, alleging that the third party is or may be liable for all or a part of any damages won by the original plaintiff against the original defendant.

The pleadings discussed to this point, that is the complaint, answer, counterclaim, and cross-claim, occur between the original plaintiff(s) and defendant(s). **Third-party practice (impleader)** permits the original defendant to file a third-party complaint against a person not yet named a party to the lawsuit. This complaint alleges that the third party is or may be liable for all or part of any damages won by the original plaintiff against the original defendant. This process is like a cross-claim, except that it is against a previously unnamed party. The pleading filed by the original defendant against this new party is called a third-party complaint, and the original defendant becomes the third-party complainant. The newly named person becomes the third-party defendant.

TASK

Prepare the third-party summons and a third-party complaint; file the third-party action with the clerk of court; have it served on the third-party defendant.

PURPOSE

The purpose of third-party practice is to litigate all the claims arising from a single set of circumstances. Third-party practice is governed by Rule 14 of the Federal Rules of Civil Procedure and parallel state rules. Rule 14 gives the person who is defending against a claim the right to bring in a third party. A third-party complaint essentially says, "If I am going to be held liable in this action, then so are you because you are at fault." For example, Ms. Forrester is suing Mercury Parcel for the injuries suffered in the pedestrian accident. Mercury Parcel may choose, in turn, to sue the van dealer or manufacturer for defects that contributed to or caused the accident. One of the advantages of such a suit is that one jury or one judge may hear all sides and render a more uniform decision. A third-party action may be based on *indemnification,* a theory that says if B is found liable, C owes B for the amount of the judgment. Or it may be based on *joint liability,* meaning B and C share the liability. Title 28 U.S.C. should be consulted to see what parties and claims may be heard by the federal court when the parties or claims do not have an independent source of federal jurisdiction.

PROCEDURE

The original defendant drafts a third-party complaint, files it with the clerk of court, and then serves a third-party summons and a copy of the complaint on the new party. A copy of the original complaint is attached to the third-party complaint.

Rule 14 gives the third-party plaintiff the right to implead another party without leave of court if the third-party complaint is filed within ten days after the answer. If it is filed after the ten days, a motion to implead must be filed to obtain the court's permission.

The third-party complainant must get personal jurisdiction over the other party, following the same procedure for service of process of the complaint outlined in Chapter 5 and Rule 4. A small filing fee may be required in some states. Independent subject matter jurisdiction is not required.

The third-party defendant may respond to the third-party complaint as any other defendant, including Rule 12 motions, counter- and cross-claims, and even a third-party action. Any claim against the original plaintiff may be asserted. The original plaintiff may implead as the respondent to any counterclaim [Rule 14(b)].

Follow these steps in preparing and filing a third-party action:

1. Obtain all necessary information on the third-party defendant.
2. Draft a motion for a third-party complaint unless the action is filed within ten days of the answer [Rule 14(a)]. Check state and local rules for variations in procedure.
3. Draft a third-party summons and third-party complaint.
4. File with the clerk of court using the summons and complaint as exhibit A.
5. On notice that the motion is approved, serve the third-party summons and a copy of the third-party complaint in the same manner that the original complaint is served (Rule 4). Attach a copy of the original complaint.
6. Note the calendar for the due date for the third party's answer.

Exhibits 6:16, 6:17, and 6:18 are examples of the third-party summons, complaint, and motion. They are based on forms 22A and 22B in the appendix to the Federal Rules of Civil Procedure.

EXHIBIT 6:16 ■ Summons Against Third-Party Defendant

[Fed. R. Civ. P. Rule 14]

UNITED STATES DISTRICT COURT FOR THE SOUTHERN DISTRICT OF _____

Civil Action, File Number _____

A.B., Plaintiff

v.

C.D., Defendant and Third-Party Plaintiff   Summons

v.

E.F., Third-Party Defendant

To the above-named Third-Party Defendant:

You are hereby summoned and required to serve upon _____, plaintiff's attorney whose address is _____ and upon _____, who is attorney for C.D., defendant and third-party plaintiff, and whose address is _____, an answer to the third-party complaint which is herewith served upon you within 20 days after the service of this summons upon you exclusive of the day of service. If you fail to do so, judgment by default will be taken against you for the relief demanded in the third-party complaint. There is also served upon you herewith a copy of the complaint of the plaintiff which you may but are not required to answer.

_____
Clerk of Court

[Seal of District Court]
   Dated: _____

EXHIBIT 6:17 ■ Third-Party Complaint

[Fed. R. Civ. P. Rule 14]

[*Title of Court and Cause*]

1.   Plaintiff A.B. has filed against defendant C.D. a complaint, a copy of which is hereto attached as "Exhibit A."
2.   (*Here state the grounds upon which C.D. is entitled to recover from E.F., all or part of what A.B. may recover from C.D. The statement should be framed as in an original complaint.*)
   WHEREFORE C.D. demands judgment against third-party defendant E.F. for all sums that may be adjusted against defendant C.D. in favor of plaintiff A.B.

Signed: _____
Attorney for C.D.,
Third-Party Plaintiff
Address: _____

EXHIBIT 6:18 ■ Motion to Bring in Third-Party Defendant

[FED. R. CIV. P. Rule 14]

[*Title of Court and Cause*]

Defendant moves for leave, as third-party plaintiff, to cause to be served upon E.F. a summons and third-party complaint, copies of which are hereto attached as Exhibit X.

_____
Attorney for Defendant
C_____ D_____
Address: _____

AMENDING AND SUPPLEMENTING THE PLEADINGS

PURPOSE

The parties to the lawsuit are permitted by the Federal Rules and the rules of adopting states to amend and supplement their pleadings freely. Amendments are generally used to repair defective pleadings that may have omitted necessary elements of a cause of action, improperly or inadequately alleged subject matter jurisdiction, or used language that is too general or states evidence. An amendment might even be used to change a defense or other legal theory.

A supplemental pleading allows a party to add facts that have occurred since the original pleadings were filed. For example, Ms. Forrester may want to supplement her pleadings if her injuries resulted in blindness or a stroke after the original pleading was filed; or a farmer who is suing a contractor for failure to complete a barn by winter may lose some cattle as a consequence after the complaint is filed. Federal Rule 15(d) authorizes supplemental pleadings.

Rule 15 of the Federal Rules of Civil Procedure states that permission to amend pleadings should be given freely. The purpose of the rule is to make it easy for parties to correct procedural oversights and bad drafting so the issues and evidence are accurately reflected in the pleadings. If amendments and supplements were not freely permitted, the parties would be hamstrung in their efforts to present the best possible case on clearly defined issues, and cases would be dismissed for procedural errors rather than tried on the real substance or merit. If, in the judgment of the court, the change to the pleading will significantly prejudice the other party, however, the motion to amend or supplement the pleading will be denied.

PROCEDURE

A party is permitted to amend a pleading without court permission any time before the responsive pleading is served. If no responsive pleading is required, and if the action is not on the trial calendar, the pleading may be amended within twenty days after the pleading is served. Otherwise pleadings may be amended only with leave of the court or with written consent (stipulation) of the opponent [Rule 15(a)].

It is necessary to respond to an amended pleading either within the remaining period to respond to the original pleading or within ten days of service of the amended pleading, whichever period is longer, unless otherwise ordered by the court [Rule 15(a)]. Response to a supplemental pleading is required only on order of the court [Rule 15(d)].

When leave of court is required to amend a pleading, the request is made by motion. Because of the policy to freely allow amendments to conform to the evidence, such motions can be brought any time, even after judgment [Rule 15(b)]. An amended pleading dates from the filing of the original pleading when *relation back* is permitted by the applicable state or federal statute of limitations law and as long as the claim or defense asserted in the amended pleading arose out of the conduct, transaction, or occurrence set forth in the original pleading [Rule 15(c)]. This avoids statute of limitations problems, especially for a party that filed the original pleading just before the deadline. If a party tries to amend the pleading with an entirely new claim based on a different fact situation, however, this new pleading will not date from the original.

In addition, a pleading may be amended to change the name of the party against whom the claim is brought. What happens if the statute of limitations runs out between the time the complaint is filed and the amendment is made? Federal Rule 15(c)(3) permits the amendment to date back to the filing of the original complaint if several conditions exist. The amendment must stem from the occurrence set out in the original complaint, and the new party must have notice of the action in time to defend against it and within the original time limit to serve the summons and complaint. Check state rules for variations.

The amended pleading should combine the amended language plus what remains of the original pleading. Pleading one complete, amended document is easier for the court and the parties than referring to both the original document and the amended one. The amended pleading should be captioned "Amended" or "Supplemented" for clarity.

Amended and supplemental pleadings are served on the adverse party's attorney by mailing or delivering a copy of the pleading to the attorney or as otherwise directed in Rule 5. These pleadings should be filed with the clerk of court. Most state jurisdictions freely permit the filing of amended pleadings; local rules, however, should be consulted.

Exhibit 6:19 is an example of an amended pleading,[7] and Exhibit 6:20 shows the format for a notice of motion and a motion to amend the complaint.[8]

EXHIBIT 6:19 ■ Amended Complaint

[FED. R. CIV. P. Rule 15(a),]

[*Title of Court and Cause*]

The plaintiff in accordance with Rule 15(a), Federal Rules of Civil Procedure, amends the complaint in this action as follows:

[*State amended pleadings.*]

———————————————
Attorney for Plaintiff

Address: ———————————

Source: Reprinted with permission of West Group.

EXHIBIT 6:20 ▪ Notice of Motion and Motion for Leave to Amend Complaint

[FED. R. CIV. P. Rule 15(a)]

[*Title of Court and Cause*]

To Attorney(s) for the Defendant _____ :

   Please take notice that the plaintiff in the above-entitled case upon the affidavit of C_____ D_____ hereto annexed as Exhibit A, will at Room _____ , United States Courts and Post Office Building, City of _____ on the [*date*], at the hour of _____ o'clock _____.M., or as soon thereafter as the court will hear counsel, move for an order permitting the plaintiff to file her proposed amendment to her complaint, a copy of which is hereto annexed as Exhibit B and herewith served upon you.

   Dated: [*date*].

_____

Attorneys for Plaintiff

Address:_____

Phone:_____

Source: Reprinted with permission of West Group.

MOTION FOR JUDGMENT ON THE PLEADINGS

TASK

You may be asked to draft a motion for judgment on the pleadings when all the required pleadings have been filed and if the supervising attorney believes the opponent's claim or defense is by law inadequate. The pleadings are normally closed after the filing of the complaint, answer, and reply to the counterclaim. Once the pleadings are closed, Rule 12(c) and parallel state rules permit the filing of a motion for judgment on the pleadings.

PURPOSE

The purpose of the motion is to end the litigation. In effect the motion says, "Even if what the opponent says is true, no claim is stated on which relief can be granted," or conversely, "No adequate defense is stated, and therefore I should win." For example, even if Ms. Forrester's allegations in her complaint are considered to be true, if Richard Hart and Mercury Parcel could show that the statute of limitations had run prior to the action being filed, the defendants' motion would be granted.

   On the other hand, if Richard Hart and Mercury Parcel's only defense is not recognized in the state, then the court is within its authority to grant the motion for the plaintiff. Their motion is to be considered without the assistance of the affidavits and matter outside the pleadings. If outside matter is presented with the court's permission, Rule 12(c) requires the motion to be considered a motion for summary judgment (discussed in the next section). A motion on the pleadings often results in an amendment to the pleadings rather than dismissal.

   The motion is drafted, filed, and served in the same manner as other motions discussed in this chapter.

Motion for Summary Judgment

TASK

Draft a motion for summary judgment and the necessary supporting documents.

PURPOSE

A successful motion for summary judgment wins the case without the necessity of a trial. The motion does more, however, than a motion to dismiss or a motion for judgment on the pleadings, because it asks the court to look behind the pleadings at additional evidence. This evidence can be affidavits, statements made under oath by parties and witnesses (called depositions and interrogatories), admissions of facts, and stipulations of facts. Only admissible evidence is considered. A motion for summary judgment and the supporting evidence must allege two things: that there is no genuine issue of material fact (no crucial questions of fact that must be answered by a jury at trial) and that, according to the law, the movant is entitled to judgment [Rule 56(c)]. If the opponent's evidence can show a genuine issue of fact, the motion is denied.

A summary judgment might be granted in the following situation. Ann Forrester files a complaint for negligence against Hart and Mercury Parcel. The defendants' answer admits all the allegations, but as a defense, states that Forrester signed a release freeing the defendants from all liability. Since defenses are deemed controverted, there appears to be a factual issue: was a release signed? If, after filing a motion for summary judgment, the defendant can prove that the release exists or present affidavits of witnesses who read the release and saw it signed, the court can grant summary judgment. There is no longer an issue of fact because the evidence proves the release was signed. As a matter of law, the release bars recovery. If the plaintiff could prove facts to the contrary or show that the release was only a partial release, then the motion would be denied, or at best granted in part. Whether the party opposing a motion for summary judgment must rebut the movant's evidence varies in state practice. If a party cannot rebut the motion because the evidence needed is not yet available, the court may not grant the motion and has the option of granting a reasonable continuance until the evidence is available [Rule 56(f)]. Keep in mind that, under Federal Rule 12(b) and parallel state rules, a motion to dismiss for failure to state a claim shall be treated as a motion for summary judgment if the court permits presentation of matters outside the pleadings.

PROCEDURE

Rule 56(a) states that any party seeking to recover on a claim, counterclaim, or cross-claim may, after twenty days following commencement of the action, move for summary judgment or do so after service of a motion for summary judgment by the adverse party. Any party defending against a claim, counterclaim, or cross-claim may move for a summary judgment any time. State rules and time requirements may vary. Either party may move for a summary judgment against the other. This is called a *cross-motion.*

The motion must be served at least ten days (more than the five days normally required in motion practice) before the hearing on the motion, and the opponent must file responding affidavits at least one day prior to the hearing [Rule 56(c)].

The documents required to file the motion are typical of those required for most motions: the motion itself, the notice of motion, attached affidavits plus exhibits, a memorandum of law in support of the motion, and an order for the court to sign. The motion is filed and a copy served on the opponent. Proof of service is filed with the clerk of court. Following are examples of the motion (Exhibit 6:21),[9] notice of motion (Exhibit 6:22)[10] and an affidavit in support of the motion for summary judgment (Exhibit 6:23).[11]

EXHIBIT 6:21 ■ Motion for Summary Judgment by Plaintiff

[Fed. R. Civ. P. Rule 56(a)]

[Title of Court and Cause]

Plaintiff, by his attorneys and pursuant to Rule 56 of the Federal Rules of Civil Procedure, moves the Court to enter summary judgment for the plaintiff on the ground that there is no genuine issue as to any material fact, and the plaintiff is entitled to judgment as a matter of law.

In support of this motion, plaintiff refers to the record herein including the amended complaint, the answer thereto, the defendants' amendment to the answer, plaintiff's annexed affidavit sworn to the ___ day of _____, _____, and _____.

_____
Attorney for Plaintiff

Address: _____

Source: Reprinted with permission of West Group.

EXHIBIT 6:22 ■ Notice of Motion and Hearing on Motion for Summary Judgment

[Fed. R. Civ. P. Rule 56(a)]

[Title of Court and Cause]

Sir:

Please Take Notice, that upon the complaint herein, the affidavits of _____, sworn to *[date]*, ____, and the affidavit of _____, sworn to *[date]*, ____, and [the annexed statement in accordance with Rule 9(g) of the General Rules of this Court], the undersigned will move this Court at a motion part thereof, to be held at Room ____, United States District Courthouse, _____, _____, on the ____ day of _____, ____, for an order granting plaintiff summary judgment pursuant to Rule 56 of the Federal Rules of Civil Procedure, on the ground that there is no genuine issue as to any material fact, and that plaintiff is entitled to judgment as a matter of law.

Dated: _____

_____
Attorney for Plaintiff

Address: _____

To: _____ *[Address]*

Source: Reprinted with permission of West Group.

EXHIBIT 6:23 ■ Affidavit in Support of Motion for Summary Judgment—General Form

[Fed. R. Civ. P. Rule 56(e)]

State of _____

   ss.

County of _____

   _____, being first duly sworn, deposes and says:

   I am _____, and have personal knowledge of the facts herein set forth.

   This affidavit is submitted in support of the plaintiff's [*or* defendant's] motion for summary judgment herein, for the purpose of showing that there is in this action no genuine issue as to any material fact, and that the plaintiff [*or* defendant] is entitled to judgment as a matter of law.

   [*State all the evidentiary facts within affiant's personal knowledge in support of motion.*]

[*Jurat*]

                                          _____

Source: Reprinted with permission of West Group.

KEEPING A PLEADING RECORD

Pleadings require good record keeping. A quick glance in the file should tell the reader exactly what pleadings have been filed, served, and replied to, and the applicable dates. A pleadings log in each file can provide this information. Exhibit 6:24 is an example of a pleadings log that can be regularly updated as each pleading is exchanged.[12]

EXHIBIT 6:24 ■ File Pleading Log

Title of Case _____   Client _____

       _____   File No. _____

Our Pleading	Date Filed	Date Served	Opponent Acknowl. of Service	Opponent Response Due	Opponent Pleading	Date of Service	Our Response Due
Summons and complaint Reply to counter-claim					Answer and counterclaim		

PLEADINGS, MOTIONS, AND TIME LIMITS

Exhibit 6:25 displays the most common pleadings in approximate chronological order, their purpose, any applicable time limit, and the pertinent federal rule. It continues through discovery, pretrial, and posttrial tasks, time limits, and rules, so make a note to return to this chart as you learn about those phases of litigation.

EXHIBIT 6:25 ■ Pleadings, Motions, and Time Limits

Pleading/Act	Purpose If Not Clear	Due	Federal Rule	State Rule/Due
PLEADINGS/PARTIES				
Complaint				
Service of summons and complaint	For personal jurisdiction	120 days after filing complaint	4, 4(m), 5	
Request for Entry of Default and Judgment of Default	To prevent defendant's response after time limit for answer, to get judgment concluding case and awarding remedy	Entry may be sought on first day after expiration of time limit for answer. Judgment sought as soon after as possible. Notice of hearing on application for default—three days prior to hearing when required.	55, 54(c)	
Motion to Set Aside Default Judgment		In reasonable time and not more than one year after judgment	55(c), 60(b)	
Motions Attacking Complaint or Action (in general)	To dismiss action for lack of subject matter jurisdiction, personal jurisdiction, improper venue, insufficiency of service, failure to state a claim, and failure to join a party, or to make complaint more definite or to strike language, or for *forum non conveniens*	Within time permitted to answer complaint, which depends on method used for service of process. Could be 20, 60, or 90 days. Twenty days generally; motion to dismiss for lack of subject matter jurisdiction can be made any time, including on appeal.	12(a), (b), (e), (f), 28 U.S.C. § 1406(a), 28 U.S.C. § 1404	
Notice of Motion plus Affidavit		Served at least five days before hearing unless ex parte	6(d)	

(continued)

EXHIBIT 6:25 ■ Pleadings, Motions, and Time Limits *(continued)*

Pleading/Act	Purpose If Not Clear	Due	Federal Rule	State Rule/Due
Responsive Motion plus Affidavit		Served not later than one day before hearing on motion, generally, or pursuant to local court rule	6(d)	
Amendment to Pleadings (generally)	To correct errors, vagueness, or other inadequacies	Prior to service of a responsive pleading or within twenty days after service if no responsive pleading is permitted. If in response to order to make more definite, ten days after notice of order.	15(a), 12(e)	
Answer	To admit, deny, or state defenses to plaintiff's allegation; may include counterclaim and motions attacking complaint	Twenty, sixty, or ninety days, depending on method used for service of process (U.S. has sixty days) or in ten days after decision on motion attacking complaint	12(a)	
Answer in Response to Amended Complaint		In remaining time to respond to original or within ten days, whichever is greater	15(a)	
Counterclaim	To state a claim defendant has against plaintiff, usually arising out of same transaction alleged by plaintiff	At same time answer is served or as permitted by court	13	
Cross-Claim	To state a claim against a party on the same side of the action and may allege that the party is the one fully or partially liable for claim alleged in complaint or counterclaim	With answer, reply to counterclaim, or other appropriate pleading	12(b)	
Reply to Counterclaim or Cross-Claim	To admit, deny, or state defenses to allegations in counterclaim or cross-claim. May include motions attacking these pleadings	Twenty days after service of answer or twenty days after service of notice of order to reply to counter-claim or as otherwise directed (U.S. has sixty days)	12(a)(2)	

EXHIBIT 6:25 ▪ Pleadings, Motions, and Time Limits *(continued)*

Pleading/Act	Purpose If Not Clear	Due	Federal Rule	State Rule/Due
Third-Party Complaint	To bring in third party who may be liable to one of the original parties for the claim or counterclaim brought against the original party	Ten days after service of original answer (counterclaim) or by leave of court	14(a)	
Third-Party Answer	To attack, or to admit, deny, or state defenses to the third-party complaint (may include counter and cross-claims)	Twenty days after service of answer	14(a), 12(a)	
Motion to Dismiss: Not Real Party in Interest	To attack jurisdiction of court and to avoid harassment of defendant by parties having no right to claim	Within time permitted for regular response to complaint	17(a), 12(a), (b)	
Motion to Join a Party	To add either plaintiffs or defendants for the purpose of adjudicating all claims of all parties arising from same or series of transactions	In reasonable time after action begins	19, 20	
Motion to Add Interpleader	To add a party to resolve all possible claims against a third party	In reasonable time after action begins	22	
Motions Regarding Class Actions	To certify a group of plaintiffs as a class or to dismiss or compromise	As soon as practical after start of action	23(c)(1)	
Motion to Intervene	To permit party to enter lawsuit so can protect interest or where statute permits intervention	In reasonable time after start of action	24, 5	
Motion for Substitution of a Party	To permit continuation of action by substituting a party in the case of death, incompetency, transfer of interest, or resignation of office	Ninety days after death, etc., made part of record	25	

(continued)

EXHIBIT 6:25 ■ Pleadings, Motions, and Time Limits *(continued)*

Pleading/Act	Purpose If Not Clear	Due	Federal Rule	State Rule/Due
Motion for Enlargement of Time	To gain extension from original date pleading is due	In time within which pleading is originally due or after if due to excusable neglect	6(b)	
Motion for Judgment on the Pleadings	To get final judgment in case based solely on the pleadings	After pleadings closed but not so late as to delay trial	12(c)	
Motion of Application for Seizure of Property (Writ of Attachment)	To secure property so that if suit is successful, judgment can be paid. Also final remedy to collect judgment	After filing of lawsuit (generally) or after judgment	64 (incorporating state law)	
Motion or Application for Injunctions including Temporary Restraining Order, Preliminary Injunction, and Permanent Injunctions	To prevent irreparable damage to persons or property involved in the original action, to require another party to do some act or to refrain from some act	After filing of lawsuit (temporary restraining order good for up to ten days unless extended by court for good cause); after ten days must secure preliminary injunction	65	
Motion for Summary Judgment	Seeks final judgment based on pleadings and supporting affidavits (may come after discovery). Alleges no genuine issue in case.	Plaintiff: twenty days after filing complaint or after being served with such motions by adverse party. Defendant: Any time after action filed. Notice: Served ten days prior to hearing on motion	56	
DISCOVERY				
Parties' Planning Meeting	To decide on a plan for disclosure and discovery	As soon as practical and at least 21 days prior to 16(b) scheduling conference	26(f)	
Planning Meeting Report		Within 14 days after parties' planning meeting	26(f)(4)	

EXHIBIT 6:25 ■ Pleadings, Motions, and Time Limits *(continued)*

Pleading/Act	Purpose If Not Clear	Due	Federal Rule	State Rule/Due
Initial Disclosure		Within 14 days of 26(f) meeting unless otherwise stipulated or ordered. At least 90 days before trial if expert witness information.	26(a)(1)(E) and (2)(C)	
Pretrial Disclosure	Witnesses, documents, exhibits, and other information for trial	At least 30 days prior to trial. Objection to admissibility within 14 days after disclosure.	26(a)(3)(C)	
Petition for Deposition Before Action or Pending Appeal	To preserve testimony or other evidence before action or appeal started	Notice to each party due twenty days before hearing on petition	27(a)(1–2)	
Notice to Take Deposition (notice to all other parties)	To gather evidence from the oral or written statements of others	After parties' 26(f) meeting	26(d), 30(a), 30(b)(1)	
Motion to Enlarge or Shorten Time for Taking Deposition			30(d)(2)	
Notice to Take Deposition on Written Questions	Requested when oral deposition impractical	After parties' 26(f) meeting; cross questions within fourteen days of service of original questions; redirect and recross questions within seven days of service of follow-up questions	31(a)	
Objections to Form of Written Deposition Questions		In time permitted for response as stated above and in five days after service of the last question	32(d)(3)(C)	
Interrogatories	To discover evidence through written questions to any party	After parties' 26(f) meeting; limited to twenty-five interrogatories	26(d), 33(a)	
Answers or Objections to Interrogatories		Within thirty days after service of questions; must be written	33(b)(3)	

(continued)

EXHIBIT 6:25 ■ Pleadings, Motions, and Time Limits *(continued)*

Pleading/Act	Purpose If Not Clear	Due	Federal Rule	State Rule/Due
Request for Production of Documents and Things and Entry to Land	To inspect documents (writings, photos, data collections, etc.) and land to gather evidence	After parties' 26(f) meeting	26(d), 34(a)(b)	
Response to Request for Production, Etc.		Within thirty days after service of request. Objection waived if no written responses served.	34(b)	
Motion for Order to Submit to Physical or Mental Exam	To require a party to submit to exam when condition in question (injury, emotional illness, other) relates to cause of action or damages	After parties' 26(f) meeting	26(d), 35(a)	
Request for Admission(s)	To get opponent to admit to certain facts so they do not have to be proven at trial by separate evidence	After parties' 26(f) meeting	36(a)	
Answer or Objection to Request for Admission		Within thirty days after service of request	36(a)	
Duty to Supplement Discovery Responses	To keep discovery current	Seasonably	26(a)(1) and (2), (e)	
Motion to Compel Discovery	To get court to order party to provide discovery	On reasonable notice to all parties and all persons affected and after attempt to resolve	37(a)(d)	
Motion for Protective Order	To get order permitting party to not respond to certain aspects of discovery or to prevent abuse of discovery by opponent	In reasonable period of time and after attempt to resolve	26(c)	
Motion to Enforce Subpoena	To require person to appear and/or produce documents for examination	Any time after objection to subpoena is made and upon notice to person commanded to produce	45(c)(2)(B)	

EXHIBIT 6:25 ■ Pleadings, Motions, and Time Limits *(continued)*

Pleading/Act	Purpose If Not Clear	Due	Federal Rule	State Rule/Due
Objection to Subpoena for Production and Inspection	To change or stop the enforcement of subpoena	Before time for compliance with subpoena or within 14 days after service of subpoena	45(c)(2)(B)	
PRETRIAL				
Demand for Jury Trial		To all parties any time after action starts but no later than ten days after the last pleading directed to such issue. Check local rules.	38(b)	
Motion for Involuntary Dismissal	To dismiss action for failure of plaintiff to prosecute	120 days after filing of action absent service of summons and complaint	41(b), 4(m)	
Consolidation of Actions or Separation for Trial	To combine actions for the sake of judicial economy or to provide separate trials where combined trial would cause prejudice or inconvenience	In reasonable time before trial	42(a)(b)	
Motion for Voluntary Dismissal	So plaintiff or parties can agree to action dismissal	By notice of dismissal at any time before service by adverse party of an answer or motion for summary judgment, whichever occurs first, or by filing stipulation signed by all parties appearing in action	41(a)(1)	
Motion to Use Deposition at Trial	To use deposition as testimony at trial	Reasonable time before trial and on reasonable notice	32(a)(3)	
Motion in Limine	For protective order against prejudicial questions or statements by adverse party	Pursuant to scheduling order and usually a reasonable time before trial or reasonable time after selection of jury	16(b)	

(continued)

EXHIBIT 6:25 ■ Pleadings, Motions, and Time Limits (*continued*)

Pleading/Act	Purpose If Not Clear	Due	Federal Rule	State Rule/Due
Motion to Exclude Evidence	To exclude evidence for a variety of reasons	Pursuant to scheduling order and usually a reasonable time before trial or as matter arises at trial	16(b)	
Offer of Judgment	To settle case by defendant offering to accept judgment for a specified amount	Any time more than 10 days before trial. Ten days to accept offer.	68	
TRIAL				
Motion for Judgment as a Matter of Law (Directed Verdict)	To have court enter judgment for moving party for failure of opponent to prove prima facie case	Any time before submission of case to jury	50(a)(2)	
Renewal of Motion for Judgment as a Matter of Law (JNOV)	To have court enter judgment contrary to that returned by jury on basis jury verdict goes against weight of evidence (may be joined with motion for new trial)	Within ten days after entry of judgment	50(b)	
POST-TRIAL				
Motion for New Trial or to Alter or Amend Judgment	To have judgment set aside and new trial ordered because of error or other injustice at first trial	Within ten days after entry of judgment	59, 52(b)	
Response to Motion for New Trial/ Affidavits	To oppose motion for new trial	Within ten days after service of motion or twenty more days with leave of court	59(c)	
Motion to Correct Clerical Errors in Judgment		Any time	60(a)	
Motion for Stay of Execution of Judgment Pending Post-Trial Motions		Within ten days after entry of judgment or with motion for post-trial relief	62(b)	

EXHIBIT 6:25 ■ Pleadings, Motions, and Time Limits *(continued)*

Pleading/Act	Purpose If Not Clear	Due	Federal Rule	State Rule/Due
APPEAL				
Notice of Appeal	To notify all parties of appeal	Within thirty days after judgment or order; sixty days if U.S. or officer or agency	Rule 4(a) of Appellate Procedure	
Stay on Appeal	To prevent execution of judgment until appeal decided	At filing notice of appeal or soon after	62(d)	

SUMMARY

Chapter 5 emphasizes the role of formulating and filing a case for the plaintiff; Chapter 6 emphasizes the defense, how to attack the weaknesses in the complaint or action, how to remove a case to federal court, and how to respond in the form of an answer to the complaint.

The defendant has twenty days or more to respond to the complaint, depending on jurisdiction and method of service. The first likely response includes a host of motions to have the complaint dismissed or modified. These motions are your first introduction to what today has become an extensive motion practice. Motions drafted by the parties to the action request the court for an order directing the other side to comply, backed up with contempt of court or other sanctions for failure to do so. Because they can result in specific court action against one or more of the parties, motions are critical to sound representation.

The first motions to be filed in a case seek orders dismissing or modifying the complaint [Rule 12(b)]. These motions can attack jurisdiction, service, or venue; or they may attack a complaint for stating an incomplete, inaccurate, or misconceived premise. Your tasks are to review the complaint and spot its weaknesses, and to research and draft the motion and supporting documents, including memoranda of law and affidavits. If the motion is successful, the complaint may be dismissed or simply amended. If the latter, then the defendant must file the answer.

If the case is filed in state court but could be heard in federal court, the defendant may choose to have the case removed to federal court, which is accomplished through the drafting and filing of a Notice of Removal.

The defendant must answer the complaint regardless of removal. The answer is the formal pleading that states the defendant's specific admission, denial, or other responses to each of the plaintiff's assertions in the complaint. What determines the needed detail in the response is whether the jurisdiction is a notice pleading or a code (fact) pleading jurisdiction.

The answer must include affirmative defenses, such as the expiration of the statute of limitations, if the defense plans to assert these defenses at trial. In addition, counterclaims that the defendant has against the plaintiff should be asserted with the answer. Cross-claims against co-parties can be included in the answer after the counterclaim or may be filed as separate documents. To litigate all the claims arising from a single set of circumstances, the parties may bring in nonparties as third-party defendants. These are persons who may be liable to the defendant for part or all of the plaintiff's claim, or may be liable to the plaintiff for part or all of the defendant's counterclaim.

The filing of each of the pleadings and motions mentioned in this chapter follows strict time deadlines that, if not met, may result in default, the loss of the right to assert or claim a defense, or the loss of the case. One of your important roles is knowing each of the time limits and then seeing to it that they are met. It also involves noting when the other parties fail to meet their deadlines.

Pleadings may be liberally amended or supplemented under Rule 15 as long as the time limits for doing so are followed. When the pleadings are closed after the filing of the complaint, answer, and reply to counterclaim, either party may file a motion for judgment on the pleadings. A judgment on the pleadings essentially asserts that even if what the adversary says is true, there is no claim or there is no defense. A motion for summary judgment is similar, but goes further by asking the court to look behind the pleadings to consider additional evidence. Because of the importance of each of these pleadings and motions and their respective time deadlines as set out in state and federal rules, it is helpful for you to keep an accurate and timely pleading record.

WORKBOOK

System Folder Assignments, other exercises, a chapter outline, a review test, and other study aids are located in the accompanying workbook.

HELPFUL WEB SITES

http://www.westlawlitigator.com
  introductory page on a wide variety of information and services for litigators (subscription)

http://www.courtlink.com
  electronic access to federal and state court records (subscription service)

QUESTIONS FOR STUDY AND REVIEW

1. What is a motion? State the purposes of motions in general.
2. What does it mean to preserve an issue for appeal?
3. What are the requirements for a motion under federal and your state rules? Identify the particular rules that apply.
4. What is a notice of motion and what purpose does it serve? Do the Federal Rules permit it to be combined with the motion?
5. What is the purpose of a supporting affidavit in motion practice? A supporting memorandum of law? What is the difference between the two?
6. Describe the detailed procedure for filing and serving motions. What federal and state rules apply?
7. What time deadlines must be heeded in motion practice? State the applicable rules.

8. Have you developed a checklist for drafting and filing motions?
9. What is a motion to dismiss? What purpose does it serve?
10. What is a demurrer? What purpose does it serve?
11. What method should you use to determine the weaknesses in a complaint subject to a motion to dismiss the complaint? Explain how the method works.
12. Be able to draft the necessary documents to obtain an order dismissing the complaint.
13. Explain the procedure, applicable rules, and time deadlines for filing and serving a motion to dismiss in both federal and your state courts.
14. What are the other Rule 12(b) motions? Must they be made separately?

15. What are the other motions attacking the complaint? State their purposes.
16. Be able to draft (a) a motion to strike and (b) a motion to make more definite and certain. What are the applicable rules?
17. If your state makes use of the special demurrer or the bill of particulars, be able to draft either.
18. When may an action be removed to federal district court?
19. What is the correct procedure and what form is needed to remove an action to federal court?
20. What is the formula for calculating time limit due dates?
21. What is the purpose of the answer? When must it be filed? What rule is applicable?
22. Be able to list style and content considerations for drafting an answer, including those that apply to denials.

23. What are the components of an answer? Be able to define each of them.
24. What is the procedure for locating the possible defenses to a claim?
25. Be able to draft an answer, including all the possible components.
26. What is the purpose of the following: third-party practice, amending and supplementing the pleadings, a motion for judgment on the pleadings, and a motion for summary judgment?
27. Be able to draft the documents needed for third-party practice, amending and supplementing the pleadings, a motion for judgment on the pleadings, and a motion for summary judgment.
28. What time deadlines apply to the variety of pleadings covered in this chapter?

▣ KEY TERMS

affiant	bill of particulars	demurrer	(memorandum of points
affidavit	brief	memorandum of law	and authorities)
answer	counterclaim	motion	third-party practice
argumentative denials	cross-claim	order	(impleader)

▣ ENDNOTES

1. Adapted from WEST'S FEDERAL FORMS, § 1101, v. 2.
2. Adapted from CAROLE A. BRUNO, PARALEGAL'S LITIGATION HANDBOOK 51 (1993).
3. Memo from J. Burton to J. McCord (March 27, 1986).
4. VETTER, SUCCESSFUL CIVIL LITIGATION: HOW TO WIN YOUR CASE BEFORE YOU ENTER THE COURTROOM 43–47 (1977).
5. NAT'L L.J. (June 1985), last page.
6. BRUNO, *supra* note 2, 43.

7. Adapted from WEST'S FEDERAL FORMS, § 2717, v. 3.
8. *Id.*, § 2701.
9. *Id.*, § 4723, v. 4.
10. *Id.*, § 4722.
11. *Id.*, § 4726.
12. Suggested by J. Warm in a memo to J. McCord (March 24, 1986).

 For additional resources, visit our Web site at **http://www.westlegalstudies.com.**

Discovery and Electronic Discovery: Overview and Interrogatories

OVERVIEW OF DISCOVERY

INTRODUCTION

Discovery is the process in a lawsuit involving the exchange of information, exhibits, and documents between parties according to specific rules of procedure. That information helps form the evidentiary basis for both sides of the lawsuit. The exchange involves the following procedures or devices listed in Federal Rule of Civil Procedure 26:

1. Disclosure: giving to the opponent a broad spectrum of relevant information about the case without a specific request or use of other discovery devices
2. Interrogatories: written questions submitted to a party
3. Deposition: sworn oral testimony of a witness or litigant taken prior to trial
4. Production of documents, tangible items, or entry to property for inspection
5. Expert's report and opinion: the name, subject matter, and substance of the report of scientists and other experts to be used at trial
6. Medical examinations: requirement upon motion that a party submit to a physical or mental examination by a doctor chosen by the opposing party
7. Request for admission: asking the opponent to admit certain facts in writing, which then do not have to be proven at trial

Employ these devices more or less in proportion to the complexity of the case and the amount in dispute. Small cases use discovery sparingly, large cases extensively. These chapters emphasize the full use of discovery, including the discovery of electronically stored information. Read the discovery section of Exhibit 6:25 for a helpful overview of the discovery devices and the rules and time limits that pertain to each. Discovery is an essential area of paralegal practice. Learn it well.

PURPOSE OF DISCOVERY

Justice is served when a case is tried on its merits (the evidence) rather than on some tactic of surprise or deception. "Trial by ambush" is no longer accepted. The rules of discovery attempt to achieve this result by making it possible for both sides in a lawsuit to be informed about the evidence and witnesses that will be presented by the opponent. More information should result in better preparation by both sides, which in turn provides the trier of fact with better information for ascertaining the truth. Despite these laudatory goals, discovery is expensive, comprising about fifty percent of the cost of litigation.[1]

More practical purposes exist as well. Discovery helps reveal whether there is a basis for the lawsuit or its defense. Therefore, discovery may lead to summary judgment or voluntary dismissal, ending the lawsuit and saving the time, expense, and anguish of a trial. The early access to information provided by discovery is more likely to lead to an early settlement based on a more accurate assessment of the case. Discovery also serves to identify undisputed facts, leaving for trial only those issues clearly in conflict. Fewer issues may result in a shorter, less expensive trial.

Another purpose of discovery is to gather information from the opponent that can strengthen one's own case or allow one to be better prepared to refute the accuracy of the evidence presented by the other side. For example, if a witness says one thing at a deposition and another at trial, the earlier statements can be used to weaken the inconsistent trial testimony.

Discovery also helps preserve evidence. If a witness gives testimony at a deposition and is later unavailable for trial, the court might permit the prior testimony to

discovery
The process in a lawsuit involving the exchange of information, exhibits, and documents between parties according to specific rules of procedure.

be entered at trial. Electronically stored information, which might be destroyed in the normal course of business, must be preserved for discovery.

PRESERVING EVIDENCE FOR DISCOVERY: THE PRESERVATION LETTER

preservation letter
A letter sent to the opposing party requesting preservation of evidence.

A party may need to act prior to discovery and, occasionally, as soon as litigation is contemplated to see that the opponent preserves potentially important evidence, particularly where the discovery of electronically stored information is contemplated. Early action is important not only because e-stored information is easily altered or lost, but also because the prospective opponent may not anticipate the need to preserve the evidence nor know what needs to be preserved and where it is located. The **preservation letter** accomplishes this end. It also alerts the opposing party to possible sanctions for carelessly or willfully losing evidence. Read the sample preservation letter for electronically stored information in Exhibit 7:1 to understand the focus and necessary detail of the letter.[2]

EXHIBIT 7:1 ▪ Sample Preservation Letter

[LAW FIRM]

[date/address]

Re: Notice to Preserve Electronic Evidence
[Legal Matter]

Dear _____ :

Our law firm represents [name] in the above legal matter in which you [your business] are [is] [will be] named as a defendant. This letter requests your immediate action to preserve electronically stored information that may contain evidence important to the above legal matter. Briefly, the matter involves [short statement of facts in case].

This notice applies to your [company's] on- and off-site computer systems and removable electronic media plus all computer systems, services, and devices (including all remote access and wireless devices) used for your [company's] overall operation. This includes, but is not limited to, e-mail and other electronic communications; electronically stored documents, records, images, graphics, recordings, spreadsheets, databases; calendars, system usage logs, contact manager information, telephone logs, internet usage files, deleted files, cache files, user information, and other data. Further, this notice applies to archives, backup and disaster recovery tapes, discs, drives, cartridges, voicemail and other data. All operating systems, software, applications, hardware, operating manuals, codes, keys and other support information needed to fully search, use, and access the electronically stored information must also be preserved.

The importance of immediate action cannot be overstated. Electronically stored information is easily corrupted, altered, and deleted in normal daily operations. Even booting a drive, running an application, or reviewing a document can permanently alter evidence. An important method for preserving data in its original state is to have a forensic image (mirror image or clone image) made of pertinent hard drives of both office and home computers used for business and of network servers. This image captures all current data, including the background or metadata about each document. Simply copying data to a CD-ROM or other common back-up medium is not adequate. For each captured image file, record and identify the person creating the image and the date of creation. Secure the file to prevent subsequent alteration or corruption and create a chain of custody log. Once the forensic data image file is created, the pertinent computer or other device can be placed back into operation.

[If known, identify any key persons', officers', supervisors', and employees' computers to which special attention for forensic imaging must be directed.]

This preservation notice covers the above items and information between the following dates: [state dates]. Follow the above procedures to preserve electronic information created after this notice.

Current law and rules of civil procedure clearly apply to the discovery of electronically stored information just as they apply to other evidence, and confirm the duty to preserve such information for discovery. You [company] and your officers, employees, agents, and affiliated organizations must take all reasonable steps to preserve this information until this legal matter is finally resolved. Failure to take the necessary steps to preserve the information addressed in this letter or other pertinent information in your possession or control may result in serious sanctions or penalties.

Further, to properly fulfill your preservation obligation, stop all scheduled data destruction, electronic shredding, rotation of backup tapes, and the sale, gift or destruction of hardware. Notify all individuals and affiliated organizations of the need and duty to take the necessary affirmatives steps to comply with the duty to preserve evidence.

Sincerely,

[attorney/address]

A good preservation letter should be as specific to the case and narrowly drawn as your knowledge of the opponent's e-storage system permits and reasonableness dictates. Consult with your office's information technology person or a consultant to provide you with the necessary technology guidance before sending your first preservation letter. Discuss the letter with your supervising attorney and plan how the legal team can effectively respond to the opponent's questions about the technology addressed in the letter. Send the letter by certified mail, return receipt requested.

MANDATORY DISCLOSURE

Introduction

Mandatory **disclosure** is the procedure automatically triggered early in a case requiring a party to give (disclose) to the opponent a broad spectrum of information pertinent to the case. It is designed to focus the attention of opposing lawyers on the details of the case at an early stage in the litigation to facilitate fairness and efficiency in the handling and resolution of the dispute.

disclosure
The procedure automatically triggered early in a case requiring a party to give to the opponent a broad spectrum of information relevant to the case.

Initial Disclosure

Within ninety days after the defendant has made an appearance in the case and within 120 days after the complaint has been served on the defendant, the court holds a scheduling conference with the attorneys to establish a time frame for the case and to issue a scheduling order [Rule 16(b)]. At least twenty-one days prior to the scheduling conference or the date that a scheduling order is due from the court, sooner if practicable, the attorneys must hold a meeting to discuss and establish a plan for disclosure and discovery in the case [Rule 26(f)]. Within fourteen days after the attorneys' planning meeting, unless otherwise stipulated or directed by the court, the *initial disclosure* of information must occur. This disclosure is automatic; it eliminates the need to start the process with a motion or request for discovery submitted to the court. Initial disclosure is defined by Federal Rule of Civil Procedure 26(a)(1) (as amended 2006).[3] It requires the parties to disclose the following information to the other parties:

(a) The name, address, and phone number of persons likely to have discoverable information that the disclosing party may use to support its claims or defenses, unless solely for impeachment, identifying the subjects of the information

(b) The production or description of relevant documents, electronically stored information, and tangible things in the possession, custody, or control of the disclosing party that may be used to support its claims or defenses, unless solely for impeachment

(c) A computation of damages, with the source of information on the nature and extent of the injuries made available to the other party for inspection and copying

(d) Any insurance agreement likely to cover the damages, made available for inspection and copying

This initial disclosure is designed to eliminate the need for an initial set of interrogatories or other early discovery devices. Occasionally, the new disclosure process occurs later in the case than some discovery opportunities under the former rules or current state rules. This delay may cause some information to be lost or a witness's memory to fade. A good paralegal is alert to such possibilities early in the case, and notifies the attorney that disclosure on that particular information needs to occur ahead of the normal schedule.

Note that the first item (a) encompasses persons with discoverable information as well as persons likely to have discoverable information. Also, the duty to disclose no longer includes information favorable to the opponent. Instead, the duty to disclose is confined to what a "party may use to *support* its claims or defenses" [emphasis added]. The phrase "claims or defenses" strictly narrows disclosure from the former language ("relevant to disputed facts") to that which the disclosing party intends to use. "Use," as defined in the advisory committee's notes, includes any use at a pretrial conference, to support a motion, or at trial.

Mandatory disclosure is not required in eight types of cases including administrative appeals, habeas corpus petitions, and actions by the United States to recover student loans. Also, the parties may stipulate to forgo mandatory disclosure, or a party's objection to mandatory disclosure may prevent disclosure until the court rules on the objection. Mandatory disclosure is also required of newly added parties. To move the process along, initial disclosure "must" be made based on what is reasonably available at the time. An incomplete investigation or the failure of the other party to properly disclose does not excuse a party from the obligation to disclose under this rule.

> "In saying what is obvious, never choose cunning; yelling works better."
> —CYNTHIA OZICK, 1928– .

Disclosure of Information on Expert Testimony

Rule 26(a)(2) requires the disclosure of information on expert testimony in the case. This rule provides for disclosure of the following information:

(a) The identity of any expert (Federal Rules of Evidence 702, 703, or 705) who may be used at trial

(b) A written report prepared and signed by the expert witness, which includes a complete statement of all of the opinions to be expressed, the reasons for the opinions, the data or information relied on, the expert's qualifications and publications in the last ten years, the expert's compensation, and other cases the witness has testified at or been deposed for in the last four years

The disclosure of expert-related information must occur as directed by the court or by stipulation between the parties. In the absence of such direction, this disclosure must occur at least ninety days before trial unless it pertains to a rebuttal expert. If the latter, disclosure must be made within thirty days after disclosure of the other party [Rule 26(a)(2)(C)]. Complying with disclosure requirements regarding expert witnesses continues to be a problematic area in practice, especially regarding what attorney work product, if any, must be revealed to comply with Rule 26(a)(2)(B). Special cooperation and frequent communication between opposing sides is crucial to having this part of disclosure work effectively.

Pretrial Disclosures

Pretrial disclosures, as distinguished from initial disclosures, must be made at least thirty days prior to trial [Rule 26(a)(3)]. Pretrial disclosures include the following information regarding evidence for trial, unless it will be used strictly for impeachment purposes:

(a) The names, addresses, and phone numbers of each witness designated as "expected" to be or "may" be called at trial
(b) The designation of witnesses who will testify by deposition with a transcript of the pertinent testimony unless stenographically recorded
(c) The identification of each document or exhibit, including summaries of other evidence, labeled as "expected" to be used or "may" be used at trial

Within fourteen days after the receipt of pretrial disclosures, a party must serve and file a list disclosing objections to the use under Rule 32(a) of any deposition proposed in (b) and any objection and grounds for the objection to the admissibility of materials stated in (c). Objections not disclosed are waived, unless the failure to disclose is excused for good cause or the objection is pursuant to Rule of Evidence 402 (relevance) or 403 (undue prejudice).

Disclosure Procedure, Certification

All disclosures under these provisions must be in writing, signed by the attorney, and served on the other party [Rule 26(a)(4)]. Include the attorney's address. Note that the filing of disclosure and discovery documents in court is prohibited until the material is used in the proceeding or the court orders filing [Rule 5(d)]. Further, Rule 26(g) adds Rule 11–type requirements and certification. The attorney's signature certifies that the disclosure is complete and correct to the best of the signer's knowledge [26(g)(1)]. When applied to discovery, the signature certifies that any discovery request, response, or objection is consistent with the rules and warranted by existing law or a good faith argument for the extension, modification, or reversal of existing law; is not interposed for an improper purpose such as to harass, unnecessarily delay, or needlessly increase the cost of litigation; and is not unduly burdensome or expensive regarding the needs of the case, previous discovery, the amount in controversy, and the importance of the issues at stake [Rule 26(g)(1)(2)].

Any discovery request, response, or objection shall be stricken if it is not signed or promptly corrected on notice of the defect [Rule 26(g)(2)]. An attorney or the party represented may be sanctioned by the court for making a certification in violation of the rules [Rule 26(g)(3)].

SCOPE OF DISCOVERY

Introduction

The courts liberally apply the rules of discovery, including those on disclosure, to carry out the rules' laudatory purposes. Some important limitations apply to what may be discovered, however. The limitations are defined in Rule 26(b) and parallel state rules.

Relevance [26(b)(1)]

Any matter that is relevant to a claim or defense of any party of the lawsuit and is not protected by one of the limitations discussed here must be disclosed and is discoverable [Rule 26(b)(1)]. Recall that information is relevant, and thus admissible for trial, if it is of consequence to the determination of the action and tends to prove or refute a fact of consequence to the lawsuit. The broad purpose of discovery, however, reaches beyond relevant information that is admissible for trial purposes to include information that "appears reasonably calculated to lead to the discovery of admissible evidence." The Advisory Committee Notes state that the emphasis on discovering admissible evidence takes allowable discovery beyond a strict limitation of relevance to a claim or defense to encompass, for example, evidence to be used to impeach a witness. Although such impeachment evidence, strictly speaking, may not be relevant to the claim or defense, it is admissible and, therefore, discoverable.

Rule 26(b)(1) creates two different areas of discovery. In the first, the attorneys are charged with and limited to carrying out discovery consisting of matters relevant to the claim or a defense to the claim. In the second, the court manages any discovery that goes beyond the claim or defense and can, on a showing of good cause, order discovery that is "relevant to the subject matter" of the action. This subsection emphasizes the court's authority to prevent unnecessarily broad and sometimes voluminous discovery requests. As a matter of practice, the legal teams for each party need to determine when the court should be brought into the process and concerning what material.

Privilege [26(b)(1)]

The rule of privilege, discussed in Chapter 3, that protects some information from being admissible for trial (attorney-client privilege and others) also protects that same information from discovery [Rule 26(b)(1)]. Therefore, privileged information may be withheld from disclosure and any other discovery. A party withholding privileged information, however, must provide a list (or privilege log) to the other party [Rule 26(b)(5)(A)]. The list must identify the document or other information along with a description of its nature so the other party can "assess the applicability of the privilege or protection."

When a discovery issue arises regarding whether a particular communication is privileged, Rule 501 of the Federal Rules of Evidence indicates that where a case in federal court relies on state law for its determination, such as in diversity cases, the state rule defining privilege controls [*Jewell v. Holzer*, 899 F.2d 1507, 1513 (6th Cir. 1990)]. If, however, the case involves both federal and state claims, then privilege is normally defined by the federal case law interpreting Rule 501 [e.g., *Hancock v. Hobbs*, 967 F.2d 462, 466–467 (11th Cir. 1992)].

Trial Preparation Materials [26(b)(3)]

The other major limitation on the scope of discovery is the attorney's work product or trial preparation materials exception. It bears repeating that documents and tangible things prepared in anticipation of litigation or trial may be discovered only if the party wanting discovery can show a substantial need for the materials in preparation for trial, and that obtaining the information any other way would cause undue hardship. This rule protects the work of the attorney as well as the work of the attorney's agents [Rule 26(b)(3)]. This rule especially protects from disclosure the mental impressions, conclusions, opinions, and legal theories of the attorney. As in the case of privileged information, the party withholding the trial preparation material must provide a 26(b)(5)(A) list to the other party. Failure to do so can result in the loss of any work product protection for the item not listed. Although Rule 26 leaves the federal judge some discretion, the protection afforded trial preparation materials is absolute in some states. Rule 26(b)(3) also provides that a party may obtain a copy of any statement made by that party or by a nonparty without any special showing of need. Should discovery disputes arise, federal law defines trial preparation materials in all cases in federal court [*Toledo Edison Co. v. G. A. Technologies, Inc.*, 847 F.2d 335, 338–341 (6th Cir. 1998)].

Time and considerable experience are required for a paralegal to learn the delicate boundaries of what is protected and what is not. Sanctions for failure to comply with these rules, as well as court orders and procedures to protect material requested under these rules, are discussed in Chapter 9.

Procedure When Produced Information Contains Privileged or Trial Preparation Material [26(b)(5)(B)]

The 2006 Federal Rule amendments that address electronic discovery issues recognize how difficult and costly it is in the electronic information age to prevent completely the production of protected information. Rule 26(b)(5) was amended with a new subsection (5)(B) to provide remedial procedure in such circumstances. The producing party may notify any recipient party of what produced information is later claimed to be privileged or protected trial preparation material and the basis for that assertion. The longer the time between the production and the notice, however, the more likely it is the court may find that any privilege or protection claimed has been waived. The recipient party must "promptly return, sequester, or destroy" the specified information and may not use or disclose it. The recipient party may challenge the claim of protection by presenting the pertinent information to the court under seal for determination of the issue. If the recipient disclosed the information prior to notification of the claim, the recipient must "take reasonable steps" to recover it. The information for which the protection is claimed must be preserved by the producing party until the question is resolved. It remains for the court to determine whether the inadvertent or other production of the information waives the privilege or protection.

Trial Preparation: Experts [26(b)(4)]

An opposing party may depose an expert who will testify at trial only after the expert's 26(a)(2)(B) report has been disclosed to the opponent. The party requesting the deposition must pay the expert a reasonable fee for the deposition or the expert's response to any other discovery device [Rules 26(b)(4)(A) and (C)]. An expert employed by the opponent but not expected to testify at trial may be deposed or requested to answer interrogatories. If so, the party requesting discovery must pay a fair portion of the expert's fee and expenses [Rules 26(b)(4)(B) and (C)].

Court Discretion and Other Limits [26(b)(2)(A–C)]

The federal court may change the number of interrogatories or depositions or other discovery devices sought if the following conditions are present [26(b)(2)(A)]:

- The discovery sought is unreasonably burdensome, cumulative, or duplicative, or is obtainable from a more convenient and less expensive source
- The party seeking discovery has had ample opportunity to obtain the information sought
- The discovery is unduly burdensome or expensive, taking into account the needs of the case, the amount in controversy, limitations of the parties' resources, and the importance of the issues at stake in the litigation [Rule 26(b)(2)(C)]

New language was added to Rule 26(b)(2) addressing the difficulty of producing some kinds of electronically stored information. Rule 26(b)(2)(B) permits a responding party not to produce requested electronically stored information when it is "not reasonably accessible because of undue burden or cost." That party, however, must "identify" for the requesting party those specific sources of information. Some examples of e-information that may not be reasonably accessible include backup tapes not indexed or easily searched, residual but fragmented data from previous deletions, and other data that can only be searched by very expensive and time-consuming forensic processes. The party asserting that the requested information is not reasonably accessible must convince the court of that fact. Despite that showing, the court may, for good cause shown by the opponent, still order production. In making that decision, the court must consider the three conditions in 26(b)(2)(C) stated above. Check your state rules for similar limits on discovery.

PARTIES' PLANNING MEETING

Discovery may not start until the parties hold a planning meeting [Rule 26(d)]. The planning meeting is governed by Rule 26(f). The parties shall meet as soon as practicable and at least twenty-one days before a scheduling conference is held or a scheduling order is due under Rule 16(b). The meeting should cover:

- the nature and basis for the claims and defenses asserted
- the possibility of a prompt resolution of the case through a settlement or other resolution
- disclosure or arrangement for disclosure as required in Rule 26(a)(1)
- any issues concerning the preservation of discoverable information, including electronically stored information
- the plan for discovery, including interrogatories, depositions, and other devices
- the parties' plans concerning
  1. disclosures and changes to be made in the timing, form, or requirements for disclosure under 26(a) or a local rule
  2. subjects in which discovery is needed, a date for completion of discovery, whether discovery should be conducted in phases or limited to particular issues
  3. disclosure or discovery issues regarding e-stored information, including in what form(s) it should be produced
  4. issues about claims of privilege or protection of trial-preparation material, including whether the parties agree on how to assert such claims

after production and on asking the court to include any agreement in an order (the Committee Note to this item encourages the parties to consider an agreement on what post-production protocol, if followed, will avoid the waiver of the pertinent privilege or protection)

5. what limitations on discovery imposed by the Rules or local rules should be changed and what other limitations should be adopted

6. any other orders to be entered by the court regarding protective orders or matters under the Rule 16 pretrial and management conference.

The attorney for each party and any unrepresented party must meet and attempt in good faith to agree on a plan. The plan must be submitted in writing to the court within 14 days of the meeting. The times for holding the parties' planning meeting and for submitting the report may be altered by the court if needed to comply with an expedited schedule for Rule 16(b) conferences. The form for the Report of Parties' Planning Meeting, Federal Form 35, is in Exhibit 7:2. Some judges have developed their own report forms to ensure a thorough meeting and reporting of that meeting by the parties.

EXHIBIT 7:2 ▪ Form 35. Report of Parties' Planning Meeting

[Caption and Names of Parties]

1. Pursuant to Fed.R.Civ.P. 26(f), a meeting was held on (date) at (place) and was attended by:

(name) for plaintiff(s)

(name) for defendant(s) (party name)

(name) for defendant(s) (party name)

2. Pre-discovery Disclosures. The parties [have exchanged] [will exchange by (date)] the information required by [Fed.R.Civ.P. 26(a)(1)] [local rule _____].

3. Discovery Plan. The parties jointly propose to the court the following discovery plan: [Use separate paragraphs or subparagraphs as necessary if parties disagree.]

Discovery will be needed on the following subjects: (brief description of subjects on which discovery will be needed)

Disclosure or discovery of electronically stored information should be handled as follows: (brief description of parties' proposals).

The parties have agreed to an order regarding claims of privilege or of protection as trial-preparation material asserted after production as follows: (brief description of provisions of proposed order).

All discovery commenced in time to be completed by (date) . [Discovery on (issue for early discovery) to be completed by (date) .]

Maximum of _____ interrogatories by each party to any other party. [Responses due _____ days after service.]

Maximum of _____ requests for admission by each party to any other party. [Responses due _____ days after service.]

Maximum of _____ depositions by plaintiff(s) and _____ by defendant(s).Each deposition [other than of _____] limited to maximum of _____ hours unless extended by agreement of parties.

Reports from retained experts under Rule 26(a)(2) due:

from plaintiff(s) by (date)

from defendant(s) by (date)

Supplementations under Rule 26(e) due [time(s) or interval(s)].

4. Other Items. [Use separate paragraphs or subparagraphs as necessary if parties disagree.] The parties [request] [do not request] a conference with the court before entry of the scheduling order.

(continued)

EXHIBIT 7:2 ■ Form 35. Report of Parties' Planning Meeting *(continued)*

The parties request a pretrial conference in (month and year).
Plaintiff(s) should be allowed until (date) to join additional parties and until (date) to amend the pleadings.
Defendant(s) should be allowed until (date) to join additional parties and until (date) to amend the pleadings.
All potentially dispositive motions should be filed by (date). Settlement [is likely] [is unlikely] [cannot be evaluated prior to (date)] [may be enhanced by use of the following alternative dispute resolution procedure: _____].
Final lists of witnesses and exhibits under Rule 26(a)(3) should be due
  from plaintiff(s) by (date)
  from defendant(s) by (date)
Parties should have _____ days after service of final lists of witnesses and exhibits to list objections under Rule 26(a)(3).
The case should be ready for trial by (date) [and at this time is expected to take approximately (length of time)].[Other matters.]
Date: _____

SUPPLEMENTING DISCLOSURE AND DISCOVERY [RULE 26(E)]

The parties are under a continuing obligation to supplement or correct any disclosure or discovery information if they learn the information given is incomplete or incorrect in some material respect [Rule 26(e)]. This duty encompasses information previously provided by experts in depositions. Supplementation is to be made at "appropriate intervals" for disclosure and "seasonably" for discovery and must be made no later than thirty days before trial.

Because paralegals work so closely with discovery information, they are frequently the ones in the law firm who know when responses need updating. A good paralegal notices outdated or inaccurate information and calendars regular reminders to seek supplementation of discovery from the opponent and to reciprocate.

ETHICAL CONSIDERATIONS FOR DISCOVERY AND DISCLOSURE

Preserving the benefits of discovery (including disclosure) demands vigilance, honesty, and cooperation. The paralegal and attorney who fail to adhere to the relevant ethical standards do a disservice not only to their profession, but also to the fairness that is the goal of discovery. The relative newness and complexities of electronic discovery only intensify the need to understand and conform to applicable ethical standards.

Numerous ethical provisions apply directly or indirectly to discovery. Several are worth noting. ABA Model Rule of Professional Conduct 1.1 requires competent representation consisting of the "legal knowledge, skill, thoroughness and preparation reasonably necessary for the representation." Although most lawyers and paralegals are comfortable with their competency in conducting discovery in the traditional context, many are far less comfortable with, and even fearful of, taking cases involving e-discovery. Comment 2 to Model Rule 1.1 sensibly states that Rule 1.1 allows attorneys to take cases where new areas of expertise will be required, if the attorney and legal team are diligent and thorough about acquiring the reasonably necessary skill and knowledge. Practically speaking, some preparation prior to accepting a case involving e-discovery is necessary to make a realistic assessment of the level of expertise needed and the time and cost involved in the case and in acquiring the requisite level of competency to handle it. You must be prepared to have a frank discussion about this issue with your supervising attorney who otherwise might blindly assume that you have the requisite knowledge and skill to compensate for the attorney's lack thereof.

Model Rule 3.4, previously discussed in Chapter 3, addresses fairness to the opposing party and counsel. It lists serious unethical actions that prevent an open and fair fact-finding process, including unlawfully altering, destroying, or obstructing access to evidence, inducing others (including paralegals) to do so, and other equally injurious acts. Some of these acts are crimes. Disobeying an obligation imposed by the rules for strictly obstructionist reasons is unethical. Rule 3.4(d) adds that a lawyer shall not "make a frivolous discovery request or fail to make a reasonably diligent effort to comply with [an opponent's] legally proper discovery request." The ethical standards set in Model Rule 3.4 are further buttressed by the anti-obstructionist certification by signature in Civil Procedure Rule 26(g)(1)(3), previously discussed. Most state ethics codes have provisions similar to those in Rule 3.4.

Model Rule 1.4 regarding communication with a client is by inference important to discovery in general and to electronic discovery in particular. Under 1.4, an attorney must take reasonable steps to consult with and inform the client about the means to accomplish the client's objectives and the status of the matter to the "extent reasonably necessary" for the client to make informed decisions [Model Rule 1.4(a) and (b)]. In the discovery context, this means the legal team must not only understand the ramifications of the lawsuit and the necessary scope of discovery and disclosure (competence), but also take the required steps needed to alert the client to the significance of each step of the discovery process and what information and action is required from and by the client to comply. This obligation of communication is invoked early in the process, even in anticipation of litigation, and is necessary to prevent destruction of evidence (spoliation). The lack of competence regarding how and where electronic information is stored and the ethical and other duties related to its preservation and discovery, and the failure to make timely and adequate communication of such to the client can result in severe and costly sanctions.

In *Zubulake v. UBS Warburg LLC*, 229 F.R.D. 422 (S.D.N.Y. 2004), sanctions, including an adverse jury instruction on willful destruction of evidence, led to a $29 million jury award. In *Metropolitan Opera Assoc., Inc. v. Local 100, Hotel Employees and Restaurant Employees International Union,* 212 F.R.D. 178 (2003), the court granted Metropolitan Opera's motion for judgment due to opposing counsel's willful and bad faith failure to comply with discovery. Practical suggestions on how you can help your attorney meet ethically mandated discovery obligations are discussed in document production in Chapter 9.

Other areas of ethical concern are the attorney work product (trial preparation materials) and attorney-client privilege. As discussed earlier, careless review and screening of materials and electronically stored information by a paralegal or an attorney may result in the improper revelation of a client's confidences or secrets in direct violation of the code of ethics [Model Rule 1.6(a)]. This rule covers information gained before and after the representation and does not require the client to indicate what is to be held secret; nor does it ask the lawyer to speculate what is embarrassing or detrimental. The rule does permit a lawyer to make disclosures when authorization is implied. The example given in the commentary to Rule 1.6 applies directly to the discovery process and states that a lawyer may disclose information by admitting facts that cannot properly be denied.

You must strive to identify any confidential or protected information and consult with the attorney prior to disclosing that information to anyone outside the firm. This is critical.

The American Bar Association has established ethical guidelines that recognize the likelihood that confidential information will be inadvertently sent to opposing parties at one time or another. When it happens, the attorney or paralegal receiving the information should avoid reading the information or sharing it with anyone else [Formal Opinion 92-368 (1992)]. If part of the confidential information is read, any unexamined part should not be read. The attorney receiving the confidential information should contact the attorney who inadvertently sent it and determine the best way to return it. This is a matter between attorneys, and a client need not be notified before the item is returned. The opinion strongly implies that inadvertently revealed confidential information should not be used by the receiving party. The Federal Rules of Civil Procedure discussed in the preceding section of the chapter reflect an approach consistent with the ABA's.

In *Stephen Slesinger Inc. v. The Walt Disney Co.*, 2004 WL612818, Calif. Super. Ct., Slesinger's case looked strong, partly because the court found that Disney had destroyed records and made false and evasive discovery responses. Unsatisfied, Slesinger's private investigator trespassed onto Disney property and found numerous privileged and protected documents in Disney's dumpsters. The documents were distributed among Slesinger's attorneys. The court found Slesinger's conduct so egregious that it dismissed Slesinger's once promising suit.

DISCLOSURE TIME FRAME SUMMARY (FEDERAL)

1. Parties' planning meeting: as soon as practical, but at least twenty-one days before court scheduling conference.
2. Court scheduling conference/date for scheduling order: as soon as practical, but within 90 days of first appearance of defendant and within 120 days since complaint served on defendant.
3. Written report to court of parties' planning meeting: within fourteen days after parties' planning meeting.
4. Objections to disclosure: at parties' planning meeting and set out in planning report.
5. Disclosure (of persons likely to have supporting discoverable information; copy or description of supporting documents, data, and tangible things; calculation of damages and supporting materials; and applicable insurance agreements): unless otherwise stipulated, ordered, or properly objected to, within fourteen days after parties' planning meeting.
6. Disclosure from party served or joined after parties' planning meeting: unless otherwise stipulated or ordered, within thirty days after served or joined.
7. Disclosure of expert testimony: unless otherwise stipulated or ordered, at least 90 days prior to trial or date set to be ready for trial. If solely to rebut previously disclosed evidence: within thirty days after opponent's disclosure.
8. Response to notification from party that information produced is subject to claim of privilege or protection: "promptly."
9. Pretrial disclosure (of witnesses, expected trial testimony of witness by deposition, and documents or exhibits): unless otherwise directed, at least thirty days before trial.
10. Objections to use of evidence at trial disclosed in step 8: within fourteen days after disclosure or will be waived.

"Arguments derived from probabilities are idle."

—PLATO, *PHAEDO*, C. LATE 4TH CENTURY B.C.

PARALEGAL'S DISCLOSURE CHECKLIST

☐ Review case file, pleadings, complexity, and so on.
☐ Give special attention to e-disclosure and discovery needs [26(b)]:
  ○ Unless previously done, consult with attorney and meet with client regarding assessment of client's e-information storage system, if pertinent to case.
  ○ Unless done, communicate to client disclosure and discovery requirements and the need to preserve evidence, including e-stored information (discussed further in Chapter 9).
  ○ Identify any pertinent e-stored information "not readily accessible," use log and record basis for conclusion.
  ○ Consult with attorney on preferred method of dealing with post-production claims of privileged or protected information.
  ○ Discuss with attorney the need for a protective order to:
    ■ preserve opponent's pertinent information or
    ■ legitimately protect aspects of client's information from disclosure and discovery (discussed further in Chapter 9).
☐ Get date for court scheduling conference/order.
  ○ Calculate other deadlines based on this date.
  ○ Modify according to subsequent plan, stipulation, or court order.
☐ Meet with the supervising attorney to determine desired depth and amount of disclosure and discovery needed and any objections to disclosure.
☐ Assist the attorney in arranging the parties' planning meeting
  ○ Assist at meeting.
  ○ Draft agreed plan (Exhibit 7:1), stipulations, and objections as directed.
  ○ Submit the parties' planning report to court if so directed.
☐ Using the investigation plan (Chapter 3) or similar approach, identify, gather, and organize the supporting evidence to be disclosed as set out in Rule 26(a). Remember to include any pertinent e-stored information.
☐ Review each item to be disclosed to raise any concerns about client confidentiality and/or attorney work product. Do this throughout the disclosure and discovery process.
☐ Format materials to be disclosed as directed. They must be written, unless court orders "otherwise" [26(a)(4)].
  ○ Include signature line and attorney's address.
☐ Give formatted materials to supervising attorney for final review and signature.
☐ Serve disclosure materials on all parties.
☐ Upon receipt of disclosure materials from the other parties, review these materials carefully to see that all disclosure requirements have been met.
☐ Prepare disclosure of any expert witness, accompanying report, and other materials as set out in Rule 26(a)(2). Review parallel materials from other parties.
☐ Using the pertinent steps outlined above, serve and promptly file with the court all pretrial discovery, including witnesses to be called, exhibits and other evidence described in Rule 26(a)(3). Do at least thirty days before trial.
☐ In consultation with the supervising attorney, prepare any objections to pretrial material disclosed by the other party within fourteen days of its receipt.
☐ Check calendar dates periodically to see whether supplementation of previously submitted disclosure is needed. Supplement as required [Rule 26(e)].
☐ Use a tracking log for all disclosure and discovery.

INTERNATIONAL DISCOVERY

Under 28 U.S.C. § 1782(a), a person located in the district of a U.S. district court may be ordered to provide testimony or produce information, including documents, for use in a proceeding in a foreign or international tribunal. The order may be made pursuant to the request of the foreign tribunal or upon the application of any interested party. The U.S. Supreme Court has given this statute a broad interpretation that facilitates discovery and cooperation in international legal matters [*Intel Corp. v. Advanced Micro Devices Inc.*, 1261 S.Ct. 2466 (2004)].

INTERROGATORIES

TASK

Mr. White wants you to draft a set of interrogatories in the next three days to be answered by a yet-unidentified officer at Mercury Parcel Service, Inc.

PURPOSE OF INTERROGATORIES

interrogatories
A discovery device consisting of written questions submitted to another party and answered by that party in writing and under oath.

Interrogatories are a discovery device consisting of written questions submitted to another party and answered by that party in writing and under oath. They are authorized in Federal Rule 33 and parallel state rules. The person submitting (propounding) interrogatories, or other matters, for consideration by another party or the court is the "proponent." The replying party is the "respondent." Interrogatories provide a relatively inexpensive way to gather information from the opposing party. Useful information on the parties, witnesses, documents and records, evidence, and leads thereto can be obtained through questions such as the following:

- State the name and address of each person who has knowledge concerning . . .
- Identify and give the location of each document or record in your possession regarding . . .

The answers to the questions can aid in drafting other interrogatories or in preparing for depositions, and can provide the supporting information for summary judgment.

Interrogatories have some outstanding advantages. They are relatively inexpensive and the answering party cannot say "I do not know" or "I have forgotten." The rules impose a duty on the answering party to seek out the answer if the information is in the possession or control of that party. Interrogatories are especially helpful in "piercing the corporate veil" to gain information about internal structure, policies, and records of a corporation or agency.

PROCEDURE

Interrogatories must be carefully planned and drafted. They may be served by any party on any other party following the parties' discovery planning meeting [Rule 26(d)]. State rules may permit service with or following the service of the summons and complaint. Rule 33(a) permits a party without leave of court or written stipulation to serve no more than twenty-five interrogatories (counting each question and discrete subpart separately) on any other party. Leave to serve more interrogatories may be granted by the court if dictated by the needs of the case and the other principles stated in Rule 26(b)(2) [Rule 33(a)]. The number of interrogatories allowed by state courts varies. Check your local rules. Each question of the interrogatory must be answered separately and completely, or objections noted in lieu of the answer. The answers to the interrogatories must be returned within thirty days of service of the interrogatories unless otherwise agreed to by the parties or ordered by the court. State time limits may vary.

Answers to the interrogatories must be verified by the party, or by a designated official or agent in the case of a corporation or other entity. The answers, however, are actually drafted by the attorney and the paralegal.

In some cases it is not fair to place the time-consuming and difficult burden solely on the responding party to search through documents and locate the exact information. Rule 33(d) (Option to Produce Business Records) is designed to reduce or transfer that responsibility when the burden of locating the answer is about the same for the proponent as it is for the respondent. It permits the responding party to identify the specific business documents and records, including e-stored information, where the information is likely to be found and giving the requesting party the opportunity to review the documents and locate the specifically requested information. The danger for the responding attorney in allowing the opponent to access and examine a block of the client's business information, including computerized information, is the unintended revelation of privileged or protected material. In such circumstances, the responding party may choose to carefully screen the block of information first or not invoke the 33(d) option.

If a party objects to a question or refuses to answer, the requesting party can seek the assistance and sanctions provided by Rule 37(a)(4). The scope of the interrogatories is the same as that for any discovery device as set out in Rule 26(b)(1) and the Rules of Evidence. Although interrogatory practice is similar in most jurisdictions, become familiar with your local practice.

PLANNING INTERROGATORIES

Introduction

Interrogatories can be extremely useful as a discovery tool if they are planned carefully. If they are not planned carefully, the opponent may pose valid objections that preclude or delay discovery or produce information so general that it is useless.

Interrogatories are generally used to obtain the following information:[4]

(a) Identities of persons who provided statements
(b) Identities of persons interviewed
(c) Facts elicited from a person interviewed who is now unavailable
(d) Identity of documents, witness statements, e-stored information, and physical evidence, including the nature, condition, location, and custody
(e) Information on all correspondence written by, read by, or mentioning a specific party, witness, or other person involved in the case
(f) Summary explanations of technical matter, data, and documents
(g) Transactions relating to the parties prior or subsequent to the events of the case
(h) Similar incidents related to the case involving the parties or others
(i) Information on the business or corporation including its organization, principal place of business, and other relevant data
(j) Information on the finances, related records, and status of the business or party
(k) Licenses relevant to party's business or conduct
(l) Identities of experts who will testify at trial and their opinions and bases for each opinion
(m) Insurance coverage, if permitted by state rule
(n) Data on time, speed, distance, and other relevant measurements, tests, or estimates

(o) Information on property and other assets for purposes of pre- or post-judgment collections

(p) Jurisdictional facts

(q) Protected work product where sufficient cause exists

The applicable discovery rules determine, in part, how the interrogatories can and should be used. For example, if the applicable rules include a substantial mandatory disclosure provision, as does federal Rule 26(a)(1), interrogatories serve more as a follow-up than as an initial discovery device, their focus depending on information obtained through disclosure. This narrowed use corresponds to the Rule 33 limit of twenty-five interrogatories, which gives the court, up front, control to prevent the deliberate drowning of an opponent in a sea of interrogatories.

Interrogatories are normally done in several sets. One set, for example, may be submitted early in the litigation to obtain leads for further investigation and discovery, and another set may be submitted later to obtain detailed information on a particular subject. Be aware of any limitations on the total number of questions that may be submitted. If the limit seems unworkable due to the complexity of the case, the supervising attorney may choose to move the court to expand the limit. [Rule 33(a)].

Determining Objectives of Interrogatories

A significant step in the planning of interrogatories is determining what information suitable for interrogatories is needed from the opponent. Ultimately the attorney will decide this issue, but you will often have responsibility for initiating the work. The following steps provide a guideline for this task.

(a) Keep the task clearly in mind, noting any special directions. In this case the task is to draft interrogatories to be submitted to Mercury Parcel Service.

(b) Review the case file including the pleadings and any other documents exchanged, as well as information obtained through informal investigation. Note areas that need clarification or more information. Review the complaint, answer, and counterclaim found in Chapters 4 and 6. Also review the information obtained in the informal investigation stages found in Chapter 3.

(c) Review or determine the elements of the cause of action according to the method outlined in Chapter 3. Also, know the elements of any alleged defense and counterclaim.

(d) Review the broad goals to be accomplished against the defendant at trial. In this case, one goal is to show that Mercury Parcel is Richard Hart's superior and is, therefore, liable for the negligent actions of Mr. Hart, its agent. Interrogatories would be needed, depending on what information was produced in any previous mandatory disclosure, to establish agency and to establish the following facts:

That Mercury is a business
That Hart was in the employ of Mercury on the date of the accident
That Mercury owned the vehicle driven by Hart
That Hart was working within the scope of his employment
That Mercury had insurance to cover Hart and the vehicle

A further goal is to establish that Mercury was liable as a matter of its own fault. By applying imagination, one might produce the following possibilities for Mercury's negligence:

That the van was defective

That regular maintenance was ignored

That complaints of defects were ignored

That a pattern of poor maintenance procedures existed

That maintenance reports were falsified to cover up poor or hurried maintenance procedures

That drivers were asked to work unusually long shifts

That Hart was asked to work an unusually long shift

That hiring procedures disregarded or did not adequately screen for poor driving records

That training of drivers was inadequate or non-existent regarding special circumstances, such as dangerous weather and road conditions

(e) Determine what information, including electronically stored information, is needed to reveal evidence or lead to evidence that supports such theories. The specific elements of the cause of action should be used as focal points for ideas on what information, witnesses, records, procedures, and so on might reveal evidence supportive of the proffered theories. Under each element, the following may prove helpful:

Duty of Care
- Laws or regulations imposing standards of care, such as a mandatory program for maintenance and vehicle and driver safety
- Records that must be kept to prove compliance with legal requirements
- The names of those responsible for recording and storing these records
- The existence of a company policy on maintenance or a regular maintenance program and records verifying such
- The existence of drivers' schedules, in-out reports, mileage, and so on
- The existence, quality, and use of a safety program and safety library
- The existence of any internal or external memos, letters, e-mails, and other communications indicating awareness of problems, failure to act, and other errors and omissions

Breach of Duty
Specifically on the van operated by Hart on the day of the accident:

- Maintenance records since the vehicle was purchased
- Source of purchase (new or used vehicle), name and address of previous owner(s)
- Records containing drivers' complaints or notes on performance
- Names and addresses of mechanics or others who worked on the vehicle
- Records relating to the history of maintenance and repair
- Maintenance and repair records for all vehicles covering the eighteen months prior to the accident
- Names and addresses of all persons responsible for implementing and supervising vehicle maintenance and repair
- Names and addresses of all drivers who operated the van
- Record of Richard Hart's driving schedule one month prior to the accident
- Dispatch logs for one month prior to the accident through the date of the accident
- Records of road hours put in by all drivers eighteen months prior to accident

- Names and addresses of all drivers employed within the last eighteen months prior to accident
- The existence of any internal or external communications pertinent to the previous items

Breach Was Substantial Cause of Injury
- Possible expert witness to testify at trial denying that any defect caused or contributed to the accident (depending on applicable disclosure rule)
- Possible expert witness to testify at trial that no defect existed at the time of the accident (depending on applicable disclosure rule)

The previous lists are by no means exhaustive, but illustrate the type of brainstorming process helpful in developing goal-related questions.

(f) Consult form or "canned" interrogatories as a reference. Although determining your own specific objectives will lead to better-focused and more useful interrogatories, the form interrogatories can act as reminders of goals or specific objectives that you may have missed. Form interrogatories are often available in the firm's form files or in the case folder of a similar case. The advantage to the latter is that the answers to the questions are available and can tell the drafter if the questions were too easily avoided or otherwise unproductive. Form interrogatories may also be found in the law library, in books written specifically on interrogatories and arranged by topic, or in various litigation practice manuals and form books. Remember, however, that form interrogatories are good sources for ideas but not so good for the final product. Form interrogatories that will meet the drafter's specific needs are rare.

(g) Once you have set out the goals and specific related objectives, organize them by topic. One approach is to use the elements of the action and defenses as topics. Another is to follow the paragraphs in the pleading. No one method is best. Each law firm or each case may require a different approach. The following list contains frequently used topics in particular types of actions.

Contract
- Identification of parties, addresses, background
- Events leading up to breach of contract
- Details of the breach
- Events following the breach
- Communications between parties
- Documents relating to breach, location, and other evidence
- Defenses raised
- Damages
- Basis for calculation of damages
- Witnesses/statements
- Elements, information, documents, and so on related to counterclaim

Personal Injury Case
- Identification of parties, addresses, background
- Jurisdictional matters (for example, determination of diversity of citizenship)
- Duty of care
- Breach of duty
- Damages/basis for calculation
- Breach is substantial cause of damages

- Defenses
- Documents and related information
- Witnesses/statements
- Elements, information, documents, and so on related to counterclaim

Products Liability
- Parties, addresses, place of business, and so on
- Product's purchase and use
- Advertising, warranties, representations, operator's manual, posted cautions, and so on
- Events leading to injury
- History of product/similar incidents and claims
- Product testing and related reports
- Details of injuries or damages (emotional, mental, and physical)
- Basis for calculations of damages
- Witnesses/statements
- Documents
- Defenses

Based on these three types of cases, one might construct a list of common categories:

- Parties, addresses, background, and so on
- Events leading up to injury or incident
- Injury
- Damages
- Basis for damages
- Witnesses/statements
- Related documents
- Defenses
- Elements, information, documents, and so on related to counterclaim

Regardless of the topics suggested here, usually other topics or subtopics are unique to the case and require special attention.

(h) E-Interrogatories: Determine what information you need on the opponent party's computer system. This is necessary for locating the relevant stored information and exchanging it in a form that you and your attorney can use. Here are some ideas on what to request:

- Kind of network used and its configuration
- Operating system used
- Details on machines (hardware) used
- Applications (software) used, including any that are custom-made
- Backup system used
- When backup media is overwritten
- System's administrator (other key technicians)
- Whether home computers are used for business
- Whether laptops, notebooks, cellphones, pagers, or other digital devices are used for business
- Whether any digital copier is connected to network
- Any remote access
- E-mail application used

- Firewall application used
- Any e-mail server
- Internet network provider
- Where e-mail is stored[5]
- Any user and administrator manuals not commercially available[6]
- Any archive of obsolete or returned e-files
- Key personnel, managers, executives, supervisors using computers

Interrogatories may be a valuable discovery device, but they are not without pitfalls. Interrogatories should not be used to cover an area exhaustively; their primary function is to get background information, determine the existence and location of evidence, and to elicit leads to other evidence. Determining the detailed content of the evidence is best left to other discovery devices such as depositions and document production. Using interrogatories exhaustively will likely elicit valid objections for length, scope, and harassment, and achieve unsatisfactory results. The practice will also engage the parties in a costly and inefficient paper war.

DRAFTING INTERROGATORIES

Review Rules and Examples

Although most jurisdictions have similar rules on the style and format for interrogatories, consult the local rules and acquire examples of interrogatories used in that particular jurisdiction. They will serve as important guides to drafting. Also consult state and federal annotated versions of the rules of procedure, such as the United States Code Annotated®, to obtain judicial rulings on the form, limits, scope, and successful objections to interrogatories and other discovery devices.

Introductory Paragraphs

After the case caption, an introductory paragraph should be drafted. Formats vary, but generally state to whom the interrogatories are directed, that an answer is required within a specified period of time, and the appropriate state or federal rule. For example:

> Plaintiff hereby requests defendants to answer under oath, pursuant to Rule 33 of the Federal Rules of Civil Procedure, the following interrogatories within thirty days of the date service is made upon you.

The introductory paragraph addressed to a corporation or other company might appear as follows.[7]

> [Caption]
>
> To _____ Company, Defendant:
>
> The plaintiff, pursuant to Rule 33 of the Federal Rules of Civil Procedure, requests that the following interrogatories be answered under oath by any of your officers competent to testify in your behalf who know the facts about which inquiry is made, and that the answers be served on plaintiff within thirty days from the time these interrogatories are served on you.

Definitions and Abbreviations

The interrogatories should be preceded by a section on definitions and abbreviations to provide clarity and make it unnecessary to define terms repeatedly throughout the questions. Definitions also reduce the number of questions and subquestions needed. For example, if "identity" has been defined in the case of a document to include type, date, author, recipients, and other matters, specific questions addressing each of those points are avoided. An example of such a section follows.[8]

I. Definitions

1. As used herein, the words "document" or "documents" include any written, printed, typed, [electronically stored] or graphic matter of any kind or nature however produced or reproduced, now in the possession, custody, or control of a defendant, or in the possession, custody, or control of the present or former officers, agents, representatives, employees of a defendant or any and all persons acting in its or his/her behalf, including documents at any time in the possession, custody, or control of such individuals or entities, or known by the defendants to exist.

2. As used herein, the words "identify," "identity," or "identification" when used in reference to a natural person mean to state his or her full name and present or last known address, and his or her present or last known position and business affiliation; when used in reference to a document mean to state its date, its author, the type of document (e.g., letter, memorandum, telegram, chart, photograph, sound reproduction, etc.), or, if the above information is not available, some other means of identifying it, and its present location and the name of each of its present custodians. If any such document was but is no longer in your possession or subject to your control, or in existence, state whether it (a) is missing or lost, (b) has been destroyed, (c) has been transferred voluntarily or involuntarily to others, or (d) is otherwise disposed of, and in each instance, explain the circumstance surrounding and authorization for such disposition thereof and state the date or approximate date thereof.

3. The words "you" and "your" mean the defendants, their present or former members, officers, agents, employees, and all other persons acting or purporting to act on their behalf, including all present or former members, officers, agents, employees, and all other persons exercising or purporting to exercise discretion, making policy, and making decisions.

(Include any abbreviations or acronyms [ABA for example] if appropriate.)

Instructions

The inclusion of a section of instructions has become increasingly common, especially in more complex cases and when local rules do not proscribe the desired procedure. These instructions provide the opposition with some guidance and allow the questioner to shape the form of the answers. An example follows:[9]

II. Instructions

1. To the extent that information sought by any Interrogatory can be furnished by reference to the Answer furnished to another Interrogatory, appropriate reference will be acceptable to the plaintiff. However, a separate answer should be accorded to each Interrogatory, and Interrogatories should not be joined together and accorded a common answer.
2. Each Answer should be preceded by identification and verbatim quote of the Interrogatory to which the Answer regards.
3. If any Interrogatory is objected to by you as inquiring into privileged matter, set forth fully in the objection the facts which form the basis for your objection.
4. If any document, report, study, memorandum, or other written material is withheld or not identified under claim of privilege, furnish a list identifying each such document for which the privilege is claimed, together with the following information: date, author, sender, recipient persons to whom copies were furnished, together with their job titles, subject matter of the document, the basis on which the asserted privilege is claimed, and the paragraph or paragraphs of these Interrogatories to which the document responds.
5. (Add others as needed.)

Another typical instruction reads: Divulge in your Answer all pertinent information in your possession, or in possession of the corporation, or your attorney's agents, investigators, employees, or other representatives.

If you are requesting production of electronically stored information, an instruction on the form in which you want the information produced is important. For example, you might encourage that e-stored information be produced on CD or DVD. If so, include a detailed instruction requiring that each CD or DVD contain an index that identifies each document or item and its assigned identification (Bates stamp) number; describes its content; references the specific interrogatory to which it responds; states the format it is in; lists a detailed physical or electronic location of the original document; states, if not the exact original, what subsequent generation it is; requires that it should be in its metadata format; identifies the pertinent application and version of creation; and, if created in proprietary metadata format, requires that a copy of the software and user manual be included.[10]

Questions: The Body of the Interrogatories

General Background One or more questions on the general background of the person or corporation being questioned frequently follow the introductory paragraph. For example:

What is your:	What is:
full name	the full name of the corporation
age	the date and place of incorporation
current address	the corporation's principal place of business
marital status	the type of corporation
employment address	
employment position	
education	

When the number of interrogatories is limited, it may be best to define the term "background" or "identity" to include all of the details set out in the preceding lists. Then only one question needs to be asked. "What is your background?" or "Identify your corporation."

Pleadings   Good interrogatories elicit information based, in part, on the most recent pleading of the opponent. Since the pleading states factual allegations to show that the elements of the cause of action exist or are denied or state a defense, the opponent has the right to discover the underlying basis of the alleged facts: the who, what, when, where, why, and how (the five Ws and an H) of the factual allegations. Therefore, the pleading in question should be reviewed carefully and interrogatories should be drafted to acquire information on each allegation. For example, assume the complaint alleges the following in paragraph 3:

> Defendant operated vehicle in a negligent manner by failing to keep a proper lookout and by operating said vehicle at an excessive rate of speed.

The defendant should draw upon the five Ws and an H to formulate questions to elicit information that is clear and complete. For example:

> Regarding paragraph 3 of Plaintiff's Complaint, describe and explain all the specific facts on which you rely to support your contention that the defendant failed to keep a proper lookout.
> Regarding paragraph 3 of Plaintiff's Complaint, describe and explain all the specific facts on which you rely to support your contention that the defendant "operated vehicle at an excessive rate of speed."

On the other hand, the plaintiff should draft questions to elicit information that forms the basis for the defendant's answer. For example, assume defendant's answer to paragraph 3 was "Denied," an appropriate interrogatory would be:

> Regarding paragraph 3 of Defendant's Answer, describe and explain all the specific facts on which you rely to support your denial of the allegation that defendant failed to keep a proper lookout.

In another paragraph of the complaint, assume that the following allegation is made:

> As a consequence of Defendant's negligence, Plaintiff has incurred numerous expenses for doctor bills, hospital bills, nursing care, and medications to the sum of $17,000.

In a section on damages in the interrogatories, the defendant might request the following information:

> In regard to paragraph 8 of Plaintiff's Complaint, identify each doctor, hospital, source of nursing care, and medication and all records related thereto to support the allegation that Plaintiff incurred expenses "to the sum of $17,000."

Basic Areas of the Case   The next section of the interrogatories goes beyond the pleadings and focuses on areas not yet addressed by the questions on the pleadings. Use the ideas generated in the brainstorming process to mold questions for this section. Recall the ideas and areas for inquiry implicating Mercury Parcel in the negligence apart from the negligence of Mr. Hart. The ideas generated in the planning stage might take the following form in the drafting stage. Some of the ideas generated under duty of care were: laws or regulations imposing standards of care such as a mandatory program for maintenance and vehicle and driver safety, records that must be kept to prove compliance with legal requirements, the names of those responsible for recording and storing these records, and the existence of a company policy on maintenance or a regular maintenance program/records indicating such.

Interrogatories based on these points should then be drafted:

1. Identify any corporate or department policies or mandatory programs regarding;
    a. Regular maintenance of your delivery vehicles
    b. Repair of your delivery vehicles
    c. Driver safety (including training, required breaks, limits to operating hours, vehicle safety checks, precautions on ice, speed, etc.)
    d. The maintaining of records on a.–c.
2. Identify all types of records kept by your company on a.–c. in interrogatory no. 1.
3. Identify all records and communications (both oral and written) on a.–c. in interrogatory no. 1 specifically pertaining to Mr. Hart and the van operated by Mr. Hart that was involved in the accident of February 26, ____.

Because "identify" has previously been defined, it is not necessary to repeat all the requests associated with the term "identify." Following this method, you should be able to continue drafting pertinent questions to cover all the necessary points for each element of the cause of action.

It is also appropriate in many jurisdictions to ask questions about insurance coverage (company, coverage, limits), the existence of physical things (evidence), persons with knowledge of the facts, witnesses and exhibits to be relied on or "may" be relied on, and the identity of persons who helped prepare the interrogatories or acted as consultants. Keep in mind that the information needed depends on whether initial disclosure is required.

Opinions and Legal and Factual Contentions   Rule 33(c) and parallel state rules permit questions calling for "an opinion or contention that relates to fact or the application of law to fact." The information gained in the answer to such a question reveals the opponent's position on a key point of possible contention and calls for the opponent to reveal the facts and other evidence relied on to support the contention. If the answer to an interrogatory reveals the matter is not contended, or the opponent is without evidence to support the contention, the area could be a productive one for the party seeking the answer. An example of such a question appears as follows:

> Do you contend that Defendant Hart was not operating the van at an excessive rate of speed at the time of the accident? If so, what are the facts and the evidentiary basis relied on to support the contention?

This type of question is often reserved until the end of the discovery period to gain maximum information and avoid responses like "not sure yet," or "investigation still continuing," or "not available at this time." This type of question can be more effective than a request for admission because it calls for the basis of the contention.[11]

Electronically Stored Information   As previously stated, to ignore e-discovery today is likely to be serious malpractice and invoke costly sanctions. Involving an information technology expert is helpful, if not essential, to avoid oversights and the loss of data. See Exhibit 7:3 for an example of interrogatories needed for e-discovery.

> " . . . answers are not obtained by putting the wrong question and thereby begging the real one."
>
> —FELIX FRANKFURTER, *PRIEBE AND SONS V. UNITED STATES*, 332 U.S. 407, 420 (1947).

Concluding or Summary Interrogatories   Consider adding one or more general interrogatories to cover any oversights and prevent the opponent from later using evidence at trial that should have been elicited in the interrogatories. For example:

> Do you have any additional information relevant to the subject of this lawsuit not set out in your previous answers? If so, please state that information.

DRAFTING TECHNIQUES

The following list provides some specific pointers for drafting well-written interrogatories.

- Test the appropriateness of the question by asking whether the information requested will lead to evidence that is admissible. There is no restriction that the information requested be admissible, only that it be reasonably calculated to lead to admissible evidence.
- Draft the question as concisely and precisely as possible. Keep it simple and easy to understand. If you do, the answer will be more to the point.
- Avoid an excessive number of questions.
- Number the questions sequentially with extra sets starting where the last set left off.
- Use the following techniques when the number of interrogatories is severely limited.[12]
  1. Avoid numbering or lettering sublistings.
  2. Do not make your subtopics conspicuous; avoid "and," "or," "the," semicolons, and colons. For example, do not write "Please state the names, addresses, and phone numbers of the defendant's employers for each job held by the defendant during 1980, 1981, 1982, 1983, 1984, and to the present." Write "Please identify all the defendant's employers beginning with 1980."
  3. Reduce lengthy phrases to a single word or class. For example, instead of asking the defendant to "list all repairs to the wheels, brakes, engine, exterior, hood, etc.," ask the defendant to "list all repairs to the car."
  4. Ask singular questions that require multiple answers rather than the other way around. For example, instead of saying, "State the name of the corporate president, vice president, and associate vice president," say, "Identify each corporate officer by name and office held."
  5. Use multiple-choice questions if appropriate, unless you do not want to suggest the answer: "State whether the bonds in question are Series E bonds, Series F bonds, or Series Y bonds."
- Draft interrogatories in the correct verb tense. "Who had custody of the documents?" is a different question and may elicit quite a different answer than "Who has custody of the documents?" The careful drafter must be sure the correct question is being asked. If it is not, lost time and a permanently lost answer may be the consequence.
- Phrase questions to determine whether an answer is based on firsthand knowledge and whether impediments to accuracy exist. Since secondhand knowledge is less reliable and likely to be excluded as hearsay, for evidentiary reasons, the questions should be phrased to determine whether knowledge is first or secondhand.[13] "Did you personally observe ice on the road?"
- Questions should also be devised to determine the ability of the party to observe the facts.[14] "Was there anything obstructing or limiting your view of the pedestrian? If so, explain the nature of the obstruction or limiting

factor, and how it affected your view of the pedestrian. Are you required to wear glasses with corrective lenses when you drive? Were you wearing your glasses at the time of the accident?"

- Keep in mind, however, that the deposition may be a better time to ask some of these questions because the answers will be more spontaneous. If answered in the interrogatories, the answer will be carefully planned and probably more self-serving than a deposition answer. The most appropriate discovery device for each type of question needs to be weighed carefully.
- Avoid questions that allow a yes or no answer unless you include a follow-up.[15] Questions that permit the answering party to respond yes or no rarely provide much useful information. Normally such a question should be followed by others that require more detail or an explanation of the answer.
- Evaluate and proofread the questions. The purpose of an interrogatory is to force the opponent to relinquish information that you need. It should be drafted to restrict the answering party's ability to provide an uninformative though truthful answer. Evaluate each question drafted to see if it is sufficiently restricted by trying to see how the question could be evaded. If it leaves room for evasion, it requires redrafting to elicit more specific answers. It is essential to go through this evaluation process prior to giving the interrogatories to the attorney for review. Further, proofread the interrogatories carefully to eliminate typos, misspellings, grammatical mistakes, and so on. Such mistakes, if left uncorrected, create a negative impression of your abilities and may result in confusion, unresponsive answers, and the time-consuming and embarrassing process of asking the opponent to stipulate to a correction.

Exhibit 7:3 contains sample interrogatories for electronic discovery.[16] Exhibit 7:4 contains sample interrogatories for an auto accident case.[17] These interrogatories are drafted in the context of mandatory disclosure.

CONCLUDING MATERIAL, FINAL PREPARATION, AND SERVICE OF INTERROGATORIES

The opponent should be advised of the continuing obligation to supplement the answers to the interrogatories. This notice can be given in the instructions or as a reminder at the end of the interrogatories. Here is an example:

> Please note that you have a continuing obligation to supplement your answers to these interrogatories as information is acquired by you, your agents, attorneys, or representatives.

After the attorney has reviewed the interrogatories, make all final corrections. Make sure that copies are prepared for each defendant, the court (if needed), and the client's file.

The interrogatories should end with a signature line for the attorney and the address of the firm or office. Prior to service, obtain the attorney's signature. Some firms enter interrogatories onto CD-ROM, using software compatible with that used by the opponent. The opponent receives the disk, copies the interrogatories, enters answers, and returns a completed CD, saving time and paper. E-mail and e-mail with attachments are the most efficient ways to deliver such information. Check local court rules and consult your supervising attorney, however, before using electronic delivery of discovery devices.

Effect service pursuant to Rule 5 of the Federal Rules and parallel state rules that permit service by mail or in person to the opponent's attorney. Execute the

EXHIBIT 7:3 ▪ Sample Interrogatories for Electronic Discovery

UNITED STATES DISTRICT COURT
DISTRICT OF [Jurisdiction]

Court File No.:

_____,

Plaintiff,

INTERROGATORIES TO [Party Name]

v.

_____,

Defendant.

I. Definition. The definitions below will apply to the interrogatories requested in this document

A. *Application* An application is a collection of one or more related software programs that enable a user to enter, store, view, modify or extract information from files or databases. The term is commonly used in place of "program," or "software." Applications may include word processors, Internet browsing tools and spreadsheets.

B. *Backup* To create a copy of data as a precaution against the loss or damage of the original data. Most users backup some of their files, and many computer networks utilize automatic backup software to make regular copies of some or all of the data on the network. Some backup systems use digital audio tape (DAT) as a storage medium. Backup Data is information that is not presently in use by an organization and is routinely stored separately upon portable media, to free up space and permit data recovery in the event of disaster.

C. *Deleted Data* Deleted Data is data that, in the past, existed on the computer as live data and which has been deleted by the computer system or end-user activity. Deleted data remains on storage media in whole or in part until it is overwritten by ongoing usage or "wiped" with a software program specifically designed to remove deleted data. Even after the data itself has been wiped, directory entries, pointers, or other metadata relating to the deleted data may remain on the computer.

D. *Document* phonorecords, Fed.R.Civ.P. 34(a) defines a document as "including writings, drawings, graphs, charts, photographs, and other data compilations." In the electronic discovery world, a document also refers to a collection of pages representing an electronic file. Emails, attachments, databases, word documents, spreadsheets, and graphic files are all examples of electronic documents.

E. *Hard Drive* The primary storage unit on PCs, consisting of one or more magnetic media platters on which digital data can be written and erased magnetically.

F. *Mirror Image* Used in computer forensic investigations and some electronic discovery investigations, a mirror image is a bit-by-bit copy of a computer hard drive that ensures the operating system is not altered during the forensic examination.

G. *Network* A group of computers or devices that is connected together for the exchange of data and sharing of resources.

H. *Operating System (OS)* The software that the rest of the software depends on to make the computer functional. On most PCs this is Windows or the Macintosh OS. Unix and Linux are other operating systems often found in scientific and technical environments.

I. *Spoliation* Spoliation is the destruction of records which may be relevant to ongoing or anticipated litigation, government investigations or audits. Courts differ in their interpretation of the level of intent required before sanctions may be warranted.

J. *Software* Coded instructions (programs) that make a computer do useful work.

(continued)

EXHIBIT 7:3 ■ Sample Interrogatories for Electronic Discovery *(continued)*

II. Documents and Data.

   A. *Individual/Organizations Responsible* Identify and attach copies of all company organizational and policy information including:

      1. Organizational charts;

      2. A list of the names, titles, contact information, and job description/duties for all individuals (or organizations) responsible for maintaining electronic process systems, networks, servers, and data security measures; and

      3. A list of the names, titles, contact information, and job description/duties for all individuals employed in the following departments (or their equivalents) for [Plaintiffs/Defendants/Third Party]:

         a) Information Technology;

         b) Information Services;

         c) Incident Response Teams;

         d) Data Recovery Units; and

         e) Computer Forensic or Audit/Investigation Teams.

   B. *Relevant Products/Services* Identify and attach copies of all documents related to (including marketing, selling, leasing, sharing or giving to another party) the computer system, programs, software, hardware, materials, tools or information that [Plaintiffs/Defendants/Third Party] uses or has used in relation to the sale or use of [Product/Service]. This includes all electronic data and necessary instructions for accessing such data relating to:

      1. The pricing of [Product/Service] in the United States and internationally;

      2. Customer invoices for [Product/Service], including the customer names/addresses, purchase volume, prices, discounts, transportation changes and production information;

      3. E-mail sent or received by [Plaintiffs/Defendants/Third Party] to customers relating to [Product/Service];

      4. Accounting records relating to [Product/Service], including work-in-progress reports, billing records, vendor invoices, time and material records, cost completion reports for each of [Plaintiffs/Defendants/Third Party] customers;

      5. Construction and development information relating to web pages offering sale of [Product/Service] to the public;

      6. Internal reports, sales reports, customer backlog reports, supplier backlog reports and operation reports related to [Product/Service];

      7. Financial reporting information on a monthly and annual basis including profit and loss statements, branch costs, contribution margins and corporate overhead relating to [Product/Service];

      8. Budgeting, projection and forecasting information relating to [Product/Service]; and

      9. Sales booked, gross profit dollars and percentage for the sales booked, net sales shipped, and gross and net profit dollars and percentages for [Product/Service].

   C. *Networks* As to each computer network, identify the following:

      1. Brand and version number of the network operating system currently or previously in use (include dates of all upgrades);

      2. Quantity and configuration of all network servers and workstations;

      3. Person(s) (past and present, including dates) responsible for the ongoing operations, maintenance, expansion, archiving and upkeep of the network; and

      4. Brand name and version number of all applications and other software residing on each network in use, including but not limited to electronic mail and applications.

   D. *Hardware* Identify and describe each computer that has been, or is currently, in use by [Plaintiffs/Defendants/Third Party] (including desktop computers, PDAs, portable, laptop and notebook computers, cell phones, etc.), including but not limited to the following:

EXHIBIT 7:3 ■ Sample Interrogatories for Electronic Discovery *(continued)*

    1. Computer type, brand and model number;

    2. Computers that have been re-formatted, had the operating system reinstalled or been overwritten and identify the date of each event;

    3. The current location of each computer identified in your response to this interrogatory;

    4. The brand and version of all software, including operating system, private and custom-developed applications, commercial applications and shareware for each computer identified;

    5. The communications and connectivity for each computer, including but not limited to terminal-to-mainframe emulation, data download and/or upload capability to mainframe, and computer-to-computer connections via network, modem and/or direct connection; and

    6. All computers that have been used to store, receive or generate data related to the subject matter of this litigation.

E. *Software* Identify and describe all software programs that have been, or are currently, in use by [Plaintiffs/Defendants/Third Party] including, but not limited to, the following:

    1. Titles;

    2. Version Names and Numbers;

    3. Manufacturers;

    4. Authors and contact information; and

    5. Operating systems that the programs were installed on.

F. *Operating Systems* Identify and describe all operating systems that have been, or are currently, in use by [Plaintiffs/Defendants/Third Party] including, but not limited to, operating systems installed during [time period] for the following individuals:

    1. [Name & Job Title]

G. *E-mail* Identify all e-mail systems in use, including but not limited to the following:

    1. All e-mail software and versions presently and previously used by you and the dates of use;

    2. All hardware that has been used or is currently in use as a server for the e-mail system including its name;

    3. The specific type of hardware that was used as terminals into the e-mail system (including home PCs, laptops, desktops, cell phones, personal digital assistants, etc.) and its current location;

    4. The number of users there has been on each e-mail system (delineate between past and current users);

    5. Whether the e-mail is encrypted in any way and list passwords for all users;

    6. All users known to you who have generated e-mail related to the subject matter of this litigation; and

    7. All e-mail known to you (including creation date, recipient(s) and sender(s)) that relate to, reference or are relevant to the subject matter of this litigation.

H. *Internet Use* Identify any Internet policies and procedures in use, including but not limited to the following:

    1. Any Internet Service Providers (ISP) that [Plaintiffs/Defendants/Third Party] has provided its employees and the method used to access the Internet;

    2. The names and titles for all individuals who had Internet access;

    3. Any Internet hardware or software documentation that is used to provide Internet access to the above individuals during [time period];

    4. Internet use/access manuals, policies and procedures, including limitations on Internet access and use; and

    5. All Internet-related data on the electronic processing systems used by [Plaintiffs/Defendants/Third Party] including but not limited to, saved Web pages, lists of Web sites, URL addresses, Web browser software and settings, bookmarks, favorites, history lists, caches, and cookies.

(continued)

EXHIBIT 7:3 ▪ Sample Interrogatories for Electronic Discovery *(continued)*

I. *Other Electronic Data* Identify any other electronic data in use, including but not limited to the following:

    1. Activity log files contained on [Plaintiffs/Defendants/Third Party] network and any equipment needed to access the log files;

    2. Manual and automatic records of hardware and equipment use and maintenance;

    3. The names of Internet newsgroups or chat groups that [Plaintiffs/Defendants/Third Party] subscribes to; include the name and title of the individuals subscribing to each group as well as any information necessary to access the groups, including passwords; and

    4. Any portable devices that are not connected to [Plaintiffs/Defendants/Third Party] network and that are not backed up or archived.

J. *Data Transmission* Describe in detail all inter-connectivity between the computer system at [opposing party] in [office location] and the computer system at [opposing party # 2] in [office location #2] including a description of the following:

    1. All possible ways in which electronic data is shared between locations;

    2. The method of transmission;

    3. The type(s) of data transferred;

    4. The names and contact information of all individuals possessing the capability for such transfer, including list and names of authorized outside users of [opposing party's] electronic mail system; and

    5. The name and contact information of the individual responsible for supervising inter-connectivity.

K. *Data Security Measures* List all user identification numbers and passwords necessary for accessing the electronic processing systems or software applications requested in this document. During the course of this litigation, you must supplement all security measures with updated information, if applicable. Include:

    1. Computer security policies;

    2. The name(s) and contact information of the individual(s) responsible for supervising security; and

    3. Information about each applications security settings, noting specifically who has administrative rights.

L. *Supporting Information* All codebooks, keys, data dictionaries, diagrams, handbooks, manuals or other documents used to interpret or read the information on any of the electronic media listed above.

III. Backup Protocols.

A. *Current Procedures* As to data backups performed on all computer systems currently or previously in use, identify and describe the following:

    1. All procedures and devices used to back up the software and the data including, but not limited to, name(s) of backup software used, the frequency of the backup process, and type of tape backup drives, including name and version number, type of media (i.e. DLT, 4mm, 8mm, AIT). State the capacity (bytes) and total amount of information (gigabytes) stored on each tape;

    2. The tape or backup rotation, explain how backup data is maintained, and state whether the backups are full or incremental (attach a copy of all rotation schedules);

    3. Whether backup storage media is kept off-site or on-site. Include the location of such backup and a description of the process for archiving and retrieving on-site media;

    4. The name(s) and contact information for the individual(s) who conduct(s) the backup and the individual who supervises this process;

    5. A detailed list of all backup sets, regardless of the magnetic media on which they reside, showing current location, custodian, date of backup, a description of backup content and a full inventory of all archives,

    6. All extra-routine backups applicable for any servers identified in response to these Interrogatories, such as quarterly archival backup, yearly backup, etc., and identify the current location of any such backups, and

    7. Any users who had backup systems in their PCs and describe the nature of the backup.

EXHIBIT 7:3 ▪ Sample Interrogatories for Electronic Discovery (*continued*)

B. *Backup Tapes* Identify and describe all backup tapes in your possession including:
1. Types and number of tapes in your possession (such as DLT, AIT, Mammoth, 4mm, 8mm);
2. Capacity (bytes) and total amount of information (gigabytes) stored on each tape; and
3. All tapes that have been re-initialized or overwritten since commencement of this litigation and state the date of said occurrence.

IV. Spoliation of Electronic Evidence.

A. *Document Retention and Destruction Policies* Identify and attach any and all versions of document/data retention or destruction policies used by [opposing party] and identify documents or classes of documents that were subject to scheduled destruction.
1. Attach copies of document destruction inventories/logs/schedules containing documents relevant to this action.
2. Attach a copy of any disaster recovery plan.
3. Also state:
  a) The date the policy was implemented;
  b) The date, if any, of the suspension of this policy *in toto* or any aspect of said policy in response to this litigation;
  c) A description by topic, creation date, user or bytes of any and all data that has been deleted or in any way destroyed after the commencement of this litigation. State whether the deletion or destruction of any data pursuant to said data retention policy occurred through automation or by user action; and
  d) Whether any company-wide instruction regarding the suspension of the data retention/destruction policy occurred after or related to the commencement of this litigation. If so, identify the individual responsible for enforcing the suspension.

B. *Document Destruction* Identify any data that has been deleted, physically destroyed, discarded, damaged (physically or logically), or overwritten, whether pursuant to a document retention or destruction policy or otherwise, since the commencement of this litigation. Specifically identify those documents that relate to or reference the subject matter of the above referenced litigation.

C. *Organizations or Individuals Responsible for Maintaining the Document Retention and Destruction Policies* List the job title, description, business address, telephone number, and e-mail address of any individuals or organizations that are/were responsible for creating, implementing or retaining any and all versions of your document retention or destruction policies.

D. *Meetings or Documents Discussing Document/Data Destruction* Identify with specificity any meetings or conversations referencing document spoliation in relation to this action.
1. Identify and attach any and all related meeting minutes/notes from [time period here].
2. List the job title, description, business address, telephone number, and e-mail address of any individuals or organizations that are/were responsible for retaining the meeting minutes/notes.

E. *Data Wiping* For any server, workstation, laptop, or home operating system that has been "wiped clean", defragmented, or reformatted such that you claim that the information on the hard drive is permanently destroyed, identify the following:
1. The date on which each drive was wiped, reformatted, or defragmented;
2. The method or program used (i.e., WipeDisk, WipeFile, BurnIt, Data Eraser, etc.).

F. *Data Recycling* Identify the person(s) responsible for maintaining any schedule of redeployment or circulation of existing equipment and describe the system or process for redeployment.

Source: Reprinted with permission of Kroll Ontrack, Inc., http://www.krollontrack.com.

EXHIBIT 7:4 ■ Sample Interrogatories to Defendant (Auto Accident)

State of _____
County of _____
Civil Court Branch

Dennis Diamond

                    Plaintiff,

        v.   CIVIL ACTION NO. _____

Janet McDonald

                    Defendant,

INTERROGATORIES TO _____

Pursuant to section _____, _____ hereby submits the following interrogatories to _____. These interrogatories are to be answered by _____ under oath and served on the attorney for _____ within _____ days.

INSTRUCTIONS AND DEFINITIONS

A. Supplement your answers to these interrogatories as information is acquired by you, your agents, attorneys, or representatives.

B. Precede each answer with a verbatim restatement of the pertinent interrogatory.

C. Answer each question completely with all information possessed by you or your attorneys, investigators, agents, employees, and representatives.

D. The term "accident" as used here, means the incident that is the basis of this lawsuit, unless otherwise specified.

E. The term "identify" when applied to an individual . . . [add other instructions and definitions as needed.]

F. [Consider adding request for opponent party to sign and return an attached HIPAA compliant authorization form for release of protected information when applicable to case or counter claim.]

INTERROGATORIES

1. State your full name, address, date of birth, marital status, and all former names or aliases.
2. Identify each person you consulted to provide information for your answers to these interrogatories.
3. State your occupation, wages, and dates of employment in reverse chronological order for the last ten years, identifying each respective employer beginning with the present.
4. State whether you were driving for your business, employer, or personal reasons at the time of the accident.
5. State in detail the purpose of your trip on the day of the accident, your complete itinerary with dates, times, locations, mileage covered between locations, passengers, purpose of stops, whom you saw, and what you did at each location.
6. Identify all persons known to you or your attorneys possessing personal knowledge of the facts and circumstances of and surrounding the accident including any eyewitnesses, medical witnesses, and others, and describe the pertinent knowledge and likely testimony of each party.
7. Identify all persons or organizations, other than your attorneys, who investigated the cause and circumstances of this accident for you and/or your employer, and state whether a written report of such was submitted, and, if so, identify the current custodian of any such report.

EXHIBIT 7:4 ■ Sample Interrogatories to Defendant (Auto Accident) (*continued*)

8. Identify the make, model, year, registration number, license number, fleet number (if applicable), and owner of the vehicle you were operating at the time of the accident, and, if the owner is a person or entity other than you, state whether you had permission to operate the vehicle.

9. State whether you have made any oral or written statements regarding the accident, and identify the date of each statement, its substance, the person to whom the statement was given, and, if written or recorded, the current custodian of each statement.

10. State whether you, your attorneys, employer, insurance carrier, or anyone acting on your or their behalf obtained written or recorded statements from any person regarding the accident, and, if so, identify each person giving a statement, the date of each statement, its substance, the person to whom the statement was given, and the current custodian of the statement.

11. State whether you, your attorney, employer, insurance carrier, or anyone acting on your or their behalf have or know of any photographs, videos, motion pictures, maps, drawings, diagrams, measurements, surveys, or other depictions regarding the accident, the scene of the accident, and the persons and vehicles involved, and, if so, state what each item purports to depict and identify the person who created the item and the current custodian of the item.

12. State the facts of the accident specifying speed, position, directions, condition, and location of each vehicle and any pertinent light, traffic, weather, road, visibility, mechanical defects, or other conditions.

13. Describe in detail all evasive steps taken by you to avoid the accident.

14. State whether you contend that plaintiff's or any other person's actions or omissions caused or contributed to the accident, and state the facts that support each contention.

15. State whether you consumed any alcoholic beverages, drugs, or medications within the twenty-four hours preceding the accident, the nature of the substance, where obtained, when consumed, and in what amount, and identify any person having knowledge as to the consumption of each item.

16. Identify any physician whose care you were under at the time of the accident, the pertinent illness or condition, the nature of treatment, and prescribed medications.

17. State whether you had any physical, mental, emotional, or other disability, disease, impairment, limitation, or restriction at the time of the accident, and identify any pertinent physician or health care professional who diagnosed each such condition.

18. State whether you had a valid driver's license, including any specialized driver's license, permit, or certifications, at the time of the accident, and list the issuing state, expiration date, license or permit number, and any restrictions on the license or permit and the nature of the restrictions.

19. State whether your driver's license has ever been revoked or suspended, and, if so, provide full details.

20. Identify all insurance policies covering the vehicle you were operating at the time of the accident, the insurance company, policy owner, policy number, coverage type, amount of coverage (including upper and lower limits), and the effective dates of coverage.

21. List all prior motor vehicle accidents in which you were involved, whether persons and/or property were involved, the name of the other driver or property owner, the accident's location, date, time, and outcome of the matter.

22. List violations of all motor vehicle or traffic laws or ordinances with which you have been charged in the State of _____ or in any other jurisdiction.

23. State whether you have been convicted of any crime other than a traffic offense, and state the nature of the offense, the date, county and state or federal court, and any sentence received.

24. State whether the plaintiff had any conversation with you after the accident, and, if so, state the substance of the conversation and identify any persons present during that conversation.

25. State whether at the time of the accident you had any eye condition that impaired your vision or required corrective lenses and, if so, state the nature of the impairment, your visual rating, the date and results of your last eye exam, whether you were wearing corrective lenses at the time of the accident and identify your eye doctor or other person who prescribed treatment or the corrective lenses.

certificate of service, sometimes called proof of service or certificate of mailing. Although many courts require the filing of interrogatories or other discovery documents, the federal courts prohibit it [Rule 5(d)]. If filing is not required, place the original interrogatories and the certificate of service in the file. This is important to preserve the record should a discovery dispute arise later. If filing is required, file the original interrogatories and the certificate of service with the clerk. Check to see if e-filing is permitted in any applicable state court. An example of the certificate of service follows.

Exhibit 7:5 is a checklist for planning and drafting interrogatories.

CERTIFICATE OF SERVICE

A copy of PLAINTIFF'S CONTINUING INTERROGATORIES SET ONE was served on Defendant Mercury Parcel Service, Incorporated's attorney, Lynn Ott, located at 518 S. Maple Street, Cincinnati, Ohio, by U.S. Mail this 21st day of November, _____ .

_____

Arthur White
Attorney for Plaintiff
(address)

> "The heaviest thing that is, is one Et cetera."
>
> —JOHN FLORIO, *FIRSTE FRUITES*, 1578.

ANSWERING INTERROGATORIES

NOTE DEADLINE, REVIEW CASE FILE

Ms. White comes to you and says, "Here are the interrogatories in the Forrester case. Please begin preparing answers to these questions. We have thirty days to respond. Let me know if you need any help." First calendar the deadline. Rule 33(b)(3) requires answers to be served in thirty days unless otherwise ordered by the court or agreed to by the parties. State rules vary. Failure to answer on time waives any objections to the questions, except questions that are grossly improper or call for privileged information or an expert's opinion [*Bohlin v. Brass Rail, Inc.*, 20 F.R.D. 224 (S.D.N.Y. 1957)]. An enlargement of the time limit for responding may be needed. If so, Consult Rule 6(b) or parallel state rules. In some jurisdictions a stipulation between parties to enlarge the time is adequate. In other jurisdictions, a court order is required.

Become thoroughly familiar with the facts and all the evidence and sources of evidence that might be called on in answering the interrogatories. This will make answering easier and give you confidence that the facts and evidence support the answers.

REVIEW POSSIBLE OBJECTIONS

Before reading the interrogatories, have firmly in mind what kinds of objections can be raised to any particular question. Then read through the interrogatories and note questions believed to be objectionable. These common types of objections are

EXHIBIT 7:5 ■ Checklist for Planning and Drafting Interrogatories

☐ Planning the Interrogatories
  ○ Have the attorney's directions for the task firmly in mind.
  ○ Review the file, especially the pleadings, and all related information discovered to date.
  ○ Review the elements of the claim, defense, counterclaim, and so on.
  ○ Determine the goals to be accomplished.
    ■ Review the pleadings for areas needing more detail or explanation.
    ■ Brainstorm on each element of the claim, defense, counterclaim, and so on, to develop useful theories of liability and areas of inquiry.
    ■ Determine what must be discovered (witnesses, documents, physical evidence, etc.) and the likely leads to it.
    ■ Assess the initial need for and scope of interrogatories on the opponent's electronic information storage system.
  ○ Acquire and read form interrogatories for suggested areas of inquiry, format, and questions.
  ○ Organize areas of inquiry by logical topics.
  ○ Avoid pitfalls.
    ■ Do not try to cover entire areas exhaustively if other methods of discovery are available and better lend themselves to the specific objective.
    ■ Keep brief to avoid setting off a paper war.
    ■ Avoid forcing the other side to prepare their case.
☐ Drafting the Interrogatories
  ○ Acquire the civil practice rules for interrogatories and locate samples of interrogatories in the jurisdiction for the particular case.
  ○ Draft an introductory paragraph stating to whom the interrogatories are directed, applicable rules, and time required for a reply.
  ○ Provide a definition and abbreviation section.
  ○ Provide an instruction section so the answer and any objections will be placed in a format most useful to the questioner.
  ○ Draft questions that focus on finding out more about the basis for the allegations in the opponent's pleadings.
  ○ Draft questions that cover the theories of liability and defenses thereto as they relate to the elements of the offense.
  ○ Draft questions calling for opinion and legal and factual contentions [Rule 33(b)].
  ○ Draft questions covering the e-storage system and the information stored.
  ○ Draft concluding or summary interrogatories.
  ○ Include notice of continuing obligation to update answers.
  ○ Provide for attorney's signature and certificate of service.
☐ Specific Drafting Techniques
  ○ Ask whether the question elicits information that is likely to lead to admissible evidence.
  ○ Keep questions concise, precise, and easy to understand.
  ○ Avoid excessive questions.
  ○ Number questions and sets of questions sequentially.
  ○ If the number of interrogatories is limited:
    ■ Do not number or letter subdivisions.
    ■ Avoid making subtopics conspicuous: avoid "and," "or," "the," semicolons, and colons.
    ■ Reduce lists to single word or class.
    ■ Ask singular questions that require multiple answers.
    ■ Use multiple-choice questions where appropriate.
  ○ Use correct verb tense.
  ○ Phrase questions to determine if answers are based on firsthand knowledge and if impediments to accuracy exist.
  ○ Avoid questions that permit yes or no answers unless more detail is requested.
  ○ Phrase questions to restrict evasiveness in the answer.
  ○ Proofread carefully prior to submitting to attorney for review.
  ○ Final Preparation and Service of Interrogatories
  ○ Make all final corrections.
  ○ Get attorney's signature.
  ○ Prepare copies for each opponent and the court, if the court requires filing.
  ○ Serve copies on the opposing attorney by mail or in person.
  ○ Execute the certificate of service and file it and the original interrogatories with the court clerk.

based on the definition of what is discoverable found in Rule 26(b)(1) and limitations stated in 26(b)(2):

Irrelevant: A question is objectionable if its ultimate aim is to elicit evidence information that is not relevant to the issues in the case.

Privileged: A question that calls for information protected by the attorney-client, husband-wife, and like privileges is objectionable.

Work product (trial preparation materials):   If a question calls for the mental impressions, conclusions, legal theories, and like matters related to the attorney's preparation for trial, it need not be answered. Objectionable questions typically ask for the names of witnesses that will be called at trial and for the names and opinions of experts who are hired as consultants and not as trial witnesses. The work product objection, however, is often invoked too broadly and abused.

Vague, ambiguous, and unintelligible: Occasionally a question is so unspecific or worded so unclearly that it requires the answering party to guess at the meaning of the question. Such a question is objectionable. This objection may also apply to the instructions.

Too broad: A question can be so inclusive that its limits are excessive. For example, a question calling for the names of all the documents gathered over the last twenty years pertaining to the incident in question is so sweeping in its coverage that it is overly burdensome, while also calling for irrelevant material. Questions requesting information covering an unduly lengthy time span are objectionable. The scope of the question must be reasonable.

Unduly burdensome: Paragraph (c) of Rule 26 allows a party to seek a protective order from unduly burdensome or expensive discovery requests. It is a valid objection to a particular interrogatory or an entire set of interrogatories. If a question or set of questions requires a response that is excessively detailed, costly, time-consuming, or embarrassing relative to the opponent's need for the requested information, then the question or set of questions is objectionable.

> "Beware the half truth; you may have gotten the wrong half."
> —Anonymous

Questions can also be too numerous, call for previously disclosed information (unreasonably cumulative or duplicative), be premature or too late, call for a scientific opinion from a lay person, call for purely legal conclusions, or for information that is just as easily obtainable by the other side. The last point is especially true if the information is not in the answering party's custody or is in the public domain. Requesting the attachment of documents or other evidence is objectionable if a request for production of documents and things (Rule 34) has not been submitted; therefore, interrogatories are often submitted with a Rule 34 production request.

Some common objections that are *not valid* are that the information is already known by the opponent; the question calls for inadmissible evidence (it may); the question seeks an admission (it may); the information is better obtained at deposition (so what!); the question seeks factual opinions, conclusions, and legal contentions (it may); and "it's no business of the questioning party."[18]

There are some strategic concerns to have in mind. Although the decision to object is the realm of the attorney, keep in mind that it is sometimes better to answer an objectionable question than to have to request the court for a protective order, especially if the information to be revealed does not hurt the answering party or might improve their case in the eyes of the opponent.[19]

REVIEW QUESTIONS

Copy the interrogatories so your working notes can be written or electronically entered on the copy. Read each definition, instruction, and question thoroughly, noting any observations. These observations might include questions, ideas on where to gather information, possible objections, or a note that an objectionable question might be answered without harm to the case. Make sure the instructions are consistent with the applicable rules of discovery and do not ask for more than the opponent is entitled to know.

Before attempting to answer the questions, confer with the attorney to discuss the questions and your notes. As each question is approached, note any comments, suggestions, or possible sources of information from the attorney.

GATHER AND RECORD INFORMATION

Interrogatories are directed to a party (the client), and that party has the duty to respond. The client and the client's agents, representatives, investigators, information technology staff, and attorney will provide much of the information needed to answer the interrogatories. It is well-accepted practice for the attorney to take this information and, with your help, mold it into the answers for the client. The client should become involved as early as possible in the interrogatory process. Before contacting the client, however, review the file and note what information you already have. That way you will not ask the client to do unnecessary work. Copy each question as a separate page and send the questions to the client with a cover letter and instructions. Some firms will ask the client to answer the questions and return them to the firm, as requested in the letter in Exhibit 7:6. Other offices prefer to have the client come in to go over each question and possible answer. Check with your supervising attorney to see which procedure is preferred. Make sure your client understands the process and do what you can to reduce the client's anxiety over what may be unfamiliar ground.

Prepare a working copy of each question and its comments on a separate page. Organize the pages so that all information gathered can be kept in order with the appropriate question. This method prevents loss and simplifies the task of drafting answers to the questions.[20]

The primary source of information must be the party requested to answer the interrogatories. In the case of a corporation or agency, it must be those officers or employees, either individually or collectively, who have the knowledge to answer the questions. Generally, a party (including a corporation) is not responsible for investigating information or records beyond that party's possession or control. In theory, such information is equally obtainable for the opponent and is, therefore, not the responding party's duty to provide.

If you have become familiar with the case, it should not be difficult to determine where the information will come from. Some of the techniques discussed in Chapter 3 on investigation might be drawn on to answer interrogatories properly. Do not overlook your client's electronically stored information.

When gathering information, keep in mind that the answer should be based on thorough investigation; it does not, however, require the searching of every possible nook and cranny. Also, the questions require a reasonable interpretation, not an irrational or hypertechnical one.[21]

EXHIBIT 7:6 ■ Letter to Client on Answering Interrogatories

WHITE, WILSON & MCDUFF
ATTORNEYS AT LAW
FEDERAL PLAZA BUILDING, SUITE 700
THIRD AND MARKET STREETS
LEGALVILLE, COLUMBIA 00000
(111) 555-0000

November 1, _____

Ms. Ann Forrester
1533 Capitol Drive
Legalville, Columbia 00000

Dear Ms. Forrester:

I have enclosed a set of questions called "interrogatories" submitted by the attorney for Mercury Parcel Service. The rules of the court require your full cooperation in answering each of the questions. We are permitted to assist you. Our office has the information to answer questions 1, 2, 8, 9, and 10. We need information from you to draft answers to 3, 4, 5, 6, 7, and 11.

We must have the information and your answers no later than November 15. Failure to return the answers when they are due may be harmful to your case. On receipt of this information and your answers, we will integrate them into our draft and return the answers for your review and verification before a notary public. Should it be necessary to have you come to the office to discuss your answers, we will inform you.

Please begin gathering all the documents and other information needed to answer the questions identified above. When writing answers to the questions, keep the following in mind:

1. Answer all questions completely but concisely.
2. Always be truthful.
3. Do not try to withhold information or be evasive. For example, if asked about witnesses (and you know of three), name all three; or, if you are asked about prior injuries, lawsuits, or criminal convictions, state them with identifying dates, times, location, etc. Any evasiveness is a serious matter and can definitely affect the outcome of the case.
4. Look up all dates, amounts, times, and other information requested.
5. You are not required to make an unreasonable search or incur unreasonable expense. If you do not have access to the information, you are not required to provide it. State any reasons for not answering a question.

After answering the questions, return them in the enclosed envelope.

Thank you for your assistance. If you have questions, please let me know.

Sincerely,

Terry Salyer
Paralegal
White, Wilson & McDuff

REVIEW TECHNIQUES FOR ANSWERING INTERROGATORIES

- Answer each interrogatory separately and fully in writing under oath.
- Precede each answer with a restatement of the applicable question. This technique is called *engrossing* the question.
- State the reason for any objection and answer any part of the question that is not objectionable.

- Write the answer clearly and concisely. Avoid confusing answers that lead the opponent to the answers of several previous questions or to answers in other documents (depositions) incorporated by reference.
- Draft objections by stating with particularity the nature of the objection and its basis, which may be done in the interrogatory or separately. Here is an example of how an objection would appear in the answer to an interrogatory:

  > Defendant objects to this interrogatory because it requests information that is irrelevant and cannot reasonably lead to evidence that is admissible on any issue in this action.

- Answer ethically with accurate and complete information; do not be evasive or deceptive. If an interrogatory asks for the name and location of a person, it would not be adequate to state only his first name and "I do not remember where he lives."
- Disclose as little harmful information as possible, but not by deliberate concealment or unreasonable interpretation of the question.
- Place the client in the best possible light without distorting or misrepresenting the facts.
- Consider using the alternative option to produce business records found in Rule 33(d), which places the burden on the opposing party to search or audit your client's records. In such cases one need only identify the documents available, which should not be done, however, if other information sensitive or harmful to the client will be revealed.
- Review your office's or your own interrogatory answer bank for previous answers to parallel questions, especially for routine interrogatories. Regularly expanding and consulting such a bank of boilerplate responses can save time if used prudently. Computerizing the answer bank permits rapid copying and pasting.
- Use the following techniques for answers you are unable to complete or are unsure of:[22]

  Indicate that supplements will follow.
  State "on information or belief" or "based on secondhand information."
  State according to person Y or records in office X.
  Indicate that you do not know the answer but received information that _____.

- Consider attaching as an exhibit a document or business record inquired about if to do so will be helpful and if it is subject to document production under Rule 34 or parallel state rule. (See Chapter 9 for guidelines on producing documents and electronic information.)

DRAFT ANSWERS AND HAVE THEM REVIEWED, SIGNED, AND SERVED

Draft the answers, incorporating the information gathered for each question. The attorney should then review the answers. Once prepared in final form, the person answering the interrogatories (usually the client, or in the case of a corporation, a representative of the corporation) must carefully review each answer for accuracy and sign the document under oath, usually in the presence of a notary public. If objections have been made, the attorney must sign as well. Attach any necessary exhibits. Prepare a certificate of service and effect service according to Rule 5, or as dictated by state rules.

UPDATE ANSWERS

In most jurisdictions, the answering party has a continuing obligation to supplement or amend responses to questions as additional information or inaccuracies in the answers previously submitted are discovered. A good way to do this is to simply replace the out-of-date page of the former answer with a revised one. The new page should restate the question accompanied by the complete new answer.

Exhibit 7:7 is an example of a defendant's answer to a plaintiff's first set of interrogatories submitted under Rule 33.

EXHIBIT 7:7 ■ Answer to Interrogatories

[Case Caption]
DEFENDANT UNITY DELIVERY SERVICES, INC.'S ANSWERS TO PLAINTIFF'S
FIRST SET OF INTERROGATORIES
INTRODUCTION

A. The enclosed responses are intended for and restricted to use in this case only.
B. No enclosed answer should be taken as an admission to the existence of any facts for purposes of trial.
C. [*Others*]

ANSWERS

INTERROGATORY NO. 1

Identify the physician(s) who conducted the company's annually required physical exams of Donald Jordan (defendant driver) and the dates of the last two exams.

ANSWER

Walter P. Hayes, M.D., 1644 W. Endover Ave., South Town, Columbia 11000, phone: (500) 000-0000. Exams were held on June 15, ___ and April 28, ___.

INTERROGATORY NO. 2

State Rodney Robert's (your disclosure material, page 3) qualifications at the time he worked on the van in question, and the dates, hours, and nature of the work performed, and identify any records and documents not previously disclosed that record what was done on the van, including any of Mr. Robert's comments and assessments concerning repairs made or that should be made.

ANSWER

Mr. Roberts worked on the van in question on September 2, ___, for 2.2 hours. He was an apprentice mechanic at that time, having been employed at that job for seven months. He had previous vocational training at Warton County Tech. On September 2, Mr. Roberts gave the van a forty-point safety inspection, changed the oil, and replaced the air filter. A parts department form 3510 reflects any parts ordered by a mechanic for a vehicle. The daily work order form was disclosed previously.

INTERROGATORY NO. 3

What company correspondence exists for the three-year period immediately preceding the accident regarding your policies or proposed notices on driver health and safety?

ANSWER (OBJECTION)

Defendant corporation objects to interrogatory 3 because it is too broad in scope, the burden or expense of the proposed discovery outweighs its likely benefits, and it covers material that is protected by defendant corporation's attorney-client privilege.

INTERROGATORY NO. 4

State defendant driver Donald Jordan's traffic record for the last five years.

EXHIBIT 7:7 ■ Answer to Interrogatories (continued)

ANSWER/OBJECTION

To defendant corporation's knowledge, Mr. Jordan has no violations in the last three years, but objects to interrogatory no. 4 insofar as it requests information that is in the custody of the Columbia Division of Motor Vehicles and is as easily obtainable by plaintiff as it is by defendant.

INTERROGATORY NO. 5

State the number of vans of the same make and model as the van in question purchased by your company in the last three years.

ANSWER (OBJECTION)

Defendant corporation objects to interrogatory no. 5 because the information requested is irrelevant to issues in this action and is not likely to lead to the discovery of admissible evidence.

INTERROGATORY NO. 6

State each fact on which you rely to support your allegation in paragraphs 3 and 4 of your counterclaim that plaintiff assumed the risk of injury and caused the accident in question.

ANSWER

1) Plaintiff was intoxicated at the time of the accident and 2) plaintiff entered the road and thumbed her nose not only at defendant driver, but also at the driver of a vehicle that passed seconds earlier.

Date_____   _____
                        Barbara J. Lane, CEO
                        Unity Delivery Service, Inc.

Date_____   _____
                        Lincoln Case, Attorney
                        789 Courthouse Square
                        Legalville, Columbia 00000
                        Phone: (111) 111-1111

ANALYZING THE ANSWER AND COMPELLING A RESPONSE

When the opponent's answers to interrogatories are received, promptly read each answer, carefully noting the opponent's objections and any deficits in completeness, responsiveness, or clarity. Prompt review of e-discovery information is particularly important in the event the information cannot be accessed or searched as contemplated. Inform the attorney of each objection and defect. If the attorney believes some clarification or other action is needed, the following options are available:

1. The attorney will handle the matter at this point.
2. You will be directed to contact the opponent's attorney or paralegal and request more information, possibly offering an extension of time. This action should be followed by a confirming letter identifying the incomplete answer, acknowledging the extension of time granted, and stating that the time for a Motion to Compel Further Answers will be assumed tolled until the opponent files a corrected response or does not make a correction within the allotted time.[23]
3. You will draft a motion to compel [to be discussed (Rule 37)] and have it filed and served. Certification that a good faith effort was made to resolve the matter with the other party is required in federal and many state courts.

"... the law is not the place for the artist or the poet. The law is the calling of thinkers."

—OLIVER WENDELL HOLMES, "THE PROFESSION OF THE LAW," SPEECHES, 1934.

SUMMARY

Your work often focuses on the stage of litigation called discovery—the formal process of investigation that invokes the cooperation of all parties in producing and exchanging information so that facts can be determined, evidence revealed, and issues narrowed before the matter goes to trial.

The discovery process continues to evolve in federal and state courts. Federal Rule 26(a) makes mandatory an initial disclosure process for all parties. Mandatory disclosure, and similar state provisions, requires each party to disclose information about parties, witnesses, records, experts, and other information early in the lawsuit and without court order.

The scope of discovery encompasses any matter, not privileged, that is relevant to the claim or defense of any party, including any information appearing to be reasonably calculated to lead to admissible evidence [FED. R. EVID. 26(b), as amended]. Information relevant to the subject matter of the action, a broader category of discovery, is discoverable by court order only. Pay special attention to any differences in the scope of discovery in your state rules.

Only those discovery requests that are unreasonable, unduly burdensome, unnecessary, or seek privileged information or protected work product information may be excluded. Cooperation and honesty in discovery are important ethical requirements.

The tools employed for discovery vary depending on the magnitude of the case and the financial strength of the client. The available tools include interrogatories; depositions; requests to produce and inspect documents, land, and other things; requests for physical and mental examination; request for admission; and use of the Freedom of Information Act.

You must be adept at employing and responding to each of these tools to gain the maximum benefit for your client within the scope, limits, and ethical standards applied to discovery. Discovery is an area quite suitable for the talents of the paralegal. When exercised knowledgeably, these discovery talents are extremely valuable to the law firm, the client, and you.

▣ WORKBOOK

System Folder Assignments, other exercises, a chapter outline, a review test, and other study aids are located in the accompanying workbook.

▣ HELPFUL WEB SITES

http://www.abanet.org/litigation/discoverystandards.html
    ABA Civil Discovery Standards, including e-discovery, revised (2004).

http://www.uscourts.gov
    Latest Federal Rules of Civil Procedure on discovery with committee notes, proposed amendments.

http://www.westlaw.com, www.lexis.com, www.findlaw.com
    Federal discovery rules, Advisory Committee Notes, some state rules; access to numerous discovery and disclosure forms.

▣ QUESTIONS FOR STUDY AND REVIEW

1. Define the term *discovery* and describe its purposes in the context of litigation practice.
2. List and define the seven discovery devices set out in the Federal Rules of Civil Procedure.
3. What is the function of a preservation letter? What are its benefits? What makes a good preservation letter?
4. In general, what kinds of information must be provided under the federal disclosure rule and under your state rule? How does your state rule differ from the federal rule?
5. When must mandatory disclosure occur? What must occur before an opposing party can depose an expert under this rule?
6. Is the fact that a party's investigation is incomplete or the other party has failed to disclose as required a legitimate excuse to withhold disclosure under the rule?
7. What must be disclosed under initial disclosure? "Pretrial" disclosure?
8. When must objections to the disclosure of any item occur?
9. What is the scope of discovery as defined by Federal Rule 26(b) and parallel state rules?
10. Has your state adopted the Federal Rules of discovery? If so, cite the statute or rule numbers.
11. What are the specific limits on discovery?
12. What is the procedure for resolving post-production claims of privilege or protected trial preparation materials [Fed. R. Civ. P. 26(b)(5)(B)]?
13. If your state does not have disclosure, under what circumstances are the facts known and opinions held by experts discoverable?
14. What reason is permitted for not producing some requested electronically sorted information under Fed. R. Civ. P. 26(b)(2)(B)?
15. What does the obligation to update discovery consist of? Can you play a key role here? Explain.
16. What are the important ethical rules that apply to discovery? What is their significance?
17. What are interrogatories, their purpose and advantages? What federal and state rules govern interrogatories? What is the limit on the number of interrogatories for federal and your state practice?
18. What kinds of computerized information do interrogatories need to uncover?
19. What are the basic procedures that must be followed when utilizing interrogatories?
20. What are the specific steps in planning a set of interrogatories?
21. What kinds of information lend themselves to exploration through interrogatories?
22. What are the typical divisions of and types of questions that make up a set of interrogatories? Explain their usefulness.
23. Be able to draft a set of interrogatories or any specific portion thereof.
24. What are the basic reasons discovery requests are objectionable under Rule 26(b)(1)? Explain each objection.
25. What are the steps to be followed in preparing answers to interrogatories?
26. What should you do on receipt of the opponent's answers to a set of interrogatories?

▣ KEY TERMS

disclosure

discovery

interrogatories

preservation letter

▣ ENDNOTES

1. *Committee Focuses on Discovery to Provide Greater Justice*, THE THIRD BRANCH, May 1999, 11.
2. Sources include: Craig Ball, The Perfect Preservation Letter, http://www.craigball.com (2005); SETEC Investigations, Preservation Letter Template, www.setecinvestigations.com/lawlibrary/legaltools.php(2006); KrollOnTrack, Sample Preservation Letter—To Opponent or Third Party, www.krollontrack.com/library/sampleopponent.pdf (2006).
3. The discussion of Rules 16, 26, 33, 34, and 37 in the discovery chapters is based on the proposed amendments to those rules expected to take effect on December 1, 2006. Verify the effective amendment date at http://www.uscourts.gov (click on Federal Rule Making, then Rules Amendments Completed).
4. ROGER S. HAYDOCK, DAVID F. HERR, JEFFREY W. STEMPEL, FUNDAMENTALS OF PRETRIAL LITIGATION, 367–368 (4th ed. 2000).
5. Sharon D. Nelson, Esq. and John W. Simek, *Don't Let Electronic Evidence Bury Your Firm*, LEGAL ASSISTANT TODAY, May/June 2004, 65.

6. William C. Gleisner III., *Electronic Evidence in the 21st Century*, WIS. LAWYER, July 2004, 54.
7. Adapted from WEST'S FEDERAL FORMS, § 3512, v. 3A, with permission, West Group.
8. *Id.*, adapted from § 3513.10, with permission, West Group.
9. *Id.*, with permission, West Group.
10. Gleisner, supra, note 6, expanded online version of article at www.wisbar.org/wislawmag/2004/07/gleisner.html (link to Model Discovery Standards).
11. NALA, MANUAL FOR LEGAL ASSISTANTS, 232 (4th ed. 2005).
12. HAYDOCK, *supra* note 4, 381–2.
13. STATSKY, TORTS: PERSONAL INJURY LITIGATION 218 (1982).
14. *Id.*
15. *Id.*
16. Sample Interrogatories (2006), http://www.krollontrack.com/legalresources/sample.aspx.
17. Some interrogatories in Figure 7:4 suggested in W. Smith, *Form Interrogatories in Personal Injury Actions*, 32 INS. COUNS. J. at 453, 458 ff. (July 1965) (now DEFENSE COUNSEL Journal) and Plaintiff's Interrogatories to Defendant, Miller & Zois, LLC, www.millerandzois.com/auto-accident-interrogatories-to-defendant.html.
18. HAYDOCK, *supra* note 4, 385–386.
19. *Id.*, 386.
20. NALA MANUAL, *supra* note 11, 235.
21. HAYDOCK, *supra* note 4, 389.
22. Adapted from HAYDOCK, *supra* note 4, 391–2.
23. NALA MANUAL, *supra* note 11, 241.

 For additional resources, visit our Web site at **http://www.westlegalstudies.com.**

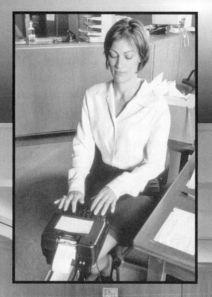

Discovery: Depositions

DEPOSITIONS

INTRODUCTION

deposition
A discovery device permitting a party's attorney to question a witness or party spontaneously and under oath before trial, and to record the testimony.

deponent
A witness or party giving testimony under oath and recorded before trial.

Chapter 8 continues the discussion of discovery devices and related paralegal tasks. Its focus is deposition practice, including the important art of summarizing depositions. A **deposition** is a significant discovery device permitting a party's attorney to question a witness spontaneously (including parties) before trial. The witness, called a **deponent,** is under oath and generally must respond orally to the questions, much as a witness responds to questions at trial. The advantage of the deposition is its spontaneity; the disadvantage is its relatively high cost.

The deposition is a commonly used discovery device with many purposes. Depositions are used to discover information or lead to information based on the deponent's testimony and any accompanying physical evidence. They are used to find out more information about the opponent's case, to further explore points raised in the interrogatories and pleadings, and to evaluate the witness and the opposing attorney. Because the answers offered at the deposition may be used later in court, depositions have purposes related to their potential use at trial. Federal Rule of Civil Procedure 32 and parallel state rules allow depositions to be used to impeach the trial testimony of the deponent. If the deponent testifies at trial that the van was going twenty-five miles per hour, but said at the deposition that it was going fifty-five miles per hour, the earlier answer may be used to throw doubt on the reliability of the trial testimony. Likewise, if a party takes the stand at trial, the party's answers at the deposition may be used as an admission of key facts or for impeachment of the party [Rule 32(a)(2)]. Further, if a witness is unavailable for trial (dead or out of the country, for example), that witness's deposition may be offered into evidence at the trial as if the witness were present [Rule 32(a)(3)].

The well-prepared legal team may also use the deposition less as the broad information-gathering tool that it has been in the past and more as a sharply focused device to support the team's theory of the case. Such an approach is more likely to lead to an earlier resolution of the case, while reducing the opponent's opportunities to exploit unfocused and unsupportive deposition testimony at trial.

SCOPE AND LIMITS OF THE DEPOSITION

"Human nature constitutes a part of the evidence in every case."

—ELISHA R. POTTER, *GREEN v. HARRIS*, HRI 5, 17 (1875).

One real advantage of the deposition over interrogatories is that persons besides the parties may be deposed: bystanders, experts, document custodians, character witnesses, and the like. Rule 30(c) requires that the deposition, examination, and cross-examination be conducted in accordance with the Federal Rules of Evidence. In all other respects the scope is the same as that for other discovery devices [Rule 26(b)].

A deposition may be taken without leave of court [Rule 30(a)(1)], but not until the parties' planning meeting, unless otherwise ordered or agreed to by the parties [Rule 26(d)]. Leave of court is needed to depose an imprisoned person or if (absent a written stipulation of the parties) the limit of ten depositions per party is exceeded, the deponent has already been deposed, or a party seeks to take a deposition before the parties' planning meeting [Rule 30(a)(2)(A, B, and C)]. An exception to the last condition allows the deposing party to certify in the notice of the deposition that the deponent is expected to leave the country and needs to be examined before then [Rule 30(a)(2)(C)]. To reduce costs and inconvenience, a deposition is limited to a seven-hour day (including any needed examination of documents by the deponent) unless otherwise authorized by the court or stipulation [Rule 30(d)(2)]. Many state rules limit the length of a deposition or give the court power to do so. Additional time may be granted by the court, especially if the deponent impedes or delays the examination. Such impediments can lead to court sanctions [Rule 30(d)(2)]. If at any time during a deposition a deponent believes the examination is being conducted in bad faith or to annoy, embarrass, or oppress the deponent or a party, the court, upon motion, may suspend the deposition and invoke sanctions under Rule 37(a)(4) [Rule 30(d)(3)].

TYPES OF DEPOSITIONS

Three types of depositions are set out in the federal and parallel state statutes. They are depositions on oral exam, depositions on written questions, and depositions before the action is filed. The most commonly used of the three is the deposition on oral examination (Rule 30), and for that reason will constitute the primary basis for discussion in the following section.

Depositions on written questions are an underused device providing for direct questions from one party and cross questions from the opposing party to be read to the deponent who orally answers the questions in the presence of a person authorized to administer oaths. This relatively low-cost procedure is governed by Rule 31 and is used primarily to gain information on noncontroversial matters or on documents from a person *other than a party*.

The third type of device is the taking of a deposition before the action and is governed by Rule 27. The purpose of this device is to preserve testimony that may be unavailable later. Such a situation might arise when a witness or party is gravely ill and may not be available to testify at the trial, or when a witness will be out of the country for a long time. In circumstances such as these, a person may, with court permission, take the deposition of a person before an action is filed. Rather strict requirements set out in Rule 27 must be met before the court will grant permission. If you are asked to assist the attorney on depositions of written questions or depositions before trial, check Rules 31 and 27 and parallel local rules for any limitations or special procedures that must be followed.

PROCEDURE

The party conducting the deposition must set a time and place and arrange for a person authorized to administer oaths and able to record the testimony. Notice of the deposition is then sent to each party. The witness is subpoenaed by the court and must be present at the designated time and place. The other parties may also attend and ask questions. At the deposition the officer swears in the witness, and the attorney requesting the deposition asks the witness questions. The opponent may cross-examine. All questions and answers are recorded by the officer, a court reporter, or other recording device. The record may be reviewed by the witness and certified as accurate.

If the deposition is conducted by written questions, the requesting party must serve the questions on every other party along with the notice of the deposition. The notice must identify the deponent and the officer, usually a court reporter [Rule 31(a)(3)]. Within fourteen days after service of the questions, a party may serve cross questions on all other parties. Questions in response to cross questions (redirect questions) must be served on all parties within the next seven days, and recross questions in seven days thereafter [Rule 31(a)(4)].

PRELIMINARY TASKS

Determine Whom to Depose

Organize Information to Identify Potential Deponents   The attorney decides who should be deposed, but a well-informed paralegal can be helpful in organizing the material needed to make that decision.

To identify potential deponents, extend the case analysis process discussed in Chapter 3 on investigation and in Chapter 7 on preparing for disclosure and interrogatories. Thoroughly review the facts of the case, the key elements, the pleadings, information gained through investigation, and especially the opponent's answer to any interrogatories.

After reviewing the information, organize it in a format favored by your supervising attorney. This could be a summary, outline, or chronology of the facts of the case. Important points to include are the parties and attorneys, the court, the issues in the case as indicated by the pleadings and any disclosure and discovery to this point, and the evidence and its source such as witnesses or documents pertinent to each issue. After the supervising attorney reviews this summary, it may help to have the attorney identify the theory of the case if not previously discussed.

Next, sift through the summary of the case for material that points to persons who can provide needed evidence as testimony or documents. From this information, prepare a list of potential deponents, describing each person's role in the case, what evidence they need to address, and what documents or other information pertains to the deponent or the deponent's testimony. Developing a list of potential deponents is a detailed process requiring thoroughness. Both the process and the result, however, can be interesting and exceptionally helpful.

Your understanding that the basis for deciding whom to depose is both practical and tactical is also helpful to the attorney who must decide if the expected information is worth the expense of the deposition. Little benefit is derived from deposing friendly witnesses or opposition witnesses who are very old or ill, or those who have previously provided a favorable statement.

Designated Corporate or Agency Deponent   The difficulty of determining what person in a corporation or government agency is the best person to depose has been eliminated by Rule 30(b)(6) and parallel state rules. Upon proper notice to the corporation or agency, including a reasonably particularized description of the desired information to be covered in the deposition, the corporation or agency must designate a person with the pertinent knowledge to testify at the deposition. A nonparty organization must be informed by subpoena of its obligation to designate such a person. The deposition questions cannot be limited to the matters stated in the notice [*Cabot Corp. v. Yamulla Enterprises*, 194 F.R.D. 499 (M.D. Pa. 2000)].

Expert Witnesses   Disclosure leads to the early identification of experts and the information they will provide. In planning which experts to depose, the timing of the deposition may be a strategic matter. Examining the opponent's experts before the opponent's case theory is set may increase the likelihood of inconsistencies and uncertainties in the expert's testimony, which can be exploited later at trial. Conversely, delaying the depositions of your own experts until your legal team's case theory is developed reduces the opposition's opportunities to exploit the deposition testimony at trial.

Conduct a Preliminary Interview

The list of persons to be deposed is narrowed by conducting preliminary interviews. Paralegals are frequently assigned this task. The purpose of the interview is to determine whether the person possesses information worth an expensive deposition. It might also reveal that the person is gravely ill or will soon be leaving the country, thus influencing the decision on whether to depose. The information gained can also help your attorney develop a case theory early in the process, which can better focus decisions regarding depositions and other discovery. Before conducting such an interview, obtain from the attorney a clear idea of what is needed from that particular witness. Then proceed in the manner described in Chapter 3 on investigation and interviewing, keeping in mind the ethical restrictions on making direct contact with a represented party. Occasionally a brief phone call may be all that is necessary to make the determination.

COORDINATE THE DEPOSITION

Arrange for Site and Necessary Components

Time   Set up the time for the deposition after consulting the applicable rules and any Rule 16 scheduling order and getting your attorney's approval. Allow adequate time for any special preparation, as in the case of deposing an expert witness. Keep in mind that a deposition cannot be used against a party (1) who on notice of the deposition and after due diligence is unable to obtain counsel for the deposition, or (2) who received less than eleven days notice of the deposition and promptly filed a motion for a protective order under Rule 26(c)(2) requesting that the deposition not be held or be held at a different time or place and that is still pending at the time of the deposition [Rule 32(a)(3)]. Then check with the attorney, the client (if attending), the parties, and possibly the person to be deposed to determine a mutually convenient date. Taking the time to coordinate the date may be time-consuming, but it will save rescheduling and paperwork in the future. Be sure to have the deposition calendared into the deadline system.

Site   In most instances, the site for the deposition is a standard one often used by the firm: a conference room at the office, or if a more formal atmosphere is sought, a room at the courthouse. Occasionally a deposition must be taken in another jurisdiction. In such circumstances, a law firm in that area might permit use of a room, or a clerk of court in the foreign jurisdiction may be able to arrange for a room. If an overnight stay is required, a conference room at a hotel may be convenient. In determining the location for the deposition, remember that the plaintiff can be required to attend a deposition in the jurisdiction where the action was brought. Other persons must be deposed in the jurisdiction where they live and work or within 100 miles of where they live, work, or conduct business [Rule 45(b)(2)]. Occasionally the deposition of a doctor is taken in the doctor's office. Regardless of the location, a suitable room should be reserved well in advance. Suitability may depend on atmosphere, adequate space, power outlets, and convenience to refreshments, meals, and rest rooms.

Method of Recording   The party taking the deposition must arrange to have the deposition recorded and bears the cost of the recording. Depositions can be stenographically recorded (typed) or recorded by audio or videotape [Rule 30(b)(2)]. The notice of the deposition must state the method to be used. At its own expense, another party can employ an additional, alternative means of recording. Many law firms use the stenographic recording for making objections, preparing deposition summaries, and for use at trial. Audio and videotape are more appealing to a jury when used at trial as compared to the dry reading of a typed deposition. Some vendors can synchronize the audio portion of a digital video recording with the typed deposition transcript. Then the use of split-screen technology allows a jury to see and hear the deponent while highlighted portions of the transcript appear simultaneously in the other window.

Videotaping a deposition provides the jury with the nearest thing to a real picture of a since-deceased individual, of a laboratory demonstration conducted by an expert witness, or testimony describing a thing or location inaccessible or inconvenient to the jury. Some disadvantages accompany the use of video, such as improper camera angles, bad or misleading lighting, and poor sound quality. Consequently, in arranging a video deposition or reviewing a stipulation for video recording, make sure that the camera is inobtrusive, the operator is well trained, the lighting and setting are fair, the audio is of high quality, and that the camera angles are fair but sufficiently varied for interest. The camera operator should not totally exclude the examiner from view. Two cameras permit a split-screen image of the witness as the dominant view and the examiner as the smaller view. Some attorneys and paralegals use a computer-networked, stenographically recorded system. Such a system produces an immediate copy of the deposition on the attorney's or paralegal's computer screen and allows simultaneous highlighting and annotating. Several companies offer real-time Internet transcript services that permit, for example, a paralegal in New York to monitor a deposition in Seattle and provide immediate research and other assistance to the attorney conducting the deposition.

Rule 30(b)(7) permits a deposition to be taken by phone or other electronic device, such as satellite television, if the parties so stipulate or the court so orders. Some state rules do not accommodate such technology. Where permitted, these methods can result in considerable savings in cost and time. It would be difficult by phone, however, to evaluate such a deponent as a potential witness unless the deponent were simultaneously videotaped. Telephone depositions are not common. If the deposition is on written questions, it is still necessary to reserve a site and to have the answers recorded.

Consult with your attorney about the method for recording the deposition. Strategy may determine whether videotaping is more or less advantageous than traditional transcription.

Oath Officer   Regardless of the type of deposition or the method used to record the deposition, a person is needed to administer the oath and take testimony. Normally, this person is a certified court reporter authorized to administer oaths. Otherwise, the court can appoint a person to administer the oath [Rule 28(a)]. Some court reporters are also trained in audio and videotaping techniques and can perform these services. If not, you need to locate a person trained in the needed technology.

The clerk of court and the law firm are likely to have a list of court reporters and video operators available for recording depositions and administering oaths. Not all lists cover all situations, however, and since it normally falls to the paralegal to locate a court reporter and other technicians, you need some resources to do so. You can contact paralegals you know in the area where the deposition is to be held. They or their attorneys may be able to help. They may also offer a conference room for the deposition. The National Court Reporters Association (800-272-6272) provides lists of qualified court reporters and sells a directory. Some commercial companies locate out-of-town court reporters and legal videographers.

See the Helpful Web Sites at the end of the chapter. It is wise to choose a court reporter certified either by the state in which they practice or by some reputable national organization.

Deposition Tracking Logs Two types of logs can help you prevent costly and embarrassing oversights in coordinating depositions. A Deposition Arrangements Checklist for each deposition lists all the arrangements to be made, those completed, and those pending; and the Log of Items Sent to Witness helps you track all materials sent to a witness, such as an expert witness, in preparation for a deposition.[1]

Prepare and Serve Notice of the Deposition

After the arrangements are made, you must serve notice of the deposition on the deponent and each of the other parties as required by Rule 30(b)(1). If a party or a person designated to represent a party is to be deposed, service of the notice of deposition is all that is needed, and failure to attend is subject to sanctions under Rule 37(d). A nonparty deponent must be subpoenaed, as discussed later.

   The notice must state the time and place, the name of the attorney conducting the examination, the name and address of each person to be deposed, and the method of recording the testimony [Rule 30(b)(1)–(2)]. If the name of the person is not known, Rule 30(b)(1) permits a general description sufficient to identify the person or his or her class or group. If the deponent is a business, association, or agency, the notice should describe in some detail the matters that the examination will cover [Rule 30(b)(6)]. If documents, books, papers, or tangible things are requested to be brought to the deposition, they should be designated in the notice to take deposition. An example of a Notice of Taking Deposition appears in Exhibit 8:1.[2]

EXHIBIT 8:1 ▪ Notice of Taking Deposition of a Witness Including Reference to Materials Designated in Attached Subpoena

[FED. R. CIV. P. Rule 30(b)(1)]

[*Title of Court and Cause*]

TO: [*Attorney for Plaintiff*]
    [*Law firm*]
    [*Address*]
   PLEASE TAKE NOTICE that pursuant to Rule 30 of the Federal Rules of Civil Procedure, Plaintiff will take the oral deposition of _____ before a notary public or other authorized officer by stenographic means on [date], at _____ P.M. and thereafter from day to day until completed, at the offices of [*law firm name and address*]. Defendant requests that deponent bring to said deposition all documents described in the attached ADDENDUM to Civil Subpoena.

                                                    _____
                                                    Attorney for Defendant
                                                    Address: _____

Source: Reprinted with permission of West Group.

The notice should be drafted and served on the deponent, all parties, and the court reporter. A certificate of service should be executed. If the deposition is rescheduled or other changes occur, draft a letter notifying the deponent, all parties, and the court reporter.

Subpoena the Deponent

subpoena

A document pursuant to a court order that commands a person to appear to testify.

subpoena duces tecum

A document pursuant to a court order that commands a person to appear with certain books, documents, electronically stored information, or tangible things.

Obtain the Subpoena   A **subpoena** is a document issued by the clerk or officer of the court commanding a person (nonparty) to be present and, if indicated, bring physical items to a specified place at a designated time. Failure to comply with the subpoena may result in contempt of court and appropriate penalties. Subpoenas are the documents used to require attendance of witnesses at depositions and at trial. Rule 45 of the Federal Rules and parallel state rules set out the requirements for a subpoena and its service. Of the two types of subpoenas, the most common is a subpoena for a person to give testimony. The second type is a **subpoena duces tecum,** which requires a person to appear and produce books, documents, electronically stored information, or tangible things [Rule 45(a)(1)(C)]. Because parties to an action do not have to be subpoenaed, it is appropriate to serve a Rule 34 request for production of documents with the notice of the deposition. It serves the same function as the subpoena duces tecum for nonparties. If a Rule 34 production is requested, the other party must receive notice thirty days before the date of the deposition [Rule 30(b)(5)].

In the federal system a nonparty deponent must be deposed within 100 miles of where that person resides, works, or regularly transacts business in person [Rule 45(c)(2)(B)(ii)]. Although some court decisions say the 100-mile limit should be calculated by a straight line, the cautious practice is to figure it according to the actual driving mileage. If the deponent is located in the district where the case is pending, the subpoena is issued by that court. If not, the subpoena must be issued by the court in the district where the deponent is located. Federal subpoenas may be served anywhere in the district of the issuing court or anywhere outside the district if it is within 100 miles of the place of the deposition or anywhere in the state where state statute or court rule permits service of a subpoena issued by a court of general jurisdiction sitting in the place of the deposition [FED. R. CIV. P. 45(b)(2)]. Generally, a deponent in a state action may not be required to go beyond the county of residence, work, or personal transaction of business. Check your state rule.

To obtain a subpoena for a deponent, provide the appropriate clerk of court with a copy of the notice to take deposition and proof of service on the parties. In the federal system the subpoena must be issued by the clerk in the district where the deposition is to be taken or by the attorney [Rule 45(a)(3)]. In some states it is issued where the action is pending. Consult local rules. The clerk will sign the subpoena *in blank* in most jurisdictions, which means that you will need to fill in the necessary information.

Following the dictates of Rule 45, be sure that the following information is on the subpoena: the name of the issuing court; the title and docket number of the action and the court in which it is pending; the name of the paralegal's attorney; the witness's name and address with directions for the witness to attend and give testimony; and the date, time, and place for the deposition. The caption of the subpoena must state the name of the issuing court. This is easy to overlook if the issuing court is different from the court where the action is pending. If done incorrectly, neither court has jurisdiction to enforce the subpoena. Indicate whether the production of documents is commanded. In addition, Rule 45(a)(1)(D) requires that the text of sections (c) and (d) of Rule 45 be set out in the subpoena. These sections define the duty of an attorney to not abuse the subpoena process and on what basis and how one objects to a subpoena. Note that Rule 45 now requires a deposition subpoena to state the method for recording the deposition [FED. R. CIV. P. 45(a)(2)(B)]. Add the details just mentioned and designate the documents or physical evidence to be produced, inspected, copied, tested, or sampled. If the items are numerous or require a lengthy description, a rider may need to be attached to the subpoena. Rule 45(c)(2)(A) does not require the personal presence of a person subpoenaed to produce documents and things.

Revisions to Rule 45 address electronically stored information. A subpoena duces tecum may designate the form in which e-stored information should be produced. If it does not so designate, the responding person must produce the information in the form or forms in which it is normally maintained or in a reasonably usable form [Rule 45(d)]. Other provisions similar to those added to Rules 26 and 34 address how to deal with privileged information, the right to refuse production of e-stored information as not reasonably accessible because of undue burden or cost, and the right to object to or compel the requested production [Rule 45(c) and (d)]. An example of a combined subpoena and subpoena duces tecum appears in Exhibit 8:2.

HIPAA and Subpoenas The HIPAA privacy regulations and parallel state laws impact deposition and subpoena practice. Keep in mind that you must comply with any stricter respective state requirements, as well as HIPAA. If you need to obtain medical information from a health care provider for discovery, the simplest procedure is to get the patient's signed authorization, as previously discussed. If a request for the authorization is refused, a subpoena is needed. A subpoena signed by a judge fulfills HIPAA requirements, because the subpoena is a court order [45 C.F.R. § 164.512(e)]. In jurisdictions where judges do not sign subpoenas, however, HIPAA and the health care provider require written assurance that the patient has been notified of the intent to subpoena the records, the medical professional, or both, and that the patient has been given sufficient time to object to the release of the protected information [45 C.F.R. § 164.512(e)]. In practice, this requires that a "notice letter" be sent to the party's attorney containing:

- reference to the governing HIPAA and state provisions;
- the intent to obtain the party's medical records by subpoena duces tecum;
- the health care provider(s) to be subpoenaed;
- copies of the subpoenas to be issued; and
- a date by which written objection must be communicated.[3]

If an objection is raised, the attorneys must resolve the issue.

Once the date for objection has passed or any objection has been resolved, then the subpoena with a copy of the notice letter and a cover letter must be sent to the provider's record custodian. The cover letter along with a copy of the notice letter gives the provider the assurance that HIPAA requirements have been met. The Sample Cover Letter to the Records Custodian in Exhibit 8:3 sets out the necessary assurances.

Another HIPAA option for subpoenaing medical records is the qualified protective order [45 C.F.R. § 164.512(e)]. A qualified protective order specifies that the protected records will be used for a qualified purpose, such as litigation in the pertinent case, and will be returned to the provider or be destroyed at the end of the defined use. When the subpoena is sent to the provider, this option requires an accompanying cover letter, similar to Exhibit 8:3, that assures the records custodian that the parties in the pertinent legal action have agreed to a qualified protective

EXHIBIT 8:2 ▪ Subpoena for Taking Oral Testimony and Production of Documents (Duces Tecum)

A088 (Rev. 1/94) Subpoena in a Civil Case

Issued by the
UNITED STATES DISTRICT COURT
DISTRICT OF _____

V.

SUBPOENA IN A CIVIL CASE

Case Number:[1]

TO:

YOU ARE COMMANDED to appear in the United States District court at the place, date, and time specified below to testify in the above case.

PLACE OF TESTIMONY	COURTROOM
	DATE AND TIME

YOU ARE COMMANDED to appear at the place, date, and time specified below to testify at the taking of a deposition in the above case.

PLACE OF DEPOSITION	DATE AND TIME

YOU ARE COMMANDED to produce and permit inspection and copying of the following documents or objects at the place, date, and time specified below (list documents or objects):

PLACE	DATE AND TIME

YOU ARE COMMANDED to permit inspection of the following premises at the date and time specified below.

PREMISES	DATE AND TIME

Any organization not a party to this suit that is subpoenaed for the taking of a deposition shall designate one or more officers, directors, or managing agents, or other persons who consent to testify on its behalf, and may set forth, for each person designated, the matters on which the person will testify. Federal Rules of Civil Procedure, 30(b)(6).

ISSUING OFFICER'S SIGNATURE AND TITLE (INDICATE IF ATTORNEY FOR PLAINTIFF OR DEFENDANT)	DATE

ISSUING OFFICER'S NAME, ADDRESS AND PHONE NUMBER

(See Rule 45, Federal Rules of Civil Procedure, Parts C & D on next page)

[1]If action is pending in district other than district of issuance, state district under case number.

EXHIBIT 8:2 ■ Subpoena for Taking Oral Testimony and Production of Documents (Duces Tecum) *(continued)*

A088 (Rev. 1/94) Subpoena in a Civil Case

PROOF OF SERVICE		
	DATE	PLACE
SERVED		

SERVED ON (PRINT NAME)	MANNER OF SERVICE

SERVED BY (PRINT NAME)	TITLE

DECLARATION OF SERVER

I declare under penalty of perjury under the laws of the United States of America that the foregoing information contained in the Proof of Service is true and correct.

Executed on _____
DATE

_____
SIGNATURE OF SERVER

_____
ADDRESS OF SERVER

Rule 45, Federal Rules of Civil Procedure, Parts C & D:

(c) PROTECTION OF PERSONS SUBJECT TO SUBPOENAS.

(1) A party or an attorney responsible for the issuance and service of a subpoena shall take reasonable steps to avoid imposing undue burden or expense on a person subject to that subpoena. The court on behalf of which the subpoena was issued shall enforce this duty and impose upon the party or attorney in breach of this duty an appropriate sanction which may include, but is not limited to, lost earnings and reasonable attorney's fee.

(2) (A) A person commanded to produce and permit inspection and copying of designated books, papers, documents or tangible things, or inspection of premises need not appear in person at the place of production or inspection unless commanded to appear for deposition, hearing or trial.

(B) Subject to paragraph (d) (2) of this rule, a person commanded to produce and permit inspection and copying may, within 14 days after service of subpoena or before the time specified for compliance if such time is less than 14 days after service, serve upon the party or attorney designated in the subpoena written objection to inspection or copying of any or all of the designated materials or of the premises. If objection is made, the party serving the subpoena shall not be entitled to inspect and copy materials or inspect the premises except pursuant to an order of the court by which the subpoena was issued. If objection has been made, the party serving the subpoena may, upon notice to the person commanded to produce, move at any time for an order to compel the production. Such an order to comply production shall protect any person who is not a party or an officer of a party from significant expense resulting from the inspection and copying commanded.

(3) (A) On timely motion, the court by which a subpoena was issued shall quash or modify the subpoena if it

(i) fails to allow reasonable time for compliance,
(ii) requires a person who is not a party or an officer of a party to travel to a place more than 100 miles from the place where that person resides, is employed or regularly transacts business in person, except that, subject to the provisions of clause (c) (3) (B) (iii) of this rule, such a person may in order to attend trial be commanded to travel from any such place within the state in which the trial is held, or

(iii) requires disclosure of privileged or other protected matter and no exception or waiver applies, or
(iv) subjects a person to undue burden.

(B) If a subpoena

(i) requires disclosure of a trade secret or other confidential research, development, or commercial information, or
(ii) requires disclosure of an unretained expert's opinion or information not describing specific events or occurrences in dispute and resulting from the expert's study made not at the request of any party, or
(iii) requires a person who is not a party or an officer of a party to incur substantial expense to travel more than 100 miles to attend trial, the court may, to protect a person subject to or affected by the subpoena, quash or modify the subpoena, or, if the party on whose behalf the subpoena is issued shows a substantial need for the testimony or material that cannot be otherwise met without undue hardship and assures that the person to whom the subpoena is addressed will be reasonably compensated, the court may order appearance or production only upon specified conditions.

(d) DUTIES IN RESPONDING TO SUBPOENA.

(1) A person responding to a subpoena to produce documents shall produce them as they are kept in the usual course of business or shall organize and label them to correspond with the categories in the demand.

(2) When information subject to a subpoena is withheld on a claim that it is privileged or subject to protection as trial preparation materials, the claim shall be made expressly and shall be supported by a description of the nature of the documents, communications, or things not produced that is sufficient to enable the demanding party to contest the claim.

EXHIBIT 8:3 ■ Sample Cover Letter to Records Custodian (Subpoena/HIPAA)

Dear Records Custodian:

Please find enclosed a subpoena duces tecum for you to provide us with a certified copy of the complete medical file on ____(patient)____.

This letter is to assure you of our compliance with the privacy requirements of the Health Insurance Portability and Accountability Act [45 C.F.R. § 164.512(e)]:

1. a copy of the letter that provided notice of our intent to subpoena the patient's medical records;
2. sent with sufficient time ___(a specified deadline)___ to give the patient the opportunity to object to the subpoena; and
3. our assurance that no objection has been raised by the specified deadline, which has expired.*

Please send a certified copy of the requested records to the address specified on the subpoena and bill us to get prompt reimbursement of your cost in producing the records.

Thank you,

_____
Counsel

*Note: Some states may have additional requirements and/or may require that the custodian receive a Notice to Take Deposition with an option to produce the records without having to appear.

---

order or the attorney seeking the records has requested the protective order from the court [45 C.F.R. § 164.512(e)(1)(iv)].

If a provider still refuses to release the medical records, the final option for the party seeking the records is to get a court order for their release. Similar procedures must be followed when a treating physician is to be deposed. A Notice to Take Deposition must be added to the process and all parties notified.

Attach Fees   Before serving the subpoena, determine if it is necessary to attach witness and mileage fees. The Federal Rules require that such fees be tendered at the time of service of the subpoena to have a valid subpoena (28 U.S.C. § 1821). Determine the distance to be traveled by the deponent and calculate the round trip mileage. A call to the federal clerk of court will give you the most recent witness fee and the mileage allowance. Prepare a check and attach it to the subpoena for service. The procedure is the same for most states. Some states require a witness fee only for witnesses from outside the county where the deposition is to be taken.

Serve the Subpoena   The subpoena and attached fee must be personally served on the deponent. Because a subpoena can be unnerving to its recipient, it may be a good idea, if your attorney approves, to warn the witness and explain why the subpoena is necessary. This explanation might keep a witness in your camp. In the federal system a subpoena may be served by a person not a party and not less than eighteen years of age. Service in state cases is performed by a sheriff, special bailiff, or any person of legal age (check local rules). Paralegals are frequently asked to serve subpoenas. Professional servers are available in some areas. When delivering the subpoena or directing someone else to do so, make sure the server fully understands the correct way to serve a subpoena. Consult local rules, but in most instances, the subpoena must be personally handed to the deponent and the deponent told what the subpoena is, where the deponent is to go, and what is expected of the deponent. The server must then acknowledge service in writing on a copy of the subpoena or execute an affidavit of service.

When service is to be on an out-of-town deponent, it is best to call the local clerk of court for the correct procedures and, if necessary, call each day to ensure issuance of the subpoena and service on the witness.[4] If a person objects to the commands of the subpoena, objections must be served on the deposing attorney within fourteen days of service of the subpoena, or on or before the deposition if it is scheduled in less than fourteen days from service.

In the case of a deposition, the objecting party must move the issuing court for an order to quash or modify the subpoena [Rule 45(c)(3)(A)]. A detailed list on subpoena practice is in Chapter 11 under Subpoena Witnesses.

PREPARE FOR DEPOSITION

Draft Questions or an Examination Outline

Although the attorney will determine what questions will be asked the deponent, you can provide considerable assistance by drafting a proposed set of questions or a detailed outline for the examination, indicating each point to be addressed. The outline may be better because it is less time-consuming, often more complete, easily amended, and provides flexibility during the examination. Adequate preparation is important.

Carefully review all file information, paying particular attention to those areas for which the witness can provide proof, information, or leads, including any documents or physical items that can or need to be introduced through this witness or otherwise impact on the witness's testimony. Pay special attention to answers to interrogatories or admissions from this case or other cases made by the witness. If the witness is a party, these items just mentioned will permit you to eliminate some areas of questioning, especially if the other party has already admitted certain facts. Make notes.

Meet with the attorney, review the notes, and determine as specifically as possible what the attorney wants from this witness. For example, the attorney for Ms. Forrester may wish to examine Mr. Hart to determine his version of the facts, lock him into that version, and establish any breaches in company policy or defects in the vehicle that may have contributed to the accident. The attorney may want to depose the head of Mercury Parcel's maintenance shop to produce his records of repairs on the van, explain the shop procedures and policies to see if they were followed in this case, or reveal any problems or defects in the van. Or the attorney for Mercury Parcel might want to depose Ms. Forrester to lock her into her story, assess how high the jury sympathy factor will be, probe her attitude on any negligence on her part, or to hear her description of her injuries and pain. Or Mercury's attorney may want to depose Ms. Forrester's surgeon and other doctors to get detailed assessments of injuries, possible causes, treatment, and prognosis. Since the witness has been previously identified, you will find that it is easier than you might think to determine what the witness needs to be asked and what can be eliminated. The discussion with the attorney ought to make clear the objectives and areas of examination.

> "Sir Rowland: You must know better than I do, Inspector, how very rarely two people's account of the same thing agrees. In fact, if three people were to agree exactly, I should regard it as suspicious. Very suspicious, indeed."
>
> —AGATHA CHRISTIE, SPIDER'S WEB, 1956.

Look at similar witness examinations from other office files or form depositions. Several publishing companies have published detailed deposition outlines to cover a variety of types of witnesses. Go to the law library and find what is available. An example of a deposition outline appears in Exhibit 8:4.[5]

EXHIBIT 8:4 ■ Deposition Outline/Checklist (Plaintiff—Automobile)

PRELIMINARY INFORMATION

Title of Case _____

Court Number _____

Deponent's Name _____

Place of Deposition _____

Date _____ Time _____

Lawyer(s) for Plaintiff(s)_____

_____

_____

_____

Lawyer(s) for Defendant(s)

_____

_____

_____

_____

Lawyers in Attendance

_____ for _____

_____ for _____

_____ for _____

_____ for _____

_____ for _____

Type of deposition: Evidence or Discovery _____

Is signature waived? _____

Is witness sworn? _____

Is a statement made for the record (e.g., the type of deposition or the rules by which it is being conducted)?

_____

Make the following statement:

"If I ask any question that you do not understand, please tell me and I will rephrase it. Do you understand?"

IDENTIFICATION OF DEPONENT

Name _____

Address _____

City & State _____

Bus. Phone _____ Home Phone _____

Names and addresses of people who will always know of deponent's whereabouts:

_____

_____

Has deponent ever used an alias? _____

If yes, explain: _____

Has deponent ever been convicted of a crime?

_____

If yes, explain: _____

_____

Has deponent been a party or witness in a lawsuit?

_____

If yes, explain: _____

_____

_____

Social Security Numbers (last 4 digit) _____

Driver's License Number _____

Selective Service Number _____

Height _____ Weight _____ Sex _____

Color of eyes _____ Color of hair _____

Race _____ Citizenship _____

Date of birth _____ Place of birth _____

Mother's maiden name _____

Further Details: _____

_____

_____

EXHIBIT 8:4 ▪ Deposition Outline/Checklist (Plaintiff—Automobile) *(continued)*

Names and Addresses of Parents, Brothers and Sisters

Name _____ Relationship _____

Address _____

City & State _____

Name _____ Relationship _____

Address _____

City & State _____

Name _____ Relationship _____

Address _____

City & State _____

Name _____ Relationship _____

Address _____

City & State _____

Others: _____

_____

_____

_____

_____

_____

_____

_____

CHILDREN

Name _____ Birth Date _____

Name _____ Birth Date _____

Name _____ Birth Date _____

Name _____ Birth Date _____

Name _____ Birth Date _____

Others: _____

_____

_____

_____

Who supports the children? _____

Educational background of deponent: _____

_____

Other special training: _____

_____

_____

Residence Addresses for the Past Ten Years

Address _____ Dates _____

City & State _____

Address _____ Dates _____

City & State _____

Address _____ Dates _____

City & State _____

Address _____ Dates _____

City & State _____

Address _____ Dates _____

City & State _____

Marital Status _____

Spouse's full name _____

Maiden name _____

Any other marriages? _____

If yes, explain: _____

_____

_____

Military Service Experience: _____

Injuries in service: _____

_____

Prior traffic convictions: _____

_____

_____

_____

Has driver's license ever been revoked? _____

If yes, explain: _____

Does deponent have restrictions on driver's license?

_____

If yes, explain: _____

_____

Does the deponent carry liability insurance? _____

Name of company _____

Policy number _____

Liab. limits _____ Med. limits _____

Effective period _____

Did the deponent settle with any other person involved in this occurrence? *(continued)*

EXHIBIT 8:4 ■ Deposition Outline/Checklist (Plaintiff—Automobile) *(continued)*

_____

If yes, explain: _____

_____

_____

Was any reimbursement received for medical expenses, loss of income, property damage, or Workmen's Compensation, or other? _____

If yes, explain: _____

_____

Were any oral or written statements given? _____

If yes, explain: _____

Were income tax returns filed in the past five years?

_____

Where? _____ Jointly? _____

Does the deponent have copies? _____

Is deponent acquainted with or related to any party in this suit?

_____

If yes, explain: _____

_____

_____

_____

EMPLOYMENT BACKGROUND

Name of employer _____

_____

Address _____

City & State _____

Job description: _____

_____ Rate of pay _____

Immediate Supervisor _____

_____

Employment for the Past Ten Years

Employer _____ Dates _____

Address _____

City & State _____

Job description: _____

Employer _____ Dates _____

Address _____

City & State _____

Job description: _____

Employer _____ Dates _____

Address _____

City & State _____

Job description: _____

If not employed for the past ten years, was deponent ever employed?

_____

Explain: _____

_____

Further Details: _____

_____

DETAILS OF DEPONENT'S VEHICLE

Make _____ Model _____

Year _____ Color _____ No. of doors _____

Unusual accessories on car: _____

_____

Owner's name _____

Address _____

City & State _____

Approximate mileage on car at time of accident

_____

When did car last have repairs? _____

Where were repairs performed? _____

_____

Nature of last repairs before accident? _____

_____

Approxmate mileage on tires at time of accident

_____

Condition of:

Tail lights _____	Tires _____
Headlights _____	Horn _____
Turn signals _____	Steering _____
Windshield _____	Wipers _____
	Brakes_____

EXHIBIT 8:4 ▪ Deposition Outline/Checklist (Plaintiff—Automobile) *(continued)*

When was the last safety check before the accident?
_____

Was the auto ever in a previous accident? _____
If yes, explain: _____
_____

What portion of the vehicle was damaged as a result of the above previous accident?
_____

Was the car repaired after the previous problem?
_____

If so, where and what was the cost of repair?_____

In how many previous accidents had this automobile been involved?
Details: _____
_____

OCCUPANTS IN DEPONENT'S CAR

L.F.(1)
Name _____ Age _____
Address _____
City & State _____
Bus. Phone _____ Home Phone _____

M.F. (2)
Name _____ Age _____
Address _____
City & State _____
Bus. Phone _____ Home Phone _____

R.F. (3)
Name _____ Age _____
Address _____
City & State _____
Bus. Phone _____ Home Phone _____

L.R. (4)
Name _____ Age _____
Address _____
City & State _____
Bus. Phone _____ Home Phone _____

M.R. (5)
Name _____ Age _____
Address _____
City & State _____
Bus. Phone _____ Home Phone _____

R.R. (6)
Name _____ Age _____
Address _____
City & State _____
Bus. Phone _____ Home Phone _____

Others
_____
_____

Did driver ask passengers to wear seatbelts?_____
_____

Which passengers were wearing seat belts? _____
Did passengers have a clear view of the accident?
Explain: _____
_____

What were passengers doing before impact (e.g., sleeping, talking, drinking, touching controls, yelling, etc.)? _____
_____

Did any passengers warn the driver of impending danger?
_____

Explain: _____
_____

Did any passengers complain of the driving? _____
Explain: _____
_____

Was anyone giving directions to the driver? _____
Explain: _____
_____

(continued)

EXHIBIT 8:4 ■ Deposition Outline/Checklist (Plaintiff—Automobile) *(continued)*

Were any occupants injured? _____

If yes, what did deponent notice about injuries to other occupants?

_____

_____

DESCRIPTION OF ACCIDENT SCENE

Diagram

Other Diagram—Draw Below

_____

Location of accident: _____

_____

Number of driving lanes for each road: _____

Number of parking lanes for each road: _____

Direction of each road: _____

_____

Describe each road (e.g., level, hilly, divided, etc.).

_____

_____

Type of surface (e.g., dirt, gravel, asphalt, brick, concrete, blacktop, etc.):

_____

Condition of roads (e.g., holes, icy, dry, wet, etc.):

_____

Were lanes marked?

Explain: _____

_____

_____

Type of area (e.g., residential, business, rural, etc.):

_____

Describe structures located at or near scene (e.g., building at each corner).

_____

_____

_____

Was there anything obstructing the driver's view (e.g., stop signs, caution signs, arrows, etc.)?_____

Explain: _____

_____

_____

Describe the traffic controls and location of each (e.g., stop signs, caution signs, arrows, etc.).

_____

_____

_____

What was the speed limit? _____

Where was the speed limit sign? _____

Were traffic signals functioning? _____

Were there artificial lights at the scene? _____

State the approximate width of each street: _____

_____

Is the deponent familiar with the accident scene?

_____

Explain: _____

_____

_____

DETAILS SHORTLY BEFORE OCCURRENCE

Where was deponent going at time of accident?

_____

_____

EXHIBIT 8:4 ■ Deposition Outline/Checklist (Plaintiff—Automobile) (*continued*)

Where was the deponent coming from? _____
_____

What route was taken? _____
_____
_____

At what time was the deponent to arrive at his destination?
_____

Was the deponent early or late? _____
Explain: _____
_____

What was the last stop made before the accident, other than for traffic?
_____
_____

Was the deponent talking to anyone in the car?
_____

If so, state to whom and the nature of the conversation.
_____
_____

Was the deponent:
　　Smoking? _____ Drinking? _____
Did he have both hands on the wheel? _____
When is the last time before the accident that the deponent had anything of an alcoholic nature to drink? Explain: _____
_____
_____

State the names and addresses of all persons present with the deponent at all times during the five hours preceding the occurrence.
_____
_____
_____

Was the deponent under medication at the time of the occurrence?
_____

Explain: _____
_____
_____

When was the last time prior to the accident that the deponent slept and how much sleep did he have?
_____
_____
_____

Was the deponent:
　　Sleepy? _____ Emotionally upset? _____
　　Ill? _____ Other? _____
If yes, explain: _____
_____
_____
_____

During the 24-hour period before the accident, did the deponent consume—
　　A tranquilizer? _____ A narcotic? _____
　　A prescription? _____ Aspirins? _____
If yes, explain: _____
_____

Did any passengers pay for the ride or share expenses?
Explain: _____
_____

Was the driver acting as agent for anyone? _____
List details (business trip, etc.). _____
_____
_____

Did driver have the owner's permission to drive car?
Details (e.g., express or implied consent):
_____
_____
_____

DETAILS OF OCCURRENCE

In what direction and on which street was the deponent traveling?
_____
_____

What was the direction and street for the other car(s)?
_____
_____

(*continued*)

EXHIBIT 8:4 ■ Deposition Outline/Checklist (Plaintiff—Automobile) *(continued)*

Other traffic present: _____

_____

_____

When the deponent first became aware of the other vehicle, how many feet was he from the point of impact? _____

How many seconds from point of impact? _____

What was his speed at this time? _____

In which lane of traffic was he? _____

Did he change lanes within one block of the point of impact?

_____

Explain: _____

_____

Did the deponent perform any maneuver to

avoid the impact? _____

Explain: _____

_____

Did the deponent try to signal or warn the other party of danger?

_____

Did he:

    Sound the horn? _____

    Use flashing lights? _____

    Other? _____

What was the deponent doing when he first became aware of danger (e.g., talking, looking the opposite way, etc.)?

_____

When the deponent first saw the other car, where was it (lane, direction of travel, distance from point of impact, etc.)? _____

_____

_____

What was the other car's speed? _____

Did the other car warn the deponent by:

    Sounding the horn? _____

    Flashing lights? _____

    Other: _____

_____

How many feet from the intersection was the deponent when he could first see the other car?

_____

Did the deponent look for the other car at the first possible point he could see it? _____

Explain: _____

_____

Did the other driver do anything to indicate he saw the deponent? _____

Explain: _____

_____

Did the deponent take evasive action at the point when he first observed the other car? _____

Explain how many seconds elapsed between the time he saw the car and the time he reacted. _____

How many feet did he travel? _____

Did the deponent apply his brakes? _____

How far (feet) from the point of impact? _____

What was the speed of the deponent:

    One block from the point of impact?   _____

    1/2 block from the point of impact?   _____

    100 feet from the point of impact?   _____

    50 feet from the point of impact?   _____

    At the point of impact?   _____

What was the speed of the other vehicle:

    One block from the point of impact?   _____

    1/2 block from the point of impact?   _____

    100 feet from the point of impact?   _____

    50 feet from the point of impact?   _____

    At the point of impact?   _____

Did deponent use:

    Hand brake? _____ Shift gears? _____

Did the brakes decrease the speed? _____

Describe the point of contact on the deponent's auto:

_____

_____

_____

Describe all remaining contact points: _____

_____

_____

EXHIBIT 8:4 ■ Deposition Outline/Checklist (Plaintiff—Automobile) *(continued)*

Describe all damage to deponent's auto: _____
_____
_____

In relation to the intersection, describe the exact point of impact (use intersecting point of lanes in which cars are):
_____
_____

Where did the deponent's vehicle come to rest in relation to the point of impact?
_____
_____

Describe the point of contact concerning the other auto(s):
_____
_____
_____

Describe remaining contact points: _____
_____

Was there debris to mark point of impact? _____
Explain (e.g., broken glass, vehicle parts, dirt or mud, water or radiator fluid, gas, oil, or grease, etc.):
_____
_____
_____

In which direction was each car facing at the final resting point? _____

Was there anything about either automobile which may have caused or contributed to the accident? _____
Explain: _____
_____

Was there anything about the road or its surface that may have caused or contributed to the accident?
_____
Explain: _____
_____
_____

Describe the location of each party to this suit after the cars came to their final resting places: _____
_____

Was anyone removed by ambulance? _____
Who? _____
_____
_____

Was first aid rendered at the scene? _____
To whom? _____
_____

By whom? _____
_____

Nature of treatment: _____
_____
_____

Was there any evidence of drinking at the scene?
_____
Explain: _____
_____

Did any person at the scene appear:
   To be intoxicated? _____
   To have been drinking? _____
Who? _____
_____

Did the deponent talk to anyone at the scene? _____
If yes, to whom and what was said: _____
_____
_____
_____

What conversation(s) did the deponent overhear at the scene? Between whom was the conversation and what was said? _____
_____
_____
_____

POLICE INVESTIGATION

Did police respond? _____
What police department? _____
_____

(continued)

EXHIBIT 8:4 ▪ Deposition Outline/Checklist (Plaintiff—Automobile) *(continued)*

How many police cars? _____

How many policemen? _____

Was a traffic citation issued? _____

To whom? _____

_____

What was (were) the charge(s)? _____

_____

Court date: _____

What was the disposition of the traffic hearing (e.g., plea of guilty, found guilty or not guilty)?

_____

(e.g., court reporter, tape recorder)?

Details: _____

_____

_____

Were photographs taken? _____

Details: _____

_____

Did the police take measurements? _____

How (e.g., tape measure, walking, etc.)? _____

_____

Further Details: _____

_____

_____

_____

_____

_____

_____

WITNESSES

Were there any occurrence witnesses? _____

If Yes, List

Name _____

Address _____

City & State _____

Bus. Phone _____ Home Phone _____

Name _____

Address _____

City & State _____

Bus. Phone _____ Home Phone _____

Name _____

Address _____

City & State _____

Bus. Phone _____ Home Phone _____

Name _____

Address _____

City & State _____

Bus. Phone _____ Home Phone _____

Others: _____

_____

_____

_____

Describe where witnesses were: _____

_____

_____

_____

_____

_____

Describe deponent's conversation with witnesses:

_____

_____

_____

_____

Did any witnesses arrive later? _____

Explain (e.g., passing motorist, friends, etc.): _____

_____

_____

_____

_____

Were any people in the immediate area? _____

Explain (e.g., gas station attendant, mailman, people waiting for a bus, etc.):

_____

_____

_____

EXHIBIT 8:4 ■ Deposition Outline/Checklist (Plaintiff—Automobile) *(continued)*

Did any articles appear in the newspapers? _____
Explain: _____
_____
_____

Further Details: _____
_____
_____
_____
_____
_____

INJURIES AND MEDICAL INFORMATION

Description of injuries: _____
_____
_____
_____

Name of treating Dr.: _____
Address _____
City & State _____
Phone No. _____

Names and Addresses of Specialists

Name _____ Specialty _____
Address _____
City & State _____
Phone No. _____
Name _____ Specialty _____
Address _____
City & State _____
Phone No. _____
Name _____ Specialty _____
Address _____
City & State _____
Phone No. _____

Name of Hosital _____
Address _____
City & State _____
Phone No. _____

Describe medical treatment received together with dates, and identify doctors giving treatment.
_____
_____
_____
_____
_____

PRIOR MEDICAL HISTORY

Prior Injuries

Date _____ Where? _____
Details: _____
_____
_____

Date _____ Where? _____
Details: _____
_____
_____

Prior Hospitalization

Date _____ Where? _____
Details: _____
_____

Date _____ Where? _____
Details: _____
_____

Date _____ Where? _____
Details: _____
_____

Does deponent have any physical or mental illnesses or is he being treated for any condition?
_____
Explain: _____
_____
_____

Any prior claims or lawsuits? _____
Explain: _____
_____
_____

(continued)

EXHIBIT 8:4 ▪ Deposition Outline/Checklist (Plaintiff—Automobile) (*continued*)

DAMAGES TO DATE

Hospital _____ $ _____

Ambulance Service _____ $ _____

Private Nurses _____ $ _____

Dr. _____ $ _____

Dr. _____ $ _____

Dr. _____ $ _____

Dr. _____ $ _____

Drugs & Prescriptions _____ $ _____

X-rays _____ $ _____

Loss of Income _____ $ _____

Property Damage _____ $ _____

_____ $ _____

_____ $ _____

_____ $ _____

_____ $ _____

Total To Date $ _____

Further Details: _____

_____

_____

_____

_____

_____

_____

_____

ATTORNEY'S APPRAISAL OF DEPONENT

Physical description, general appearance and characteristics, handicaps, or impairments—hearing, eyesight, speech, etc. _____

_____

Does the deponent describe the accident in a clear, rational and understandable manner? If not, why not? _____

_____

Does the deponent show any marked tendency to engage in conjecture and speculation? _____

_____

Can the deponent be easily confused, swayed, or led? _____

_____

Do deponent's normal activities and past experiences qualify with respect to estimating speeds, distances, etc.? State the qualifications, if any._____

_____

General attitude—favorable, unfavorable, or passive?

_____

_____

General Impression: From your observations of the deponent, state whether the deponent's appearance, personality, and demeanor shall normally invite belief or disbelief in his version of the accident or occurrence, as the deponent tells it.

_____

_____

_____

Submitted by: _____

Name of Attorney

Source: Reprinted with permission of the author, Alan E. Morrill.

The outline in Exhibit 8:4 can be adapted to a particular witness and set of facts. If no sample is available, check the objectives carefully and brainstorm topics and subtopics that must be covered. In most circumstances, it is necessary to get detailed information on the witness's background (including possible areas for future impeachment), and then on the details of the event, documents, or other matters relevant to the case. Remember that in a deposition the attorneys have more latitude in the types of questions they may ask than they have at trial. The scope is confined to what is relevant to the case, is admissible evidence, or might reasonably lead to admissible evidence. Therefore, hearsay may be legitimate, as is the identification of other possible witnesses, documents, and physical evidence. In deposition preparation it is probably better to err on the side of going too far rather than being too cautious.

One of the best techniques for generating questions for an outline is to sit down with your notes, form depositions, and a tape recorder, and dictate every question you can possibly think of to elicit the desired information. You will be surprised once you get rolling how many useful questions you can generate. Trying to write the questions in longhand or on a word processor takes too long and is not as productive as the tape recorder. Have a working document typed that you can edit and add to as needed.

As you are going through materials and generating questions, be sure to write down each document that needs to be gathered for your attorney for use or to be introduced at the deposition. A possible format for the outline appears in Exhibit 8:5.[6]

EXHIBIT 8:5 ■ Sample Deposition Outline

CASE: Smith v. Jones
DEPONENT: Albert Smith-Plaintiff

DEPO DATE: 6 Jan 1990
LOCATION: 1421 6th Avenue, Sacramento

ATTYS: E. Gibson for Jones
       N. Mason for Smith

Items to Cover	Testimony	Exhibit Desc. & No.
ID: Name, Address, & Telephone	Albert Smith 2130 "I" Street Sacramento 777/333-2222	
SSN	238-45-9726	
Age, DOB	47, 9/14/50	
Education	Wilson HS, Sacramento, 1968 Stanford, BS Math, 1972 UCLA, MS Math, 1974	
Employment	Stanford, Asst. Prof, Math Dept; 1973-1974 State of CA Dept of Highways Statistician; 1974-present	

Docs reviewed prior to deposition	Accident report
	Statistics on accidents in location of
	   accident in this matter
	Report of raw data on which statistics
	   are based
		Acc. Report, Exh. 1
		Statistics, Exh. 2
		
		Raw data docs, Exh. 3

Source: Reprinted with permission of Delmar Learning, a division of Thomson Learning: www.thomsonrights.com.

The advantage of such an outline form is that it lists the questions or topics on one side and permits comments, notations, documents that need to be introduced, or evaluation of the answer on the other side. This format will help the attorney at the deposition. It also permits highlighting of questions that the attorney may choose to use out of chronological sequence to elicit a more spontaneous and less planned answer from the deponent.

Once the outline is in good draft form, it should be reviewed by the attorney. Amendments should be added, and a final outline prepared. Extra copies should be made for the form file if there are no other good examples.

Gather and Prepare Documents and Exhibits

Each of the documents or photographs the attorney plans to introduce for authentication or needs for reference should be gathered and placed in separate, clearly labeled manila folders. Sufficient copies of each document should also be in the folder, allowing the attorney to mark up one copy as needed or to give copies to the other attorneys at the deposition. Other physical items requiring introduction should be gathered.

Some exhibits may need to be located, purchased, or prepared. Preparation of exhibits will be discussed later in the chapter on preparing for trial. Most attorneys agree that witnesses have an easier time and are more accurate if they refer to a diagram or some other visual exhibit. These should also be organized in the order they will be needed by the attorney.

Set Up Witness Files

A good witness file is particularly important to conducting a good deposition. You can begin to organize a witness file as it becomes clear that a particular witness will play a role at deposition and probably later at trial. The file should be organized prior to the scheduled deposition of the witness and should contain the following:

A witness information sheet (see Chapter 3)

The deposition outline or questions

Documents by or concerning the witness arranged chronologically or as needed at the deposition

An extra set of documents that you or the attorney may mark on during the deposition

Discovery information gained through interrogatories, admissions, or other requests

Allegations in the pleadings

Notice of deposition, subpoenas, and certificate of service

The witness file should be arranged according to the specifications of the supervising attorney. A small three-ring binder with all pertinent documents placed loosely at the back in separate, clearly labeled folders seems to aid organization and quick access. A separate witness file should be maintained for each witness to be deposed or later examined at trial.

Assist in the Preparation of the Client or Witness for Testimony

Preparing clients or witnesses for deposition testimony is extremely important, because what they say, how effective they appear, and how certain they are of the facts may well determine whether the case is settled in the client's favor or heads for a full-blown expensive trial. Further, if the case does go to trial and the witnesses' answers are not well thought out, there is considerable likelihood that the opponent will use the deposition to show inconsistencies and inaccuracies that will harm the witnesses' credibility in the eyes of the jury.

You can play an important role in seeing to it that the witnesses do the best job they can. In many law offices the paralegal's role is primarily one of communication, keeping the witness informed on what to expect and when to expect it. This task involves timely correspondence, phone calls, and coordinating meetings with the attorney. In some offices the paralegal is used even more effectively by working directly with the witness. In this case the client or witness comes to the office where the paralegal assists the attorney by addressing the witness's anxiety, counseling on testifying techniques, and answering questions. Frequently the firm takes the witness through a mock examination. The paralegal can help by having questions ready that are likely to be asked by the opponent.

The experienced paralegal occasionally participates in questioning the witness during the mock examination.

You may have the responsibility of informing the client or witness what to expect and how to handle the deposition, which is frequently accomplished through a letter, brochure, or video on testifying. Many law firms use commercial products for this purpose; others develop their own list of suggestions. Check with the office.

There are numerous ways you can assist at a preparation conference: making suggestions to the witness, observing the witness in mock examination and noting weak or ineffective areas, doing the questioning while the attorney notes problems, and other possibilities. You may need to be assertive at this stage in suggesting ways to render assistance.

Exhibit 8:6 is a sample letter that serves two purposes; first, it shows the form of a letter that many paralegals are called on to draft and send to clients, and second, it covers the most significant tips that should be passed on to a client, whether by letter or in a conference at the office. Some attorneys would rather not send out detailed instruction letters to clients. Such letters may be used against the client or attorney, so they prefer to handle such things in an office visit. Check with your supervising attorney. The proposed letter can be used as a checklist on what to tell the client at such an appointment.

A letter such as in Exhibit 8:6 should be followed by an appointment with the attorney, possibly including yourself. At that time any additional directions can be conveyed. If given responsibility for guiding the witness, keep in mind some matters of concern:

- It is unethical for an attorney or attorney's agent to tell a client what to say to answer questions, either at deposition or at trial. To do so greatly influences the witness, and may unintentionally lead to perjury or cause the witness to believe that you or the attorney condones such dishonesty. Even if you or the attorney knows a particular answer is true, specific answers should not be suggested. Any breach of this ethical standard is extremely serious and the slightest implication of impropriety can be damaging to the case and the reputation of the attorney. This admonition applies to the substantive part of an answer. It does not, however, apply to a nonsubstantive preface to an answer. For example, it is not uncommon for an attorney to ask a question that states facts not yet proven. Rather than have the deponent answer the question as if the facts were true, it would not be unethical to coach the client to say, "assuming your facts are correct," as a preface to a substantive answer.

"Challenging an expert and questioning his expertise is the lifeblood of our legal system—whether it is a psychiatrist discussing mental disturbances, a physicist testifying on the environmental impact of a nuclear power plant, or a General Motors executive insisting on the impossibility of meeting Federal antipollution standards. . . . It is the only way a judge or jury can decide whom to trust."

—DAVID L. BAZELON, CHIEF JUDGE, U.S. COURT OF APPEALS, *DALLAS TIMES HERALD*, MAY 13, 1973.

EXHIBIT 8:6 ■ Letter to Client Regarding Deposition

WHITE, WILSON & McDUFF
ATTORNEYS AT LAW
FEDERAL PLAZA BUILDING, SUITE 700
THIRD AND MARKET STREETS
LEGALVILLE, COLUMBIA 00000
(111) 555-0000

Ms. Ann Forrester
1533 Capitol Drive
Legalville, Columbia 00000

November 1, _____

Dear Ms. Forrester:

As we previously discussed, the time has come when you will need to testify about the accident and your injuries at a deposition. We will work with you to prepare for the deposition. Mr. White will be with you and is confident you will do just fine.

The deposition is scheduled for Wednesday, December 2, _____, at 10:00 a.m. in room 202 in the Federal District Court Building at Third and Race Streets. Parking is available at the Municipal Parking facility behind the courthouse. Please be there by 9:30 a.m.

A deposition is an examination of a witness under oath by the opposition and in the presence of a court reporter. The examination is to determine the witness's version of the facts, the evidence in support of those facts, and the location of the evidence and names and addresses of persons having information about the evidence. It is an important stage in the lawsuit because the other side will be evaluating you as a witness, including your appearance, ability to recall facts, truthfulness, etc. Depositions produce evidence that might lead to a settlement of the case. They may also be used at trial to test the consistency and credibility of a witness. Therefore, good preparation on your part is important. It will give you confidence.

In preparing for the deposition, please keep the following in mind:

1. Depositions are occasionally postponed, and if so, you will be informed.
2. Chronologically review the facts of the case up through your current medical status; anticipate questions on dates, times, directions, distances, speeds, weather, clothes, events, injuries, medical treatments, expenses, witnesses, statements, etc. If you do not know distances and the like for sure, reasonable approximations are acceptable. A return to the scene of the accident to check distances, obstructions, and other details before your deposition might be helpful.
3. Be sure you have informed your attorney of all matters about the incident and those that reflect on your own honesty and credibility. Do not allow your attorney to be surprised to your detriment.
4. Expect the opponent's attorney to do most or all of the questioning. Your attorney will object when it is necessary.
5. Dress neatly, be pleasant, and speak up.
6. Listen to each question carefully. If you do not understand the question, *do not guess at its meaning,* simply state you do not understand.
7. Think about your answer; do not blurt out answers. Be cautious of a series of questions in quick succession that intend to lead you to the answer your opponent desires. Answer thoughtfully at your own pace.
8. Above all, tell the truth. You will be under oath and should avoid giving in to the temptation to fill in gaps of information. Do not guess. Should you want to correct an earlier answer, simply indicate your desire to do so. The attorney will assist you.

Exhibit 2:2 ■ Checklist Form: Automobile Accident (*continued*)

9. If you are asked, "Did you speak with your attorney about testifying today?" answer "yes." There is nothing wrong with speaking with your attorney about testifying. If the question is, "Did your attorney tell you what to say?" the correct answer is, "He told me to tell the truth." Other than that, your attorney will not tell you what to say.

10. While testifying, it is preferable that you not seek guidance from your attorney. You must answer the question as best you can. If your attorney feels a question is improper, an objection will be stated. An objection is a signal to you to stop answering.

11. A common technique of adverse attorneys is to remain silent after your answer. They frequently do this in the hope that you will feel compelled to add more information. It can be damaging information. Therefore, resist the temptation to add information and to fill silences.

12. Avoid discussing your case and any aspect of your testimony with anyone other than your attorney. Casual conversation about your case can be damaging.

13. You may be asked at the deposition to sketch a diagram of the accident scene. If you try some practice sketches, you should not have any difficulty with this.

14. During the deposition you may be given documents, diagrams, photographs, or other items to identify. Be sure to examine such items carefully to see that they accurately reflect what they intend to reflect before you agree to their accuracy.

15. Be prepared to describe your injuries and medical treatment in detail. Do not exaggerate or understate.

16. Be prepared to discuss any injuries you suffered or claims you made before this accident.

17. Bring any documents that you have been requested to bring.

18. Be prepared to discuss changes such as loss of pay, property damage, and other out-of-pocket expenses.

19. It is not necessary to memorize possible answers and is probably better if you do not.

In summary, you will do the best job at your deposition if you are well prepared, thoughtful, deliberate, and truthful. I will be contacting you soon to set up a time when you and Mr. White can meet to discuss the deposition. Meanwhile, if you have any questions or concerns, please feel free to contact me or Mr. White.

Very truly yours,

Terry Salyer
Paralegal

- In going over questions that might be asked the witness, watch for questions that call for privileged information or the attorney's work product. Such matters should be called to the attention of the attorney so the client can be instructed accordingly and any necessary protective orders can be sought.

- When working with a witness as opposed to a client, many of the same suggestions apply. One additional suggestion is to stress to the witness the importance of impartiality. If the witness appears too sympathetic to the client or too eager to help, it may cause the jury to question the reliability of the witness and possibly discount the testimony.

- It is not a good idea to have witnesses, including clients, review documents and recorded statements prior to depositions or trial. The other side is entitled to a copy of a document that a witness has reviewed to refresh his or her memory of the events. Such a document can be damaging and especially useful to the opposition for impeaching the friendly witness.

The best approach is to try to get the client to recall facts by asking questions and discussing information rather than having the client read the document.

- A set of form deposition questions can be used to simulate the deposition. An attempt to anticipate unusual questions that will likely be asked by the opponent is usually well worth the effort.

ATTEND AND REVIEW THE DEPOSITION

You may be asked to attend the deposition with the supervising attorney. This may depend on the complexity of the deposition and whether the cost of a paralegal's attendance is justified. Some insurance companies will not pay for the paralegal to attend. Ideally, you should have the opportunity to attend one or more depositions prior to doing any deposition work. That experience provides a better understanding of the entire process and leads to a better job of assisting the attorney and the witness in all steps of deposition practice.

At the deposition your most important role is to listen carefully. If your attorney is doing the questioning, follow along on the outline of questions. The paralegals for both sides should take notes on significant information, contradictions, objections, and observations about the effectiveness of the witness and opposing counsel. Listening and observing carefully are important factors because the supervising attorney will occasionally be too distracted to be a good listener. You should be able to make suggestions, catch topics or questions that have been missed, and detect evasiveness, inconsistencies, or lies. You can also make sure information and documents are quickly retrieved when needed, that the law is researched on a point that arises in the deposition, or that an important phone call is made. Keep in mind that a paralegal may not question the deponent. To do so is the practice of law. It is generally acceptable for a paralegal to be the only person from the office to attend a deposition if the paralegal's only role is to observe, listen, and take notes.

It is also important for you to understand the rules governing procedure at the deposition. Federal Rule of Civil Procedure 30(b)(4) calls for the oath officer to start the deposition by entering into the record preliminary information about the oath officer, date, time and place of the deposition, deponent, administration of the oath, and the parties. The parties may agree to have one of the attorneys do this preliminary task.

Objections made to the qualifications of the oath officer, the manner of taking the deposition, the evidence presented, conduct of any party, or any other aspect of the proceeding shall be entered into the record by the officer [Rule 30(c) and parallel state rules]. Objections shall be concise, nonargumentative, and shall not suggest an answer to the deponent [Rule 30(d)(1)]. The deposition continues, however, subject to the objections. A deponent may be instructed not to answer only if to preserve a privilege, to enforce any court-imposed limits on the deposition, or to present a motion regarding conducting the deposition in bad faith or for unreasonably annoying, embarrassing, or oppressive questioning [Rule 30(d)(1) and (3)]. The appropriate court may stop or limit the deposition if serious bad faith or similar violations occur, and may impose any necessary sanctions. Once stopped, a deposition cannot resume except by court order [Rule 30(d)(3)].

If a deponent or a party wants to review the transcript, that request must be made before the deposition is completed, and the request is entered into the record [Rule 30(d)]. Under the Federal Rules, unless this request is made, a party or deponent waives the right to review and list changes in the form or substance of the testimony.

At the end of the deposition, the oath officer shall record that the deposition is complete and place any important stipulations into the record, such as who will have custody of the transcript.

Immediately following the deposition, compare notes with the attorney and draft a summary of the deposition based on those notes and other impressions. This summary allows discovery to progress and avoids having to wait for the typed transcript before other discovery decisions are made.

Following the deposition, the court reporter will prepare the transcript. If the deponent or a party requested to review the transcript, the oath officer notifies the deponent that the record is ready, then the deponent has thirty days in which to review the transcript or recording [Rule 30(e)]. If the deponent wants to submit changes in the form or substance of the deposition, that must be done in a signed, written statement detailing the changes and the reasons for the changes. The officer certifies that this review was requested and appends the changes to the transcript or recording. Your state procedure may vary.

Where state rules require it, check to see that the deponent signs the transcript. If the deponent refuses to sign it, the court reporter should sign it and state the reason why the witness would not sign. Verify that the court reporter has certified in writing that the witness was duly sworn by the officer and that the deposition is a true record of the testimony given by the witness [Rule 30(f)]. The deposition is then sealed and filed with the court or sent to the attorney who arranged for the transcript or recording. That attorney has the duty to protect the integrity of the transcript or recording. The officer is required to keep a copy so the other parties can request and receive copies as well. On request of a party, documents and things produced for inspection during the deposition should be marked as exhibits and attached to the deposition following the procedures outlined in Rule 30(f)(1). Verifying that the requirements have been met assures the deposition's effective use at trial if needed.

On receipt of the deposition transcript, review it carefully. Any questions omitted by the attorney should be noted so they can be asked through interrogatories or at trial. Inconsistencies in a witness's testimony should also be noted. For example, in one part of the transcript the witness might say the van was traveling at thirty-five to forty miles per hour and twenty pages later say it seemed like less than thirty. Such inconsistency can be used to impeach the witness. The review may also reveal inaccuracies or omissions in the reporting.

DIGESTING DEPOSITIONS AND OTHER DOCUMENTS

INTRODUCTION AND DEFINITION

Whether you are confronted with medical records, depositions, trial transcripts, a party's written statement, commercial records, expert reports, or other documents, it is critical to reduce the volume of information to a format that affords the attorney a concise and accurate summary with a handy reference for locating the complete language in the original documents. To that end, this section focuses on digesting (summarizing) documents, using depositions as the primary example. The methods used to digest depositions are applicable to most other documents. Once each deposition or each significant document is summarized, the information on each point can be organized under topical headings. Such a format permits evidence

"A word must become a friend or you will not understand it. Perhaps you do well to be cool and detached when you are seeking information, but I remind you of the wife who complained, "When I ask John if he loves me, he thinks I am asking for information."

—Sir Edward Coke, *Case of Swans*, 7 Rep. 15, 17 (1592).

from one or more witnesses to be compared, evaluated for evidentiary weight, and examined for inconsistencies and weaknesses.

Paralegals practice the art frequently and soon become good digesters. Digesting depositions can become tedious at times, but the task's overall importance to the success of the client's case cannot be overstressed. The attorney with good digests in hand at trial will be more organized, knowledgeable, decisive, and effective.

PURPOSES FOR DIGESTING DEPOSITIONS

Deposition digests are used for the following purposes:[7]

1. Condense large amounts of material
2. Index testimony and topics
3. Facilitate questioning and cross-examination of witness at trial
4. Lay foundation for production or admissions for discovery
5. Identify items for follow-up investigation or discovery
6. Verify key or disputed facts
7. Reveal inconsistencies in evidence or testimony
8. Review for trial or additional depositions
9. Support summary judgment and other motions
10. Include relevant facts or testimony in briefs
11. Cross-reference topics, witnesses, evidence
12. Bring new attorneys or paralegals up to speed on a case
13. Inform client
14. Prepare correspondence, settlement brochures, and material relevant to pretrial and other hearings

TECHNIQUES FOR DIGESTING DEPOSITIONS

Being a good digester takes language skills, time, and experience. Doing a good digest, however, even the first time, is not difficult. Here are some techniques for a good start in this area.

1. Study the file to grasp the claim, defenses, issues, and legal theories.
2. Ask the attorney to provide the outline of the questions used at the deposition that gives an overview and suggestions for topical headings, and guidance on the type of digest and indexes desired, location of examples of similar summaries, desired detail, paraphrased or ellipsis format (see number 13 below), time frame, cost, need of extra assistance, key issues, key individuals, and any other special requests.
3. Skim the entire deposition first; develop a feel for its scope, importance, issues addressed, and topics for digest headings.
4. Draft a topical outline or tentative table of contents for the digest, placing topics in the order raised in the deposition, for example:
   - Personal background
   - Education
   - Prior injuries
   - Other information (repeat headings where necessary)
5. Schedule blocks of time to do actual digesting so you will not lose sight of the continuity of the entire deposition and forget what topics have previously been addressed.
6. Handwrite, type, dictate, or better yet, compose on the word processor. The last affords immediate editing while the deposition is fresh in mind, not

always the case when written or dictated drafts take days to be typed. If your office computerizes depositions by full text, make another computer copy of the deposition and do your editing and summarizing on the computer. Delete irrelevant information, leaving only the most essential information to work with. If the depositions are not computerized, make a photocopy and delete unnecessary language and take notes on the photocopy.

7. Be as concise as possible. Eliminate unnecessary words: article adjectives such as "the," "an," "a"; previous or proper nouns if the reference is clear; exchanges between attorneys; and false starts in questioning or answering by the attorneys or deponent. Reduction quotas, such as one digest page for every ten pages of transcript, are not particularly helpful.[8]

8. Use abbreviations and short forms as much as possible, but be sure they are clear: re = regarding; ex = exhibit; 12/3/01 = December 3, 2001; w/ = with; w/o = without; ∴ = therefore, ≅ = approximately, and so on.

9. Be accurate about what witnesses said. Use the witnesses' key words. Avoid distortion for the sake of obtaining a briefer phrase or having the digest coincide with your own understanding of the material. *Do not interpret!*

10. Use subheadings frequently and write in short paragraphs.

11. Use page and line number references in the margins and/or in a paragraph of summarized material, indicating where the full text of the summarized information can be found in the original transcript.

12. Utilize the "sheet" or "slip" method of recording. The sheet method condenses several pages of transcript into a single sheet of letter-size paper. Sheets are topically labeled as the topics arise in the deposition; as pertinent information is read it is summarized onto the appropriate topic sheet. The slip method employs index cards (slips) to record each new piece of information, noting the original line and page number as well as topic on the card. The individual cards provide greater flexibility, permitting the cards to be organized sequentially by page or by topic or according to some other need before typing.[9]

13. Utilize the "paraphrase" or the "ellipsis" method of summary. The paraphrase method is a concise restatement in paragraph form of what the witness said. The ellipsis method is a chronological listing of significant statements in sentence fragments preceded by ellipsis points (. . .). An example of each appears in Exhibit 8:7, a sample deposition digest form.

14. Include, in addition to the obvious, all dates exactly as mentioned, all exhibits by name and number with attached exhibit list referring to pages where the exhibit is identified, court reporter's notes on the witness's behavior, substantive objections, admissions, stipulations, document requests, and any notes by the attorney or yourself on the effectiveness of the witness.[10]

> ". . . the lawyer's vacation is the space between the question put to a witness and his answer!"
>
> —RUFUS CHOATE, 1799–1859, IN SAMUEL GILMAN BROWN, *THE WORKS OF RUFUS CHOATE*, 1862.

TYPES OF DEPOSITION DIGESTS AND INDEXES

The prior techniques can be applied to create various types of deposition digests. Deposition digests (summaries) have a variety of names and formats. Eventually, you will need to choose the format that works best for you in a particular situation. Here are some formats for your consideration.

The *chronological* (sequential or page/line) summary condenses the deposition in the order that matters were raised. Each summarized fact or answer is referenced to its page and line in the transcript. Appearance of exhibits and the deponent's comments on them are also noted. The chronological digest should have a table of

EXHIBIT 8:7 ■ Deposition Digest (Chronological)

DEPOSITION DIGEST

CASE: Smith v. Jones Dixon Sup Crt #234 567
DEPONENT: Albert Hackston
DATE: 7/25/01

Page: Contents
Atty: G. Baker
L/A: N. LUONO

TABLE OF CONTENTS/TOPICAL INDEX

Topic	Page	Lines
1. Personal Data	1	6–12
2. Education		
High School	2	6–8
On-the-job Training	2	17–20
	10	3–5
3. Employment History		
Prior to Employment w/Plaintiff	5	
Employment w/Plaintiff	6	1–4
	11	17–20
	33	12–17

DEPOSITION DIGEST (CHRONOLOGICAL)

DEPONENT: Albert Hackston   Page 1

Pg.	Ln.	Topic	Summary	Exhib/Notes
1	6–12	Personal Data	Born 6/1/60, Detroit, MI, married, 2 children, lives at 1400 North Ave., Detroit	Speaks very softly
2	6–8	Education	Finished H.S. 77	
	17–20		OJT 1 year Army	Most recent training
3	10	Safety Training	(*Paraphrase method*) Hackston had read the instructions in detail and received 4 hours of OJT before operating the machine. In June 1999 he watched the disassembly and reassembly of the machine. It was frequently serviced and he specifically recalled preventive maintenance was performed on Sept. 8, '99.	
3	10	Safety Training	(*Ellipsis method*) . . . he had read the instructions in detail.	
	13		. . . he had 4 hours of OJT before using it.	
	18		. . . saw the apparatus disassembled and reassembled in June 1999 . . .	
4	6		. . . he was present when preventive maintenance was performed Sept. 8, '99	

EXHIBIT 8:7 ▪ Deposition Digest (Chronological) *(continued)*

DEPOSITION DIGEST
DEPONENT: Albert Hackston   Page: Exhibit Index

EXHIBIT INDEX

EXHIBIT NUMBER	DESCRIPTION
1	Ch. 3, "Safety," ST 3 Trng. Man'l dated 5/10/98
2	St 3 Operating Instructions dated 9/20/98
3	OJT Training Certificate dated 2/19/99

Source: Reprinted with permission of Delmar Learning, a division of Thomson Learning: www.thomsonrights.com.

contents or topical index that states the topics as they arise in the deposition with appropriate page references. These can be made easily from the information on the sheets or the slips. Exhibit 8:7 is an example of the format for a chronological deposition digest beginning with a table of contents or topical index and ending with an exhibit index.[11]

The *topical* (category, subject) digest is organized by topics and subtopics. Each of the deponent's answers that addresses a particular topic, regardless of where it appears in the transcript, is collected under that topical heading. These answers may then be organized as they appear in the transcript. The slip method of recording lends itself particularly well to this type of summary. An appropriate table of contents should be prepared. Sample pages from a topical deposition digest appear in Exhibit 8:8.

An increasing number of court reporters prepare transcripts that condense several pages of deposition transcript into one. If this practice is the case in your jurisdiction, you may need to adapt the traditional page/line emphasis according to what your attorney prefers. In addition, many court reporters provide indexing services. With a list of topics (key words) provided by you, the reporter can compile an index showing on what page that topic is mentioned.[12]

The *narrative* digest incorporates the paraphrase method of complete sentences and may be organized by topic, witness, or other categories depending on the attorney's needs. Narrative digests are particularly good to send to a client such as an insurance company so the client can get an understanding of the nature of the evidence in the case.[13] An example of a page from a narrative digest arranged by topic is in Exhibit 8:9.

DIGEST AIDS FOR COMPLEX CASES

If there are numerous deponents, you may be asked to perform several tasks to assist the attorney in trial preparation as well as at the trial. First, a master topical digest can be developed to collect the comments of all deponents on a particular topic under the respective topical heading. This type of digest facilitates a quick review of all evidence, including exhibits, from all deponents on a particular key point. A master topical digest should also include references to page, line, and deponent.

EXHIBIT 8:8 ■ Page Extracts from Topical (Subject) Deposition Summaries

TOPICAL DEPOSITION SUMMARY

Case: FORRESTER v. MERCURY PARCEL

Case File No. _____   Page 1

Deponent: Ann Forrester   Attorney: L. Ott

Date: 12/10/___   Paralegal: C. Sorenson

TOPIC: INJURIES

Page	Line	Summary	Exhibits/ Notes
38	3	Date of accident 2/26/___ ... she felt sharp pain at point of impact.	
	6	... pain was extreme in hip, lower abdomen, and upper left leg.	
39	1	... she felt nauseated.	
53–54	28–1	Date: 3/10/___ ... after two weeks in hospital the leg felt numb and she could not move it. etc.	

TOPIC: EMPLOYMENT

Page	Line	Summary	Exhibits/ Notes
62	7	... she said she rarely missed work before the accident.	
66	12	... believed she would have been promoted by now to master teacher.	
71	2	... does not see how she can return to teaching with her current disabilities. etc.	

The preparation of more complex cases can also be assisted by the compilation of subindexes that list all deponents, all exhibits, or are organized by topic.

AUTOMATED DEPOSITION SUMMARIES

Many court reporters now provide depositions and other transcripts on disk. The transcript can then be downloaded to the law office computers, dramatically enhancing the paralegal's ability to summarize, annotate, index, locate, and otherwise manipulate the information. Software specifically for summarizing transcripts and other information is readily available. Programs such as *Summation iBlaze®*, *Concordance*, and others make digesting more interesting and efficient, and are

EXHIBIT 8:9 ▪ Deposition Digest (Narrative)

DEPOSITION DIGEST (NARRATIVE/TOPICAL)

CASE: Johns v. Brown No. Civ 880050   Page 1
DEPONENT: Catherine Johns

                                                             Atty: H. Ray
DATE: 7/16/01   Plgl: C. Borden

Background

Catherine Johns is 34 years old, residing at 1437 Oak St., Legalville, Columbia, is divorced and has one child, Edward, 10. (pages 1–2)

She has a master's in business administration from Columbia State and her high school diploma from East Legalville H.S. (3)

Employment

She worked for two years after high school for Columbia Foods as a secretary from 1993–95. She has worked for Fairmont Computers as a market analyst from 2000 to the present, earning $30,000 per year. (4–5)

The Accident

On May 3, 2000, Johns was driving to work, proceeding north on Holiday Blvd. in Legalville at 7:40 A.M. She was wearing a seat belt. She drove a 1999 Chevrolet Camaro and was 200 feet from the intersection of Holiday and East Twenty-third St. when defendant, Harold Brown, suddenly backed out of his driveway at 3201 Holiday Blvd. in his 2000 Buick Le Sabre. (9, 32)

Johns "swung car to left" but the back of Brown's car hit hers in the Camaro's left front. (10–11)

Johns' car "lurched" into oncoming traffic lane, crossed lane avoiding car driven by Walter Forth, went up curb and "smashed" into Roy's Hot Dog Stand and stopped. (11–12, 23)

Injuries

Johns hit her head on the steering wheel, breaking her nose and cheekbone. Ligaments in her left knee were severed, and she suffered muscle damage and internal injuries to the stomach lining causing internal bleeding. (14, 27)

Johns was rushed to Mount Sinai Hospital where she was admitted and operated on to correct fractures, stop internal bleeding, and repair ligaments in knee. Minor plastic surgery was performed on her nose by Dr. Kizar on 7/2/00. (15, 28)

One year after accident Johns still needs cane to walk. The fractures have healed satisfactorily but chewing is limited and painful, and one obvious scar remains on her nose. (16, 28–30).

Loss of Employment

(narrative continues)

designed to utilize the summarizing formats already discussed, and others. This software enables the paralegal to monitor live depositions on-line, annotate and mark the deposition in real-time, access multiple depositions and other document depositories simultaneously, download documents, and, of course, summarize the deposition. See the Web site addresses at the end of this chapter to access more information about software and on-line services.

Exhibit 8:10 is an excerpt from the transcript (absent page and line numbers) of a deposition of Mr. Hart.

EXHIBIT 8:10 ■ Deposition of Richard Hart

UNITED STATES DISTRICT COURT FOR THE EASTERN DISTRICT OF COLUMBIA

ANN FORRESTER
  and
WILLIAM FORRESTER,
               Plaintiffs

     v.
RICHARD HART
  and
MERCURY PARCEL SERVICE, INC.,
              Defendants

Civil Action, File No._____

Cincinnati, Ohio, Wednesday, January 12,_____

    Pretrial examination of Richard Hart held in the offices of Ott, Ott & Knudsen, 444 Front St., Cincinnati, Ohio, at 10:00 A.M. on the above date before Bernadette Schaffer, Certified Court Reporter and Notary of Ohio.

    APPEARANCES:
    Arthur White
White, Wilson & McDuff
Attorneys for Plaintiffs

    Lynn Ott
Ott, Ott & Knudsen
Attorneys for Defendants

(signature and certification omitted)

    Richard Hart, after having been duly sworn, was examined and testified as follows:

By Mr. White:

Q. Please state your full name.
A. Richard Hart
Q. Your residence?
A. 1223 Penny Lane, Cincinnati, Ohio.
Q. How long have you lived there?
A. Eight years.
Q. Where did you live prior to that?
A. 4313 East Wickland St., Columbus, Ohio.
Q. How long did you reside there?
A. Seven years.
Q. Are you married?
A. Yes.
Q. Your wife's full name?
A. Jessica Marie Hart.
Q. When were you married?
A. Seventeen years ago. June 19_____.
Q. Do you have any children?
A. Yes, two boys.
Q. What are their names and ages?

EXHIBIT 8:10 ■ Deposition of Richard Hart *(continued)*

A. Brett is sixteen and Jerome is fourteen.

Q. When and where were you born?

A. August 13, 19_____, I am forty-one.

Q. Where?

A. Oh, ah . . . Columbus, Ohio.

Q. How far did you go in school?

A. I graduated from high school.

Q. Where did you attend high school?

A. Taft High in Columbus.

Q. What, if any, schooling have you had since high school?

A. I was trained as an ambulance driver by the army and took a truck driving course about twelve years ago.

Q. When were you in the army?

A. Twenty years ago, 19_____ to 19_____, for two years.

Q. How extensive was your training?

A. A few weeks each year.

Q. Where was your training?

A. Fort Oglethorp, Georgia.

Q. Did you ever have any special training for driving on ice and snow?

A. No, but I have lived in Columbus most of my life and we get plenty of winter weather.

Q. Where was the truck driving course?

A. In Cincinnati.

Q. What was the name of the school?

A. The Cincinnati Vocational Institute.

Q. How long was the course?

A. Six weeks.

Q. Did you learn how to drive vans at this school?

A. No, it was for large rigs.

Q. Did they give you any special training for winter driving?

A. They were supposed to, but we never got to it.

Q. Have you ever received any formal training for driving in wintery weather?

A. No.

Q. Not even with Mercury Parcel?

A. No.

Q. What is your current occupation?

A. Route man.

Q. Would you explain what a route man is?

A. O.K. I drive a truck—or van—and deliver parcels and things to people and stores over a certain route.

Q. What route do you cover?

A. We cover several different ones—sometimes we fill in for a guy that's sick.

Q. Are you assigned to the Legalville, Columbia route very often?

A. Oh, sure.

Q. Have you ever made deliveries on Capitol Drive outside of Legalville before?

A. No . . . possibly . . . I'm not sure.

Q. Would any records of your deliveries indicate whether you had been out there before?

A. They might. It's probably been years ago.

Q. How long ago?

A. Maybe five or six years ago . . . I don't know.

Q. What records might show that?

A. We have to fill out a record of delivery form—it has addresses on it.

(continued)

EXHIBIT 8:10 ■ Deposition of Richard Hart (*continued*)

Q. Do they show every delivery?

A. Yes.

Q. Does this form have a number?

A. I think so. It . . . it's a Form 30.

Q. Who is your current employer?

A. Mercury.

Q. Do you mean the Mercury Parcel Service?

A. Yes.

Q. How long have you worked for them?

A. Let's see, two years in Columbus and eight years in Cincinnati. Ten years.

Q. Is this full-time employment?

A. Yes.

Q. Have you worked in any capacity other than route man for Mercury?

A. No.

Q. How much do you earn an hour?

A. $10.35 an hour.

Q. How many hours per week?

A. Usually 40 . . . unless we need to work overtime.

Q. How often do you work overtime?

A. Every so often when someone is sick or we have a lot to deliver . . . or if we volunteer to put in some extra time.

Q. Where did you work prior to working for Mercury?

A. I worked as an ambulance driver for the town of Jackson just outside Columbus. There was always trouble getting adequate funds to keep the service going, so I quit and went with Mercury.

Q. What is the address for that service?

A. If it's still there—it is Route 3, Highway 95, Jackson, Ohio.

Q. How long did you work for the ambulance service?

A. Six years.

Q. Have you had a good driving record?

A. Yes.

Q. Have you had any accidents either on or off the job?

A. Well, yes. I think most folks do.

Q. When did you have the accidents?

A. Well, I had one two years ago in Cincinnati, and . . .

Q. Were you driving for Mercury at the time of the accident?

A. Yes, I was.

Q. What happened?

A. I was trying to exit off I-75 and a guy was trying to enter I-75. They cross there. I thought he was by me and he slowed down. I ran into his left side. No one was hurt, thank goodness.

Q. Were any citations issued by the police?

A. No.

Q. Have you had any other accidents?

A. Yes, I had one about five years ago in Columbus.

Q. What happened?

A. My family and I were heading for downtown Columbus to see a Fourth of July parade. I was in a line of stopped traffic. The line began to move. I turned to say something to my wife. The car in front of me stopped and I rammed into it. An elderly lady got hurt but my insurance company paid for her doctor bills.

Q. Were any citations issued?

A. Yes, I got a ticket for inattentive driving.

EXHIBIT 8:10 ▪ Deposition of Richard Hart *(continued)*

Q. Any other accidents?

A. Not that I recall.

Q. Have you received any other traffic citations?

A. Well, a few over the years.

L. Ott: Let the record reflect that I object to this question on the grounds that it is not relevant to the accident in question.

Mr. White: Counselor, if there is a pattern of reckless driving, then I believe it is relevant. Your objection is noted. May I proceed?

L. Ott: Yes.

By Mr. White:

Q. What were those citations for?

A. Mainly for speeding.

Q. How many in the last five years?

A. Oh, not too many.

Q. More than five?

A. I guess so.

Q. Six?

A. I think about six.

Q. Where have most of these violations occurred?

A. In the Cincinnati area.

Q. How many occurred on the job?

A. Oh, about half, I'd say.

Q. Mr. Hart, do you recall the accident you had on February 26, _____?

A. Yes, I do.

Q. Were you working for Mercury Parcel at the time of the accident?

A. Yes.

Q. When did you start work that day?

A. I was on the night shift and started at 11:00 P.M. on the twenty-fifth. I was supposed to be back in the barn by 7:00, but I was about two hours behind schedule because of the weather.

Q. So normally on night shift you work from 11:00 P.M. until 7:00 A.M.?

A. Yes.

Q. Were you driving the entire time the night of February 25 to 26?

A. Well, not constantly. We do stop and get out of the truck to deliver the packages or letters. However, because most of the deliveries were in Legalville, and due to the weather, I guess I was driving more than usual.

Q. Did you take any breaks?

A. Yes, the union says we're to get two breaks and a paid half-hour lunch break. That night, though, I only took a break at 3:00 A.M. By lunchtime and the second break I was too far behind to stop.

Q. Other than the weather, did anything else occur that was unusual that night?

A. Not that I recall.

Q. Were you having any mechanical trouble with the truck—like braking or steering problems?

A. Not really. Oh, the van pulls to the left a little when you brake hard, but I knew that and was able to allow for that when I stopped.

Q. How long had that problem existed?

A. Oh, about two weeks. I mentioned it to them about a week before the accident but told them it wasn't too serious.

Q. Who do you mean when you say "them"?

A. A couple of the mechanics at the barn—Mercury's shop.

Q. Can you name them?

A. Well, I think I told Arnie Hanson and I might have told Johnny Sloan . . . I'm not sure about Johnny.

Q. Is there a regular procedure for reporting problems with a vehicle?

(continued)

EXHIBIT 8:10 ■ Deposition of Richard Hart (*continued*)

A. No, not really . . . well, there is a form that we're supposed to fill out, but if it is not too serious, we just mention it to one of the mechanics.

Q. What does the mechanic do then?

A. If they can find the time, they'll look at it. If not they wait till their next regular servicing of the van.

Q. Had the problem of pulling to the left been worked on at the shop?

A. No, I don't think so.

Q. Do you always drive the same van?

A. Yes, almost always.

Q. Did you fill out a form on the braking problem?

A. No.

Q. Describe the weather conditions that night.

A. The roads were wet from melting snow at the beginning of the evening, but by mid-shift—say 3:30 A.M.—the roads began to freeze in spots. You had to be careful.

Q. Had you done any slipping that night?

A. Occasionally . . . but nothing serious.

Q. Was there a lot of ice on the roads?

A. Here and there.

Q. What was the road like just before the accident?

A. Well, it wasn't too bad. There were occasional patches of ice, but not too bad.

Q. Was there enough ice to slow you up some? In other words, did you reduce your speed?

A. Oh, maybe five or ten miles an hour . . . but not much. The road really wasn't too bad.

Q. How fast were you going just prior to the accident?

A. Well, I had just looked and I was going at about thirty-five miles per hour.

Q. What do you mean you "just looked"?

A. Well, I looked at the speedometer to check my speed.

Q. Why?

A. Well, I'm not sure . . . I think I was thinking about how late I was going to be getting back home.

Q. Were you anxious to get back to Cincinnati?

A. Yes, it had been a long night.

Q. Were you tired?

A. A little—because of the weather, I think.

Q. Couldn't you have stopped for a break?

A. I could have, but I didn't. I was late enough the way it was.

Q. Had you had any other long shifts that week?

A. The last shift had been snowy, so I was about an hour late that night.

Q. How much sleep did you get the following day, the twenty-fifth?

A. About six hours, I think. My son had a basketball game that afternoon, so I didn't get to sleep quite as much as I usually do.

Q. Are there any company rules about how much sleep you are to have before your shift?

A. No.

Q. Are there any company rules about taking a break if you become tired?

A. Oh, they tell us to pull over if we are real tired, but I felt OK.

Q. How do they tell you to pull over? Is that a rule, or do they mention it at meetings? How is this done?

A. Well, anyone who drives knows that, but I think there are some safety rules posted in the shop.

Q. Do you read those rules?

A. Not really. They're nothing most drivers don't already know.

Q. Are there any limits on how many hours you are supposed to drive at any one time?

A. I think the rule is around seven hours of actual driving time.

Q. How many hours of actual driving time did you drive that night?

EXHIBIT 8:10 ▪ Deposition of Richard Hart *(continued)*

A. Oh, I'd say about eight, maybe nine.

Q. And had the accident not occurred, you would have had nearly two more hours of driving?

A. Yes.

Q. Is there any penalty for driving over the limit of hours?

A. Not that I know of.

Q. On bad weather nights, or if you're late for any other reason, do you get paid overtime?

A. Only if the extra hours are unavoidable, such as for bad weather.

Q. Would you please describe the road you were driving at the time of the accident?

A. The road was quite narrow, hilly, and curvy.

Q. What was the posted speed limit on that road?

A. I'm not sure.

Q. Would you characterize the road as tricky?

A. Oh, maybe a little . . . but I have driven a lot of roads worse than that.

Q. You mentioned before that you looked at your speedometer just before the accident. What happened next?

A. Well, I looked up and suddenly there was this lady stepping out onto the road.

Q. You looked at your speedometer just before the accident occurred?

A. Yes, I glanced at it—only for a split second.

Q. Had you seen the woman before you looked at the speedometer?

A. No.

Q. Why not?

A. Well, she was hidden by a rise in the road. See, there is a dip in the road where the lady was at. I was coming over the hill just before the dip. You can't see to the bottom of the dip. And that's where the lady was.

Q. What happened then?

A. I thought she would stop, but she just kept looking ahead and kept walking into the road.

Q. What do you mean she just kept looking ahead?

A. Well, when I came over the hill she was barely onto the road. I thought she would see or hear me and stop, but her head was tucked down into her coat and she just kept walking.

Q. Did you sound your horn?

A. No.

Q. What did you do?

A. I hit the brakes.

Q. Then what?

A. The truck began to pull to the left . . . it began to fishtail back and forth. I pumped the brakes to keep control. The lady looked up then, but hesitated and then went the wrong way. I couldn't avoid her. I was trying to get control of the van and then I heard the thump. I felt sick—I knew I'd hit her.

Q. What happened then?

A. The van was crossing the middle of the road. I saw the woman fall off from my side of the van. I tried to hold the van under control, but it went into the ditch and hit a tree.

Q. How hard did the van pull to the left when you applied the brakes?

A. It started that way almost immediately. I think it might have been the same problem I described before, or it might have been the ice. I don't know

(Assume that the examination went on to cover what happened after the accident, damages to the van, Mr. Hart's injuries, etc. The opposing counsel would have an opportunity to ask questions, and then the deposition would conclude.)

Mr. White: I have no other questions.

(Witness excused)

(Deposition concluded)

OTHER FOLLOW-UP TASKS

As discovery progresses you can enhance your value to the litigation team by keeping the file current. Important information from documents, interrogatories, digests, investigation, research, and other sources should be regularly integrated into a case summary that includes specific source location references. This process not only better preserves critical information about the case over a long period of time and facilitates a quick review of the case, it also helps identify specific areas of the case that need attention.

SUMMARY

Deposition practice is an indispensable area of paralegal knowledge. Understand what a deposition is, what it can be used for, and what the rules of civil procedure require when taking depositions. Tasks include setting up the deposition, locating a court reporter, sending out notices and subpoenas, assisting witnesses and the attorney in preparing for the deposition, attending the deposition, summarizing it, and performing other follow-up tasks.

Deposition digests come in several formats adaptable to the special needs of a case. Computer software specifically for summarizing depositions and other documents greatly enhances your ability to work efficiently and effectively.

Knowing the issues in a case and what testimony is necessary to prove or refute proof of these issues is the key to good digesting. Condensing large documents and transcripts of testimony down to concise summaries that are well indexed to the originals saves countless hours when planning strategy, negotiating, preparing for trial, and appealing a case.

▣ WORKBOOK

System Folder Assignments, other exercises, a chapter outline, a review test, and other study aids are located in the accompanying workbook.

▣ HELPFUL WEB SITES

http://www.ncraonline.org
   National Court Reporters Association; service for locating court reporters and videographers

http://www.deponet.com
   service for locating and scheduling court reporters, process servers, and legal videographers

http://www.livenote.com
http://www.reallegal.com (DepoStream)
http://www.I-Dep.com
   These sites provide real-time transcript services.

http://www.mapquest.com
   can be used to calculate 100-mile limit for subpoenas for deponents

http://www.dataflight.com
   current information on *Concordance* deposition and LiveNote-compatible products

http://www.summation.com
   current information on the *Summation iBlaze®* deposition product

▣ QUESTIONS FOR STUDY AND REVIEW

1. What is a deposition? What is the purpose of a deposition?
2. What are the advantages and disadvantages of a deposition?
3. How many kinds of depositions are there, and what are their unique functions?
4. What is the time limit on the length of a deposition in federal cases? Your state's cases?
5. What is your role in the deposition process?
6. Identify and give the purpose and benefits of the two types of deposition tracking logs.
7. How do you obtain a subpoena for a deponent? What is the appropriate clerk? What should be included on the subpoena?
8. What are the HIPAA-imposed assurance procedures and pertinent documents that must be employed when using a subpoena to get protected medical information?
9. When are witness and mileage fees required under Rule 45?
10. What should you do to plan and draft an outline for taking a deposition?
11. What should be included in a witness file for the attorney?
12. Why is it important to prepare friendly witnesses or clients for deposition testimony?
13. What are some of the most significant things a witness can be told in preparing for the deposition?
14. What are significant ethical and other considerations that you need to be aware of in working with witnesses?
15. What is your most important role at the deposition? Why?
16. Why should the deponent's signature on the certified copy of the deposition not be waived in most instances?
17. What should you check for on receipt of the record of the deposition from the court reporter?
18. What do you look for when reviewing a deposition?
19. Draft a sample outline for the attorney conducting a deposition.
20. What is the purpose of digesting litigation documents?
21. What skills are needed to be a good digester?
22. What are the important uses of a deposition summary?
23. List the techniques for digesting depositions.
24. Prepare examples of several types of deposition digests.
25. Name two computer products for digesting depositions.

▣ KEY TERMS

deponent	deposition	subpoena	subpoena duces tecum

▣ ENDNOTES

1. Carla Fredrick Lown, *Basic Steps to Avoid the Most-Dreaded Phone Call*, FACTS & FINDINGS, Nov. 2004, 46.
2. WEST'S FEDERAL FORMS § 3429, v. 3A (5th ed.), Notice of Taking Deposition.
3. Anne K. Guillory and Philip Grossman, *A Year in the Life of HIPAA*, KENTUCKY BENCH & BAR, July 2004, 11, and *Defendant's Model Notice Letter for Subpoenas*, LOUISVILLE BAR ASSOCIATION, http://www.loubar.org/HIPAA/.
4. Memo from J. Schuller to J. McCord (March, 1986).
5. Selected from ALAN E. MORRILL, *Deposition Checklist Plaintiff—Automobile*, TRIAL DIPLOMACY 200–11 (2d ed. 1972).
6. NATIONAL ASSOCIATION OF LEGAL ASSISTANTS, MANUAL FOR LEGAL ASSISTANTS, 250 (3d ed. 1999).
7. Piatz, *Organizing and Digesting Depositions*, LEGAL ASSISTANT TODAY, July/Aug. 1990, 45.
8. Hardwick, *Deposition Summaries*, LEGAL ASSISTANT TODAY, Nov./Dec. 1986, 36–37.
9. NATIONAL ASSOCIATION OF LEGAL ASSISTANTS, MANUAL FOR LEGAL ASSISTANTS, 243 (2d ed. 1992).
10. Piatz, *supra* note 7, 47–48.
11. Adapted from NALA MANUAL FOR LEGAL ASSISTANTS, 407, 409 (1st ed. 1979).
12. Clark, *The Art of Summarizing Depositions*, LEGAL ASSISTANT TODAY, Sept./Oct. 1993, 144–145.
13. Piatz, *supra* note 7, 47.

 For additional resources visit our Web site at **http://www.westlegalstudies.com.**

Discovery: Document Production and Control, Medical Exams, Admissions, and Compelling Discovery

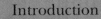

INTRODUCTION

This chapter covers requests for production of documents and things and entry upon land for inspection and other purposes, the related process of document management, and request for physical and mental examination. The section on medical record analysis illustrates techniques a paralegal can use to analyze discovery or other information in a highly technical field. Following this section, we take a look at the request for admissions. In addition, you will find that you can use federal and state freedom of information requests and their benefits as a device that is independent of the formal discovery process. The Federal Rules covering the subject of discovery also contain provisions for compelling discovery, and courts may make use of applicable sanctions against uncooperative parties. The final section suggests how to organize the client's file with the information accumulated through investigation and discovery.

PRODUCTION OF DOCUMENTS AND THINGS AND ENTRY UPON LAND FOR INSPECTION AND OTHER PURPOSES

INTRODUCTION

Production of documents and things is a request made of one party by the other to physically produce and permit the requesting party to inspect, copy, test, or sample documents, electronically stored information, physical evidence, and land and buildings, and is governed by Federal Rule of Civil Procedure 34. Its purpose is to make evidence available to both sides to assess its value and to prevent surprise at trial. More specifically, the requesting party uses the device not only to discover what evidence the other side has, but also to locate evidence damaging to the other side that supports any theories propounded by the requesting party. The request for production and inspection is particularly valuable in business cases and for accessing any tests or information used to form the basis for the testimony of the adversary's expert witnesses. Information discovered in this manner can be valuable in preparing for depositions, settlement proposals, or trial. With the Rule 26(a) disclosure of documents provision or similar state rules, the request for documents and things is more a narrow, follow-up device than a sweeping discovery tool.

Documents may be produced in the context of interrogatories [33(c)], depositions [30(f)(1)], and subpoenas (Rule 45). Rule 34 and parallel state rules, however, are the primary means to require production of documents from another party and, therefore, are the focus of this section.

SCOPE

Rule 34(a) defines the scope of the request and includes the following evidence:

(. . . writings, drawings, graphs, charts, photographs, sound recordings, images, and other data or data compilations stored in any medium—from which information can be obtained—translated, if necessary, by the respondent into reasonably usable form) or to inspect and copy, test, or sample any tangible things which constitute or contain matter within the scope of Rule 26(b) and which are in the possession, custody or control of the party upon whom the request is served; or (2) to permit entry upon designated land or other property in the possession or control of the party upon whom the request is served for the purpose of inspection and measuring, surveying, photographing, testing, or sampling the property or any designated object or operation thereon, within the scope of Rule 26(b).

"... but we find the law, as well as many other pursuits, requires much perseverance and patience to obtain the object; it is well for us that we do not always foresee the degree that it is necessary."

—Susannah Farnum Copley, letter to her daughter, March 15, 1805.

The scope of the rule covers not only tangible (physical) information such as paper documents, but also any type of e-stored information. The request, however, cannot be unreasonably burdensome, oppressive, or unduly disruptive, such as when going to observe the internal workings of a business or manufacturing plant [Rule 26(b)(2)]. Businesses are not expected to disclose commercially valuable trade secrets. Of course, privileged and work product materials and information that are irrelevant or cannot reasonably be expected to lead to admissible evidence are beyond the reach of the rule. Rule 34 contains no specific limits on the number of requests or documents that may be requested; it is, however, objectionable to be unreasonable in the number requested or the period of time (dates) covered by the request. Reasonableness is dictated by the type, value, and complexity of the case.

PROCEDURE

In many nondisclosure jurisdictions the request for production and inspection can be made with the service of the summons and complaint, or at any time after the action starts. Where Rule 26(a) or similar disclosure is in effect, production of documents and things cannot be requested until at or after the parties' discovery planning meeting, unless authorized by the court or otherwise stipulated. The request can be made to any other party. Third persons can be asked to produce documents and things or submit to an inspection through the subpoena duces tecum [Rule 45(a) and 34(c)].

The request may be served directly on the other party without leave of the court and must state the items to be inspected either by individual item or by category with reasonable particularity. It shall also specify a reasonable time, place, and manner for conducting the inspection and any related activities, such as copying or testing. The form or forms in which e-stored information is to be produced may be specified as well [Rule 34(b)].

The responding party must file a reply within thirty days of receipt of the request. A longer period may be in effect in nondisclosure jurisdictions. A shorter or longer period may be required by the court or agreed to by the parties in writing, subject to the restrictions in Rule 29. Rule 29 states that only the court can extend the time specified in Rules 33, 34, and 36 if the requested extension would alter the date for completion of discovery, hearing a motion, or starting a trial. The reply must be written and shall indicate, with respect to each item or category, compliance or any objection (including objection to the requested form for producing e-stored information), specifying the particular part or section of the request objected to and the reasons [Rule 34(b)]. If the form for producing e-stored information is not indicated in the request or is objected to, the responding party must state in which form it intends to produce the information. Any unobjectionable part of an item or category objected to must be produced or made available for inspection. One may not withhold a set of documents because one of the documents requested is objectionable [Rule 34(b)]. The requesting party may move for a court order under Rule 37(a) if they think the refusal or objection is improper. Most states have either parallel or similar procedures, but it is always wise to check.

Unless otherwise agreed or ordered, documents shall be produced either as they are kept in the usual course of business or organized and labeled according to the categories in the request [34(b)(i)]. Unless specified in the request or otherwise agreed or ordered, e-stored information must be produced in a form (or forms) in which it is ordinarily maintained or that is "reasonably usable" [34)b)(ii)]. A party may not take usable information and produce it in a form "that removes or significantly degrades" that usability [Committee Note, Civil Rule Amendments 2006, Rule 34, Subdivision (b)]. To reduce the burden of production, the producing party need only produce any item of e-stored information in one form [Rule 34(b)(iii)].

The cost of complying with a request to produce documents and things in the federal system is generally borne by the producing party [*Oppenheimer Fund Inc. v. Sanders,* 437 U.S. 340 (1978)]. Where costs are particularly burdensome, such as in large e-discovery cases, courts are increasingly inclined to shift some of the costs to the requesting party [*Rowe Entertainment Inc. v. The William Morris Agency Inc.,* 205 F.R.D. 421 (S.D.N.Y. 2002). Shifting any costs should be considered, however, only regarding data described as inaccessible, such as fragmented, "deleted", or damaged data or that on storage or archival back-up tapes [*Zubulake v. UBS Warburg LLC,* 217 Fed. R. D. 309 (S.D.N.Y. 2003)]. Inaccessible data is usually the most expensive to produce.

Practically speaking, attorneys informally work out cost issues according to local practice and the amount in controversy, the resources of the respective clients, and the degree of significance of the issues. It is common for the requesting party, once the information is produced, to pay for such things as copying the information, developing negatives of photos, and like procedures that facilitate the requestor's subsequent analysis and use of the material in preparing for trial.

INITIAL PREPARATION FOR PRODUCTION AND INSPECTION REQUEST

Decide what to request, keeping in mind the facts of the case and the legal theories gained through a review of the file. Give particular attention to the answers to interrogatories or deposition questions that identify pertinent documents. It might be useful to determine the types of documents or things often used in a particular industry or business. Clients may help here, or experts, or persons in similar businesses and trade and professional associations. The law office's or client's technology manager may be helpful in an e-discovery case. In a highly complex or technical matter, a consultant may be needed. If disclosure has occurred, focus on documents and things missed in or suggested by the initial disclosure. Review the Rule 26 discovery plan. Consider the opponent's cost and likely benefit of each item requested. For electronically stored information, the cost hierarchy, from least expensive to most expensive, runs as follows:

Active Data: e-mail and other information currently accessible on computers, network, and the like (the least expensive)

Metadata (data about data): hidden data, information on author creation and alteration; similar information on e-mails including recipient and blind copies, plus other information

Replicant Data: automatically generated data such as backup files, audit logs, Internet access, and system crash fragments

Backup Data: backup tapes and discs

Residual Data: fragmented data such as that from deleted files and corrupted files (the most expensive to produce).[1]

Determine, as well, whether the office has adequate resources, both in technology and personnel, to handle and analyze the information to be requested. In particularly voluminous cases, the cost of hiring an outside vendor should be weighed. Consult with the attorney to arrive at a mutual list of specific items or categories of items that should be requested.

> "The picture cannot be painted if the significant and the insignificant are given equal prominence. One must know how to select."
>
> —Benjamin N. Cardozo, 1870–1938, quoted in "Law and Literature," *Selected Writings of Benjamin Nathan Cardozo*, Margaret E. Hall, ed., 1947.

Frequently the production and inspection occurs in a room in the office of the attorney whose client has possession of the documents. In some cases it involves arranging to go to a particular building to inspect machinery, observe a production process or a test, or copy computerized data forensically. If so, a time and manner of inspection of copying should be agreed on that is reasonable and not disruptive, which may require setting a time outside normal business hours; otherwise, most requests are timed for normal business hours. Production and inspection may simply be a process of exchanging a CD-ROM or sharing access to an on-line document bank.

DRAFTING THE REQUEST FOR PRODUCTION AND INSPECTION

A good sample of a request, preferably in a similar case, should be obtained for reference. Office copies or the standard form books and electronic sources should be consulted. Exhibit 9:1 is a general form for a Request for Production [Form 24, Fed. R. Civ. P.]. Some practitioners include, at the beginning of the request, a definitions section similar to equivalent sections in interrogatories. In drafting a request, remember the following guidelines:

1. Describe the items or categories with sufficient specificity so that a person of average intelligence has enough information to know what must be produced. The standard is flexible and is determined by how much the requesting party can reasonably be expected to know and whether the respondent has sufficient knowledge to determine what is requested. Phrases such as "financial records" or "all correspondence between" have been found to be inadequate descriptions.[2] More specificity in name, topic, and time is required.

EXHIBIT 9:1 ■ Request for Production, Inspection, and Copying of Documents, and Inspection and Photographing of Things and Real Property—General Form

[Fed. R. Civ. P. Rule 34]

[*Title of Court and Cause*]

Plaintiff A_____ B_____ requests defendant C_____ D_____ to respond within _____ days to the following requests:

    (1) That defendant produce and permit plaintiff to inspect and to copy each of the following documents:
[*Here list the documents either individually or by category and describe each of them.*]
[*Here state the time, place, and manner of making the inspection and performance of any related acts.*]

    (2) That defendant produce and permit plaintiff to inspect and to copy, test, or sample each of the following objects:
[*Here list the objects either individually or by category and describe each of them.*]
[*Here state the time, place, and manner of making the inspection and performance of any related acts.*]

    (3) That defendant permit plaintiff to enter [*here describe property to be entered*] and to inspect and to photograph, test, or sample [*here describe the portion of the real property and the objects to be inspected*].
[*Here state the time, place, and manner of making the inspection and performance of any related acts.*]

_____
Attorney for Plaintiff

Address: _____

Source: Reprinted with permission of West Group.

2. Organize the request by the type of evidence requested (see Exhibit 9:1) and include a paragraph on the continuing obligation of the respondent to produce pertinent documents that come into the respondent's possession after the original production date.
3. Include an instruction that directs the producing party to designate clearly what documents and things produced respond to each respective item of the request, if your request is pursuant to a rule that does not specify how the information should be produced.
4. Regarding electronically stored information, apply the knowledge gained from your e-discovery interrogatories (Exhibit 7:3) and any subsequent deposition of the other party's technology manager; identify the form in which you want the data produced, such as in native format (which includes metadata), paper or electronic form, and other considerations; and confine the request to cover a reasonable period of time.

Assume Mercury Parcel has indicated in its answer to Ms. Forrester's interrogatories that the following items do exist: rules and regulations of the Interstate Commerce Commission on the required maintenance of vehicles used in interstate commerce, copies of Form ICC-2010 needed to report compliance with those rules on a quarterly basis, Form ICC-2010A used to record regular maintenance information on a specified vehicle, and Form ICC-2015 for recording specific complaints and resulting repairs to a specific vehicle. Also assume that the answer revealed that the van was vehicle number 23 and that photographs had been taken of the van and the accident scene. Although more records might be available, these examples should be sufficient for purposes of illustration. Assume Mr. White has asked you to draft that request. After reviewing the file and forms and consulting with the attorney, you might draft a form that looks like Exhibit 9:2.

EXHIBIT 9:2 ■ Example of a Production and Inspection Request Form

UNITED STATES DISTRICT COURT FOR THE EASTERN DISTRICT OF COLUMBIA

ANN FORRESTER,
                         Plaintiff

        v.   Civil Case, File No. _____

MERCURY PARCEL SERVICE, INC.,
                         Defendant

PLAINTIFF'S REQUEST FOR PRODUCTION AND INSPECTION OF DOCUMENTS, THINGS, AND REAL PROPERTY

According to Rule 34 of the Federal Rules of Civil Procedure, Plaintiff requests Defendant Mercury Parcel Service to respond within thirty days to the following requests:

1. That Defendant produce and permit Plaintiff to inspect and to copy each of the following documents:
  a. The specific rules and regulations of the Interstate Commerce Commission requiring regular safety checks, maintenance, and repair of vehicles used in interstate commerce.
  b. Defendant's file copies of all Form 2010s submitted to the ICC between Feb. ____ and Jan. ____.
  c. All Form ICC-2010As recording the regular maintenance and safety checks on van number 23 over the two-year period preceding the accident on February 26, ____.

(continued)

EXHIBIT 9:2 ■ Example of a Production and Inspection Request Form *(continued)*

d. All Form ICC-2010As for all other Defendant's delivery vehicles over the two years preceding the accident.

e. All Form ICC-2015s recording complaints and needed repairs and subsequent repairs made to van number 23 for the two years preceding the accident.

f. All Form ICC-2015s on all other vehicles for the two years preceding the accident.

g. All photographs or negatives thereof that Defendant had taken of the accident scene and the damage to the van. Plaintiff will inspect and copy these items at the office of Plaintiff's attorney on November 1, ____ at 9:00 A.M., or at any other reasonable time and place convenient to counsel in this action.

_____

Arthur White
Attorney for Plaintiff
(address)
(phone number)

The wording in Exhibit 9:2 can be customized to encompass electronic forms of the requested information, plus any memos or e-mails that address maintenance of van number 23 or other matters related to the ICC reports.

SERVICE OF THE REQUEST FOR PRODUCTION

The request should then be signed by the attorney, and you should serve the request by mail and execute the appropriate certificate of mailing. A copy should be kept for the file. Follow the filing dictates of Rule 5(d) as previously discussed or any applicable local rules, including those governing e-filing. The response date should be noted on your calendar and in the deadline calendar so that the failure of the other party to respond will not go unnoticed. The attorney should be informed if no reply is forthcoming so remedial measures can be taken.

PREPARING FOR PRODUCTION OF DOCUMENTS AND THINGS

INTRODUCTION

This section focuses on the significant procedure and techniques for preparing for the production of documents and things. We start, however, on what the law firm must do, even before there is a request for production, to protect the client from accusations of spoliation and potentially costly sanctions.

SPOLIATION AND THE DUTY TO PRESERVE EVIDENCE: PROTECTING THE CLIENT FROM SANCTIONS

spoliation
The destruction or loss of evidence, including the failure to preserve it.

As noted in Chapters 3 and 7, a party has the duty to preserve evidence, even if it is harmful. Correspondingly, **spoliation** is the destruction or loss of evidence, including the failure to preserve it. Spoliation can be intentional or careless, and can so negatively impact on the laudatory aims of discovery as to warrant serious judicial sanctions. Protecting the client and the law firm from accusations of spoliation, made even more difficult with e-information, is a paramount concern for the legal team.

A client's duty to preserve evidence is clear, but the exact time at which the duty arises is not. Case law and good practice suggest that the duty to preserve arises when the party becomes aware or should have become aware that there is a real potential for litigation. At that time, a client must prepare to produce documents and things in a manner consistent with the obligation to preserve evidence and avoid spoliation. Your awareness of the following guidelines, which are specific to the preservation of e-information, will enhance your value as a litigation paralegal:

1. Have the client—particularly businesses, organizations, and institutions—develop a comprehensive ongoing *document retention policy*. The policy should address active and archival e-storage systems; what types of information are necessary, practical, and reasonable to retain in the ordinary course of business; what can and should be routinely destroyed (e-shredding); proper use and storage of e-mail, instant messaging, and voice mail; proper use of portable devices such as stick drives, hand helds, and laptops; proper business use of home computers; what applications and programs provide useful access and search functions; who will manage, monitor, and enforce the policy; security; and other considerations. Include a section on the special response required for litigation. Inform the client and the client's technology person or staff why it is important that the policy be developed with an eye toward litigation.

2. Fully inform the client of the duty to preserve evidence and the consequences of spoliation.

3. When the potential for litigation is real, the attorney should promptly notify the client. Include in the notice process a *litigation hold letter* that is similar in content to the model preservation letter in Chapter 7. The letter advises the client immediately to implement a *litigation hold order*. The order informs employees of the potential for litigation and directs them to take prompt steps to preserve and not destroy evidence. Some parties shut down their entire computer system so a mirror image copy can be made of all data. This, of course, is extremely costly, usually includes volumes of unneeded information, and is seriously disruptive to the client's operations. The better practice may be to continue with routine backup and destruction processes while a previously designated litigation response team quickly begins to narrow down what must be preserved.[3] The response team should consist of the attorney, the paralegal overseeing discovery, and, at least, the client's technology manager. Your legal team must anticipate, as well as you can at this early stage, the cause of action and related legal issues. Promptly interview key employees to determine who created relevant information, who received it, and what computer applications and equipment were involved. The technology people then identify where it is electronically stored and how best to locate, isolate, and preserve the information in a usable form. Establish a chain of custody log and address security issues. Choose a method to review for privileged and protected information. This process should reasonably balance discovery requirements with fiscal responsibility.[4]

If the client is an individual, such as Ms. Forrester in her personal injury case, the preservation of her e-stored information, which should not be ignored, is likely to be a far less complicated undertaking.

In addition to drafting document production and inspection requests and assisting in the earliest efforts to protect your client from spoliation sanctions, you must also know how to prepare documents either for initial disclosure or to respond to a production request. Mr. White has asked that you oversee the production of a sizable number of documents pursuant to a request for production submitted by the adverse party in one of our cases. The following material suggests a variety of techniques and steps for performing this task.

The purpose of production is to provide the opponent an opportunity to review documents pertinent to the case to determine if and how the documents support the

> "He who must search a haystack for a needle is likely to end up with the attitude that the needle is not worth the search."
>
> —ROBERT H. JACKSON, BROWN V. ALLEN, 344 U.S. 443, 537 (1953).

facts to be alleged at trial. From the point of view of the person producing the documents, the more practical objectives are to locate and produce documents thoroughly, accurately, and efficiently. In order to do this effectively, the documents must be well organized and easy to retrieve. The entire process should interfere as little as possible with the daily business needs of the client or the client's employees.

TASK AND PROCEDURE

Background

Initial Steps Checklist for Preparing for Production of Documents and Things

(a) Review the case thoroughly.
- Completely review the file.
- Understand the cause of action, the elements that must be proved, defenses, and the corresponding evidence requirements.
- Draft a brief summary of these things and ask your supervising attorney to review it for accuracy and omissions.
- Develop a sense of what is at stake and the complexity of the case.

(b) Review the opponent's request for production.
- Note the items requested, possible objections, privilege concerns.

(c) Meet with the client and key personnel.
- If applicable to the type of case and if the information has not been gathered previously, determine:
  - how the client's business or organization is structured.
  - its chain of command.
  - the departments most relevant to the case.
- Go over the document request with the client's technology manager and any documents custodian to find out:
  - what kinds of documents (electronic or paper) are responsive to the request.
  - likely volume.
  - who created them.
  - where they are stored.
  - how they are accessed.
- This is a good time to have your attorney remind the custodians of the duty to preserve evidence and, possibly, the need to issue a more specific litigation hold order.

(d) Develop a document production plan.
- Using the information gathered above and working closely with your supervising attorney, a technology manager, perhaps an experienced paralegal, and a consultant (if needed), plan for the entire production process. Lack of a plan leads to confusion and spiraling costs.
- Address the complexity of the case:
  - the extent of both paper and e-information sought
  - the expertise level needed to implement and manage the production
  - the time required for the project
  - the human and technology resources needed
  - whose staff and equipment will be used to produce (the law office's, the client's, or outsourced)
  - the ability of both the law office and the client's staff to pull employees off what they normally do to work on the production

❑ where the information will be stored and secured

❑ access policies

❑ how attorney client privilege and other protected information will be screened

❑ who will be on the production team

❑ what the chain of command will be

❑ what policies and procedures (such as those for coding and classifying relevant documents) will be implemented

❑ what logs must be kept

❑ in what form documents will be produced

❑ how the chain of custody will be maintained

❑ who will be the designated expert to testify should chain of custody, spoliation, or other production and technical issues arise

❑ who will serve as liaison to the other party to work out production issues

❑ what procedures will be the least disruptive to the client's operations

❑ what quality control will be needed to see that the established policies and procedures are followed

❑ after looking at comparative costs and production times, will the production be paper, electronic, or a combination of the two

❑ is production better done in-house or by an outside litigation production vendor

■ Estimate costs (in large e-information cases, this may require expert assistance):

❑ Screen representative samples of documents for

❑ types of documents requiring screening

❑ page length and data space of documents

❑ time required to review, code, and log documents manually or electronically[5]

❑ Once you know how many boxes of documents you have, time to do a project and employee needs can be estimated according to the following procedure.[6] Note how many boxes of documents have been located to be produced plus an estimate of the number of boxes to be produced by other parties. Most standard storage boxes contain about 2,000 pages. You can check this by filling one of your empty storage boxes with reams of copying paper. Estimate the average document size, say seven pages. Divide the number of pages (2,000) by seven to get the number of documents per box (286). Assume you have fifty boxes of documents or the electronic equivalent, which equals 14,300 documents.

14,300 documents	×	5 minutes each	=	71,500 minutes
71,500 minutes	÷	60 minutes	=	1,192 hours
1,192 hours	÷	8 hours	=	149 days
149 days	÷	30 days/deadline	=	5 coders
14,300 documents	÷	30 days	=	477 documents/day
477 documents	÷	5 coders	=	95 documents per coder per day

❑ Also, consider the following:

1. 2,000 pages (1 box) is about 650 megabytes of data.

2. 1 G.B. (gigabyte) of data is approximately 45,000 to 50,000 pages (25–30 boxes).

3. 1 CD-ROM holds 15,000 pages.
4. 1 DVD holds 7 CD-ROMs of data.
5. 1 double sided, dual layer DVD holds 15.9 GB.
6. 1 typical case production takes six to twelve weeks.[7]

As a general rule, the greater the number of documents and data to be produced, the more efficient and economical it is to create and use an all-electronic, searchable database. Also, the more complex the case is, the greater the need for experience and expert assistance.

Locate Documents

The difficulty in locating documents varies with the particular case. Locating the medical records on Ms. Forrester's injuries and treatment and her employment records is relatively easy. Locating all the records pertaining to the manufacture, maintenance, and operation of the van driven by Mr. Hart could be more difficult. Much more difficult is locating all pertinent documents and the full gamut of electronically stored information generated by a large multinational corporation with numerous subsidiaries and branch offices.

For locating both paper and e-stored information, meet with the client and key personnel and follow section (c) of the Initial Steps Checklist. The document retention policy, if one exists, may tell you what is most likely to have been retained or destroyed. The likely flow of memos, e-mails, reports of problems and comments and discussion of such reports or problems is important. Whether the information is active, metadata, residual data, or archival data provides insight into how difficult and costly it will be to recover. Prepare a detailed list of potentially relevant information, subject matter, type of data, and the specific location or likely location of the information. Develop an atmosphere of cooperation. Be sensitive to the need for keeping disruption of the office routine to a minimum, and express appreciation for any help extended to you and the production team.

Pull Files and Documents

Pulling Paper Manually

By this stage the document production team, if one is called for, should be in place and trained. In coordination with each of the client's designated document custodians and carefully following the guidelines set up by the attorney or the document production team leader, pull the files or individual documents likely to contain the responsive information. For each relevant file, do the following:

- Pull the file and fill out a file checkout card or leave a temporary replacement sheet or file cover indicating by whom the file has been pulled, for what case, its next location (office or room number), and the date. When in doubt whether to pull a file, the best practice is to pull it.
- Check with the custodian to see if the file is so critical to daily operations of the office that an immediate copy of the file or of certain documents needs to be made for the convenience of the office. If so, have the document or file photocopied. Tape a legend reading: "Copy: original in case file _____ v. _____" to the photocopy machine so it will appear on each copy. This provides notice that the new file is a copy and indicates where the original can be located.
- Label each file or document as it is pulled to indicate its place in the case file. For example, the first file pulled for the *Forrester* case could be labeled F-1 indicating that it is now in the first file folder of the *Forrester* case.

| EXHIBIT 9:3 ■ Document Production Original Source Log |

New File No.	Description	Source
F-1	Maint. form 20's _____	Merc. Parcel Rm 108 drawer 31 Ralph Johnson
F-2	Maint. form 20's _____	Merc. Parcel Rm 108 Dr. 31 R. Johnson
F-3	Driver Hour Logs ____	Merc. Parcel Rm 108 Dr. 81 Betty Robinson

- On your laptop, prepare a log of each file pulled. The log should contain at a minimum the source of the file, a description of the file (exact title is best), the new working file number (F-1, F-2) assigned to it, and the custodian. The log might also contain other information as indicated in Exhibit 9:3, which shows an original source log.
- The original source log provides immediate information on the source of the document or file and is invaluable when the files or documents are returned.
- If any files cannot be found, this fact should be noted in the log, and a memo so indicating should be addressed to the case file and attached to the log. Such a memo protects you from accusations of sloppy work and the firm from possible sanctions from the court for failure to comply with a discovery order.
- Log books, journals, or other unique items should be specially noted to indicate their unique nature for easier identification in the future.
- Remove the pulled files and documents to a separate office or screening room with limited access to ensure control over the documents and enhance the efficiency of additional screening. When dealing with a large number of documents, place the files into file boxes and label them—for example, Box 1 files F-1 to F-50, Box 2 files F-51 to F-100, and so forth.
- As a courtesy, inform the custodian what documents have been removed.

Converting Paper to Electronic Files (Imaging)

Some law offices strive to be paperless. All documents are created and stored electronically; all incoming paper documents (correspondence, contracts, memoranda, etc.) are scanned into the computer. This same process is invaluable to document production. Electronic conversion of paper documents prevents loss, eliminates filing cabinets or boxes, greatly enhances portability, quickens retrieval, speeds copying and organization into folders of related files for a particular purpose, and facilitates access by multiple parties at any time.

In this process, done in-house or by a vendor, the paper document is scanned and converted into a "read only" electronic document, meaning that the text cannot be edited. Many office photocopiers now double as digital scanners. When equipped with the right software, scanners can produce the document in PDF or TIFF format. A more dated process is to scan paper or a digital image with an optical character reader (OCR). Despite regular upgrades, these readers are relatively slow and prone to interpretation errors regarding character recognition and formatting. Once the documents are converted to digital files, they can be processed like any other electronically stored information.

"Pulling" Electronically Stored Information

The client's potentially responsive e-stored information must be "pulled" or captured with great care. Capturing data is often the costliest stage of e-discovery and requires intense scrutiny to "ensure complete compliance with the request, as well as the integrity of the data."[8] Close cooperation among the firm's technology manager, the client's technology manager, and any expert consultant is imperative. A big stakes case may require data to be captured by an expensive forensic expert. That is not necessary in most cases, however.

Here is a sensible approach for a typical (assuming there is such) e-discovery case.[9]

- Verify that any routine or other destruction of potentially relevant e-stored information has stopped.
- Capture mirror images of the data, including residual data, on each pertinent person's pc and portable devices. This can be done with commercially available applications such as Norton Ghost or True Image.
- Expand the capture to other likely data sources, but only after the team has thoroughly weighed what is likely to be found, the hierarchy of usefulness, and the realities of difficulty and cost of capture.
- Keep a source log and expand the information to include the method of capture.
- Once the data is captured, secure it.

Screen Pulled Files and Documents

Objectives of the Screening Process

This next stage lies at the heart of good document control and production. It requires the review of each piece of paper or electronic page for its relevancy to the request and for any privileged or sensitive material. Although laborious at times, the importance of the process cannot be overstated. Some high profile cases have completely turned on the hero paralegal's ability to find and recognize a key piece of evidence hidden among thousands of pages of a document review. The objectives and guidelines for this step of the document production process should be specific.

The objectives of this step normally include the following:

- To identify documents that are responsive to each particular request for production
- To number those documents, if so directed, for easy identification and retrieval
- To identify documents that are privileged or sensitive to avoid disclosure of that information
- To classify documents for rapid identification, retrieval, and return
- To prepare documents for photocopying or other electronic recording
- To have documents readied for review by the attorney

Screening Paper

The tasks for manual paper screening involve the following:

- Aim to pass through all documents once and to record all necessary information at that time. If several people are reviewing, logs should be maintained by each person to show who has reviewed what.
- Place the files and documents on their sides in boxes. As each relevant document is identified, the document should not be removed from the file but placed in an upright position so it protrudes from the file. See Exhibit 9:4.

EXHIBIT 9:4 ■ Place Documents in an Upright Position

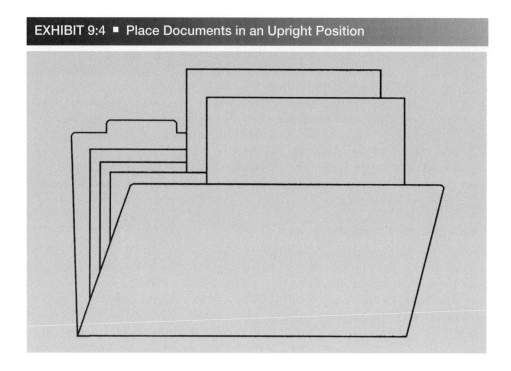

- Number each document page in sequential order as the pages are turned up. Since these are the original documents and need to be preserved in their original state, a decision must be made by the attorney if numbering and other notations should be penciled on the document or a Post-it label used on which to record the necessary information. If the Post-it labels are the type that reliably stay on and can be removed without damaging the original document, this method is probably the best. Some firms number the documents directly; others do not. Some firms still use a manual Bates stamping device. Others use a computerized Bates numbering system, bar codes, and computer-generated labels. Numbering now saves much time later. In large-volume cases this entire process may be contracted to a private vendor.
- Indicate the number on each document, the set and paragraph of the production request to which it responds, the numbered source file in which it belongs (F-1, F-2), how many copies of the document are needed, and to which cross files the copies of the document should go. The files normally kept include three files of original documents: one as numbered, one of privileged and other undiscoverable documents, and one of unresponsive documents. Copies of all the files and documents are made to be returned to the original custodian. Additional copies of the numbered documents go into cross files: chronological files and files sorted by production request set and paragraph. Some firms also want copies of the documents sorted into files by issue and by person. Systems may become even more detailed than this. With all of the sorting, cross referencing, and photocopying, the benefits of converting paper to digital data quickly become apparent.
- Indicate whether the document is privileged or contains work product or other sensitive material. In such cases a colored cover sheet should be placed in front of the document so it can be readily identified and pulled when necessary.

"And how, milord, can we expect these twelve poor mutts on the jury—

The Judge: What is a mutt?

Sir Ethelred: Milord, a mutt—

The Judge: Sir Ethelred, no doubt you know best the lines of advocacy most likely to advance the interests of your clients; but is it quite wise to describe the jury as 'mutts,' which, though I am not familiar with it, I judge instinctively to be a term of depreciation?

Sir Ethelred: Milord, 'mutt' is a relative term. The Prime Minister, if he were requested to transpose a

- Index the documents. The number of indexes maintained will depend on what the supervising attorney has requested. A master index should record the number of the document, subject matter on the document, and its nature (memo, letter, tax return, phone log, etc.), the new file number, the date of the document, the author of the document, the recipient of the document, whether the document is privileged or otherwise undiscoverable, the set and item of the production request that it responds to, and eventually whether the document was produced to the adversary. If other files, such as personality files, are requested, information such as names of persons mentioned or receiving copies or drafts of the document might be included. This master index can then be used to create other indexes. Even if screening paper is done manually, indexes are best done electronically.

Use a Standardized Numbering System

A standardized or uniform numbering system will prove most efficient and can be adapted to most cases in the office. Many attorneys set up a numbering system as it occurs to them in a particular case, resulting in confusion for others not privy to its logic. Further, such haphazard systems often prove inadequate as the case expands, or result in telltale gaps in the numbering system as privileged or attorney work product documents are removed. The method used by many law firms is the decimal system. The numbers become a shorthand description of the document, and the system can be used for all appropriate cases. Here is how the system works.[10]

First, an estimate of the number of documents involved must be made. The number of documents equals the degree of digits needed for numbering. Ninety-nine (99) or fewer documents is a second-degree case, 100–999 documents equals a third-degree case, 100,000 documents equals a sixth-degree case, and so forth. The number of digits needed for numbering is based on the formula: degree + 3 = digits needed. Therefore, a third-degree case is simply calculated: degree = 3 + 3 = 6 digits. A sixth-degree case calculates: 6 + 3 = 9 digits (xxx,xxx,xxx).

The first digit refers to the first assigned category or grouping. In many firms this first grouping is the *role* the document will play in the proof process according to the elements of the case and related factors. A sample group one in a negligence case might appear as follows:

Group I, Role in Case

1. Jurisdiction (to establish or challenge)
2. Parties (to identify)
3. Existence of duty
4. Breach
5. Causal connection to damage/injury
6. Damages
7. Defenses
8. Others

If the first document to be numbered for production (or the first to be received in response to a request for production) pertains to the existence of a duty, the first digit will be numbered 3xx, xxx, xxx. In other words, anyone familiar with the categories will know at a glance the expected role the document will play in the case. The other digits, as you will see, provide similar information at a glance. This information will be based on categories carefully planned by the attorney. The categories will generally be the same for all negligence cases or all products liability cases. The attorney-paralegal team, however, can alter these categories as the unique nature of a case dictates.

A document might play several roles. In that case, number it for its major role, but also number a reference insert page according to the secondary role, which refers the searcher to the original numbered document. When the documents are sorted by categories, this additional numbering will prevent a document with dual purposes from being overlooked and may make an extra copy of a lengthy document unnecessary.

The second digit may be designated to show the *source* of the document. Group two, therefore, might appear as follows:

Group II, Source of Document

1. Ms. Forrester
2. Dr. Harris
3. Mr. Hart
4. Mercury Parcel Service
5. Others

If the first document came from Ms. Forrester, the numbered document would appear as 31x, xxx, xxx. Other groupings for remaining digits could include the *type* of document (correspondence, memo, others), *production mode* (how produced—with pleadings, pursuant to a request for production, subpoena duces tecum, etc.), *potential for evidentiary exclusion* (admissible, privilege, hearsay, etc.), and any other grouping predetermined by the attorney.

The order in which the document was pulled or received can be indicated by using the right-hand digits in the number. If your first document is numbered by all its categories and appears at 318,720,001, it would be recorded on the general index as the first document. The next document (whatever its categories would indicate) would end in xxx,xxx,xx2 and would be the second document entered into the general index. If there are numerous groupings, digits may have to be added to accommodate the sequential numbering. If the document is multipaged, pages are indicated simply by inserting a decimal and the page number. The ninth page of your first document would be numbered 318,720,001.9. This uniform decimal system is computer-compatible.

Screening the Captured Electronically Stored Information

The process of screening the captured e-information loosely parallels the process for screening paper documents. Whether done by a person or by automated software or a combination thereof, each document must be reviewed for relevance to the document production request and for privileged and protected information. The final production set must ultimately be numbered, coded, and indexed like the paper documents, but with the assistance of software designed for these document management tasks. This software offers far more fields, numbering options, indexing and cross-indexing options, and other benefits over the manual paper process. Whether in small or large volume, the documents are placed into a separate discovery data bank where they can be retrieved quickly and further organized into groups responsive to each item of the document request. The documents can be kept in their native format or converted to PDF, TIFF, or other form agreed on by the parties.

A document production company is often the best approach in large volume cases. They can automatically filter data to eliminate all duplicate files, application and system files, unneeded file types, dated material that falls outside any specified date range, and other data not pertinent to the case. Additional filtering can be done by keywords and even concepts. This filtering process can narrow the original captured data by as much as 75 to 80 percent and reduce the cost of production

musical composition in A flat major into the key of E minor would readily confess himself a mutt in relation to that particular task.

The Judge: Very well, Sir Ethelred. Proceed.

Sir Ethelred (turning to the jury): How, I say, can you poor mutts be expected to get a grip of this colossal conundrum without the assistance of any documents at all?"

—A. P. HERBERT, *UNCOMMON LAW,* 1936.

by up to ninety percent or more.[11] The savings in temporary staff and hours of document review can be dramatic.

Once reduced, metadata and text can be extracted and the documents converted to a universally usable form. This much leaner database can be returned to the production team for final review, numbering, indexing, privilege checking, and so on. The final production data can then be provided to the requesting party in CD, DVD, or other form. Some attorneys agree to have the final production set of documents placed on an online repository. This permits both sides to access the production set securely from any place at any time. These services often facilitate searching and manipulating the documents into subsets by issues, names, witnesses, and other criteria. Any final production data set can be downloaded into document management and litigation support software for retrieval, organization into subsets, searching, further narrowing to a trial set of documents and exhibits, and other functions.

Have the Attorney Review the Documents

Once the production set (whether paper, electronic, or both) is ready, have your supervising attorney verify that the documents are responsive to the production requests, that all privileged and other protected documents have been identified, that the paper documents have been kept in original format (stapled, bound, paper-clipped), that the electronic documents have been kept in native form or in a form agreed on by the attorneys, and that any necessary paper copies will be prepared. Your supervising attorney will also appreciate anything you can do to red-tag or point out documents that stand out as particularly significant to the case.

Extract Privileged Documents

Each of the privileged or sensitive documents should be extracted from the original file and placed in a separate paper or electronic folder. If the document is paper, pull the colored privileged document sheet as well. A sheet of paper with the document's number on it should be substituted in the original file.

Recall that Federal Rule 34(b) requires a party to produce any unprotected and relevant information from the same document that contains privileged or otherwise protected information. Therefore, once the privileged information is identified, it must be removed from the original document that will be produced. The process of editing out irrelevant, privileged, or protected information from the text of a document is called **redaction.** A brief notation indicating that the document has been redacted and why should be entered on the document. Return the redacted version of the document to the production set. Maintain an original (unredacted) version of the document in a secured folder.

Keep in mind that Rule 26(b)(5)(A) requires the disclosing or producing party to inform the other party of any material otherwise discoverable that is withheld from discovery because it is privileged or is attorney's work product. Either the master index, referred to previously, or a privileged/work product index can be used to create a privileged/work product log for the other party. This entire extraction, redaction, and return process must be done in very thorough consultation with your supervising attorney.

Have Documents Copied

Determine how many copies of each paper document are needed. Usually four or five are necessary: one to replace the originals in the files of origin, one to duplicate the original file, one for a chronological file, one for each item of the response

redaction
The process of editing out irrelevant or privileged information from the text of a document.

request, and any other need such as a person or issue file. The person making copies substitutes a sheet in the original file indicating what documents are being copied and by whom. The copies should contain a legend indicating that they are a copy of the original and where the original can be found, as described previously. The copies should be in the same format, paper-clipped, stapled, and so on, as the original. Unless it is impractical, an entire document should be copied even if only one page of the document is responsive. All oversized, reduced, and otherwise nonreproducible or altered documents should be noted. Any bad copies should be destroyed. The copies should then be sorted into expandable file folders or boxes as initially indicated on the original. The originals should be placed in an original document file in numerical order as they were identified. A copy of the originals should be reinserted in the files of origin, and they may be returned to their custodians and refiled. A letter of return to the custodian should be drafted and the copy placed in the case file. The custodian should be directed to keep the files in their original state. It is wise to request a receipt. If a case is small, it may be adequate just to set up a three-ring binder and place the copied documents into the needed categories or according to the sets of the discovery requests with a simple table of contents at the front.

Prepare Documents for Examination

A copy of the documents should be arranged and noted according to the set and item of the request they pertain to or as they are kept in the normal course of your client's business. Some firms prefer to renumber the documents at this time. (This renumbering is not necessary with the decimal numbering system.) Others wait for the examination and number only those documents selected by the opponent. Either way, an index showing the original number of the document, the item to which it responds, that it was produced, and if it was selected by the adversary should be kept. Be sure to keep a copy of all documents produced to the opponent.

For electronic information, document management or litigation support software facilitates the ultimate arrangement of the production set, that is, either in subsets corresponding for each item of the opponent's production request or as the e-information is kept in the ordinary course of the client's business. Make sure that you retain at least one exact duplicate of what is produced to the opponent.

Retrieve the Documents

During the case it may become necessary to retrieve a particular document or several documents, which could be necessary to prepare for a deposition, to find documents for an expert to review, to prepare for the examination of a witness, or to make a critical rebuttal point at trial. Using the indexes that have been prepared, you can retrieve the pertinent documents efficiently with one or more of the following: the date of the document, the name of the author or recipient, the number of the document, the issue that it pertains to, key words, concepts, and so on. A check-out system for all paper documents should be carefully maintained.

It is in search and retrieval that document management and litigation support software saves enormous amounts of time and facilitates numerous trial preparation and presentation functions.

The Legal Technology Resource Center (LTAC) of the American Bar Association tests lawyer software and can provide assistance in choosing a program. Periodicals such as *Law Office Computing, Law Technology News,* and *Legal Assistant Today,* and periodicals specifically devoted to e-discovery can also help.

Return the Documents and Retain Indexes

At the close of the case, usually after all appeals have been exhausted, the original paper documents may be returned to their original locations. The return of each document or identifiable group of documents should be logged and receipted. Any of the client's original documents filed with the court or in the possession of the other parties should be retrieved and returned. All copies should then be shredded or burned.[12] All the indexes, return letters, and receipts should be kept in the case file.

If your task is to review the documents sent by the opponent in response to a request for production submitted by your firm, a similar system of selecting and organizing can be used.

Quality Control

Every document production system requires regular checking either by the attorney or an experienced auditor or litigation manager. Checks should be made to see that the uniform terminology, coding, and other systems are being followed and that test retrievals produce the anticipated results.

Security

Once the data is computerized, precautions should be taken to protect it. As mentioned earlier, original hard-copy documents should be placed in a room with limited access. Make a backup copy of the final production set, whether paper or electronic, in case something happens to the originals. The backup should be stored in a completely separate and well-protected location. Some law offices store backup sets in more than one secure off-site location. If the documents are in an online repository, the vendor provides security. All originally mirrored and collected data and duplicates should be placed in locked facilities or otherwise secured to prevent and detect any unauthorized access to and use of the information. Should any document be challenged, its chain of custody must be verifiable. Of course, extracted privileged, protected, and privacy information must be secured as well. As attorneys and paralegals work with the documents in preparation for trial, the usual protection of computer data should be in place, such as passwords, firewalls, virus protection, locked server rooms, wireless use prohibition, encryption, e-mail attachment metadata removers, and access shut-offs for those unexpectedly extended step-out-of-the-office moments.

An increasing number of law offices and their clients are seeking highly technical security advice to protect the integrity of their computer data.

PRODUCTION PROCEDURE

REPLYING TO A REQUEST FOR PRODUCTION AND INSPECTION

A party must respond to a request for production in writing and within thirty days of service of the request, unless ordered by the court or otherwise agreed to by the parties. Again, state rules may vary. Before drafting the response, review each item of the request once more. For each item of the request, outline:

- What documents or information responsive to that item, if any, were located in the search of information
- Any objection and the reasons for the objection [Rules 26(b) and 34(b)] (failure to object may waive the objection)

EXHIBIT 9:5 ■ Response to Request for Production—General Form

[FED. R. CIV. P. Rule 34]

[*Title of Court and Cause*]

_____

Attorney for Plaintiff

Address: _____

In response to plaintiff's request to produce and for inspection in the above-entitled action, served upon plaintiff [*date*], ____, the inspection and related activities requested will be permitted at [*if a different place than requested*] with respect to each item and category as requested [add "with the exception of Items as follows, _____, to which inspection defendant objects, respectfully on the following grounds:" list each request objected to, the objection and the reasons_____][or, the inspection and related activities requested are objected to on the ground that _____].

Yours, etc.

_____

Attorney for Defendant

Address: _____

Source: Reprinted with permission of West Group.

- In what form or forms the opponent wants the information produced and in what form or forms it is best for your client to produce the item
- What differences or concerns need to be worked out with the other party prior to seeking a protective order [Rules 26(c) and 37(a)(2)(B)]
- What process is best for the client and the opponent for delivering the information or conducting any inspection, copying, testing, or sampling of the information

Prior to raising an objection in the response, it is good practice to research case law on what kind of information courts have protected from production. Only the specific part of the document that is objectionable may be excluded from production [Rule 34(b)].

Go over your outline with your supervising attorney and identify who will do what in negotiating differences and arrangements with the other side. Cooperation with the opponent can greatly simplify the production and reduce the number of subsequent problems. The written response can be easier to draft following such negotiations.

Then draft the response to the request for production. A general form for the response is shown in Exhibit 9:5.[13] The preferred practice is to respond specifically to each enumerated item in the request for production by restating the item requested, then adding your response or objection and the explanation for the objection [Rules 26(b)(5)(A) and 34(b)].

Here are a few examples of how to respond to a specific, enumerated request.

> *Request:* All Form ICC-2012s referred to in defendant's answer to plaintiff's interrogatories.

Answer: Defendant will produce these documents, copies of which are included with this response.

Or,

Answer: Defendant will produce the documents requested for the two years prior to the accident, but objects in so far as the request is for documents from an unlimited time period, which is unduly burdensome [FRCP 26(b)].

Or,

Answer: Defendant will not produce these documents because the request was served after the court order staying discovery.

Have the attorney review and sign the response. Serve the response on the other parties and execute the return of service. Calendar any dates and times scheduled for the examination of the documents and other information.

ASSISTING AT THE PRODUCTION, EXAMINATION, OR INSPECTION

In many smaller cases, production is handled informally between the law offices. Requested documents are copied, logged as submitted to the other party, and exchanged. Some productions still occur in the traditional on-site manner, however. Paralegals frequently oversee the on-site production of documents or play an important role in examining the documents produced by the other party.

If your task is to oversee the examination of your client's documents, arrange for the location and remind those concerned of the time and place. Normally, production is held at the responding party's law office, the client's place of business, or a storage facility. See that the room is secure and has a phone and a copying machine. Check with your supervising attorney and the other party regarding any use of scanners at the production. Review the case, the request, and the written response so you know what is to be produced. Verify that the documents to be examined, whether paper or electronic, have been properly indexed as previously indicated, and that the nature of the documents, time periods, and other factors are responsive to, and do not exceed, the bounds of the request. Determine if there are any documents in a foreign language, and notify the examining party accordingly. Schedule any technical assistance for the examiner, such as when specialized proprietary software is needed for the review. Arrange the documents *according to how they are kept in the client's usual course of business or organized and labeled to correspond to the categories in the request* [Rule 34(b)]. Any attempt to obscure or bury key documents or produce them in a form that is less usable than the original form is unethical and subject to sanction. Take a note pad or laptop and a numbering or tabbing device, know where to reach your supervising attorney, and be ready to stay for the duration of the examination. If you use a commercial copying service, consider having the other party billed directly for its copies. During the examination, see that the documents are kept in order and that none are removed from the room. Keep a log of all documents chosen by the opponent and note if special attention is given to any particular document. Strictly avoid conversation about the case or judgments on the value of any of the documents. If issues come up, do not leave the room. Use the phone to call the attorney. When breaks are needed, ask all persons to leave the room and lock the door. In the alternative, phone out for someone else to fill in for you. Immediately after the examination, summarize anything noteworthy, and give the summary to your supervising attorney. Then proceed with any needed follow-up, such as photocopying selected documents, copying them to a CD, and getting them to the opponent.

If your role is examining the documents, prepare by reviewing the file and the specifics of the request for production and the response. Have the issues of the case and the examination objectives clearly in mind. Seek suggestions from your supervising attorney on what to look for and what the client's budget will allow for copying, scanning, photographing, testing, or whatever method best suits the particular examination. Make sure the method of copying is clear to both sides and that the necessary equipment and technical support will be available. Determine cost allocation and billing procedures. Inquire whether any of the documents are in a foreign language and the number, which may necessitate the hiring of a certified translator.[14]

Take a laptop or note pad, a tagging or numbering device in case none is provided by the opponent, and a small tape recorder. The laptop or tape recorder facilitates efficient recording of observations and descriptions of documents, especially if they cannot be numbered or copied. At the examination, methodically work through the documents, noting type, date, author, addressee, pages, and attachments. Pay special attention to any extraneous marks or handwriting. Such scribbles can provide valuable insights, or even evidence, against the opponent. See that all documents requested are produced and that the opponent provides a list of each document not produced under the claim of privilege or other objection. Note and index each document you want and have documents copied or see that arrangements are made to have them copied later and delivered to your office. If a vendor or others will be responsible for copying your selections:

- Consider bringing a hand-held scanner for those especially important documents to ensure against loss in the copying process.
- Be certain they know the specific date by which you need the documents.
- Send a follow-up verification letter.
- Calendar the return date.[15]

For budgetary reasons, copy only useful documents. If in doubt as to whether to copy a particular document, it is best to copy it. Immediately after the examination, summarize your notes and taped comments and share them with your supervising attorney. The summary will also help you recall what you were thinking at the time of the examination, which can be beneficial when you review the documents later.[16]

In the rarer instance of being given direct access to the other party's computer system for purposes of examination, testing, or sampling [Rule 34(a)(1)], a qualified technician will be needed to make a complete examination of the e-system, deal with viruses, detect tampering or changes since the date of the preservation hold, extract meta- and residual data, and properly duplicate the selected information. In this process, it is essential that the technician know the agreed on protocol involving the exposure of privileged or protected information.

ANALYZING DOCUMENTS PRODUCED BY THE OPPONENT

The documents produced by the opponent need to be analyzed immediately. Apply the same processes described earlier (preparing the client's documents for production) to number, code, digest, index, scan where needed, retrieve, and review the documents. Employ document management and good litigation support software to make full use of your opponent's information, including deposition transcripts, video, photos, and the like, not only for discovery, but also for trial preparation.

The documents should be reviewed for compliance with the original request. Are the time periods requested covered? Are all of the pertinent attachments referred to in the document properly attached? Are the objections appropriate? Are there gaps in the records or chronology? Have items been lost or destroyed? Is an additional request for production necessary; for example, do you need to request production in native format (including metadata) of a suspicious document that was initially produced in PDF or TIFF? Concerns raised by the analysis should be discussed with the attorney. An expert may be needed to help interpret highly technical material. If any points of concern cannot be resolved in discussion with the other party, a Rule 37 motion to compel discovery may be needed. Compelling discovery is covered later in this chapter.

REQUEST FOR PHYSICAL AND MENTAL EXAMINATION

PURPOSE AND SCOPE

Rule 35 and parallel state rules permit an adverse party, with good cause, to have the other party submit to a medical examination. The exam is requested to confirm the opponent's allegations of mental or physical injury and to prevent fraudulent claims. The exam may be to confirm a child's blood type in a paternity action, the permanency of a physical injury in an automobile accident, or the mental capabilities and awareness of a person who may be claiming incapacity in a contract challenge.

The request may reach parties and persons who are in the custody or legal control of a party. For example, a mother suing for paternity may need to bring the child for a blood test, or a guardian ad litem may be requested to produce an incompetent person to have injuries examined that the guardian alleges disabled that person in an automobile accident. Co-parties may also be reached under the rule.

According to Rule 35(a) an examination may be ordered if two tests are met: (1) the alleged condition is in controversy (i.e., the nature and extent of the condition is at issue), and (2) good cause exists to have the examination. In this context, good cause refers to a legitimate need to confirm the injury or to discover information likely to have a direct bearing on the case. Because of the potential for abuse, and the obvious and sometimes painful intrusion into the privacy of the person subject to examination, the courts tend to interpret "good cause" rather strictly and deny motions for medical examinations if the information can be acquired through less intrusive means. Medical examinations are most routinely ordered in personal injury cases.

PROCEDURE

Attorneys for the parties are usually quite cooperative regarding such exams. Often a phone call and a confirming letter are all that is needed to secure the examination. However, a request to a party to undergo an exam does not require the party to undergo the exam. If an informal overture is rejected or ignored, a motion for a court order is required. A refusal to submit to the exam in violation of a court order may result in dismissal of the case [Rule 37(b)]. The party subject to the exam may object or seek a protective order.

Once the exam is completed, a physician's report is prepared for the party requesting the exam, who then is responsible to forward a copy of it to the examined party if requested.

SET UP THE EXAM

You may be asked to perform several tasks in conjunction with the Rule 35 examination. Contacting the other party's attorney to see if there are any objections to the exam and proceeding informally will be the initial task. Consult with the supervising attorney to see if a confirming letter or a more formal stipulation is appropriate, or if a motion is required.

Contact the physician to discuss the purpose of the exam and the method of payment. Schedule an appointment and convey this information to the party to be examined.

DRAFT THE DOCUMENTS

Draft the necessary documents. An example of a motion for compulsory physical examination appears in Exhibit 9:6.[17]

The motion may require a notice of motion, an accompanying affidavit, and/or a proposed order for the judge. Check local practice. The motion should be reviewed by the attorney, signed, and served on the other party. After the exam, obtain a report from the doctor and consult with the supervising attorney. When the report is approved, send a copy to the opposing party if requested or as directed by your attorney. Pay the doctor and record the expense so it can be added to the client's bill.

EXHIBIT 9:6 ■ Motion for Compulsory Physical Examination

[FED. R. CIV. P. Rule 35(a)]

[*Title of Court and Cause*]

Defendant, _____, moves the court for an order requiring the plaintiff, _____, to submit to a physical examination [to be made by _____ describe examiner or examiners, or by a competent _____ describe type of examiner or examiners designated by the court, at _____ or as the court shall order,] for the purpose of determining the exact nature and extent of his [or, her] injuries, if any, and the disabilities, if any, resulting therefrom [or for an order requiring the plaintiff _____, the Guardian of _____ to produce _____, for whose injuries the above entitled action is brought, to submit, etc, or include appropriate designations of the party and person under his legal custody and control].

The ground of this motion is that there is a controversy between the plaintiff and defendant as to the physical injuries, if any, sustained by the plaintiff [or _____], and the disability, if any, resulting therefrom, and that the physical examination of the plaintiff [or_____] is necessary in order that the defendant, _____, may be in a position to defend as to the claimed injuries of the plaintiff [or _____], as is more fully shown in the affidavit of _____ hereunto annexed as Exhibit A [designate record and any other supporting documents].
[Date]

                                    _____
Attorney for Defendant

Address: _____

Source: Reprinted with permission of West Group.

INFORM THE CLIENT

If your party is subject to the exam, tell the client as soon as it is determined that the exam should be taken. Although the client may have been forewarned of a possible exam, the reality of it calls for further explanation, support, and instruction, which may be done by letter as in the Exhibit 9:7 example. In the alternative, the client might be instructed on these points at the office. In some circumstances you may be asked to accompany the client to the exam. In a Colorado case, a judge ruled that a paralegal could attend the Rule 35 physical exam of the paralegal's client. The court ruled that the exam was more adversarial than medical, giving rise to the need of the paralegal to protect the client from overreaching and unfair questioning.[18]

EXHIBIT 9:7 ▪ Notice to Client of Physical Examination

WHITE, WILSON & McDUFF
ATTORNEYS AT LAW
FEDERAL PLAZA BUILDING, SUITE 700
THIRD AND MARKET STREETS
LEGALVILLE, COLUMBIA 00000
(111) 555-0000

December 15, _____

Ms. Ann Forrester
1533 Capitol Drive
Legalville, Columbia 00000

Dear Ms. Forrester:
You may recall I mentioned in our initial interview the possibility that the other side in this case may request an examination by a doctor of their choosing to confirm the existence and extent of your injuries. Lynn Ott has contacted me to request such an exam.

The exam is scheduled for January 23, _____, at 1:30 in the afternoon. The examining physician is Dr. Melissa Ward, whose office is at 1644 Fountain Drive near exit 103 off I-275 in Legalville. Please make arrangements to be at Dr. Ward's office at the appointed time.

The exam will consist of a routine examination of your injuries, brief strength and movement tests, and a discussion with the doctor about your injuries and disabilities. The exam should last about an hour.

Before going to the examination, you may choose to make a list of your injuries, treatments, pain, disabilities, and current status. A review of your injury diary should help you.

You should cooperate fully in the exam and be sure neither to overstate nor understate the progress of your condition.

Mr. White believes the exam will be beneficial to your case. If you have any concerns, please let me know.

Very truly yours,

Terry Salyer
Paralegal

REQUEST THE REPORT

Following the exam, check with the supervising attorney on whether to request a copy of the report. Once the report is requested by the examined party, Rule 35(b)(2) says all privilege regarding other examinations of that party pertaining to the condition in question is waived. Normally this waiver of privilege would not be a problem, but in some unusual cases it may be. You may be asked to review and summarize the report noting any significant findings or comments for the attorney.

REVIEWING AND INTERPRETING MEDICAL RECORDS AND OTHER TECHNICAL DOCUMENTS AND REPORTS

INTRODUCTION

Most litigation paralegals review and summarize medical, commercial, industrial, scientific, and other technical records and reports that come into the case file as the result of a request for a medical examination, initial disclosure, document production, or other investigation. This can be exciting not only when you come upon information critical to your client's case, but also because you are learning entirely new areas of knowledge. Steps for dealing with such material are as follows:

1. Start the process of review as soon after receipt of the information as is practical.
2. Review the case file for the facts and issues.
3. Check each document against the list of requested documents to see if all are present. If not, note any absence and explanation for the attorney.
4. Read each document to categorize it and check its completeness, legibility, and accuracy. Missing words, letters left out of an abbreviation, misused words, and any other inaccuracies should be noted to avoid misreading or inaccurate conclusions. Certain documents providing critical information should be summarized.
5. Interpret each technical document by translating it into plain English.
6. Digest each document by summarizing the most significant information. Note inconsistencies or anything unusual. Highlight things that are particularly important to a determination of the issues.

The following section describes how this methodology is applied in the particular example of interpreting medical records.

MEDICAL RECORD INTERPRETATION

Resources

Assume that you have received the medical records for Ann Forrester. The hospital has sent each record that you requested. It is now your job to read that record, verify its accuracy, and understand it so that you can summarize it in lay terms for the benefit of the attorney. The stumbling block, however, is that you cannot interpret what you do not understand. Therefore, it becomes your task to educate yourself. In the case of medical records, as is true of many other technical documents, the

> "A phrase begins life as a literary expression; its felicity leads to its lazy repetition; and repetition soon establishes it as a legal formula, undiscriminatingly used to express different and sometimes contradictory ideas."
>
> —FELIX FRANKFURTER, *TILLER, EXECUTOR V. ATLANTIC COAST LINE RAILROAD CO.*, 318 U.S. 54, 68 (1943).

major obstacle is the terminology and abbreviations. To overcome this obstacle, you need specialized dictionaries and other guides. A good medical dictionary is an essential for litigation paralegals working in personal injury cases. It is a good idea to create a concise, working glossary of obscure or technical terms raised in a particular case for quick reference for the duration of the case. An electronic version of the glossary is convenient for such a task and provides organizational flexibility and mobility.

Some reports use abbreviations or codes that may not be readily found in a dictionary. The people who work regularly with such documents have a code key or some other guide to abbreviations. For example, a tactful request to the medical records librarian of a hospital usually produces a list of abbreviations used by that hospital. Medical report abbreviations are somewhat standardized, but each hospital or each form may have its own peculiarities. Professional associations often have uniform abbreviations or code guides. Diagrams on human anatomy and physiology should be obtained. They are available in basic biology or nursing textbooks, as well as in appropriate sections of the medical or law library. Much of this information is also available online.

You should have a guide to pharmaceutical (drugs) and therapeutic terminology. The *Physician's Desk Reference*, is an excellent reference for medicines, their purposes, and side effects. A current guide to medical tests and procedures is also helpful. Another good source is *Paralegal Medical Records Review* by Kristyn S. Appleby and Joanne Tarver. See the list of investigative resources in Chapter 3 for relevant on-line sites. Equipped with such resources, you should have little difficulty interpreting and summarizing hospital and physician's records. Many other technical fields have similar references.

The Mini-Guide

Having acquired the necessary dictionaries and other resources, it may be worthwhile to create a mini-guide that can be used repeatedly as a quick reference when interpreting technical records. An example of such a mini-guide, *A Mini-Guide for Interpreting Medical Records*, is located in Appendix D. Please review the *Mini-Guide* at this time. The mini-guide method is adaptable to any technical field.

One paralegal confirms the importance of preparation and attention to detail in document review in a car accident case. In medical reports from immediately after the accident and ten days later, the paralegal found statements that the plaintiff was alert with no loss of consciousness or signs of head or face trauma. Then the paralegal found inconsistencies.

> The next sets of records . . . were for treatment received one year after the accident, at which time the plaintiff was complaining of headaches and double vision. In these records, the plaintiff related to two different physicians (a neurologist and an ophthalmologist) that he had lost consciousness for a long period of time and had woken up in the ambulance on his way to the hospital. In addition, he stated that he was very bruised around both eyes. By pointing out these inconsistencies in my summary ("This statement is not supported by the medical record") I was able to provide information to the attorney to use as he saw fit.[19]

Once the record is translated, it can be summarized or digested in the same manner that depositions are digested. Some medical or other specialized records can be provided in electronic form or can be converted. Commercial vendors and consultants are available to assist when working with such records.

REQUEST FOR ADMISSION (RULE 36)

PURPOSE AND SCOPE

A request for admission is a document that sets out statements on specific facts, opinions, or the application of law to facts for the other party to admit or deny. Once admitted, the matter cannot be controverted. The purpose of admissions is to clarify which matters are no longer in dispute and, thus, unnecessary to prove at trial. This device is authorized by Rule 36 of the Federal Rules and parallel state rules. By narrowing the issues and related areas of proof, admissions can reduce the amount of time devoted to investigation and discovery, as well as the number of witnesses needed for trial. The need for the trial itself can be eliminated by clarifying the desirability of a settlement or possibility of a summary judgment. In short, it aims to achieve efficiency and frugality. The request for admission generally follows other discovery devices. It is not a request for information like a deposition or an interrogatory, but a confirmation of the truthfulness and accuracy of the previously discovered information. Requests for admission are a productive but often underused discovery device.

The scope of the request is defined by Rule 26(b) and for all practical purposes is the same as for the other discovery devices. The request may be directed to any other party in the lawsuit, and its use is limited solely to the particular lawsuit. In addition to facts, opinions, and application of law to facts, the request may seek admission on the genuineness of documents, photographs, exhibits, and physical evidence (things). When an admission should be forthcoming, failure or refusal to admit can lead to significant sanctions.

PROCEDURE

The steps in requesting admission include the following:

1. The request for admission with pertinent documents attached must be served on the responding party with copies to other parties.
2. The request may not be made prior to the Rule 26(f) discovery planning meeting unless ordered by the court or stipulated to by the parties. Check local rules.
3. The response must be made within thirty days or *matters are deemed admitted* unless extension of time is requested and granted.
4. The party responding may choose to seek a Rule 26(c) protective order on any particular matter. If so, other parties must be notified, the motion argued, and order entered.
5. The party responding may withdraw an answer and amend it with leave of the court. A timely withdrawal is granted if the original response is inaccurate and has not prejudiced the other party's case. If a party relied on the truthfulness of a response, and as a result did not pursue an expert opinion or evidence at that time available but now lost, the withdrawal can be denied.
6. The party requesting admission may accept the opponent's replies and objections or seek an order compelling either an answer or an expanded answer through a motion to determine the sufficiency of the response [Rule 36(a)].
7. Motions for court-imposed sanctions may be made if a denial is ruled improper or the challenge to an objection improper. The court may then require the other party to pay for costs of having to bring or argue a motion or for having to prove the matter at trial when it should have been admitted

[Rules 36(a) and 37(c)(2)]. The court will not order sanctions if the request was held objectionable at the time of the 36(a) motion, or the admission sought was inconsequential, or there were reasonable grounds to believe the refusing party would prevail on the unadmitted issue at trial, or for other good reason not to admit.

PREPARING THE REQUEST FOR ADMISSION

Your role in working with requests for admissions can range from simply keeping track of what has been admitted and what has not, to a more intensive involvement, including the drafting of questions and answers for such requests. The following is a list of suggested steps in assisting the attorney with requests for admissions:

1. Review the pleadings, interrogatories, depositions, statements, and other relevant information if it is not fresh in your mind.
2. Prepare a list of admissions you need from the opponent. In the *Forrester* case it would be helpful if Mercury Parcel admitted that Mr. Hart was their employee and on duty at the time of the accident, or that Mr. Hart had exceeded the recommended number of shift hours just prior to the accident, if discovery had so revealed. Depending on the nature of the case, the list could become quite lengthy.
3. Seek suggestions and comments on the list from the attorney.
4. Draft a set of requests, keeping the following suggestions and techniques in mind:
   a. Check to see if court rules impose any limits on the number of admissions that may be requested. The Federal Rules have no such limitations.
   b. Locate a form for requests for admissions to learn format, types of questions, style, detail, and other matters that will help in visualizing the task.
   c. Set forth each point in a separate request or clearly delineated subsection. Combining points can be confusing and may lead to evasive or misleading answers.
   d. Write brief and concise questions that elicit yes or no or otherwise brief answers. Eliminate unnecessary qualifiers from the questions.
   e. Avoid use of incorporations by reference unless it is the only alternative.
   f. Number questions sequentially and from the end of one set of requests to the beginning of another.
   g. Research any request formats that raise questions of appropriateness.
   h. Request admissions that relate to facts, statements or opinions of fact, or of the application of law to fact. Include admissions regarding the genuineness of documents or other physical evidence including diagrams and exhibits [Rule 36(a)].

An example of a request for admission of a fact:

> Please admit:
> That Mr. Hart was driving said vehicle on the date of said accident.

An example of a request eliciting an admission of an opinion:

> Please admit:
> That Defendant Hart was tired at the time of the accident.

An example of a request relating the application of law to fact:

> Please admit:
> That Defendant Hart was acting in the scope of his agency to Defendant Mercury Parcel at the time of the accident.

Agency and its scope are defined by law; therefore this question requires the application of legal principles on agency to the specific facts of the case.

An example of a request related to a document:

> Please admit:
> That Exhibit 5, a form MSA dated June 12, _____, signed by Mr. Hart:
> a. is an accurate copy of the original document,
> b. is kept in the ordinary course of Mercury Parcel Service's business,
> c. is a document used for drivers to report complaints about Mercury Parcel's vehicles.

This example demonstrates how a document should be identified and how a question on one item can be broken down to elicit admissions on each important subpoint. These points, if admitted, not only establish the copy of the document as a true copy, but also seek an admission that will lay the necessary foundation for the document to be admitted into evidence at trial. If admitted, these points will eliminate the need of a special witness to lay the foundation.

Usually a copy of the document is also included as an exhibit for review by the opponent; however, attaching the document is not necessary if the other party has the original document or a copy acquired through discovery. The description of the document must be sufficiently detailed to enable the other party to determine what document is addressed.

5. Have the request for admission reviewed, signed, and served on all parties.

Exhibit 9:8 is the form for a request for admissions based on Official Form 25 of the Federal Rules of Civil Procedure.

RESPONDING TO A REQUEST FOR ADMISSION

1. Calendar the necessary response date figured on the basis of thirty days, otherwise deemed admitted.
2. Review the request thoroughly and the particular case file as needed.
3. Consult with the supervising attorney on how to respond to each request.
4. Draft the response keeping the following in mind:
   a. Answer each question unless told to do otherwise. Failure to answer means the item is admitted.
   b. Engross questions and then add the corresponding response for purposes of convenience and clarity.

EXHIBIT 9:8 ■ Federal Form 25: Request for Admission Under Rule 36

[Caption]

Plaintiff A.B. requests Defendant C.D. within _____ days after service of this request to make the following admissions for the purpose of this action only and subject to all pertinent objections to admissibility which may be interposed at the trial:

1. That each of the following documents, exhibited with this request, is genuine. (Here list and describe each document.)

2. That each of the following statements is true. (Here list the statements.)

Signed: _____
Attorney for Plaintiff
Address: _____

    c. Answer with one of the following choices: admit, deny, qualify, object, move for extension of time, or move for a protective order.

    d. You must admit if you believe the matter is at least substantially true; however, if you have a reasonable doubt, such as when the veracity (truthfulness) of a witness is doubted, a denial is permissible.[20] Misspellings and other minor inaccuracies are not sufficient grounds for denial unless they go directly to the substance of the dispute.

    e. If an item is denied, you must state "denied," not "refuse to admit" or "not accurate."[21]

    f. You may admit in part and deny in part, but be clear.

    g. You may qualify a response and say, "Cannot admit or deny," as long as you give adequate reasons such as, "After reasonable inquiry, there is insufficient information to admit or deny" [Rule 37(c)].[22]

    h. If an objection is made, the reason must be stated.

    i. You may object if a specific question does not fall within the usual scope of discovery. The most common objections are irrelevancy and privilege. Other acceptable objections may include vagueness, trade secrets, compound question, and others.[23] Typical invalid objections include: request presents issue for trial, disputable matter, factual opinion, mixed question of law and fact, other party already knows the answer, and requesting party has burden of proof.[24]

5. Have the draft reviewed, typed, signed, and served on all parties.

    Exhibit 9:9 is the form for the Response to Defendant's Requests for Admissions.[25]

EXHIBIT 9:9 ■ Response to Defendant's Requests for Admissions

(Caption omitted)

The Plaintiff, _____, in answer to the Defendant's request for admissions served on the _____ day of _____, ____, in the above stated matter, says:

    1. Denied. However, Plaintiff admits that, apart from the fact that the premiums were waived by the terms of the policies on account of Plaintiff's then existing total and permanent disability, premiums would have become due as set out in that statement.

    2. Admitted.

    3. Admitted in part and denied in part. Plaintiff admits that the check referred to in Statement No. 2, when deposited by the Defendant, was not honored by the bank. Plaintiff denies that the check was not paid thereafter.

    4. Plaintiff objects to Request No. 4, which request is as follows: _____. The objection is: _____. (State as ground for objection that the requested admission is privileged, irrelevant or otherwise improper.)

    5. Plaintiff can neither admit nor deny Request No. 5, which request is as follows: _____. This is because Defendant refused to permit Plaintiff to review the document in question pursuant to a proper request for production, and without said production, Plaintiff does not have the knowledge to admit or deny the request.

                                     _____

                                     Attorney for _____

                                        (address)

Source: Reprinted with permission of West Group.

REVIEW OF AND REPLY TO RESPONSE

1. List all admissions, denials, objections, or improper responses.
2. Consult with the supervising attorney concerning the response and the list you made on it.
3. Draft motions to test the appropriateness of answers or objections as instructed.
4. Keep a record of all costs related to proving points denied by the other party for recovery if denial is shown to be improper.

AMENDING RESPONSES

If a response is discovered to be untrue because of inaccuracies or change in facts, you may be requested to draft a motion for a court order to withdraw the answer and to submit an amended response [Rule 36(b)]. The paralegal on the other side may have to draft a response to the motion demonstrating that the client would be prejudiced by the withdrawal. A party may be prejudiced, for example, if he or she had stopped discovery on an issue or failed to seek witnesses because of reliance on the admission.

OBJECTIONS, COMPELLING DISCOVERY, AND SANCTIONS

OBJECTING TO DISCOVERY: PROTECTIVE ORDERS

A discovery request may go too far. It may request privileged information or attorney work product, be unduly expensive, or be excessive in some other way. When this happens, it is necessary to object to the specific question or request. If after a good faith attempt to resolve the matter between the parties, the requesting party persists, the resisting party may by motion request a protective order from the court. This motion must be accompanied by a certificate stating that the party requesting the protective order made a good faith attempt to resolve the issue with the other party. The court has the duty to protect a party or person from annoyance, embarrassment, oppression, or undue burden or expense. It is empowered to provide these remedies set out in Rule 26(c):

1. Deny the requested disclosure or discovery
2. Grant discovery on specific terms and conditions, including time and place
3. Grant discovery but by a different method than requested
4. Grant discovery provided certain items are not inquired into, or if the scope of the inquiry is limited
5. Grant discovery but only in the presence of certain individuals named by the court
6. Grant discovery provided the deposition is sealed and opened only by court order
7. Deny discovery of trade or commercial secrets, or grant discovery in a limited way
8. Grant discovery only if parties simultaneously file specified information or documents in sealed envelopes to be opened as directed by the court

The court has the power to deny the motion and order the resisting party to permit the discovery. If the motion is denied and justice requires, the court may order the resisting party to pay the costs and attorney fees incurred by the party seeking discovery [Rules 26(c) and 37(a)(4)]. The protective order may be sought in the district where the case is pending or in the district where the discovery is sought.

COMPELLING DISCOVERY

The federal discovery rules and those in most states are designed to encourage cooperation in the mutual discovery process with a minimum of court involvement. Despite the emphasis on cooperation, the court must sometimes become involved. When one of the parties refuses to respond or cooperate in disclosure or a request for discovery, the other party can invoke the power of the court to compel that party to produce the information or give valid reasons for not doing so.

A party may seek the aid of the court when the other party does not provide the required disclosure or answer questions in interrogatories or a deposition, when a corporation or other entity fails to designate the person who will provide the required interrogatory or deposition answers, when a party does not permit the inspection of documents, or when a party provides an evasive or incomplete answer [Rule 37(a)(2) and (3)].

MOTION, ORDER, AND SANCTIONS

When a party has failed to cooperate, the adverse party may file a motion requesting an order to compel disclosure or discovery. The court may then order the uncooperative party to pay the costs (reasonable expenses) and attorney fees incurred by the other side in bringing the motion, unless the failure was substantially justified or if the moving party did not make a good faith attempt to resolve the matter with the other party. Conversely, if a motion to compel is filed, denied, and found to be without substantial justification, the filing party may be ordered to pay costs, including attorney's fees [Rule 37(a)(4)].

If the motion is filed, and the court orders compliance but the party does not comply, the court may impose a number of severe sanctions. The court in the district where the deposition is taken may fine the uncooperative deponent for contempt of court if the person has refused an order to be sworn in or to answer a deposition question [Rule 37(b)(1)]. If a party or the designated person for an entity fails to obey an order to permit discovery, the court may impose certain sanctions:

a. Order that the matter or evidence sought be considered proved for the benefit of the party requesting the order;
b. Order the uncooperative party not to oppose certain claims or defenses or not to introduce designated matter into evidence;
c. Order the pleadings or parts thereof be stricken;
d. Stay (stop) further proceedings until the order is obeyed;
e. Dismiss the action, or any part thereof;
f. Render a default judgment against the disobedient party;
g. Find the party in contempt of court;
h. Order sanctions a, b, and c, when there is a refusal to submit to a medical exam, unless the party can show that the person to be examined cannot be produced [Rule 37(b)(2)(A-E)].

In lieu of or in addition to these sanctions, the court may impose the payment of costs, including attorney's fees, unless such failure to respond is substantially justified [Rule 37(b)(2)]. Also, when a party breaches the duty to preserve potentially discoverable information, an *adverse jury instruction* can be given the jurors.

This instruction permits the jury to infer that the lost information was damaging to that party.

In addition, Rule 37(c)(1) sanctions for failing to disclose information required by Rule 26(a) or 26(e)(1) or failure to comply with the continuing duty to disclose, unless there is substantial justification or the failure to disclose is harmless, include not being able to use the undisclosed evidence or witness at trial or other hearing; having to pay reasonable expenses caused by the failure, including attorney's fees; and the other sanctions set out in (a) through (f) in the preceding list. These sanctions do not require a motion.

As mentioned in the section on requests for admission, if a party receives a request for admission and fails to admit the genuineness of any document (or e-stored information) or the truth of any matter as requested under Rule 36, and the other party proves the genuineness or truth of the matter, the court on motion may order the refusing party to pay the other party's expenses in proving the matter [Rule 37(c)(2)].

If a party or an officer, director, or managing agent of a party or a designate for a corporation or other entity fails to appear at the deposition after receiving proper notice, or fails to serve answers or objections to interrogatories after proper service, or to serve a written response to a properly served request for inspection, the court may on motion impose the sanctions previously mentioned in (a) to (f), including payment of costs [Rule 37(d)].

If pursuant to Rule 26(f) a party requests a discovery conference to set up a discovery plan and the other party fails to participate in good faith in the framing of a discovery plan, the court may impose the payment of costs incurred by the other party, including attorney's fees, due to the failure to cooperate [Rule 37(g)].

Rule 37(f) recognizes that the standard operation of e-information systems can lead to the non-culpable loss of discoverable information. Under subsection (f), a party is protected from court sanctions if the information is "lost as a result of the routine, good faith [non-culpable] operation of an electronic information system." Routine overwriting and other loss of data in the normal operation of the system are acceptable. Conversely, once a party is aware of the duty to preserve discovery information in the context of particular litigation, routine loss of potentially relevant data is not acceptable.

Local rules may provide different procedures and sanctions and should be consulted.

PROCEDURE FOR COMPELLING DISCOVERY

When the opponent has not provided disclosure or responded to a request for discovery or has objected to a request for discovery, the supervising attorney should be informed. If, after the required good faith effort to resolve differences, the decision is made to compel disclosure or discovery and seek sanctions, draft the necessary documents to file the motion to compel discovery. The documents include the motion, certification of attempt to resolve, the notice of motion, usually a memorandum of law, the desired order, and the certificate of service. Before you draft the motion, however, the attorney must decide what court should receive the motion. A motion for an order to compel a party may be filed in the court where the action is pending; if to compel a nonparty, the motion should be made in the court in the district where the discovery is sought [Rule 37(a)(1)]. The caption should be drafted accordingly. An adaptable form for a motion to compel appears in Exhibit 9:10,[26] the affidavit in support of the motion is Exhibit 9:11,[27] and a proposed order to compel in Exhibit 9:12.[28]

EXHIBIT 9:10 ■ Motion to Compel Production, Inspection, and Copying of Documents in Case of Objection or Failure to Respond Plus Rule 26(c) Certification—General Form

[FED. R. CIV. P. Rules 34(b), 37(a)]

[*Title of Court and Cause*]

Defendant, _____, moves the court for an order requiring plaintiff, _____, to produce and to permit defendant to inspect and to copy or photograph each of the following documents [*here list the documents and describe each of them*]. This motion is made on the ground that the defendant served a written request upon the plaintiff for production, inspection, and copying or photographing the above-mentioned documents, a copy of which is attached hereto as Exhibit A, and that the plaintiff objected to said production by a response, a copy of which is attached hereto as Exhibit B [*or* and that plaintiff has failed and refused to respond to defendant's request as required by Rule 34, Federal Rules of Civil Procedure]. The documents requested by defendant contain relevant and material evidence in the above-entitled action and their production is necessary for defendant to prepare for trial, as indicated in Exhibit C hereto attached.

Attorney for Defendant

Address: _____

Certification of Attempt to Resolve [Rule 26(c)]

I [*attorney's name*], attorney for [*defendant, plaintiff*], certify that prior to filing this motion to compel discovery I made a good faith attempt to resolve this discovery issue as follows:

1. [*Briefly state facts and dates of attempt and failure to resolve.*]

2. _____

Date _____

_____

Attorney for   _____
Address:
Phone:

Source: Reprinted with permission of West Group.

EXHIBIT 9:11 ■ Affidavit in Support of Motion to Compel

[FED. R. CIV. P. Rules 34, 37(a)]

[*Title of Court and Cause*]

[Venue]

_____, being first duly sworn, on his oath states:

That he is one of the attorneys for the above named defendant and he makes this affidavit in support of the Motion for Production of Documents and Things for Inspection, Copying and Photographing which is attached hereto; that the production of the documents, papers, statements and things requested is made in good faith; that he has been informed and therefore believes that the matters and things so sought in said motion are competent as evidence in said cause and are especially competent by reason of the fact that, _____; that the facts sought to be elicited are facts necessary to be shown and produced in said cause in the furtherance of justice and in securing all the facts competent upon the issues to be tried.

EXHIBIT 9:11 ■ Affidavit in Support of Motion to Compel (*continued*)

The motion herein made is made in good faith and the affiant as one of counsel for defendant desires to inspect said documents solely for the purpose of establishing facts to be used as evidence in the above-entitled cause and affiant does not intend to use said information for any other purpose or to convey the same to any other party or persons.

Dated this _____ day of _____, ____.
[*Jurat*]

Source: Reprinted with permission of West Group.

EXHIBIT 9:12 ■ Order That Interrogatories Concerning Personal Jurisdiction Are Answered and That Personal Jurisdiction is Established

[FED. R. CIV. P. Rule 37(b)(2)]

[*Title of Court and Cause*]

Ready for decision is the plaintiff's motion to impose sanctions for failure to comply with order of the court, filing _____.

On [*date*], ____, an order was entered, filing _____, requiring the defendants to file answers to designated written interrogatories on or before [*date*], ____. No such filing has been made to the present day, and no motion has been made for an enlargement of time in which to comply with the order.

Sanctions under Rule 37(b) of the Federal Rules of Civil Procedure are therefore appropriate.

It appears to the court that the unresolved issues to which the interrogatories went are those designated in Exhibit C of the order on pretrial conference, filing _____, as:

"1. Personal jurisdiction on The _____ Company, a _____ corporation.

(a) Was The _____ Company, a _____ corporation doing business in _____?

(b) Was the involvement of The _____ Company substantial enough to give this court jurisdiction over this defendant?"

Those questions will now stand as answered in the affirmative, and personal jurisdiction waived by that defendant.

It may be that the interrogatories are relevant to other issues described in the order on pretrial conference. If so, the plaintiffs may make a showing brief or otherwise pointing out what other issues, and consideration will be given to imposition of further sanctions.

IT IS SO ORDERED.

1. That the motion to impose sanctions for failure to comply with the order of the court, filing is granted to the extent that it hereby is determined: That the defendant The _____ Company, a _____ corporation, was doing business in_____ and its involvement was substantial enough to give this court jurisdiction over that defendant; that personal jurisdiction over the defendant The _____ company, a _____ corporation, is deemed admitted and established and the issue of personal jurisdiction over the defendant is waived by that defendant;

2. That the defendant The _____ Company shall pay within fifteen days of the date of this order to the plaintiffs' counsel the amount of $_____ as the expense of obtaining this order; and

3. That because The _____ Company, a _____ corporation, is now known as _____ Corp., wherever in this order there is reference to _____ Company, a _____ corporation, it is applicable to _____ Corp.

[*Date*]

United States District Judge

Source: Reprinted with permission of West Group.

A copy of the motion and supporting documents should be reviewed by the attorney and served on the attorney for the adverse party. All documents plus proof of service should be filed with the appropriate clerk of court. These procedures and the required documents may vary in state practice.

THE FREEDOM OF INFORMATION ACT

DEFINITION AND PURPOSE

In addition to the formal discovery devices covered in Chapters 7, 8, and 9 and the informal investigation devices covered in Chapter 3, paralegals can enhance the client's case by accessing government sources of information. In 1976, the Freedom of Information Act, 5 U.S.C. § 552 (FOIA) was passed to provide the general public access to the records of many government agencies. The public policy underlying the law is that a more informed public will enhance the accountability and performance of government agencies and officials. Such openness is deemed desirable and consistent with our democratic form of government. Several states have passed similar laws.

The FOIA might be helpful in a suit against a particular government agency or in a suit against a private party. The Consumer Products Safety Commission, for example, might be able to provide information on the safety record of the make of van involved in Ms. Forrester's accident, on the type of extension cord used by the campground in Case II, or on the all-terrain vehicle that led to the death of Sean Coleman in Case III.

Use of the FOIA offers some advantages over most other discovery devices:

1. It is not necessary to file an action or order to gain access to the information. In the examples just given, a request for information about faulty products could be submitted well before the filing of the action, and could be useful in determining whether the manufacturer of the product in question should be joined as one of the defendants in the case.
2. Because the law is not oriented toward litigation, the Rule 26(b) prerequisite of relevancy does not apply. Consequently, one can go on "fishing expeditions" regardless of relevancy in the hope of turning up something useful.
3. Access is available to anyone with a bona fide request.
4. The request is not restricted to information from a party as is true of some discovery devices; therefore, the range of information that can be obtained is greater.

PROCEDURE AND LIMITS

The requesting party invokes the FOIA by submitting a request to the pertinent agency through that agency's designated information officer. The request must demonstrate that the information requested is in the records of an agency covered by the act. Specific exemptions to the disclosure requirement are listed in section 552(b) of the act:

- Properly classified national defense or foreign policy documents
- Internal personnel rules and practices
- Material specifically exempted from disclosure by statute
- Trade secrets and commercial or financial information obtained from a person which are of a privileged or confidential nature

- Inter- and intra-agency communication (letters and memos) otherwise not available through discovery in actions against an agency
- Personnel, medical, and similar files of a private nature
- Law enforcement records and information if disclosure would impede investigation, violate personal privacy, or permit circumvention of the law
- Reports related to the regulation or supervision of financial institutions
- Geological and geophysical information on oil and natural gas wells

Once the request is submitted, the agency must indicate within 20 days whether it will comply or deny the request [§ 552(a)(6)(A)(i)]. That decision may be appealed, and if so, a determination must be made within twenty days [§ 552(a)(6)(A)(ii)]. If the agency upholds the decision to withhold the information, the administrative remedies are exhausted and relief must be sought in federal district court.

A reasonable fee for producing the information will be charged. The agency may waive the fee, however, if release of the information is likely to contribute significantly to public understanding of the operation or activities of government and is not primarily in the commercial interest of the requester [5 U.S.C. § 552(a)(4)(A)(iii)].

THE ROLE OF THE PARALEGAL

Your task as paralegal regarding a request for information under the FOIA will be to draft the request. Exhibit 9:13 is a form that can be used as a guide when drafting the document.[29] FOIA forms can usually be found at the Web site of the applicable agency.

You may also be called on to research the likely availability of particular information and whether it is accessible under the act. Agency Web sites now post information of public value that is likely to be requested, so you may find what you need with a simple search. Excellent resources on making FOIA requests are a Bureau of National Affairs pamphlet entitled, "The Freedom of Information Act: Business Uses" and the extensive Department of Justice information at http://www.usdoj.gov/04foia.

ORGANIZING FILES

INTRODUCTION

You see yourself sitting next to your supervising attorney at counsel's table at a dramatic point in the trial. The attorney turns to you and whispers, "I need the follow-up medical report from Dr. Grimes!" Your eyes shift to a dog-eared folder swollen beyond its capacity with corners of various pages slipping toward chaotic freedom. You begin to perspire as you feverishly page through the documents. Your attorney helps by loudly whispering, "Hurry up! Hurry up!"

As you fly through the folder, it creeps toward the edge of the table, and suddenly papers come flushing out like water through a broken dam as the file and its contents spread over the floor.

Then you wake up from the nightmare and swear that you will never let that happen to you.

The documents gathered and analyzed in discovery and investigation, plus the pleadings and other materials, must be organized in the case file. This document management is essential for efficient use of the information and to reduce the risk

EXHIBIT 9:13 ■ Freedom of Information Act (FOIA) Sample Request Letter

Agency Head [*or* Freedom of Information Act Officer]
Name of Agency
Address of Agency
City, State, Zip Code

Re: Freedom of Information Act Request

Dear _____:

This is a request under the Freedom of Information Act.

I request that a copy of the following documents [or documents containing the following information] be provided to me: [*identify the documents or information as specifically as possible*].

In order to help to determine my status to assess fees, you should know that I am [*insert a suitable description of the requester and the purpose of the request*].

[*Sample requester descriptions:*

a representative of the news media affiliated with the _____ newspaper (magazine, television station, etc.), and this request is made as part of news gathering and not for a commercial use.

affiliated with an educational or noncommercial scientific institution, and this request is made for a scholarly or scientific purpose and not for a commercial use.

an individual seeking information for personal use and not for a commercial use.
affiliated with a private corporation and am seeking information for use in the company's business.]

[*Optional*] I am willing to pay fees for this request up to a maximum of $_____. If you estimate that the fees will exceed this limit, please inform me first.

[*Optional*] I request a waiver of all fees for this request. Disclosure of the requested information to me is in the public interest because it is likely to contribute significantly to public understanding of the operations or activities of the government and is not primarily in my commercial interest. [*Include a specific explanation.*]

Thank you for your consideration of this request.

Sincerely, _____

_____
Name
Address
City, State, Zip Code
Telephone number [Optional]

Source: Reprinted with permission of West Group.

of loss or misplacement. A variety of methods can be used for organizing a client's file. More than likely you will use the method preferred by your supervising attorney. The following systems are only two methods of organization. Should you be asked to set up a system for organizing client files, law office management books will provide a variety of other methods from which to choose. The Association of Records Managers and Administrators, Inc. (http://www.arma.org) provides numerous aids. Case management software that allows an entire case file to be stored and updated electronically, Internet access, and laptop computers and mobile printers for in-court access and printing may soon make the hard-copy case file an endangered species. Even electronic files, however, need some organizational structure.

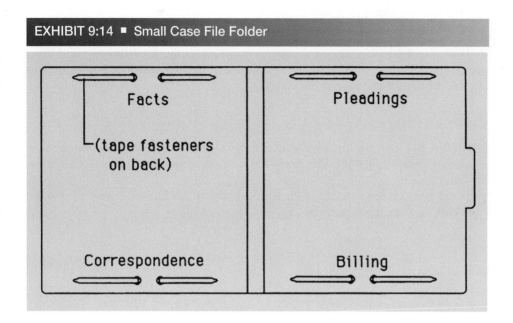

EXHIBIT 9:14 ■ Small Case File Folder

Facts

(tape fasteners on back)

Pleadings

Correspondence

Billing

SMALL CASE FILE

The documents needed in most small case files can be neatly organized into one manilla folder.[30] By attaching some of the documents at the top and some at the bottom of each of the two flaps of the folder, four general categories of file documents can be maintained. Four common file categories include pleadings, correspondence, factual items, and billing documents. The folder would appear as indicated in Exhibit 9:14.

The fact section should include such things as client background sheet [see Exhibit 2:1], client interview or summary, accident reports, contracts, pertinent business records, medical reports and authorizations, witness statements, medical bills, damage estimates, and so on. The client data sheet can contain a checkoff section indicating what was done last in the case and what should be done next. This section can be a separate form (see Exhibit 11:2) that can be standardized and computerized for ease of updating and determining the status of a case at a glance. The subcategories of the fact section may be organized into subgroups and placed in chronological or reverse chronological order and tabbed with gummed labels.

The pleadings section should contain the complaint, answer, motions, affidavits, memoranda of law, proofs and acknowledgments of service, requests for admissions, and other documents filed in the case. These documents are normally filed in chronological order and may also be tabbed and color-coded for plaintiff's and defendant's pleadings.

The correspondence section consists of all letters, memos, and other correspondence, which may be divided and tabbed in subgroups and filed in reverse chronological order. Some firms use special colored carbons to allow quick identification of correspondence originating from their offices.

The billing section should include all items that will go into the client's bill: records of travel, phone calls, conferences, witness fees, filing fees, service of process expenses, time slips, and others. Having these items organized in such a manner facilitates figuring the bill and provides the basis for status reports requested by the client.

A current index of each section of the folder should be kept at the top of one leaf of the folder for quick reference.

This type of file provides some organization, allows the file to be updated in an organized way, and should reduce the amount of time needed when the supervising attorney says, "Hurry up!"

LARGE CASE FILE

When the case involves lots of documents or outgrows the small case file, a more involved system is called for. The following method is one of several ways that it can be done.[31]

The first step is to gather all of the documents and file folders that pertain to the case, and separate these materials into six broad divisions:

- Correspondence, bills, and miscellaneous
- Pleadings
- Transcripts
- Photographs
- Documents and exhibits
- Medical records (or other relevant category)

The second step is to take the "correspondence, bills, and miscellaneous" material and make file folders assigning the following file numbers and titles:

Correspondence, Bills, and Miscellaneous: Numbers 10-99

- 10 Correspondence
- 20 Bills
- 30 Research
- 40 Investigations
- 50 Miscellaneous memos and notes
- 60 Deposition summary and notes
- 70 Answers to interrogatories summaries
- 80 Witnesses (background, memos, statements, etc.)
- 90 Miscellaneous (as needed)

Each of the subcategories can be further broken down as needed:

10 Correspondence

- 10.1 Client (to or from)
- 10.2 Insured (to or from)
- 10.3 Plaintiff's counsel (to or from)
- 10.4 Co-defendant's counsel (to or from)
- 10.5 Court (to or from)
- 10.6 Miscellaneous

If folders need to be broken down further, then use 10.1(a), (b), (c), and so on. The other categories in the division should then be broken down into logical and relevant subdivisions.

The "pleadings" division should be assigned the number 100 and subdivided accordingly. Pleadings are placed in chronological order in their subdivision and numbered in red. For example, the complaint would have a 1 in its lower right corner, the answer a 2, and so forth.

Pleadings: Numbers 100–199

110 Complaints, answers, related motions, and other related pleadings

120 Discovery pleadings to plaintiff and plaintiff's responses

121 Interrogatories to plaintiff

122 Plaintiff's response to interrogatories

123 Requests for admissions to plaintiff

124 Plaintiff's responses to admissions request

125 Requests for production and so on

130 Discovery pleadings to defendant and defendant's responses

131 Interrogatories to Defendant

132 Defendant's responses to interrogatories and so on

140 Notice of depositions and related pleadings

150 Open (to be used as specific case dictates)

160 Open

170 Pretrial/trial pleadings

180 Miscellaneous pleadings by plaintiff

190 Miscellaneous pleadings by defendant

The remaining divisions should be numbered and subdivided in like fashion. As the file folders are being created for each subdivision, a detailed index should be made of each division and the contents of each category and each subcategory. The master index should show the divisions and subdivisions with their assigned numbers. The subsequent sheets of the index should be assigned to each subfile, and as new items are placed in the subfile, a description of the item should be entered on the appropriate subfile index sheet. Exhibit 9:15 is an example of how the master index sheet might appear, and Exhibit 9:16 shows the subfile index sheet.

EXHIBIT 9:15 ▪ Master File Index Sheet

Case: *Forrester v. Mercury Parcel Service* Case File No. _____

File No.	Categories
0–99	Correspondence, bills, miscellaneous
10	Correspondence
20	Bills
30	Research
100–199	Pleadings
110	Complaints, answers, motions, and other related pleadings
120	Discovery pleadings to plaintiff
200–299	Transcripts
210	Depositions of plaintiff's witnesses
220	Depositions of defendant's witnesses
230	Trial transcripts
300–399	Photographs

EXHIBIT 9:16 ■ Subfile Index Sheet

Case: *Forrester v. Mercury Parcel Service* Case File No. _____

File No.	Subtitled Components
10.1	Client (to or from)
(a)	6/26/__ letter from seeking our representation
(b)	7/11/__ letter to setting up interview
(c)	7/13/__ letter to describing items to bring
(d)	7/20/__ letter to accepting case
10.2	Insured (to or from)
(a)	9/01/__ letter to requesting payment of damages
(b)	9/20/__ letter from stating not responsible for damages

The index can be kept and regularly updated as the first file in the case or as a three-ring binder to facilitate the rapid retrieval of needed documents. All the subfiles of the case can then be expandable case files in numerical order.

These index sheets kept at the top or front of a case file provide a quick overview of where everything is filed, and a more detailed log of the current holdings in each file. When kept current, such an index is a great organizer and time saver. If the case is going to be particularly voluminous, there are advantages to using the uniform decimal numbering system discussed earlier in the chapter.

SUMMARY

This chapter concludes the three-chapter discussion on disclosure and discovery. You have now been introduced to one of the most significant areas of litigation practice and paralegal responsibility.

Interrogatory and deposition practice were covered in the previous chapters. The focus of Chapter 9 is the production of documents and electronically stored information in disclosure and by request for production of documents and things, request for medical exam, and request for admission. Each of these procedures requires paralegals to know the applicable rules of procedure and the forms and techniques for seeking and providing the necessary information. The awareness of when and how to compel disclosure and discovery and to protect the client against improper discovery provides the weapons and armor needed to ensure that the system works for you and the firm's clients.

Further, techniques for organizing and analyzing large amounts of information, including the application of the latest computer technology to the tasks, can make an otherwise overwhelming discovery process manageable. When exercised knowledgeably and ethically, these discovery skills are extremely valuable to the client, the firm, and our system of civil justice. This knowledge plus experience will help make you an indispensable member of the litigation team.

▣ WORKBOOK

System Folder Assignments, other exercises, a chapter outline, a review test, and other study aids are located in the accompanying workbook.

▣ HELPFUL WEB SITES

http://www.lawtechnology.org
  ABA Legal Technology Resource Center

http://www.workshare.net
  information on DeltaView document comparison
software

http://www.lawofficecomputing.com
  reviews and articles on law office technology

http://www.usdoj.gov/atr/cases/f1900/1979.htm
  U.S. reply to Microsoft Corporation's Opposition to Plaintiff's Motion to Compel Production of data bases

▣ QUESTIONS FOR STUDY AND REVIEW

1. What is the definition, purpose, and scope of the request for production of documents and things?
2. What are the procedural steps and time requirements involved in the production of documents?
3. In what form should e-stored information be produced? What are the concerns regarding the format of such material?
4. How do you determine what documents and things should be requested for a production of documents and things?
5. What are the most expensive types of e-information to produce? The least expensive? Who pays for the production?
6. Know the requirements and techniques for drafting a Request for Production, Inspection, and Copying of Documents and its response.
7. What are three steps to prevent spoliation of evidence and its sanctions?
8. What are the primary initial steps in production of documents and things?
9. Who is often the most helpful person in locating documents?
10. What is often the most expensive stage of e-discovery? Why?
11. What steps need to be followed in pulling document files, both electronic and paper?
12. Describe the objectives and each step in screening the pulled files or documents, both electronic and paper.
13. What cross files are normally kept in preparing for document production?
14. What is the decimal document numbering system, and how does it work? What are its advantages?
15. Why is it important to have the attorney review the tabbed documents before copying?
16. What should be done with poor or extra photocopies of documents for production?
17. What steps should be followed and indexes kept at the examination stage?
18. What steps are important when returning documents that have been produced to the original custodian?
19. What security techniques should be taken to protect computerized data?
20. What is the procedure for replying to a request for production and inspection? What rules apply?
21. List important techniques for assisting at the production, examination, or inspection.
22. If your client is producing documents in a foreign language, what is your related responsibility to the receiving party?
23. When you hire a vendor to copy documents for production, what does the vendor need to know?
24. What should you look for when analyzing documents produced by the opponent?
25. What is the purpose of a Rule 35 mental or physical exam? What nonparties may be reached through this rule, and what showing is needed for such a request to be granted?
26. What are the procedures and tasks you perform in working with requests for compulsory medical examination?
27. What are your objectives in reviewing and interpreting discovery documents?
28. What techniques should be employed in reviewing and interpreting discovery documents?
29. What resources are recommended for reviewing medical reports?
30. What is the definition, purpose, and scope of Rule 36 requests for admissions?
31. What are the steps in the procedure for requesting admissions and responding to them?

32. Describe in detail your role regarding requests for admissions.
33. Be able to draft a request for admissions and its response.
34. Under Rule 37, when can a party seek the aid of the court to compel disclosure and discovery?
35. What sanctions can be imposed on a party by the court for failure to cooperate and adequately comply with a disclosure or discovery request, or for failure to comply with a court order compelling discovery?
36. What is the procedure for compelling discovery and the role of the paralegal?
37. What is the Freedom of Information Act? Why is it potentially useful to you as a litigation paralegal?
38. What materials are excepted from the FOIA?
39. What must be demonstrated to be granted a FOIA request, and what procedure must be followed to have such a request approved?
40. How do you organize a small case file, and what kinds of documents go in each subsection?
41. How do you organize a large case file?

◉ KEY TERMS

redaction   spoliation

◉ ENDNOTES

1. Daryl Teshima, *7 Deadly Sins of Electronic Discovery*, LAW OFFICE COMPUTING, June/July 2003, 80.
2. UNDERWOOD, A GUIDE TO FEDERAL DISCOVERY RULES 222 (2d ed., 1985).
3. Kevin F. Brady and Matthew I. Cohen, *Achieving a Useful Litigation Hold*, NAT. LAW JRNL. July 25, 2005, S7.
4. *Id.*, S8.
5. Teshima, *supra* note 1, 81.
6. Miró, *Ten Thousand Documents and Counting: The Mechanics of Project Control and Data Base Design*, LEGAL ASSISTANT TODAY, Mar./Apr. 1996, 41, 43–44.
7. Items 1, 3, 4, and 6 are from Lovett, *Data Bases That Help Win Cases*, NAT'L. L.J., Jan. 29, 1996, C1–C3; item 2 is from Terry Carter, *Thrifty Litigation*, ABA JRNL., Aug. 2005, 38; and item 5 is from David A. Saraceno, *The New Disk in Town: Using DVD Recordable Technology in the Practice of Law*, LAW OFFICE COMPUTING, June/July 2003, 86.
8. Alan Kays, *Electronic Discovery*, FACTS & FINDINGS, Aug. 2003, 41.
9. Teshima, *supra* note 1, 82–83.
10. The discussion of the numbering system is based on LIPSON, ART OF ADVOCACY: DOCUMENTARY EVIDENCE, § 7; and Bender's Forms of Discovery, § 4.09(6)(6).
11. Juhnke, *Where Litigation Support Ends and Electronic Discovery Begins*, NATIONAL PARALEGAL REPORTER, Dec. 2002/Jan. 2003, 31.
12. NALA MANUAL FOR LEGAL ASSISTANTS, 298 (4th ed., 2005).
13. WEST'S FEDERAL FORMS, § 3557, v. 3A.
14. Oliver Gierke, *Dealing With Foreign Language Documents:*

Tips for Translation, Production, and Organization, LEGAL ASSISTANT TODAY, Nov./Dec. 2005, 73.
15. Elissa A. Santo, *Document Reviews*, FACTS & FINDINGS, Feb. 2004, 40.
16. Several suggestions in this section are from a memo from J. Burton to J. McCord (March 27, 1986).
17. WEST'S FEDERAL FORMS, § 3601, v. 3A.
18. *Boulder Colorado Judge Rules to Allow Paralegals to Attend R. 35 Examinations*, NFPA ALERT, July 1989.
19. Appleby, *A Guide to Reviewing and Summarizing Medical Records*, LEGAL ASSISTANT TODAY, Sept./Oct. 1990, 26, 27.
20. ROGER S. HAYDOCK, *et al.*, FUNDAMENTALS OF PRETRIAL LITIGATION, 457 (4th ed., 2000).
21. *Id.*
22. *Id.*, 458.
23. *Id.*, 439–459.
24. *Id.*
25. Adapted from Forms § 3632 and § 3635, WEST'S FEDERAL FORMS, v. 3A, with permission of West Group.
26. WEST'S FEDERAL FORMS §§ 3559, v. 3A.
27. *Id.*, § 3560.
28. *Id.*, § 3721.5.
29. WEST'S LEGAL FORMS, § 19.2, v. 28 (3d ed., 1997), with permission of West Group.
30. Suggested in part by Weitzel, *Who's Coming to Dinner? The Bread and Butter of Your Files*, TEX. B.J. 31 (May 1968).
31. This section based on TREAT, ed., UNIFORM FILING SYSTEM, LITIGATION AIDS (National Association of Legal Assistants, June 1984).

 For additional resources visit our Web site at **http://www.westlegalstudies.com.**

CHAPTER

10

Settlement and Other Alternative Dispute Resolutions

INTRODUCTION

The purpose of litigation is to resolve disputes. Going to trial is one method of resolving the differences between parties. Most cases, however, never go to trial. They may be negotiated and settled, or the parties may seek some alternative form of resolution as required by contract or court process, or by choice. This chapter focuses on settlement as the primary method of resolving a case, but it also addresses other resolution procedures including arbitration, mediation, summary trials, and related processes that are growing in importance. As in trial preparation, the paralegal organizes information and prepares it for presentation in alternative dispute resolution. Paralegals with appropriate training can also have a more direct role in alternative dispute resolution by working as mediators and arbitrators.

SETTLEMENT

INTRODUCTION

Definition and Purpose

settlement
The process whereby both sides review strengths and weaknesses of a case and reach a mutual agreement on how to dispose of the case.

Settlement is the process whereby both sides review strengths and weaknesses of a case and reach a mutual agreement on how to dispose of the case. Approximately ninety-eight percent of all federal civil cases are settled or resolved without a trial. A case may be settled at nearly any stage of the litigation process, with some cases being disposed of before a complaint is filed, most before trial, some at trial, and a few during appeal.

Cases are settled for a variety of reasons, the most obvious being to save time, trouble, and expense. Settlement is encouraged in our system. If cases were not settled at the rate they are, our courts would be overloaded even worse than they are, and the endless litigation that lasts over several generations as portrayed in Dickens's *Bleak House* would be a reality. Settlement removes the uncertainty of the outcome of a trial, eliminates or reduces adverse publicity, and ends the fear of the ordeal of trial.

Settlement is based on a combination of factors: amount of damages, ability of the defendant to pay, insurance coverage, ease with which liability and damages can be proven, nature of the injury (permanency, horror factor, disability), sympathy for the plaintiff, whether the plaintiff needs to be paid right away or can hold out through trial, amount of verdicts in similar cases in the same area, respective ability of attorneys, attitude of the judge, desire of either party for vindication, and others. Though most of these matters are assessed by the attorney, an alert paralegal often spots things otherwise overlooked that might make a difference.

> "A lean agreement is better than a fat judgment."
>
> —PROVERB, IN ROSALIND FERGUSSON, *THE FACTS ON FILE DICTIONARY OF PROVERBS*, 1983.

Role of the Paralegal

The primary role of the paralegal is to gather, organize, and draft materials to help the attorney evaluate the case and present it in negotiation to the other side. If a settlement is reached, it generally falls to the paralegal to draft the necessary settlement documents.

Ethical Considerations

Both attorneys and paralegals must remember that the decision to accept a settlement is up to the client. ABA Model Rule 1.2 states, "A lawyer shall abide by a client's decision whether to accept an offer of settlement of a matter." This language incorporates the spirit of the old code, which is still the ethical standard in some states.

Regardless of confidence in the facts or fairness of a case, a paralegal *may not make settlement offers, accept offers, or counsel the client on the advisability of accepting a settlement.* Take caution in discussing such matters with the client and in conveying advice of the attorney. It must be crystal clear that the paralegal is not giving the advice, and the information conveyed must be accurate.

Take care when discussing matters with an adverse attorney, paralegal, or others, since a client's opportunity for settlement may be adversely affected if information is unwittingly revealed. Settlement précis and brochures (to be discussed in this chapter) or other items prepared for review by the opponent or an insurance adjuster must not reveal harmful information. Confidential information must be protected, and should be revealed only with the client's permission and approval of the attorney.

Throughout the process, you may be expected to keep the client readily informed of the progress in negotiation and any proposals. Professional ethics require the attorney to keep the client informed (Model Rule 1.4a and b).

PREPARING FOR SETTLEMENT

Introduction

The importance of the preparation needed to conduct and ultimately reach a negotiated settlement is generally underestimated. Attorneys and paralegals alike tend to focus on the trial and frequently establish all preparation timetables accordingly. Since so many cases are settled, however, timetables and preparation need to be geared to the settlement process as well. An important by-product of preparation for settlement, if done correctly, is that it becomes a significant part of the preparation for trial.

The paralegal contributes to two significant stages in settlement: the attorney's evaluation of the case and the presentation of the case for settlement. If the opponent's side is presenting the case for settlement, the paralegal's work will help prepare the attorney to evaluate the opposition's proposal.

Evaluation of the case involves a thorough look at all the elements that make up a case, such as liability, damages, ability to pay, and others. Presentation of the settlement involves organizing information in an economical, informative, and persuasive format to convince the opponent that the claim is a good one and worth settling.

Early Investigation and Collection of Information

Introduction A thorough early investigation is important because settlement can come early in the litigation process. To assist in the attorney's preparation, you need to collect and summarize the following information from the beginning of the action.

Party's Social or Business Background Note age, race, sex, personality, family, education, character, occupation, income, benefits, advancement potential, lifestyle, activities, and interests both before and after the accident or claim. Determine whether your plaintiff is receiving or about to receive Medicaid or Medicare assistance. If so, the federal and state governments may have claims against any monetary settlement or judgment received by your client. The courtroom effectiveness of witnesses should also be evaluated. For a commercial plaintiff, note reputation, age, income, and status before and after the alleged injury. Comparative wealth of parties in both commercial and personal injury cases is also important.

Party's Medical Condition   Note prior injuries and their possible implications for injuries caused by the accident (may reduce or, in rare cases, increase the amount of damages); details of injuries from accident; diagnosis; post-accident impediments such as shock, unconsciousness, embarrassment (these often explain statements or actions inconsistent with allegations of injuries);[1] unwillingness to admit disability; causal relationship between alleged wrong and injury; treatment required (emergency, surgery, tests, hospital care, home care, checkups, other medical consultations); progressive stages of healing; hideous nature of injury or effects; temporary injuries and disability; permanent injuries and disability; disfigurement; psychological and emotional injury; effect on personality and happiness; prognosis; need for future medical care (nursing care, prosthetic devices); pain and suffering (at time of injury, during medical treatment, permanent); change in life expectancy because of injuries; occupational implications of injuries; effect on hobbies, interests, and home life; all out-of-pocket expenses for medical bills, travel for treatment, and prosthetic devices; and projection of future medical care and related out-of-pocket expenses. Collect all the items (bills, medical reports, witness statements, etc.) necessary to prove or disprove these factors. Consider if the injured party has the three strikes: has not seen a doctor, has not lost work, has not used home remedies.[2]

Party's Commercial Condition   Note the value of land and other property involved; replacement value of property; value of property after injury; income before injury and after; loss of markets; loss of customers; loss of opportunity; loss of profits; past, present, and future losses; loss of rents; loss of business reputation; loss of the entire business; cost of any delay caused by injury; cost of finding alternatives for lost services or property; attempts to mitigate damages; and relationship of the alleged wrong to the injuries. Collect all evidence to prove these factors.

Special Areas of Investigation   You can assist by investigating other items as well. Research can be conducted on the recent verdicts rendered by juries or judges in the jurisdiction where the case will be tried. If this research is done very early in the case, it may help determine the best venue for the client. For example, rural juries are likely to produce lower awards than urban juries. Recent verdict information can be obtained from the clerk of court or from other attorneys in the vicinity. Some good sources on jury awards and amounts of damages include: the American Trial Lawyers Association's *ATLA Law Reporter,* the damages section of *West's Digests,* and sections on jury verdicts, damages, and settlements in *American Law Reports.* Such information is also available through Westlaw, Lexis, and other electronic services. Noteworthy is a recent study conducted by the National Center for State Courts (NCSC) that concludes that jury verdict reporting services regularly overstate both the average frequency of plaintiff victories and the amount of the awards.[3] This information will help the attorney determine a fair settlement range in a particular jurisdiction.

Expert witnesses (including doctors) to be relied on should be researched on their reputation, background, intelligence, and courtroom abilities. Their friends, colleagues, and attorneys who have dealt with them can be helpful here.

The trial judge's attitude and previous decisions in similar cases should be researched. Other attorneys and paralegals can provide insights.

The opponent's lawyer needs to be assessed as well. If the adverse attorney is a good trial lawyer, tough minded on negotiations, and takes lowest offer to mean lowest offer, then settlement requests may differ from those of an experienced lawyer who starts high but caves in fast, and never goes to trial. Attorneys, clerks of court and assistants, and, in some cases, paralegals may be helpful in giving such information.

The track record of the insurance company in settling cases for the defendant and for how much may also be valuable.

Life expectancy statistics, vocational opportunities for the client, estimated inflation trends that may affect the cost of a child's college education, future medical care, estimated lost income and benefits, and basic cost of living (vocation experts and economists may need to be consulted) are areas that may need to be researched. Most of this kind of information can be obtained through the help of a reference librarian in most libraries or through pertinent online services.

Costs of litigation, trial, and attorney's fees should also be researched and collected if the attorney does not have a basis for this.

Communicate with Client and Insurance Adjuster[4]

Continue to send to the client copies of letters and documents that will keep the client informed of the status of the case as well as items needing attention. In personal injury cases, track the client's medical treatment schedule so you can request resulting records and follow up with the client if medical appointments are missed. Gaps in treatment can appear to show an improvement in the client's condition and, therefore, can affect the level of damages.

Especially if settlement is being negotiated before a complaint is filed, initiate a positive and professional relationship with the defendant's insurance adjuster. Provide the plaintiff's identification information and regular updates on your client's condition, treatment, and current subtotal of medical bills, enclosing authenticated copies of the bills and medical progress reports. Respond promptly to the adjuster's requests for other information or documentation. If the insurer's investigators have taken written or recorded witness statements, request copies from the adjuster.

If the statute of limitations deadline is near and a complaint must be filed, the insurance adjuster may turn the case over to an attorney for litigation, possibly narrowing the chances for settlement, so time is important in completing settlement tasks.

Calculating Damages

The most important settlement objective in most cases is a dollar amount the plaintiff claims to deserve from the defendant. You can be of considerable assistance by recording and calculating the dollar amount of the damages. For a review of the types of damages (general, special, and exemplary), see the remedies section of Chapter 4. All bills, expenses, receipts, and so on should be collected and categorized. Damages should be itemized to ensure they are clear, accurate, reviewable, and believable. Exhibit 10:1 is an example of a form that can be used to list and calculate damages in personal injury and other cases.[5] Read the form carefully and note each category of damages so you will know what to look for in this and future cases.

It may be useful to note that in some state courts and in some federal actions for personal injury, survival, and wrongful death, the "loss of enjoyment of life" (LOELs, hedonic damages) is separated from "pain and suffering," and in other jurisdictions

EXHIBIT 10:1 ■ Damage Summary and Worksheet

Plaintiff _____ Date of Accident _____

Case _____ v. _____ Case No. _____

Attorney _____ Prepared by _____

                                                                    Date _____

I. Damage Totals

                                                     Special Damages   _____

                                                     General Damages   _____

                              Other Special and Exemplary Damages   _____

                                                                     _____

                                                     Total Damages   _____

ITEMIZATION

II. Special Damages

   A. Special Damages (Medical)

1. Ambulance Service: Name _____ Date _____

                              Amount _____

2. Hospital: Name _____ Address _____

         Date _____ Service, Test, or Treatment _____

                              Amount _____

         Name _____ Address _____

         Date _____ Service, Test, or Treatment _____

                              Amount _____

   (add as needed)

3. Doctor: Name _____ Address _____ Date _____

         Purpose or Treatment _____ Tests _____

                              Amount _____

   (add as needed)

4. Pharmaceutical:

         Pharmacy _____ Address _____ Date _____

         Medication or Prosthetic Device _____ Purpose _____

                              Amount _____

         Pharmacy _____ Address _____ Date _____

EXHIBIT 10:1 ▪ Damage Summary and Worksheet *(continued)*

Medication or Prosthetic Device _____ Purpose _____

Amount _____

(add as needed)

5. Travel for Medical Purposes:

Purpose _____ Date _____

Mileage _____ × _____ ¢/mile = $ _____ Lodging $ _____

Meals $ _____ Airfare, cabs, etc. $ _____

Amount _____

(repeat as needed)

6. Home Care (Nurse or Attendant):

Purpose _____ Date(s) _____

Amount per day _____ × no. of days _____

Amount _____

(add as needed)

7. Psychologists and Physical Therapists:

Name _____ Address _____

Purpose _____ Date _____

Amount _____

(add as needed)

TOTALS $ _____

TOTAL PAST MEDICAL COSTS $ _____

8. Future Medical Expenses:
   a. Special

☐ Hospitalization: no. of days _____ × cost _____ Amount _____

☐ Doctor: Purpose _____ $ _____

☐ Surgery: Type _____ $ _____

☐ Therapy: Type _____ $ _____

☐ Travel: Purpose _____ miles _____ × _____ ¢/mi. $ _____

Airfare, etc. _____ $ _____

☐ Pharmacology: Nature _____ $ _____

☐ Nurse: Cost/wk. _____ × no. of wks. _____ $ _____

☐ Other: _____ $ _____

(continued)

EXHIBIT 10:1 ▪ Damage Summary and Worksheet *(continued)*

   b. Daily: Itemize current daily needs: nurse, equipment, medications, etc.

     Item: _____ Purpose: _____ Daily Cost $ _____

     Item: _____ Purpose: _____ Daily Cost $ _____

                                                    Total _____

(add as needed)

   Total Daily Cost _____ × _____ Days/yr. × _____ Years + Special Costs + that figure × _____ % for growth in medical costs = gross expenses × _____ % for present cash value* = $ _____

                              TOTAL FUTURE MEDICAL EXPENSES $_____

*Present cash value (present value discount) reduces the future gross expense to a current lump sum, which if invested will provide for the total gross expenses when needed. The percentage of reduction is usually based on projected annuity tables or average yields for savings accounts or U.S. bonds over a reasonable historical period.

   B.   Special Damages (Economic Loss)

1. Current Wage _____ Date returned to work _____

2. Units (hours, days, months, etc.) or percentage of annual income lost _____

                                       Total wages lost to date _____

3. Lost fringe benefits, bonuses, perquisites _____

_____

(list if needed)   Total benefits lost to date _____

                         Total lost wages and benefits to date _____

4. Lost Household Services to Date:
   (Market value of household chores: bookkeeper, parent [care giver, tutor, chauffeur], maid, cook, decorator, gardener, etc.) $_____/wk. × no. of weeks _____ = $_____

5. Lost other considerations: _____

_____ $ _____

              Total Lost Wages, Benefits, Household Services to Date _____

6. If the person's income is reduced by any disability, for example a need to change to a job with less pay, then that loss should also be added. $_____

7. Future Economic Loss
   a. Future Wages (if complete disability or death):

   Most recent normal year's wages $_____ × years of work expectancy** _____ (including any remaining portion of current year) + that figure × compounded annual growth rate*** of _____% = gross wage loss $_____

Gross wage loss $_____ less _____% reduction to present cash value = $_____

☐ If the person has partial disability, gross wage loss can be computed by applying the same formula to the percentage of current yearly wage lost because of disability. If death, reduce gross wage loss by the percentage of annual wage actually consumed by that person. See family expenses over a period of several years.

**Years to age of retirement or Department of Labor Statistics for work life in specific occupations or may be set by state law.

EXHIBIT 10:1 ■ Damage Summary and Worksheet (continued)

***Based on average % raise over same number of past years as work expectancy years for that person or industry standard. Consult Department of Labor statistics but usually between 4–8%. Adjust figure upward if raises show marked increase in recent years. Note: Provide alternative set of figures if promotion, career change, or other variable is likely.

  b. Future Fringe Benefits:

Annual fringe benefit $_____ × ____ years of work expectancy + that figure × compounded annual growth rate for benefits of _____% = gross benefits loss

$ _____

Gross benefits loss $ _____ less _____% reduction to present cash value =

$ _____

☐ Annual growth rate for benefits is usually higher than wages. See Department of Labor statistics for occupation. Adjust if recent rise in %.

  c. Future Investments (if applicable)

  Amount of annual income placed in savings or other investments $_____ × compounded annual growth rate _____% (based on average return over past years)

Total Lost Future Investment Income $_____

(reduced to present cash value if necessary)

  d. Future Household Services

  Annual Lost Market Value for each service (bookkeeper, cook, maid, painter, gardener, child-care giver, etc.) _____ Annual cost × _____ yrs. life expectancy = $_____ + that figure × _____% annual growth rate in cost of household services‡ =

Total Future Household Services $_____

Life expectancy: based on readily accessible projections (consult reference librarian or insurance sources).
‡Annual growth rate for household services is often tied to projections based on history of consumer price index adjusted for any recent increases. The percentage usually ranges from 3–5%.

  e. Adjustments for Income Taxes: Consult with Attorney
  f. Adjustments for Inflation:
  (Being allowed more frequently. See published reports from trustees of Federal Old Age and Survivors Insurance and Disability Insurance Trust Funds for inflation projections and what that means in real wage increases.)

Total Future Income Loss $_____

  C. Special Damages (Property)

1. Personal Property:

Item _____

Destroyed: Market Value $_____ less salvage $_____ = $_____

Damaged: Cost of restoration $_____ or if cannot be restored, value before damage $_____ less value after damage $_____ plus costs to attempt to preserve or restore $_____ = $_____

  Other Property:
List: Portraits, heirlooms, pets, etc., with appraiser's valuation or some other reasonable standard

$_____

Appliances, furniture, clothing, worth at time of loss $_____

(continued)

EXHIBIT 10:1 ■ Damage Summary and Worksheet (*continued*)

2. Real Property (land, buildings):

Item _____

If permanent: value before damage $_____ less value after $_____ plus interest to date =

$_____

If temporary: reduction to rental or other profit value $_____ plus injury to crops, buildings, improvements $_____ plus restoration costs $_____ plus any applicable interest =

$_____

(consult local law)

Total Property Damages $_____

Total Special Damages $_____

III. General Damages

Pain and Suffering: fear, humiliation, inconvenience, anxiety, horror of injury, pain, discomfort; loss of companionship, status stimulation of job, enjoyment of life's experiences; and other subjective factors caused by injury. Briefly summarize: _____

_____

_____

_____

Standard: as estimated by party or reasonable person as fair.

Value per day $_____ × no. days/yr. _____ × yrs. of life expectancy _____ × _____% inflation factor if allowed = $_____

Consortium: value per day $_____ × no. of days per year _____ × yrs. of life expectancy × _____% inflation factor if allowed = $_____

Note: Review current jury verdicts for reasonable estimates. Check local statutes for any limits on awards. Most states do not require a reduction to present cash value for pain and suffering.

Total Pain and Suffering and General Damages $_____

IV. Other Special and Exemplary Damages

1. Funeral Expenses $_____

2. Exemplary:

   Punitive $_____

   Attorney's Fees $_____

3. Miscellaneous Damages $_____

Total of other Special and Exemplary Damages $_____

TOTAL DAMAGES $_____

it is still an element of pain and suffering. The decision in *Kansas City Southern Railway Co. v. Adams*, 2001WL107864 (Miss. 2001, *unpublished opinion*) drew a clear line between LOEL, limitations on "ability to enjoy the pleasures and amenities of life," and pain and suffering, the "physical and mental discomfort caused by injury, such as anguish, distress, fear, humiliation, grief, shame, and worry." It also affirmed that expert testimony on LOEL meets evidentiary standards; some other jurisdictions reject such testimony. Most states bar hedonic damages in wrongful death suits and when the injured person is comatose on the theory that the person cannot feel anything, so enjoyment of life is irrelevant. Loss of companionship is recoverable for the family, however. Connecticut, Georgia, New Mexico, Mississippi, and federal civil rights suits under 42 U.S.C. 1983 allow hedonic damages in wrongful death suits, and New York and some other states allow them for comatose patients.[6] Plaintiffs try to separate the LOELs; defendants fight that separation.

A damages summary and worksheet similar to Exhibit 10:1 can be devised for a commercial case stressing actual and anticipated damages. Pulling a file from a previous case where such damages applied can help in devising the worksheet.

Spreadsheet programs or damage calculation software can be used to enter and calculate damages and update them regularly. They also can be used to explore variables and make the calculation of annuities, interest, and other settlement figures much easier. A damage calculation Internet search will give you names of consulting and accounting services offering damage calculations in several fields.

When asked to review the damage claims of the other side, employ a similar process to test the thoroughness and accuracy of the opponent's proposal. In either case, all arithmetic should be double checked, and all the supporting documents should be reviewed for accuracy and applicability. Forward the damage sheet to the attorney for review and amendment.

Verify that the following items are also gathered and readied to support or contradict a settlement claim: all doctors' summaries, discovery summaries, photographs, videos, charts, diagrams, legal memoranda, witness statements, accident reports, and any other material needed to help convince the other party.

PRESENTING THE SETTLEMENT REQUEST

Introduction

The gathered and summarized information can now be evaluated by the attorney to determine the strength of the case and a fair settlement. The settlement request usually comes from the plaintiff and is presented to convince the defense that this settlement is fair and reasonable and in their client's best interests. The actual form in which the case is presented depends to a large degree on the amount of damages. It makes little sense to prepare a settlement brochure costing $500 in a $1,200 lawsuit. There would be nothing left for the client after attorney fees and other expenses. In this kind of case, a small narrative summary sheet or letter outlining the key information may suffice. A large case may justify a more detailed version of the summary, called a **settlement précis.** In the big cases involving many thousands of dollars, a thorough settlement brochure may be prepared.

A settlement letter, précis, or brochure needs to be as convincing as possible. In marshaling the facts of the case, it must stress the obviousness of the opponent's liability; the serious and sympathetic nature of the injuries; the amount of damages that have been and will be incurred; but most of all, the presentation must stress how the accident has torn up the life of the injured person as a productive or potentially productive individual. If liability is likely to be proven, it is the human

settlement précis
A brief presentation of the client's case designed to persuade the opposing party to settle the case on terms satisfactory to the client.

factor that will impress the jury and affect the amount of their award. A settlement presentation, therefore, can use the leverage of a potentially sympathetic jury to move the defendant to settle.

Settlement Précis or Letter

The précis or demand letter must be brief and should cover the following: the identification of the plaintiff; the facts of the case that reflect the liability of the defendant; the theory of liability; the injury and past, current, and future medical consequences; all expenses; a summary of the evaluation; and a proposed figure for settlement. Exhibit 10:2 is an example of a settlement précis.[7]

The précis can be reduced to an even more concise statement, if appropriate.

EXHIBIT 10:2 ■ Settlement Précis—Illustration

Social history—Sharon Williams was born July 10th, 1994, the fourth of four children born to John and Virginia Williams. The family lives at 2305 Grand Vista, Columbus, Missouri. Mr. Williams is employed as a machinist at Eagle Air Craft Co. A position he has held for six years.

Sharon is a student in the second grade of Middleton Grade School. She is a member of Girl Scout Troop 378 and is a member of the YMCA girls' swimming team.

Medical History—Sharon had a normal prenatal history and a normal birth. She has been attended by Dr. Grant Fry, a pediatrician, from birth. She has suffered from the childhood diseases of chicken pox and measles. She has never suffered any disability to her lower limbs and has never sustained any injuries to her legs, back or spine. Dr. Fry's medical report is attached.

Facts of Accident—On April 5, 2001, Sharon was en route from her home to school. The attached police report confirms that the day was clear and warm and the streets were dry. Sharon was by herself and crossing Grand Avenue at its intersection with Washington Street moving westwardly from the southeast to the southwest corner approximately six feet south of the south curb line and within the designated crosswalk. Grand Avenue is forty feet wide with two lanes of traffic moving in each direction. It is straight and level and surfaced with asphalt. There were no cars parked within sixty feet of the intersection. A sign located one hundred feet south of the intersection on Grand has the legend "Caution Children." Police report confirming the description of the scene of the accident is attached.

Sharon was struck by the northbound automobile of defendant at a point five feet from the center line. The attached photographs show the following:

Photo 1: skid marks ten feet long, blood on street

Photo 2: damage to left head light

Sharon states that when she left the southeast corner of the intersection the light was in her favor. She never looked at the light again. She walked at a normal pace until she was hit. She was looking forward and never saw or heard the defendant's automobile. The accident occurred at 8:35 A.M. The school is two blocks away and convenes at 8:45 A.M.

A statement taken from the defendant, a copy of which is attached, acknowledges that he didn't see the plaintiff until she was fifteen feet from him and that his automobile came to a stop twenty feet after impact.

Theories of Recovery

The plaintiff has three theories of recovery:

1. That defendant violated a red light.
2. That defendant failed to keep a lookout.
3. That defendant failed to exercise the highest degree of care to bring his automobile to a stop or slacken after plaintiff came into a position of immediate danger.

The proof of the first theory is supported by plaintiff's testimony that when she left the curb the light was green for westbound traffic. By reason of the plaintiff's age the court may not permit her to testify. In that event, the defendant's failure to keep a lookout could be submitted as an alternate theory of recovery. Defendant has acknowledged that he didn't see plaintiff until he was fifteen feet away from her and she was already in his path. This would place Sharon at least twelve feet from the curb. The court will judicially notice that the pace of walk is approximately two or three miles an hour or 2.9 to 4.4 feet per second. *Wofford v. St. Louis Public Service Co.,* Mo., 252 S.W.2d 529. Sharon was in the street and visible to defendant for almost three seconds before the accident. At defendant's acknowledged speed of twenty-five miles per hour he was traveling at approximately thirty-six feet per second or was approximately one hundred feet away when he should have seen Sharon. He was further alerted by the warning sign as he approached the intersection.

By reason of her age, it is questionable whether Sharon would be held responsible for her own actions. *Malott v. Harvey,* 199 Mo. App. 615, 204 S.W. 940; *Quirk v. Metropolitan St. Ry. Co.,* 200 Mo. App. 585, 210 S.W. 103.

In the event Sharon could be held accountable for not maintaining a proper lookout, a third theory of recovery is available: defendant's failure to stop or slacken after plaintiff came into a position of immediate danger. By defendant's admission he came to a stop twenty feet after the impact and he did not attempt evasive action until he was fifteen feet from Sharon, therefore his overall stopping distance was thirty-five feet. A jury could find that by reason of Sharon's obliviousness that she was in immediate danger as she approached the path of the vehicle and when defendant's automobile was more than the thirty-five feet that was available to bring his vehicle to a stop.

The skid marks indicate that no slackening took place until the defendant's vehicle was within ten feet of the impact. The damage to the automobile indicates it was the left front headlight which struck Sharon. Sharon was within two feet of safety beyond the path of the car when she was struck. Moving at 4.4 feet per second, in one-half second she would have escaped injury. From this the jury could assume that a failure to slacken at an earlier time was the proximate cause of the injury.

Medical

The police report states that Sharon was "bleeding about the face and mouth" and complaining of "pain in the right hip." She was taken by police cruiser to Welfare Hospital where it was discovered that she had suffered the loss of a front upper left tooth which was permanent, a laceration of the lip necessitating six stitches, and a bruise of the right hip. Portions of the hospital record are attached. She was examined by her pediatrician Dr. Fry who referred her to Dr. William Jones, a dentist, for examination. He confirms the loss of the permanent tooth and outlines the dental prostheses which will be needed throughout her growth stage and into adulthood. His report is attached. The stitches were removed after six days by Dr. Fry leaving a hair line scar one-fourth inch long near the upper lip.

Expenses

Emergency room Welfare Hospital	$550
Dr. Grant Fry	$150
Dr. William Jones	
Examination	$175
Anticipated Treatment	$4,000

Analysis of Evaluation

Actual out-of-pocket expenses total $875 with anticipated costs for dental prosthetic devices throughout Sharon's growth period adding $4,000 for a total of $4,875. The loss of the tooth is permanent and will necessitate special prophylactic care to maintain the prosthetic devices which must be employed. The scar above the lip is discernible and will be permanent.

It is anticipated that a jury verdict could fall within the $60,000 to $70,000 range. If the case could be settled without further legal procedure I would recommend a settlement of $45,000.

Source: Adapted and reprinted with permission of West Group.

Settlement Brochure (Demand Package)

The settlement brochure is the product of a serious commitment of time and money. Brochures are unlikely to be used unless injuries are serious and the liability of the defendant is sufficiently clear. It does little good to "sell" the pain and suffering of a client if the opponent has a good shot at disproving liability at trial. Many firms cut costs by using their own computer desktop publishing to print brochures or produce them on CD-ROM or DVD. The decision to commit resources to a brochure rests with the attorney, but you should be prepared to give impressions and evaluations of the case if asked.

The brochure is an orderly, dramatic, and persuasive presentation of the facts, statements, reports, and exhibits in the case. When done well and prepared early in the case, it tells the other side that this is a case to be taken seriously, that the plaintiff is thorough, organized, and likely to win. In addition, the preparation of the brochure forces the attorney to evaluate the case early in the process, identify its strengths and weaknesses, and see where more investigation or evidence is needed. It also facilitates the preparation of the trial brief (see next chapter) for the pretrial conference or trial. The fact that the plaintiff has set everything out in the case can be used as evidence of the plaintiff's desire to deal openly and in good faith from the start. A juror may decide to vote for higher damages if it appears that the defendant could have avoided the time-consuming trial by settling weeks or months before.

Paralegals with good communication skills can increase their value to the law firm by being able to organize and draft an effective settlement brochure. It not only can be of tremendous assistance to the attorney, but also may be the tool that wraps up the case.

The brochure should be organized to include the following areas:

> (a) The facts of the case as supported by the evidence
> This section includes summaries of the cause of action; details of the accident, witnesses, and reports; photos of the accident scene, vehicle, and injured party; dramatic newspaper clippings; and other evidence to support the claim.
> (b) The personal history of the plaintiff
> This section introduces the client and makes a statement as to who this person is, what kind of life he or she has had, what the person has enjoyed, what joy the client has brought to others, what services he or she has provided others, employment, earnings, service and professional organizations, stature in the community, religious affiliation, education, awards, recognition, services to family, letters of citation, evidence of advancement, future prior to accident, and other "get-to-know-this-person" facts and evidence. One or several carefully selected before-the-accident photos can be effective here.
> (c) The prior medical history of the plaintiff
> This section is a concise summary of the plaintiff's medical history prior to the accident. Any previous injuries or medical conditions, even if they tend to reduce the damages, should be candidly presented. This promotes credibility and makes the brochure more effective. Previous medical reports should be included if relevant and if they clearly define the extent and limits of previous problems.
> (d) Injury and its present and long-term effects
> This section should graphically depict the fear, pain, and anguish of experiencing the accident. The injuries should be described in detail and be supported by physician's reports, hospital summary sheets, records of surgery, tests, treatment, therapy, photos, and reference to videos of healing progress.

"The main object of conciliation lies in reaching a solution to a case based upon morals and with a warm heart."

—Confucius, *Analects*, c. 500 b.c.

The current and future status of the client should also be described, supported by physician reports on the prognosis of the injured party. This section should evoke sympathy and meaningfully portray the pathetic physical and social existence faced by the plaintiff. One or two letters written by a friend, family member, or co-worker in their own words can provide an effective personal account of the impact of the injury on the life of the plaintiff.[8]

(e) The economic and related psychological impact of the injury

The brochure describes how the injury affects future employment and that impact on the plaintiff and the plaintiff's family. The economics of disability, reduced status, lowered self-esteem, continual problems, and the like should be thoroughly covered.

(f) Damages

The special, general, and exemplary damages are summarized and explained where necessary. Copies of all bills, checks, receipts, and so on are included to substantiate the claims.

(g) Evaluation of claim

The brochure ends with a summary reiterating the most significant aspects of the claim and statement of a proposed settlement figure.

Some attorneys feel that any pertinent legal memoranda and such questions as the legal issues in the case, evidentiary matters, and itemized damages should be included. Others believe the brochure is not the place for such arguments. Some attorneys also like to include copies of the pleadings, enclosing at least the complaint, summons, and answer, or go so far as to include the pertinent jury instructions. It can be effective to show that pertinent law clearly and persuasively supports your position, but be sure to discuss these items with the attorney before you draft a brochure.

The brochure should be honest and professional. It should not be overblown, simplistic, or unduly sentimental. How much it should reveal is sometimes a difficult question. A brochure should be forthright, but it can be a disadvantage if it only succeeds in better preparing the opposition to rebut creative and imaginative arguments. Supporting medical reports and witness statements should at least appear to be objective. If they show a strong bias for the plaintiff, they may simply alert the opponent to the fact that the attending physician has lost objectivity and is vulnerable to attack. These questions are addressed by the supervising attorney, but, again, an alert paralegal can point out areas that may have been overlooked and can contribute to an improved brochure.

Exhibit 10:3 is an example of a settlement brochure. Although it does not strictly follow the category arrangement previously proposed, most of these elements are contained in this sample.[9]

It is a common practice to include a cover letter that sets a date after which the offer will be withdrawn and a date for return of the brochure. A statement is included that the brochure is the property of plaintiff's counsel and that there are restrictions on its use. A request for the acknowledgment of receipt of the brochure and an agreement to abide by the restrictions is accompanied by a proposal to meet and reach a mutually agreed-upon settlement.[10]

Video: "Day in the Life"

An increasingly persuasive settlement and trial aid is a digital video of the injured party that tastefully and graphically demonstrates the injuries, treatment, progress, and likely future of the victim. These videos have been named "Day in the Life" videos

EXHIBIT 10:3 ■ Settlement Brochure

UNITED STATES DISTRICT COURT FOR
THE _____ DISTRICT OF _____ _____ DIVISION

_____,
Plaintiff

v.   Civil Action, File No. _____

_____,
Defendant

SETTLEMENT BROCHURE

_____
Plaintiff's Attorney

_____
Address

_____
Phone

Note: (Optional)

The exhibit, statements, and reports incorporated in this brochure are submitted for settlement purposes only. They are not to be copied or reproduced in any fashion. In the event this case is tried, none of the contents of this report, neither facts, representations, nor opinions are to be used without plaintiff's permission. (Some offices place a legend on each page of the brochure so it cannot be used by the other party.)

Index (or Table of Contents)

EXHIBIT 10:3 ▪ Settlement Brochure *(continued)*

Settlement Brochure

page 1

I. Description of Accident

Photo of Accident

News Clipping

News Clipping

News Clipping

(continued)

EXHIBIT 10:3 ▪ Settlement Brochure (*continued*)

Settlement Brochure

Police Report   page 2

(Own summary could be substituted)

Settlement Brochure

Witness Statements or Summary   page 3

Settlement Brochure

Photo of Injuries   page 4

Settlement Brochure

Photos of Plaintiff Today   page 5

(Showing scars, limitations, wheelchair, etc.)

Settlement Brochure

                                                                                       page 6

II. Memorandum on Admissibility of Photographic Evidence

III. Personal History of Plaintiff

Catherine Brown was born June 8, 1974, and at the time of the accident was twenty-six years of age. She was reared in Texas where she completed four years of high school at Lockhart, Texas, and four years of college at Southwest Texas State College. On March 13, 1996, she was married to Fred Brown and his change of employment necessitated a move before her last semester of college could be completed.

On January 29, 1997, Catherine gave birth to her only child, Carl Robert.

Upon arrival in the Kansas City area Catherine enrolled in the Music Conservatory of the University of Missouri—Kansas City and graduated with a B.M.E. in music in 1998. She served as a substitute music teacher in the public schools of Kansas City in the Spring of 1999 and in the fall of that year was hired as Music Director of the R-7 School District in Center City, Missouri, at a salary of $24,800 for the school year.

Catherine's responsibility included the directorship of three bands and two choirs. In addition she served as a sponsor for the Pep Club and Cheerleaders. Her outside activities included membership in the Mu Phi Epsilon Music Sorority and the Center City Music Club.

IV. Medical History of Plaintiff—Summary

Prior to the date of the accident, June 16, 2000, Catherine Brown was in excellent health. She had never suffered any physical disability and her only hospitalization was for the birth of her son.

The accident was unusually violent. The loaded gravel truck struck the vehicle in which plaintiff was a passenger with such force that the automobile was carried seventy-six feet and seven inches beyond the point of impact. The side on which plaintiff was sitting was literally "run over." (See attached photo from police report.)

The injuries, detailed in the hospital record and medical reports which follow, consisted primarily of the following:

disfiguring lacerations of face;

multiple fractures of the jaws;

fracture of clavicle with loss of bone;

multiple fractures of the pelvis;

fracture of radius and ulna right arm;

fracture of left forearm;

severe cerebral contusion.

V. Medical History and Physical Report by Initial Attending Physician

[Date]

BROWN, Catherine.

CHIEF COMPLAINT: Auto accident.

PRESENT ILLNESS: The patient is a 26-year-old Gravida I, Para I, Aborta O, white female who was involved in an auto-truck accident. The patient was brought immediately to the Emergency Room of General Hospital at which time the patient was admitted through the Emergency Room by Dr. Smith. The patient was then seen by this doctor in the Intensive Care Unit at which time the patient presented with a blood pressure systolic between 80 and 90. The patient had a very rapid pulse of 120. The patient was cool and appeared to be in shock.

PHYSICAL EXAMINATION:

NEUROLOGICAL: The patient was confused as to time and place with episodes of incoherence. The pupils were dilated and extremely sluggish but were reactive. Fundoscopic examination revealed the discs to be sharp. There was no evidence of papilledema. Cranial nerves appeared to be intact. There was no evidence of motor or sensory loss of the extremities. The patient had obvious multiple fractures.

(continued)

HEENT: Tympanic membranes were intact. There was no evidence of fluid or blood in the auditory canals. Posterior pharynx was clear. Oral cavity: The patient had palpable fractures of the mandible bilaterally.

NECK: Supple with no palpable masses or tenderness. No bruits. Thyroid was not palpable.

CHEST: Lungs were clear on auscultation and percussion. The patient had palpable fractures over the right chest.

ABDOMEN: No palpable masses or tenderness. Bowel sounds hypoactive. No CVA tenderness. Patient had a mild suprapubic tenderness.

EXTREMITIES: Symmetrical. The patient had marked deformity of the right forearm and wrist area with marked swelling. The patient also had deformity of the left forearm with some swelling. Pressure applied to the pelvic cage caused excruciating pain. Peripheral pulses in all extremities were grade III and equal bilaterally.

SKIN: The patient had multiple large facial lacerations that covered the entire right face, forehead and parietal area. The patient also had a laceration of the right submandibular area, and left face at the outer canthus of the mouth. The patient had multiple abrasions over the upper extremities and a large laceration over the dorsum of the left hand with no evidence of tendon involvement.

IMPRESSION: Shock syndrome secondary to blood loss and multiple fractures; fracture of the right radius and ulna; right thoracic fractures; pelvic fractures; severe cerebral contusion; multiple lacerations.

DISPOSITION: Patient will be treated for shock syndrome with intravenous fluids, plasma expanders, antibiotics, and patient will the have splinting of the extremities and lacerations closed.

DIAGNOSIS: Compound fracture right and left body of the mandible. The patient sustained the injuries in an auto accident.

RECOMMENDATIONS: Closed reduction by the application of maxillary and mandibular arch bars.

Thank you for this consultation.

[*Signed*]

_____

C. A. Jones, M.D.

VI. Operative Record of Initial Attending Physician

[*Date*]

BROWN, Catherine.

PRE-OP DIAGNOSIS: Auto accident with shock syndrome, multiple facial lacerations, laceration of the left lower lip, laceration of left hand, open fracture of the clavicle, fracture of radius and pelvic fractures, cerebral concussion, moderate, severe.

SURGEON: C. A. Jones

OPERATIVE PROCEDURE: The patient was placed in the supine position. Utilizing 1% Xylocaine diluted to 1/2% the patient had local infiltration and field blocks for closure of lacerations. The patient had multiple lacerations around the right eye, eyebrow and scalp. The patient also had a through and through laceration of the left lower lip and mouth. The patient had multiple small lacerations on the left arm and dorsum of the left hand. All the lacerations were infiltrated and thoroughly scrubbed with Betadine and Betadine solution. The patient then had excision of the margins of the lacerations. The patient had a moderate amount of skin loss on the right temporal area which required undermining of the scalp flap for primary closure. This was repaired with interrupted 4–0 chromic suture and 5–0 nylon suture. Through and through laceration of the left lower lip was repaired with closing the subcutaneous tissue beneath the submucosa of the oral cavity with interrupted 3–0 chromic. The wound was thoroughly irrigated with Saline. The subcutaneous tissue and muscle tissue was then approximated with interrupted 4–0 chromic. The skin was closed with interrupted 5–0 nylon. The subcutaneous tissue and muscle tissue was then approximated with interrupted 4–0 chromic. The skin was closed with interrupted 5–0 nylon suture. The lacerations on the hand and arm were handled in a likewise manner. The patient also had an open comminuted fracture of the right clavicle with a portion of the bone sticking up through the skin and remaining attached by a piece of periosteum. The bone had apparently been ground into the dirt. It was therefore thought advisable and with consultation by Dr. Peterson that this portion of the clavicle should be excised and removed. The wound was opened and thoroughly irrigated with approximately two liters of saline solution. The wound was then closed with interrupted 3–0 chromic and interrupted 4–0 nylon suture. All the wounds were then bandaged with Garamycin and 4 × 4 dressings. The patient also had an obvious fracture of the forearm. The forearm was thus splinted due to severe edema at that time; it was felt that casting was not indicated. The arm was splinted with a posterior splint and Ace bandage.

The patient was then returned to surgical ICU for further followup. Post-operative condition was guarded.

[Signed]

_____

C. A. Jones, M.D., Surgeon

VII. Consultation Report by Doctor Johnson, Orhopedic Surgeon

[Date]

BROWN, Catherine.

This 26-year-old woman was seen in consultation with Dr. Jones. The initial care had been provided when the patient came into the hospital by Dr. Jones for a compound fracture of the right clavicle and thoracic fractures. The patient also had fractures of the pubis which were also treated by Dr. Jones. I saw the patient at Dr. Jones' request for treatment of a fracture of the right distal radius, and this was treated with a closed reduction 6/18/00, and immobilized in a long arm cast.

Review of x-rays of the right clavicle revealed satisfactory position of the fracture of the clavicle and also fractures of the right pubis were in satisfactory position. The patient was treated with bed rest for the fractures of the pubis. The patient responded quite nicely to this.

Because of persistent pain in the forearm, left, x-rays were taken several weeks following the accident and these revealed a cracked fracture of the distal ulna. Although it was a good position it was felt that immobilization in a short arm cast was indicated and this was applied. At the time of discharge the patient was instructed to return to my office to be followed as an outpatient as treatment for fractures of the right radius and ulna and the left ulna.

[Signed]

_____

A. B. Johnson, M.D.,
Consultant

VIII. Operative Record of Doctor Smith, Oral Surgeon

[Date]

BROWN, Catherine.

OPERATIONS: Closed reduction and application of maxillary and mandibular arch bar with manual reduction.

PRE-OP DIAGNOSIS: Compound fracture of the right and left body of the mandible.

SURGEON: A. B. Smith.

OPERATIVE PROCEDURE: The patient was brought to the operating room in satisfactory physical condition. General anesthesia was induced. The patient was intubated through the right nares and draped in the usual manner for an intra-oral procedure. Mouth and throat were thoroughly cleansed. Deep throat pack was placed. Following this a maxillary arch bar was ligated to the remaining maxillary teeth. After this had been accomplished manual reduction of the fracture sites was accomplished, circumferential wires were placed around the teeth on either side of the fracture site. After this had been accomplished a mandibular arch bar was ligated to the mandibular teeth thus holding the fracture sites in good alignment. Deep throat pack was removed.

(continued)

EXHIBIT 10:3 ▪ Settlement Brochure *(continued)*

Elastids will be placed this evening or in the morning. Dr. Johnson then continued with his part of the procedure, reduction of the right arm.

[*Signed*]

_____

A. B. Smith, D.D.S.

IX. X-ray Interpretation

[*Date*]

BROWN, Catherine.
RIGHT FOREARM EXAM including the ELBOW AND WRIST REGION with multiple views with a metal splint in place reveals recent fracture of the distal one-third of the shaft of the radius approximately 2 inches from the wrist joint. There is minimal comminution. The fragments are not widely displaced or separated. There is very slight anterior angulation.
There is also a fracture of the ulna slightly more than one cm. from the distal end with minimal displacement of these fragments. There is no dislocation.
RIGHT SHOULDER REEXAM WITH AP VIEW shows the lateral fracture fragments of the clavicle to be displaced completely inferiorly in relation to the medial fragment. The major fragments are separated approximately one-half cm. The fracture fragments of the right 2nd rib are separated almost one-half cm. There is little callus formation in the fracture region but the fragments are not stabilized by bony union. There are also fractures of the right 5th and 6th ribs posteriorly in good position.
LEFT FOREARM EXAM reveals a fracture in the ulna about 7 cm above the wrist joint. The fragments are in close opposition with less than 1/2 cm. displacement and no significant degree of angulation.
PELVIS EXAM WITH FILMS MADE AT THE BEDSIDE reveals recent fractures of the superior and inferior pelvic rami and the symphysis pubis on the right side. The fragments show only minimal displacement. There is no dislocation. There is also irregularity in the right side of the sacrum due to fracture in this region with minimal impaction of the fragments.
The sacroiliac joints are not disrupted.
RIGHT FOREARM AND ELBOW reading including with reading of the films of night before examination of the Rt Arm.
EXAMINATION OF THE SKULL AND MANDIBLE WITH MULTIPLE VIEWS reveals recent fracture of the body of the mandible on the left side. The anterior fragment is displaced medially one cm. No other definite fracture of the mandible is seen at this time. There is no apparent fracture of the skull or depression. The sella turcia is regular.
RIGHT CLAVICLE AND CHEST EXAM reveal the markedly comminuted fracture near the mid portion of the right clavicle. The major fragments are separated almost one-half inch. There is complete inferior displacement of the lateral major fragment. There is no definite rib fracture or lung injury.
RIGHT FOREARM EXAM with AP AND LATERAL VIEWS with films made at the bedside shows fracture of the radius 2 inches from the distal end with minimal comminution, and approximately 10 degrees anterior angulation of the fragments. The fragments are not widely displaced. There is also a fracture of the ulna approximately one cm. from the distal end with minimal comminution and slight impaction of these fragments. There is no dislocation.

[*Signed*]

_____

Radiologist

X. Discharge Summary

[*Date*]

BROWN, Catherine.
PRESENT ILLNESS: The patient is a 26-year-old white female who was involved in an auto-truck accident. The patient was apparently struck broadside by the truck and carried out through a field. The patient was brought

EXHIBIT 10:3 ▪ Settlement Brochure (*continued*)

to the Emergency Room for treatment. The patient was admitted through the Emergency room by Dr. Smith, who initiated treatment. The patient was then seen in ICU with a blood pressure of 60 to 90 systolic. The patient was confused as to time and place. Neurological examination revealed both pupils to be extremely dilated and sluggish. Discs were sharp. The patient was able to move all extremities. The patient also had multiple facial lacerations and fractures of the extremities.

PERTINENT PHYSICAL FINDINGS: Revealed multiple facial lacerations involving the right face and right temple area. There was no palpable skull fracture. The patient had bilateral fractures of the mandible, fractures of both forearms and pelvic fracture. The patient was also seen in consultation by Dr. Peterson, Dr. Johnson and Dr. Smith. Patient initially had closure of the facial lacerations, repair of lacerations of the lower lip and left hand. The patient had an open fracture of the right clavicle which was debrided. A small portion of bone was removed. The wound was thoroughly irrigated and closed. The patient had splinting of both forearms. The patient was treated vigorously for shock with intravenous fluids, vasopressors, and blood. The patient was also started on massive doses of antibiotics. The patient became more responsive 36 hours after admission at which time the patient then had maxillary fractures and fractures of the radius and ulna bilateral corrected. The patient was then treated with bed rest for four weeks due to large pelvic fracture. The patient's hospital course following the first four days of admission was unremarkable except for slow progression of activity. The patient was ambulated on the 3rd week post-admission. At the time of the discharge the patient was ambulatory without assistance, however, the patient had a wide base gait due to instability of the pelvis. The patient's forearms were in plaster splints. The patient's maxillas were still wired. The patient was on a full liquid diet. The facial lacerations had healed well with minimal amount of scar defect. The patient was given a one week return office appointment for followup examination. The patient was discharged from the hospital on Keflex 250 mgms q.i.d.

FINAL DIAGNOSIS:
(1) Shock syndrome, secondary to multiple fractures and blood loss
(2) Fracture of right radius and ulna
(3) Fractures of left ulna
(4) Fracture of right clavicle and right second rib, anteriorly
(5) Multiple pelvic fractures
(6) Severe cerebral contusion
(7) Multiple facial and extremity lacerations

[*Signed*]

———————————————
C. A. Jones, M.D.

XI. Medical Report of Doctor Anderson, Orthopedic Surgeon

[*Date*]
Re: Catherine Brown
(including history, previous injuries, physical exam, summary and prognosis)

XII. Medical Report of Doctor Holt, Plastic Surgeon

James P. Holt, M.D.

Plastic and Reconstructive Surgery Maxillo-facial Surgery

[*Date*]

Mr. James W. Jeans, Attorney
U.M.K.C. Law Building
5100 Rockhill Road
Kansas City, Missouri 64110

(*continued*)

EXHIBIT 10:3 ▪ Settlement Brochure *(continued)*

Dear Mr. Jeans:

The following is a medical report on Catherine Brown, a 26-year-old music director, who was seen in my office on December 9, 2000, for evaluation of scars resulting from injuries in an automobile accident on June 16, 2000.

The patient states that she was hospitalized for over a month in Joplin, Missouri, with fractures of the pelvis, jaw, right forearm, left forearm, right clavicle and ribs.

She has multiple atrophic scars running from the eyebrow and temple to above the ear (4–5 inches in total length), a scar at a right angle to the mandible and lower part of the ear (3–4 inches) which is also atrophic, a transverse atrophic scar of the lower lip (2 inches) with a ridge inside the labial mucosa, a scar of the dorsum of the right hand (3 inches), two scars of the radial aspect of the wrist (1 inch) and a scar of the right lower neck (1 1/2 inches).

There is sensitivity around the right temple and clavicle and over the right wrist due to the injuries and scarring. She has some limitation of supination at the wrist and difficulty in abduction of the right fifth finger. These limitations interfere with playing the piano which is her professional activity.

My recommendation in this case would be a revision of the scars mentioned above which would require hospitalization and general anesthesia. The surgical fee for the procedures over the entire areas could be estimated at $5,000–$7,000 not to include the cost of hospitalization, anesthesia, surgical suite, laboratory fees, etc. After the initial revision, it is possible that a dermabrasion procedure might further minimize the scarring after a period of 4–6 months.

In any event, regardless of the improvement that could be obtained from the surgery, the patient would still undoubtedly have permanent, visible scarring and some cosmetic disfigurement in the areas enumerated.

[*Signed*]

‾‾‾‾‾‾‾‾‾‾‾‾‾‾‾‾
James P. Holt, M.D.

XIII. Medical Expenses

The cost of the medical services necessitated by the injuries incurred in the accident are itemized as follows:

General Hospital	$25,846.27
Dr. Smith	2,000.00
Dr. Chess	600.00
Dr. Johnson	1,200.00
Dr. Jones	4,500.00
Misc.	525.00
Dr. Murphy	560.00
Dr. James Holt	150.00
Total	$35,381.27

In addition Dr. Holt, the plastic surgeon, estimates $5,000–$7,500 for surgical fees for remedial surgery plus a like amount for hospitalization, anesthesiologist, etc. It appears fair to state that total medical will approximate fifty thousand dollars.

XIV. Effects of Injuries

The effects of the injuries upon Catherine Brown and her family have been pronounced. She has lost weight, has been moody and depressed and has been unable to resume her activities in music. Although rehired in 2001 at $26,000 (as evidenced by the employment contract) because of her physical and emotional effects of her injury she was unable to satisfactorily perform her duties and was not rehired. In addition her private music lessons (which accounted for approximately $150 per month) had to be discontinued.

EXHIBIT 10:3 ■ Settlement Brochure (*continued*)

Fred Brown, at the time of the accident, was working toward a master's degree in Counselor Education at U.M.K.C. His wife's need for constant attention and encouragement has delayed the completion of his education and has worked a real hardship on the family. Even though Catherine is no longer employed in the Bronaugh area, they continue to live there because they secure their present housing by Fred doing farm chores for the owner. He must commute over 100 miles to Kansas City for his schooling and work forty to sixty hours on the farm for house rent and living money.

XV. Evaluation of Claims

The injuries speak for themselves and anyone so victimized would be entitled to a substantial sum for the resulting pain and disability. For Catherine Brown the effects were particularly disabling. The loss of strength, flexibility, and dexterity of her right hand has seriously impaired her capacity as a musician and thus has affected her earning potential. The effects of the disfiguring facial scars on this 26-year-old woman have been aggravated by the fact that her employment brings her before the public as well as numerous students. Although future plastic surgery may ameliorate some of the disfigurement of the skin, others will remain. The contour of the jaw and teeth have been permanently altered. The loss of bone in the clavicle has resulted in a permanent postural change.

We evaluate the damages for Catherine Brown as follows:

Medical expenses to date	$35,381.27
Medical expenses projected	15,000.00
Loss of earnings school year 2001	26,000.00
Loss of earnings private lessons to date at $150 per month	2,250.00
	$78,631.27

Future loss of wages depends on the hirability of a physically impaired candidate suffering from permanent head injuries manifested by "nervousness, irritability, anger, fatigue, memory changes, forgetfulness, headaches, concentration difficulties." The impairment of Catherine's earning capacity is a fact—only the amount is uncertain. A strong argument could be advanced that a fair estimate could be figured at $5,000 a year or a total of $190,000 until her work expectancy of sixty-five.

If permanent disability and future pain and suffering were to be evaluated on the same basis of $5,000 for each year of expectancy, one could argue an additional $280,000 for the expected life span. A total of these sums is $548,631.27.

This computation is advanced as an example of jury argument that could be legitimately advanced with, in my opinion, a good chance of acceptance. I appreciate that for settlement purposes the sum of $548,631.27 is not a valid figure—but it does represent the degree to which each of the parties is exposed as individual or joint tort-feasor. Add to this the loss of consortium claim of the husband and the injury to the son and that exposure, again in my judgment, exceeds $750,000.

The plaintiff is assured of recovery against someone. The nature of the accident, the extensiveness of the injury, and the "jury appeal" of the plaintiff lead one to conclude that a jury would be generous in evaluating the case. Our settlement demand for all claims is $525,000.

Source: Adapted and reprinted with permission of West Group.

because they focus primarily on one day in the life of the injured party. Recently, for example, a law office assigned a paralegal to videotape the progressive stages in the medical treatment of an accident victim. This videotaped record provided credible, otherwise unobtainable documentation of the pain and suffering of the client and strikingly illustrated that the healing process was going to take a long time with recovery clearly doubtful. The recordings were edited into a concise and powerful presentation by the paralegal. The cost was minimal. The "Day in the Life" video or DVD can include much of the settlement brochure including photographs, television commentary, and newspaper clippings.

Some firms video family and friends as well. Their out-of-court comments on what impact the serious injuries have had on the plaintiff's life and on their own can be moving.[11]

Calendaring

It is important to calendar dates the attorney has designated to initiate settlement or follow up on a demand letter or a brochure. Continue to inform the client of the progress in settlement negotiations.

ROLE OF THE DEFENDANT'S OR INSURANCE COMPANY'S PARALEGAL

The process of preparing for settlement on behalf of the defendant or an insurance company is, in many respects, the same as preparing for settlement for the plaintiff. Although the defense rarely, if ever, prepares a settlement précis or brochure, you may be asked to draft a letter proposing settlement and summarizing significant elements of the case from the defendant's perspective. Further, you will often be responsible for organizing and summarizing the information that arrives for the case. If the plaintiff submits summarized medical reports and witness statements rather than copies of the original, it may mean that there are some weaknesses in those reports. The originals should always be obtained, using discovery if more informal means have not been productive. The same process of researching jury verdicts, assessing pain and suffering, and submitting final summaries for attorney review are employed. You should inform the attorney if there appears to be a need for an independent medical exam or special surveillance of the adverse party.

Calendar the date indicated by your supervising attorney to respond or initiate the settlement process. Note in your calendar when tasks must be done in preparation for that date.

PREPARING FOR THE PRETRIAL CONFERENCE

Federal Rule of Civil Procedure 16, individual state rules, local practice, and the preference of a particular judge determine what happens at the pretrial conference. In some jurisdictions the conference is mandatory, and the judge is active in trying to settle the case. In other jurisdictions the conference must be requested, and the judge may refrain from any involvement in settlement discussions.

A pretrial conference is normally conducted in the judge's chambers and is attended by the attorneys for the parties and the judge. Clients may be required to attend. Traditionally the conference is a discussion by the attorneys of the facts in the case, the evidence to prove those facts, the issues remaining in the case, when and how long trial will be, and, if possible, whether settlement is in the offing. Federal Rule 16 now requires a more extensive pretrial conference process involving more than one meeting in many cases. In this context the pretrial conference takes on the important role of facilitating the overall planning and management of the progress of the case beginning at a much earlier point in the litigation (within 90 days of the defendant's first appearance or within 120 days of serving the complaint on the defendant, whichever is shorter). Rule 16 describes the pretrial process.

Rule 16. Pretrial Conferences; Scheduling; Management

a. Pretrial Conferences; Objectives.　In any action, the court may in its discretion direct the attorneys for the parties and any unrepresented parties to appear before it for a conference or conferences before trial for such purposes as

1. expediting the disposition of the action;
2. establishing early and continuing control so that the case will not be protracted because of lack of management;
3. discouraging wasteful pretrial activities;
4. improving the quality of the trial through more thorough preparation, and;
5. facilitating the settlement of the case.

b. Scheduling and Planning.　Except in categories of actions exempted by district court rule as inappropriate, the district judge, or a magistrate judge when authorized by district court rule, shall, after receiving the report from the parties under Rule 26(f) or after consulting with the attorneys for the parties and any unrepresented parties by scheduling conference, telephone, mail, or other suitable means, enter a scheduling order that limits the time

1. to join other parties and to amend the pleadings;
2. to file motions; and
3. to complete discovery.

The scheduling order may also include:

4. modifications of the times for disclosures under Rules 26(a) and 26(e)(1) and of the extent of discovery to be permitted;
5. provisions for disclosure or discovery of electronically stored information;
6. any agreements the parties reach for asserting claims of privilege or of protection as trial-preparation material after production;
7. the date or dates for conferences before trial, a final pretrial conference, and trial; and
8. any other matters appropriate in the circumstances of the case.

The order shall issue as soon as practicable but in any event within 90 days after the appearance of a defendant and within 120 days after the complaint has been served on a defendant. A schedule shall not be modified except on a showing of good cause and by leave of the district judge or, when authorized by local rule, by a magistrate judge.

c. Subjects for Consideration at Pretrial Conferences.　At any conference under this rule consideration may be given, and the court may take appropriate action with respect to

1. the formulation and simplification of the issues, including the elimination of frivolous claims or defenses;
2. the necessity or desirability of amendments to the pleadings;
3. the possibility of obtaining admissions of fact and of documents which will avoid unnecessary proof, stipulations regarding the authenticity of documents, and advance rulings from the court on the admissibility of evidence;
4. the avoidance of unnecessary proof and of cumulative evidence, and limitations or restrictions on the use of testimony under Rule 702 of the Federal Rules of Evidence;
5. the appropriateness and timing of summary adjudication under Rule 56;

6. the control and scheduling of discovery, including orders affecting disclosures and discovery pursuant to Rule 26 and Rules 29 through 37;
7. the identification of witnesses and documents, the need and schedule for filing and exchanging pretrial briefs, and the date or dates for further conferences and for trial;
8. the advisability of referring matters to a magistrate judge or master;
9. settlement and the use of special procedures to assist in resolving the dispute when authorized by statute or local rule;
10. the form and substance of the pretrial order;
11. the disposition of pending motions;
12. the need for adopting special procedures for managing potentially difficult or protracted actions that may involve complex issues, multiple parties, difficult legal questions, or unusual proof problems;
13. an order for a separate trial pursuant to Rule 42(b) with respect to a claim, counterclaim, cross-claim, or third-party claim, or with respect to any particular issue in the case;
14. an order directing a party or parties to present evidence early in the trial with respect to a manageable issue that could, on the evidence, be the basis for a judgment as a matter of law under rule 50(a) or a judgment on pretrial findings under Rule 52(c);
15. an order establishing a reasonable limit on the time allowed for presenting evidence; and
16. such other matters as may facilitate the just, speedy, and inexpensive disposition of the action.

At least one of the attorneys for each party participating in any conference before trial shall have authority to enter into stipulations and to make admissions regarding all matters that the participants may reasonably anticipate may be discussed. If appropriate, the court may require that a party or its representative be present or reasonably available by telephone in order to consider possible settlement of the dispute.

d. Final Pretrial Conference.   Any final pretrial conference shall be held as close to the time of trial as reasonable under the circumstances. The participants at any such conference shall formulate a plan for trial, including a program for facilitating the admission of evidence. The conference shall be attended by at least one of the attorneys who will conduct the trial for each of the parties and by any unrepresented parties.

e. Pretrial Orders.   After any conference held pursuant to this rule, an order shall be entered reciting the action taken. This order shall control the subsequent course of the action unless modified by a subsequent order. The order following a final pretrial conference shall be modified only to prevent manifest injustice.

f. Sanctions.   If a party or party's attorney fails to obey a scheduling or pretrial order, or if no appearance is made on behalf of a party at a scheduling or pretrial conference, or if a party or party's attorney is substantially unprepared to participate in the conference, or if a party or party's attorney fails to participate in good faith, the judge, upon motion or the judge's own initiative, may make such orders with regard thereto as are just, and among others any of the orders provided in Rule 37(b)(2)(B), (C), (D). In lieu of or in addition to any other sanction, the judge shall require the party or the attorney representing him or both to pay the reasonable expenses incurred because of any noncompliance with this rule, including attorney's fees, unless the judge finds that the noncompliance was substantially justified or that other circumstances make an award of expenses injust.

Paralegal tasks in preparation for pretrial conference are to make available to the attorney all needed information and supporting documents, and to place the conference time in the docket control and reminder systems.

A pretrial preparation checklist should contain the following:

Pretrial Conference Preparation Checklist

1. Docket conference date and reminder dates for yourself and the attorney.
2. Enter reminder dates to inform the client of upcoming conferences, their significance, and whether the client should plan to be present. Check with the attorney.
3. Determine rules of pertinent jurisdiction and expectations of the assigned judge. Most courts publish their local rules; call the judge's deputy clerk for clarification. Summarize for the attorney.
4. See that the client has signed all needed documents authorizing the attorney to enter into stipulations and to settle the case (see example following this checklist).
5. Have available for the attorney summaries of the following:
   - The facts, acts, and omissions that form the basis of the claim
   - Any specific statutes or ordinances that have been violated
   - Documents, photos, diagrams, and other tangible evidence that will be entered into evidence at trial
   - All witnesses (names, addresses, and area of testimony), including expert witnesses
   - All injuries, damages, and monetary amounts
   - All points of factual and legal contention
6. Gather and organize all documents and other evidence needed by the attorney to submit to the other side for stipulations.
7. Gather all needed records, bills, and other documents, and evidence to support claim.
8. Gather and organize all motions to be made or that are pending in the case.
9. Gather and organize any briefs, memoranda to the court, or other summaries of the law, or any points of contention.
10. Confer with the attorney to see that all that is needed is prepared.

In order for the attorney to negotiate in good conscience and to be in a position to make an offer to settle and to agree to settle at the most opportune time, the client must sign a written authorization for the attorney to negotiate and settle the lawsuit. Some firms incorporate an authorization in the fee agreement. Prior to signing, the client should be fully informed as to the likelihood of settlement negotiations, a realistic settlement figure, and what is given up when settlement is elected. If the authorization has not been obtained earlier, it should be obtained by the time of the pretrial conference. Exhibit 10:4 is an example of a general authorization.[12]

Some attorneys and courts require the preparation of a pretrial statement following the pretrial conference. It includes an overall summary of the items mentioned in the previous checklist. If you have summarized the damages as previously indicated and prepared a settlement précis or brochure, the preparation of a pretrial statement should be relatively easy. The only new wrinkle is to determine the exact format preferred by the attorney or the court requiring the statement.

Some courts require the pretrial statement (memorandum) to be prepared jointly, furthering the opportunity for settlement. This may be followed by a pretrial order

EXHIBIT 10:4 ■ Power to Settle Personal Injury Claims

For me and in my name to represent me in any negotiations with _____, or his attorney, with reference to his claim for damages against me on account of personal injuries received in a collision with my automobile on or about the _____ day of _____, hereby authorizing my said attorney either to compromise said claim for such amount as he may deem best, or to defend action thereon in the courts, if he deems that necessary to protect my interests.

Source: Reprinted with permission of West Group.

drafted by the judge or one or more of the parties. Because the required format varies with the jurisdiction, it is best to locate a local example of these documents. The following is an outline of one format. The pretrial order generally follows the same format as the pretrial memorandum.

[Caption]
PRETRIAL MEMORANDUM

Pretrial Conference
    Attorneys, date, location, etc.
Statement of Uncontested Facts
    Agreed times, events, damage, etc.
Contested Issues of Fact
    Disputed facts: Speed of vehicle, signature on document, intent of contract, etc.
Contested Issues of Law
    Disputed application of rules of law, defenses, and other matters for the judge to decide.
Witnesses
    A list of witnesses with their position, title, and relationship to case to be called by each party.
Exhibits
    A list and brief description of each exhibit to be presented at trial. In some jurisdictions this is added as an appendix; in others it is placed in the body of the memorandum with a column for any objections to the exhibits, i.e.,

Exhibit   Objections

Other Categories
    Other categories that may be included, depending on the jurisdiction and nature of the case, include a statement of agreed damages or special damages, attached jury instructions and any objections to them, and a statement of any agreed findings of fact and conclusions of law.

    Respectfully Submitted this _____ day of_____
    By:

_____
Attorney for Plaintiff
_____
Attorney for Defendant

SETTLEMENT CONFERENCE

A settlement conference is a meeting between the parties to discuss settlement of the case. Its purpose is, therefore, more narrow than the pretrial conference. A settlement conference may be part of the extended pretrial conference procedures under Rule 16 and parallel state rules, or it may come after a pretrial conference or occur as the parties or the court deem necessary. A party may request a settlement conference, or the court may order it. A magistrate judge or other judge particularly skilled in settlement may conduct the settlement conference. Procedures, settlement conference statements, and local rules vary.

Your role in preparing for a settlement conference incorporates many of the tasks previously discussed in this chapter. The objective is to see that your supervising attorney has all needed material organized for quick, logical access. Settlement conference material includes identification of all remaining issues and supporting authority; highlighted parts of crucial reports, records, medical bills, and transcripts; key statements of experts and other witnesses; and important photographs, diagrams, and exhibits. As in the case of a pretrial conference, preparation is the key.

SETTLEMENT FORMS

RELEASES AND SETTLEMENT AGREEMENTS

Once the parties have agreed to settle, there are several forms that you may be asked to draft or review for accuracy. One such form is the **release.** A release is a document executed by the plaintiff or claimant that frees the defendant from any further obligations or liability stemming from the incident causing the damages in return for consideration (money). The document ends litigation on the matter between the two parties. Two common types of releases are set out in Exhibit 10:5, an easily adapted example of a release for personal injury, and Exhibit 10:6, a mutual release used when both sides in a lawsuit have claims against the other.[13]

release
A document executed by the plaintiff or claimant that frees the defendant from any further obligations or liability stemming from the incident causing the damages in return for consideration (money).

EXHIBIT10:5 ▪ Release and Settlement of Suit for Personal Injuries

Received of the City of _____ the sum of _____ dollars ($_____), lawful money, to me in hand paid, the receipt of which is hereby acknowledged, the same being in full payment, satisfaction and discharge of any and alll claims, demands or causes of action, of whatsoever nature which I or my heirs, executors, administrators, personal representatives, successors or assigns, may now or hereafter have against the City of _____, its officers, agents or servants, its successors and assigns, for damages for or by all reason of all personal injuries, all pain and suffering, damage to property, all losses and expenses, of whatsoever character, sustained as a result of an accident which occurred to me on or about the ____ day of _____, about _____ o'clock, _.M., at or near _____ Avenue, on which date and at which time and place I was injured when attempting to board a bus, and especially from the cause or causes of action set forth in a petition filed by me in the Court of _____, _____ County, _____, in an action entitled "_____ vs. City of _____," Case No. _____ on the docket of said Court, in which entry may be made "Settled and dismissed at defendant's costs. No record."

I hereby certify that this release is fully understood by me and is entirely satisfactory.
In Witness Whereof, *etc.*

Source: Reprinted with permission of West Group.

EXHIBIT 10:6 ■ Mutual Release of All Claims and Demands

_____, of _____ and _____, of _____, each hereby releases the other from all sums of money, accounts, actions, suits, proceedings, claims, and demands whatsoever which either of them at any time had or has up to this date against the other for or by reason of or in respect of any act, cause, matter, or thing whatsoever.

Signed and sealed on _____ at _____.

_____ [_Seal_]

_____ [_Seal_]

Source: Reprinted with permission of West Group.

Releases may be general in nature or specific, tied to a particular claim or injury. It is a good idea to consult local law on what must be included in a valid release. Some states, for instance, do not require consideration. In some circumstances a covenant not to sue is executed, which is not a release of past wrongs but simply an agreement not to sue on a claim in return for consideration. Exhibit 10:7 is an example of a covenant not to sue.[14] This type of release is also called an indemnification agreement or hold harmless agreement.

Settlement agreements are often used in more complex cases and provide a more detailed description of the settlement than a typical release from liability. The **settlement agreement** is a contract between the parties setting all the terms, conditions, and obligations of the parties, including how the action will be dismissed. If requested to draft such an agreement, review local examples of the document and ask the attorney for specific guidelines. Exhibit 10:8 is an example of a settlement agreement.

An issue generating increased debate is whether settlement agreements should be permitted by the courts to be secret (or sealed) and whether such agreements should be permitted to contain restrictions on parties, particularly plaintiffs, from providing information to government investigative bodies.[15] On one hand, secrecy encourages settlements, while opening secret settlement provisions to public scrutiny may discourage them. On the other hand, anti-secrecy proponents argue that there is strong public policy in support of revealing settlement information that might prevent additional harm to the public or facilitate health and safety investigations of public agencies. It is likely that courts will increasingly scrutinize what settlement information can be sealed or subjected to revelation prohibitions.

settlement agreement
A contract between the parties setting all the terms, conditions, and obligations of the parties, including how the action will be dismissed.

STIPULATION AND ORDER FOR DISMISSAL

Once an action has been filed and settlement agreed upon, the parties generally have two options for finalizing the settlement. The first is a stipulation and order for dismissal; the second is a consent decree and order.

A stipulation and order for dismissal notifies the judge that the case has been settled and the parties want an order dismissing the action. Under Federal Rule 41(a)(1) and parallel state statutes, the plaintiff without order of the court may file a notice of dismissal at any time before the opponent has filed an answer or a motion for summary judgment, whichever occurs first. If later than this, the

EXHIBIT 10:7 ■ Covenant Not to Sue (with Reservation of Rights as to Others)

COVENANT NOT TO SUE

In consideration of _____ dollars ($_____) paid to me by _____, of _____, and _____, of _____, individually and as a partnership doing business as _____, at _____ and _____ Indemnity Company, of _____, receipt of which I hereby acknowledge, I hereby covenant not to sue _____ or _____, individually or as a partnership doing business as _____, or _____ Indemnity Company, and refrain forever from instituting, pressing, collecting or in any way acting or proceeding upon any and all claims, judgments, debts, causes of action, suits and proceedings of any kind at law or in equity which I ever had, now have or may have against any of the aforementioned covenantees or their legal representatives, successors or assigns, arising out of the following matters: _____

_____

I have received the consideration of $_____ in full payment for this covenant not to sue, notwithstanding any injuries or damages sustained, whether known or unknown.

This instrument is not intended as a release or discharge or nor as an accord or satisfaction with any person whomsoever, but only as a covenant not to sue by which each covenantee hereby purchases peace and is hereby given peace upon any and all claims and matters whatsoever which have been or may be made against covenantees by me. I acknowledge that covenantees in making payment of the consideration for this covenant have done so solely to obtain peace and do not thereby admit any liability on account of any of the above-described matters but expressly deny all of such liability whatsoever.

I hereby expressly reserve the right to proceed against or sue _____ of _____ or _____ of _____ or any other person or persons against whom I may have or assert any claim on account of damages arising out of the above-described matters. Nothing contained in this instrument shall in any way tend to release or discharge or be construed as releasing or discharging _____ or _____, or any other person or persons against whom I may have or assert any claim on account of damages arising out of the above-described matters.

Signed and sealed on _____.

_____ [Seal]

Witness:

_____

Source: Reprinted with permission of West Group.

EXHIBIT10:8 ■ Settlement Agreement

SETTLEMENT AGREEMENT

[*Name of first party*] of [*address*], hereafter referred to as _____ and [*Name of second party*] of [*address*], hereafter referred to as _____ in order to settle the controversy between them designated as _____ v. _____ civil case file number _____ filed in the [*name of court*] by the dated signatures below, HEREBY AGREE AND INTEND TO BE LEGALLY BOUND BY THE FOLLOWING TERMS:

1. (Here state in detail each term, condition, and covenant agreed to by both parites: amount, time, and terms of payment; nature and extent of releases that will be executed and delivered; when and how the action will be dismissed; how court costs and legal fees will be handled; whether goods or documents

(*continued*)

EXHIBIT10:8 ■ Settlement Agreement *(continued)*

will be exchanged or discharged; what collateral, if any, will be used to insure the agreement; and any other items suggested by the attorney.)

(Seal)   (First Party)

Attest _____   by _____
                                                    Party (or duly authorized officer)

                                                    _____
                                                    Address

                                                    Date _____

(Seal)   (Second Party)

Attest _____   by _____
                                                    Party (or duly authorized officer)

                                                    _____
                                                    Address

                                                    Date _____

without prejudice
In the dismissal of a case, the understanding that the action may be brought again.

with prejudice
In the dismissal of a case, the understanding that the action may not be brought again.

adjudication on the merits
A judgment by the court deciding the issues of an action, precluding that action from being brought again.

parties may file a stipulation for dismissal signed by all the parties that have appeared in the action. Such a dismissal is normally **without prejudice,** meaning the action may be brought again. A signed release is important in this case, since it serves as a defense to the action being brought again. If requested, however, the court may dismiss the action **with prejudice,** meaning it may not be brought again. The case is treated as an **adjudication on the merits,** as if the court had considered and decided all remaining issues. One advantage to this process is that the parties do not have to make public the terms of the settlement. If one of the parties breaches the agreement, the court may impose sanctions. Exhibit 10:9 is an example of a stipulation and order for dismissal. Local rules and examples should always be consulted.

CONSENT DECREE AND ORDER

The parties may instead choose a consent decree and order. This method differs from the stipulation for dismissal by including the details of the settlement and by asking the judge to review and approve the terms of the settlement. A number of states require any settlement on behalf of a minor to be approved by the court. Judgment is entered according to the terms as approved. Exhibit 10:10 is an example of a stipulation and consent decree and order.

SETTLEMENT DISTRIBUTION STATEMENT

The attorney or firm should give the client a settlement distribution statement that clearly itemizes the amount of the settlement and how it will be distributed. The drafting of such a statement is not difficult and can be instrumental in avoiding unnecessary conflicts and misunderstanding with the client both now and in the future. Also, to avoid misunderstandings and the appearance of impropriety, settlement checks cannot be deposited in the law firm's bank account before distribution to the client. Exhibit 10:11 is an example of a settlement distribution statement.

EXHIBIT 10:9 ■ Stipulation and Order for Dismissal

IN THE UNITED STATES DISTRICT COURT FOR
THE _____ DISTRICT OF _____

_____   Plaintiff

v.   Civil Action, File No. _____

_____   Defendant

STIPULATION AND ORDER FOR DISMISSAL

On this _____ day of _____, it is stipulated between counsel for Plaintiff and counsel for Defendant that this action be dismissed *[with or without prejudice]* regarding all claims and counterclaims of the parties and without costs to the parties, and that an order consistent with this stipulation be entered without further notice to the parties.

_____
Attorney for Plaintiff
_____
Address
_____
Attorney for Defendant
_____
Address

So Ordered

_____, Judge United States District Court of the _____ District of _____

Date _____

OTHER ALTERNATIVE DISPUTE RESOLUTIONS: ARBITRATION, MEDIATION, AND SUMMARY TRIALS

INTRODUCTION

Paralegals are becoming increasingly involved in assisting attorneys and clients in preparing for alternative dispute resolution (ADR) processes. These processes include various forms of arbitration, mediation, summary trials, and others. The remaining portion of this chapter focuses on these procedures and the role of the paralegal in assisting in these processes.

The interest in and use of alternative dispute resolution continues to grow dramatically. Three primary reasons explain the increasing use of these systems. Alternative dispute resolution keeps many cases out of an already overcrowded court docket, which not only relieves pressure on our courts, but also allows thousands of ADR cases to be resolved more quickly than if they had been adjudicated in the

EXHIBIT 10:10 ▪ Stipulation and Consent Decree and Order

(Caption omitted)

STIPULATION AND CONSENT DECREE

The parties to this action, having agreed to settle this case, hereby consent to the entry of the following order.

This order and stipulation shall not be interpreted as an admission of wrongdoing by either party.

   THE PARTIES, BY THEIR ATTORNEYS, STIPULATE THAT THIS CASE SHALL BE SETTLED BY CONSENT DECREE AS FOLLOWS:

   1. The Defendant, _____, shall pay to the Plaintiff, _____, the agreed upon sum of $_____ for all injuries, pain and suffering, and damages, past, present, and future sustained from [*state accident or other source of claim*] on [*date*]   .

   2. The Defendant, _____, shall pay the sum in the following manner: _____.

   3. The Plaintiff, _____, shall pay to the Defendant, _____, the sum of $_____, for all damages, past, present, and future, incurred by the Defendant as a consequence of [*restate accident as source of claim*] as alleged in Defendant's counterclaim against Plaintiff.

   4. The Defendant shall pay the costs of this action in the sum of $_____

   5. The parties will pay their own attorney's fees.

   6. At the time of compliance with all terms of the stipulation and decree, the above captioned action shall be dismissed with prejudice.

For Plaintiff,   For Defendant,

_____   _____
Attorney for Plaintiff   Attorney for Defendant

_____   _____
Address   Address
Date _____

(Caption omitted)

ORDER

Having reviewed the above entitled case and the Stipulated Consent Decree freely entered into by both parties to this action as evidenced by the signature of their respective counsel, the Court ORDERS, ADJUDGES, and DECREES that the Stipulation is approved, as set forth and attached hereto, so ordered this _____ day of _____.

_____
Judge, United States District
Court for the _____
District of _____

EXHIBIT 10:11 ▪ Settlement Distribution Statement

WHITE, WILSON & McDUFF
ATTORNEYS AT LAW
FEDERAL PLAZA BUILDING, SUITE 700
THIRD AND MARKET STREETS
LEGALVILLE, COLUMBIA 00000
(111) 555-0000

SETTLEMENT DISTRIBUTION STATEMENT

CASE: _____ vs. _____   CLIENT: _____

    Civil Case No. _____

    Court _____

Total Gross Settlement (received from _____) $_____

    Less Attorney's Expenses (Itemized)

        Travel $_____

        Printing $_____

        Doctors' Report Fees $_____

        Medical Records Fees $_____

        Phone Calls $_____

        Court Costs and Filing Fees $_____

        Photocopies $_____

        Others $_____

                            Subtotal $_____ $_____

Less Attorney's Fee (figured by percentage of gross in contingency fee
case or by itemized billing entries)

                                              $_____

                    Total Net Settlement Due Client $_____

courts. Complex trials can go on for months or over a year. ADR hearings usually are completed in several hours, a day, or, in complex cases, a series of one- or two-day sessions over several months.

Second, because ADR takes less time and is less formal with relaxed standards of evidence, procedure, and location than a court procedure, it also saves parties a considerable amount of money. Costs may be waived for indigency in some cases. A greater fee in large commercial cases is still a bargain.

Third, ADR processes are less adversarial and confrontational than a trial and substantially reduce the emotional trauma and bitterness associated with trials. Cases involving family law, business associates, employers and employees, landlords and tenants, and a host of other kinds of disputes are better served by a process that stresses reconciliation, common ground, and the mutual desire to get the matter over with as congenially as possible.

At one time ADR was reserved for small cases. Today, however, cases involving millions of dollars and complex technical issues have been resolved through alternative dispute resolution. An increasing number of courts require ADR in at least some types of cases. Some states, require ADR in all civil cases. All federal courts have been required to have mandatory ADR programs since 1998. In 1991, the Administrative Dispute Resolution Act amended the Administrative Procedure Act of 1946 specifically to authorize and encourage the use of ADR processes in federal agencies. In 1996, President Clinton signed an executive order requiring all U.S. government lawyers to use alternative dispute resolution when warranted. (Incidentally, this same order called for a greater use of nonlawyer representatives in federal administrative agency practice.) Although satisfaction with ADR generally runs high, concerns exist, particularly in regard to arbitration.

ARBITRATION

arbitration
An alternative dispute resolution process consisting of the submission of a dispute to a neutral decision maker.

Arbitration is an alternative dispute resolution process consisting of the submission of a dispute to a neutral decision maker. It is, generally speaking, a private contractual process that is encouraged by state and federal law. Most states have adopted a version of the Uniform Arbitration Act. The Federal Arbitration Act (9 U.S.C. § 10) applies to arbitrations when they are part of contracts involving interstate commerce.

Although the parties surrender decision-making power to the arbitrator, they have considerably more control over the process than they do in litigation. They can determine whether the award will be binding or advisory, and they can select the time, place, the arbitrator (who may or may not be an attorney), the conditions that invoke arbitration, the procedures, and even the standards for the arbitrator's decision. The terms of the arbitration are set out in a formal agreement and signed by each party. Parties are bound by the agreement as they would be by a contract. The parties pay the arbitrator's fee, a filing fee, and expenses. The losing party frequently covers the prevailing party's filing fee. Arbitrators and guidelines for arbitration are available through various arbitration associations, including the American Arbitration Association and the Society of Professionals in Dispute Resolution.

The procedure in voluntary arbitration is initiated by a "demand for arbitration," a "statement of claim," or some similar document. This document sets out the dispute, a remedy, and the amount of the award sought. It serves the same purpose as a complaint, but is generally more informal in nature. The "demand" is usually accompanied by a "submission agreement" signed by both parties agreeing to the arbitration. Alternatively, the claim may be filed with the arbitration association, which serves the claim on the opposing party. A reply may be required.

A list of arbitrators may be sent to the parties who, generally, can cross out the names of a specified number of arbitrators. The arbitrator is then selected from the remaining names.

A form of discovery is also available: Documents, information, and depositions are exchanged when deemed necessary by the arbitrator. Generally, thirty days are permitted for the response to such requests. A hearing date is set, and notice is given allowing approximately forty-five days for preparation.

The hearing is similar to a trial but more informal. Opening arguments are given, witnesses are heard, some cross-examination is allowed, and evidence is presented. The rules of procedure and burdens of proof are more relaxed; for example, hearsay evidence is generally not objectionable. The complaining party may be given the choice on whether to go first or last in closing arguments.

Sometimes summary briefs are requested after the hearing. The decision is usually rendered within thirty days. An appeal to the courts is available, but generally the court's latitude in overturning a decision is limited to the grounds stated in the Federal Arbitration Act (9 U.S.C. § 10) and similar statutes. Generally they are as follows:

1. The award was obtained by fraud or corruption.
2. The arbitrator was obviously partial or corrupted.
3. The arbitrator was guilty of misconduct or some obvious abuse of fairness or discretion, or otherwise exceeding delegated powers.

The standard of proof in arbitration varies depending on the type of case. It can be as indefinite as "the party whose evidence is most persuasive viewed as a whole."[16]

Despite the success of arbitration or because of it, concerns have developed. One such concern stems from the expanded use of mandatory arbitration clauses in a variety of commercial and employment contracts. For individuals, if you want the job, merchandise, credit card, mortgage, service, or other contracted benefit, you must agree to arbitration, rather than litigation, as the means to resolve any claim against the employer or the merchant. These clauses are criticized for being a product of unequal bargaining power where there is no practical alternative for the weaker party and where the clauses contain additional obstacles that make it difficult or often too costly to pursue a claim or seek judicial relief.[17] Despite these concerns, courts have largely upheld mandatory arbitration clauses, even extending enforcement of the Federal Arbitration Act to employment contracts [*Circuit City Stores, Inc. v. Adams,* 121 S.Ct. 1302 (2001)].

Other concerns include the lack of hard data on whether arbitration, especially in complex commercial cases, actually saves money and time; whether individuals have adequate information on which to base their choice of an arbitrator; whether arbitration agreements can prohibit class actions; and whether dissatisfaction with aspects of arbitration, especially mandatory arbitration, is leading to increased and more frequently successful court challenges.[18]

Here is an example of a voluntary arbitration case.[19]

> "We should get away from the idea that a court is the only place in which to settle disputes. People with claims are likely people with pains. They want relief and results and they don't care whether it's in a courtroom with lawyers and judges, or somewhere else."
>
> —WARREN E. BURGER, ADDRESS, AMERICAN BAR ASSOCIATION, NEW ORLEANS, *LOS ANGELES TIMES,* AUGUST 27, 1978.

EXAMPLE OF VOLUNTARY ARBITRATION

Velda Bruno was a senior typist for Midwest Phone Systems. On December 18, 1985, she was discharged from her job. Her discharge letter said that she had proved "unable to perform the word processing job for which she was hired." Bruno protested her discharge to the Communications Workers Union that represented Midwest Phone employees. Union and management representatives were unable to resolve the dispute informally. The union argued that Bruno was fired hastily and for insufficient reasons after being transferred to a word processing job from a typing job where she performed satisfactorily. Midwest Phone argued that Bruno's job performance had been continuously substandard, that she had been disciplined regularly, and that the discharge was a logical consequence of her failure to improve her performance.

When attempts at informal resolution failed, the union sent a demand for grievance arbitration to Midwest Phone. The collective bargaining agreement between the Communications Workers and Midwest Phone provided for arbitration of disputes arising out of employee suspension or discharge by the company. Midwest Phone's reply to the demand made it clear that the two parties would be unable to resolve the dispute themselves. Attorneys for the company and the union met and drafted an agreement to govern the arbitration. Their "submission agreement" covered the following points:

1. *Parties.* Midwest Phone Systems and Communications Workers Union.
2. *Relevant contract provision.* Article 12, section 12.1(e) on "suspensions and dismissals" provides that "the Arbitrator shall determine whether the suspension or dismissal was for just cause, but the judgment of the Arbitrator may be substituted for that of the Company only if the Arbitrator finds that the Company acted without making a reasonable investigation or that it acted upon evidence that would not have led a reasonable person to take such action."
3. *Issue.* Was Velda Bruno discharged on December 18, 1985, for just cause? If not, what is the remedy?
4. *Arbitrator.* Alfred Wong was named arbitrator.
5. *Time and place of hearing.* The hearing was to be in the conference room of the Airport Holiday Inn in Minneapolis, Minnesota, beginning at 9:30 A.M., February 10, 1986.
6. *Report of the proceedings.* The parties agreed to share the cost of a stenographic record of the hearing.
7. *Procedures.* The hearing was to be closed to the public; witnesses were to be sworn; the order of presentation of evidence was established; each side was to make an opening statement and closing argument; each side was to offer rebuttal and surrebuttal evidence; all witnesses could be cross-examined and re-examined; each side would submit a post-argument brief to the arbitrator; and each side would provide the other with copies of exhibits ten days prior to the hearing. The parties also agreed that the arbitrator would be given authority to determine any other procedural issues that might arise at the hearing.
8. *Expense of arbitration.* Each party agreed to pay one-half of the arbitrator's expenses and fee.
9. *Decision of the arbitrator.* The arbitrator was to submit a signed copy of the decision and award as soon as possible following the hearing but no later than forty-five days after the hearing.

The submission agreement was signed on January 13, 1986. The parties gave themselves a relatively short time to put together their cases. Prior to the hearing, Midwest Phone moved to compel production of personal notes that Bruno previously had given to the union and to a civil rights agency. Arbitrator Wong denied the motion on the grounds that the information should be regarded as a work product of the grievant, her union, and its counsel, and hence was not subject to examination by Midwest Phone. Ten days before the hearing counsel for the union and the company exchanged copies of their exhibits.

The hearing commenced at 9:30 A.M. on February 10.

Company's case   The company put on its case first. It called five witnesses: the head of the personnel department and Bruno's first and second-level supervisors at the different facilities where she worked. They testified that Bruno had been hired on October 8, 1983, as a senior typist assigned to the company's word processing center in the company's main building. Bruno passed the typing test given by the company, typing between 90 and 100 words per minute with two errors on an electronic typewriter. She worked with three other employees in a separate room, away from other clerical help and clients. After about three months on the job, her first supervisor testified, Bruno suffered a broken wrist and was unable to type for about two months. During that time she answered telephones at various offices in the company's buildings. When she returned to a typing job in March 1984 she was sent to another word processing center in a satellite facility. At the second center she was trained on Vydec word processing equipment, which displayed typewritten material on a cathode-ray tube, enabling typists to edit material before storing it on a floppy disk or printing it onto paper.

In April, Bruno met with her first-level supervisor at the satellite facility, who informed her that her job performance was not satisfactory. Bruno was told that she had missed 31 percent of the due dates on her jobs and that she had not advised her supervisor early enough that she would not be meeting her deadlines. Bruno was given an opportunity for additional training prior to her six-month evaluation.

In June, Bruno received her six-month evaluation. Her typing evaluation was "satisfactory," but she received an "unsatisfactory" quantity rating on work produced. Bruno's supervisor said she apparently still found it easier to retype some jobs than to make corrections on the word processing equipment. She was given two months to improve her performance.

Bruno's supervisor testified that in August she still was not producing adequate quantities of work. The first-level supervisor reported Bruno's lack of progress to the second-level supervisor who informed Bruno that her performance would be subject to monthly evaluations and that if she did not improve within six months, she would be discharged.

By January 1985, Bruno's supervisors testified, her work had improved considerably. The threat of discharge was lifted. In February 1985, however, one of Bruno's jobs was returned because of improper formatting on a list of telephone extension numbers. Shortly thereafter, her first-level supervisor testified, she neglected to index a job to facilitate future use of stored material. A few weeks later her supervisor discovered that the second page of a job had been stored on the same track as the first page, thereby erasing the first page. The company continued to have problems with Bruno. She would make some improvement, then lapse into errors. In June, for example, she stored four pages of material on a disk but could not locate them. Her first-level supervisor found that she had written the wrong information on the index sheet, which is why she could not locate the work.

By July, Bruno and her first-level supervisor were having serious communications problems. Her first-level supervisor at the satellite facility testified that Bruno became so defensive about her errors that she tried to hide them and would not communicate candidly. The first-level supervisor again notified the second-level supervisor. In August, Bruno received the first warning notice from her second-level supervisor: If her work performance did not improve she would receive a second warning in late October and would be terminated before the end of the 1985 calendar year.

Bruno's first-level supervisor testified that after the first warning Bruno became even more defensive. In September, the company agreed to transfer Bruno to another work unit on the assumption that she might be able to perform more adequately under a different first-level supervisor. The new unit also used Vydec equipment. Bruno's first-level supervisor in the new work unit testified that Bruno had severe problems operating the printers in that unit and that because of her problems her production never came up to acceptable levels. Bruno received her second warning letter in late October.

In mid-November, according to her supervisor's testimony, Bruno missed three job deadlines and improperly stored two jobs. The improper storage made it impossible for weekend typists to find and complete the jobs. In December, Bruno was discharged.

On cross-examination, Bruno's counsel elicited testimony that Bruno's job performance on her typing job before her broken wrist was well above average and that neither her supervisors nor her clients had anything negative to say about her work. Cross-examination also revealed that although the unit to which Bruno was assigned in September 1985 did use Vydec equipment, it was an updated version of the equipment Bruno had worked on previously. The printing system was almost entirely different, and storage and retrieval processes were substantially changed. The company's testimony lasted approximately a day-and-a-half.

Union's case   The union called only one witness. Velda Bruno testified that she had been a typist for eighteen years at a local construction company before going to work for Midwest Phone. Prior to that she had been at home with her children for approximately fifteen years. During her tenure with the construction company she had consistently won merit promotions and pay increases. During that time she had worked on IBM Selectric typewriters and had learned to use electronic typewriters as well.

Bruno testified that she applied to work for Midwest Phone when the construction company went out of business. During her interview she was told that she would be required to work on the company's electronic typewriters and that she would be working in a separate typing unit with three other employees in the word processing center. Bruno also testified that in January 1984, three months after she was hired, she slipped on the ice on the way to work and broke her wrist. She was unable to type for two months. She was replaced by another typist and answered telephones until March 1984. When she was ready to resume her typing duties, Bruno testified, she was told that the company had been unable to find a temporary replacement for her while her wrist healed, that it had therefore hired a permanent replacement, and that she was being assigned to another word processing unit in a satellite building in another part of town. Bruno testified that she agreed to the transfer in order to keep her job, and that after she reviewed her contract with the company she realized that as a senior typist she was required to work on word processing equipment if asked.

When Bruno reported to her new job location she found that her hours would be 7:00 A.M. to 4:00 P.M. She received eight hours of training on the equipment. Bruno testified that her new typing duties involved primarily statistical typing, whereas her previous typing had been primarily manuscripts and letters.

Bruno admitted on both direct and cross-examination that she found the transition to her new job very difficult. Her new job required her to work in a large room with 30 other typists, on new equipment, doing very different work than she was accustomed to doing. She admitted that her production levels were lower than those of other employees and that she had trouble storing jobs on the Vydec equipment. Furthermore, she had trouble retrieving materials that had been stored by night and weekend typists. She testified that she found her first-level supervisor hard to work with and that she seemed to like to criticize Bruno's work in a loud voice in front of the other typists. Bruno said she became increasingly nervous about losing her job. When she received her first warning notice she was unable to sleep and finally requested a transfer, thinking that a different work unit might be better. She said the working conditions in the second unit were better and that she liked her new first-level supervisor very much, but that it was difficult to adjust to the new Vydec equipment. Printers, for example were located in a separate room, rather than being connected to individual terminals. While that made the work place quieter, it did require typists to call up their jobs for printing and Bruno had difficulty learning the technique. As a result, her production rates dropped even further. She received no training in storage and retrieval on the new machines. She did receive a manual but could not understand it and was afraid she would be criticized if she asked too many questions.

On cross-examination Bruno was asked specifically about the jobs that had been returned to her, the material that she had lost through improper storage, and her failure to complete three jobs on time. She said that in each instance the jobs returned to her for correction had not been her original work product but that she could not prove that to her supervisor because the indexing cards on those jobs apparently had been lost. She said she felt terrible about the work she lost and that she thought it was the result of being new to the equipment and nervous about the possibility of losing her job. With respect to the jobs she failed to complete on time, Bruno explained that her work hours were 7:00 A.M. to 4:00 P.M. and that two of the jobs were called late because they were not done by her quitting time, even though she had been able to have them on her clients' desks by 8:00 A.M. the next day, their starting time. She said she received no complaints from her clients. The third late job had been marked "Rush" and on that day Bruno said she stayed late to get it done. Nonetheless, the job was called late because it was not ready at her regular quitting time.

Bruno's testimony and cross-examination took approximately three hours. Counsel for both sides then waived closing arguments, agreeing to summarize their arguments in the post-hearing briefs that were to be submitted to the arbitrator within five days of the hearing. The hearing was closed.

Arbitrator's award   Arbitrator Wong studied post-hearing briefs from each side (each approximately 25 pages long, summarizing its position based on the testimony) and reviewed some of the testimony given at the hearing. Approximately three weeks after the close of the hearing he delivered his opinion and award to the parties. The opinion addressed the issue submitted by the parties: "Was Velda Bruno discharged for just cause? If not, what is the appropriate remedy?" In a 27-page opinion Wong summarized relevant facts, including a chronological account of the events that led to Bruno's discharge, and a short statement of the positions of the parties. He included a short statement about the burden of persuasion and a statement that in his opinion, Midwest Phone had the burden of proving by a preponderance of the evidence that Bruno was discharged for just cause.

Wong concluded that although there were isolated instances of satisfactory performance on Bruno's part, her overall performance was not satisfactory and that Midwest Phone had just cause to take disciplinary action against her. Under the circumstances, however, discharge was not a reasonable penalty and should be set aside. Bruno had a good work record for eighteen years with another employer and for three months with Midwest Phone. However, Bruno did not successfully make the transition from typist on electric and electronic typewriters to the company's word processing equipment, a transition a senior typist was expected to be able to make according to the contract between the union and Midwest Phone. Hence, Wong concluded that Bruno should not be reinstated to the position of senior typist in the word processing center. Wong ordered a 30-day disciplinary suspension for Bruno without pay, and reinstatement with back pay and no interest as a typist at a reduced grade at one of the company's secretarial departments, assigned to tasks and equipment more commensurate with her former secretarial experience, training and background. In arriving at this conclusion, Wong cited as authority opinions from four other reported arbitration proceedings.

At the end of the month Arbitrator Wong submitted his bill to Midwest Phone and the union. The total included his travel and hotel expenses, stenographic assistance, research and $485 per day, his fee as an arbitrator. He spent a total of three days on the case. The company and the union each paid half of the bill, in addition to splitting the costs of renting the conference room.

Another form of arbitration is court-annexed arbitration. It is controlled by the court in which the action is filed and, if the arbitration is not successful, the case may still be tried by that court. Procedurally, a complaint is filed in court as it would be in any lawsuit. The defendant answers the complaint. Court personnel screen the filings and assign certain cases to the arbitration process. The assignment may be challenged by a party not wanting to go to arbitration or, if a case is not assigned to arbitration, a party or the parties may request that it be so assigned.

The arbitrator or panel of arbitrators are generally selected by the court or by the parties from a court list. Arbitrators are usually attorneys and normally paid by the court. In some jurisdictions they are expected to work hard to facilitate a settlement prior to the hearing. The hearings may be quite trial-like and formal or informal where each side simply states its case and no witnesses testify. A decision is rendered in as little as a week in some programs. The award is entered as the court's judgment.

If a party is unsatisfied with the decision, that party may request that the case be tried in a *trial de novo* (a trial as in any other case and as if no previous hearing had been held). Usually, however, such a request is discouraged by disincentives such as the requirement of a party to pay the other party's court costs and attorney's fees if it does not do significantly better at trial than it did under the arbitration award. This requirement helps prevent abuse of arbitration as just another pretrial discovery tool, and upholds its purpose in freeing court dockets. Appeals are often limited.

Arbitration is also important to the global market. Since the vast majority of international business agreements now contain an arbitration clause, paralegals practicing in international business law need to consult the International Arbitration Rules of the American Arbitration Association, the Rules of Arbitration of the International Chamber of Commerce, or the Arbitration Rules of the United Nations Commission on International Trade Law, depending on the system being used. The collection and presentation of evidence in international arbitration hearings is not usually covered by these rule systems, however. In 1999, the International Bar Association approved its updated *IBA Rules on the Taking of Evidence in International Commercial Arbitration*, balancing the requirements of differing legal cultures and clarifying the limits of discovery and use of witnesses.[20] Web sites for these organizations are listed at the end of this chapter.

MEDIATION

mediation

An alternative dispute resolution process incorporating a neutral person (the mediator) who facilitates a mutual resolution of the dispute.

Mediation is an alternative dispute resolution process incorporating a neutral person (the mediator) who facilitates a mutual resolution of the dispute. The parties reach their own decision as to how to resolve the matter. Arbitration focuses on a somewhat adversarial fault-finding process of presenting evidence to decide a case and render an award; mediation focuses on common ground, how the parties can conduct themselves in the future (not how they conducted themselves in the past), and conciliatory compromise to resolve the dispute. In a 1999 survey, lawyers stated their overwhelming preference for nonbinding mediation over binding arbitration, because of savings in both time and money.[21]

Generally, the two types of mediation are voluntary and mandatory. In voluntary mediation the parties realize that they are unable to resolve a dispute on their own or, at least, realize that they need assistance. They seek assistance through mediation programs or mediation associations. Mandatory mediation is generally imposed in specific types of cases by statute or by court order. Its purpose is to require the parties to mediate their differences before exercising their right to a trial or to other procedures, such as a strike in labor disputes. In either case the agreement is strictly voluntary with few if any sanctions for going ahead with other dispute resolution processes, including litigation if mediation fails. Voluntary mediation provides more party control over the process—selection of mediator, objectives, written agreement—than does mandatory mediation.

Procedurally, the processes used in the two types of mediation are similar. First, the parties select a mediator or are assigned one by the court or under a procedure established by the controlling statute. The parties meet with the mediator to gain an understanding of the goals of the process and how it works, and to establish some rules within which the mediation will be conducted. Where arbitration may have more formal and sometimes set rules of procedure, mediation is far more flexible with rules often created according to what will best serve the parties. For example, arbitration normally sets some standard or burden of persuasion. There is no such burden in mediation. Once the rules are formulated, then the parties or their representatives meet together or individually with the mediator in private to set out some facts and to propose solutions. Generally, these discussions are considered confidential and cannot be used as evidence in court. When these discussions are completed, the effort focuses on the drafting of a mutually agreed plan to resolve the dispute. This agreement is to be the agreement of the parties' own work and ideas and not an agreement imposed on the parties by the mediator. Indications are that parties stick more readily to the terms of a mediated settlement because the terms are their own. Sometimes the parties will be able to agree on all issues, other times only on some—but even then progress has been made. When the parties cannot agree, the process returns to more formal remedies such as litigation. Many agreements provide for further mediation if disputes on clarifying terminology or some other matter arise later. An attempt at mediation is not a step in litigation and does not interrupt the tolling of the statute of limitations, however, so timing is important [*Gallagher v. Cook*, 775 So. 2d 79 (La. App. 2000)].

Mediation programs are growing, keeping numerous cases out of court, and preserving congeniality and civility in what might otherwise be far more seriously estranged relationships. While mediation lends itself well to family, neighborhood, and consumer disputes, it is now being more widely used in complex labor, environmental, and intellectual property cases.[22] The American Bar Association joined forces with the American Arbitration Association and the Association for Conflict Resolution to develop the Model Standards of Conduct for Mediators (2005), uniform ethical guidelines.

A hybrid form of dispute resolution is med-arb. **Med-arb** is a combination of mediation and arbitration methods in which the matter is first mediated, then any unresolved issue is decided by the same or a different person who serves as an arbitrator. This approach incorporates the best features of a nonconfrontational process while still providing a decision to better ensure finality of the matter. Here is a case example of med-arb.[23]

med-arb
A combination of mediation and arbitration; the matter is first mediated, then any unresolved issue is decided by the same or a different person who serves as an arbitrator.

EXAMPLE OF MED-ARB

John Cotesworth, Evan Handy, and Cynthia Paul attended veterinary school together in the mid-1960s. During school they were best friends and decided to go into partnership together in a small town in the Midwest when they graduated. Because they were such close friends they decided to run their practice on a very informal basis. They each contributed money to buy equipment and supplies, rent a clinic, and advertise their services. Handy's father had been a veterinarian and gave them a lot of good advice, some equipment, and his patient list when he retired. Cotesworth, Handy, and Paul agreed to share profits equally.

For almost fifteen years the practice went quite smoothly. The clinic developed an excellent reputation in the community and each of the veterinarians was highly respected and well known. Paul served three terms as mayor, Cotesworth was active in United Way, and Handy was named Citizen of the Year in 1984 for his work with senior citizens.

In May 1986, the three started to have problems. Cotesworth and his wife were divorced after several months of a child custody battle. Cotesworth's ex-wife remained Cynthia Paul's best friend. Paul found it increasingly hard to work with Cotesworth given what his former wife told her about him. Handy, who had always been a social drinker, occasionally showed up for work intoxicated or hung over and sometimes was unable to perform even routine surgeries. Cotesworth had no patience with Handy's drinking and would refuse to speak to Handy for several days after Handy had come to work intoxicated. Soon the personal problems started having professional ramifications. Cotesworth felt that because he was single Paul and Handy expected him to do most of the weekend emergency work but were unwilling to compensate him for it. Paul felt that both Cotesworth and Handy assigned the temperamental cases to her because of her diplomacy with people and her ability to calm nervous animals. By mid-year the three veterinarians could barely speak to one another and realized that they should stop trying to work together.

Every time Cotesworth, Handy, and Paul tried to discuss the best way to end their partnership they got into serious arguments. None was content with a three-way split. Paul and Cotesworth felt they had contributed much more than their share of time to the practice, while Handy contended they should not be allowed to benefit from all the help they had received from his father when they were starting their practice. Neither Cotesworth nor Paul wanted to stop practicing veterinary medicine, although Handy readily admitted that he was ready for a career change. Both Cotesworth and Paul wanted the equipment and the clinic; Handy said he would rather sell his share to anybody else than Cotesworth and Paul.

Cotesworth finally consulted his lawyer about the best way to dissolve the partnership. His attorney asked to see a copy of the original partnership agreement in order to study the provisions for dissolution. Cotesworth explained that when the three had started out they were best friends and that they had operated all these years without a partnership agreement.

Cotesworth's lawyer listened to her client's explanation of the problem confronting the veterinarians and explained med-arb. The three could try to negotiate a settlement to their dispute with the aid of a neutral mediator. Lacking agreement, the mediator either could offer an opinion or could turn the dispute over to an arbitrator. Cotesworth's lawyer gave him a list of three people in the community who practiced mediation.

Cotesworth, Handy, and Paul interviewed the three mediators and agreed that one would be acceptable. They agreed that they did not want everyone in the town to know about their problems and concluded that the mediator should be authorized to arbitrate the dispute if they were unable to resolve their dispute.

The mediator spent several hours with the three explaining mediation and establishing ground rules. Achieving agreement on a process was a big step. In addition to agreeing on a process, they agreed to meet twice a week for two hours until they either came to agreement or reached stalemate.

The three veterinarians stayed in mediation for almost five weeks. Sometimes they met together; sometimes the mediator met with them individually or in pairs. The mediator was able to get them to talk about what had happened to their friendship as well as the best way to dissolve the partnership. Cotesworth finally understood that Paul had been angry with him because of his divorce and comments from his ex-wife. He thought she disapproved of the way he had handled a case several months ago and was holding a grudge. Cotesworth and Paul both came to a better understanding of Handy's drinking problem, apparently precipitated by the fact that he no longer liked veterinary medicine but thought he was too old to make a career change. Cotesworth and Handy listened to Paul's resentment about being given the most difficult patients. All were able to acknowledge how important their friendship had been over the years.

Through mediation Cotesworth and Paul were able to agree that they both wanted to continue to practice veterinary medicine in the same town and that they did not want to be in competition with one another. They knew, however, that they would never be close friends as they once had been. They agreed to retain a lawyer to draw up a formal partnership agreement.

Despite their progress in mediation, the three were not able to agree how much Handy should be paid for his share of the partnership. That issue eventually was turned over to the mediator, now arbitrator, for a decision. Cotesworth and Paul then agreed on what percentage of the award each of them should pay Handy. Handy used his share of the settlement to relocate in another community to work with a group of cattle breeders.

Before leaving arbitration and mediation, brief mention of some related concepts may be helpful. One is *collaborative law*, a process where attorneys for disputing parties agree in writing to work diligently for a negotiated settlement to the dispute. If no settlement is reached, the attorneys will refer their client to another attorney for litigation of the matter. The aim is to increase the likelihood of settlement by committing the parties and their agents to the sole purpose of settlement.

Another is the *high-low agreement*, where the parties agree to no more than a maximum (high) award and a set minimum (low) award, regardless of the jury's verdict or the arbitrator's decision. The high-low agreement removes some of the uncertainties of the final result. For example, if a plaintiff sees the potential that a jury may find the plaintiff partly responsible for an accident or more responsible than the defendant, the low part of the agreement assures the plaintiff that the very least awarded will be enough to cover hospital bills, attorney fees, and other expenses. If the verdict is more than the agreed low but less than the agreed high, the plaintiff will get the amount of the verdict. For the defendant, if the verdict goes beyond the agreed high, the plaintiff gets the agreed high and no more.

Finally, Federal Rule of Civil Procedure 68 and equivalent state rules are relevant to both the discussion of settlement and arbitration. Under Rule 68, more than 10 days prior to trial, the defendant may serve the plaintiff with an *offer of judgment*— an offer to allow entry of judgment against the defendant for a specified amount. If the plaintiff refuses the offer, and the result after trial is not more favorable to the plaintiff than the offer of judgment, the plaintiff must pay the defendant's costs incurred after the offer. The rationale for the rule is to encourage another thoughtful analysis of the case and possible settlement before accruing the added costs of trial. The Rule 68 approach of shifting the costs of trial to an unreasonable party is not just limited to civil court actions, but also applies to arbitrations in some states.[24]

EARLY CASE ASSESSMENT

Some federal courts have implemented early case assessment or early neutral evaluation programs. These programs attempt to head off the substantial expense of discovery by having a neutral court employee, an appointed attorney with pertinent

"One utterance of [Oliver Cromwell] has always hung in my mind. It was just before the Battle of Dunbar; he beat the Scots in the end, as you know, after a very tough fight; but he wrote them before the battle, trying to get them to accept a reasonable composition. These were his words: "I beseech ye in the bowels of Christ, think that ye may be mistaken." I should like to have that written over the portals of every church, every school, and every court house, and may I say, of every legislative body in the United States."

—LEARNED HAND, IN IRVING DILLIARD, *THE SPIRIT OF LIBERTY*, 1960.

expertise, or a different judge facilitate the exchange of only the information that is key to resolving the dispute. After this minimal exchange, the parties may enter mediation for a resolution of the case. These programs have been quite successful in settling cases before expensive discovery occurs.[25]

SUMMARY JURY TRIAL

summary trial
A nonbinding, abbreviated trial before a summary jury to see whether either side's case merits a real trial; encourages settlement of especially large cases.

Courts also utilize the **summary trial.** Used most often in expensive, complex trials, its purpose is to let both sides try the key points of their respective cases before a small jury in an abbreviated format. The purpose of a summary trial is to get at the results quickly, and then encourage the parties to settle the case on the basis of the additional information. Summary trials have a way of pointing out theories and evidence that will not work in fact, despite their appeal on paper. When this happens, settlement often occurs and much time and money are saved. The summary trial verdict, however, is not binding, and the case may still go to a full trial.

ROLE OF THE PARALEGAL IN ALTERNATIVE DISPUTE RESOLUTION

You may find that a case you are working on goes to arbitration, mediation, or some other ADR procedure. Or an attorney in the office becomes the arbitrator or mediator in a case and requires your assistance. In such circumstances your role will be similar to the role you normally play in preparing for settlement—that is, gathering facts, cooperating with the other side on a form of discovery, and drafting and filing necessary documents to start an action and present it at a hearing. You may work with witnesses in some cases, research the client's best choice of arbitrators or mediators, and research and draft summaries of evidence that can be similar to settlement packets or briefs. Most of your tasks in ADR are similar in technique to what you do in trial or settlement preparation, only abbreviated for alternative dispute resolution.

In some instances experienced paralegals may serve as layperson mediators. Should you become involved in assisting in a mediation or arbitration process, keep in mind that forms and procedures and names of arbitrators and mediators can be obtained from sponsoring associations such as the American Arbitration Association, Neighborhood Justice Forums, the Federal Mediation and Conciliation Service, National Academy of Arbitrators, local and federal courts, chambers of commerce, landlord/tenant associations, and others. The entire area of alternative dispute resolution, including efforts to negotiate a settlement, can be an exciting endeavor, especially when you realize that your work has resulted in the resolution of a conflict without the cost in time, money, and emotional trauma often associated with a court trial.

SUMMARY

Chapter 10 focuses on the resolution of civil cases without trial. Under the umbrella of alternative dispute resolution (ADR), this chapter addresses settlement, procedures that encourage settlement such as pretrial and settlement conferences, the summary trial, early case assessment, and the alternatives to litigation offered by arbitration and mediation. You serve the client in each procedure by gathering and organizing pertinent information and by drafting persuasive and other necessary documents.

Settlement is the traditional method of ending a case through the negotiation and agreement of the parties. It is facilitated by summarizing the collected facts and carefully totaling the damages. You may be asked to prepare a presentation of this summary in the form of a settlement request. The request can be brief in small cases or involve the preparation of a detailed settlement brochure in more complex cases. The request, regardless of size, normally includes a summary of the facts and the evidence to support those facts, background of the injured party, description of injuries or damage, impact or consequences, a summary of the actual cost in dollars of the damages, and a proposed settlement amount. It becomes the task of the defense paralegal to examine such proposals with a fine-tooth comb and to note weaknesses, inaccuracies, and inconsistencies in the settlement request.

The pretrial conference is a meeting of the opposing lawyers in the case and the judge. Its purpose is to decide what issues remain to be tried and whether the parties can reach a settlement. Again by utilizing a system and checklist approach, you can assist the attorney in preparing for the conference. The process for a settlement conference is similar. If a settlement agreement is reached, the necessary releases, covenants, settlement agreement, and other documents must be drafted and filed. Some courts—in complex cases in which settlement has not been reached—use abbreviated summary trials to identify additional motivation for settlement.

Disputes are being resolved at an increasing rate through arbitration and mediation to keep costs down, reduce the time for ending a dispute, minimize adversarial confrontation, and keep large numbers of cases off the court trial dockets. In arbitration the parties ask a neutral third party to decide the dispute; in mediation the parties utilize a third party to help them work together to come up with a solution to their dispute. Med-arb, combines the best features of both arbitration and mediation to bring a dispute to a conclusion. Collaborative law, high-low agreements, and Rule 68 offers of judgment also enhance the dispute resolution effectiveness.

▣ WORKBOOK

System Folder Assignments, other exercises, a chapter outline, a review test, and other study aids are located in the accompanying workbook.

▣ HELPFUL WEB SITES

http://www.juryverdicts.com
  National Association of State Jury Verdict Publishers; some also provide settlement reports, statistical analysis, and other research

http://www.morelaw.com/index.asp
  recent verdicts and settlements, list of expert witnesses

http://www.adr.org
  American Arbitration Association, rules, roster of arbitrators and mediators, forms, ethics, ADR procedural guides, education and training resources

http://www.iccwbo.org/index_court.asp
  International Chamber of Commerce, International Court of Arbitration, rules, statistics, cost calculator

http://www.uncitral.org
  United Nations Commission on International Trade Law

http://www.ibanet.org
  International Bar Association

http://www.acrnet.org
  Association for Conflict Resolution

http://www.mediate.com
   articles, resources, lists of mediators

http://www.adrr.com
   ADR resources and links

http://www.cybersettle.com
   online service for settling with insurance companies

http://www.clicknsettle.com
   online service for settlement negotiation, arbitration, or mediation

QUESTIONS FOR STUDY AND REVIEW

1. What is a settlement?
2. What percentage of civil cases are settled?
3. Why are cases settled? What factors must be taken into consideration?
4. What is your role in the settlement process?
5. What are the ethical considerations applicable to the settlement process? Why are they important?
6. What must be investigated and summarized in preparing for settlement? Why is this information necessary?
7. What kinds of information needed in preparing for settlement and in evaluating a case can be obtained from a reference librarian or on-line service?
8. During the settlement process, what are the goals of communication with clients? With insurance adjusters?
9. What formulas and processes are utilized to calculate various kinds of damages?
10. How do hedonic damages differ from pain and suffering?
11. Be able to prepare a damage summary and worksheet.
12. What is included in a settlement brochure and a settlement letter or précis? What is the difference between the two and the primary reason for the difference?
13. What is the definition and purpose of a pretrial conference? What Federal Rule applies? What state rule applies?
14. What things should you do to assist the attorney in preparing for the pretrial conference?
15. What is an authorization to negotiate (compromise), and why is its execution by the client important?
16. Be able to draft each of the settlement forms.
17. What are the contents and what is the purpose of a release? A settlement agreement?
18. What is ADR and its advantages and disadvantages?
19. Be able to define the following terms and explain their differences and similarities: voluntary arbitration, court-annexed arbitration, voluntary mediation, mandatory mediation, summary trial, collaborative law, high-low agreement, offer of judgment, early assessment program.
20. In general, explain the paralegal role in ADR processes.

KEY TERMS

adjudication on the merits	mediation	settlement agreement	with prejudice
arbitration	release	settlement précis	without prejudice
med-arb	settlement	summary trial	

ENDNOTES

1. JEANS, TRIAL ADVOCACY, 2nd ed., 510–515 (1993).
2. *Id.*, 522–523.
3. Paula Hannaford-Agor and Thomas Cohen, *Treading on Uncertain Ground: The Reliability of Jury Verdict Reporter Statistics*, National Center for State Courts, cited in Leonard Post, *Study Finds Inflated Jury Reports*, NAT. L. JRNL., May 23, 2005, 11.
4. Melynda Hill-Teter, *Building the Perfect PI Settlement Demand Package*, LEGAL ASSISTANT TODAY, July/Aug. 1998, 71–72.
5. Some of the formulas used in the Economic Loss section of the worksheet suggested by Stone, *Quantifying Damages in Tort Cases*, 14 TRIAL 444–49 (1978).
6. Marcia Coyle, *Updating "Hedonic" Damages*, NAT'L L.J., April 9, 2001, A1, A15.
7. JEANS, *supra* note 1, 550–553.
8. Hill-Teter, *supra* note 4.
9. JEANS, *supra* note 1, 554–573.
10. Werchick, *Trials*, 4 AM. JUR. 374.
11. Donelson, *Settle or Take It to Court? The Paralegal's Role in Preparing a Case for Settlement*, LEGAL ASSISTANT TODAY, May/June 1994, 90, 92.
12. WEST'S LEGAL FORMS, § 28.223, v. 30 (3d ed., 1997).
13. *Id.*, § 30.66, v. 30 (3d ed. 1997) and § 12.34 v. 10 (rev. 2d ed., 1994), with permission of West Group.

14. *Id.*, § 12.54 v. 10 (rev. 2d ed., 1994), with permission of West Group.

15. David Hechler, *Secrecy in Settlements as a Public Safety Issue,* NAT. L. JRNL., Jan. 12, 2004, 1, 3, and *Bill Hits Confidentiality,* NAT. L. JRNL., Jan. 19, 2004, 6.

16. LEESON & JOHNSTON, ENDING IT: DISPUTE RESOLUTION IN AMERICA 53 (1988).

17. Richard Bales, *An Introduction to Arbitration,* KY BENCH & BAR, March 2006, 16.

18. David Hechler, *Arbitration Not Such a Sure Thing?,* NAT. L. JRNL., May 2004, 1, 10.

19. LEESON & JOHNSTON, *supra* note 16, 54–58; reprinted from ENDING IT: DISPUTE RESOLUTION IN AMERICA with permission. Copyright 1988 Matthew Bender & Company, Inc., a member of the LexisNexis Group. All rights reserved.

20. Terry F. Peppard, *New International Evidence Rules Advance Arbitration Process,* WIS. LAW. , March 2000, at 19–21, 56.

21. Lisa Brennan, *What Lawyers Like: Mediation,* NAT'L L.J., Nov. 15, 1999, A1, A10.

22. *Id.*, A10.

23. LEESON & JOHNSTON, *supra* note 16, 151–153; reprinted from ENDING IT: DISPUTE RESOLUTION IN AMERICA with permission. Copyright 1988 Matthew Bender & Company, Inc., a member of the LexisNexis Group. All rights reserved.

24. Jessica Case, *Seeking to Shift Costs: Rule 68 in Arbitration Context,* KY. BENCH & BAR, March 2006, 19.

25. WOLF AND SNAPP, *Novel Early Assessment Program Cuts Costs,* NAT'L L.J., April 29, 1996, B9–B10.

 For additional resources visit our Web site at **http://www.westlegalstudies.com.**

Trial Preparation and Trial

Trial Preparation

Assistance at Trial

Summary

TRIAL PREPARATION

INTRODUCTION AND TRIAL PREPARATION CHECKLIST

Late yesterday afternoon Mr. White said that despite all our efforts, it did not appear that the *Forrester* case was going to settle, and that we should begin our final preparation for trial. The trial date, set at the pretrial conference, is two months from yesterday. It will be your job to perform much of the preparation and to assist Mr. White at trial. Good trial work is based on thorough preparation; much of that responsibility rests in your hands.

Use the trial preparation checklist (Exhibit 11:1), adapting it to the unique features of each case. The remaining materials will help explain what must be done at each step on the checklist. Study the checklist, carefully noting each task.

EXHIBIT 11:1 ▪ Trial Preparation Checklist

At Least Three Months Prior to Trial

☐ If a trial has not yet been set, check with the attorney and file any request or praecipe needed to have trial date set.

☐ Calendar the trial date, unless done previously, and check for any scheduling conflicts.

☐ Check case status sheet and calendar more frequent updatings right up to trial.

☐ Check to see that all required disclosure to date has been completed, including exchange of expert witness names and written report (federal rules).

☐ Check time deadline chart and confirm that key dates are calendared and that litigation team members are reminded.

☐ Meet with team to assess need for special exhibits and technology at trial.

At Least Six Weeks Prior to Trial

☐ Meet with litigation team to review case status and establish countdown work schedule.

☐ Review the case status sheet and keep it updated in the file. Inform the attorney of any depositions, discovery, or other steps needing completion or updating.

☐ Review the facts of the case to determine if there is a need to amend the pleadings.
    ☐ Keep the client fully informed. Meet as needed.
    ☐ Prepare witnesses' statements or witness sheets.
    ☐ Highlight important facts both for and adverse to client.

☐ Review pretrial order to determine if the issues have been narrowed.
    ☐ List documents, exhibits, and witnesses needed on each point, including refutation of the opponent's key points and evidence.

☐ See that legal memoranda have been completed on all questions of law including any likely questions relating to the admissibility of evidence or any motions likely to be made at trial.

At Least Three Weeks Prior to Trial

☐ Prepare a list of all witnesses needed; confirm with the attorney and have subpoenas prepared and served.

☐ Conduct the jury investigation.

☐ Conduct an investigation of the judge, the opposing attorney, and the community if not previously done.

☐ Prepare any exhibits, diagrams, audiovisual aids.

(continued)

EXHIBIT 11:1 ■ Trial Preparation Checklist (*continued*)

At Least One Week Prior to Trial

- ☐ Verify the court date.
- ☐ Complete the trial notebook.
- ☐ Verify service of all subpoenas.
- ☐ Prepare client and witnesses for testimony.
- ☐ Make final arrangements for the following:
  - ☐ Lodging of the client, witnesses, and staff as needed.
  - ☐ Payment of lost wages for witnesses if committed by the attorney.
  - ☐ Transportation of all files, documents, audiovisual equipment, computer terminal, and other items needed at trial.
  - ☐ Petty cash needed for parking, meals, phone calls, and so on.

One Day Before Trial

- ☐ Meet one last time with the trial team.
- ☐ Meet with the client.

PRELIMINARY TRIAL PREPARATION TASKS

You should confirm the exact trial date and time if available. Some judges, however, do not set specific times. They follow a docket list for a one- or two-month period, and as cases set for trial are either settled or tried, the client's case moves up on the docket. Where such a system is used, the attorney can normally guess the approximate day of the trial, but you need to keep the attorney and all witnesses informed as the court docket progresses. Court dockets are often accessible online. The date and time must be calendared with related reminder dates for the completion of various tasks prior to the trial.

Well before trial verify that all disclosure to date, as set out in the applicable rules or in the court's scheduling order, is complete. About ninety days before trial is a good time for the litigation team to meet to review the status of the case and to assess the need for the preparation of trial exhibits and other courtroom presentations, especially if the presentation will be high tech.

Although trial preparation time frames vary with the complexity of the case, at least six weeks prior to trial check the case status sheet to verify that all necessary investigation and discovery are complete. Exhibit 11:2 is an example of a case status sheet.

The case status sheet, or its computerized equivalent, should be set up early in the case and reviewed monthly, and possibly weekly within the last six weeks before trial. The attorney should be informed on any matters that are outstanding, so the necessary action can be taken.

Review the file, the case evaluation sheets, summaries and digests of information, witness sheets, and so on to see that all is in order and the issues are clearly in mind. Case management and litigation support software, as previously noted, enhance this preparation process. A discussion with the attorney and other litigation team members at this point to verify the issues (possibly narrowed by the pretrial conference), and to review the evidence, exhibits, and documents needed for each issue would be helpful in better completing the tasks to follow.

EXHIBIT 11:2 ■ Case Status Sheet

Trial date: Case name and no.:
Client: (plaintiff, defendant)   Defendant:
Attorney: Court:
Paralegal: Date filed:
Date client interviewed: Judge:

PLEADINGS AND MOTIONS ON PLEADINGS

Description	Date filed and served	Response date	Check if met	Hearing date
Complaint				
Motion to dismiss				
Answer and counterclaim				
Motions				
Reply				
Amended pleadings (list)/dates filed/response date				

Default: Date: Judgment for default: Date

Jury trial demanded   ☐ yes   ☐ no

INVESTIGATION

Signify investigations to be conducted and witnesses to interview

                                                              ☐ Done/date:
                                                              ☐ Done/date:
                                                              ☐ Done/date:

DISCOVERY

Interrogatories

	Date served	Due date	Response date served	Motion to object or compel
Plaintiff's				
Defendant's				

Depositions (by plaintiff)

Deponent/date	Notice/fee	Subpoena/fee	Location	Court reporter	Done
					☐
					☐
					☐

Depositions (by defendant)

					☐
					☐
					☐

Request for Production of Documents and Things (Plaintiff's)

Describe	Served	Due	Answer/served	Objections/motions	Conducted	Copies delivered
					☐	☐
(Defendant's)						
					☐	☐

(continued)

EXHIBIT 11:2 ■ Case Status Sheet (continued)

Request for Mandatory Physical Examination   ☐ yes   ☐ no
Person examined: Date: Physician:
Request for Admissions (Plaintiff's)
Served   Due   Answer/served   Objections/motion to compel

☐
☐
☐

(Defendant's)

☐
☐
☐

MOTIONS

Describe   Notice   Served   Response   Argued   Result

CASE EVALUATED

Plaintiff's damages: Total:
Other notes:

PRETRIAL CONFERENCE

Date: Judge:
Preparation (describe):   Done
☐
☐

Notes on result:

SETTLEMENT

Settlement précis or brochure   ☐
Date: Terms:
Releases/settlement agreement   ☐
Stipulation, consent decree, order for dismissal   ☐
Settlement distribution statement   ☐

FINAL PRETRIAL

Witness   Address   Subpoenaed   Fees
Jury Investigation   ☐
Preparation of Exhibits and Diagrams

☐
☐

EXHIBIT 11:2 ■ Case Status Sheet *(continued)*

Preparation of Trial Notebook (Proof chart, voir dire questions, witness sheets, legal research, motions, jury instructions, etc.) ☐

Preparation of Witnesses, Including Experts ☐

Final Arrangements (Lodging, meals, parking, petty cash, transportation of trial materials) ☐

Trial Date: Verdict/Date: Judgment/Date:

Motions:	Served	Reply due	Reply	
				☐
				☐

APPEAL

Notice filed:			☐
Order transcript and preparation of record			☐
File brief:	Plaintiff/date	Defendant/date	
Oral argument:	Date:		
Court Decision			
Motion for reconsideration:			☐
Bill of costs			☐

The attorney should pinpoint the need for any further research on legal questions as well, in preparation for motions either before or during trial and to deal with objections or arguments that might arise at trial. These items should be researched and any memoranda or rough drafts should be completed. The writing of some of these may be assigned to you depending on the personal preference of the attorney. Memorandum preparation is good work for paralegals well versed in research skills. Offering to do this kind of work is one way to enhance your value to the law firm.

SUBPOENA WITNESSES

The client and friendly witnesses should be informed as soon as possible about the trial date and when they will be expected to testify. Client and witness preparation sessions should be calendared at this time so the client or witness can be notified of the trial and preparation session dates. The availability for trial of each witness should be determined.

The attorney should be consulted to finalize the list of witnesses to be called on behalf of the client. Some attorneys prefer to subpoena only the witnesses who are not considered friendly; however, the best practice is to subpoena all the witnesses needed for your case. Do so unless instructed otherwise. Some witnesses prefer to be subpoenaed so that it can be made clear that they have been ordered to testify, especially if the witness has a business or friendly relationship with both parties of the lawsuit and wants to remain, or at least appear, neutral. A subpoena also gives the witness something to show an employer for the absence from work. It is a good idea to explain to each witness the necessity of serving them with a subpoena.

Subpoenas for trial are obtained and served in the same way they are obtained and served for depositions. The following are important points to remember:

1. Service of subpoenas is covered in Rule 45 and parallel state and local rules.
2. Local rules and procedures for the issuing and service of trial subpoenas should be reviewed.
3. Clerk of court issues the subpoena signed and sealed but otherwise blank in most state courts. Attorneys can issue subpoenas in federal court [Rule 45(a)(3)].
4. In most jurisdictions any person over eighteen years of age can serve subpoenas. Professional process servers may be used.
5. It is best to read the subpoena to the person being served.
6. The subpoena is not valid until it is personally served on the witness, the required witness and mileage fees are tendered, and the return of service is completed and filed with the court (28 U.S.C. § 1821). Normally only the first day's fee plus round trip mileage is tendered.
7. Check with the clerk for amount of fee and mileage.
8. If a subpoena is issued on behalf of the United States or its officer or agency, fee and mileage need not be tendered.
9. Subpoenas reach to the boundaries of the state for both state and federal court trials. Hardship exceptions may be made in some circumstances. Subpoenas are valid outside the federal district to within 100 miles of the place of trial or as specifically authorized by the pertinent federal statute [Rule 45(b)(2)].
10. A witness in a foreign country is subpoenaed pursuant to 28 U.S.C. § 1783.
11. A subpoena duces tecum must describe documents with reasonable certainty—that is, so they can be identified without an extensive search. Wording such as "every" or "all" is suspect.
12. If a subpoena is directed to a corporation, it is best to name the corporate official in charge of the specific documents.
13. Subpoenas are generally valid for the date or dates entered on them and for the remainder of the trial unless the person subpoenaed is dismissed by the court or the party that subpoenaed the person.
14. Subpoenas remain in effect for continuances and postponements.
15. Subpoenas need to be reissued if there is a change of venue.
16. A subpoena can be challenged as insufficient, oppressive, or unreasonable through a motion to quash, vacate, or modify.

At least one week prior to trial, verify that all subpoenas have been served. Occasionally a subpoena will have to be obtained at the last minute of the last working day before trial. In such a situation, the relationship that you have nurtured with court personnel will pay off. Keep a record to show that all subpoenas have been obtained, served with amounts of fees paid, and returns have been filed with the clerk, if required.

"A fox should not be of the jury at a goose's trial."

—Proverb, Thomas Fuller, *Gnomologia,* 1732

JURY INVESTIGATION

Introduction

Regardless of the size of the case, if a jury has been requested, some investigation of the jury will be needed. The extent of that investigation depends on the nature and size of the case. The degree that you will be involved varies, but this area is another in which you can assume responsibility.

The purpose of the jury investigation is to gather the best possible information on each prospective juror and that juror's likely response to the issues in the case. The information will guide the attorney during voir dire, when the jurors are selected at trial. The overall purpose is to rid the jury of those persons biased against or not likely to be sympathetic with your client, and to shield or protect the selection of those individuals who are likely to favor your client.

Exhibit 11:3 is a juror data sheet. It can serve as a summary sheet for the attorney before and at trial, as well as your checklist in determining what information should be gathered. Check with the attorney to see if special concerns or information is needed in addition to that requested on the following form.

EXHIBIT 11:3 ▪ Juror Data Sheet

Case: File no: Court: Date:

Attorney: Paralegal:

Juror no. _____ Name: Aliases:

Overall Evaluation: Good _____ Bad _____ ? _____

Place and date of birth: Race: Ethnic group:

Address:

Previous addresses (list most recent first):

Grew up at:

Home phone: Work phone:

Employment (list most recent first):

Occupation: Employer: Address: Phone: Dates:

Present annual income:

Highest level of education completed: Date:

Health:

Marital status: single: married: divorced: widowed: remarried:

Immediate family

   Parents: Age: Occupation/education:

   Where lived most of life: Current address

   Spouse: Age: Occupation/education:

   Children: Age: Occupation/education:

   Grandchildren: Age: Occupation/education:

(continued)

EXHIBIT 11:3 ■ Juror Data Sheet (*continued*)

Juror's political affiliation: Rep ( )   Dem ( )   Ind ( )

                                   Liberal ( )   Middle of road ( )   Conservative ( )

Juror's professional and service associations:

  Veteran:

  Religious affiliation: Active: Inactive:

Hobbies and activities:

Friends and relatives:

Financial concerns in case:

Relationship to parties:

Prior jury service: Where: When:

  Type of case: Verdict: Foreperson:

Previous or current litigation: Plaintiff: Defendant:

  Where: When: Type: Outcome:

Close family or friend involved in litigation: Plaintiff: Defendant:

  Where: When: Type: Outcome

Prior experiences related to trial and issues: (for example, ever injured in an accident, ever at fault in accident, etc.)

Assessment of opinion on: Issues:

  Source of information: Survey: Fellow workers: Other:

Assessment of jury leadership potential and strength of personality:

  Source of information:

     Record of juror on current panel:

     Overall evaluation: Good: Bad: ?:

     Explanation:

     Additional comments:

Sources for Juror Information

The amount of information a paralegal is asked to gather and the money that can be spent gathering it is proportional to the size and significance of the case. The following sources are listed in approximate order from the least expensive to most expensive. Choose appropriate methods in consultation with the attorney.

    a. *Jury Panel List.*   A list of the names of all jurors for the upcoming term can be obtained from the clerk of court's office. This list may not be available in some jurisdictions.

    b. *Juror Information Sheets.*   These forms are filled out by each juror providing a minimum of information on background, marital status, education, occupation, previous jury service, and litigation. They may be copied or reviewed in the clerk's office and are a good source of information with minimal copying cost and inconvenience. The American Bar Association recommends that judges permit lawyers to expand the jury information sheet with jury questions, especially in complex cases (ABA Civil Trial Practice Standards, Standard 1, 1998). Such questions go beyond the typical limited background information to solicit views and experiences that could impact a case or trial strategy. Useful in the Forrester case, for example, would be questions about the juror's opinion of proper training for truck drivers, whether the juror had ever had to care for a seriously ill or injured person, whether the juror ever worked for an insurance company or conducted claims evaluations, and on the importance of partial but lesser fault to assigning liability in an unrelated accident scenario.[1] Juror information sheets or questionnaires can be customized for any type of litigation. The key is determining what out of a list of possibilities are the most critical things to learn.

c. *Internet Research.* With a juror's name and background, including affiliations, search that person's name, Web site, and sites of relevant organizations for valuable, inexpensive information.

d. *Voter Registration Lists.* Available in the county clerk's offices, these lists provide information on political party affiliation where such information is required by law.

e. *Co-workers, Friends, Others.* Sometimes your co-workers, attorneys, paralegals, relatives, friends, and others may be able to recognize the names of people on the jury list and provide valuable information. It is not uncommon in a small town for a few people to know practically everyone. Sometimes a friend of a friend can tap into that information. If attorneys or paralegals in another firm have recently had experience with this jury panel, they might also be willing to provide some insights. The client might be able to help, or have friends or relatives that can help.

f. *Clerk of Court Personnel.* If you are on particularly good terms with one or more of the local clerk's staff, that person might prove helpful.

g. *Jury Files Kept by Law Firms.* Some law firms keep extensive records on jurors. Information on particular jurors may often be purchased from these firms.

h. *Professional Jury Services.* Usually in big cities, these services compile extensive background information on prospective jurors and conduct a thorough investigation of specific jurors on request. These services can be valuable, but are expensive.

i. *Jury Surveys.* These extensive phone surveys are more or less scientifically based. If the law firm does not have the internal expertise, a consultant on surveying techniques should be employed to guarantee an accurate random sampling of the prospective community and to assure that questions are worded to elicit accurate and meaningful responses. Such a survey reaches only qualified jurors; their religion, occupation, and other background is recorded. The responses can then be evaluated by types or categories of persons, providing some information on how that type of person would vote as a member of the jury. Depending on how it is done and who does it, a survey like this can be quite expensive to conduct and to analyze, but can be useful for general guidance. If you are asked to conduct such a survey, a good source to consult is *Jurywork: Systematic Techniques*, 2nd ed., prepared by the National Jury Project in cooperation with the National Lawyers' Guild and National Conference of Black Lawyers.

    j. *Employment of Psychologists and Other Experts.*   Some firms may choose to send a synopsis of the case to a psychologist, social scientist, or other jury selection consultants to evaluate and give advice on what type of person should be chosen and what type should be avoided. This process can be helpful but expensive. Nationally recognized resources include The National Jury Project, The Jury Research Institute, and Decision Quest.

    k. *Mock Juries.*   Some firms employ mock juries or focus groups. A scaled-down version of the trial is held or a summary of the key issues is presented to persons who represent the expected composition of the jury. After their decision, the jurors are questioned at length about why they decided as they did and what impressed them the most and the least. This simulation helps the firm make decisions on what jurors to select, what theory of the case works best, and how to improve their presentation.

When investigating jurors, remember that it is unethical to have any direct contact with a juror. Take every precaution to avoid having jurors become aware that they are being investigated. This awareness not only might disturb some jurors, but also can cause reactions potentially damaging to the firm and the client.

All the information on a particular juror should be recorded and summarized for quick reference by the attorney. Be prepared to add your own evaluation of the juror to such a summary sheet, if requested. Summary sheets will be used at trial.

Some scientific research reports the following information about potential jurors.[2] Those surveyed tended to mistrust large corporations and politicians. Seventeen percent said they could not be impartial to a gay or lesbian defendant, three times as many as those who said they could not be impartial to other minorities. Many believed that personal injury litigants often seek to blame others for their own carelessness, and seventy-five percent said they would do what they believed was right rather than follow the judge's instructions on the law. The surveys reveal a higher mistrust of the system, especially the criminal system and police officers among those studied who were poor and African American or Latino.

Ancillary Investigation

The judge, opposing counsel, and the community should be researched if not already done in preparation for settlement. See the resources listed in Chapter 10 on verdict and settlement research. It is important to know the judge's practice on jury information sheets, extent of voir dire, preferred jury instructions relevant to the respective type of case, and other trial practices. It is also important to determine if the judge permits jurors to take notes at trial, have mid-trial discussions about the case, ask questions of the witnesses, take evidence and instructions into the deliberation room, and other modern jury practices. In this regard, it is useful to review the ABA's Principles for Juries and Jury Trials, American Jury Project (2005).

PREPARING DEMONSTRATIVE EVIDENCE

Introduction

Imagine for a moment a hushed courtroom at a dramatic moment in a trial where a jury will decide whether the tobacco industry is liable to a class of plaintiffs for making cigarettes more addictive. Then the plaintiffs' paralegal presses a button and in mid-air, before the jurors, appears a stunning 3D holographic image of a human brain. In real time, the hologram shows how quickly nicotine invades the brain and causes addiction. Jurors return a $600 million verdict for the plaintiffs. This has already occurred in a state courtroom.[3]

Jurors learn more and retain more when they can read something, hear about it, and see it. Generations X (born 1966–1981) and Y (born 1982 and later), raised with e-technology and expecting its use, now comprise up to forty percent of jurors.[4] According to work conducted at the William and Mary School of Law, called the Courtroom 21 Project, the competent use of demonstrative technology contributes to juror understanding and efficient trials.[5]

Further, today's courtrooms are rapidly becoming high-tech. Therefore, the legal team of the twenty-first century, including the paralegal, not only must understand the importance of demonstrative evidence in general, but also must apply it competently to effectively represent a client. Like the competent use of e-discovery, the competent use of e-technology in the courtroom may be required for the ethical practice of law. Of course the maxim applies that the bigger and more important the case, the larger and more justified is the expense.

In addition to use at trial, demonstrative devices can play an important role in interviewing, depositions, settlement negotiations, mock trials, and focus groups.

Evidentiary Concerns

Some evidentiary foundation is essential to the use and admission of demonstrative evidence (see Chapter 3). Diagrams for purely illustrative purposes need only be a fair representation of what is depicted. On the other hand, if a diagram or scale model is presented as evidence to be taken to the jury room, it must be accurate: drawn to scale and based on accurate measurement and timely observation. Local rules may vary on what is admissible as demonstrative evidence and what is not, and should be thoroughly researched according to the type of item to be prepared (photo, video, diagram, document, computer animation, etc.).

Technology

As the use of the holographic image in the tobacco case indicates, technology is dramatically changing trial presentations. Computer software enables the creation of colorful charts, graphs, and diagrams, and the recording of photos, audio material, and videos. Software like PowerPoint and similar programs colorfully highlight key presentation points in the form of sequential "slides." Anything computer-generated or recorded can be vividly projected, using a laptop computer, a television, or a liquid-crystal large-screen projector. High-powered software such as InData Director Suite™, Sanction II™, and other programs facilitate the integration of audio, video, animation, and PowerPoint-type slides into an efficient and precise trial presentation. Documents and transcripts can be displayed on a split screen with carefully edited clips of a witness's deposition or other video. With a properly wired court, some witnesses who might otherwise be unavailable to testify can do so by two-way conference technology. Similar technology can be used to access foreign language interpreters, especially for rare or less common languages.

Physical evidence including documents can be viewed on a large screen by the use of color video document cameras, which can zoom in on an important detail such as a particular paragraph in a document or the serial number on a key piece of evidence. Microscopic video cameras can expose minute detail, revealing otherwise hidden defects. The paralegal who understands presentation technology and, better yet, learns how to operate it can be instrumental to the success of the litigation team.

The minimum courtroom presentation equipment list includes an LCD large-screen projector with a minimum of 2000 lumens (brightness), a regular movie screen or multifunction white board or TV monitors, document camera (Elmo, Dean, others), VCR, DVD player, laptop with corresponding trial presentation software, an all-in-one printer-scanner-photocopier, cables, cords, power strips, and a bar code reader (wand). With a list of trial exhibits and the corresponding paste-on bar code tags, the lawyer or paralegal simply scans the bar code of the needed item on the list, and the exhibit is instantly projected. Some courtrooms are equipped with all or most of these items, some are not. In the latter situation, it is necessary to provide your own equipment, rent equipment, or hire a presentation technology vendor.

A variety of audiovisual aids can be used at trial to help the jury understand your client's viewpoint in the case.

- *Diagrams.*   Diagrams are probably the most often used audiovisual aid. They can depict almost anything and, if kept simple, can be inexpensively created. The diagram of the site of an accident, for example, is frequently used in automobile injury cases. Witnesses can use the diagram to identify streets and the location of witnesses, traffic signals, obstructions, and vehicles before, at the time of, and after the accident.

   The preparation of diagrams does not require any special artistic ability. To make an effective diagram, keep it simple; strive for reasonable accuracy; make it concise and readable by using short titles and descriptions, horizontal wording, letters easily seen from the required distance, and clear lines. Keep in mind how the jury will see it.

   If you choose not to use computer software to make the diagram, the art department of a bookstore or school supply store can provide the necessary materials. If you tell the clerks what you are trying to do, they may have suggestions for techniques and products that can simplify your job. Some universities have an instructional media department with personnel who specialize in preparing audiovisual aids. They can provide sound, free advice on a variety of techniques and equipment. Professional services are available that provide diagram preparation or preprinted diagrams. Several companies specialize, for example, in medical diagrams of every part of the human body.

- *Charts and Graphs.*   Charts and graphs also lend themselves to simple construction by the paralegal. Follow the guidelines mentioned for diagrams to make graphs and charts that convey complex and hard-to-picture data in an easily understood manner. For example, a vertical bar graph may better dramatize the decreasing ability of an intoxicated person to react to emergencies than a simple reference to a percentage.

- *Timelines.*   A timeline is a form of diagram or chart that graphically portrays a single sequence of events or shows the relationship between two or more independent lines of conduct or occurrences. Although timelines have always been important to help jurors visualize a chain of events, timeline software has greatly simplified their creation and enhanced presentation quality.

- *Animation.*   Digital animation can provide a moving recreation of events such as those leading up to, during, and immediately after a traffic accident or a work injury. Animation can show various viewpoints and is particularly effective when demonstrating obscured and unsafe viewpoints. Professional vendors are available but are expensive and need a lot of lead time.

"If you want to win a case, paint the Judge a *picture* and keep it simple."

—JOHN W. DAVIS, ANNUAL MEETING OF SCRIBES (THE AMERICAN SOCIETY OF WRITERS ON LEGAL SUBJECTS), AUGUST 21, 1955.

- *Models.* Models are often used to display parts of the body, buildings, equipment, and a variety of other items. Construction of scaled, admissible quality models usually requires professional skill. Companies that construct, sell, and rent models advertise in trade journals. Costs are usually quite high for such services. Computerized models create the illusion of three dimensions and can be manipulated to show various perspectives. Such models are expensive but effective. Holographic imaging is the cutting-edge technology for model presentations.
- *Photographs.* Photographs of injuries, damages, individuals, equipment, settings, and other items can be extremely helpful. The paralegal with minimal training can be the photographer, or professionals can be employed. Blown-up photographs can be particularly dramatic if allowed by the court. Digitized photos can be projected onto a large screen, and key features zoomed for emphasis.
- *Slides.* Simply another form of photograph, slides have largely been replaced by the use of digital photography and scanners. Film is still used where the highest professional quality is needed. It is expensive.
- *Video.* Video is relatively inexpensive and does not always require a professional technician. Some firms use professional video services if the case justifies it. Large screen projectors greatly enhance video presentations, making a "day-in-the-life" video or a video clip a powerful piece of evidence. When the defense in a medical malpractice trial claimed that the victim was in a persistent vegetative state and could not feel pain, and therefore did not deserve compensation for pain and suffering, a "day-in-the-life" video showed otherwise, resulting in a record verdict for the victim and also for her husband for loss of consortium.[6]

Be an opportunist and make yourself even more valuable to the law office by seeking training in the effective operation of trial presentation technology. The American Bar Association's THE LAWYERS' GUIDE TO CREATING PERSUASIVE COMPUTER PRESENTATIONS, 2nd edition, is a useful resource. As trial approaches, visit the trial courtroom well in advance to determine the most advantageous placement of displays, the adequacy of lighting and electrical hookups, and the availability of teleconferencing and court-supplied electronic and audio-visual equipment. Be ready for technical problems. Have an extra projector lamp, a backup laptop containing a duplicate of the presentation, a set of video tapes should you not be able to run the digital video clips, and hard copy backups of each exhibit. Learn the judge's rules and preferences on the use of technology and what electronic exhibits, if any, will be allowed in jury deliberations. Review the relevant ABA standards.

ABA Standards

The American Bar Association's Civil Trial Practice Standards address the use of technology for trials. Standard 15 urges judges to have adversaries view all demonstrative evidence before trial to facilitate objections and save time at trial. Judges are encouraged to rule on admissibility of demonstrative evidence well ahead of trial to avoid significant expenditures on ultimately unusable presentations. Standard 21 suggests that all matters submitted to the court be in computer-readable format for ease of use, and Standard 24 states that parties should agree to use the same equipment to save courtroom space. Also, to help focus juror attention, Standard 24 urges judges to permit the presentation of properly edited video material.

TRIAL NOTEBOOK

Introduction

A trial notebook (often notebooks) consists of everything an attorney needs at the trial organized for easy and quick retrieval. The information it contains ranges from names of everyone involved in the case to a court opinion in support of admission of evidence. In some respects it is an outline of each step that must be taken to try the case, complete with indexes and cross-indexes. Trial notebooks are critical to successful courtroom litigation. If well prepared, they can make the difference between winning and losing and, regardless of the outcome, assist the attorney and the paralegal in being organized, effective, and confident.

Mr. White has asked that a trial notebook be assembled for the *Forrester* case. It is your job to put it together. The following material will help guide you in that process.

Begin organizing the sections of a trial notebook from the beginning of the case. This provides several advantages: (1) organization of case materials with indexes for quick retrieval of original documents, (2) paralegal control over the case materials with a checkout system for materials that have to be removed from the notebook, (3) easy reduction and editing of materials as issues narrow, and (4) quick preparation for settlement, pretrial conferences, meetings with the client or witnesses, and other procedures.

If prepared in hard copy, the trial book should consist of one or more loose-leaf three-ring binders, preferably of different colors, for standard 8 1/2-by-11-inch paper. If some 14-inch pages must be used, they can be reduced in the copying process to the standard size. Plenty of tabbed dividers will be needed to place between major sections and their subsections. Increasingly, paralegals prepare trial notebooks electronically. This is done using standard word processing software or software designed specifically for the purpose. Electronic trial notebooks are easily customized, edited, and updated. They provide organizational structure, effortless duplication, quick retrieval, and are conveniently loaded into the trial laptop.

The actual contents and order of a trial notebook vary according to the type of case and the preference of the attorney. A lot of time can be saved by asking the attorney for a detailed outline of what is wanted in the notebook, or by preparing an outline of the notebook and asking the attorney to express preferences on the outline.

Read Exhibit 11:4 for a detailed outline of the basic structure of a trial notebook. The sections are arranged chronologically as they would come up at trial. Such an arrangement allows the attorney and the paralegal assisting at trial to work methodically through each section as needed. Each attorney has an organizational preference, however, so consult your supervisor. You can provide assistance by preparing the overall structure of the trial notebook and many of its components.

Legal Research

You can do much of the trial brief section of the trial notebook. Initial background research on evidence, elements of a cause of action, the appropriateness of a jury instruction, and the composition of concise memoranda and lists of legal authorities for the attorney's perusal are tasks a paralegal can handle competently. These may have to be edited, expanded, or changed in other ways, but your winnowing will form a sound base for further work.

EXHIBIT 11:4 ■ Outline of Trial Notebook

Page or tab number	Divisions

Section One: Reference

    1. Table of contents (complete last)

    2. Persons and parties at trial

        a. Court, courtroom, judge, clerks, bailiff: name, phone, office e-mail

        b. Own staff at trial: attorneys, paralegals, others: names, phone numbers, e-mail, motel, etc.

            (1) Firm's office numbers for assistance

            (2) Client

            (3) Witnesses   Names, addresses, phone numbers, affiliations

            (4) Expert witnesses

            (5) Others

        c. Opponent's staff at trial and witnesses, experts, phone, affiliation, etc.

    3. Case summary: factual and legal issues

    4. Proof chart: elements and proof in case

EXAMPLE OF PROOF CHART

Plaintiff's elements and facts to prove	Source of proof
Negligence:	
Excessive speed	Wit: Schnabel "between 45–50 mph" Statement
	Client: "over 45" deposition p. 26 (Tab____)
	Photo: skidmarks, test. of Officer Timms
Inattentiveness	Hart's test.: "looking at speedometer" deposition p. 35 (Tab____)

Same for defendant's proof

Section Two: Pleadings and Pretrial

    1. Major pleadings as amended: complaint, answer, defenses (all tabbed and color coded to separate plaintiff's from defendant's with key sections highlighted)

    2. Alternative method: (Simply summarize pleadings stating allegations, admissions, and denials. Highlight remaining issues.)

    3. Any pretrial order could go here

Section Three: Last-Minute Motions

    1. Any remaining pretrial motions with supporting authorities

    2. Authority to oppose any expected last-minute motions by the opposition

Section Four: Voir Dire (Jury Selection)

    1. Jury challenge chart: (usually eighteen to twenty boxes on standard sheet of paper to enter no. and name of each juror, plus attorney's and paralegal's notes on suitability)

(continued)

EXHIBIT 11:4 ■ Outline of Trial Notebook *(continued)*

    2. Profiles of jurors most and least wanted (predetermined by jury investigation)

    3. Outline of voir dire questions: (if the attorney is permitted to conduct voir dire—if not, proposed questions for the judge to ask jurors with copies for the judge and opponent. Questions are usually drafted by the attorney or an experienced paralegal with attorney review. There are numerous sources on conducting voir dire.)

    4. List grounds and authority for challenges for cause (a challenge for cause is a request to remove a juror for lawful reasons such as inability to be impartial)

    5. List of authorities on any anticipated jury issues (including legality of any voir dire questions)

    6. Jury panel chart (usually twelve boxes to place names and comments about jurors finally selected to hear the case)

    7. Blank loose-leaf sheets to write notes on voir dire or to record any objections

Section Five: Opening Statement

    1. Complete text

    2. Alternative: outline (both drafted by attorney. Use large orator's type.)

Section Six: Outline of Order of Proof and of Opponent's Proof

Section Seven: Witness Examination

    1. Own witnesses: direct examination (tabbed subsections for each witness in the order they will be called by the attorney). Each witness subsection should include:

        a. A synopsis of witness information, whether subpoenaed and interviewed

        b. An outline or chronological list of the questions that will be asked on direct examination on each critical issue. Use wide margins so notes can be added

        c. Notations of what exhibits will be introduced by the witness with inserted copies of the exhibits

        d. Notations inserted on any references to diagrams or other audiovisual aids

        e. Conflicting testimony of witness (references to prior statements, depositions, interrogatories, admissions)

        f. Questions to rehabilitate witness, especially if harmful cross-examination by opponent is expected

        g. Summaries of any statement, letters, memos, or depositions with key quotations highlighted. Cross-indexed to section containing copy of full statement, deposition transcript, memos, etc.

        h. Copies of subpoena with proof of service

    2. Opponent's witnesses: cross-examination (Some attorneys prefer an entirely separate, different colored notebook for dramatic effect.)

        a. Similar structure to item 1 above with emphasis on conflicting and inconsistent statements, testimony, or other impeachment material

        b. Inserted copies of necessary exhibits, criminal records, etc.

EXHIBIT 11:4 ■ Outline of Trial Notebook *(continued)*

Section Eight: Exhibits (sometimes kept as separate book)

      1. Exhibit log

EXAMPLE OF EXHIBIT LOG

Ex. no. (as premarked or as assigned at trial)	Descript. or title of exhibit	Whether introduced, accepted or rejected. Notes.
<u>Own ex.</u> (in order of introduction)	Title	Introduced ( ) Accepted ( ) Rejected ( ) Notes:
P-1 (Plaintiff)		
<u>Opponent's ex.</u>	Title	Introduced ( ) Accepted ( ) Rejected ( ) Notes:

      2. Each exhibit in expected order of introduction (may be separated by identifying tabs, including exhibit no. if premarked by clerk

      3. Each exhibit section should include:

         a. Exhibit summary sheet paper-clipped to exhibit (includes brief description of exhibit and significance, case file location or code no., witness needed for introduction, foundation, brief statement of authorities on admissibility

         b. Exhibit

            (1) Marked copy for judge, opponent, one for each juror if desired, one for witness section, one for exhibit section

            (2) If oversized, specially indexed to separate container or if cannot be hole punched, place in three-hole plastic envelopes

         c. Place exhibits in box if there are too many for notebook.

      4. List of all audiovisual props and accessories indexed to specially numbered containers if necessary.

Section Nine: Trial Motions and Authorities

(Any motions such as for dismissal or for directed verdict. Reminders to make motions should be placed at chronologically appropriate places and cross-indexed to this section. Consult with the attorney for what and where.)

Section Ten: Jury Instructions (Charge to Jury)

      1. Attorney's copy of all instructions proposed to be read to the jury. (Should contain complete language of instruction, one instruction per page, plus any legal authorities supporting its use. Each should contain a checkoff for given, modified, or refused. Have enough copies for all parties and the judge.)

      2. Opponent's proposed instructions with checkoff

      3. Final copy of instructions read by the judge

      4. If no jury, copy of request for findings of fact and conclusions of law for the judge

Section Eleven: Proposed Verdict Form (General, Special, General with Interrogatories)

(Optional section depending on detail of verdict desired by attorney. Necessary copies for judge and opponent. Section for supporting authorities.)

(continued)

EXHIBIT 11:4 ▪ Outline of Trial Notebook *(continued)*

Section Twelve: Closing Statement

    1. Text or outline of closing statement (orator's size print)

    2. Props or list of props

    3. Notepad for recording items to add as trial progresses

Section Thirteen: Law Section

    1. Trial memo or brief covering the law on all significant questions of law concerning the issues, evidence, motions, and other anticipated objections or conflicts

    2. Geared to the judge's bench book (legal authority book)

    3. Should include points and responses to law likely to be argued by opponent

    4. May include concisely typed copy of the Rules of Evidence and pertinent Rules of Procedure with authorities

    5. Cross-indexed to relevant sections in notebook

Section Fourteen: To Do, Notes, and Reminders

    1. List of items to do before trial in completing notebook, serving subpoenas, gathering exhibits, etc.

    2. Reminders of motions to make, whether to poll jury, and others

    3. Notepad for items that come up at trial that should be commented on, argued, noted for appeal, etc.

Motions

The attorney will have a good idea of what standard motions are likely to be needed just before and during trial. Many of these motions, such as a motion to dismiss or a motion for a directed verdict (called a motion for judgment as a matter of law in the federal system), require grounds that can be stated generally. The attorney will be able to fill in needed details as more specific reasons develop at trial. Authorities that generally state the legal standards necessary to grant or deny the motion can be cited. Therefore, you can prepare a skeletal or general version of the motion, along with an accompanying order. See Chapter 6 on motion drafting. Exhibit 11:5 and Exhibit 11:6 contain examples of several common trial motions to include in the trial notebook.

in limine
A motion filed for protection against prejudicial questions and statements at trial.

You might be assigned the tasks to draft a motion **in limine.** This motion asks the court for protection against prejudicial questions and statements. It is usually made when the attorney realizes that the opponent is likely to ask questions of a witness or refer to matters that will prejudice the jurors, making a fair trial difficult to achieve. An example of a motion in limine appears in Exhibit 11:7.

Voir Dire Questions

You can research possible voir dire questions. A trial attorney generally has these in mind, but each case has its own peculiarities. Furthermore, new ideas and approaches are always being developed along with a current body of literature that you can review and digest into a list of questions with supporting legal authority for the attorney's consideration.

EXHIBIT 11:5 ■ Motion for Mistrial

(*Caption*)

MOTION FOR MISTRIAL

_____ (Plaintiff/Defendant) respectfully moves this court for an order declaring a mistrial in this action and discharging the jury from further consideration of this case.

As grounds for said motion, _____ (Plaintiff/Defendant) states that [*state grounds*]. Consequently, it is impossible for _____ to receive a fair trial by the jury.

This motion is made on the basis of all records, files, and proceedings in this case.

Date _____

Attorney for _____

Address _____

_____

EXHIBIT 11:6 ■ Motion for Directed Verdict

At Close of All Evidence
(*Caption*)

MOTION FOR DIRECTED VERDICT

_____ (Plaintiff/Defendant) respectfully moves this court, at the close of all the evidence in this case, to instruct the jury to return a verdict in favor of _____.

As grounds for said motion, it is asserted that [*state grounds*].

Date _____

Attorney for _____

Address _____

_____

EXHIBIT 11:7 ■ Motion in Limine

For Order Prohibiting Reference During Trial to Insurance Payments Received by Plaintiff
(*Caption*)

MOTION IN LIMINE

The Plaintiff respectfully moves this Court to order counsel for the Defendant to avoid any reference during the course of trial to any compensation received or likely to be received by the Plaintiff from the Plaintiff's insurance carrier for his/her hospital and medical expenses.

Grounds for this motion are that reference to such insurance payments would be improper and prejudicial, and that such prejudice could not be corrected by any court ruling or admonition of the jury.

Date _____

Attorney for plaintiff _____

Address _____

_____

Jury Instructions

Not unlike voir dire questions, jury instructions can be researched, revealing new ideas and cases where jury instructions favorable to the client's position have been given and upheld as proper. Jury instructions or charges are read to jurors by the judge and cover a review of the evidence, burden of proof, the pertinent law, and application of the law to the facts in this case. If your client's case will be tried by a judge who permits jurors to take printed jury instructions into the jury room for deliberations, this phase of preparation becomes even more important.

Most states have a standard jury instruction source book used by judges in the state. Many of the federal courts use standardized instructions as well. Extensive, annotated collections of jury instructions are now available on CD-ROM. The instructions are organized by topic, so it is not difficult to find those covering each area of the case. Research into other case files, periodical literature, recent books on the topic, and recent case law may reveal instructions better suited to the client than the standard instructions. From these, you can draft a set of instructions to be reviewed by the attorney and altered or expanded where necessary. These special instructions, when supported by good legal authority, can give the attorney that needed edge. Exhibit 11:8 is an example of how jury instructions can be worded to approach the same facts, but from slightly different viewpoints. Which instruction do you believe is preferable for Ms. Forrester?

Witness Questions

You may be asked by your attorney to draft proposed questions for witnesses at trial, or to draft an outline of topics to be covered in direct or cross-examination. Apply the pertinent techniques discussed in Chapter 8 on preparing for a deposition. If this task is not assigned, you can propose to do it.

Juror Notebooks

Some judges have permitted parties to give notebooks to jurors for use at trial, especially in complex cases (ABA Civil Trial Practice Standard 2). This notebook consists of exhibits, photos, expert witness resumes, glossaries, and other useful information. If asked to prepare a juror notebook, consult your attorney about content and how polished it should look.

Noting Special Details

While working on a case, you will undoubtedly become very familiar with its facts and evidence. Use that familiarity to identify those special details and pieces of reality that will help sway a jury. Note these for the lawyer. If you are able to attend the trial, hearing reference to something you contributed will be very satisfying.

PREPARING THE CLIENT AND WITNESS FOR TESTIFYING AT TRIAL

Task

Your role in assisting the attorney to prepare a witness for testifying can go beyond that of preparing a witness for a deposition. Trial means some new challenges for the witness, and you can be an instrumental part of the legal team preparing the witness for trial.

Most obvious is the task of communicating more frequently with the client or witness as the trial date approaches. Inform the client of the trial date, appointments

EXHIBIT 11:8 ▪ Jury Instructions

JURY INSTRUCTION
Instruction no. _____

Crossing between intersections, not in marked crosswalk, last clear chance
1. Although the Plaintiff had the duty to yield the right of way to vehicles on the highway, the Defendant had the duty to exercise ordinary care for pedestrians and others, including the duty of keeping a proper lookout. If you are satisfied from the evidence that immediately prior to the accident it was no longer possible for the Plaintiff, by exercise of ordinary care for his/her safety, to avoid the Defendant's vehicle, while the Defendant still had time, by the exercise of ordinary care, to discover the Plaintiff's danger and avoid the accident, you will find for the Plaintiff; otherwise you will find for the Defendant.
2. Definition of ordinary care from other standard instructions.)
3. (Damages from other standard instructions.)

Authorities (List relevant statutes and cases.)

ALTERNATIVE JURY INSTRUCTION
1. It was the Defendant's duty while operating his/her vehicle to exercise ordinary care for others, including:
   a. keeping a lookout for others close enough to pose a danger
   b. keeping vehicle under reasonable control
   c. driving at a reasonable and prudent speed as dictated by speed limits and conditions of the road

If you are satisfied from the evidence that the Defendant failed to comply with one or more of these duties, and that such failure was a substantial factor in causing the accident, you will find for the Plaintiff; otherwise you will find for the Defendant.

2. If you are satisfied from the evidence that the Defendant complied with all of these duties and that the Plaintiff moved into the path of the Defendant's vehicle so suddenly that the Defendant could not avoid the accident, you will find for the Defendant.
3. (Add definition of ordinary care from other standard instructions.)
4. (Add standard instruction on damages.)

Authorities

at the office, and those things that the witness will need at trial. The client or witness may need to be reminded to review their deposition several weeks before the trial and again just before a final preparation session with the attorney.

You can take witnesses to the courtroom to familiarize them with the surroundings and procedures: where they should report the day of the trial, what they should and should not wear, what to do when called to the stand, where the witness box is, what it is like to sit in the witness box, how important it is to address the jury and speak up, how to refer to diagrams and other props and still communicate with the jury, how to look at the attorney asking the question and turn to the jury to answer it, what it feels like to be in the jury box, and how important it is for the jury to see and hear. The need for any special accommodations for the witness should be reviewed. A brief dry-run direct examination can be conducted here. Learn how to set the stage. Such efforts will give the witness confidence and reduce a lot of unnecessary anxiety. Witnesses will greatly appreciate it.

Most attorneys try to prepare the client and most important witnesses, even in the simplest of cases. The preparation can range from a rather brief, informal discussion about the case and things to keep in mind, to a complete courtroom-like direct and cross-examination with a critique of the witness's performance. In such circumstances, most attorneys prefer to do the fine tuning with the witness, but you can still play an important role by observing, noting behavior or idiosyncracies, listening for inconsistencies, and relating any impressions to the attorney. The facilities also have to be readied and witnesses made comfortable just as in preparing for the first client interview.

Critiquing witnesses must be done tactfully because of the anxious state most witnesses are in. You can help here by saying a few words of encouragement and letting them know that they will do fine.

Videotaping the witness during mock testimony can be helpful. You can do the taping and review it with the witness. Witnesses frequently note and comment on their obvious mistakes and distracting mannerisms that need to be worked on. On the other hand, most people will be pleasantly surprised that they were more effective and confident than they thought. Videotape presentations on how to be an effective witness can also be prepared for viewing by each witness. This could prove to be a great time saver when used repeatedly.

With the proper guidelines and authorizations from the attorney, you can help locate and enlist the expert witness. All the necessary data on the expert's qualifications should be gathered and placed in a summary format for the attorney. The expert might suggest publications, evidence, props, testing devices, and audiovisual material that need to be gathered and organized for trial or mock testimony. Summaries of the facts, theories in the case, and other relevant information may also have to be gathered and prepared for the expert. Caution regarding confidentiality is in order here, however, because no attorney-client privilege exists between the attorney and the expert. The expert can benefit from a trip to the courtroom as well. Experts need to be told not to get defensive during cross-examination, that they are there to give an opinion based on their best work and what they consider the best principles and theories of their area of expertise, despite contrary opinions of other experts and authors. Experts must also be guided tactfully to avoid appearing condescending or pompous, and cautioned against using jargon. Mock sessions with an expert can be helpful, and their time on the "stage" should be well orchestrated down to the finest detail.

The attorney may give you permission to inform some witnesses that, for their convenience, they will be called to court only at the time they will be needed, even if that is not the time listed on the subpoena. Witnesses should be fully informed of their place in the trial and how other witnesses are likely to testify. The client should be well informed as to the theory of the case.

You may be asked to produce a list of suggestions for testifying. In addition, knowing the primary tips for a trial witness will help in setting-the-stage visits to the courtroom and in critiquing witnesses. Exhibit 11:9 is a list of common suggestions provided to a witness. Such a list should not be given a witness without the direction of the attorney and should be reviewed thoroughly by the attorney for any additions or deletions.

An Ethics Reminder

Remember that any attempt to have a witness conceal evidence, give misleading testimony, or lie is a serious ethical violation. It is best, therefore, to avoid even the appearance of impropriety. If any questions do arise, consult the attorney immediately. Also, keep in mind that just because an attorney tells you to do something,

EXHIBIT 11:9 ■ Guidelines for a Witness's Trial Testimony

☐ Dress neatly in clothing that helps you feel secure.

☐ Arrive at court one half hour before the designated time.

☐ Do not discuss your testimony or the case with or in the presence of others.

☐ Look at the attorney asking the question, then look at the jury when answering.

☐ Speak up.

☐ Try to be as relaxed as possible. Remind yourself that you are not there to match wits or to outsmart someone, but you are there simply to tell the truth as best you can. Let the chips fall where they may.

☐ Do not try to memorize your testimony. If you have reviewed the facts in your own mind, and anticipated likely questions, your answers will be informed but spontaneous.

☐ Listen to the opening statements of the attorneys to better understand the opposing theories and where your testimony will fit. Be prepared, however, if you are not a party, that you may be sequestered (set off in a separate room) so your testimony will not be influenced by the testimony of others.

☐ Listen to each question very carefully. Do not try to answer if you do not understand the question or a term in the question. Ask for clarification.

☐ Do not guess at an answer. If you do not know, say so, and do not be led into guessing or agreeing with the cross-examiner when you really do not know.

☐ Do not look at the attorney for help, guidance, or approval. Once on the stand, all responses should be your own.

☐ Pause if a question seems inappropriate; give your attorney a chance to object.

☐ Do not continue to answer a question if your attorney objects.

☐ Do not get trapped by the opposing attorney into a yes or no answer even if the attorney says "Just yes or no." State what needs to be said. You have the right to answer a question fully.

☐ Avoid qualifying your answer with "maybe," "I think," "to tell you the truth," or "honestly."

☐ Your attorney will give you a chance to explain your side fully, but if the opponent gives you an opening, take it.

☐ Do not overexplain. State your point clearly and briefly and let it be.

☐ If you are a party, be prepared to be called by the opposition for cross-examination during their presentation of the case.

☐ If you are asked by the opposing attorney whether you remember saying something, agree only if you do remember it. If you do not, or are not sure, ask to see the statement. If refused, make it clear that you will have to guess.

☐ If asked, "Is that everything that occurred?" give yourself an out by saying, "That is all I recall at this time."

☐ Visit the scene prior to testimony, review photos, videotape, and diagrams; note any current changes or differences from the original scene.

☐ Review the statements or testimony of other likely witnesses.

☐ Have an understanding of the case, the theories of both sides, and the order of presentation.

☐ Bring all records and documents requested.

☐ Do not fabricate or mislead.

☐ If you have spoken with the attorney before testimony and the opponent asks, "Have you spoken with attorney so-and-so prior to testifying?" state "Yes." There is nothing improper about this as long as you have been instructed to tell the truth.

☐ If you have been reimbursed for lost wages or travel to testify or have been paid as an expert witness, acknowledge this when asked. Witnesses are frequently reimbursed and experts are paid for their time and experience. They are not paid to mislead or state something other than their well-founded, expert opinion.

☐ If an expert witness, do not readily accept other authorities as sole authority in the field.

☐ Avoid jargon and technical language.

☐ Do not get defensive if challenged by the opposition; relax and avoid a battle of egos or wits.

☐ If an expert, testimony should be extremely well prepared and planned.

☐ Be ready to show how measurements and calculations were made.

especially if you know it is improper, you are not relieved from exercising independent judgment based on a sound knowledge of professional ethics.

ADDITIONAL PREPARATION

The paralegal is often charged with supervising the following arrangements:

- All hotel reservations for the trial team
- All transportation to the trial site
- Parking and payment for parking, including change when necessary for parking meters
- A prearranged system for meals and payment
- A system for collecting receipts for all expenses
- Arrangements and cash for emergency copying, phone calls, etc.
- Delivery of all trial materials, diagrams, files, equipment, etc., to court

ASSISTANCE AT TRIAL

INTRODUCTION

Some law firms have a paralegal do much of the background preparation for the case and then make the mistake of failing to utilize the knowledge and skills of that paralegal at trial. The firms that utilize paralegals at trial realize the tremendous benefits that can be derived from such assistance.

Before we discuss the role of the paralegal at trial, become familiar with the key stages in trial procedure, as outlined in Exhibit 11:10.

DECORUM AT TRIAL

Discuss courtroom decorum with your supervising attorney so you know what is expected of you. Additionally, here are a few reminders. Dress for your role as the professional representative of both your client and the law firm. Dress conservatively, yet comfortably. Assume that you will be observed by client, judge, jury, court personnel, and others in the court. Reflect confidence in and support for your client, witnesses, and colleagues. Place your cell phone on standby or vibrate, or as directed by the judge. Be aware of whether any personal electronic devices are likely to interfere with other courtroom technology. Use such devices only during court recesses, unless absolutely unavoidable. Avoid any personal interaction with jurors, because such contact could lead to accusations of improperly trying to influence the jury.

JURY SELECTION

voir dire
The questioning of potential jurors by the judge (and attorneys in state court) to reveal disqualifying information in the process of selecting an impartial jury.

challenge for cause
The attorney's request to remove a potential juror on the grounds of bias or other reason.

peremptory challenge
The authority of an attorney to strike the name of a potential juror without having to express any reason for the strike; limited in number.

To begin jury selection, names are drawn from the jury pool to form the potential jury panel. The judge in federal court and the judge and attorneys for each side in state court question the potential jurors during **voir dire** to reveal bias or personal interest in the case. When voir dire reveals information that disqualifies a juror, the attorney makes a **challenge for cause** to strike that person from the panel. The challenge must be based on grounds, and is decided by the court. Each side also may make a certain number of **peremptory challenges** to strike jurors without justification by the attorneys. These challenges reduce the panel to the required number of jurors.

EXHIBIT 11:10 ▪ Stages in Trial Procedure

1. **Jury Selection (Voir Dire):** Initial selection and questioning of prospective jurors by the judge and possibly the attorneys to choose an impartial jury. Attorneys exercise challenges for cause and a predetermined number of peremptory strikes to eliminate unwanted jurors.

2. **Opening Statements:** Introductory remarks by the opposing attorneys on the case and what they will be proving. The defendant's attorney may reserve the opening statement for later.

3. **Plaintiff's Case in Chief:** The attorney presents the plaintiff's case through direct examination (questioning) of the plaintiff's witnesses. Physical evidence is also presented through the appropriate witnesses. Defendant's attorney may cross-examine each of the plaintiff's witnesses.

4. **Defendant's Motion for Dismissal or Directed Verdict:** The defendant may move for dismissal of the action or a directed verdict requesting the judge to dismiss the case on the grounds the plaintiff has failed to prove the allegations sufficiently. If the plaintiff, in the judge's opinion, has met the requisite burden of proof, it is a **prima facie case** (sufficient to prove a claim prior to any rebuttal), and the case will continue. If the evidence is inadequate, the judge will dismiss the case.

5. **Defendant's Case in Chief:** Presentation of evidence through the defendant's witnesses. The plaintiff may cross-examine.

6. **Plaintiff's Rebuttal:** Presentation of any witnesses or evidence by the plaintiff to rebut any new items raised in the defendant's case in chief.

7. **Defendant's Rejoinder:** Presentation of any witnesses or evidence by the defendant to rebut evidence offered in the plaintiff's rebuttal.

8. **Motion for Directed Verdict** (called a motion for judgment as a matter of law in federal court): Motion by either side stating that the other side has failed to prove or sufficiently rebut the evidence such that, as a matter of law, the verdict is clear. If granted, the judge enters the verdict and the case ends.

9. **Conference to Determine Jury Instructions:** Attorneys argue and judge decides what jury instructions should be given the jury. The conference takes place in chambers.

10. **Closing Arguments:** Attorneys review the evidence, summarize the case, and request the jurors to enter a verdict in favor of their client. In most civil cases the defendant closes first and then the plaintiff. Some jurisdictions have plaintiff, defendant, then plaintiff's rebuttal if needed.

11. **Instructions or Charge to Jury:** Judge reads instructions to jury on their duties and the law governing their decision.

12. **Jury Decides Case:** The jury adjourns to the jury room, deliberates, and reports its verdict to the judge.

13. **Motion for Judgment Notwithstanding the Verdict (JNOV)** (a renewal of the motion for judgment as a matter of law): Either party may move the judge to enter a judgment contrary to the jury's verdict on grounds the verdict is against the great weight of the evidence.

14. **Motion for New Trial:** Either party may move for a new trial based on serious errors occurring at trial. If granted, the case will have to be retried.

15. **Entry of Judgment:** The court enters judgment consistent with the jury verdict or JNOV. From this judgment, the unsatisfied party may appeal.

prima facie case
The minimum evidence sufficient to prove a case, prior to any rebuttal by the defense.

As each person's name is called as a potential juror, you can quickly note on the jury selection charts (or electronic equivalent) the juror's name and previous assessment of that person as good, bad, or intermediate for the case. Transfer key, relevant facts about the person to the chart for the attorney. At this point, all the jury investigation performed earlier pays off. As the juror answers voir dire questions, enter significant responses on the chart.

Paralegals are frequently asked to note their observations of both verbal and nonverbal actions of the potential juror during voir dire. Much popular literature, including quasi-scientific articles, has been written about body language and ways to tell if a person is being truthful. Some attorneys place stock in these articles and train paralegals in such techniques. The truth is, however, that most such techniques should be applied with great caution. Only the most obvious clues, requiring simply an observant eye, prove useful. A good paralegal is cautious and conservative in the use of even the obvious. The human mind is extremely complex and often does not reveal the experience or belief system behind the behavior. Common sense should serve as a guide. For example, if the attorney asks a juror a question and the juror turns away from the attorney and starts fidgeting, it may be a better than 50 percent chance that the juror does not care much for the attorney. Or, if on questions regarding racial or ethnic prejudices a juror keeps referring to a certain group as "those people," it is probable that the person chooses to be distanced from the subject and is likely to be prejudiced. Even the most noticeable clues, however, are not foolproof; do not rule out manipulation by the knowledgeable juror.

During the questioning, keep track of the voir dire questions on a copy of the voir dire outline from the trial notebook so questions overlooked can be pointed out to the attorney. The attorney can use information recorded on the jury selection chart to make challenges for cause and to strike jurors. You may be consulted. Once the final panel is selected, fill in a chart showing these jurors.

Occasionally, paralegals are asked to observe potential jurors unobtrusively where they gather and take breaks. Every so often a paralegal overhears a juror say something that provides insight as to their suitability for the case. For example, if in the rest room a prospective juror was heard to say that she had a reliable cousin who felt Ms. Forrester was akin to the wrong end of a horse, it would certainly affect the attorney's decision to strike that juror. Stranger things have happened.

SHADOW JURY[7]

A group of citizens who reflect the cross-section of the community represented in the jury and who are hired to sit in the public area of the courtroom and to give their impressions of the trial is called a shadow jury. These people listen to evidence the jury hears, leave the courtroom whenever the actual jury is excused, and receive no outside information about the case, just like the empaneled jury. The shadow jury renders no verdict, however, but reports to a consultant at the end of each day. This information gives the attorney an idea of what the jury is thinking, what points need to be clarified, what weaknesses need to be shored up.

Jury consultants charge substantial fees for managing shadow juries, but paralegals can do the work for much less cost to the client. In either case, shadow juries are a good investment when a large amount of money is at stake.

Setting up a shadow jury includes the following steps:

1. Decide the number of jurors needed (three to six is recommended) and costs (fees can be based on an hourly wage for temporary work or a flat payment per day), with guidance from your supervising attorney and client.

> "The charge is prepared; the lawyers are met, The judges all ranged (a terrible show!)."
>
> —John Gay, *The Beggar's Opera*, 1728.

2. Choose individuals who reflect the jury pool in age, gender, race, educational background, and other factors important in your community. Observe the jury selection process in another case to learn typical jury characteristics.
3. Recruit shadow jury participants from the student body of local colleges, employment agencies, teachers or other seasonally unemployed people, and members of the jury pool who were excused.
4. Have the shadow jurors sign an agreement to avoid news and information about the case, and not to discuss the case with anyone but the paralegal or consultant in charge. This stipulation maintains their effectiveness as a reflection of the true jury. The agreement should include a pledge not to speak to any regular jury member or court personnel. Tell the shadow jurors what will be expected of them, and give them instructions as to how they are to respond if questioned by the judge or opposing counsel.
5. Set up a location for the debriefing of the shadow jury each day. This site should be neutral if you do not want to reveal which side has employed them.
6. Set up a process for payment of fees and for communication in case of illness or other emergency.
7. Determine who will debrief the shadow jurors. Some attorneys prefer to do this themselves. In other cases, the debriefer should not be identifiable as a representative of one of the parties, but should always be knowledgeable about the case and should attend the trial to be familiar with significant events of the day.
8. Debriefing the jury individually allows comparison of opinions. Debriefing the group together may show the effects of group dynamics on the jury's decision. Which approach to use should be decided before the trial.
9. Prepare questions that elicit general impressions, irritations, or distractions; opinions about the case in general, attorneys, witnesses, experts, and testimony that are confusing or unbelievable; and questions about evidence or case theories.
10. Do not use leading questions or reveal facts or evidence not yet presented. The exercise is more beneficial the closer it approximates the reflections of the actual jury.
11. Present the information to the attorney, noting significant areas to be considered, for example, in the closing argument.

WITNESS CONTROL

You can help during trial by keeping track of witnesses, notifying them when to appear, meeting them, and reducing their anxiety. Sometimes it is necessary to arrange for the witness's payment, lodging, and transportation. Occasionally a witness will have to be found and subpoenaed during trial.

DOCUMENTS AND EXHIBITS

You can also serve as custodian of exhibits, equipment, and other trial materials. In such cases you must see that everything is ready that will be needed that day at trial, and that each item is stored in a secure place at the end of the day. If others are to serve as custodians, you should have a list of who has what and where the items are stored.

> "It is the duty of a Judge to make it disagreeable to counsel to talk nonsense."
>
> —JOHN SINGLETON COPLEY, THE YOUNGER, ENGLISH JURIST, QUOTED IN JOHN CAMPBELL, *LIVES OF LORD CHANCELLORS*, 1849.

> "Law is not justice and a trial is not a scientific inquiry into truth. A trial is the resolution of a dispute."
>
> —EDISON HAINES, QUOTED IN LAURENCE J. PETER, *PETER'S QUOTATIONS*, 1977.

EXHIBIT AND WITNESS LOGS

During testimony you should keep track of each exhibit that is presented by both sides. This record serves as a guide to what has been presented, objected to, and accepted. It also tells you when the attorney needs a reminder to present an exhibit. Refer to Section 8 of the Trial Notebook (Exhibit 11:4).

Witness logs should also be maintained to show what witnesses have been called and whether they have deviated significantly in their testimony from previous statements, or as otherwise anticipated. Outlines of questions for each witness can be followed as a check to make sure the attorney has not forgotten important questions. It is not unusual during the course of trial for the attorney to ask the paralegal, "Have I forgotten anything?" See Section 7 of the Trial Notebook.

TRIAL NOTES

Take notes at the trial. The attorney is frequently too busy to note or even observe some significant comment or action. These notes should be particularly detailed when your supervising attorney is cross-examining the opponent's witnesses. A good technique is to use a fresh spiral notebook with lined paper. Each page should be numbered ahead of time. A summary-outline of the proceedings can be recorded on the left page, with detailed notes on a particular witness's answer or other important notes on the right page. This provides a systematic means to take notes. Key entries at vital stages in the proceedings will be easier to locate when reviewing the notes. Notes should be kept on what the attorney specifies before trial; most commonly that includes the name of the case, judge, court reporters, and staff; all parties, attorneys, experts, and others. Indicate what witnesses have been called, by whom, and the essence of their testimony. Note exact quotations if particularly significant. Record the exhibits entered through each witness. Note all objections and judge's rulings, and the times of all recesses, conferences before the bench, conferences in chambers, and times trial resumed. Much of this process can be done on an in-court laptop computer. Many courts are now equipped with instant or real-time transcript reporting technology, providing attorneys and paralegals with an immediate on-screen copy of the typed testimony. Key portions can be highlighted and reviewed in conjunction with your notes.

TRIAL DAY REVIEW MEETINGS

Frequently the entire trial team gathers each evening to discuss the day's events and next day's strategies. Your notes of the day can be compared to the attorney's notes and recollections. Items can be noted for follow-up or emphasis in the closing arguments. You can offer suggestions when appropriate and receive instructions on what to do for the following day, which might involve last-minute subpoenas, arranging for transportation, or doing some last-minute legal research on a point expected to be argued the following day. Motions may need to be put into final form, or at least readied for the attorney's submission.

WHEN THE PARALEGAL MUST TESTIFY

Sometimes it becomes necessary for the paralegal to testify at trial. Such testimony is commonly used to prove that something was mailed on a specified date, that a photo is authentic, or that a chain of custody has been maintained to preserve certain evidence. The better practice is to refrain from involving the paralegal, but sometimes it is unavoidable.

When asked to testify, you should review the suggestions given to any witness. The attorney can prepare you through questions, since a review of actual documents to refresh recollection will make the documents accessible to the opposing attorney for cross-examination and can result in the revelation of attorney-client privilege.

Your testimony should be kept to a minimum, advocacy should be left aside, and the testimony should be professional and truthful. Any commitment to the client or the attorney cannot and does not supersede the commitment and responsibility to the truth.

VERDICT

The **verdict** is the final decision of the jury regarding the questions of fact submitted to it by the judge. Typically, there are three types or forms of verdict:

1. *General verdict:*   The jury simply indicates whether it finds for the plaintiff or defendant and, if for the plaintiff, the amount of the award.
2. *Special verdict:*   The jury states its findings on a list of questions of fact submitted by the judge, from which the judge decides which party prevails. Special verdict questions may address the percent of fault of the respective parties [Rule 49(a)].
3. *General verdict with interrogatories:*   The jury enters a general verdict based on its required answers to one or more prerequisite questions of fact. Whether the answers to the interrogatories are consistent with the general verdict determines whether the court enters a judgment consistent with the general verdict, enters a judgment notwithstanding the general verdict, sends the jury back to reconsider the inconsistencies, or orders a new trial [Rule 44(b)].

Prior to the judge's submission of the verdict document to the jury, each party has the opportunity to request what type of verdict it wants submitted to the jury. The paralegal can play a role in researching what form of verdict would be best and what legal authority supports the submission of that form, and drafting the necessary documents. The documents and supporting authority are placed in Section Eleven of the Trial Notebook.

verdict
The final decision of the jury regarding the questions of fact submitted to it by the judge.

POLLING THE JURY

At the completion of trial, the jury may be polled to see if the verdict stated is in fact agreed to by that particular juror. Polling is usually done when the attorney is surprised by the verdict. The attorney may ask the jurors about what witnesses were the most significant, what evidence had the most impact, and why they decided the way they did. You can assist by suggesting topics to be covered and taking careful notes during the polling.

FINDINGS OF FACT AND CONCLUSIONS OF LAW

In some states, in cases with no jury, the prevailing party has the duty of drafting the court's **findings of fact and conclusions of law.** This document summarizes the key evidence on the necessary elements of the cause of action and the judge's conclusion that form the basis of the judgment. The paralegal is often asked to draft this document for the attorney's review. You should consult several pertinent examples of findings of fact and conclusions of law before drafting the document. It is submitted to the court, signed by the judge, and distributed to the parties. Exhibit 11:11 is a skeleton form for drafting findings of fact and conclusions of law.

findings of fact and conclusions of law
The document that contains the court's judgment summarizing the key evidence on the elements of the cause of action and the judge's conclusions that form the basis of the judgment.

EXHIBIT 11:11 ▪ Findings of Fact and Conclusions of Law

(*Caption*)

FINDINGS OF FACT AND CONCLUSIONS OF LAW

The above entitled action, having been tried before this court without a jury on [*date*], with _____ appearing as the attorney for _____, and _____ appearing as the attorney for _____, and having heard the evidence in this case and the arguments of counsel, this court, being fully advised herein, makes the following findings of fact and conclusions of law:

Findings of Fact

(In separately numbered paragraphs state each finding of fact.)
From the foregoing facts, the court concludes

Conclusions of Law

(In separately numbered paragraphs state each conclusion of law.)

By the Court

_____

Judge

Dated _____

Summary

Preparedness through organization continues to be a common thread that defines much of your responsibility as a paralegal. Preparing the litigation team for trial is not only crucial to success at trial, but also involves some of the most interesting and creative tasks that you may be asked to perform. You have learned to develop and utilize a checklist such as the Trial Preparation Checklist. You have learned the importance of and techniques for serving subpoenas, conducting jury investigations, creating demonstrative evidence, drafting motions in limine and motions to be used at trial, and preparing witnesses to testify. You have become familiar with the components and organization of an effective trial notebook.

Paralegals, as we have seen, also play an important role at trial by knowing each stage of the trial and anticipating how they can be of best use at each stage, by observing and recording information at jury selection, by coordinating witnesses and maintaining control over documents and exhibits, by taking careful notes for daily trial review, and other tasks. Although these tasks require energy and diligence, your hard work will be rewarded at the moment of victory. One outstanding paralegal describes how she felt after her hard work made a significant contribution to a favorable verdict for her firm's client:

> It was the most incredible feeling . . . The last time I felt like that was when they told me it was a girl . . . I was literally shaking . . . I've been doing this for eight years and you never get used to it; I hope I never do.[8]

◉ WORKBOOK

System Folder Assignments, other exercises, a chapter outline, a review test, and other study aids are located in the accompanying workbook.

◉ HELPFUL WEB SITES

http://www.abanet.org/litigation/civiltrialstandards/home.html
  ABA's Civil Trial Practice Standards, with commentary (must download)

http://www.njp.com
  National Jury Project, an array of fee services regarding jury selection

http://www.jri-inc.com
  Jury Research Institute, articles and services on juries

http://www.astcweb.org
  American Society of Trial Consultants

http://www.abanet.org/juryprojectstandards/principles.pdf
  ABA principles for juries and jury trials

◉ QUESTIONS FOR STUDY AND REVIEW

1. What are the trial preparation tasks to be performed by the paralegal well before trial? In the last six weeks before trial?
2. What is the importance of a case status sheet?
3. What steps must be followed in subpoenaing witnesses?
4. How can you help in conducting a jury investigation? What information should be gathered and from what sources?
5. What purpose does the juror data sheet serve?
6. What benefits are derived from diagrams and other audiovisual aids?
7. List and describe current technology and some typical audiovisual aids used in the courtroom.
8. What are the rules in your jurisdiction on the admissibility of and proper foundation for demonstrative evidence, including diagrams?
9. Whom might you consult when preparing your own diagrams and charts?
10. What is a trial notebook? List and define its key components.
11. What aspects of the trial notebook can you draft?
12. What is a juror notebook?
13. What are jury instructions? What should you do to prepare a draft set of instructions for the attorney?
14. How can you assist the attorney in preparing the client or a witness for trial testimony? What ethical considerations must be kept in mind?
15. How can you assist the attorney at voir dire and other stages of the trial?
16. Define three types of verdicts.

◉ KEY TERMS

challenge for cause
findings of fact and
  conclusions of law

in limine
peremptory challenge
prima facie case

verdict
voir dire

◉ ENDNOTES

1. Robert B. Hirschorn, *Jury Selection in Civil and Criminal Trials* (accompanying materials), presented at the Kentucky Bar Association Annual Convention, June 24, 2004, 98.
2. See the reports of studies done jointly by DECISION QUEST and THE NATIONAL LAW JOURNAL: Peter Aronson, David E. Rovella, and Bob Van Vorts, *Jurors: A Biased, Independent Lot*, NAT'L L.J., Nov. 2, 1998, A1, and Bob Van Vorts, *Voir Dire Tip: Pick Former Juror*, NAT'L L.J., Nov. 1, 1999, A1.
3. Leonard Post, *Clearing the High-Tech Hurdle*, NAT. L. J. Aug. 22, 2004, 1, 17, regarding the Louisiana state court case of *Scott v. American Tobacco*, No. 96-8461 (Orleans Parish, La., Dist. Ct.).

4. Lisa Brennan, *Pitching the Gen-X Jury*, NAT. L. J., June 7, 2004, 1.

5. Frederick I. Lederer, *Courtroom Technology: The Courtroom 21 Project: Creating the Courtroom of the Twenty-first Century*, 43 JUDGES JOURNAL 39, Winter, 2004.

6. Margaret Cronin Fisk, *55M for Med-Mal Sets Mark*, NAT'L L.J., June 19, 2000, A10.

7. This section is based on Lana J. Clark, CLA, *Litigation Tips*, FACTS & FINDINGS, Feb. 1996, 5, 30-31.

8. Arnold, *A Once in a Lifetime Case*, NAT'L PARALEGAL REP., Winter 1989, 24 [quoting Jill Burton of Brown, Todd, and Heyburn in Louisville, Kentucky].

 For additional resources, visit our Web site at **http://www.westlegalstudies.com.**

Post-Trial Practice from Motions to Appeal

INTRODUCTION

This chapter covers the procedures employed after the verdict is rendered. Here you will learn the function, procedure, and forms for four post-trial processes: post-trial motions for judgment notwithstanding the verdict and a motion for a new trial, the proper filing of the judgment and bill of costs, enforcing a judgment, and appealing the case.

With experience, a good paralegal should be able to perform each of these tasks. Keep in mind, however, that not all law offices will readily delegate all of these tasks to the paralegal. It falls to you to earn the confidence of the law firm and, in many situations, to *make* the opportunity and reach out for enhanced responsibility.

POST-TRIAL MOTIONS

Even if the court has entered judgment in the case, the party against whom the judgment has been entered may move to have the judgment set aside.

Under Rule 50 of the Federal Rules of Civil Procedure and like state rules, a party who has moved for a motion for judgment as a matter of law (a motion notwithstanding the verdict) at the close of all the evidence may file a renewed motion for judgment as a matter of law. The motion must be filed within ten days after judgment has been entered [Rule 50(b)]. A proposed revision of this rule eliminates the requirement that the motion be renewed at the close of all the evidence and runs the ten day filing period from the "discharge of the jury" rather than from the entry of judgment (Dec. 2007). The motion asks either that the judgment be set aside, combined with a motion for a new trial, or that judgment be entered in accordance with the previous motion for judgment as a matter of law. A motion for a new trial may also be filed separately. Generally speaking, a motion for judgment as a matter of law is granted if the weight of the evidence is contrary to the jury's verdict; in other words, if there is only one reasonable conclusion as to the verdict.

A motion for new trial must be filed within ten days of the entry of judgment (Rules 50 and 59). Typically, this motion alleges procedural errors (improperly admitted or excluded evidence, improper argument by opposing counsel, prejudicial jury instructions, etc.), a verdict contrary to law, excessive or inadequate damages, and other grounds. The motion must be supported by affidavit. The opposing party has ten days in which to file responsive affidavits. Failure of a party to renew a motion for judgment as a matter of law [Rule 50(b)] and a motion for a new trial (Rule 59) deprives the appellate court of the authority to review such matters on appeal [*Unitherm Food Systems Inc. v. Swift-Eckrich Inc.*, 126 S.Ct. 1609 (2006)].

remittitur
A post-trial motion in which the defendant requests the court to reduce a jury award because of an error in determining the award or because the award is unreasonably excessive.

additur
A post-trial motion in which the plaintiff requests the court to increase a jury award.

Post-trial motions also include motions for remittitur and additur. **Remittitur** is a post-trial motion in which the defendant requests the court to reduce a jury award because of an error in determining the award or because the award is unreasonably excessive. If the plaintiff agrees to the remittitur, there is no new trial. Remittitur is used in both state and federal post-trial practice [FED. R. CIV. P. 59(a)]. **Additur** is a post-trial motion in which the plaintiff requests the court to increase a jury award. Although additur is used in a number of states, it is not used in the federal system since the Supreme Court declared it a violation of the Seventh Amendment in *Dimick v. Schiedt*, 293 U.S. 474 (1935).

Your role in post-trial motion practice can be significant. Immediately after trial, review with the attorney the copious notes you took at trial. From these notes the attorney develops theories on which the motion can be based.

Research the applicable local rules of procedure and the legal standards and authority for the motion in the pertinent jurisdiction. After a review of the authorities

EXHIBIT 12:1 ■ Renewal of Motion for Judgment as a Matter of Law (State: Motion for Judgment Notwithstanding the Verdict)

UNITED STATES DISTRICT COURT

THE _____ DISTRICT OF _____

_____ DIVISION

ABC

    Plaintiff   Civil Action File No._____

    v.

XYZ

    Defendant

RENEWAL OF MOTION FOR JUDGMENT AS MATTER OF LAW

[Plaintiff or Defendant] ABC having, at the close of all the evidence, moved this court for judgment as a matter of law, which motion was denied, and subsequently a verdict was entered for [plaintiff or defendant], [plaintiff or defendant] ABC now renews his/her motion for judgment as a matter of law pursuant to Rule 50(b), Federal Rule of Civil Procedure.

This motion is made on the grounds that [*state specific grounds for each point*].

Dated_____   Respectfully submitted,

                                          _____

                                          Attorney
                                          Address:
                                          Phone:

[*Notice*]

Source: Reprinted with permission of West Group.

with the attorney, draft the motion and any supporting affidavit, brief, or memorandum required by local rules. Filing dates should be entered in the deadline control system. Once in final form, the motion and supporting documents are served on the opponent and filed in court. Exhibit 12:1 is a sample motion for judgment as a matter of law and Exhibits 12:2 and 12:3 are examples of motions for new trial.[1]

JUDGMENT AND BILL OF COSTS

Another task performed by the litigation paralegal is the preparation and filing of the bill of costs. Federal Rule 54(d) and parallel state rules provide that costs shall be awarded to the prevailing party unless otherwise directed by the court. The prevailing party files a bill of costs with the clerk of court. A copy is sent to the opposing attorney. The opposing attorney may object to all or part of the bill. If either party is dissatisfied with the clerk's determination, a motion for court review may be served within five days of the clerk's taxation of costs.

Taxable costs allowed by 28 U.S.C. § 1920 include such things as filing fees, printing fees, pleadings, witness fees, and other items. A standard fee is usually established by the clerk of court, who can provide the necessary information. Generally, attorney's fees are not recoverable. There are exceptions, however, mainly in the form of statutes, including the Americans with Disabilities Act, the Privacy Act, and various civil rights acts. The recovery of attorney's fees under these acts is sought by a separate motion. Check local

---

EXHIBIT 12:2 ■ Motion for New Trial in Nonjury Case

IN THE UNITED STATES DISTRICT COURT
FOR THE _____ DISTRICT OF _____ _____ DIVISION

ABC

      Plaintiff

     v.   Civil Action No. _____

XYZ   Judge _____

      Defendant

MOTION FOR NEW TRIAL IN NON-JURY CASE

Plaintiff ABC moves the Court to set aside the Findings of Fact, Conclusions of Law and Judgment pursuant to Rule 52(b) Federal Rules of Civil Procedure, and to grant Plaintiff a new trial pursuant to Rule 59(a), Federal Rules of Civil Procedure on the grounds that:

1. The Court erred in ruling that * * *
2. The Court erred in admitting the following evidence offered by the Defendant over objection of Plaintiff * * *
3. The Court erred in excluding evidence of Plaintiff * * *
4. The Court erred in admitting the following exhibits over objection for the following reasons * * *
5. The Court erred in excluding the following exhibits * * *
6. The Judgment is contrary to law in that * * *

                   Respectfully submitted,

                   _____

                   J. Doe, Attorney for Plaintiff

         [*Add Proof of Service*]

Source: Reprinted with permission of West Group.

EXHIBIT 12:3 ■ Motion for New Trial in Jury Case

IN THE UNITED STATES DISTRICT COURT FOR
THE _____ DISTRICT OF _____ _____ DIVISION

ABC

      Plaintiff

     v.   Civil Action No. _____

XYZ   Judge _____

      Defendant

MOTION FOR NEW TRIAL IN JURY CASE

Defendant XYZ moves the Court pursuant to Rule 59(a), Federal Rules of Civil Procedure, to set aside the verdict of the Jury returned herein on _____ and the Judgment entered on _____ and to grant a new trial on the grounds that:

1. The verdict is contrary to the law as follows * * *
2. The verdict is contrary to the evidence as follows * * *
3. The evidence in this case is totally insufficient to support a finding of validity, enforceability and infringement.
4. The verdict of the jury herein is excessive and appears to have been given under the influence of passion and prejudice as follows * * *
5. The Court erred in permitting the following testimony over objection of Defendant XYZ * * *
6. The Court erred in refusing to allow witnesses to answer Defendant's questions as follows * * *
7. The Court erred in admitting the following exhibits for the following reasons * * *
8. The Court erred in excluding the following exhibits for the following reasons * * *

                   Respectfully submitted,

                   _____

                   J. Doe, Attorney for Plaintiff

         [*Add Proof of Service*]

Source: Reprinted with permission of West Group.

rules. In every respect, however, costs must be reasonable under the circumstances. What to include in the bill and what is necessary to support the charge is set out in Federal Form AO133. Some state courts provide similar forms. A supporting brief or memorandum may be required. Exhibit 12:4 is the federal form for a bill of costs.

It is advantageous from the start of the action to dedicate a section of the case file in which to note bills and costs and collect receipts and other pertinent records.

EXHIBIT 12:4 ■ Bill of Costs

United States District Court

DISTRICT OF

BILL OF COSTS

V.

Case Number:

Judgment having been entered in the above entitled action on _____ against _____,
Date

the Clerk is requested to tax the following as costs:

Fees of the Clerk ....$ _____
Fees for service of summons and subpoena .... _____
Fees of the court reporter for all or any part of the transcript necessarily obtained for use in the case .... _____
Fees and disbursements for printing .... _____
Fees for witnesses (itemize on reverse side) .... _____
Fees for exemplification and copies of papers necessarily obtained for use in the case .... _____
Docket fees under 28 U.S.C. 1923 .... _____
Costs as shown on Mandate of Court of Appeals .... _____
Compensation of interpreters and costs of special interpretation services under 28 U.S.C. 1828 .... _____
Other costs (please itemize) .... _____

TOTAL $ _____

SPECIAL NOTE: Attach to your bill an itemization and documentation for requested costs in all categories.

DECLARATION

I declare under penalty of perjury that the foregoing costs are correct and were necessarily incurred in this action and that the services for which fees have been charged were actually and necessarily performed. A copy of this bill was mailed today with postage prepaid to:

_____.

Signature of Attorney: _____

Name of Attorney: _____

For: _____   Date: _____
Name of Claiming Party

Costs are taxed in the amount of _____ and included in the judgment.

_____ By: _____

Clerk of Court   *Deputy Clerk*   *Date*

(continued)

EXHIBIT 12:4 ■ Bill of Costs *(continued)*

WITNESS FEES (computation, cf. 28 U.S.C. 1821 for statutory fees)							
NAME AND RESIDENCE	ATTENDANCE		SUBSISTENCE		MILEAGE		Total Cost Each Witness
	Days	Total Cost	Days	Total Cost	Days	Total Cost	
						TOTAL	

NOTICE

Section 1924, Title 28, U.S. Code (effective September 1, 1948) provides:

"Sec. 1924. Verification of bill of costs."

"Before any bill of costs is taxed, the party claiming any item of cost or disbursement shall attach thereto an affidavit, made by himself or by his duly authorized attorney or agent having knowledge of the facts, that such item is correct and has been necessarily incurred in the case and that the services for which fees have been charged were actually and necessarily performed."

See also Section 1920 of Title 28, which reads in part as follows:

"A bill of costs shall be filed in the case and upon allowance, included in the judgment or decree."

The Federal Rules of Civil Procedure contain the following provisions:

Rule 54 (d)

"Except where express provision therefor is made either in a statute of the United States or in these rules, costs shall be allowed as of course to the prevailing party unless court otherwise directs, but costs against the United States, its officers, and agencies shall be imposed only to the extent permitted by law. Costs may be taxed by the clerk on one day's notice. On motion served within 5 days thereafter, the action of the clerk may be reviewed by the court."

Rule 6 (e)

"Whenever a party has the right or is required to do some act or take some proceedings within a prescribed period after the service of a notice or other paper upon him and the notice or paper is served upon him by mail, 3 days shall be added to the prescribed period."

Rule 58 (In Part)

"Entry of the judgment shall not be delayed for the taxing of costs."

This will prevent loss and oversight of such items and ease the task of preparing and filing the bill of costs at this stage. You may be asked, as well, to review and determine the accuracy of a bill of costs submitted by the opposing party.

ENFORCEMENT OF THE JUDGMENT

INTRODUCTION

One of the perplexing quirks in civil procedure is that the winner of a judgment, the **judgment creditor,** often must go back into court to force the **judgment debtor** to comply with the judgment. Although not a difficult process, it is time-consuming and adds additional expense to the lawsuit.

judgment creditor
The winner in civil cases in which money has been awarded.

judgment debtor
The loser in civil cases in which money has been awarded.

More than likely, the judgment debtor will cooperate and make arrangements to pay. It may be a lump-sum payment in cash, a structured payment involving investments and annuities, installments secured by promissory notes and collateral, or some other method.

If, at the beginning of a lawsuit, the plaintiff fears that the defendant will try to hide or even transfer assets to avoid loss through judgment, the judgment creditor can seek court action to seize the property to satisfy a favorable judgment. Federal Rule 64 permits such procedure in accordance with the remedies and procedures available in the state in which the federal district court sits. Some typical prejudgment remedies include *attachment, garnishment, replevin,* and others. Some of these same remedies are available after judgment and will be discussed later in this section. Prejudgment remedies are less popular today than a few years ago, and courts are unlikely to grant them unless there is a good reason. If the action involves the title to specific property, a notice of **lis pendens** may be filed by the plaintiff. It places all other buyers of that property on notice that the plaintiff has claimed a right to that property depending on the outcome of the case. Exhibit 12:5 is an example of a notice of lis pendens.

lis pendens
Record to notify potential buyers that the plaintiff has asserted a claim against that property in a lawsuit.

EXHIBIT 12:5 ■ Notice of Lis Pendens

STATE OF _____   CIRCUIT COURT   COUNTY _____

_____
                              Plaintiff

      v.   Civil Case File No. _____

_____,
                              Defendant

NOTICE OF LIS PENDENS

NOTICE IS HEREBY GIVEN that an action has been filed in the above entitled court by _____, Plaintiff against _____, Defendant for an action [*state type of action such as "to quiet title".*]

This action affects title to real property in _____ County as described below:

(Provide legal description of property.)

Date _____   Attorney for Plaintiff _____

                                         Address _____

                                         Phone _____

The focus of this chapter, however, and the more common concern of the paralegal, is locating and obtaining assets after the judgment has been entered and the debtor refuses to cooperate.

LOCATING THE ASSETS OF THE JUDGMENT DEBTOR

judgment proof
Description of a party who has no assets with which to pay a judgment.

Prior to taking any action, the judgment creditor must determine whether the debtor has any assets. Most likely, this was determined to some extent in the early stages of the case. Few attorneys are willing to put forth the effort to win a case, only to find at the end that the defendant has no assets and is, for all practical purposes, **judgment proof.** Whether at the beginning or end of the case, you need to gather this information.

A Guide to Locating Assets[2]

Your objective is to compile a list of every asset that the judgment debtor has. As you search for assets, you will want to obtain the following basic information for each asset:

A description of the asset. Be specific as to quantity, color, size or other measurements, function, component parts, or any other data relevant to the kind of asset in question.

Location. Where is the asset? Give the exact addresses and names of people who have possession of the asset, including, of course, the judgment debtor.

How did the judgment debtor obtain his/her interest in the asset? If by purchase, how much was paid, when acquired, etc.?

What is the current fair market value of the asset? If the asset were sold on the open market, how much would it probably bring?

When tracking assets in an attempt to obtain the above information, it is useful to think of the various categories of assets that are possible:

1. Personal property—Real property
2. Property solely owned by the judgment debtor—Property in which others also have an interest
3. Tangible property—Intangible property
4. Property in the possession of the judgment debtor—Property in the possession of a third person
5. Property in the state where the judgment was rendered (forum state)—Property in another state (foreign state)
6. Property the judgment debtor currently has—Property that will be received in the future
7. Property the judgment debtor currently has—Property that the judgment debtor disposed of since the litigation began or just before it began
8. Property that is exempt from creditor collection—Property not protected by exemption

Any single asset may fall into a variety of categories.

Personal/Real Property. Personal property would include cash, bonds, securities, uncashed checks, cars, trucks, boats, jewelry, clothing, business inventory, equipment, pension rights, insurance policies, debts owed the judgment debtor (e.g., accounts receivable), etc.

Real property: current residence, vacation home, fixtures on the land, buildings (business or personal use), etc.

Solely Owned/Others with Interest. The judgment debtor may own many assets in his/her own name without anyone else having a property interest in the asset. On the other hand, there will usually be assets in which others will also have a property interest. For example,

- a spouse may jointly own a bank account or a home
- a spouse may have a dower or community property interest in assets acquired during the marriage
- an associate may have an equal partnership interest in a business
- a tenant will have a property right to remain on land owned by the judgment debtor as landlord
- the government may have a tax lien on property because of nonpayment of taxes
- a bank or some other creditor may have a security interest in property, e.g., the property was used as collateral in order to obtain a mortgage or borrow money in some other way
- a neighbor has an easement over the judgment debtor's land allowing the neighbor to use the land for a limited purpose

The following are some basic property terms with which you should be familiar. They all involve assets in which more than one person has a property interest:

Joint tenancy: individuals (called joint tenants) own the entire property together. They do not own parts of it; each individual owns all of the property. When one joint tenant dies, the property does not pass through the decedent's estate. The property passes immediately to the surviving joint tenants. This principle is known as the right of survivorship. (A joint tenant is not a tenant who rents an apartment; these are totally separate concepts of tenance.)

Tenancy by the entirety: a joint tenancy in which the joint tenants are husband and wife.

Tenancy in common: individuals (called tenants in common) own a portion or a share of the whole property. There is no right of survivorship. When one tenant in common dies, his/her interest in the property passes through his/her estate and does not go to the surviving tenants in common.

Lien: a claim against property usually created to secure payment of a debt. The holder of the lien can force the sale of the property when the debt is not paid. The proceeds from the forced sale are used to satisfy the debt.

Mortgage: in some states, a mortgage is simply a lien of property used to secure the mortgage debt.

Tangible/Intangible Property. angible property: having a physical form, which can be seen or touched, e.g., land, car, equipment.

Intangible property: a "right" rather than a physical object, e.g., the right to receive money from an employer, the right to the exclusive use of an invention, the right to have money repaid with interest, etc. These rights may be described in documents that are tangible, e.g., a stock certificate, a promissory note, a patent, but the rights represented by these documents are intangible.

Possession of Judgment Debtor/Possession of Others. Very often the judgment debtor will have assets in the possession of other persons or institutions. Banks and employers, for example, often hold money that belongs to the judgment debtor, which will be turned over upon request or when a set date arrives. Insurance companies, unions and government agencies also hold ("possess") assets (often called benefits), which will be given to the judgment debtor at a certain time or upon the happening of a designated condition, e.g., retirement.

A bailment exists when someone else's goods are being held for use, repair or storage, e.g., furniture in storage, a borrowed or rented car, a car in a repair shop. The person holding the property (called the bailee) may or may not be receiving a profit for holding the goods of the other (called the bailor).

Garnishment is the process of trying to reach the assets of the debtor (here the judgment debtor), which are in the possession of a third party, in order to satisfy the debt.

"Once a lawyer was arguing a case before three lord justices in the court of appeal, dealing with an elementary point of law at inordinate length. Finally, the master of the rolls, who was presiding, intervened. "Really," he protested, "do give this court credit for some intelligence." Quick as a flash came the reply. "That is the mistake I made in the court below, my lord."

—ANONYMOUS, IN ARCHIBALD EDGAR BOWKER, *A LIFETIME WITH THE LAW,* 1961.

Property in Forum State/Property in Foreign State.   The forum state is the state that rendered the judgment for the judgment creditor against the judgment debtor. A foreign state is any other state in the United States or any other country in the world. The judgment debtor may own land or other assets in a foreign state as well as in the forum state.

Current Property/Future Property.   Many of the judgment debtor's assets will already be in his/her possession. Other assets, however, may be on their way to the judgment debtor through the mail or other means of shipment. Some assets will not be received until the occurrence of a designated event or condition, e.g., a request for the asset is made by the judgment debtor, a certain age is reached, retirement, death, a designated date has arrived, etc.

Assets the judgment debtor has a right to receive in the future can usually be *assigned* to someone else so that the latter will be entitled to receive the asset. An assignment is simply a transfer of rights from one person to another.

Current Property/Property Recently Disposed Of.   The great fear of a judgment creditor is that the judgment debtor will voluntarily render him/herself judgment proof by giving away, destroying, or otherwise disposing of the assets before the trial is over. The judgment creditor may or may not have obtained protection against this by the kind of pretrial attachment referred to above. Even if no such protection was obtained, the judgment creditor may be able to invalidate any transfers of assets made by the judgment debtor just before and during the trial on the ground that they were sham transfers, or were made with the intent to defraud the judgment winner.

Exempt Property/Nonexempt Property.   All the assets owned by the judgment debtor are not fair game to the judgment creditor. By law, certain property is exempt, e.g., a designated percentage of the judgment debtor's salary, clothes, the tools of one's trade or profession, some furniture. Such property cannot be reached by the judgment creditor to satisfy the judgment debt.

How then does the judgment creditor go about locating the assets of the uncooperative judgment debtor that fall into one or more of the eight categories of assets? There are some formal procedures that can be of assistance in discovering assets. Before discussing these, some thoughts will be presented on *informal* investigative techniques.

The judgment creditor has just been through a trial and perhaps an appeal with the judgment debtor. A good deal is already known about him/her. This data must be organized and evaluated at two levels. First, the data contains specific information on the possible assets and liabilities of the judgment debtor. Second, the data tells you a lot about the life style of the judgment debtor. One's life style is an excellent clue to assets and liabilities. You are interested in liabilities or other debts because the kind and extent of liabilities one assumes is often an indication of one's assets. The assumption is that someone with a lot of liabilities probably has a lot of assets to cover those liabilities. Someone who rarely gets into debt probably has very little to risk. Of course, you also want to know if the judgment debtor is over his/her head in liabilities since there may be little or nothing left for the judgment creditor to reach.

---

postjudgment interrogatory
A method to discover the assets of the judgment debtor through written questions to be answered under oath.

The power of the court can also be called upon to aid in locating assets of the judgment debtor. These more formal methods utilize devices designed for pretrial discovery to gather information important to the post-trial resolution of the case.

The least expensive method is the **postjudgment interrogatory.** The paralegal draws in part on the process of informally locating assets to design a set of questions for the judgment debtor to answer. The number of postjudgment interrogatories may be limited by local rules. Exhibit 12:6 is an example of interrogatories for the purpose of discovering assets.[3]

EXHIBIT 12:6 ▪ Interrogatories in Aid of Judgment

[Caption]

INTERROGATORIES IN AID OF JUDGMENT

Because you have failed to pay the full amount of the judgment against you entered in favor of [*creditor*], [*creditor*] has the right to attempt to enforce that judgment by a judicial sale [*sheriff's sale*] of your assets. [*Creditor*] also may inquire concerning the existence and location of those assets.

Pursuant to the applicable [*state*] Rules of Civil Procedure you are required to make full and complete answers to the questions set forth on the following pages. These answers must be made in writing, under oath, within thirty (30) days after service upon you and sent to counsel for [*creditor*]; [*attorney's name and address*]. Please attach additional sheets if necessary to completely answer questions.

Should you fail to answer, the court may enter an order imposing sanctions against you.

If you do not understand your duty to answer these questions, you should consult a lawyer. If you do not have or know a lawyer, then you should go to or telephone the office set forth below to find out where you can get legal help.

[Lawyer Referral Service address and telephone number]

1. State whether you are currently employed. If so, state whether you are paid weekly, semi-monthly, bi-weekly, monthly, or in some other fashion. If you are self-employed, state the name of your business, address, nature of your business and annual income.
   ANSWER:

2. *ACCOUNTS:* State whether or not you maintain any checking or savings accounts. If so, state the name and location of the banks or savings and loan association or building and loan association or credit union and the branch or branches thereof, the identification (account) numbers of each account, and the amount or amounts you have in each account. If you maintain any of these jointly with another person, give their name and address. Also provide the above information with respect to any such bank accounts which were maintained and which were closed within the past twelve (12) months.
   ANSWER:

3. *REAL ESTATE:* Do you have an ownership or interest in any real estate anywhere in the United States? If so, set forth a brief description thereof, including the lot size and type of construction; the location, including the state, county, and municipality; the volume and page number of the official record; and state further whether you own it solely or together with any other person or persons and give their full names and addresses. If any of the above properties are mortgaged, supply the names and addresses of the lender[s], the date and amount of the mortgage, where it is recorded, the monthly payments and the balance now due.
   ANSWER:

(continued)

EXHIBIT 12:6 ■ Interrogatories in Aid of Judgment (*continued*)

4. *DEBTS, NOTES & JUDGMENTS:* State the names and addresses of any and all persons whom you believe owe you money and set forth in detail the amount of money owed, the terms of payment and whether or not you have written evidence of this indebtedness, and if so, the location of such writing. Also state if the matter is in litigation, and if so, give full details. If you hold a judgment or judgments as security for any of these debts, state where and when the judgment was recorded; and the county, number and term where the judgment is recorded. If you hold this judgment jointly with any other person or persons, give their name and address.
ANSWER:

5. *INSURANCE:* State whether or not you are the owner of any life insurance contracts. If so, state the serial or policy number or numbers of said contract, the face amount, the exact name and address of the insurance company, the named beneficiary or beneficiaries and their present address. If you own this insurance jointly with any other person or persons, give their name and address.
ANSWER:

6. *MORTGAGES:* State whether you own any mortgages against real estate owned by any other person in the United States. If so, state whether or not you own this mortgage with any other person or persons and, if so, supply their full names and addresses. State further the names and addresses of all borrowers and the state and county where said mortgage is recorded together with the number of the volume and the page number.
ANSWER:

7. *AGREEMENTS:* State whether you have any agreements involving the purchase of any real estate anywhere in the United States. If so, state with whom this agreement is made, and state whether or not any persons are joined with you in the agreement. Supply full names and addresses of all parties concerned. If the agreement is recorded, provide the state and county of recordation, volume and page numbers.
ANSWER:

8. *STOCKS, SHARES OR INTERESTS:* State whether or not you own any stocks, shares or interests in any corporation, or unincorporated association or partnership, limited or general and state the location thereof. Include the names and addresses of the organizations and include the serial numbers of the shares or stock. If you own any of the stock, shares or interests jointly with any other person or persons, give their names and addresses.
ANSWER:

9. *GOVERNMENT, MUNICIPAL OR CORPORATE BONDS:* State whether or not you own individually or jointly any corporate or governmental bonds including U.S. Savings Bonds. If so, include the face amount, serial numbers and maturity date and state the present location thereof. If you own any of these bonds jointly with any other person or persons, give their names and addresses.
ANSWER:

10. *SAFETY DEPOSIT BOXES:* State whether or not you maintain any safety deposit box or boxes. If so, include the names of the bank or banks, branch or branches, and the identification number or other designation of the box or boxes. Include a full description of the contents and also the amount of cash among those contents. If you maintain any of these jointly with another person, give their full name and address.
ANSWER:

11. *TRANSFERRED ASSETS AND GIFTS:* If, since the date this debt to [*creditor*] was first incurred, you have transferred any assets (real property, personal property, chose in action) to any person and/or, if you have given

EXHIBIT 12:6 ■ Interrogatories in Aid of Judgment (*continued*)

any gift of any assets, including money, to any person, set forth, in detail, a description of the property, the type of transaction, and the name and address of the transferee or recipient.
  ANSWER:

12. *INHERITANCE:* State whether or not, to your knowledge, you are now or will be a beneficiary of or will inherit any money from any decedent in the United States, and state the place and date of death, the legal representative of the estate, and the location of the court where the said estate is administered or to be administered.
  ANSWER:

13. *ANNUITIES:* State whether you are a beneficiary of any trust fund, and if so, state the names and addresses of the trustees and the amount of the payment and when the payment is received.
  ANSWER:

14. *PERSONAL PROPERTY:* Set forth a full description of all furnishings and any other items of personal property (including jewelry) with full description, value and present location. State also whether or not there are any encumbrances against that property and if so, the name and address of the encumbrance holder, the date of the encumbrance, holder, the date of the encumbrance, the original amount of that encumbrance, the present balance of that encumbrance and the transaction which gave rise to the existence of the encumbrance. If you own any personal property jointly with any other person or persons, give their names and addresses.
  ANSWER:

15. *RENTAL INCOME:* State whether you are the recipient, directly or indirectly, of any income for the rental of any real or personal property; and if so, state specifically the source of payment, the person from whom such payments are received and the amount and date when those payments are received.
  ANSWER:

16. *MOTOR VEHICLES:* State whether or not you own any motor vehicles. Include a full description of such motor vehicles including color, model, title number, serial number and registration plate number. Also show the exact name or names in which the motor vehicles are registered, the present value of those motor vehicles and their present location and place of regular storage or parking. State also whether or not there are any liens or encumbrances against those motor vehicles and if so, the name and address of the encumbrance, the present balance of the encumbrance and the transaction which gave rise to the existence of the encumbrance.
  ANSWER:

17. *PENSION:* State whether you are a participant in or the recipient of any pension or annuity fund, and if so, state specifically the source of payment, the person to whom such payments are made, the amount of the payments and date when those payments are received.
  ANSWER:

18. *OTHER ASSETS:* If you have any asset or assets which are not disclosed in the preceding seventeen interrogatories, please set forth all details concerning those assets.
  ANSWER:

_____
Attorney for Plaintiff

post-trial request for production of documents
Method to obtain documents that will help in locating the assets of the judgment debtor.

post-trial deposition
Device used to discover the assets of the judgment debtor through oral examination under oath.

supplementary proceedings
The methods used to acquire information about the judgment debtor to enforce a judgment; for example, the post-trial deposition.

supersedeas bond
Bond filed by the judgment debtor to secure the amount of the judgment while the execution of that judgment is stayed pending post-trial motions.

execution
The process of carrying out or enforcing a judgment.

Postjudgment interrogatories, however, have disadvantages. The debtor can draft answers carefully to provide as little information as possible. If the debtor refuses to answer, the court must be asked to compel an answer, causing further delay.

As is true in discovery, the interrogatories could be joined with a **post-trial request for production of documents,** or the request could be submitted independently. The request can obtain a variety of documents including copies of tax returns, financial records and reports, bank statements, insurance policies, certificates of title, deeds, loan applications, mortgages, and others.

A more expensive and time-consuming process is the use of the **post-trial deposition.** This procedure is known as a *creditor's examination.* It can be used to bring the judgment debtor or other individuals knowledgeable of the debtor's finances into a setting where they can be questioned under oath about the location of the debtor's assets. Being able to question the debtor and others directly provides the opportunity for flexibility and immediate pursuit of newly raised areas of inquiry. Draft a list of those to be deposed and have them subpoenaed as approved by the attorney. Assist in preparing post-trial depositions in the same way you prepare for the discovery deposition. These procedures are referred to as **supplementary proceedings** and may be used before any action is filed to enforce a judgment or as part of separate actions to collect on the judgment. Sanctions can be imposed for failing to comply with these devices, including the contempt powers of the court. State rules and statutes should be carefully consulted before using any of these devices.

OBTAINING THE ASSETS OF THE JUDGMENT DEBTOR

Introduction

With a detailed list of the debtor's assets and consultation with the attorney, all that remains is the selection of an appropriate procedure and the drafting of the relevant documents. The easiest and least expensive collection method is to write a letter to the debtor. Keep in mind that the Federal Fair Trade Debt Collections Practices Act (15 U.S.C. § 1692) applies to attorneys. If the letter is to collect the judgment for a personal or consumer debt (as opposed to a business debt), consult the federal statute and locate form letters specific to collecting that type of debt. Exhibit 12:7 is an example.[4] Exhibit 12:8 is an example of a follow-up letter.[5]

If the letters fail, procedures used to enforce a judgment include execution, garnishment, and domestication of a judgment. None of these actions may be taken, however, as long as any stay has been granted by the court on the execution of the judgment. Under Federal Rule 62 and parallel state rules, an automatic stay is imposed for the first ten days after judgment, and the court may grant longer stays in its discretion, including a stay pending the outcome of an appeal. The judgment debtor may have to post a **supersedeas bond** to secure the amount of the judgment during the stay. Absent a stay, enforcement actions may be taken.

Execution

Execution is the process of carrying out or enforcing a judgment. Some judgments are self-executing. For example, a divorce decree or a quiet title action requires no further action. Some judgments require the transferring of title or a deed. When the party obligated to execute the transfer refuses to do so, the court may, on application, appoint a trustee to execute the necessary documents. In other states the court has the power to order done that which the judgment says should have been done. The court order has the effect of the deed when properly recorded.[6]

EXHIBIT 12:7 ▪ First Letter to Judgment Debtor

JONES & SMITH
ATTORNEYS AT LAW
100 MAIN STREET
ANYWHERE, U.S.A. 00000
(000) 000-0000

[*date*]_____

Mr. Henry I. Judgment-Debtor
110 North Sycamore Street
Anywhere, U.S.A. 00000

Dear Mr. Judgment-Debtor:

A judgment was entered against you in the _____ Court of _____ on [*date*], _____ in favor of our client _____ , in the amount of $ _____ . This amount is still owing to our client on account of the judgment.

Please call this office to make arrangements for payment of this amount. By making such arrangements now, you will avoid the inconvenience, embarrassment, and expense of further legal action against you to collect the judgment.

We trust you will give this matter your immediate attention.

Very truly yours,

JONES & SMITH

By _____

Attorneys for _____

cc: [*Client*]
     Clerk, _____ Court

Source: Reprinted with permission of West Group.

A writ of execution is a device used to enforce a judgment for money. Both federal courts and the individual state courts rely on the procedure set out in the rules and statutes of that state. Check the local practice for the correct procedure. Most states have a local source book on the forms and procedures for collections.

Typically, the judgment creditor has a list of the property of the defendant needed to satisfy the judgment. A writ of execution is obtained from the court specifying the property to seize and sell **(levy).** A public officer, usually the sheriff, locates the property and physically or constructively seizes it. Only the property needed to satisfy the judgment may be seized. A procedure carefully outlined in state law is followed by which the property is sold. Some delay in the sale is common to give the debtor a chance to receive notice of the levy. The property is sold at auction or other sale, and proceeds are used to pay off the costs of execution, the judgment, and any interest accrued on the principal of the judgment since entry of the judgment. Any remaining proceeds are returned to the judgment debtor. Exhibit 12:9 is an example of a writ of execution.[7] They are often available in preprinted form from the court.

levy
To seize and sell property of the judgment debtor as specified by the court to satisfy the judgment.

EXHIBIT 12:8 ■ Follow-Up Letter to Judgment Debtor

JONES & SMITH
ATTORNEYS AT LAW
100 MAIN STREET
ANYWHERE, U.S.A. 00000
(000) 000-0000

[*date*]____

Mr. Henry I. Judgment-Debtor
110 North Sycamore Street
Anywhere, U.S.A. 00000

Dear Mr. Judgment-Debtor:

Enclosed is a certified copy of the judgment which was entered against you in the _____ Court of _____ on [*date*], ____ in the amount of $ _____ . We have not yet received any response to our letter to you dated _____, asking you to make arrangements for payment of this amount. Therefore, our client _____ has instructed us that, unless we hear from you by [*date*], ____, we are to take further legal action against you. Such legal action may include seizure and sale at public auction of your nonexempt personal property, including your automobile; garnishment of a portion of your wages from your employer; and issuance of a subpoena to compel you to testify in court concerning all your assets, in default of which you may be arrested and punished by fine or imprisonment for contempt of court.

Please pay to our office not less than $ _____ by [*date*]____. Otherwise, we will have no choice but to take further legal action against you.

Very truly yours,

JONES & SMITH
By _____
Attorneys for _____

cc: [*Client*]

Source: Reprinted with permission of West Group.

---

receivership
Placement of the assets of a business or an individual under the control of a court-appointed receiver who will protect those assets to pay a debt.

garnishment
The process of trying to reach the assets of a judgment debtor that are in the possession of a third party in order to satisfy the judgment.

In some cases, such as where the judgment debtor owns business property, placing the property into **receivership** may be preferable to selling it. In this procedure, the court appoints a receiver who sees to it that the judgment is paid out of the regular income of the business until the debt is satisfied. It allows the debtor to maintain the business beyond payment of the debt unless the court orders the sale of the property.

Garnishment

Garnishment is used to obtain property of the debtor held by or owed to the debtor by a third person. Property typically garnished includes money in bank accounts or wages regularly owed the debtor. The judgment creditor generally applies for a writ of garnishment. The writ is served with a summons by the sheriff or some other public official on the third person **(garnishee),** and directs that person to disclose

---

EXHIBIT 12:9 ■ Writ of Execution for Specific Property (or Its Value)

IN THE _____ COURT OF _____

_____,
Plaintiff

v.   No. _____

_____,
Defendant

WRIT OF EXECUTION

The State of _____ to the Sheriff of _____ County:

On [*date*], in this case plaintiff _____ recovered a judgment against defendant _____ for the title and possession of the following property with costs of suit, which to date amount to $_____:

Property	**Valued at**
	$

Therefore, you are commanded to seize the above described property and deliver possession of it to the judgment creditor _____ and to cause to be made the sum of $_____ for payment of the costs adjudged against the judgment debtor _____ and the further costs of executing this writ from property the judgment debtor owns subject to execution.

And in case a delivery of the above described property or any part of it cannot be had, you are further commanded to cause to be made the value of such undelivered property from property the judgment debtor owns subject to execution.

Bring the money [and the property] together with this process, showing how you have executed it, before this Court at _____, within _____ days.

Witness the Honorable _____, [Chief] Judge of the _____ Court of _____, on [*date*].

Issued on [*date*].

ATTEST: _____

Clerk of the _____
Court of _____
[*Seal*]

Source: Reprinted with permission of West Group.

---

the amount of money being held by the garnishee. The garnishee usually has twenty days to respond to the summons. Once the amount is determined, an order for garnishment is requested and a writ issued for seizure of the property or for a lien on the property preventing its transfer to the debtor. When wages are involved, federal law exempts 75 percent of the employee's disposable earnings. Disposable earnings are all earnings less withholding taxes, Social Security, and other lawful deductions. Exhibit 12:10 is an example of an application and affidavit for a writ of garnishment.[8] Exhibit 12:11 is the writ of garnishment.[9]

garnishee
The third party who is directed to surrender property owed to the judgment debtor to satisfy the judgment.

Domesticating a Judgment

When a judgment is entered and recorded, it is good for a period of ten years in most jurisdictions. The recording of the judgment notifies all other creditors and potential buyers that a lien exists on the debtor's property. Most property will not be sold until all such liens are cleared. For a nominal fee, most judgments can be renewed. This procedure becomes particularly useful when a debtor is currently unable to pay the judgment but comes into money or property at a later date.

When the debtor has property in another jurisdiction, particularly another state, creditors can levy on that property by *domesticating the judgment*. In other words, the judgment from one state may be entered into a court in another state,

EXHIBIT 12:10 ■ Application and Affidavit for Writ of Garnishment After Judgment

IN THE _____ COURT OF _____

_____,
Plaintiff and Garnishor
v.
_____,
Defendant and Garnishee
and
_____,
Defendant

No. _____

APPLICATION AND AFFIDAVIT FOR WRIT OF GARNISHMENT AFTER JUDGMENT

_____, being duly sworn, deposes and says:

1. My name is _____; I am the _____ of plaintiff _____; and I am duly authorized to make this affidavit on plaintiff's behalf.
2. The applicant, _____, is plaintiff in Case Number _____, styled _____ v. _____, on the docket of the _____ Court of _____ ("the main suit"). The garnishee is _____, whose address is _____.
3. In the main suit, applicant has a valid subsisting judgment, rendered on [*date*], against _____ in the amount of $_____ with interest theron at a rate of __% per year until paid. There is due on the judgment the sum of $_____ which is uncollected, unpaid and unsatisfied [*or* other factual assertation]. Within my knowledge the defendant in the main suit does not have in his possession in this state property subject to execution sufficient to satisfy the judgment.
4. This writ of garnishment is not sued out to injure either the defendant or the garnishee.
5. I have reason to and do believe that garnishee _____, who resides in _____ County, State of _____, is indebted to the defendant, _____, or has possession or custody of effects belonging to the defendant. The source of my information and belief is _____.
6. [*It may be advisable to use this clause except in unusual situations.*] Applicant requests that the defendant, _____, be given notice and an opportunity to appear at a hearing before the court for the purpose of allowing him to oppose this application and to introduce evidence why the writ of garnishment applied for should not issue.
   [*OR: Alternate, for use in unusual situations*] The following facts constitute an unusual situation that justifies issuance of the writ without prior notice to the defendant and without a prior hearing: _____. Applicant requests that defendant be given notice of the issuance of the writ and an opportunity to appear at a hearing before the court for the purpose of allowing him to oppose the issuance of the writ and to introduce evidence why the writ should be dissolved.
7. Applicant requests that [after the hearing] the court issue a writ of garnishment against the garnishee, that a copy be delivered to the defendant, and for further proceeding thereon as provided by law.
8. A copy of this application has been mailed to _____ at _____ on [*date*].

_____

[*Acknowledgment*]

Source: Reprinted with permission of West Group.

and all rights will attach to that judgment as if it had been initially obtained in the foreign jurisdiction. This area is another in which a paralegal's investigation of assets can be valuable. The procedure involves locating the court that has jurisdiction over the debtor's property and filing an application in the foreign court.

EXHIBIT 12:11 ▪ Writ of Garnishment

IN THE _____ COURT OF _____

_____,
Plaintiff and Garnishor
v.

_____,
Defendant and Garnishee
and   No. _____

_____,
Defendant

WRIT OF GARNISHMENT

To: [*Name and Address*] Garnishee:

1. ___ claims that he is plaintiff in the _____ Court of _____ in cause no. _____ on the docket of that court, styled _____ v. _____, defendant, in which he has a valid, subsisting and uncollected judgment against the defendant for the sum of $_____ with interest theron at the rate of ____% per year [*date*], and costs of suit.
2. Plaintiff has applied for a writ of garnishment against you, [*Name*].
3. You are hereby commanded to appear before this court at [*date*] [*or:* on ___ ___. m. on the Monday next following the expiration of _____ days from the date of service hereof]. You must then answer upon oath what, if anything, you are then indebted to [*Defendant*] and were when this writ was served upon you; and what effects, if any, of [*Defendant*] you have in your possession, and had when this writ was served; and what other persons, if any, within your knowledge, are indebted to [*Defendant*], or have effects belonging to [*Defendant*] in their possession. Answer as the law directs.
4. The officer serving this writ is directed to serve a true copy also on _____, defendant in the main action.

Dated and issued on _____.

ATTEST: _____
Clerk of the _____
Court of _____

_____
Judge Presiding

Source: Reprinted with permission of West Group.

The application includes statements that enforcement of the judgment is not barred by the statute of limitations in either state, that no stay of execution on the judgment is in effect, that the judgment remains unsatisfied, that no other action based on the judgment is pending, and that no judgment based on the original judgment has been previously entered in the foreign state. In addition the name and address of the debtor and the judgment creditor are included. An authenticated, **exemplified,** or otherwise certified copy of the original judgment should be attached.[10]

Under Article 4, § 1 of the U.S. Constitution, the foreign state must give "full faith and credit" to the judgment of a sister state. Once domesticated, the judgment can be entered with the foreign state in the same fashion as the original state.

exemplified
Authenticated as a true copy, as an official transcript to be used as evidence.

The judgment debtor may challenge the judgment on the basis that the original court lacked jurisdiction or that the judgment has been paid. The burden of proof, however, rests with the judgment debtor. There is no retrial of the original issues. Judgment may be ordered in a similar manner in foreign countries, but in such cases the procedures may vary somewhat.

Transferring federal court judgments for enforcement is quite simple. Title 28 U.S.C. at § 1963 permits the registering of a judgment from a federal court in any other federal court. Once registered, the judgment is treated as a local judgment.

Keeping Track of Collections of Judgment

Each case file should have a sheet kept at the front or top of the file that indicates the case, court, judgment, attorney, and the progress in collecting the judgment. If the judgment was not paid soon after its entry, a file record sheet should indicate all types of enforcement action taken and what has been collected on each action to date. You may decide to computerize the file record sheet.

You may also choose to keep a master list of all cases in which judgments have not been satisfied. Calendar all judgment expiration dates so that renewals of those judgments can be sought if the judgment remains unsatisfied. Review the unsatisfied judgment list with the attorney on a periodic basis to see if additional action needs to be taken.

APPEAL

INTRODUCTION

question of law
A point requiring the application or interpretation of statutes and case law, to be decided by a judge; for example, whether a statute is constitutional.

question of fact
A point decided on evidence; for example, whether the traffic light was red.

The purpose of an appeal is to ask a higher court to review the decisions of the trial judge that the person appealing believes are erroneous. The appellate court will review questions of law only, not questions of fact decided by the trial court judge or jury. A **question of law** is a point requiring the application and interpretation of statutes and case law. For example, was the statute in question constitutional? Did the lower judge erroneously instruct the jury on the burden of proof? On the other hand, a **question of fact** is a point decided on evidence. For example, was the traffic light red, or was the contract signed? In some issues, such as whether the verdict goes against the weight of the evidence, the appellate judge must review the evidence, but the question remains a question of law—whether the verdict was so erroneous that, as a matter of law, it must be reversed. Appeal has also become an effective tool against large jury awards.

Most parties choose not to appeal because appeals are expensive, and the majority of appellants are unsuccessful. The appeal, however, is an important part of our checks and balances system that guarantees a person the right to have a lower court's decision reviewed if there is a reasonable basis for the appeal. If the party did not raise an issue by objection or motion at the trial, the issue is waived for purposes of appeal.

The person bringing the appeal is called the appellant; the person defending against the appeal is called the appellee or respondent. Appellate procedure generally involves the following stages. The appellant must file a notice of appeal that is conveyed to all the other parties. The appellant is responsible to see that a transcript of the pertinent aspects of the trial is ordered, prepared, and sent to the appellate court. Briefs are filed by both parties, stating the facts, the issues to be addressed, and the arguments and authorities on the issues. Oral arguments are presented by all parties during which the judges may ask questions. The judges meet to discuss the case, and an opinion is written. The appellate court may affirm, modify, or reverse the judgment of the trial court. Even if the appellate judges rule that the trial judge was in error, the appellate court will not alter the judgment unless the error substantially affected the verdict in the case. A lesser degree of error will be declared **harmless error.**

    The study of appeals in all their complexity is beyond the scope of this text, so the following discussion is simply an overview of the fundamentals in the process.

harmless error
An error found to have occurred at the trial court by the appellate court, but insufficient to substantially affect the verdict of the case, and therefore, insufficient to overturn the verdict.

APPELLATE PROCEDURE CHECKLIST

Appellate procedure is fairly standardized in the federal courts, but it varies among states. Research the applicable state rules and adhere to them. Following is a list of the significant procedural steps and deadlines for the Federal Rules of Appellate Procedure (FRAP). These rules are amplified further by the local rules (LRs) and internal operating procedures (IOPs) of each respective circuit of the U.S. Court of Appeals.

- ☐ Consult with the attorney for go-ahead on the appeal.
- ☐ Develop a case appeal log for recording compliance with all requirements of the appellate process.
- ☐ File a petition for leave to appeal from *interlocutory order* pursuant to 28 U.S.C. § 1292(b). (Appellee has seven days after service of petition to file opposition, FRAP 5.)
- ☐ For post-trial appeals, verify that a judgment or order has been entered [FRAP 4(a)(7); FRCP 58, 79(a)].
- ☐ Draft a notice of appeal (see following form).
- ☐ File the notice of appeal within thirty days of entry of judgment or order, or within sixty days if the United States or an officer or agency thereof is a party [FRAP 3, 4(a)(1)]. Pay fees.
- ☐ File a bond for the cost of the appeal or a supersedeas bond if the execution of judgment is stayed [FRAP 7 and 8]. Seek stay or injunction pending appeal.
- ☐ File with the court of appeals a statement naming each party represented on appeal by the attorney within ten days after filing the notice of appeal [FRAP 12(b)].
- ☐ Order a transcript of the trial proceedings (pertinent parts or pertinent videotape if so recorded) from the court reporter within ten days after filing the notice of appeal or entry of an order disposing of the last motion such as a motion for a new trial, whichever is later. File a copy of the order with the clerk of district court [FRAP 10(b)(1)]. Unless the entire transcript is ordered, file (within ten days of notice or entry of an order) a statement of issues on appeal. Notify all other parties of the issues on appeal and the parts of the transcript ordered so appellee can designate other parts of the record needed for appeal within ten days of service of the order and statement of the issues. Appellant must order the added parts within the next ten days [FRAP 10(b)(3)]. Parties may stipulate to omit certain parts of the record.
- ☐ See to it that the reporter files a transcript with the clerk of district court within thirty days of the date ordered by appellant [FRAP 11(b)]. See that the record is complete (pleadings, exhibits filed in district court, transcript or parts thereof, and certified copies of docket entries), prepared by the clerk, and submitted by the clerk of court to the court of appeals.

"The young judge spends the first third of his life in fear that he might be reversed by the court of appeals, the middle third in the conviction that the court of appeals was always wrong, and the last third not caring whether it was right or wrong."

—Patrick Devlin, English jurist, *The Judge*, 1979.

Check to see if the record is sent by the clerk. The clerk of the court of appeals will docket the case upon receipt of the notice of appeal and the docket entries (FRAP 12).

☐ Send to appellee a designation of the parts of the record to be included in the appendix within ten days of the filing of the record, unless there is an agreement on the contents (FRAP 30) or the alternative method of filing the appendix is chosen [FRAP 30(c)].

☐ File all papers with the clerk of the court of appeals by mail addressed to the clerk. Some courts of appeal permit electronic filing. All papers must arrive within the required time limit. Briefs are considered timely if mailed before expiration of the time limit [FRAP 25(a)]. Proof of service should be filed with the papers [FRAP 25(d)]. Rule 35(a) now authorizes the adoption of local appellate rules to require electronic filing. Heed rules regarding redactions for privacy and security concerns.

☐ Service on the party or the party's counsel may be personal, by mail, or by commercial carrier.

☐ File a motion for extension of time if good cause can be shown [FRAP 26(b)]. The time for filing a notice of appeal may not be extended.

☐ Draft the brief and appendix according to the strict specifications in FRAP 28, 29, 30, 32, and 32.1 (unpublished opinions).

☐ File and serve appellant's brief and appendix within forty days after the date on which the record is filed. If the brief is not filed on time, the appellee may move for dismissal of the appeal. FRAP 31 calls for filing 25 copies of the brief, but check the respective local rule because the required copies often vary.

☐ File for an extension of time, if necessary.

☐ Note the date that appellee's brief is due. (Appellee has thirty days after receipt of appellant's brief to file and serve brief. [FRAP 31(a)].

☐ Check the opponent's brief for accurate statements of fact, case holdings and citations, and accurate recitation of the record.

☐ File and serve the appellant's reply brief within fourteen days after service of the appellee's brief [FRAP 31(a)]. Double-check all case citations and citations of the record before filing.

☐ Be sure all time limits are on the docket deadline control calendar.

☐ Record notice from the clerk of court whether oral argument is to be heard, and if so, the time, place, and duration of each side's oral argument [FRAP 34(b)]. Notify the attorney and see that all deadlines are calendared.

☐ Assist in the preparation of oral argument as requested by the attorney. Prepare an oral argument notebook.

☐ Arrange delivery of any exhibits to the court set up prior to oral argument, and removal immediately after argument.

☐ Attend oral argument to assist the attorney if requested (FRAP 34).

☐ Note the receipt of opinion and judgment (FRAP 36) and convey it to the attorney.

☐ Submit an itemized and certified bill of costs to the clerk with proof of service within fourteen days after entry of the judgment. Objection to the bill of costs must be filed within ten days of service of the bill [FRAP 39(d)].

☐ Draft and file a petition for rehearing if so directed by the attorney. The petition must be filed within fourteen days after entry of the judgment, forty-five days if United States or agency or officer is a party [FRAP 40(a)]. The petition should follow the form prescribed by Rule 32(a) and served according to Rule 31(b).

☐ Consider with attorney the filing of a motion to stay the mandate (direction of the Court of Appeals based on the judgment) pending an application to the U.S. Supreme Court for a writ of certiorari [FRAP 41(b)]. The motion must be filed within twenty-one days of the entry of judgment. Note that Appellate Rule 27(d)(1)(E) requires that the typeface and type style requirements for motions must comply with rules 32(a)(5) and (6), respectively.

Exhibit 12:12 is a notice of appeal, Exhibit 12:13 is a designation of record on appeal,[11] Exhibit 12:14 is a motion for enlargement of time,[12] and Exhibit 12:15 is a notice of filing of brief.[13]

ASSISTING IN THE APPEAL

Introduction

The checklist spells out the tasks you can and should perform. This section will focus on a few tasks that require some amplification.

Deadline Control and Appeal Management

The experienced paralegal can assume the role of appeals manager. To prepare for this role, study the appellate rules meticulously and record all deadlines, formats, and procedures. If you have questions, ask the appropriate clerk of court. An appeal program sheet should be kept for each case. Overall management can be achieved by using a master sheet with all pending appellate cases and points of progress for

---

EXHIBIT 12:12 ▪ Notice of Appeal

FORM 1. NOTICE OF APPEAL TO A COURT OF APPEALS FROM A JUDGMENT OR ORDER OF A DISTRICT COURT

United States District Court for the
_____ District of _____

File Number _____

Plaintiff
v.   Notice of Appeal
Defendant

Notice is hereby given that (here name all parties taking the appeal), (plaintiffs) (defendants) in the above named case,* hereby appeal to the United States Court of Appeals for the _____ Circuit (from the final judgment) (from an order (describing it)) entered in this action on the _____ day of _____, 2 ____.

(s) _____

Attorney for _____

Address: _____

*See Rule 3(c) for permissible ways of identifying appellants.

EXHIBIT 12:13 ▪ Designation of Record on Appeal

IN THE UNITED STATES DISTRICT COURT FOR
THE _____ DISTRICT OF _____ _____ DIVISION

ABC _____
                 Plaintiff

    v.   Civil Action No. _____

XYZ _____   Judge _____
                 Defendant

DESIGNATION OF RECORD ON APPEAL

Plaintiff ABC hereby designates the following docket entries, as set forth on the docket sheet of this civil action, to constitute the record on appeal.
   [Here insert a list which includes docket numbers, date and an identification of each docket entry which is being designated]

                                    Respectfully submitted,

                                    _____
                                    J. Doe, Attorney for Plaintiff

                  [Add Proof of Service]

Source: Reprinted with permission of West Group.

EXHIBIT 12:14 ▪ Motion for Enlargement of Time—Court of Appeals

IN THE UNITED STATES COURT OF APPEALS FOR THE _____ CIRCUIT

ABC   _____,
             Plaintiff–Appellant
                v.   Appeal No. _____

XYZ   _____,
            Defendant–Appellee

Appeal From the United States District Court

For the _____ District of _____ ,

_____ Division, Civil Action No. _____

MOTION FOR ENLARGEMENT OF TIME

Appellant ABC respectfully moves for an order extending the time for filing its Brief by an additional _____ days.
   The basis for this request is that Appellant's attorney has been unable to complete the Brief within the requisite forty days because of the length of the record and because of the loss of "working days" due to legal holidays *[insert any additional reasons]*.

                                    Respectfully submitted,

                                    _____
                                    J. Doe, Attorney for Appellant
                  [Add Proof of Service]

Source: Reprinted with permission of West Group.

EXHIBIT 12:15 ■ Appellate Brief—Notice of Filing

IN THE UNITED STATES COURT OF APPEALS FOR THE _____ CIRCUIT

ABC _____ ,
    Plaintiff–Appellant
        v.
                        Appeal No. _____
XYZ _____ ,
    Defendant–Appellee

Appeal From the United States District Court

For the _____ District of _____ ,

_____ Division, Civil Action No. _____

NOTICE OF FILING OF BRIEF

Plaintiff–Appellant _____ hereby files twenty-five copies of its brief and ten copies of the Appendix and hereby serves two copies of its brief and one copy of the Appendix on Appellee.

Respectfully submitted

_____

J. Doe, Attorney for Plaintiff—Appellant

[*Add Proof of Service*]

Source: Reprinted with permission of West Group.

---

each case. Regular calendared reviews by all involved paralegals and attorneys can result in thorough and effective appellate management. With a little experience, the task will be easier and your benefit to the firm enhanced.

Research

The paralegal is frequently assigned to research potential theories for the appeal, locate authority in support of the theory, and verify the accuracy of all citations used by all parties in their briefs and oral arguments. You can frequently turn up misuse of authority by checking whether the authority cited actually stands for the principle of law being asserted, and whether the facts are as presented. Eliminating erroneous citations from one's own brief can only strengthen it, while being able to call the court's attention to misuse of authority by the opponent can be effective in challenging the overall credibility of their argument. Note that unpublished opinions issued after January 1, 2007, may be cited in federal appeals; earlier unpublished opinions may not be cited unless previously authorized by local court rule. Check state appellate rules on citing unpublished opinions.

Verifying the Record

Before the record is sent to the appellate court, review it to verify that the reporter has accurately portrayed what happened at the trial. If a partial transcript has been requested, verification of the accuracy of the key parts is particularly important. Further, determine whether everything needed in the record is ready to be sent by the clerk.

Assisting with the Appellate Brief

The appellate brief is a formal document drafted to specific standards that sets out the pertinent facts, legal questions, the legal argument addressing those questions, and legal authorities in support of that argument. The brief is often accompanied by an appendix of exhibits, relevant transcript sections, and other materials.

Each law office has a different approach to what the paralegal does here. Some firms do not use paralegals in brief preparation; others utilize experienced paralegals to prepare a full rough-draft brief that is reviewed by the attorney and then honed to a sharp edge.

If asked to research the brief, verify and update authorities on each key issue. Double-check each citation stated in the record and each citation to the record. Extract from the transcript those key lines that lie at the heart of the appeal. In addition, you may be asked to organize and write initial drafts of arguments based on the authorities. Good writing and organizational skills are needed at this stage. Observe the format and style of one or two appellate briefs previously filed in the particular court in question. If a brief of the exact same point can be found, it will substantially reduce the work (and also illustrate the value of keeping a brief bank on various topics). In reviewing these materials you will learn rules of drafting such as state your strongest argument first and use clear subheadings that state arguments. Relevance, fairness, and accuracy should characterize the statement of the facts, and crystal clarity and conciseness, the argument. Appellate handbooks and materials on brief writing provide more techniques and should be reviewed prior to writing the rough draft.

You should assume responsibility for organizing and indexing the brief. Old briefs are of great value here, but since court rules and specifications change, the latest edition of the appellate rules and specifications for briefs should be obtained. The Federal Rules of Appellate Procedure 28, 30, and 32 set the following specifications for briefs.

Rule 28 states that the appellant's brief shall contain a corporate disclosure statement (Rule 26.1), a table of contents, a table of authorities (cases listed in alphabetical order and statutes and other authorities cited to page of brief), a statement of jurisdiction, a statement of the issues on appeal, and a statement of the case including its nature, previous proceedings, and disposition. In addition, the brief shall have a statement of the relevant facts (with appropriate references to the record), a concise summary of the argument, an argument based on legal authority, a short conclusion stating the precise relief sought, and a certificate of word or line number compliance, if required by Rule 32(a)(7).

Parties shall be referred to as "plaintiff" and "defendant" or by name rather than as "appellant" or "appellee." References in the briefs to the record shall be to the pages of the brief's appendix at which those parts appear. Relevant statutes, rules, regulations, and so on, or parts thereof, shall be reproduced in the brief, in an addendum, or supplied to the court in pamphlet form [Rule 28(d-f)].

The appellee's brief shall be the same, except that statements of jurisdiction, the issues, the case, the facts, and the standard of review need not be made unless the appellee is dissatisfied with the statement of the appellant [FRAP 28(b)].

Appellant's and appellee's briefs shall not exceed thirty pages, and the reply briefs fifteen pages [unless they comply with Rule 32(a)(7)(B or (C)], excluding the table of contents, tables of citations, and any addendum. Check for the current limits on the number of words permitted. Rule 30 requires the appellant to prepare and file the appendix to the brief containing the relevant docket entries in the proceeding; relevant portions of the pleadings, charge, findings, or opinion; the judgment, order, or decision in question; and any other parts of the record for the court.

> Nothing is so easy as to be wise after the event.
>
> —CHIEF JUSTICE JERVIS, c. 1859.

Unless filing is to be deferred, the appellant shall serve and file the appendix with the brief. Ten copies of the appendix shall be filed with the clerk, and one copy shall be served on each party.

The parties are encouraged to agree as to the contents of the appendix [FRAP 30(b)]. If they cannot, the appellant shall, not later than ten days after filing the record, serve on the appellee a designation of the parts of the record that the appellant intends to include in the appendix and a statement of the issues for appeal. The appellee may, within ten days after receipt of the designation, serve upon the appellant a designation of additional parts to be included by the appellant.

The cost of producing the appendix shall initially be paid by the appellant unless otherwise agreed. If parts of the record designated by the appellee for inclusion seem unnecessary to the appellant, the appellee shall pay for including those parts. The cost of producing the appendix shall be taxed as costs in the case. If either party shall cause matters to be included in the appendix unnecessarily, the court may impose the cost of producing such parts on the party [FRAP 30(b)].

The court may permit the appendix to be filed after the brief in specific cases. In such cases the appendix may be filed twenty-one days after service of the brief of the appellee [FRAP 30(c)].

The appendix shall include a table of its contents with page references. When transcripts are included in the appendix, the transcript page shall be indicated in brackets immediately before the matter that is set out. Omissions must be indicated by asterisks. Captions, subscriptions, acknowledgments, and so forth shall be omitted.

Exhibits shall be included in a separate volume. Four copies shall be filed with the appendix and one copy served on each party [FRAP 30(c)].

A court of appeals may by rule or in specific cases dispense with the appendix and permit appeals to be heard on the original record with such copies of the record [FRAP 30(f)].

Rule 32 sets out the form of the brief. Briefs and appendices must be clearly reproduced on opaque, unglazed, white paper. Photos, illustrations, and other matter need only be a good copy of the original. Pages shall be 8 1/2 by 11 inches, double spaced, with one-inch margins on all sides. The cover of the appellant's brief should be *blue,* the appellee's *red,* an intervenor's *green,* any reply brief *gray,* and the cover of the appendix, if separately printed, *white.* The front covers, if separately printed, shall contain the name of the court; the case number; the title of the case; the nature of the proceeding; the lower court, agency, or board; the title of the document; and the names, addresses, and phone numbers of counsel. Complete requirements can be found in Rule 32 and parallel state statutes.

Exhibit 12:16 is a skeletal example of the proper order and format of an appellate brief to be filed in the U.S. Court of Appeals.

Oral Argument

The paralegal assists with oral argument by preparing an oral argument notebook in close consultation with the attorney. The notebook is organized to contain major arguments with references to supporting legal authority, applicable public policy, indexes to the most significant references in the record, major case authorities, copies of important statutes, jury instructions, and other key materials for quick reference.

You should attend the oral argument if possible. Your familiarity with the case, gained through months and years of work, can assist the attorney at significant points in the argument, especially in responding to unanticipated points made by the opposition or questions from the court.

EXHIBIT 12:16 ▪ Sample Appellate Brief

IN THE UNITED STATES COURT OF APPEALS
FOR THE _____ JUDICIAL CIRCUIT
Case No. _____

_____
_____,
      Appellant
  v.
_____
_____,
      Appellee

On Appeal from the United States District Court for the _____ District of _____
BRIEF AND ARGUMENT OF APPELLANT

(Attorney)_____
(Address)_____
Attorney for_____

(Table of Contents Page)

TABLE OF CONTENTS

(Authorities Page)

TABLE OF AUTHORITIES CITED

Cases*	Page

*In alphabetical order. [These cites are fictional for purposes of illustration.]

EXHIBIT 12:16 ■ Sample Appellate Brief *(continued)*

Rules

Statutes

Treatises

STATEMENT OF JURISDICTION

The basis for subject matter jurisdiction at the district court for the _____ district of _____ is _____. Appellate jurisdiction for . . .

STATEMENT OF THE ISSUES

The Honorable Walter F. DAVIS, Judge of the Northern District of Columbia, it is asserted made three errors at or following the trial in this case. The errors alleged are stated below:

1. _____

2. _____

3. _____

STATEMENT OF THE CASE*

*(FED. R. APP. P. 28(a)(6) "a statement of the case briefly indicating the nature of the case, the course of proceedings, and its disposition in the court below.")

This case is on appeal from the district court's ruling . . .

STATEMENT OF THE FACTS*

*(7) a statement of the facts relevant to the issues submitted for review with appropriate references to the record [Rule 28(a)(7).

In February of __, Ann Forrester, a brilliant and creative teacher and mother of two, was . . .

SUMMARY OF ARGUMENT*

*[FED. R. APP. P. 28(a)(8)]

ARGUMENT*

*[FED. R. APP. P. 28(a)(A)(B)].

I. BECAUSE THE JURY VERDICT WAS CONTRARY TO THE GREAT WEIGHT OF THE EVIDENCE, THE TRIAL COURT ERRED IN DENYING PLAINTIFF'S MOTION FOR JUDGMENT AS A MATTER OF LAW.

The law on when a motion for judgment as a matter of law is to be granted was reiterated in the recent Supreme Court case of *Abrams v. Pure Manufacturing, Inc.,* 500 U.S. 312, 33 L. Ed. 2d 419 (1995). The court stated the rule to be:

When the evidence in a case demonstrates . . .

(continued)

EXHIBIT 12:16 ■ Sample Appellate Brief (*continued*)

CONCLUSION*

*(10)a short conclusion stating the precise relief sought [FED. R. APP. P. 28(a)(10)]. Under the rule of law stated in *Abrams v. Pure Manufacturing, Inc.,* the plaintiff must prove . . .

CERTIFICATE OF COMPLIANCE*

"(11) the certificate of compliance, if required by Rule 32(a)(7)."

APPENDIX

Page of Transcript		Page of Appendix
T–1	Amended Complaint	1
T–3	Answer	4
T–110	Motion for Judgment as a Matter of Law	8
T–19–21	Relevant Testimony of Ms. Forrester	9–11

SUMMARY

In this chapter you have learned the function, procedure, and forms for post-trial practice. Paralegals often research and draft two post-trial motions. A motion for judgment as a matter of law, if granted, overturns the verdict as going against the weight of the evidence. A motion for a new trial because of procedural or other errors may be combined with the motion for judgment as a matter of law. A bill of costs is calculated and drafted by the prevailing party.

The paralegal for the prevailing party may assist the attorney in gaining the enforcement of the judgment. This process may be started in the initial stages of

---

White, Wilson & McDuff
ATTORNEYS AT LAW
FEDERAL PLAZA BUILDING, SUITE 700
THIRD AND MARKET STREETS
LEGALVILLE, COLUMBIA 00000
(111) 555-0000

MEMO TO: Terry Salyer

FROM: Isadora Pearlman

Your preliminary work in post-trial procedure has been successful; you are now ready to assist Mr. White in the appeal of Ms. Forrester's case.

Better than that, you have come to the end of your training period. Now you have the skills to assist our attorneys in the variety of litigation cases that will be assigned to you. You know how to research what you need on your own. Always remember to ask questions and strive to improve your knowledge.

You are ready to be a highly professional litigation paralegal. Congratulations and good luck!

the case to guarantee that the property or funds will be available to cover any judgment. Notice of an expected judgment against the property is filed as a lis pendens. Enforcement procedures are more commonly employed after judgments, and involve investigating the location and amount of the debtor's assets through a variety of techniques. Interrogatories, post-trial depositions, writ of execution, garnishment, and domestication of the judgment may be used.

Appeal is a complex process allowing the losing party to seek appellate review of the trial judge's decision. Your role in this step includes developing a thorough appellate checklist, drafting and filing the necessary notice and other documents, maintaining a deadline control system, researching and drafting an appellate brief, and assisting at oral argument.

■ WORKBOOK

System Folder Assignments, other exercises, a chapter outline, a review test, and other study aids are located in the accompanying workbook.

■ HELPFUL WEB SITES

http://www.uscourts.gov/rules/newrules4.html
 rules and forms in effect for federal courts, including appellate procedure

http://www.ca6.uscourts.gov
 (substitute number of desired circuit) each respective circuit of the U.S. Courts of Appeals, LRs and IOPs, plus links to forms and other information

http://www.court.state.nd.us
 sample of a state court site that includes examples of appellate briefs

http://www.ftc.gov/ogc/briefs.htm
 sample of a federal site that includes examples of briefs

http://www.law.com
 has "practice centers" for specific areas of law practice, legal news, case law, and practical tools

http://www.briefreporter.com
 commercial brief reporting service

■ QUESTIONS FOR STUDY AND REVIEW

1. What are the two most common motions to have the judgment set aside? What are they called in your state practice? Define each of these motions.
2. What is a motion for remittitur? A motion for additur?
3. Rule 59 requires that a motion for a new trial must be filed within how many days of the entry of judgment? What is the rule in your state?
4. What role can you play in post-trial motion practice?
5. What is the bill of costs? What should you include when preparing a bill of costs? What form is used for a bill of costs?
6. What is a judgment debtor? A judgment creditor?
7. To what law does a judgment creditor in federal court look to enforce a federal judgment? A state judgment in state court?
8. What is a prejudgment remedy?
9. What is a lis pendens?
10. What does it mean to be judgment proof?
11. What are the various types of property subject to execution? What is exempt in your state?
12. What are the formal methods that can be used by a judgment creditor to determine the assets of the judgment debtor?
13. Identify and describe the common procedures for enforcing a judgment.
14. What is the step-by-step process for executing on property in your state?
15. Describe the steps in domesticating a judgment.
16. On what basis may a judgment debtor challenge an attempt to enforce a domesticated judgment?

17. What procedure is followed to have a judgment rendered in one federal jurisdiction honored in another federal jurisdiction?
18. List the various ways you can assist in the appeals process.

19. Describe the key steps and time limits in the federal appellate process and in your state's appellate process.
20. What are the key components of an appellate brief?
21. What are the key components of an oral argument notebook?

KEY TERMS

additur	judgment creditor	post-trial deposition	remittitur
execution	judgment debtor	post-trial request for	supersedeas bond
exemplified	judgment proof	production of documents	supplementary proceedings
garnishee	levy	question of fact	
garnishment	lis pendens	question of law	
harmless error	postjudgment interrogatory	receivership	

ENDNOTES

1. WEST'S LEGAL FORMS, §§ 16.77 and 16.78, v. 25 (2d ed., 1984).
2. STATSKY, TORTS: PERSONAL INJURY LITIGATION, 282-86 (1st ed., 1982).
3. WEST'S LEGAL FORMS, § 24.20, v. 11, (rev. 2d ed., 1994).
4. WEST'S LEGAL FORMS, § 21.2, v. 11 (rev. 2d ed., 1994).
5. Id., § 21.3.
6. BLANCHARD AND BLANCHARD, LITIGATION AND TRIAL PRACTICE FOR THE LEGAL ASSISTANT, 577 (5th ed., 2000).
7. WEST'S LEGAL FORMS, § 17.17, v. 11, (2d ed., 1984).
8. Id., § 22.6, v. 11 (rev. 2d ed., 1994).
9. WEST'S LEGAL FORMS, supra note 8, § 17.54, v. 11 (2d ed., 1984).
10. LARBALESTRIER, PARALEGAL TRAINING MANUAL, 228 (1981).
11. WEST'S LEGAL FORMS, § 17.19, v. 25, (2d ed., 1984).
12. Id., § 17.23.
13. Id., § 17.13.

 For additional resources visit our Web site at **http://www.westlegalstudies.com.**

SYSTEM FOLDER CONTENTS

The list of system folder contents follows the text and the system folder assignments in the workbook. It is a suggested list only. The system folder is a student-created portfolio and can be created by using the following outline. A good system folder has a table of contents, for which this list can be used, or a tab system for the quick location of any part of the system. Expand the system as you choose to accommodate local practice forms or alternative methods of practice.

QUICK REFERENCE INFORMATION

I. Preliminary and frequently used information
   A. Office structure and procedure
      1. Office structure chart
      2. Timekeeping forms and procedure
      3. Deadline control forms and procedure
   B. General information
      1. Court structure, names, addresses, and phone numbers for clerks of court and other persons frequently contacted
      2. Time deadline chart/rules and formula for computing time
      3. Statutes of limitations
      4. Case roadmap
      5. Ethics
      6. Professional organization information

INTERVIEW

I. Client interview
   A. Task and purpose
   B. Interview plan
      1. Interview plan checklist
      2. Steps in interview plan
         a. Interview forms and checklists
         b. List of information for client to bring to interview
         c. Appointment confirmation letter
         d. List of ethical considerations
         e. List of interview techniques
         f. Checklist of information to be given client at initial interview
         g. Fee arrangement
         h. Release of information forms (HIPAA)
         i. Checklist for preparing interview site
         j. Sample interview summary

INVESTIGATION

I. Investigation
   A. Purposes of investigation
   B. Quick guide to evidence
   C. Investigative sources, including Internet sources
   D. Sample investigation plan
   E. Ethical Applications to Investigation
   F. Medical information
      1. List of available medical records
      2. Standardized request letter
      3. Authorization to disclose protected health information (HIPAA)
      4. Letter to doctor requesting medical summary/follow-up letter
   G. Accident scene checklist
   H. Suggestions for locating witnesses and experts
   I. Interviewing a witness
      1. Witness information cover sheet
      2. Checklist for witness interview
      3. Description of how to create interview questions
      4. Checklist of considerations for conducting a witness interview
      5. Tips for taking and drafting an effective statement (illustrative statement)
   J. Preserving evidence
      1. Accident diagram and other forms
      2. Checklist

PLEADINGS AND SERVICE

I. Drafting the complaint
  A. State and federal captions/pertinent rules including captions for multiple parties and privacy redaction
  B. Common causes of action and remedies
  C. Checklist for drafting a complaint
  D. Sample notice and fact complaints
  E. Other sample complaints

II. Injunctions/sample forms

III. Filing the lawsuit and service of process
  A. Outline of tasks and purposes
  B. Fee schedule for federal and state courts
  C. Forms
    1. Federal and state summons
    2. Federal civil cover sheet
    3. Notice of lawsuit and request for waiver of service of summons
    4. Waiver of service of summons
    5. Form USM-285: process receipt and return and equivalent state form
    6. Motion for special appointment to serve process
    7. Affidavit of return of service
    8. Consent to jurisdiction by magistrate judge
  D. Reference guide and checklists for methods of filing, e-filing, and service (add state)
  E. Checklist for locating defendants
  F. Checklist for service of process: federal and state
  G. Checklist for filing and service of documents subsequent to the complaint: federal and state

IV. Obtaining default judgment
  A. Task and purpose
  B. Checklist for default judgment: federal and state
  C. Forms
    1. Affidavit and request for default judgments
    2. Clerk's certificate of entry of default
    3. Request to clerk for entry of default judgment and affidavit
    4. Request to court for entry of default judgment and affidavit
    5. Affidavit of nonmilitary service
    6. Judgment of default
    7. Notice of application for default judgment
    8. Notice of motion for default judgment by court to defendant who has appeared in action
  D. Setting aside a default judgment/motion to set aside

V. Motions
  A. Checklists for drafting, filing, and serving motions: federal and state
  B. Motion to dismiss complaint
  C. Notice of motion
  D. Demurrer
  E. Memorandum of law in support of motion to dismiss
  F. Order for dismissal of complaint
  G. Joint application for extension of time
  H. Other motions to dismiss/Form 19 Federal Rules/Rule 12(b) motions
    1. Federal Rule 12(b) motions to dismiss: Form 19 Federal Rules
    2. Motion to make more definite and certain: Federal Rule 12(e)
    3. Motion to strike: Federal Rule 12(f)
    4. Motion for judgment on the pleadings
    5. Motion for summary judgment/notice/affidavit
  I. Other motions (add as they come up in text)

VI. Removal of state action to federal court
  A. Checklist for removal of action to federal court
  B. Notice of removal

VII. Answer, counterclaim, and cross-claim
  A. Task and purpose: answer
  B. List of style and content suggestions for answer
  C. List of suggestions for drafting successful denials in the answer
  D. Chart of forms of denial in pleadings
  E. Steps in locating affirmative defenses
  F. Sample answer, counterclaim, and cross-claim

VIII. Third-party practice pleadings
  A. Checklist for third-party complaint
  B. Third-party summons
  C. Third-party complaint
  D. Third-party motion to implead

IX. Amended pleadings
  A. Checklist of procedures and time limits for amended pleadings

B. Amended complaint

C. Motion to amend the pleadings

X. Motions for judgment on the pleadings and summary judgment: see motions

XI. File pleading log

XII. Pleadings, motions, and time limit exhibit (or place in quick reference section at beginning)

DISCOVERY

I. Discovery in general/motions to compel and for protective orders

A. Outline of definition and purpose, applicable state and federal rules on scope, limits, and sanctions

B. Preservation letter

C. Checklist of disclosure procedure

D. Report of parties' planning meeting

E. Ethical considerations and authority

II. Interrogatories

A. Outline of definitions, purpose, scope, applicable rules, and procedure for interrogatories, including time limits

B. Checklist for planning and drafting interrogatories

C. Sample interrogatories in e-discovery cases

D. Form interrogatories for auto accident case

E. Copies of any other interrogatories or types of questions

F. List of objections to interrogatories

G. Form letter to client to gather information for answering interrogatories

H. Checklist for answering interrogatories

III. Depositions

A. Outline on definition, purpose, scope, applicable rules, and procedure, including time limits

B. Checklist on preparing and serving subpoenas, including subpoena duces tecum, HIPAA procedural requirements, and sample cover letter to records custodian

C. Notice to take deposition

D. Subpoena and subpoena duces tecum

E. Deposition checklist, plaintiff, auto

F. Deposition outline

G. Format for deposition outline

H. Checklist for planning and preparing an outline for taking a deposition

I. Checklist for preparing witness files

J. Letter to client on preparing for deposition

K. List on preparing witnesses for testifying

L. Checklist for attending and reviewing the deposition

M. Digesting depositions
1. List of techniques for digesting a deposition
2. Sample digests of deposition

IV. Production of documents and things and entry upon land for inspection and other purposes

A. Outline on definition, purpose, scope, applicable rules, and procedure for requests for production, including time limits

B. Checklist for production of documents and electronic information—request, response, examination

C. Sample request for production and inspection of documents, things, and real property

D. Response to request for production

V. Request for physical and mental examination

A. Outline on the definition, purpose, scope, applicable rules, and procedure for a request for physical and mental examination

B. Motion for compulsory physical examination

C. Letter to client regarding compulsory physical examination

D. Checklist on the paralegal's role in drafting and working with requests for compulsory physical examinations

E. Guide for reviewing and interpreting documents: creating the mini-guide on any technical topic

F. Sample mini-guide for interpreting medical records

VI. Requests for admissions

A. Outline on definition, purpose, scope, applicable rules, and procedures related to a request for admissions

B. Form for request for admissions: Federal Form 25

C. Form for response to a request for admissions

VII. Objections, compelling discovery

A. Outline of definition, purpose, applicable rules, and procedures related to objections, protective orders, and compelling discovery

B. Checklist on compelling disclosure and
    discovery
C. Motion to compel
D. Affidavit in support of motion to compel
E. Order compelling discovery

VIII. Discovery through Freedom of Information Act
   A. Checklist for making a request pursuant to
       the Freedom of Information Act (both
       state and federal)
   B. Form for request pursuant to Freedom of
       Information Act

IX. Organizing files
   A. Checklist for organizing the small case file
   B. Checklist for organizing the large case file
      1. Master index sheet
      2. Subfile index sheet
   C. Alternative methods for organizing case files
   D. Case file to date

SETTLEMENT

I. Settlement
   A. Definition and factors bearing on settlement
   B. Outline of ethical considerations
   C. Checklist of items to be researched and
       summarized in preparation for settlement
   D. Damage summary and worksheet
   E. Damage calculation formulas
   F. Sample settlement précis or letter
   G. List of components of settlement brochure
   H. Related forms
      1. General authorization for settlement
          (power to settle)
      2. Release for personal injury
      3. Mutual release
      4. Covenant not to sue
      5. Settlement agreement
      6. Stipulation and order for dismissal
      7. Stipulation consent decree and order
      8. Settlement distribution statement

II. Alternative dispute resolution
   A. State statutes on ADR
   B. State forms for mandatory or voluntary ADR

PRETRIAL CONFERENCE

I. Pretrial conference
   A. Preparation checklist
   B. Applicable federal and state rules
   C. Outline for pretrial memorandum

TRIAL PREPARATION AND TRIAL

I. Trial preparation
   A. Trial preparation checklist
   B. Case status sheet
   C. Steps in obtaining and serving subpoenas
       (cross reference to section on deposition
       subpoenas)
   D. Juror data sheet
   E. Sources and methods for conducting jury
       investigations
   F. Applicable state and federal rules of evi-
       dence on demonstrative evidence
   G. List of commercial sources of demonstra-
       tive evidence
   H. List of ABA Civil Trial Practice Standards
       on technology and pretrial preparation
   I. Structure of a trial notebook
   J. Sample trial motions (also add to motion
       section)
   K. Sample motion in limine (also add to
       motion section)
   L. Jury instruction sources
   M. Sample jury instructions

II. Preparing the client and witness for trial
   A. Checklist for preparing clients, witnesses,
       and expert witnesses for trial
   B. Guidelines for witness's trial testimony

III. Trial
   A. List of tasks at trial
   B. Form for drafting findings of fact and con-
       clusions of law
   C. Verdict forms (3 types)

POST-TRIAL PRACTICE

I. Post-trial motions and pertinent rules/
    deadlines
   A. Renewal of motion for judgment as a
       matter of law (JNOV for state)
   B. Motion for new trial (place extra copies in
       motion section)

II. Bill of costs: state and federal

III. Enforcement of judgment
   A. Pertinent rules of procedure and statutes
   B. Notice of lis pendens
   C. Interrogatories in aid of judgment
   D. List of exempt assets under state law
   E. Checklist for enforcing judgments under
       state law

1. Letter to judgment debtor
2. Follow-up letter
3. Writ of execution
4. Application and affidavit for a writ of garnishment
5. Writ of garnishment
6. State garnishment forms
7. Outline of procedure for domesticating a judgment in another state and in federal court

APPEAL

I. Checklist for federal appellate procedure, including rules and time limits
   A. Notice of appeal
   B. Designation of record on appeal
   C. Motion for enlargement of time
   D. Notice of filing of brief

II. Checklist for state appellate procedure/forms

III. Outline of federal and state appellate briefs plus rules on required format, sample appellate brief format

THE SUBSTANTIVE LAW OF TORTS

- Introduction
- Sources of Tort Law
- Unintentional Torts: Negligence
- Intentional Tort
- Torts that Interfere with Economic Relationships
- Vicarious Liability

- Contribution and Indemnity
- Employer's Liability to Employees
- Strict Liability
- Product Liability
- Computer Torts
- Immunity from Suit in Tort

INTRODUCTION

The importance of learning the substantive law of torts,* or for that matter any other area of law, is that you will know the unique terminology of that area, its various causes of actions or defenses to which your client may be entitled, and its evidentiary requirements—all of which helps you to distinguish the relevant facts and information from the nonrelevant. In addition, your general knowledge of an area of law helps you to recognize issues and gives you the framework from which you can construct effective research and inquiry into issues or elements identified as relevant. The goal of this appendix is to provide you with the basic knowledge necessary to begin working effectively in the area of torts, and specifically tort litigation.

A tort is a civil as opposed to a criminal wrong for which the injured party can sue the wrongdoer for compensation. It is distinct from breach of contract and addresses harms to persons, property, rights, and economic and other relationships. Generally, torts have four common elements: (1) a legal duty of one person to another, (2) an act or omission that breaches that duty, (3) a harm, and (4) a finding that the harm was a direct result of the act or omission. Typical torts are driving recklessly and causing an automobile accident, manufacturing a product that is defective and causes injury, maliciously telling lies about a person that damages the person's reputation, and causing toxic industrial wastes to seep into the groundwater. Some torts, such as striking a person or wrongfully taking property, may also be crimes. When torts and crimes coincide, two distinct bodies of law are invoked, resulting in a government action for violation of a criminal statute and a private (or civil) action for violation of tort law.

The basic public policies underlying tort law are *fairness* (those who cause harm should bear its costs), *compensation* (an injured party ought to have access to a remedy for an injury inflicted by another), and *prevention* (holding people responsible for

---

*See "A Brief Guide to Causes of Action and Remedies" in Chapter 5 for a concise statement of the elements that must be proved in several of the torts mentioned in this appendix.

their wrongs will cause them to take steps to avoid those harms). This appendix will address the various kinds of torts and applicable defenses, and who can be held responsible for a tort.

SOURCES OF TORT LAW

Although many other areas of law, including contracts, have been substantially codified—placed into statutory form—tort law is founded in and primarily exists today as common (court-made) law. Some state and federal statutes create duties and define torts, but most of tort law and the individual torts are defined by a series of judicial opinions incorporating, interpreting, and adding to the common law. Some works such as the *Restatement (Second) of Torts* and treatises such as Prosser's *The Law of Torts* provide a general sense of tort law applicable in all jurisdictions, and they should be consulted along with existing statutes.

UNINTENTIONAL TORTS: NEGLIGENCE

INTRODUCTION

Unlike criminal law that emphasizes the intentional commission of a crime, tort law addresses unintentional, careless, or accidental harms. This substantive area of tort law is referred to as negligence law. Negligence is defined by *Black's Law Dictionary* as "The failure to use such care as a reasonably prudent and careful person would use under similar circumstances." All persons have a duty to conduct themselves in their activities so as not to create an *unreasonable* risk of harm to others. The basic elements of negligence are:

1. Duty
2. Breach of that duty
3. Injury
4. Proximate cause—the breach has caused the injury.

   In order to recover damages, the plaintiff must prove the existence of each of these elements by a preponderance of the evidence.

DUTY

A *duty* is the obligation of care exercised by one person in respect to another person as dictated by the circumstances and as imposed by common law or statute. For example, when you operate a vehicle at high speeds, you have a duty to the person in the vehicle in front of you to keep a reasonable distance between your car and the other vehicle. That distance is necessary to avoid a collision should the other vehicle have to stop quickly. The harm likely to occur under the circumstances if care is not exercised defines the duty.

   In addition, some duties are not invoked until some action is taken. A person seeing another person stranded on a ledge on a tall building has no duty to try to save the person, because doing so may get two people killed instead of one or none. If the bystander, however, elects to help the stranded person, the duty to do so in a non-negligent fashion is involved. On the other hand, a firefighter has a duty to try to rescue the stranded person, as a lifeguard has a duty to try to rescue a drowning person.

   Normally the harm must be *foreseeable*—likely and predictable. Airline baggage loaders who frequently toss luggage and packages do not have the same duty of care to those around them as they would if they were told package X contained nitro-glycerin or other explosives. Therefore, the duty is defined by the circumstances that include any predictable harm resulting from the absence of due care.

BREACH OF DUTY—STANDARD OF CARE

A *breach of an existing duty* is the failure to conform to the required standard of care. The required standard of care is that which is reasonable under the circumstances. In other words, *what would a reasonable and prudent person do under similar circumstances?* If a person's conduct conforms to that standard, there is no breach; if the person's conduct falls short, there is a breach. Driving the speed limit on a dry, sunny day may be reasonable, but doing the same thing on an ice-covered road may not be.

A physically handicapped person is held to a standard that is reasonable for a physically handicapped person. Mental illness or infirmity does not generally change the standard, however. A child is held to a standard of reasonability for children of similar age. Professionals such as physicians, engineers, lawyers, and others are held to a higher standard, i.e., that which is acceptable for a member of the profession as defined by professional competence in the community. Normally these standards are proven by expert testimony.

Businesses and other land owners must make reasonable efforts to see that their property is safe for those likely to come onto or be attracted to the property.

INJURY/DAMAGES

The third element requires that an injury actually occurs to the victim. The types of injuries that are compensated (with money) are medical bills and services related to physical injuries and disabilities, pain and suffering (distress, discomfort, emotional trauma), lost wages (only if because of some physical injury), lost enjoyment of life, and damages for injury to or destruction of land or other property.

CAUSATION

The final element of negligence is causation, proof that the injury was caused substantially by the negligent act or omission that comprises the breach of duty. Cause is shown by evidence that X's negligence is the direct cause of the injury—the factual cause.

But factual cause is not enough. The act or omission must be the legal or proximate cause as well. *Proximate cause* requires the consideration of foreseeable consequences and intervening causes. The general rule on foreseeability is that if the result is not foreseeable, then there is no liability. Liability is limited only to the harm that gave rise to the duty in the first place. A famous case on foreseeability is *Palsgraf v. Long Island R.R.,* 248 N.Y. 339, 162 N.E. 99 (1928). Railroad employees negligently caused X to drop a package containing fireworks. It exploded and caused railroad scales to fall on Mrs. Palsgraf, resulting in injuries. The court held that liability was limited to the foreseeable, i.e., that contents in the dropped package would be damaged, which defined the original duty of care. A minority of courts rule otherwise and extend liability through to the damage caused by the last falling domino.

Persons causing an accident or other damages are also liable for the harms caused by the rescuers who attempt to undo or mitigate the damage. Since the wrongdoer (*tort feasor*) has placed the person in a state of danger or injury, the wrongdoer is also responsible for the action of those who will foreseeably come and attempt to administer to the injuries or rescue the victim from the danger. Further, the tort feasor is also liable for the full extent of the injuries even if the victim was in an unpredictably weakened or vulnerable state beforehand, i.e., the person who slips on a banana peel in a store and suffers a serious heart attack because of a previous condition can recover damages for that injury in addition to the predictable and more likely injuries.

Tortious conduct may not incur liability if the cause of the injury is an *intervening* cause. This cause can be a human act or a natural occurrence (act of God) such as a tornado or lightning. The key is whether the intervening cause is a *superseding* cause. A qualifying superseding cause cannot simply be the foreseeable act of another that makes the situation worse or is the catalyst that sets off the harm. For example, if A carelessly erects a large flagpole, his neighbor bumps the pole with his lawn mower, and the pole falls injuring the mail carrier, A is still liable. The lawnmower bump is not sufficient to relieve the original tort feasor from liability; the cause is not superseding. The cause would probably be superseding if the neighbor deliberately pushed the pole onto the mail carrier, or if lightning struck the pole causing it to fall on the carrier. If the intervening event was a wind not sufficient to blow over a well-secured pole, then it would not be a superseding cause.

Normally the victim must prove each of these four elements in order to prevail in an action for negligence. In a situation where negligence is the likely explanation for the injury, a high duty of care is expected, and the defendant has exclusive control over the product or activity, the doctrine of *res ipsa loquitur* ("the thing speaks for itself") comes into play. This doctrine shifts the burden to the defendant to prove there was no negligence. In cases involving airplane accidents, the airline has an enormous duty of care implying that if almost *anything* goes wrong, it is obviously the airline's fault. Also, an injured passenger would normally not have access to evidence revealing negligence, so the burden falls to the airline to prove no negligence was involved.

WRONGFUL DEATH

Common law prevented civil actions based on negligence or willful conduct that resulted in the death of the victim. Consequently, laws have been passed called *wrongful death statutes* that permit suits by representatives of the deceased's estate for the benefit of the deceased's family and other beneficiaries. These statutes permit actions based on negligence as well as willful conduct.

DEFENSES TO NEGLIGENCE

The defenses to negligence include the following:

1. *Comparative negligence.* The doctrine of comparative negligence—which is the law in the majority of states and in Columbia (unless your instructor indicates otherwise)—permits a plaintiff who is contributorily negligent to recover, but the award is reduced proportionately by the percentage of the plaintiff's negligence. For example, if Ann Forrester stepped onto the highway without looking, then slipped as she tried to retreat, a jury might find her 30 percent negligent. If Mr. Hart was driving too fast to stop, a jury might find him 70 percent negligent. If Ms. Forrester's damages came to $100,000, the award would be reduced by 30 percent to $70,000. In some

states, Ms. Forrester would be barred from any recovery if her comparative negligence was found to exceed 50 percent. Some states still use the term *contributory negligence* for this doctrine, although it is a modified version of contributory negligence [see (3) of this list].

2. *Assumption of risk.* This defense states that plaintiffs may not recover for damages if they knowingly place themselves in danger. For example, if Ms. Forrester had decided to stay in the middle of the road and thumb her nose at any oncoming vehicle, she would be assuming the risk of injury, and Mr. Hart would have a defense to Ms. Forrester's action for negligence.

3. *Contributory negligence.* Although most states have abolished contributory negligence as a defense, its use should be understood. If the action of the plaintiff, the person suing for injuries, was a contributing factor in the accident, the plaintiff cannot recover her losses from the defendant, the person being sued. For example, if a jury found that plaintiff Ann Forrester had contributed to her own injuries by failing to look both ways before crossing the highway, she would be barred from any recovery, even if defendant Mr. Hart was found to be primarily responsible for the accident. The harshness of this rule explains why it has been abolished in many states. Assume that contributory negligence is not the law in Columbia unless your instructor indicates otherwise.

4. *Last clear chance.* This doctrine permits recovery of damages by parties who normally could not recover because of their contributory negligence. In that sense it is a defense to the defense of contributory negligence. It applies when the plaintiff, through her own negligence, is placed in the defendant's path so that the defendant has the last clear chance to avoid an accident. If the defendant does not react as a reasonable person should (is negligent), causing injury to the plaintiff, the plaintiff may recover regardless of her initial contributing negligence. For example, assume Ann Forrester carelessly ran across the ice on the road, slipped and fell, leaving her directly in the path of Mr. Hart's van. Also assume that Mr. Hart had a last clear chance to avoid the accident. If he was inattentive and did not avoid the accident, Ms. Forrester could still recover damages, in spite of her own negligence.

Intentional Tort

INTRODUCTION

All intentional torts have three common elements:

1. An offensive act
2. Intent to commit the act
3. The infringement of a victim's lawfully protected right.

The act must be purposeful and not part of a chain caused by a third party. For example, if X pushes you into Y, your act of falling into Y is not the requisite act for liability. The requisite act must also infringe on the victim's legally protected right. For example an *assault* (threat of harm) invades one's sense of well-being and security, although no discernible physical injury occurs. Because that sense of personal well-being and security has been infringed, liability attaches absent physical damage.

The requisite *intent* is the conscious decision to commit the wrongful act knowing it has harmful consequences. Intent is proven by a person's statement of intent or by circumstantial evidence. Whether the wrongdoer is a child, intends to hit A but hits B, or the harm is greater than intended makes no difference.

INTENTIONAL TORTS AGAINST PERSONS

Assault is the intentional and immediate threat or attempt to inflict injury on the victim while apparently possessing the ability to do so. No physical injury or actual contact is necessary, but generally, the tort victim must be in fear or in apprehension of harm. Words are generally an insufficient threat, but this could depend on the circumstances.

Battery is intentional physical contact on another person to cause or result in bodily injury or offensive touching. Wrongdoer A does not have to personally touch victim B—A can throw a stone that strikes B, or A can touch B's clothing or an item being carried. If A so threatens B that it is a substantial likelihood that B will be struck—and B is struck—A is liable for battery even though A intended only to threaten B. Even a physician may be held liable for battery if an operation goes beyond that which is contemplated and necessary, or causes harm from risks that were not adequately explained to the patient.

False imprisonment is the unlawful and deliberate restraining of the liberty of another. Generally the victim must be aware of the restraint or be injured by it, but the length of confinement is irrelevant. One may be unlawfully restrained by threats as well as by walls. One can be falsely imprisoned if one is at a place voluntarily and then is deliberately prevented from leaving, or no practical way to leave is provided when released, i.e., the failure to unlock the door knowing X is ready to leave. Once the plaintiff proves the intentional confinement, it remains for the defendant to prove any justification or lawful authority.

Since shoplifting has become such a national problem, and its in-store investigation so vulnerable to actions for false imprisonment, most states have passed laws giving shopkeepers the right to detain persons reasonably suspected of shoplifting for a reasonable investigative period.

False arrest is a component of false imprisonment. It is the intentional abuse of the power to arrest. It occurs when a person is arrested on knowingly trumped-up charges or is detained beyond a reasonable period for investigation and interrogation. Usually, citizens can make arrests only if they have a reasonable belief the person to be detained is the perpetrator of a felony.

Intentional infliction of emotional distress is an outrageous and extreme act that is intended to cause or recklessly causes the victim to suffer severe emotional distress. A person who secretly exhumed the body of X's husband and placed it in X's house for her to discover when she arrived home would likely be guilty of this tort. In this tort the conduct must be truly abhorrent and the distress must go well beyond normal humiliation or brief depression. There is no need to prove physical injury, but the distress should normally be manifested over a significant period of time. The need for extended psychological or psychiatric care would be such evidence.

Invasion of privacy concerns a series of rights including the right to be left alone (intrusion), the right to exclusive use of one's name and image, the right not to be placed in a false light in the public eye, and the right against unreasonable publicity of private facts [RESTATEMENT (SECOND) § 652A]. Generally the award is for mental suffering, shame, or humiliation as gauged by a person's ordinary sensibilities.

May a business conglomerate try to silence an effective critic by tapping the critic's phone, threatening him, and hiring women to entice him and place him in a compromising light? If it does, it is liable for the tort of intrusion. [See *Nader v. General Motors Corporation*, 298 N.Y.S.2d 137 (1969).] Intrusion is one of four torts under the umbrella phrase invasion of privacy.

Intrusion can consist of entry of another's dwelling, an illegal series of persistent phone calls or intrusive appearances, unauthorized blood tests, and the like.

The right to exclusive use of one's name and image prevents advertisers, for example, from misappropriating an actor's name in an embarrassing or humiliating way. Under such a theory, talk-show host Johnny Carson successfully sued a toilet company for using "Here's Johnny" to advertise its company and product [*Carson v. Here's Johnny Portable Toilets*, 698 F.2d 831 (1983)].

The right not to be placed in a false, and usually humiliating, light places liability on a person for, for example, taking a photo of a public official stepping out of a thunderstorm to shelter under the entrance of a triple-X-rated peep show and publishing it with a caption that suggests the official is a frequent customer of the show.

The fourth area of privacy addresses the *intentional and unreasonable publicity of private facts* and protects persons from the unwarranted publicity of personal or private matters. The matters could include financial concerns, revelation of embarrassing diseases, intimate relations, and similar kinds of things. The publication normally involves newspapers, television, the Internet, and other media where the revelation serves little public purpose and is normally embarrassing and humiliating. Truth, which is a defense to libel and defamation (to be discussed), is not a defense to this tort.

These torts and the entire area of the right of privacy are being reinforced by laws that secure aspects of the right of privacy. These laws give persons the right to live together as consenting, unmarried adults, the right to an abortion, the right against tampering with mail, the right against electronic eavesdropping, and others.

Fraud is the intentional deceit of another for the purpose of depriving the person of property or some other right. The tort of fraud consists of four elements:

1. a false material statement about a past or current fact known by the perpetrator to be false or in reckless disregard of the truth
2. with the intent of securing the victim's reliance on the statement
3. causing the victim to reasonably rely on the statement
4. resulting in loss or harm to the victim

Tort actions for fraud generally arise in the context of business dealings. Typical fraud is the sale of used cars whose odometers have been turned back or other misrepresentations concerning quality of performance. Fraud does not generally encompass statements of opinion such as, "This is the best value on the market," (puffing in advertising or salesmanship) or statements made from lack of information. In one of the most celebrated fraud cases, Sears was held liable for providing false information to the inventor of quick-release socket wrenches that led the inventor to believe his invention was worth far less than it was. Sears paid $10,000 in royalties for the device that brought in close to $50 million for Sears. Eventually the inventor was awarded several million dollars [*Roberts v. Sears, Roebuck & Co.*, 573 F.2d 976 (1978)].

Defamation is the intentional publishing of false information about a person that injures the person's reputation, respect, or goodwill, or which holds the person out to ridicule, scorn, or contempt. Its origin may lie in the admonition, "Thou shalt not bear false witness against thy neighbor," and its justification stems from the fact that good reputations take years to build but can be dashed on the rocks with one lie. Defamation has become a complex area of law, especially in the struggle of values between a person's right to his or her reputation and the belief in freedom of the press.

First, a party suing for damages must show that the information communicated is false and defamatory. Second, the plaintiff must show that the information was in fact communicated to others—in other words, published. *Publication* can occur in two basic ways. The first is by *slander*, which is the oral communication of the lie, but may include gestures in some circumstances. It involves stating the lie to a third person. The other form of publication, called *libel*, is the writing or printing of the lie in a manner that will communicate the information to at least one third party. Because of the greater permanency of something written, libel is considered the more serious of the two defamation torts. Printing can include pictures or signs or even a message posted on the Internet . When oral statements are recorded or preserved in a way that the danger of dissemination and repetition are similar to written words, then such oral statements are treated as libel rather than as slander.

In addition to the statement being a defamatory lie and being published in some form, the perpetrator must have intended to communicate the statement and there must exist a special harm or a statement that is actionable in and of itself regardless of any special harm.

Some of the principles or rules of defamation law are:

1. There is no action in tort if the person defamed is dead.
2. Individuals, corporations, and groups can sue for defamation if the targets are reasonably identifiable.
3. A statement is not defamatory if said in jest or humor.
4. There is no tort if only a small segment of the community would or does find the statement to be offensive.
5. The plaintiff must be able to show that he or she is the target of the statement.
6. Bookstores and libraries are not liable for libel if they are not aware the book is defamatory.
7. When newspapers and radio stations report a defamatory statement made by another, they are held liable as the primary publisher.
8. Generally the plaintiff must be able to show damages. Special damages are monetary losses such as loss of a job, loss of a promotion, loss of a business deal, or loss of sales.
9. Damages cannot be for emotional harms such as humiliation, stress, or anger.
10. No special damages need to be shown if a slanderous statement
    a. defames a person's business, business outlook, or professional qualifications,
    b. says a person committed an immoral crime (moral turpitude),
    c. says a person has a horrible and humiliating disease (venereal disease), or
    d. impugns the chastity of a woman.
11. Special damages may not have to be shown in libel cases if it is *libel on its face* (obvious). Special damages may need to be shown, however, where the statement is *libel per quod* (where other information is needed). For example, if it was published that X just married Y, that is not libelous on its face. If the community knows that X is already married to Z, however, then we have a problem.

12. To defame a public figure (movie actor, athlete, or other person of voluntary celebrity) or public official (mayor, judge), it must be shown that the publication was reckless as to the truth, malicious (with a desire to hurt the victim), or knowingly false. For ordinary persons and persons involuntarily thrust into the limelight (by being party to a lawsuit), the standard is simply negligence as to the truth.

Several defenses are unique and specific to defamation. They are as follows:

1. The victim's consent to publish.
2. The statement is true (but not if incomplete and thus misleading).
3. The publisher has an absolute privilege—participants in a trial and related procedures, legislators and public officials during the course of their official duties, and spouse to spouse.
4. The publisher has a qualified privilege—news reporter reporting false statements of another made in judicial or legislative hearing, critics of the arts but not the personal life of the artist, and statements made to public officials to facilitate their duties. An example of the latter would be reporting criminal behavior to a police officer or an employee reporting suspected theft by another employee to the manager. If these reports are made with malice then the limited privilege evaporates.

INTENTIONAL TORTS TO PROPERTY

A number of intentional torts can also be committed on property. These are trespass to land or to chattels and conversion. *Trespass to land* in common law is simply an act that encroaches upon the property right of another; in modern tort law the act must be intentional, reckless, or negligent, and if reckless or negligent, it must cause damage. The intent does not have to be to commit the harm; it simply must be to enter the land. Damages encompass all harm caused by the trespass plus any consequential harm including emotional distress. There is no need to show that the damage was done negligently. Planes and boats generally have a reasonable right of passage unless the manner of the passage becomes extreme. Trespass, however, may occur above or below the surface of the land. A trespass can also occur if A sells land to B and A fails to remove A's truck.

Trespass to chattels is strictly intentional as opposed to negligent or reckless interference with the personal property of another, including damage, alteration, use, etc. The tort feasor's belief that the article was his or hers is no defense. Generally damages must be shown, but nominal damages are awarded for dispossession—taking and depriving one of use of one's property. Return of the property plus damages is a common remedy.

Conversion is intentional trespass to chattels that permanently deprives a person of the rightful use of the property, or some similar act that justifies forcing the perpetrator to pay for the property. It is viewed as a serious trespass. Theft is a typical conversion. A taking, even if by mistake, coupled with a complete destruction of the property is a conversion. Receipt of property with knowledge the property belongs to a third party, or failure to release property owned by another when required to do so, are also conversions.

Nuisance is that which causes a substantial and unreasonable annoyance, disturbance, or other offensive interference with private or public land. A *public nuisance* adversely affects an entire community and is generally prosecuted through criminal law. Obstructing a highway, storing explosives, releasing untreated sewage, unlawful dumping, and an unreasonably noisy activity are all public nuisances. Normally the remedy is the enforcement of criminal law and not damages.

Private nuisances are generally remedied by damages, injunctions, or both and include activities that affect one or a few properties as opposed to the entire community. Obnoxious odors, seeping wastewater, the vibrations from explosions, and failure to maintain a property to the deleterious effect of a neighbor may all be private nuisances. Nuisance focuses on the harm rather than on the act and, therefore, can be remedied through various intentional, negligent, or strict liability tort actions. For example, a suit in negligence may be appropriate, or a suit for intentional trespass, or a combination of theories or causes of action.

DEFENSES TO INTENTIONAL TORTS

Although some defenses may be unique to the specific tort, as in the case of truth being a defense to defamation, there are some general defenses to intentional torts. The most obvious is the voluntary *consent* of the injured person. If there is consent, the act becomes privileged or authorized. Some privileges are created by law or exist because of the circumstances. Football players obviously are privileged to knock each other's blocks off (within accepted parameters) without expressly giving or receiving consent. Doctors are permitted to aid accident victims in an emergency. Otherwise, the consent must come from a person qualified to give consent. When a church minister revealed a man's confession of marital infidelity in a "shaming" ceremony of church discipline, the man sued for intentional infliction of emotional distress. The church argued that, by his involvement in the church, the man consented to its discipline. This consent defense won a summary judgment in the church's favor [*Smith v. Calvary Christian Church*, 614 N.W.2d 590 (Mich. 2000)].

Self-defense is the permissible use of force against others if a person reasonably believes he or she or others are threatened with immediate physical harm or improper confinement and retreat is not a viable option. The force is limited to what is reasonable under the circumstances, including retreat. Retreat is not required for persons threatened in their own dwellings. A parallel defense is available to persons defending property; however, a warning, if feasible, is required and the minimum force that is necessary to prevent trespass or to expel the intruder or an intruding object is the legal limit. Threat of force is also permissible. Force that could lead to serious bodily harm or death is never permitted to defend property.

Reasonable force or threat thereof may be employed to recover a piece of stolen property following a request to give up the property. Normally this applies in the context of hot pursuit. Generally, one may repossess land if the repossession is peaceable.

Necessity is an emergency that excuses trespass to property or conversion. A flood, starvation, or other circumstances may leave a person with little choice.

Authority of law may protect otherwise tortious behavior. For example, a store owner can generally detain suspected shoplifters, and teachers and parents may be permitted some leeway in disciplining children.

TORTS THAT INTERFERE WITH ECONOMIC RELATIONSHIPS

Some torts adversely affect business relationships. *Disparagement* is akin to defamation, but is restricted to the impact on a business relationship. It is an intentional publication of a false statement that discredits the financial status of a person, the quality of goods or services, or the saleability or title to property.

Interference with contractual relations is a general tort that permits recovery for an intentional act that interferes with the performance of a contract. In this instance, a third party such as a bank might deliberately make it difficult for a party to get the financing to finish construction on a building or other property. A potential buyer of property might harass tenants so they break leases and make a rental property less profitable, so the owner will sell the property.

Interference with an economically advantageous relationship is exemplified by the famous case of *Texaco Inc. v. Pennzoil Co.*, 728 S.W.2d 768 (Texas 1987). In this case Texaco agreed to buy Getty Oil property after Pennzoil had worked out an agreement in principle to buy the same property. Texaco was found liable for the tort of interference with an economically advantageous relationship. This tort requires a spiteful or wrongful intent.

VICARIOUS LIABILITY

The doctrine of vicarious liability imposes liability on persons who, because of a relationship, are held responsible for the torts committed by others. Thus an employer is held responsible for the torts of an employee if the employee at the time of the tort is in the course of employment or doing something on behalf of the employer. It is the doctrine of *respondeat superior*. If the job requires some use of force, such as in the case of a police officer or a private security officer, the employer is liable for excessive force. Normally, however, employers are not liable for intentional torts beyond the control of the employee. Likewise, one partner is responsible for the actions of another partner if the person was acting on behalf of the partnership. And a parent is liable for the torts of a child, but only if the child is acting on behalf of the parent. Vicarious liability has expanded in some states to include the owner of a bar for the unlawful service of minors, and for the tortious acts of patrons who have become intoxicated at a bar even if the owner was not present at the bar. The negligence of the operator of a vehicle can be applied to the owner of the vehicle if the person was driving on behalf of the owner. Vicarious liability does not extend from the independent contractor to the person employing the independent contractor.

CONTRIBUTION AND INDEMNITY

Contribution permits an injured party to sue two or more parties when the wrongdoers have indivisibly contributed to the injuries or if they have acted in agreement. The plaintiff may sue one or both for the entire amount. If one is sued for the entire amount, that defendant may in turn sue the joint tort feasor for an appropriate share of the damages.

In *indemnity* one party either has or assumes the legal obligation to pay for one or more kinds of tortious acts of the other. Contracts frequently state that one party indemnifies the other party for any damages arising from the indemnifier's actions.

EMPLOYER'S LIABILITY TO EMPLOYEES

Today most employers are covered by *workers' compensation* insurance. Thus, an employee's injury is compensated at legislated rates from an insurance fund to which the employer contributes. Negligence or fault is no longer an issue in such cases. If the employer intentionally or recklessly subjects an employee to an unreasonable risk, however, then the employee has an action in tort.

STRICT LIABILITY

Strict liability is an area of tort law that for reasons of public policy attaches liability to certain kinds of hazardous and other activities regardless of fault. Workers' compensation, discussed previously, is one area that has been statutorily made into a strict liability matter. Traditionally, however, it is the more dangerous activities that incur strict liability. An owner of animals is generally strictly liable for the injuries and trespasses caused by the animals. There are some exceptions for dogs and cats and livestock in certain circumstances. Owners of wild animals are strictly liable for injuries caused by the animals. Otherwise, any use of land or other activity that is unnatural and particularly hazardous incurs strict liability. Persons using explosives, hauling gasoline, and storing toxic waste are held to a strict liability standard. The key in strict liability is that no fault must be shown if the person engaging in the dangerous activity is aware of the risk that is being created.

PRODUCT LIABILITY

When a person is injured by a dangerous product, several theories under the broad term *product liability* may provide a remedy for the injury.

Negligence: Product liability negligence requires proof of the same basic elements required in any negligence action: duty, breach of the duty, injury, and breach being the actual and proximate cause of the injury. Negligence might occur in the design, manufacture, testing, or packaging of the product. If the product is dangerous and its danger is not obvious, the failure to place adequate warnings may provide the basis for a negligence suit. The person harmed can be anyone likely to use the product, and the manufacturer, supplier of a part in the final product, the seller, and the distributor might all be liable.

Breach of warranty: An area of commercial law (Uniform Commercial Code) stemming from the old law of torts provides a remedy for physical harms caused by defective or unfit products. *Express warranties* are promises of quality on which a buyer relies when purchasing a product. A defective product that causes injury is a breach of the promise and is actionable. Express warranties are voluntarily assumed by the manufacturer to help sell the product.

Implied warranties are warranties required by law and follow the goods. Manufacturers and sellers can avoid such warranties by expressly disclaiming them, but such a waiver is deemed unconscionable as applied to physical harm [U.C.C. § 2-719(3)]. The implied *warranty of merchantability* promises that the product is reasonably safe, is of a certain standard of quality, and is fit for its ordinary use. The implied *warranty of fitness* arises when the buyer relies on the seller's knowledge that the product is fit for a specific purpose. Breach of these warranties imposes strict liability unless the seller has expressly limited or disclaimed the warranty.

Strict tort liability: In most jurisdictions today, the manufacturers and sellers of goods are strictly liable for any defective or unfit product that is unusually dangerous and which causes physical harm. Automobiles must withstand certain standards of "crashworthiness" and cannot, for example, have a gas tank that is likely to explode in a typical rear-end collision. Defenses include assumption of risk and improper use of the product.

COMPUTER TORTS

The proliferation of computers and the Internet brings with it the necessity of updating tort principles to encompass damages incurred by both accidental and intentional misuse of new technologies. Rapidly spreading viruses can do billions of dollars in damage, with blame going to writers of the virus code, software companies whose products allow it to spread, and users who continue its spread. Questions of whether a program code causes harm, data loss is physical damage, or software is subject to products liability suits open the doors to an extensive new area of torts.*

IMMUNITY FROM SUIT IN TORT

Immunity from suit exists in several circumstances. Governmental bodies and officials are generally immune from suit (sovereign immunity) when acting in their official capacities, and the government itself is normally immune from personal injury suits unless it has granted individuals the right to sue it. In recent years the Supreme Court has broadened the Eleventh Amendment's provision of sovereign immunity to bar suits in both state and federal court against an unconsenting state by one of its own citizens [*Seminole Tribe of Florida v. Florida*, 517 U.S. 44, 116 S. Ct. 1114 (1996), *Alden v. Maine*, 527 U.S. 706, 119 S. Ct. 2240 (1999), and *Kimel v. Florida Board of Regents*, 528 U.S. 62, 120 S. Ct. 631 (2000)]. The federal government and many state governments have passed tort claims acts that do permit such suits under the theory that persons who are injured because of the wrongful conduct of others should not be denied a remedy, especially when the cost of the remedy can be borne by an entire population through taxes and the purchase of insurance. Government employees engaged in ministerial (administrative) tasks have less or no immunity when compared to those engaged in discretionary activity. For example, a judge is immune to suit when making judicial decisions but not when hiring or firing a court employee.

Family members are increasingly being allowed to sue each other for torts. Generally, however, the right of children to sue parents is limited.

---

*Christopher J. McGuire, *Old Torts Never Die—They Just Adapt to the Internet*, Nat'l L.J., Sept. 25, 2000, B15-B17.

APPENDIX C

THE SUBSTANTIVE LAW OF CONTRACTS

INTRODUCTION

The purpose of this appendix is to provide you with a basic working knowledge of the terms and principles of contract law.* This knowledge will facilitate solving assignments related to the litigation material in this text and the completion of entry-level paralegal tasks concerning contract litigation. The appendix should be particularly helpful in understanding the elements that must be proven for a successful breach of contract action, organizing a related investigation, performing legal research, drafting pleadings, pursuing discovery, and completing other significant stages of the litigation process.

Black's Law Dictionary defines a contract as an agreement between two or more parties creating reciprocal obligations to do or not to do something. If written, it sets out the agreed terms and conditions and serves as proof of the obligations. Contracts are fundamental to doing business in our world and, thus, comprise one of the most significant areas of law practice. The hundreds of thousands of contracts entered into each day inevitably result in some disputes and litigation.

The public policy (expressed societal values important to the public good) underlying contract law is that in order to conduct business and have a vibrant economy, it is essential that persons be able to rely on the promises of others. The performance (following through on the promise) of these obligations allows houses, factories, and roads to be built; goods, land, and services to be sold; and people to be employed. Each of these things contributes significantly to an orderly society characterized by an enjoyable standard of living. It is easy to see why contracts are crucial, and why public policy favors and requires their strict enforcement.

In addition to the policies favoring contract law, this appendix will explore the sources of contract law, the components necessary to form a binding contract, quasi-contracts, the statute of frauds, how contracts are interpreted, defenses to an action

---

*See "A Brief Guide to Causes of Action and Remedies" in Chapter 5 for a concise statement of the elements that must be proven in several of the contract actions mentioned in this appendix.

for breach of contract, remedies for a breach of contract, third-party beneficiaries, assignment of rights and delegation of duties, discharge of a contract, and contractual warranties.

SOURCES OF CONTRACT LAW

Whether you are drafting a contract or examining one in preparation for litigation, its legality and enforceability depend on the law that governs the particular type of contract in the particular jurisdiction in question. The sources of law to consult are the common law, the *Restatement of Contracts, Second,* state statutes on contracts including the Uniform Commercial Code (U.C.C.), and any particular provisions of federal law that apply, such as those in the Federal Consumer Protection Act of 1968 (Truth in Lending Law) or the Magnuson-Moss Warranty-Federal Trade Commission Improvement Act.

The U.C.C. has been adopted by all states in some variation and covers sales by laypersons as well as merchants. It changes some of the common law of contracts and, therefore, must be consulted if it appears to apply to the contract at hand. The most significant provisions of the U.C.C. are Article 2 (sale of goods) and the recent 2A (leasing of goods). "Goods" are defined by the U.C.C. as "all things (including specially manufactured goods) which are moveable at the time of identification (performance) to the contract." The key to whether a contract for goods is covered by the U.C.C. is that the good is moveable at the time the contract is performed and that the primary focus of the contract is this good and not a service. Therefore, the U.C.C. covers the sale of trees or crops but only if they are to be harvested. The sale of machinery, vehicles, household goods, and so on, is covered. Services such as the construction of a building, repairs to equipment, and legal services are not. Mixed contracts including both goods and services are covered by the U.C.C. if the sale of goods is the primary purpose of the contract. For example, the sale of a sofa, which includes delivery, removal of the old sofa, and setup, is covered even though the services of setup and removal are part of the contract. Determining what law applies to a particular contract requires some good background work. In some cases the parties state the applicable law in the contract.

ELEMENTS OF A VALID CONTRACT

A valid contract requires the following elements:

1. Competent parties bargaining at arm's length
2. Mutual assent including an offer and acceptance
3. Reciprocal consideration
4. A lawful and enforceable purpose
5. A form required by law
6. Absence of fraud, duress, undue influence, or mistake of fact

COMPETENT PARTIES BARGAINING AT ARM'S LENGTH

First, the parties to the contract must be *legally competent*. They must be adults (usually age eighteen) and not incapacitated by insanity or intoxication. Contracts entered into by minors or insane persons are usually *void* (not binding) or *voidable*

(able to be terminated), which means that the incompetent person can end the contract without meeting his or her contractual obligation. Some state laws hold a child liable for the value of any contractual benefit the child has received up to that point. The legal guardian for an incompetent person may enter into an enforceable contract on behalf of the incompetent. Children may also be held liable in quasi-contracts (a statutory obligation, not a contractual one) for the value of purchased necessities and/or food, shelter, and clothing. If a person is insane or intoxicated to the extent that they cannot appreciate the nature of the legal obligation and the other party is aware of the incapacity, the contract can be rescinded. Courts are less inclined to help a person who was voluntarily inebriated.

All contracts must be at "arm's length"—that is, two or more parties exercising free will and contracting in "good faith" (RESTATEMENT, SECOND § 205 and U.C.C. § 1-203). Good faith is essentially honesty at the time the contract is made and in the execution or modification of the contract.

MUTUAL ASSENT

There must be a *mutual assent,* a meeting of the minds. This manifested agreement to enter into the contract most often requires an offer and an acceptance.

Offer

An *offer* is a proposal to enter into a contract which, if properly accepted, binds the party to the terms stated in the offer. The party making the offer is the *offeror* and the person receiving the offer is the *offeree.* The essential terms of the desired contract must be included in the offer and stated with enough certainty that the existence of a breach can be ascertained. Generally, the offer must be objectively manifested. That is to say, the subjective, internalized understanding of the party is normally not relevant. A discussion between a used car dealer and buyer about how great a new paint job *would* look on the vehicle might lead the buyer to believe that a paint job *is* included in the price of the car. If such is not stated clearly in the contract, however, the dealer is not obligated to provide it. The rule is what a reasonable third person would have understood under the circumstances.

Advertisements, catalogs, and the like are usually not considered to be offers because they are unspecific as to the exact type, number to be sold, color, and other factors. They are considered invitations for the customer to make an offer. The advertising of rewards for information or the return of a lost article or pet are offers because of their specificity.

Adequate manifestation of a meeting of the minds also requires the offeree to have knowledge of the offer. It must be communicated to the offeree.

An offer can be terminated. Generally the offeror can retract (revoke) an offer any time up to acceptance. The revocation must be received by the offeree and must occur prior to a valid acceptance. Normally the offer contains a specified time when the offer expires. The date may be specified as "at noon on the thirtieth of September" or as "ten days from the receipt of this letter." If a specific date is not given, the offer expires in a reasonable time. Depending on the circumstances, a reasonable time may be six months, twenty-four hours, or by the end of a telephone conversation. An implied option to accept exists when the offeror says, "I will pay $500 for you to paint my car." Once an offeree begins painting the car, the offeree must be given the chance to complete the job.

The offer is also terminated before acceptance if the offeree rejects it, if a party or other person who is essential to the performance of the contract dies, if the object of the contract is destroyed, if one of the parties becomes incapacitated, if the offeree makes a counteroffer, or if there is a supervening illegality. A supervening illegality would occur, for example, if you offered to sell and deliver high-tech equipment to country Y, and before acceptance the U.S. government passed an act or executive order prohibiting such sales.

An *option to purchase* is a special type of contract in which the seller for a fee agrees to give a prospective buyer a specified period of time in which to accept the seller's offer. The option specifies what the terms of the sale will be should the buyer exercise the option to buy. No other offers to buy can be accepted by the seller during the option period, nor can the seller terminate the offer. If the buyer does not exercise the option to buy within the specified time period, then the sale returns to the open market.

Acceptance

An *acceptance* is the manifested consent of the offeree to enter into a contract—to accept the offer. The offer must be known to the offeree and cannot be accepted by pure happenstance or coincidence. Traditionally the manner of acceptance depends on whether the offer is for a bilateral contract or a unilateral contract. A *bilateral contract* is a two-sided contract in which the offeror promises to do or not do something in trade for a promise by the offeree to do or not do a certain thing. It is a promise for a promise. Once the offeree makes the reciprocal promise, the offer is accepted and both parties are bound by the contract.

A *unilateral contract* is more one-sided. The offeror makes a promise to do or not to do something in trade for the offeree actually doing or not doing something. These are often offers for rewards. In this case the offeree makes no reciprocal promise and, therefore, is not bound by the contract. The offeror, however, remains bound. If the offeree accepts by performing the requested act, returning the lost item, then the offeror is bound and a unilateral contract is formed. If the offeree starts and then forsakes the performance, the offeror may not sue for breach because absent a completed performance, the contract has not been formed. Unilateral contracts are less common than bilateral ones.

The differences are important in traditional contract law, because if a party mistakenly accepts an offer for a bilateral contract by an act or accepts a unilateral contract with a promise, then no contract has been formed. Both the U.C.C. and the *Restatement of Contracts, Second,* require the traditional avenues of acceptance when the offer clearly calls for a bilateral or a unilateral response. When there is confusion or no specific manner of acceptance is required, however, modern law permits the offeree to choose either manner of acceptance [U.C.C. § 2-206; RESTATEMENT (SECOND) OF CONTRACTS, § 30(2)].

Generally speaking, for an acceptance to form a contract, it must be communicated to the offeror. If the acceptance makes changes in terms, this *counteroffer* for all practical purposes becomes a new offer terminating the original offer. Both the common law and the U.C.C. seem to take a similar approach when new terms are proposed and do not require acceptance by the original offeror. If, however, the original offer is clearly accepted and the offeree is only suggesting some *optional* modification, the contract is formed on the basis of the original offer (U.C.C. § 2-207).

There are several methods by which to accept an offer. If the method (place, time, manner, medium) is specified in the offer as the only way to respond, then the acceptance must comply. Therefore, notice of acceptance by mail rather than by the required telegram is no acceptance unless acquiesced to by the offeror. If a method is suggested but not specified as the only method, another similar method true to place and time forms the contract. Section 2-206 of the U.C.C. allows "any medium reasonable in the circumstances," including face-to-face acceptance and acceptance by mail, fax, or other appropriate method.

Computers and e-commerce have expanded the methods of acceptance of contract offers. Even though the purchaser of computer software sold in a shrink-wrapped box has no access to the restrictive licensing terms that are contained inside the box, that purchaser in effect accepts those terms by tearing off the shrink wrap. Such shrink-wrap licenses were upheld in *ProCD v. Zeidenberg*, 86 F.3d 1447 (7th Cir. 1996) and *Hill v. Gateway 2000 Inc.*, 105 F.3d 1147 (7th Cir. 1997), cert. denied, 118 S. Ct. 47 (1997). Acceptance by mouse click in e-commerce was upheld in *Caspi v. The Microsoft Network*, 732 A.2d 528 (N.J. Super. 1999). In 2000 Congress made it legal to sign contracts online.

A timely acceptance is generally binding when it is mailed or otherwise dispatched. If an unauthorized or untimely method is used, the acceptance may occur when received by the offeror. The time of acceptance is important, of course, in relation to the effective time for revocation or the time of acceptance made by another party. Acceptance may also be made in specific circumstances by silence, by exercising control over received goods, or by benefiting from receipt of services.

CONSIDERATION

Consideration is an element essential to a contract and is something of value exchanged for a promise or act. It is the essence of a contract—the very reason that the parties have a meeting of the minds. The consideration must have value and that value must be reasonably determinable. The most common considerations are

1. a promise to give money, property, or service
2. an act
3. the foregoing of a legal right to do something
4. the formation, alteration, or termination of a legal relationship, like a partnership

The crux in determining if something is valid consideration is whether the party is incurring a *legal detriment*. A police officer cannot legally claim a $2,000 reward for capturing a wanted thief because the officer had the obligation to do so anyway. Doing something you are already obligated to do is not a legal detriment and, therefore, there is no consideration. The consideration does not have to be equal in value to the promise or act and is not a concern of the courts in determining the legality of a contract. Things or circumstances that fall short of being legal consideration include the following:

1. Gifts—by nature optional, free of obligation
2. Illusory promises—"I'll *consider* painting the house if you pay $250."
3. Jokes or jests (determined by the surrounding circumstances)—"Kiss me, and I'll follow you anywhere."

4. A forbearance of something illegal—"I'll stop stealing your trade secrets if you pay me $25,000."
5. Stated consideration that is nonexistent or false
6. The modification of a contract including a different obligation but no new consideration.

Renewed promises to pay a debt or other obligation previously discharged or made unenforceable by a statute of limitations or other legality are enforceable even though there is no new consideration. Similarly, a debt may be revived by partial payment. Charitable pledges are frequently enforceable even though the charity provides no consideration.

FOR LAWFUL OR ENFORCEABLE PURPOSE

A contract that promises payment for an illegal act is unenforceable. Therefore, if a wife contracts with X to murder her husband in exchange for $100,000 of the insurance money, there is no enforceable contract. Also, if the contract is contrary to public policy, it will not be enforced. For example, in many states a surrogate mother contract is unenforceable.

In some jurisdictions with blue laws, some contracts are not enforceable if entered into on a Sunday or if they are usurious or involve types of gambling. Credit or loan transactions may be enforceable only if they comply with the provisions of the Truth in Lending Law. In jurisdictions where services require a licensed technician or plumber, for example, contracts cannot be enforced if performed by an unlicensed person. But contracts made by a business that has not obtained the license required of all businesses to operate in the city are generally enforceable.

IN A FORM REQUIRED BY LAW—THE STATUTE OF FRAUDS

Modern contract law provides for oral and written contracts. Both are enforceable if all the normal requirements are met. All states have a *statute of frauds* that requires certain contracts to be in writing. If they are not written and do not meet the requirements set out in the statute, the contract is generally unenforceable.

The types of contracts included in most statutes of frauds concern substantial issues of value, time, or purpose. Types of contracts covered by a statute of frauds include the following:

1. An assumption of debts or obligations of another
2. A promise given in exchange for a promise to marry
3. Real estate contracts
4. An agreement that will take more than one year to perform
5. Leases exceeding one year in length
6. Promises to pay debts discharged by bankruptcy or barred by the statute of limitations
7. Vehicle repairs, warranties, and many other consumer transactions
8. Sale of goods exceeding a $500 price
9. Sale of securities
10. Sale of personal property exceeding $5,000

If the contract is required to be in writing, it can be any writing signed by the party charged that identifies the subject matter, terms of the contract, and mutual assent to a reasonable certainty.

ABSENCE OF FRAUD, DURESS, UNDUE INFLUENCE, MISTAKE OF FACT, AND OTHER DEFENSES

The numerous defenses to a suit for breach of contract can be pleaded individually or in the alternative. Some have been alluded to in previous sections. The following is a list of defenses.

1. Capacity to Contract
2. Undue Influence—Prevents a party to a contract from exercising free choice because the other party knowingly takes advantage of that party's innocent or weakened state of mind. The result is an unfair contract, which may occur because one party is a child; has a mental infirmity due to advanced age, alcohol, or drugs; is isolated from relatives, friends, or a spouse; or some other circumstances. It may involve a breach of a fiduciary relationship, where one party has a special position of trust in regard to another party, such as guardian-ward, lawyer-client, or principal-agent.
3. Duress—Coercive influence such as a threat of criminal action, physical harm, or the release of damaging information depriving a party of free choice at the time of entry into the contract.
4. Mistake of Party Known to Other—Occurs when one party realizes the other party has made a mistake as to party, price, or other important error. Even though the party aware of the mistake may act to take advantage of it, no contract has been formed. For example, Shifty Industries receives an offer to sell item X at a value so clearly under the going rate that it is obviously a mistake. Shifty licks its chops and greedily accepts. There is no contract because there was no legitimate offer.
5. Mutual Mistake—Where both parties have a different or erroneous idea about a fundamental term of the contract which has a material (important) impact on the contract. The understanding of the term "denim" in the contract between Briar Patch Dolls and Teeny Tiny Manufacturing (Case IV) by Briar Patch to be a certain heavy-gauge material and by Teeny Tiny to be any coarse cotton fabric could be considered a mutual mistake.
6. Misrepresentation—Where one party attempts to conceal important facts from another party. In a car sale, the dealer may be aware a car has been in an accident, but assigns a salesperson to the car who is not aware of this fact. The car is represented as having never been in an accident. This action is misrepresentation and may result in rescinding the contract of sale.
7. Fraud—Essentially a lie (not an opinion) or a reckless statement made with the intent to deceive the other party and to induce that party to enter a contract. The victim must be deceived, rely on the statement in agreeing to the contract, and be injured by the untruthful statement.
8. Unconscionability—A doctrine to prevent oppression and unfair surprise. It may focus on the procedure to contract, including the illiteracy of a party or the arcane language and fine print in a contract. It also may focus on the substance of a contract, such as particularly harsh features that leave one party without a benefit or remedy. Generally a contract that is so unjust as to shock the public conscience is declared unconscionable and voidable. *Adhesion contracts* are "take it or leave it" contracts providing consumers with no chance to bargain. These one-sided contracts are frequently found to be unconscionable.
9. Statute of Limitations—If the statutory time period for suing on a breach of contract (usually four years) has expired, then the cause of action is unenforceable.

In addition to the use of these defenses, other factors may lead to a contract being rescinded:

1. Justification—Other side has failed to produce consideration.
2. Involuntary Breach (impossibility or impracticability)—The contract cannot be performed because of no fault of the party or parties. If a party dies, the property to be sold is destroyed, or some supervening governmental action prohibits performance, the contract is essentially void. Having higher costs or greater difficulty than was anticipated to perform the contract is not an excuse.
3. Release—The party has been released by the other party from any obligation.
4. Mutual Rescission—Both parties agree to end the contract.

The following defenses to an action for breach take the position that the contract has been adequately performed:

1. Accord and Satisfaction—B owes A $500. B pays by painting A's house, to which A assents.
2. Satisfaction—Adequate performance. A delivers 999 of a contracted 1,000 items and substitutes an item of similar quality for the missing item. This action is probably adequate to be considered a compliance with the terms of the contract.

OTHER ENFORCEABLE AGREEMENTS

Oral Contract

Oral contracts are true contracts, with all the definite and specific terms of written contracts, but not in written form. In some states performance must be within one year of the agreement.

Quantum Meruit

Quantum meruit is a Latin phrase meaning "as much as he or she deserves." It is also called an implied-in-fact contract. The agreement does not contain all necessary terms of a contract, such as price, but is a mutual assent. The plaintiff can recover the reasonable value of services rendered.

Quasi-Contract, Implied-in-Law Contract, or Unjust Enrichment

Quasi-contracts, implied-in-law contracts, and unjust enrichment are not contracts, but are treated as if they were. There is no mutual assent. Elements include that the defendant inadvertently received a benefit from the plaintiff and had knowledge or appreciation of the benefit, and that it would be unfair for the defendant to enjoy the benefit without paying the plaintiff for it. Benefits do not include gifts. Aid rendered by a physician in an emergency entitles the physician to recover the actual value of the services rendered. If a landscaper contracts to work on A's property, but by mistake improves the beauty of B's property, the landscaper can claim restitution from B for the value of the work. Quasi or implied-in-law contracts focus on the plaintiff and the value of services rendered. Unjust enrichment focuses on the defendant and the value of the benefit received.

Detrimental Reliance (Promissory Estoppel)

Detrimental reliance or promissory estoppel is a cause of action that makes a party liable for a promise when another party reasonably relies on that promise and incurs financial injuries as a result of breach. Charitable pledges fall into this category. These promises that do not amount to contracts are rare in case law.

THIRD-PARTY CONTRACTS: BENEFICIARIES, ASSIGNMENT, AND DELEGATION

BENEFICIARIES

One or both parties entering into a contract may intend that a third party receive the benefit of the contract. A common example is a life insurance policy where the husband lists his wife as the third-party beneficiary. It is best if such contracts expressly identify the beneficiary. In many instances the court is left this task.

In addition, the court must also determine whether the third-party beneficiary has the right to enforce the contract and claim the benefit. Generally two classes of beneficiaries are able to do so: donee beneficiaries and creditor beneficiaries. *Donee beneficiaries* are generally given the benefits of a contract as a gift, such as the life insurance contract. It is also true if A agrees to provide legal services to X in return for X placing the fee for that service in a trust account for A's child. In such circumstances, A's child is a third-party beneficiary known by both the contracting parties. The right is significant and enforceable by A's child according to the terms of the trust. A's child, however, is not liable to X for A's promise to deliver legal services.

Creditor beneficiaries are those third parties who are owed money by one of the contracting parties and will receive it from money the other contracting party owes the original debtor. For example, A buys B's store and agrees to pay off B's creditors to the amount of $10,000 as part of the sale. B's creditors become creditor beneficiaries to the contract between A and B, and they can sue A for payment of the debt under the contract.

Both types of beneficiaries are called "intended" beneficiaries under the *Restatement of Contracts.* The key is whether the parties intended the beneficiaries to receive the performance or a part of the performance of a contract. All other beneficiaries are called *incidental beneficiaries.* They lack the degree of direct benefit from the contract that an expressly intended beneficiary has. If an airport construction company contracts to build an airport for Miami, Florida, the airline and its employees will benefit. They are not the intended beneficiaries and cannot enforce the contract as the city of Miami and the donee and creditor beneficiaries can. If most of the benefit of the contract runs to the contracting party and only a small amount runs to the beneficiary, the beneficiary is likely to be an incidental beneficiary. In this case only the original party can sue.

ASSIGNMENT OF CONTRACT RIGHTS AND DELEGATION OF CONTRACT DUTIES

A party may *assign* its rights or *delegate* its duties under a contract to a third party. Normally assignment or delegation can be done unless (1) the parties state otherwise or (2) such action would significantly alter the duty or rights of the other party to the contract. The person who assigns his or her contract rights to another is called the *assignor;* the person receiving the assignment is the *assignee.* In delegation it is *delegator* and *delegatee,* respectively. The assignee takes all rights assigned and can sue to enforce those rights, and also assumes any existing defenses that could have been asserted against the assignor. Assignments are normally sold to the assignee.

In delegation, the delegator authorizes another party or parties to fulfill all or a part of the delegator's original duty. The delegator remains responsible for performance of the overall duty, and each delegatee becomes responsible to the delegator for performing his or her part of the duty. A typical delegation of duties occurs in construction contracts where the contractor delegates some of the construction, say the plumbing and electrical work, to subcontractors. The other party to the contract to whom the duty is owed is the *obligee*.

A party may substitute another party to the contract if all parties agree. This substitution is called *novation* and discharges the original party obtaining the novation.

REMEDIES FOR BREACH OF CONTRACT

Assuming that the contract is valid and one party breaches the contract, the other party is entitled to some remedy that duplicates as closely as possible the benefits the victim would have obtained from the performance of the contract. The remedy is usually money damages. The most significant remedies follow.

1. Compensatory Damages—Normally money damages equal to the service provided or the lost benefit plus any costs such as those to cover having to pay a higher price for the goods than that negotiated under the breached contract. Compensatory damages are also called expectation or benefit of the bargain damages.
2. Reliance Damages—Damages in the amount necessary to place the injured party in a position equal to that before the contract. They cover any expenses or costs incurred for relying on the promise of the breaching party. For example, a cement company promises to be at X's construction site on a specific day. X hires a crew to be there on that day to spread and finish the cement. If the cement company breaches, it is liable for the fees X had to pay the crew for that day.
3. Restitution Damages—Damages awarded to the wronged party to equal any benefit the other party has received from the contract. These damages are usually sought when the nonbreaching party lawfully rescinds the original contract and the other party has already received a benefit, or when the original contract was not valid but one party has performed to the benefit of the other. Restitution seeks the value of the benefit already received by the other party.
4. Liquidated (Stipulated) Damages—Damages described in the language of the contract and agreed to by the parties in case one side or the other breaches the contract. The damages may be a set amount or based on some formula, and must be reasonable under the circumstances. They are frequently used where actual damages may be hard to determine.
5. Specific Performance—Requires the breaching party to perform the stated duty under the contract. For example, X pays Y $500,000 for a rare and unique copy of this textbook. Y backs out. Because of the uniqueness of the item, the court orders Y to deliver the rare copy. These damages are awarded rarely and generally when money damages are not adequate.
6. Punitive Damages—Money damages in addition to all other damages awarded to penalize the breaching party for reprehensible conduct, e.g., fraud.
7. Other Remedies—Interest, rescission of contract, replacement or repair of defective goods, and assurances that a party will perform the obligation under the contract.

INTERPRETING THE TERMS OF A CONTRACT: THE PAROLE EVIDENCE RULE AND OTHER CONSIDERATIONS

The terms of the contract do not have to be written unless the contract falls within the statute of frauds. If it is written, however, the question is whether the writing comprises all the terms of the contract or only some of its terms. If the court determines that the writing *integrates* all of the terms of the contract, no evidence of other agreements prior to or contemporaneous with the writing will be allowed to add to or modify the terms expressed in the writing. An exception applies if fraud or the like is involved. If the writing is determined by the court to be only a *partial integration* of the terms, the court can consider extrinsic evidence—both written and oral evidence—to determine the terms of the contract. Technically parole evidence is oral evidence, but in contract law it applies to both written and oral evidence.

If any contract is uncertain (*ambiguous*) as to its terms or intent, the court can consider outside evidence in the form of other writings and statements to clarify the contract. If the contract is declared unambiguous, the general rule has been not to consider outside evidence. The *Restatement, Second,* and some states encourage the use of extrinsic evidence to show the intent and understanding of the parties whenever a question arises.

WARRANTIES

Sellers of goods or services warrant as part of the contract the quality, character, or title (ownership) of the object of the contract. Actions under these collateral provisions are for breach of warranty. Warranty law is defined in most states by U.C.C. § 2-312. Additional requirements that warranties be in writing and clear language in consumer transactions are set out in the Magnuson-Moss Warranty Act.

In general, merchants and casual layperson sellers are bound by several implied (enforced by law, but do not have to be written) warranties:

1. Warranty of Merchantability or Fitness—The goods are free of defects, fit for their ordinary purpose, adequately packaged and labeled, and conform to declarations made on the package.
2. Warranty of Title—Implied promise that the seller owns the goods.
3. Warranty Against Encumbrances—The goods are free of liens, encumbrances, or other creditor's claims not known to the buyer.

Express warranties are written or oral statements by the seller, or samples displayed by the seller, that convey or state a fact about the character, quality, uniformity, and purpose of the goods. Opinions are not warranties. Express warranties are assumed voluntary by the seller as a marketing device.

A seller can disclaim all warranties, but such must be in clear language. The warranty of merchantability must be specifically disclaimed. Display of an expression such as "as is" serves as a disclaimer. Disclaimers in situations in which the buyer has little choice may be unconscionable.

A MINI-GUIDE FOR INTERPRETING MEDICAL RECORDS

Medical Prefixes and Suffixes[1]

Word Part	Definition	Word Part	Definition
a(n)-	inadequate; no; not; lack of	cutane/o	skin
ab-	away from	cyst/o	bladder; sac
acr/o	extremity; top	cyt/o	cell
ad-	toward	de-	lack of; removal
aden/o	gland	dent/o	tooth
-al	pertaining to	-derma	skin
-algia	pain	dors/o	back
angi/o	vessel	dur/o	dura mater (outermost membrane surrounding the brain.)
ante-	before		
anter/o	front		
arteri/o	artery	dys-	bad, difficult; painful; poor
arthr/o	joint	e-	out; outside; without
-asthenia	no strength	-ectomy	excision; surgical removal
-blast	immature, growing thing	edema	accumulation of fluid
carcin/o	cancer; cancerous	-emesis	vomit; vomiting
cardi/o	heart	-emia	blood condition
caud/o	tail	encephal/o	brain
cephal/o	head	endo-	with; within
cerebr/o	brain	enter/o	small intestine
cervic/o	cervix; neck/ neck of uterus	epi-	above; on
chondr/o	cartilage	eso-	inward
-clast	breakdown	-esthesia	sensation
coccyg/o	coccyx; tailbone	eu-	normal; good
col/o	colon; large intestine	ex-, exo-, extra-	out; outside; outward
cortic/o	cortex; outer layer	fibr/o	fibers; fibrous tissue
crani/o	skull	-flux	flow

Word Part	Definition	Word Part	Definition
gastr/o	stomach	-lysis	breakdown; separation
-gen	producing	mamm/o, mast/o	breast
-genesis	development; production	maxill/o	maxilla; upper jaw
gloss/o	tongue	medi/o	middle
gonad/o	gonads; sex glands	-megaly	enlargement
-grade	to step; to go	men/o	menstruation; month
-gram	record; writing	mening/o	membrane; meninges
gynec/o	female; woman	multi-	multiple
hem/o, hemat/o	blood	my/o, myos/o	muscle
hemi-	half	myel/o	bone marrow; spinal cord
hepa/o	liver	myring/o	eardrum
hist/o	tissue	nas/o	nose
home/o	same	necr/o	death
hydr/o	water	neo-	new
hyper-	abnormal increase; excessive	nephr/o	kidney
		neur/o	nerve
hypo-	abnormal decrease; below normal	nulli-	none
		occipit/o	occiput (back part of head)
hyster/o	uterus		
-ia	condition; state of	ocul/o	eye
-iasis	abnormal condition; process	odont/o	teeth
		-oid	resembling
ile/o	ileum (distal portion of the small intestine	oligo-	deficient; few
		-oma	mass; tumor
ili/o	hip	oophor/o	ovary
infer/o	below; downward	ophthalm/o	eye
infra-	within	-opia	visual condition
inter-	between	orchi/o	testicle
intra-	within	orex/i	appetite
is/o	equal	ortho-	straight
-itis	inflammation	-ory, -ose, -ous	pertaining to
-ium	structure	-osis	abnormal condition
-kinesis	movement	oste/o	bone
laryng/o	larynx; voice box	ot/o	ear
leuk/o	white	oxy-	quick, sharp
lip/o, lipid/o	fat	pan-	all
lith/o	stone	para-	abnormal; beside; near
lumb/o	lower back	-partum	labor; delivery; childbirth
lymph/o	lymph (clear, watery fluid)		

Word Part	Definition	Word Part	Definition
path/o, -pathy	disease	-sclerosis	hardening
pector/o	chest	spermat/o	spermatozoa; sperm
ped/o	child	splen/o	spleen
peri-	around	spondyl/o	vertebra
-phagia	swallow; to eat	-stenosis	narrowing; stricture
pharyng/o	pharynx; throat	stomat/o	mouth; opening
-phasia	speech	sub-	tongue; under
phleb/o	vein	super/o	above; toward the head
-phobia	fear; irrational fear	supra-	above; beyond; excessive
-phonia	voice	sym-	together; with
phot/o	light	tachy-	fast
-physis	to grow	ten/o; tend/o tendin/o	tendon
-plasia, -plasm	development; formation	-therapy	treatment
-plasty	surgical repair or reconstruction	-thermy	heat
-plegia	paralysis	thorac/o	chest; thorax
pleur/o	pleura; pleural cavity	thromb/o	clot
-pnea	breathing	tom/o; -tomy	to cut
pneumon/o	lungs	trans-	across
poly-	many	-tripsy	crushing
post-	after	-trophy	development; growth; nourishment
poster/o	back		
proct/o	rectum	-ule	small
pulmon/o	lungs	ur/o	urinary tract; urine; urination
py/o	pus		
quadri-	four	uter/o	uterus
ren/o	kidney	vascul/o	vessel
retro-	backward; back; behind	ven/o	vein
rhin/o	nose	ventr/o	front
-rrexis	rupture	vesic/o	bladder
-rrhage	bursting forth	viscer/o	internal organs
-rrhea	flow; discharge	xer/o	dry
schisis	cleft; splitting	-y	process

ANATOMICAL DIAGRAMS

(The following are for illustrative purposes. You may choose to include several more in your guide.)

FIGURE A:1 ■ Human Skeleton[2]

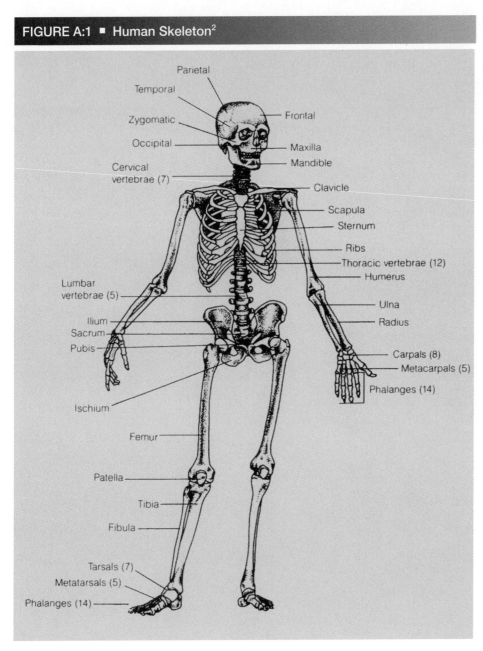

Source: Reprinted with permission of Wadsworth, a division of Thomson Learning: http://www.thomsonrights.com.

FIGURE A:2 ■ Selected Muscles of the Body—Front View[3]

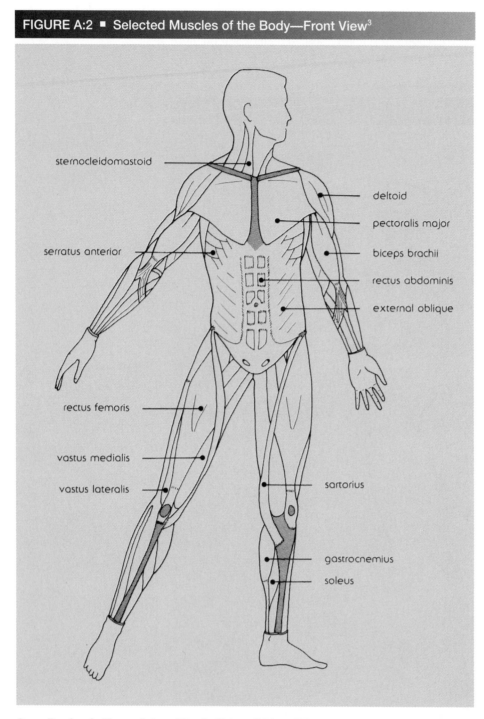

Source: Reprinted with permission of Brooks/Cole, a division of Thomson Learning: http://www.thomsonrights.com.

FIGURE A:3 ■ Selected Muscles of the Body—Back View

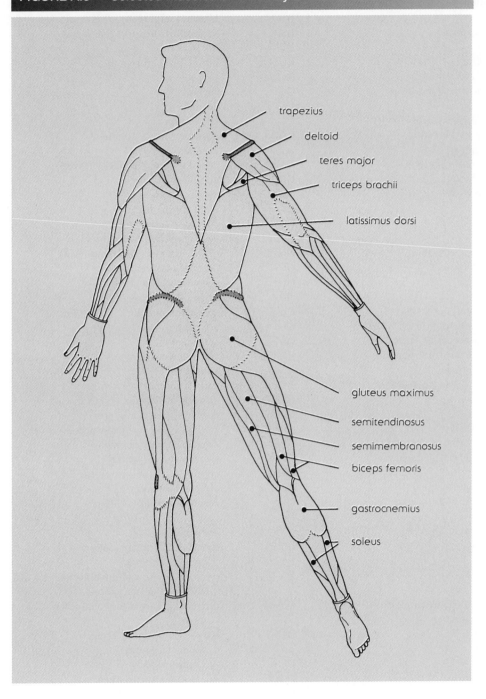

trapezius

deltoid

teres major

triceps brachii

latissimus dorsi

gluteus maximus

semitendinosus

semimembranosus

biceps femoris

gastrocnemius

soleus

COMMON MEDICAL RECORD ABBREVIATIONS AND SYMBOLS[4]

$A + SO_4$	atropine sulfate		BS	bowel sounds
aa	of each		BSO	bilateral salpingoopherectomy
Ab	antibody (lab term)		BSP	bromsulphalein test (lab term)
ablib	as desired		BTL	bilateral tubal ligation
ac	before meals		BUN	blood, urea, nitrogen
ac & hs	before meals & bedtime		bx	biopsy
ACTH	adrenocorticotropic hormone		C	carbon
AD	right ear		Ca	calcium
ADT	anticipate dismissal tomorrow		CA	carcinoma
add	add or let there be added		CAD	coronary artery disease
adv	(adverse) against		caps	capsule
AFB	acid fast bacillus (lab term)		CAR	coronary artery bypass
A/G ratio	albumin-globulin ration		CBC	complete blood count
Ag	antigen (lab term)		cc	cubic centimeters
AK	above the knee		CC	chief complaint
alb	albumin		CCU	coronary care unit
a.m.	before noon		CFT	complement fixation test
AMA	against medical advice		chart	powder paper (pharmacy term)
ANA	antinuclear antibody		CHD	coronary heart disease
anes	anesthesia		CHF	congestive heart failure
A.P.	anteroposterior		circ	circumcision
A & P	auscultation and percussion		CIS	carcinoma in situ
APAP	acetaminophen (pharmacy term)		CI	chloride
APC	aspirin, phenacetin, caffeine		cm	centimeter
APTT	activated partial thromboplastin time (lab term)		CNS	central nervous system
			c/o	complaint of
aq	(aqua) water		CO_2	carbon dioxide
AS	atropine sulfate		COAD	chronic obstructive airway disease
A.S.	left ear		COD	codeine (pharmacy term)
ASA	aspirin		CPD	cephalopelvic disproportion
ASAP	as soon as possible		CPK	creatinine phosphokinase
ASCVD	arteriosclerotic cardiovascular disease		C & S	culture and sensitivity
			CSF	cerebrospinal fluid
ASD	atrial septal defect		cu. mm	cubic millimeters
ASHD	arteriosclerotic heart disease		CVA	cerebrovascular accident
AU	both ears		Cx	cervix
AUB	abnormal uterine bleeding		CXR	chest x-ray
AV	atrioventricular		D5NS	dextrose 5% normal saline (pharmacy term)
Ax	axillary			
B	bacillus		$D5\frac{1}{2}NS$	dextrose 5% in sodium chloride 0.45% (pharmacy term)
Ba	barium			
BarB	phenobarbital (pharmacy term)		D5W	dextrose 5% in water (pharmacy term)
BBB	bundle branch block			
BCP	birth control pills		DC65	darvon compound 65 mg. (pharmacy term)
BE	barium enema			
b.i.d.	twice a day		DC	discontinue
BK	below the knee		D & C	dilatation and curettage
BM	bowel movement		DAT	diet as tolerated
BMR	basal metabolic rate		decub	decubitus
BOW	bag of water		DEM	meperidine hydrochloride (pharmacy term)
BP	blood pressure			
BPH	benign prostatic hypertrophy		diff	differential
BRP	bathroom privileges		DIP	distal interphalangeal joint
bs	blood sugar		disc	discontinue

disch	discharge	HCl	hydrochloric acid
DIV	divide	HCO_3	bicarbonate
DJD	degenerative joint disease	HCT	hematocrit (lab term)
DM	diabetes mellitus	HCVD	hypertensive cardiovascular disease
DOA	dead on arrival	HEENT	head, eyes, ears, nose, throat
DOE	dyspnea on exertion	Hgb.	hemoglobin (lab term)
DPT	diptheria, pertussis, tetanus	hs or HS	hours of sleep
dr	dram (pharmacy term)	Hx	history
Dt's	delirium tremens	i	one
DTD	send of such doses (pharmacy term)	I	iodine
dx	diagnosis	ICCE	intracapsulary cataract extraction
ECG	electrocardiogram	ICS	intercostal space
EDC	expected date of confinement	ICU	intensive care unit
EEG	electroencephalogram	I & D	incision and drainage
EKG	electrocardiogram	i.e.	that is
ELF	elective low forceps	IM	intramuscular
elix	elixir	IMP	impression
ENT	ears, nose, throat	in	inch
EOM	extraocular movements	inf	infection
EOS	eosinophils (lab term)	INH	Isoniazid (pharmacy term)
ER	emergency room	inj	injection
ESR	erythrocyte sedimentation rate	I & O	intake & output
et	and	IOL	intraocular lens
EUA	exam under anesthesia	IPPB	intermittent positive pressure breathing
Ext	extract	IQ	intelligence quotient
F	Fahrenheit	IUD	intrauterine device
FBS	fasting blood sugar (lab term)	IUP	intrauterine pregnancy
FDP	fibrin degradation products (lab term)	IV	intravenous
Fe	chemical symbol for iron	IVP	intravenous pyelogram
FFP	fresh frozen plasma (lab term)	JVD	jugular venous distention
FH	family history	K	potassium
FHT	fetal heart tone	KCl	sugar-free 10% potassium chloride
FS	frozen section	Kg	kilogram
FSH	follicle stimulating hormone	$KMnO_4$	potassium permanganate (pharmacy term)
FUO	fever of undetermined origin	KO	keep open (pharmacy term)
Fx	fracture	KUB	kidney, ureter, bladder
gal	gallon	L or l	liter
GB	gallbladder	L & A	light and accommodation
GC	gonorrheal	lab	laboratory
GI	gastrointestinal	lb	pound
gm	gram	LDH	lactohydrogenase
gr	grain	LE	lupus erythematosis
GSW	gunshot wound	LEVO	Levo Dromoran
gtt	drops	LH	lutinizing hormone (lab term)
GTT	glucose tolerance test	Li	Lithium
GU	genitourinary	LLE	left lower extremity
GYN	gynecology	LLQ	left lower quadrant
H_2O	water	LMD	local medical doctor
H_2O_2	hydrogen peroxide	LNMP	last normal menstrual period
h	hour	LOA	left occiput anterior
HAA	hepatitis associated antigen (lab term)	LR	lactated Ringers
HBP	high blood pressure	LSF	liver function studies
HCG	human chorionic gonadotropin	LSO	left salpingoopherectomy

LUQ	left upper quadrant		PE	physical exam
LVH	left ventricular hypertrophy		PERLA	pupils equal and react to light and accommodation
lytes	electrolytes (lab term)			
m	minim (pharmacy term)		PETN	peritrate (pharmacy term)
M	mix (pharmacy term)		PI	present illness
mcg	microgram		PID	pelvic inflammatory disease
MCl	midclavicular line		pm	afternoon
mEg	milliequivalents		PMH	past medical history
mft	mix and make (pharmacy term)		PMI	point of maximum impulse
mg	milligram		PND	paroxysmal nocturnal dyspnea
MGSO₄	magnesium sulfate		po	by mouth
MHFD	modified high fiber diet		Polio	poliomyelitis
MI	myocardial infarction		PORR	postoperative recovery room
ml	milliliter		postop	postoperative
mm	millimeter		pp	after eating
MOM	Milk of Magnesia		PPD	purified protein derivative
MS	morphine sulfate		preop	preoperative
MVA	motor vehicle accident		PRN	as necessary
MVI	multivitamin infusion		PROM	premature rupture of membranes
Na	sodium		PT	physical therapy
NaCl	sodium chloride		PTA	prior to admission
NAD	no acute distress		PTH	parathyroid hormone (lab term)
NaHCO₃	sodium bicarbonate		PUD	peptic ulcer disease
NB	newborn		pulv	powder (pharmacy term)
neg	negative		PVC	premature ventricular contraction
NG	nasogastric		q	every
NND	no new data		qd	every day
non rep	do not repeat		qh	every hour
Norm M	Normosol M		qhs	every hour of sleep
NPH	type of long acting insulin		q.i.d.	four times a day
NPO	nothing by mouth		qn	every night
NPTFC	no past tracing for comparison		qns	quantity not sufficient
NR BC	nucleated red blood cell (lab term)		qod	every other day
NS	normal saline		qs	sufficient quantity
NTG	nitroglycerin tablets (pharmacy term)		qsad	to make a sufficient quantity
			qt	quart
O	pint		R	respiration
O₂	oxygen		RA	rheumatoid arthritis
OB	obstetrics		RBBB	right bundle branch block
occ	occasional		RBC	red blood count
o.d.	right eye		RHD	rheumatic heart disease
OD	daily		RLQ	right lower quadrant
O&P	ova and parasites		R/O	rule out
OR	operating room		ROA	right occiput anterior
ORIF	open reduction and internal fixation		ROM	range of motion
o.s.	left eye		ROP	right occiput posterior
o.u.	both eyes		ROS	review of system
oz	ounce		RPCF	Reiter protein complement fixation (lab term)
p	phosphorus			
PA&LAT	chest posterior, anterior and lateral		RR	recovery room
Pap	papaniculaou		RTC	return to clinic
PAS	sodium (pharmacy term)		RUQ	right upper quadrant
PB	phenobarbitol		Rx	treatment
pc	after meals		sat	saturation
PC	packed cells		sc	subcutaneous

$MGSO_4$ magnesium sulfate
O_2 oxygen
$NaHCO_3$ sodium bicarbonate

sed rate	sedimentation rate	TPR	temperature, pulse, respiration
sig	let it be labeled	TSH	thyroid stimulating hormone
SGOT	serum glutamic oxalo-acetic transaminase	tsp	teaspoon
		TUR	transurethral resection
SGPT	serum glutamic pyruvic transaminase	TURP	transurethral resection of prostate
SL	sublingual	u	unit
SLR	straight leg raising	ua	urinalysis
SMA-7	SMA-6 plus creatinine	UGI	upper gastrointestinal series
sp. gr	specific gravity	UPJ	ureteropelvic junction
S-P	status post	URI	upper respiratory infection
spec	specimen	ut. dict.	as directed
ss	one half	UTI	urinary tract infection
SSE	soap suds enema	v	five
staph	staphylococcus	VD	venereal disease
stat	to be done immediately	VDRL	venereal disease research laboratory
Strep	streptococcus	VHD	valvular heart disease
SUI	stress urinary incontinence	VS	vital signs
sx	symptoms	vs	versus
T	temperature	WB	whole blood (lab term)
T & A	tonsillectomy and adenoidectomy	WBC	white blood count
tab	tablet	WNL	within normal limits
tal	of such (pharmacy term)		
TAH	total abdominal hysterectomy		
T.A.T.	tetanus antitoxin		
TB	tuberculosis		
TBA	to be admitted		
TBLC	term birth living child		
Tbsp	tablespoon		
TFS	thyroid function studies		
TIA	transient ischemic attack		
TIBC	total iron binding capacity		
t.i.d.	three times a day		
tinc	tincture		
TL	tubal ligation		
TLC	tender loving care		
TM	tympanic membrane		
TNG	nitroglycerin tablets		
TNTC	too numerous to count (lab term)		
TP	total protein		

SIGNS AND SYMBOLS

%	percent	℥	oz.
$\bar{s}$	without	Э	scruple
$\bar{p}$	after	℥^{i}	1 dram
$\bar{c}$	with	m	minim
♂	male	>	greater than
♀	female	<	less than
ɨ	one	α	alpha
ɨɨ	two	β	beta
ℨ	dram		

ROMAN NUMERALS

V=5	C=100
X=10	D=500
L=50	

FIGURE A:4 ■ Physician's Orders[5]

INSTRUCTIONS: BEFORE PLACING IN CHART, IMPRINT PATIENT'S PLATE AS INDICATED BELOW

Reynolds-Reynolds DAYTON, OHIO LITHO IN U.S.A. K8552 (8-84)

PHYSICIAN'S ORDERS
PATTIE A. CLAY HOSPITAL
RICHMOND, KENTUCKY 40475

IMPRINT PATIENTS PLATE HERE

ORDERED		ORDERS	NOTED BY/TIME
DATE	TIME		
2-26	0829	① admit ICU	
		② V/S & neuro checks q1h	
		③ I & O q1 / call if O < 30 cc/h	
		④ Tagamet 300 mg IV q6h	
		⑤ Keflen 1 Gm q6 IV	
		⑥ alt Maalox & Mylanta per nG q2h c̄ clamp x 30 min	
		⑦ nG lo int wall suction	
		⑧ IV's DSRL 125 cc/h	
		DSNS c̄ 30 meq K 100 cc/h	
		⑨ O₂ 4L n/c	
		⑩ Bucks traction c̄ 20 lb wt to Ⓛ femur	
		⑪ clean lacerations q4h c̄ betadine	
		⑫ ABG's q2h tonight	
		⑬ H & H q4h & call if Hct < 36	
		⑭ a.m. lab	
		lytes	
		CBC	
		ABG's	
		repeat KUB & chest x-ray	
		⑮ When fully alert & oriented 1 codeine 30 mg IM q6h P.R.N. pain (after 24 hours)	
		⑯ Tylenol #3 for less pain ī - īī tab	
		⑰ Tylenol 60 mg q6h T↑101 get blood cultures x 3 for T↑101	
		⑱ log roll.	
		⑲ no sx	
		⑳ Halo / clean pins c̄ betadine q6h	

"Authorization is hereby given to dispense the Generic or Chemical equivalent unless otherwise indicated by the words — NO SUBSTITUTE"

Use Ball Point

AFTER DOCTOR WRITES A MEDICATION ORDER
1. Remove first yellow copy.
2. Send yellow copy to PHARMACY.
3. After last yellow sheet is used "X" out remaining unused lines.

No. must show through hole→ before physician writes on order

Source: Reprinted Courtesy of Pattie A. Clay Hospital

FIGURE A:5 ■ Physician's Orders (Translated)[6]

INSTRUCTIONS: BEFORE PLACING IN CHART, IMPRINT PATIENT'S PLATE AS INDICATED BELOW

THE REYNOLDS & REYNOLDS CO., DAYTON, OHIO   PRINTED IN U.S.A.

PHYSICIAN'S ORDERS
PATTIE A. CLAY HOSPITAL
RICHMOND, KENTUCKY 40475

IMPRINT PATIENTS PLATE HERE

ORDERED DATE	TIME	ORDERS	NOTED BY/TIME
		1. admit intensive care unit	
		2. vital sign and alertness checks every hour	
		3. intake and output every hour. Call if output less than 30cc.	
		4. . . . every six hours	
		5. . . . 1 gram every six hours	
		6. Alternate . . . per naseogastric tube every two hours and clamp for 30 minutes.	
		7. . . . low intermittent	
		8. Intravenous fluids . . . 125cc per hour, 30 milequivalent potassium	
		9. Oxygen 4 liters nasal cannula	
		10. . . . with 20 pound weight . . . left	
		11. . . . every four hours	
		12. Arterial blood gases every two hours	
		13. Hemoglobin and hematocrit . . . hematocrit less than 36	
		14. Electrolytes Complete blood count Kidneys, Urine, Bladder and chest x-ray	
		15. . . . intermuscle every six hours as needed for pain	
		16. . . . one or two tablets	
		17. . . . temperature above 101	
		18. log rolling (technique for moving patients with spinal injury)	
		19. no suctioning	
		20. Halo (support for spine injury)	

"Authorization is hereby given to dispense the Generic or Chemical equivalent unless otherwise indicated by the words — NO SUBSTITUTE"

Use Ball Point

AFTER DOCTOR WRITES A MEDICATION ORDER
1. Remove first yellow copy.
2. Send yellow copy to PHARMACY.
3. After last yellow sheet is used "X" out remaining unused lines.

No. must show through hole→ before physician writes on order

◉ ENDNOTES

1. Adapted from Juanita Davies, *Illustrated Guide to Medical Terminology*, 435–442 (1st edition, 2006). Reprinted with permission of Thomson/Delmar Learning.
2. From INTRODUCTION TO PHYSICAL ANTHROPOLOGY, 3rd edition by NELSON/JURMAIN, 527. © 1985. Fax 800 730–2215.
3. From FITNESS AND WELLNESS: THE PHYSICAL CONNECTION, 1st edition by ROSATO, 158–159. © 1986. Fax 800 730–2215.
4. The list of abbreviations is courtesy of Pattie A. Clay Hospital, Richmond, Kentucky.
5. Form courtesy of Pattie A. Clay Hospital, Richmond, Kentucky. Data on form provided by Peggy Walker, R.N.
6. Translation provided by Peggy Walker, R.N.

GLOSSARY

Additur: A post-trial motion in which the plaintiff requests the court to increase a jury award.

Adjudication on the merits: A judgment by the court deciding the issues of an action, precluding that action from being brought again.

Admissible evidence: Evidence that may be presented in court because it complies with the rules of evidence that it must be relevant.

Affiant: The person who signs an affidavit.

Affidavit: A written, sworn statement.

Affirmative defense: Defense showing that the defendant is not liable even if the plaintiff's claim is assumed to be true and for which the defendant bears the burden of proof.

Alienage jurisdiction: A diversity jurisdiction involving foreign states and their citizens or subjects.

Answer: A formal pleading filed in response to the complaint; identifies the issues to be contested and contains a statement of what the defendant admits and denies and what defenses to the claim, if any, will be presented.

Arbitration: An alternative dispute resolution process consisting of the submission of a dispute to a neutral decision maker.

Argumentative denials: Denials that state facts suggesting a defense, but in fact are not really defenses.

Attorney's work product (trial preparation materials): The attorney's mental impressions, conclusions, opinions, or legal theories concerning a case; not discoverable.

Best evidence rule: Rule that allows only the original document or item to be admitted (exceptions are allowed for practical reasons).

Bill of particulars: A request for the opponent to make an ambiguous pleading more definite and certain.

Billable hours: The time spent on a client's case that can be billed to the client.

Brief: A document stating the relevant legal authority and how it should be applied to the issues and facts of a case.

Burden of proof: The obligation to prove the allegations; usually falls to the accuser.

Capacity: Requirements of age, competency, and so on, for a party to be allowed to sue or be sued.

Cause of action: Statement of the claim upon which relief may be granted in an action.

Chain of custody: The chronological record tracing a piece of evidence to the event that has resulted in the action, proving that it is the item in question.

Challenge for cause: The attorney's request to remove a potential juror on the grounds of bias or other reason.

Circumstantial evidence: Evidence that suggests the existence of some other occurrence or thing.

Civil litigation: The process whereby one person sues another person in a court of law to enforce a right or to seek a remedy such as financial compensation.

Class action: A suit by or against an entire class—whose members are too numerous for a joinder—represented by one or a few individuals.

Clear and convincing evidence: A higher standard of proof than preponderance of the evidence; requires that the matter be shown to be highly probable.

Complaint: The formal document used to commence a lawsuit; tolls the statute of limitations, identifies parties, and states the cause of action the plaintiff alleges against the defendant.

Concurrent jurisdiction: Authority by two courts to hear the same type of case.

Constructive service: Service of process other than direct service, such as through a newspaper of general circulation.

Contingent fee: Legal fee for representation based on a percentage of the award won by the plaintiff and allowing for no fee if the plaintiff loses.

Counterclaim: A claim asserted by the defendant against the plaintiff, often included in or with the answer.

Cross-claim: A claim by one party against a co-party in the same action.

Default judgment: Judgment rendered against the defendant for the damages specified in the claim without the case going to trial, based on the defendant's failure to respond to the complaint within the time limit.

Defendant: The party being sued for an alleged wrong.

Demonstrative evidence: Depiction or representation of something such as a photo of a scar or a diagram of the accident scene.

Demurrer: A document used in some states to dispute the sufficiency of the complaint or other pleading.

Deponent: A witness or party giving testimony under oath and recorded before trial.

Deposition: A discovery device permitting a party's attorney to question a witness or party spontaneously and under oath before trial, and to record the testimony.

Direct evidence: Evidence that is directly observable and proves the truth asserted.

Disclosure: The procedure automatically triggered early in a case requiring a party to give to the opponent a broad spectrum of information relevant to the case.

Discovery: The process in a lawsuit involving the exchange of information, exhibits, and documents between parties according to specific rules of procedure.

Diversity of citizenship: Jurisdictional requirement for U.S. District Court that all parties of a lawsuit be citizens of different states.

Documentary evidence: Paper evidence such as letters, contracts, or medical records.

Domicile: A person's true, permanent home.

Due process of law: Fair, prescribed judicial proceedings that must be followed before a person may be deprived of life, liberty, or property; guaranteed by the Constitution.

Duty: In tort law, due care owed by one person to another.

E-filing: A court-approved, Internet-based system for filing, serving, and accessing legal documents.

Electronic billing (e-billing): The posting of billing information by the law office to a secure electronic host site for instant client access.

Exclusive jurisdiction: Authority of the only court to handle a specific type of case.

Execution: The process of carrying out or enforcing a judgment.

Exemplary (punitive) damages: Damages awarded to a plaintiff beyond actual loss as punishment for conduct of the defendant that is particularly aggravated; also called punitive damages.

Exemplified: Authenticated as a true copy, as an official transcript to be used as evidence.

Fact pleading: The requirement that the body of a pleading state in detail the facts in support of each element of the rule of law or claim.

Federal questions: "[A]ll civil actions arising under the Constitution, laws, or treaties of the United States" (28 U.S.C. § 1331).

Findings of fact and conclusions of law: The document that contains the court's judgment summarizing the key evidence on the elements of the cause of action and the judge's conclusions that form the basis of the judgment.

Garnishee: The third party who is directed to surrender property owed to the judgment debtor to satisfy the judgment.

Garnishment: The process of trying to reach the assets of a judgment debtor that are in the possession of a third party in order to satisfy the judgment.

General damages: Damages that are a natural and direct result of the defendant's wrong, such as pain and suffering, humiliation, and loss of enjoyment of life.

General jurisdiction: The right to hear all types and subjects of cases rather than just a specific class.

Geographical jurisdiction: The right to hear cases that arise within a specific geographical area.

Guardian ad litem: Representative for a party who lacks the legal capacity to sue or be sued; serves for the duration of the action.

Habit: The semiautomatic, repeated response to a specific situation.

Harmless error: An error found to have occurred at the trial court by the appellate court, but insufficient to substantially affect the verdict of the case, and therefore, insufficient to overturn the verdict.

In forma pauperis: "In the manner of a pauper"; permission given to a poor person to sue without liability for costs.

In limine: A motion filed for protection against prejudicial questions and statements at trial.

In rem action: An action involving the attachment of property to resolve claims to the property.

Interpleader: The joining of those parties that have the same claim against a third party; done to limit the liability of the third party.

Interrogatories: A discovery device consisting of written questions submitted to another party and answered by that party in writing and under oath.

Joinder of parties: The uniting of parties making claims or defending against an action as co-plaintiffs or co-defendants.

Judgment creditor: The winner in civil cases in which money has been awarded.

Judgment debtor: The loser in civil cases in which money has been awarded.

Judgment proof: Description of a party who has no assets with which to pay a judgment.

Judicial notice: Admission of evidence without authentication, either a fact commonly known in the territorial jurisdiction of the court or a fact readily verifiable through undisputed sources.

Jurisdiction: The power or authority of a court to hear and decide the questions of law or fact (or both) presented by a lawsuit.

Jurisdictional amount (amount in controversy): Specific dollar amount that must be claimed in an action to meet the jurisdictional minimum of a given court.

Leading question: Question phrased in such a manner as to suggest the desired answer ("It was raining that night, wasn't it?").

Legal advice: Independent professional judgment based on knowledge of the law and given for the benefit of a particular client.

Levy: To seize and sell property of the judgment debtor as specified by the court to satisfy the judgment.

Limited jurisdiction: Authority to hear cases dealing only with specific subjects, i.e., traffic courts can hear only traffic cases.

Lis pendens: Record to notify potential buyers that the plaintiff has asserted a claim against that property in a lawsuit.

Litigation system: A detailed procedure manual that is a chronological collection of the guidelines, forms, correspondence, checklists, procedures, and pertinent law for all steps in the litigation process.

Long-arm statutes: Laws giving a court personal jurisdiction over nonresident persons or corporations in specified circumstances.

Mandatory injunction: Requirement that the defendant perform conduct specified by the court.

Material: Of consequence to the determination of the action.

Med-arb: A combination of mediation and arbitration; the matter is first mediated, then any unresolved issue is decided by the same or a different person who serves as an arbitrator.

Mediation: An alternative dispute resolution process incorporating a neutral person (the mediator) who facilitates a mutual resolution of the dispute.

Memorandum of law (memorandum of points and authorities): A document, normally shorter and less formal than a brief, stating the relevant legal authority and how it should be applied to the issues and facts of a case.

Motion: A request for a court order granting relief to the moving party.

Multijurisdictional practice: The provision of legal services in states other than the one for which the attorney is licensed.

Notice pleading: Abbreviated form of pleading authorized by the Federal Rules of Civil Procedure and parallel state rules.

Order: A directive from a judge requiring some act or restraint from some act in a lawsuit.

Original jurisdiction: The right of a specific court to hear a specific type of action first.

Peremptory challenge: The authority of an attorney to strike the name of a potential juror without having to express any reason for the strike; limited in number.

Personal jurisdiction: Jurisdiction over the person; authority to impose a binding judgment on a party, achieved with service of process.

Plaintiff: The party bringing the lawsuit.

Pleadings: Formal documents filed in a lawsuit that inform all parties of the basis for and defenses to the lawsuit; normally include the complaint, answer, counterclaim and reply, answer to cross-claim, and third-party complaint and answer.

Postjudgment interrogatory: A method to discover the assets of the judgment debtor through written questions to be answered under oath.

Post-trial deposition: Device used to discover the assets of the judgment debtor through oral examination under oath.

Post-trial request for production of documents: Method to obtain documents that will help in locating the assets of the judgment debtor.

Preponderance of the evidence: Evidence that is more convincing to the trier than the opposing evidence; meets the requirement for the burden of proof in civil cases.

Preservation letter: A letter sent to the opposing party requesting preservation of evidence.

Presumption: A mechanism that allows a jury to presume a fact is true based on indirect evidence if it might be awkward or difficult to prove by direct evidence. For example, mailing a letter creates the presumption it was received. A presumption stands unless it is rebutted.

Prima facie case: Sufficient evidence to prove a case, prior to any rebuttal by the defense.

Pro bono: Free legal services provided to those unable to afford representation.

Probative value of evidence: The degree to which evidence tends to prove or actually proves something.

Procedural law: Law that defines the rules and steps that must be followed in a lawsuit.

Professional ethics: For attorneys, the rules of conduct that govern the practice of law.

Prohibitory injunction: Order that informs a defendant to refrain from a specific course of conduct.

Proof beyond a reasonable doubt: Proof that is so strong it excludes any other reasonable hypothesis or explanation—almost a certainty.

Proximate cause: In tort law, the cause-and-effect relationship that must be established to prove that the conduct in question was the substantial cause of the injury in question.

Quasi in rem action: An action in which the court uses the property of a defendant over whom it does not have personal jurisdiction to pay a judgment against the defendant entered in an action unrelated to the property.

Question of fact: A point decided on evidence; for example, whether the traffic light was red.

Question of law: A point requiring the application or interpretation of statutes and case law, to be decided by a judge; for example, whether a statute is constitutional.

Real evidence: The thing itself, physically present as opposed to being described, such as a scar, implement, or live view of the accident scene.

Real party in interest: The one who has the right to sue by law; for example, the injured party or legal representative of that party.

Receivership: Placement of the assets of a business or an individual under the control of a court-appointed receiver who will protect those assets to pay a debt.

Redaction: The process of editing out irrelevant or privileged information from the text of a document.

Release: A document executed by the plaintiff or claimant that frees the defendant from any further obligations or liability stemming from the incident causing the damages in return for consideration (money).

Relevant: Admissible in court, of consequence to the determination of the action and tending to prove or refute a fact of consequence.

Remittitur: A post-trial motion in which the defendant requests the court to reduce a jury award because of an error in determining the award or because it is unreasonably excessive.

Removal jurisdiction: The authority of federal district courts to remove cases from state courts to federal court having jurisdiction to hear the case.

Res gestae statements: Statements that are present-sense impressions, excited utterances, or about then-existing mental, emotional, or physical conditions.

Routine (custom): The equivalent of "habit" for organizations.

Service of process: Delivery to the defendant of official notification of the lawsuit and of his or her need to respond; delivery of a copy of the summons, complaint, writs, and other documents to another party.

Settlement: The process whereby both sides review strengths and weaknesses of a case and reach a mutual agreement on how to dispose of the case.

Settlement agreement: A contract between the parties setting all the terms, conditions, and obligations of the parties, including how the action will be dismissed.

Settlement précis: A brief presentation of the client's case designed to persuade the opposing party to settle the case on terms satisfactory to the client.

Special damages: Damages that are incurred because of the defendant's wrong and the actual result of the injury, but not the necessary result, such as medical bills, lost wages, or property loss.

Specific performance: In breach of contract cases, the requirement of the offending party to fulfill specific terms of the contract regarding a unique piece of property.

Spoliation: The destruction or loss of evidence, including the failure to preserve it.

Standing to sue: Requirement that only plaintiffs who suffer or will suffer real or direct injury may sue.

Statute of limitations: Law stating the time limit in which an action must be filed. If the time limit is not met, the defendant has a defense to the action, and the case will be dismissed.

Stipulation: Formal agreement between opposing parties to a lawsuit regarding matters pertinent to the lawsuit, such as to admit certain evidence without testimony.

Subject matter jurisdiction: Authority to hear cases based on the nature or subject of those cases; for example, criminal, juvenile, civil, or appellate cases, or, in federal district courts, diversity cases involving more than $50,000.

Subpoena: A document pursuant to a court order that commands a person to appear to testify.

Subpoena duces tecum: A document pursuant to a court order that commands a person to appear with certain books, documents, electronically stored information, or tangible things.

Substantive law: Law that defines the duties owed by one person to another.

Substituted service: Any type of service of process other than actual, personal service, such as through mail, waiver, publication, or legal representative.

Summary trial: A nonbinding, abbreviated trial before a summary jury to see whether either side's case merits a real trial; encourages settlement of especially large cases.

Summons: A document issued by the court that informs the defendant of the action and requires the defendant to respond or appear by or at a designated time; when served, gives the court personal jurisdiction over the defendant.

Supersedeas bond: Bond filed by the judgment debtor to secure the amount of the judgment while the execution of that judgment is stayed pending post-trial motions.

Supplemental jurisdiction: The power of federal courts already having jurisdiction over a federal claim to hear a state claim and add parties if that claim is based on essentially the same facts as the federal claim.

Supplementary proceedings: The methods used to acquire information about the judgment debtor to enforce a judgment; for example, the post-trial deposition.

Testimonial evidence: Spoken or signed, elicited from a witness.

Third-party practice (impleader): The filing of a third-party complaint by the original defendant against a person not yet named a party to the lawsuit, alleging that the third party is or may be liable for all or a part of any damages won by the original plaintiff against the original defendant.

Unbundling legal services: The mutually agreed limitation of legal representation to one distinct step in a legal matter or process that may have numerous steps.

Venue: "Neighborhood"; the geographical area in which a court with jurisdiction can hear a case; distinct from jurisdiction.

Verdict: The final decision of the jury regarding the questions of fact submitted to it by the judge.

Voir dire: The questioning of potential jurors by the judge (and attorneys in state court) to reveal disqualifying information in the process of selecting an impartial jury.

With prejudice: In the dismissal of a case, the understanding that the action may not be brought again.

Without prejudice: In the dismissal of a case, the understanding that the action may be brought again.

Writ of certiorari: A discretionary writ that allows the Supreme Court to take only cases that, in its opinion, have sufficient national significance to warrant its attention.

INDEX